History of

AMERICA'S SPEEDWAYS

Past & Present

Allan E. Brown

AMERICA'S SPEEDWAYS
PO Box 448
Comstock Park, MI 49321
(616) 361-6229

International Standard Book Number:
0-931105-42-0

Printed in the United States of America

Cover photos:
Front: Midgets line up for a race in 1941 at Jungle Park Speedway near
Rockville, Indiana. - Bob Sheldon photo. / **Rear:** (top) Drake Olson leads a pack
of IMSA GT prototypes through turn nine at Portland (OR) International
Raceway. - David Allio photo. / (middle) The pace lap of the 1957 convertible race
at the Daytona Beach (FL) road/beach course. - Len Ashburn photo. / (bottom)
Dick LaHaie smokes the tires in his slingshot dragster. - Dick LaHaie collection
(courtesy of the Michigan Motor Sports Hall of Fame).

History of

AMERICA'S SPEEDWAYS

Past & Present

compiled, edited, and published by:
Allan E. Brown

associate editors:
Wilson Davis
Nancy Brown
Pam Smith

cover advisor:
Larry J. Feist

DEDICATED TO THE DRIVERS WHO HAVE
THRILLED AUTO RACING FANS
THE PAST CENTURY

Special thanks to: David Allio; Len Ashburn; Mike Bell; Bruce Craig; Wilson Davis; Tom DeVette; Larry Feist; Greg Fielden; Dave Franks; Christian Genest; Halifax County Historic Society; Phil Harms; Len Heyden; Robert G. Hunter; Alden Jamison; Dick Jordon; Stan Kalwasinski; Keith and Kathryn Knaack (I.M.C.A.); Don Knouse; Marty Little; Michigan Motor Sports Hall of Fame; John Mahoney; Don Radbruch; Rolland Rickard; R.A. Silvia; Bill and Susie Seith; Bob Sheldon; Bob Stoltz; Guy and Pam Smith; Norm Wagner; Crocky Wright; and the auto racing facilities that supplied us with photos from their tracks.

The USAC Silver Crown cars during the annual "Hoosier 100" at the Indiana State Fairgrounds. The cars are direct decedents of the early auto racing machines. Their basic shape can be traced as far back as 1906. Dirt track racing is one of the most popular forms of motor sports. This one-mile track is the oldest active track in the world as its first race was held on June 19, 1903. - John Mahoney photo (Len Ashburn collection).

FOREWORD

By Stew Reamer
(Founder, *Racing Promotion Monthly*
and the *RPM Promoters Workshops*,
consultant to motorsports management)

Since the turn of the century, Americans have had a love affair with two things: automobiles and sports. Combine them and you have the ultimate attraction--one so compelling that it has remained among the top three U.S. spectator sports for more than five decades, a feat accomplished largely without the gratuitous subsidization lavished upon stick and ball sports by the public media.

The largest single-day sporting event in the world is the Indianapolis 500, and in more than ten states, auto racing has produced the largest sports crowds ever assembled there. Racing's success today is an incredible bootstraps effort, its growth and success now forcing recognition. It is a beautiful sport, with rich history, and atmosphere that dazzles the senses: filled with color, sights and sounds that are present nowhere else in sports. Indeed, it is said, "There is only one sport--the rest are merely games."

Racing is also a truly unique sport; baseball, football and basketball have major leagues, where most of their attendance is counted, and minor or college leagues, with relatively small attendance. Racing is the exact opposite--an "upside down" sport. Its major-track events (Indianapolis, Daytona, Charlotte, etc.) account for only 20% of the sport's annual attendance, while 80% or more is counted at the 1000 or so weekly-schedule "grass roots" tracks across America--the tracks whose history is captured so completely and carefully in this book.

No one knows who sold the first ticket to an auto race, nor can they agree where it was held. Like the followers of other sports, we look to the historians to trace and reveal the roots of racing. Allan Brown's thorough and remarkable research marks him as one of racing's important historians. His *History of America's Speedways* publications are, and will remain, the definitive reference for those who seek to chronicle our sport. Serious racing scholars or curious fans are all in his debt.

ACKNOWLEDGEMENTS

David Allio; George Anderson; Glen Anderson; Randall Anderson; Cora Arkkelin; Len Ashburn; Mike Bandl; Henry Banks; Gene Banning; Bob Barkhimer; Dick Beebe; Mike Bell; Randy Bennett; Jack Biddison; Mike Bird; Ed Bloom; Chris Boals; Al Bochman; Larry Boos; Donna Braga; Junior Braga; Jean Brennfoerder; Frank Brennfoerder; K.C. Breslauer; Bob Brooks; Wayne Brooks; Terry Brotherton; Adrian Brown; Lawrence & Bethel Brown; Frank A. Buhrman; Eldon Butcher; Bob Byrne; Lloyd Campbell; Frank Canale; Bob Carey; Bruce Carley; Jim Carmichael; Emmett Carpenter; Duane Carter, Sr.; Denis Castelle; Joe Cawley; Walt Chernokal; Ed Chervenock; Greg Clemens; Jim Cleveland; Jon H. Clifton; Kenneth Clifton; Lance Childress; Tom Clutters; Ken Coles; John Colvin; Duke Cook; Hazel (Bell) Cotton; Bruce Craig; Art Cross; Gary Cross; Tom Curley; Jesse Cunningham; Wilson Davis; Tom DeVette; Gerald Dixon; Jack A. Donahey; Stewart Doty; Elmer Duellman; Phil Dullinger; Jim Dunham; Bob Echo; Chris Economaki; Don Edmonds; Dennis Elia; George England; Rod Eschenburg; Bill Evans; Ross Ferguson; Greg Fielden; D.A. Fischer; Dr. David Floyd; Terry Ford; Chuck Frame; Jim Franklin; Jamie Franklin; Dave Franks; Chris Funk; Andy Fusco; Ron Garske; Steve Geitgey; Christian Genest; David Gilmore; Gary Gore: John Grady; Don Grassman; Dick Greene; John Grivins; Robert Haase; C. Ray Hall; Jaxon Hammond; Bill Haglund; Phil Harms; Len Heyden; Bill Hill; Ray Hill; Hooker Hood; P.J. Hollebrand; Roscoe "Pappy" Hough; Deke Houlgate; Jim Howe; E.S. Hunter; Robert Hunter; Scott Huyett; Jack Ingram; Daryl Jacob; Gary Jacob; Alden Jamison; Larry Jendras, Jr.; Dick Johnson; Mike & Sue Johnson; Harvey Jones; Jeff Jones; Dick Jordan; Stan Kalwasinski; John Kelly; Wayne Kindness; Bob Kingen; Jerry Kinney; George Koyt; Keith & Kathryn Knaack; Ted Knorr; Al Krause; Don Knouse; Armin Krueger; John A. Lacko; Bill Ladabouche; C.J.Landry; Tommy Lane; Kenneth Larson; Robert Lawrence; Gardiner Leavitt; Dick Lee; Pete Leikam; Robert Leonard; Ernie Lethbridge; Bob Lewis; Don Lieberum; Gary Lindahl; Bill Lipkey; Marty Little; Christopher Long; George Long; Bud Lunsford; Terry Lynch; Bob Mace; Harry Macy; John Mahoney; Ken Marksman; Lyle Marsh; Tony Martin; Jimmy Mathis; Bob Mays; Lucky Mays; Don McAuley; Shirley McElreath; John McKarns; Nate Mecha; Bob Memmers; "Broadway Bob" Metzler; Len Milde; Bud Miller; Shorty Miller; Steve Mitchell; Charlie Mize; John D. Moore; Larry Moore; Bill Morris; Duke Nalon; Wayne Niedeken; Dick O'Brien; Bill Ogle; Bruce Ogle; Frank Opalka; L.D. Ottinger; Tony Palumbo; Al Paradise; Wally Parks; Andy Phillips; Lynn Phillips; Jack Poehler; Paul Plumber; Ron Plumlee; John Potts; John Printz; John Quinn; Don Radbruch; Jim Raper; Stew Reamer; Terry Reed; Thomas Reel; Bill Reser; Johnny Rice; Rolland Rickard; Charlie Roberts; Jimmy Roberts; Eddie Roche; Ray Rogers; Robert Rowan; Johnny Rogers; Slim Rutherford; Roger Rubino; Tom Saal; Tom Savage; Paul Sawyer; Al Scott; Paul Shaffer; Tom Schmeh; Gary Schmelzer; Gordon Schroeder; Mick Schuler; Gary Scott; Rick Schneider; Bill & Susie Seith; Mike Shaw; Bob Sheldon; Johnny Shipman; R.A. Silvia; Al Singer; Andy Sivi; Albert Smith; Grassy Smith; Guy & Pam Smith; Deb Snyder; John Snyder; Art Sparks; Dan Spence; Steve Stamper; Paul Starta; Richard Stafani; Jerry Stephens; Ottis Stine; Paul Stogsdill; Bob Stolze; Steve Stubbs; Jim Sullivan; Larry Sullivan; Al Tasnady; Jim Thurman; Dick Trickle; Pete Van Iderstine; Dan VanKoevering; Gary Vercauteren; Bill Vukovich, Jr.; Norm Wagner; Lyle West; Ed White; Gordon White; Ed Williams; Steve Williams; Wally Williams; Gordy Wilson; Bob Wilson; Dave Wilson; James Wilson; Tom Wilson; Kenneth Dale Wood; Bryce Woodward; Jim Woodward; Crocky Wright; John Wyckoff; Larry Yard; Grant Young.

CONTENTS

UNITED STATES TRACKS

CANADIAN TRACKS

PREFACE

There are four major spectator sports in America. They are football, baseball, basketball, and auto racing. The most exciting of these is auto racing. Auto racing is the general term used for the different types of racing and classes of cars. In fact, there is so much variety that it often becomes confusing.

Each year 50 million fans pass through the turnstiles of the 1300 auto racing facilities in operation. Auto racing is truly a unique sport, as there isn't another sport that is as intriguing or offers as much common fellowship among competitors and their fans.

The history of major auto racing was been expertly cataloged in excellent books like Albert R. Bochroch's book, *American Automobile Racing, An Illustrated History;* Greg Fielden's series of books on the NASCAR Winston Cup trail entitled *Forty Years of Stock Car Racing;* Dick Wallen's *BOARD TRACK, Guts, Gold & Glory* covering the famous board track era; and Robert C. Post's *High Performance,* detailing the roots of drag racing. All are fantastic reference sources and should be on the must-read list for every auto racing enthusiast.

This book covers over 5500 oval tracks, 500 road courses, and 700 drag strips that have been in operation at one time or another. Eighty percent of racing is on the semi-pro or amateur level. This book is saturated with information on that type of racing.

There were a number of reasons why this project was started. Researching the history of the weekly tracks can be extremely difficult. Most history books on auto racing are written on major events, a specific driver, a certain track, or a specific type of racing. Public libraries offer little help for the sports enthusiast trying to understand the perplexing world of auto racing. Hopefully this book will touch some of the interesting aspects of the sport by showing brief histories of the various tracks. The photos from the different eras will pictorially show how auto racing has progressed over the years.

Early auto racing history (other than major events) is pretty sketchy, and researching the various tracks is time consuming. With the help of many people who allowed us to go through their private collections of scrap books and photos, this publication was possible. A sincere thank you to everyone who has helped. Special thanks should go to Wilson Davis, who diligently provided many of the exact dates listed in the book. He has been working on cataloging feature winners for a number of years. The goal is to someday make this information available to all historians to help in their research. Other people who have helped tremendously include Mike Bell, Robert Hunter, and Norm Wagner. Each has researched the tracks in a number of states or provinces, and has shared his findings with us. Other fans like Don Knouse of South Dakota are researching the races in their home state. Racing enthusiasts all across the continent have helped with the research by sending updates from our previous book published in 1984.

The majority of the information was researched through the various auto racing tabloids. The earliest publications devoted to short track racing were in the early 1930's. Major events after the turn of the century were sometimes detailed in a number of publications. Finding information on the various dirt tracks after the turn of the century becomes increasingly difficult as many of the competitors in that era are deceased.

The golden era of auto racing cannot be defined by certain years. Each auto racing period was a golden era; from the barnstorming episodes of Barney Oldfield, which brought auto racing to the populous; to the famous board track era, which brought about great strides in racing car development; to the exciting dirt track era of the 1920's and 1930's; and to the jalopy and stock car days of the early 1950's. To many fans, the golden era is the first time they were introduced to auto racing. Today's auto racing spectators are fortunate to have the opportunities to witness a variety of racing throughout the continent.

The intent of this book is not to elaborate on the careers of the various drivers, but to chronicle the history of the various tracks and the different types of racing over the years. Our first edition of this book listed 4600 tracks. This edition lists over 6400 tracks, and includes dragstrips (which were not listed in the first edition). No one really knows how many tracks have been in existence, but we believe we have a pretty good handle on the current tracks.

The number of tracks varies from decade to decade. You will find a break down of the different states and the different era in statistics on page x. We were able to confirm the common belief that there were over 2000 tracks in 1950's. Surprisingly, we found that the life expectancy of most of the tracks from that era was very short as many were very primitive facilities. Most of the tracks that currently operate have been in operation for an average of 15 years or more. The largest number of the tracks are dirt tracks. Each year about forty new tracks are built, and most of them are dirt tracks. The others are dragstrips or paved ovals. Very few permanent road courses have been built in the past dozen years. They could be counted on one hand. There have been close to 1250 race tracks located at either a state or county fairgrounds.

In this book you will find articles on some of the different types of race tracks and race cars. Included is an article on the famous board tracks. These articles tell a brief history of the different types of racing and the different types of race tracks each type utilized.

A few notes on reading the information in the book might be helpful. The tracks listed in bolder print are the active tracks at the time of publication. The small "c." before a date or year stands for circa. That means the track may have run before or after that date listed. Occasionally, Wilson Davis would confirm a track ran on a certain date, but the article he read implied that racing was held before that date as well. Finding the date of a track's last races becomes more difficult as very few tracks issue press releases letting the racing fraternity know of its demise.

It is interesting to read about history, and to research it is doubly satisfying. We certainly hope you enjoy reading and referring back to this book as much as we have enjoyed producing it. - the Editor.

TRACK SURVEY

<u>UNITED STATES TRACKS</u>

overall (active)	Ovals	Drags	Road Courses
ALABAMA	85 (24)	25 (19)	7 (1)
ALASKA	14 (4)	4 (2)	1
ARIZONA	47 (11)	10 (2)	9 (2)
ARKANSAS	74 (19)	9 (4)	3
CALIFORNIA	330 (51)	60 (11)	79 (7)
COLORADO	70 (10)	11 (4)	12 (5)
CONNECTICUT	31 (4)	3	3 (1)
DELAWARE	31 (6)	2 (1)	–
DISTRICT OF COLUMBIA	5	–	–
FLORIDA	133 (27)	35 (10)	32 (4)
GEORGIA	133 (25)	31 (11)	14 (3)
HAWAII	10 (1)	4 (4)	3 (1)
IDAHO	26 (8)	4 (2)	1
ILLINOIS	266 (36)	19 (6)	12 (2)
INDIANA	232 (50)	13 (10)	7 (2)
IOWA	165 (42)	7 (3)	3 (1)
KANSAS	125 (28)	13 (6)	14 (1)
KENTUCKY	109 (25)	13 (8)	1
LOUISIANA	42 (10)	14 (3)	6
MAINE	29 (6)	3 (2)	–
MARYLAND	44 (4)	7 (5)	4
MASSACHUSETTS	52 (3)	3	7
MICHIGAN	188 (28)	17 (7)	13 (3)
MINNESOTA	121 (40)	5 (3)	4 (1)
MISSISSIPPI	54 (15)	12 (7)	1 (1)
MISSOURI	162 (26)	15 (8)	5
MONTANA	35 (7)	7 (2)	–
NEBRASKA	96 (19)	8 (2)	1
NEVADA	31 (9)	7 (3)	7 (1)
NEW HAMPSHIRE	39 (13)	2 (1)	5
NEW JERSEY	70 (4)	14 (3)	4
NEW MEXICO	36 (9)	9 (5)	4
NEW YORK	314 (37)	26 (6)	27 (2)
NORTH CAROLINA	157 (33)	26 (17)	4 (1)
NORTH DAKOTA	35 (15)	–	1
OHIO	270 (34)	24 (13)	8 (3)
OKLAHOMA	93 (22)	15 (4)	8 (2)
OREGON	65 (13)	12 (6)	5 (1)
PENNSYLVANIA	310 (53)	21 (8)	9 (1)
RHODE ISLAND	13	2	–
SOUTH CAROLINA	85 (20)	18 (7)	4
SOUTH DAKOTA	69 (15)	5 (3)	–
TENNESSEE	109 (27)	19 (15)	4 (1)
TEXAS	232 (36)	51 (17)	34 (7)
UTAH	13 (4)	4 (3)	2
VERMONT	26 (3)	–	–
VIRGINIA	77 (20)	16 (10)	2
WASHINGTON	116 (18)	11 (4)	11 (1)
WEST VIRGINIA	56 (9)	7 (4)	1 (1)
WISCONSIN	136 (37)	5 (3)	9 (1)
WYOMING	21 (6)	4 (1)	–
U.S. totals	5082 (966)	652 (275)	391 (57)

CANADIAN TRACKS

overall (active)	Ovals	Drags	Road Courses
ALBERTA	44 (9)	7 (3)	5 (2)
BRITISH COLUMBIA	62 (17)	15 (4)	6 (2)
MANITOBA	21 (6)	2 (1)	2 (1)
NEW BRUNSWICK	13 (7)	2 (1)	2
NEWFOUNDLAND	1	1	2
NOVA SCOTIA	20 (4)	2 (1)	3 (2)
ONTARIO	121 (21)	7 (3)	9 (3)
PRINCE EDWARD ISLAND	4 (1)	1 (1)	–
QUEBEC	105 (21)	13 (7)	13 (7)
SASKATCHEWAN	40 (11)	3 (1)	2
YUKON	3	–	–
Canadian Totals	434 (97)	53 (22)	44 (17)
Overall	5516 (1063)	705 (297)	435 (74)

UNITED STATES TRACKS BY DECADES

	Ovals	Dragstrips	Road Courses
1895 - 1898	8	–	3
1900 - 1909	91	–	19
1910 - 1919	274	–	27
1920 - 1929	542	–	4
1930 - 1939	1147	–	20
1940 - 1949	1245	3	14
1950 - 1959	2011	171	163
1960 - 1969	1421	367	143
1970 - 1979	1309	343	76
1980 - 1989	1269	305	92
1990 - 1994	1073	290	77

CANADIAN TRACKS BY DECADES

	Ovals	Dragstrips	Road Courses
1895 - 1898	–	–	–
1900 - 1909	3	–	–
1910 - 1919	14	–	–
1920 - 1929	16	–	–
1930 - 1939	23	–	–
1940 - 1949	29	–	–
1950 - 1959	112	3	7
1960 - 1969	168	24	14
1970 - 1979	144	26	23
1980 - 1989	159	29	22
1990 - 1994	117	26	21

ROAD RACING

Auto racing is a diverse sport with many aspects making up the sport in its entirety. There are basically three types of auto racing tracks. Road courses... which requires turning left and right during an event. Oval tracks...which generally means each driver will be constantly turning left forming a circle. The third type is dragstrips...which are straight, and the object is to go from a dead stop to as fast as possible in the required distance, which is usually one-quarter or one-eighth mile in length.

Road racing is the oldest form of auto racing in the world. These events consist of races in which the contestants have to turn both left and right during the event. These races can either be point-to-point races or share a joint start/finish line (known as closed circuits). The first contests for gasoline powered automobiles were point-to-point events held on European country roads.

What is generally considered the first organized race was held on country roads in France. Twenty-one automobiles started the Paris to Rouen reliability run on July 22, 1894. Surprisingly, 17 cars finished the 78.75 mile contest. The second European race was the Paris to Bordeaux event on June 11, 1895. In the early years of motor sports in Europe, the most prestigious events were the "Gordon Bennett Cup", which was sponsored by James Gordon Bennett, an American newspaper publisher, who was living in France. The concept of his annual races was that the winning driver's country would be next year's event site. The "Bennett Cup" races were held from 1900 to 1905. The first major closed circuit race was the Circuit des Ardennes in France in 1902 after the French government outlawed point-to-point races as being too dangerous.

In America, an endurance event was held in 1878; it could hardly be counted as a race, but rather a challenge. The State of Wisconsin in 1875 offered $10,000 for the first person to travel from Green Bay to Madison in a horseless carriage and still maintain an average speed of at least four miles an hour over the 210 mile distance. It wasn't until three years later that the money was collected when two competitors in steam-powered carriages went the distance in July of 1878. Steam automobiles had been in existence for over 70 years in America and many of them held speed records from time to time. The first mention of a steam car in America was in Philadelphia in 1805. The most famous of the American steamer cars were built by twins, Francis and Freelan Stanley. In France George Bouton won an endurance event that was held in 1887 in a steam car. The event went from Paris to Versaille and then back to Paris. Steam cars had come a long way from the time that Isaac Newton predicted in 1680 that a jet-propelled carriage would be powered by steam. Steam-powered vehicles go back as far as 1789 when Nicolas Cugnot built a steam-driven tri-cycle tractor for military purposes. His original hand-hammered copper boiler proved clumsy, and the entire car was too expensive to be practical.

AMERICA'S FIRST RACE

The first organized automobile race in North America was scheduled for November 2, 1895 in Chicago by H.H. Kohlsaat, who owned the *Chicago Times-Herald*. Nearly 100 entries were received, but only a few were ready. The actual event had to be postponed until Thanksgiving Day on the 28th, so an exhibition event was held on the original date between Charles Mueller in his father's Mueller-Benz and J. Frank Duryea in the car that he and his brother Charles had built. The Benz was one of the first gasoline powered automobiles. German Karl Benz' built his first automobile in 1888. Duryea built the first gasoline powered automobile in America in 1893. The exhibition run started at Halstad and 55th Street and headed north to Waukegan and then back to Chicago. Mueller was the only finisher of the 92 mile exhibition race and he was presented $500 for his efforts. He averaged about 10 miles per hour. The Duryea entry was forced off the road by a farm wagon.

CHICAGO-ELGIN-CHICAGO

Bad weather greeted the participants for the Thanksgiving Day Motocycle race. The name Motocycle was used by the *Times-Herald* after a contest was held to find a better name than horseless carriage. A twelve-inch snowstorm had left the roads nearly impassible, but America's first actual automobile race, known as the "Chicago Times-Herald Contest", went off as rescheduled. There were six contestants, two of the starting field were electric cars, and each left at different intervals with J. Frank Duryea being the first to leave. The second contestant ran into trouble within minutes as he skidded into the back of a streetcar and then crashed into a sleigh. A late arriving Charles Mueller didn't leave the starting line until an hour and eleven minutes had transpired since Duryea had left. Duryea was the first to complete the 54 mile run from Chicago to Elgin and back to Chicago. He did so in seven hours and fifty-three minutes in running time. Mueller was the only other finisher and he crossed the finish line a mere 24 minutes behind Duryea, but because he had started an hour late the honors went to Duryea. Duryea was awarded $2,000 for his win.

Alexander Winton in his car, nicknamed the "Bullet", on the sands of Ormond Beach (FL). He was one of the nations foremost innovators in the development of the automobile. - Photo courtesy of the Halifax County Historical Society.

OTHER EARLY CONTESTS

The point-to-point races were fast becoming popular in America. The next American race was held in New York City on May 30, 1896. The race was sponsored by the *Cosmopolitan Magazine* and consisted of starting at Kingsbridge City Hall in the Bronx and ending at Irvington-on-Hudson some 30 miles farther up along the Hudson River. Duryea showed that he had the superior car as he covered the distance in seven hours and thirteen minutes. He won $3,000 this time. In 1897, Alex Winton went from Cleveland, Ohio to New York City in ten days. Two years later he lowered that to 47 hours and 37 minutes, cutting over eight days off his initial run. In 1903 the first transcontinental crossing was made by an automobile when H. Nelson Jackson and Sewell Crocker took 64 days to go from San Francisco to New York City.

In 1900, a 50 mile race on Long Island, NY was held from Springfield to Babylon and back to Springfield. A.L. Riker in an electric car won that race at an average speed of 24 miles per hour.

Probably one of the most bizarre auto racing contests was the New York to Paris race in 1908. Six cars started this remarkable event that went from New York to Seattle and then the cars were to be loaded on a boat for the ride to Valdez, Alaska. From Valdez the cars were to be driven over frozen rivers to the Bering Seas and then over the frozen Seas to Siberia and then on east across the Asia continent until reaching Europe and the final destination of Paris. The race started on February 12, 1908 (during the winter so crossing the Bering Seas was possible), and the American entrants Monty Roberts and George Schuster in a Thomas Flyer took the early lead. Linn Nathewson replaced Roberts near Salt Lake City, and the Americans made it to San Francisco in 41 days. But upon arriving in Alaska it was learned the initial route was impassible as snow was so deep it would have been impossible to even try. So the car was loaded back on a boat and sent back to Seattle, where they boarded another boat, this one heading to Japan. The boat docked in Japan, and after a drive across Japan a boat ride to Siberia awaited the American drivers. When the Thomas Flyer drivers arrived in Asia, the only other competitors still running in the race were the two German Protos. The Protos had arrived at Vladivostok in Russia before the Thomas Flyer, but they had been assessed a penalty for shipping their car via rail from Salt Lake City to Seattle, while the Thomas crew, because they were the only ones to take the boat ride to Alaska, were given a bonus. The combination of this bonus and the Protos penalty was enough for the Thomas Flyer to win the race by 16 days even though the Protos actually arrived in Paris four days earlier. The drivers of the Thomas Flyer had completed 13,341 miles in 161 days.

HILL CLIMBS

Another type of challenge for automobiles are hill climbs. The first recorded hill climb was up Mount Washington in New Hampshire on August 30, 1899. The eight-mile "Climb to the Clouds" was won by Freelan O. Stanley in one of the Stanley Steamers.

The most famous hill climb is by far the Pikes Peak Hill Climb in Colorado which was first held in 1916. This 12.42 mile event starts near the base of Pikes Peak at an elevation of 9,400 feet and races up 156 turns on the gravel road to the top of Pikes Peak, which has an elevation of 14,100 feet. The Unser clan from Albuquerque, NM are the undisputed "Kings of the Hill" winning countless times. Wins have been recorded by the Unser brothers Jerry, Bobby and Al and their children Al, Jr. and Robby on this famous mountain.

VANDERBILT CUPS & AMERICAN GRAND PRIZES

The first really important road racing events in America were the prestigious "Vanderbilt Cup" races. William K. Vanderbilt, Jr., the great-grandson of Commodore Vanderbilt, participated in a number of auto races and speed trials including a third place finish in the 1903 Ardennes race in France. In 1904 the 28-year-old Vanderbilt became the first person to unofficially exceed 100 miles per hour in an automobile as he did 102.85 miles per hour at Ormond Beach, Florida.

In January of 1904, Vanderbilt approached the American Automobile Association (AAA) with sponsorship of the America's first International races. The first "Vanderbilt Cup" race was held on October 8, 1904. The course consisted of 30 miles of country roads on Long Island. George Heath in a Panhard was the winner at an average speed of 54.2 miles per hour in the 284.4 mile event. A crowd estimated at 200,000 people viewed the event from points along the way. The "Vanderbilt Cup" races were held on a modified Long Island course in 1905 and 1906. The crowd had grown to over an estimated 300,000 in 1906. It had become obvious that the races were far too dangerous and the lack of crowd control of spectators who were lining the edge of the track forced the race to be cancelled in 1907. In 1908 the event was moved to a special closed course circuit, called the Long Island Motor Parkway. The track was a newly built tollway and the event went off much better than the ones in the past as the crowd was able to be contained to some extent. George Robertson in a Locomobile won the 1908 race. Harry Grant in an ALCO won both the 1909 and 1910 races at the Motor Parkway, but again, an unruly crowd became a major factor as the race was moved the next year to Savannah, Georgia.

Savannah had held another major race called the "American Grand Prize" in 1908 and many people considered it better than the "Cups". When Savannah hosted the first "Grand Prize" the track was 25.13 miles in length and Louis Wagner won the 400 mile race in a Fiat. The event wasn't held in 1909, but was

Ralph Mulford winning the 1911 "Vanderbilt Cup" ran in Savannah (GA) in a Lozier. - Allan E. Brown collection.

revived in 1910 with David Bruce-Brown winning this time on a 17.3 mile course. In 1911 the "Vanderbilt Cup" race was won by Ralph Mulford in a Lozier on November 27, 1911. Three days later the "American Grand Prize" was held on the Savannah course, and once again David Bruce-Brown was victorious.

The "Grand Prize" was moved to a suburb of Milwaukee in 1912 and Caleb Bragg won the prestigious 410 mile race in Wauwatosa. Defending champion David Bruce-Brown was fatally injured in a crash during practice. Neither race was held in 1913, but both races were resurrected the following year, this time at Santa Monica, California. The following year the races were moved upstate and were held at the Panama-Pacific Exposition in San Francisco. Dario Resta in a Peugeot became the first driver to win both races in the same year. The two races returned to Santa Monica in 1917 with Resta winning the "Cup" again and Howdy Wilcox claiming the longer distanced "Grand Prize". With America and Europe entering into World War I, major road racing events came to an end in America and didn't resurface for nearly ten years.

Just after the turn of the century, other road racing events were held at Bakersfield, CA (1911 - 1915), Fresno, CA (1912 - 1916), Glendale, CA (1914 and 1915), Oakland, CA (1906 - 1910), Ontario, CA (1919), San Diego, CA (1913 - 1916), Venice, CA (1910 - 1916), Visalia, CA (1914 - 1917), Denver, CO (1909), Ormond Beach, FL (seven turn road course on the beach in 1907), Elgin, IL (1910 - 1920), Crown Point, IN (1909), Dodge City, KS (1912 and 1913), Lowell, MA (1907 - 1909), Three Rivers, MI (1910 and 1911), Longport, NJ (1905), Briarcliff Manor, NY (1908), Bridgehampton, NY (1915 - 1920), Morris Park, NY (1907), Riverhead, NY (1909), Springfield Gardens, NY (1900), Cincinnati, OH (1911), Oklahoma City, OK (1915), Medford, OR (1911), Portland, OR (1909), Fairmont Park, PA (1908 - 1911), Sumter, SC (1904), Dallas, TX (1909), and Tacoma, WA (1912 and 1913).

The starting grid for the 1937 "Vanderbilt Trophy Race" at Roosevelt Field on Long Island, New York. The German-built rear-engined Auto Unions that won the race are in the middle of the first and third row. - Bruce Craig collection.

Although road racing picked back up in Europe after the first World War, it wasn't until 1936 that the Vanderbilt races were revived. This time a specially built four-mile course was constructed at Roosevelt Field in Mineola, New York. Two major races called "Vanderbilt Trophy" races were held. Both races were dominated by Europeans their superior handling road racing cars.

Only a few road races were held during the 1920's and 1930's in America. Probably the most significant were events held in 1934 at the Sleepy Hollow Ring in Pocantico Hills, New York. These races were sanctioned by the Automobile Racing Club of America (ARCA). Some people consider this sanction the predecessor to the present day Sports Car Club of America (SCCA).

Other 1930's sports car races were held at Elgin, Illinois in 1932 and 1933, and at Long Beach, California in 1938. An unique road race was held during the 1940 New York's Worlds Fair. A three-quarter mile road course running through the Fair complex held sports car races on October 10.

SPORTS CAR CLUB OF AMERICA IS BORN

True sports cars, although very popular and plentiful in Europe, were very rare in North America until after World War II. It is said that many of our servicemen became infatuated with the sleek sports cars while on duty on the European front, and many of the small cars were imported back to America.

SCCA was incorporated on February 26, 1944 by seven sports car enthusiasts in Boston. Ted Robertson is considered SCCA's founder. One of the key players in the early years of SCCA was Miles Collier. SCCA held their first official sports car race on town roads in Watkins Glen, New York on October 2, 1948. Prior to this first SCCA race, any contest they had held was only of a rally nature. The new club continued to grow, but racing on city streets had the same problems that beset their ancestors a half-century before, mainly safety and crowd control.

The club raced on the city streets of Watkins Glen until 1952, but after a few serious accidents it became obvious that the racing was too dangerous for the spectators who were crowding too close to the circuit. So the annual race was moved to country roads near the town of Dix, and the races were held there from 1953 to 1955. Other early SCCA races were held at Broward Speedway, Florida (1949), Pebble Beach, California (1950 - 1956), Elkhart Lake, Wisconsin on country roads from 1950 - 1952, and Palm Beach Shores in Florida (1950 and 1951). Thompson Speedway in Connecticut added a road course utilizing part of its paved oval track in 1952.

The worst auto racing catastrophe in the world occurred on the sports car track at LeMans, France in 1955. Pierre Levegh crashed into a grandstand on lap 42 of the 24 hour race. His car exploded and he and 89 spectators were killed.

AIRPORTS AND ABANDONED AIR BASES

With safety a major concern, a suitable alternative for crowd control was available by using airport runways. The first road course that utilized airport runways was Mines Field in California. The airport allowed road racing to take place on some of their runways from 1932 until 1935. After 1945 there were many abandoned airfields that could be easily adapted to road courses. One of them was in Sebring, Florida. This former air base had been a training base for British pilots during World War II. The first sports car race at Sebring was held on December 31, 1950. The course, laid out on the runways and taxiways, was

6

rather blase because of its flat terrain compared to the challenges of racing on city streets, but the safety aspects and crowd control were vast improvements. Sports car racing at Sebring is still going strong and the annual "Twelve Hours of Sebring" is held there each spring. With more and more of these abandoned air bases becoming available, sports car racing flourished.

THE SAC AIR BASES

Air Force General Curtis LeMay approached SCCA president Fred Wacker and proposed holding SCCA races on Strategic Air Command (SAC) bases. LeMay, a sports car buff who owned an Allard, took the money he cleared from the races (reported one million dollars) and invested it back into recreational facilities for the enlisted men. One of the first sports car races on a SAC base was at Turner Air Force Base in Albany, Georgia on October 26, 1952. For the next three years SCCA enjoyed its relationship with LeMay, and the availability of SAC bases gave the sport much needed exposure. About 20 different SAC air bases held sports car events between 1952 and 1954. President Dwight D. Eisenhower presented the "President Cup" trophy at a race at Andrews Air Force Base. The SAC races were suspended when suspicions and congressional scrutiny unjustly accused LeMay of wrong-doing. He was later cleared of all charges.

Jim Kimberly in a 1988 cc Maserati at Sebring (FL) in the late 1950's. Kimberly was one of SCCA's early stars. - Len Ashburn photo.

PERMANENT ROAD COURSES

With the renewed interest in road racing came the first permanent road courses. These courses were built to simulate racing on country roads and were explicitly built for true road racing. The courses were also designed so crowd control could be closely monitored. One of the first permanent road courses built was Wilmot Hills near Milwaukee. It opened on May 26, 1953. It closed in 1965. Willow Springs in California opened on November 22, 1953. Road America in Elkhart Lake, Wisconsin became the next permanent road course in 1955. Watkins Glen received a permanent road course in 1956. In 1957 five major road courses were built. They were constructed in Riverside, California; Lime Rock, Connecticut; Danville, Virginia; Bridgehampton, New York; and Monterey, California. A unique road course was built in the infield of Daytona International Speedway in Florida. That sports car track, utilizing part of the high banked oval track, opened on April 5, 1959 and is the home of an annual 24 hour race. New courses were built in Portland and Seattle in 1960. Mid-Ohio was constructed in 1964. Sears Point, California and Brainerd, Minnesota opened in 1968. Road Atlanta, Georgia was new in 1970. Ontario, California was built the following year. The building of new permanent road courses stopped for a number of years. The construction of Heartland Park in 1989 was the first new major permanent road course to be built in a number of years. The newest permanent road course is Thunderhill Park, California. Thunderhill, which opened in 1993, is unusual as it was financed by contributions from club members.

SCCA GOES PROFESSIONAL

SCCA continues today as the leader in sanctioning amateur sports car racing in America. It should be noted that prior to 1961, all SCCA races were considered amateur events and the competitors were hobbyists who competed only for trophies. SCCA added a new dimension to the sport when they reintroduced professional sports car racing to the continent in 1962. The Can-Am series evolved from the United State Road Racing Championship (SCCA's first professional venture). The series used the unlimited Group 7 cars, and it became very popular with many foreign stars who competed in the series. American drivers such as Dan Gurney, Jim Hall, and Mark Donohue joined foreign drivers John Surtees, Denis Hulme and Bruce McLaren and emerged as heroes in these fleet high-powered sports cars. Surtees was the first Can-Am champion in 1966. The Can-Am series flourished for a number of years, but the series came to an abrupt halt in 1974 when fuel restrictions forced a number of tracks to cancel their Can-Am races. The energy crisis that year made for a tough year on auto racing in general. The once popular series was revived a few years later but folded again in 1986.

Jim Hall (#66) and Dan Gurney (#36) at Laguna Seca Raceway (CA). Hall's winged "Chaparrals" were some of the fastest cars in the mid 1960's. Both Gurney and Hall ran these cars in SCCA Can-Am events. - John A. Lacko photo

SCCA also sanctioned an open-wheeled, single seat division known as Formula 5000. The cars were allowed up to 5000 cubic centimeter motors (five liter) and most competitors chose U.S. built V-8 as their choice of powerplants. The series was first called the SCCA Grand Prix Championship when it began in 1967. In 1969 it was billed as the Continental Championship, but it was discontinued in 1976. The oldest SCCA professional series is the Trans-Am Tour. This circuit started in 1966. The current Trans-Am vehicles consisted of compact cars such as Ford Mustangs, Chevrolet Camaros, Dodge Daytonas, etc. Horst Kwech and Gaston Andrey in Alfa GTA's were co-champions in 1966. Other Trans-Am champions over the years include Mark Donohue (the series' only four-time champion), Parnelli Jones, Peter Gregg, Bob Tullius, David Hobbs, Wally Dallenbach, Jr., Scott Sharp, and Jack Baldwin. The first foreign cars were allowed on the Trans-Am tour in 1976.

A classic Ford against Chevy match-up. The Mustang (#15), driven by Parnelli Jones, and a Camaro (#25), driven by Lloyd Ruby, at Daytona International Speedway (FL) in a Trans-Am race. Jones and Ruby, both "Indianapolis 500" veterans, were frequent campaigners in the early years of the SCCA sanctioned Trans-Am series. - Tony Martin photo

SCCA continues to sanction amateur events as well, and the classes of race cars are broken down into different categories. Some of the current professional and amateur classes include GT1, GT2, GT3, GT4, GT5, E,F,G, and H Production, C & D Sports Racing, Sports 2000, SCCA Spec Racer, Spec Racer Ford, Shelby Can-Am, Formula Atlantic, Formula Continental, Formula Ford, Formula Vee, Formula 440, Showroom Stock GT and Showroom Stock.

SCCA versus IMSA

SCCA isn't the only professional sports car circuit in America. The International Motor Sports Association (IMSA) was formed in 1969 by John Bishop, a former SCCA official. His first concern was to enhance professional sports car racing and IMSA soon became a major sanctioning body for endurance races held in North America, including the annual races at Sebring and Daytona. IMSA does not sanction amateur events and is only concerned with the professional aspect of sports car racing. Currently IMSA runs a number of professional series for a variety of sport car classes. They include the World Sports Cars, Fire Hawk, Supreme and Supercar Series.

The city street road course in Columbus (OH) on Oct. 19, 1985. The Ford Probe IMSA GT (#7) driven by Klaus Ludwig and Doc Bundy lead the cars down Front Street, during the "Columbus Ford Dealers 500." - David Allio photo

TEMPORARY ROAD CIRCUITS

The newest craze in road course construction is the building of temporary circuits. Some of them were built on active airports, while others were in parking lots and still other circuits ran through downtown city streets. Each of these courses are made to be constructed quickly and then disassembled just as fast to avoid disrupting normal aspects of the property. Temporary circuits are very costly to erect as the guard rails (usually cement blocks called "New Jersey Barriers") have to be put into place and fencing has to be erected to protect the spectators. Temporary grandstands are then set in place. After the event, the barriers and grandstands are disassembled and either stored or rented for other functions. Because of the enormous, expense very few temporary circuits last much more than a few years. The Phoenix Grand Prix in Arizona is a prime example. The track, which consisted of racing on downtown city streets, lasted only three years (1989 - 1991). The city never drew the large crowds it needed to financially support such an expensive endeavor. The first of these new temporary courses was the Grand Prix of Long Beach in southern California. The circuit, constructed in 1975 by utilizing portions of the Long Beach Expressway, is still used today. Next came the Caesar's Palace Grand Prix which ran from 1980 until 1984. The various circuits at Caesar's Palace in Las Vegas, Nevada were built in the parking lots of the famous gambling casino. One of the most unique major temporary circuits was the Meadowland Grand Prix Circuit in East Rutherford, New Jersey. The track was built in the parking lot of the Meadowlands Sports Complex (a NFL football stadium). Another of the oldest temporary circuits is the Cleveland Grand Prix which started in 1982. The circuit is constructed each year on the Burke Airport near downtown Cleveland, Ohio. Other temporary circuits included the Grand Prix du Mardi Gras on city streets in New Orleans, Louisiana (1991 and 1992), the St. Petersburg Grand Prix, which was also on city streets in that Florida city (1985 - 1990), and the Detroit Grand Prix. The first Detroit Grand Prix was held on city streets in downtown Detroit, Michigan in 1982. The race was then moved to park roads on an island in the Detroit River called Belle Isle for the 1992 race, where it has been held ever since.

OPEN WHEEL RACE CARS

Open wheel racing is the oldest form of oval track racing. In the early days, only one type of race car existed. They were open cockpit racers, but there were several classes. The 1902 French-built Panhard is considered to be the first true race car, and from its design evolved a shape and style of car that would later be called a sprint car. The distinction between classes were by engine displacement and overall weight. Smaller cars were placed in a class called lightweights and ran shorter preliminary events. The larger and faster cars were called big cars or championship cars and were used for the longer events. Because of the lightweight's smaller size and lesser weight they were better suited for the smaller tracks. In the late 1920's, a few tracks began running a class of race car called hobos or roadsters. These cars were cut-down passenger cars. In the mid 1930's smaller versions of the big cars, called midgets, were being raced on the West Coast. They quickly became the most popular type of car in oval track racing. By the early 1950's, the jalopy race cars replaced the midgets as the most popular, and when they were later altered for more speed, they were called modifieds. As car owners continued to chop and cut the modifieds down even more, they evolved into a type of race car called a supermodified. These supermodifieds became the main weekly attraction at many tracks across the country in the 1960's. Variations of the above classes have made open wheel racing one of the most diverse types of racing in America.

SPRINT CARS

Sprint car racing is truly an American sport. The modern sprint cars (called big cars until the 1950's) evolved over the years from the early Indy cars, the speedsters, the roadsters, and the supermodifieds.

At the turn of the century, major auto racing in this nation was primarily of the road racing nature, with only a few oval track events being held, and most of them were on large one mile horse tracks. Some confusion exists as a mile was the standard distance for harness race timing and the one mile tracks were known as a one lap track, and half mile tracks were known as two lap tracks. Many of these mile long tracks were located at state fairgrounds. We have discovered 29 horse tracks that held auto races in 1906. Twenty-four of them were one mile tracks, but by 1915, the majority of dirt track racing was done on smaller half-mile tracks.

Open wheel, oval track racing dates back about 100 years. The first oval track race was at the one mile long Narragansett Park in Cranston, Rhode Island on September 7, 1896. The oldest oval track that is still active in the United States is the Indiana State Fairgrounds in Indianapolis. It held its first race on June 19, 1903. The Wisconsin State Fairgrounds was only a few months behind, as its first auto race was on September 11, 1903. The oldest half-mile track that we have on record was Branford Park in New Haven, Connecticut. That horse track held its first auto race on July 25, 1899. The oldest half-mile track that is still active is the Iowa State Fairgrounds. The first auto race at the Des Moines oval was on August 14, 1907.

BARNEY OLDFIELD

Folklore has it that oval track racing received a shot in the arm on May 23, 1906 when Barney Oldfield, along with his manager Bill Pickens, promoted a 50 mile race at the Lexington Fairgrounds in Kentucky. Oldfield was well known for his barnstorming across the country in the O.L. Wilson designed Peerless Green Dragon. The prerace publicity for this event was outstanding, including Oldfield receiving a speeding ticket for racing through the neighboring town of Versailles on his way to Lexington. Even though there were no speed limits at that time, the judge still fined him $50 for "scorching through Woodford County." One of the articles in the *Lexington Herald* mentioned how Oldfield was hoping to set new world records, and Oldfield went on to say how dangerous racing was, and how many times he had been injured. Oldfield, the 1905 AAA Dirt Track Champion, is quoted in the newspaper as saying, "The whole country is speed mad and contests between both horses and automobiles must be near the record mark before real interest is shown." The race was on a Wednesday afternoon and the excitement was so high that the judge in Lexington adjourned court early so the jurymen could go to the races. The admission price was only 50 cents, and the horse track was jammed by race time. The next day the *Lexington Herald* stated that the 2,500 grandstands seats went quickly and the track "...was filled comfortably (whatever that meant)." Rumor has it 36,000 people were on hand. The event was certainly successful, and Barney didn't disappoint the onlookers either as he set many new records. At the end of the 50 lap race he was 10 miles ahead of his nearest competitor. In *The Illustrated History Of Sprint Car Racing*, author Jack Fox said, "Maybe Barney Oldfield would come their way only once or twice but there were some young men in the area who would cut down their rickety passenger cars to try to emulate their hero. This was the real beginning of Sprint car racing."

The immortal Barney Oldfield in the Peerless "Green Dragon". He was one of the most famous figures in early American auto racing. He was known for his "barnstorming" and his match-races. - Allan E. Brown collection.

The Florida State Fairgrounds in the 1920's. - Bob Sheldon collection.

When other horse and fairgrounds tracks found out how many people these match races attracted and how much money was to be made, many of them contacted Oldfield to come to their tracks. This started a real boom for oval track racing. When not barnstorming, Oldfield was a frequent competitor on the American Automobile Association (AAA, or commonly known as Triple-A) circuit. AAA was the nation's premier auto racing sanctioning body. One of AAA's first promoters was J. Alex Sloan. Sloan was a real showman, and he understood the potential of auto racing promotion. Sloan and Pickens occasionally teamed together to present exhibition races between Oldfield and Ralph DePalma. DePalma is perhaps the winningest driver of all time with as many as 2,500 wins.

I.M.C.A. IS FORMED

On March 29, 1915 a new sanction was formed by the major state fairgrounds managers. The International Motor Contest Association (I.M.C.A.) came about because Triple-A raised their sanctioning fees considerably. Also instrumental in the birth of I.M.C.A. was Sloan, who organized the early I.M.C.A. events. The first I.M.C.A. race was at the Michigan State Fairgrounds on May 30, 1915. The 75 mile main event was won by Bill Endicott in a Maxwell. There were 60 I.M.C.A. events that first year, with the races split almost 50/50 between one mile tracks and half-mile tracks, as many of the smaller county fairgrounds had also joined the I.M.C.A. fold. It is believed that many of the early I.M.C.A. races were "hippodromed" (meaning prearranged as to who was to win), which was probably true, but in later years it certainly wasn't the case. Ernie Johnson (who ran I.M.C.A. in the late 1920's) said, "Not once, did he (Sloan) tell where to finish or ever ask me to slow down."

Another of the early I.M.C.A. promoters was Ralph Hankinson. Hankinson moved to AAA in 1926 and started a AAA fairgrounds circuit. It was probably Hankinson who convinced AAA that they should be paying more attention to dirt track racing. The contest board of AAA, in its arrogance, considered any racing other than AAA as being "outlaw". The word "outlaw" was used in AAA correspondence even before I.M.C.A. was organized in 1915.

STATE FAIRGROUNDS TRACKS

Twenty states with one mile tracks held auto racing events before World War I. They are Alabama (1906) [year of first known auto race], Arizona (1910), California (1912), Georgia (1920's), Illinois (1910), Indiana (1903), Louisiana (1910), Michigan (1899), Minnesota (1904), Missouri (1915), Montana (1915), New York (1905), North Carolina (1926), Rhode Island (1896), South Carolina (1910), Tennessee (1907), Texas (1914), Virginia (1907), Washington (1926), and Wisconsin (1903).

States with state fairgrounds with half-mile tracks that were running before World War One were Colorado (1915), Idaho (1915), Iowa (1907), Kansas (1914), Kentucky (1918), Mississippi (1903), Nebraska (1915), New Jersey (1900), North Dakota (1917), Ohio (1919), Oklahoma (1913), South Dakota (1913), Utah (1915), Vermont (1928), and Wyoming (1910's). If you were observant, you noticed that six of the above tracks opened in 1915. That was no coincidence as that was the first year the International Motor Contest Association (I.M.C.A.) ran races, and each of those six tracks inaugural auto racing events were I.M.C.A. races.

After the first World War additional state fairgrounds held auto racing, but now the majority of these were half-mile tracks including, Arkansas (1925), Delaware (1930), Florida (1921), Maine (1941), Oregon (1933), and Vermont (1928). The Nevada State Fairgrounds (1950) is the only new state to build a mile track after World War I.

Four state fairgrounds were moved for various reasons, and most were rebuilt as half-mile tracks. They include Oklahoma (1954), South Carolina (1932), and Virginia (1946). California (1978) has the distinction of being the only state that rebuilt with a one mile track.

After the first World War eight states reduced the size of their state fairgrounds from one mile tracks to smaller half-mile tracks. They were Alabama (1933), Georgia (1947), Louisiana (1931), Minnesota (1940), North Carolina (1940), Oregon (1933), Tennessee (1958), and Virginia (1929).

THE SPEEDSTERS

The Ford Model T, first introduced in 1908, made great race cars. Many a backyard mechanic modified Model T's into speedsters. These cars were very popular for short track racing. The two-seated speedsters evolved into single seat big cars. By the 1920's there were many racing parts available for the Ford engines. Of these, the most famous were the Frontenac parts built by Arthur Chevrolet. His brother Louis originally built bicycles using the Frontenac name. The brothers then built automobiles starting in 1912 using their last name, but when W.C. Durant bought them out in 1916 (Durant created the General Motors empire), the Chevrolet's were not allowed to use the Chevrolet name again. Chevrolet sold more than 10,000 of the popular "Fronty" heads. In the 1920's, smaller versions of Harry Miller's famous engines (which propelled most championship cars of that era) were installed in some of these short track big cars. The majority of the cars were still powered by the Fronty-Ford engines or similar powerplants, mainly because of the availability of the parts and the lower cost. A full race Fronty could be built for under $3,000, and was nearly as fast as a Miller costing upwards of $15,000.

Fred Offenhauser bought Harry Miller out in 1933, and in 1935 the first four cylinder Offenhauser racing engine (a direct decedent of the Miller) became the standard powerplant for front running big cars. Affectionately known as the "Offy", it continued its dominance until the early 1960's when modified Chevrolet V-8 engines became the best engine for sprint car racing. The first Chevy V-8 came off the assembly line in 1955 and was soon adapted to racing. Today, the fuel-injected Chevy V-8 can be found under the hood of most sprint cars.

Triple-A was sanctioning only a few dirt track events. That left the door open for I.M.C.A. to quickly became the major dirt track sanctioning body. We have been able to find only 14 Triple-A sanctioned dirt track races in 1917, while there were 94 race dates on the 1918 I.M.C.A. schedule. Triple-A escalated their sanctioning of dirt track racing in the 1920's, probably in retaliation of I.M.C.A.'s domination of dirt track racing. Even though I.M.C.A. was sanctioning more events, Triple-A became the most prestigious circuit. There were a number of other big car organizations in the 1930's and the 1940's including the Central States Racing Association (C.S.R.A.), which was based in Ohio, and the American Racing Association (ARA), based in California.

Big car racing was wild and exciting in the 1930's, but it was also dangerous, and only the bravest men would drive the powerful machines. With the driver's head high above the rest of the car for best visibility, the driver was exposed to potentially grave injury in case of an accident. The average life expectancy of a big car driver was seven years. In fact, in the 1930's over 200 big car drivers were fatally injured in racing accidents. It was an extremely dangerous sport.

One of the most famous tracks before World War II was Legion Ascot (CA). Here the cars are on the pace lap of a main event. Notice the large crowd in the stands. - Photo courtesy of Don Radbruch from the George Sowle collection.

ROADSTERS

In the late 1920's another form of race car, known as roadsters, started to gained in popularity. These were basically stripped down passenger cars and were the poor man's open cockpit racer. Roadsters, similar to the speedsters, and not to be confused with the offset designed Indy cars of the 1950's and 1960's, were somewhat popular until the early 1950's. Some of the top Indy car drivers of the 1950's started their careers in these roadsters, including "Indy 500" winners Troy Ruttman and Jim Rathmann. Like the sprint cars, they were very dangerous, with little protection for the drivers. The roadster name undoubtedly came from the fact that most of the cars started out as opened- topped passenger cars, called roadsters. Today, similar cars are called convertibles.

If you were a race car driver in the 1930's, 1940's or 1950's, your ultimate goal would be driving in the Indianapolis 500. To do so, you had to drive in AAA big car or midget races. If you did well in AAA (or later USAC), it might land you a ride in an Indy car. When USAC took over as the major sanctioning body in 1956 (Triple-A decided it was time to step away), USAC became the premier sprint car circuit. It remained the top sprint car sanction until the late 1970's.

The basic shape of sprint cars has remained the same since the early days of the sport. The driver sits in an upright position directly behind the engine compartment. The body is only large enough to cover the engine, driver, and gas tank (which is positioned behind the driver). The wheels remain exposed with no fenders. Even with improvements in streamlining, engine development, advanced chassis designs, and better tires, today's sprint cars look similar to, and still react somewhat like the early big cars.

Shortly after World War II ended, a few more sprint car organizations came into existence. They included the California Racing Association (CRA), and the East Coast based, United Racing Club (URC).

Bob Flock, from Atlanta, Georgia, in a NASCAR roadster from the late 1940's. Flock went on to become one of the top drivers in the NASCAR Grand National circuit. - Frank Smith photo (Len Ashburn collection)

Open Wheel Race Cars

Bobby Allen in a typical supermodified of 1960's. The photo was taken at Dorsey Speedway (MD) in 1966. - Bob Williams photo (Larry Jendras collection)

SUPERMODIFIEDS

In the mid 1950's another form of open wheel race car appeared. By combining jalopy stock cars, roadsters, and sprint cars all into one car, the new hybrid was called a supermodified. As cut-down versions of the jalopies, they kept the safety feature of a four-post roll cage, but used smaller cut-down bodies like many of the roadsters. To conserve weight, the starter and battery were removed, and the cars had to be pushed to be started, like sprint cars. The first time the name supermodified was ever mentioned in National Speed Sport News was in an article from Playland Park in Houston, Texas on May 26, 1954. Many supermodifieds were just as fast as the best sprint cars of their day, and it wasn't long before the cut-down jalopy bodies gave way to homemade bodies and eventually to sprint car bodies. A sprint car could be converted to a supermodified by just adding a roll cage. Many sprint car owners made the cage detachable with bolts, so the car could still run in sprint car races, where it was taboo to run the cages. The roll cage is a series of tubular bars that surrounds the driver's cockpit and protects him in case the car should turn over. Sprint cars, by design, are top-heavy and can easily "get upside-down".

Weekly supermodified racing spread across most of the country in the early 1960's. The class started to lose some of its momentum in the late 1960's for a variety of reasons, including the fact that short track late model stock car racing had become increasingly popular and considerably less expensive.

By the late 1960's supermodified racing was split into two categories. These were dirt track supers, which eventually evolved back into sprint cars, and the pavement supers. The lay-down Indy roadster design, with its lower center of gravity, became the way to go on the smoother asphalt tracks. By the late 1960's, Indy cars were rear-engined in design, and many of the older Indy roadsters were converted into pavement supermodifieds. A few car builders constructed rear-engined supers, but they were eventually outlawed, as not to obsolete the offset roadsters, like the English built Coopers and Lotus' did to the roadsters in Indy car racing. There are only a handful of weekly supermodified tracks left. The most famous is Oswego Speedway in upstate, New York. There are a few traveling circuits for the pavement supers including the International Super Modified Association (IMSA) and the Western States Super Modified Tour (W.S.S.M.T.). A couple of supermodified drivers have gone on to win the Indy 500. Gordon Johncock and Tom Sneva were top supermodified drivers before both went on to win the Indianapolis 500.

WINGS AND THINGS

It wasn't until the public cried for safety that all sprint car sanctions went along with the advantages of roll cages on sprint cars. I.M.C.A. was one of the last sprint car sanctions to allow the full roll cages. By the mid 1960's, many weekly dirt tracks switched from the home built supermodifieds to the full sprint cars, but they retained the roll cages. This new class was sometimes called Caged Sprints or Super Sprints.

Most modern day sprint cars have large inverted airfoils, called wings, mounted above their roll cages. The first wing was introduced by Ohio's Jim Cushman in 1958 on his supermodified. The wings not only give added down pressure on the rear wheels for better traction, but they also give better stability in the turns. Wings also tend to decrease the risk of injury in case of a serious accident. The late Jack Gunn, the promoter of Pennsylvania's famous Williams

Jim Cushman poses beside his winged supermodified. He is credited with installing the first wing on a short track race car. The main object of the wing was to force pressure on the rear wheels, thus giving the car more traction. He began winning regularly after installing the airfoil. - Allan E. Brown collection.

Grove Speedway, said in 1970, "Wings are a big safety factor, acting as a shock absorber when a car flips." Over 80% of modern day sprint car racing is done with wings attached to the cages. Racing with a wing or without a wing is drastically different, both for the drivers and the spectators. The wingless cars tend to broadslide more in the turns and many fans enjoy this type of racing action. The cars go faster with the wings, partly because the cars have better traction down the straightaways. The big difference, however, is in the cornering. A wingless car tends to lean to the outside as it slides through a corner. The centrifugal force makes the top-heavy cars react that way. The winged car will lean towards the inside, even though forces should make the cars shift to the outside. The reverse happens as the sideboards on the wings push against the wind making the top of the car lean inward. The winged cars can enter the corners faster because of this. Normally a winged car can turn a dirt track over two seconds faster than a non-winged sprint car.

The sprint cars of Roger McCluskey (#51) and Bobby Unser (#3) at Terre Haute Action Track (IN) in 1966. - Armin Krueger photo (Allan E. Brown collection)

The top sprint car circuit throughout the late 1950's and 1960's was USAC. As AAA had proclaimed, USAC considered any racing other than USAC as being "outlaw". As weekly sprint car racing began to become more popular and the prospect of going from a sprint car to an Indianapolis car was dwindling, Bud Miller from western Pennsylvania saw the opportunity to promote big-pursed "outlaw" races for sprint cars. The present day All Star Circuit of Champions, in a roundabout way, evolved out of his races. In late 1977, Ted Johnson organized a sprint car race at Boothill Speedway. Many of the best sprint car drivers from across the country ventured to Louisiana that weekend. That race, coupled with others that Johnson had promoted, led him to form the World of Outlaws. In short order, his organization surpassed USAC as the top sprint car sanction. An average season for the World of Outlaws includes racing over 100 times a year at 50 or so tracks. The "Outlaws" raced in at least 25 different states in 1994.

Over the years many well known drivers have thrilled racing fans by driving big cars or sprint cars. Louis Schneider, Wilbur Shaw, Gus Schrader, Frank Lockhart, Emory Collins, Tommy Hinnershitz, Rex Mays, Ted Horn, Jimmy Wilburn, Bobby Grim, Deb Snider, A.J. Foyt, Jerry Richert, Jim Hurtubise, Parnelli Jones, Jan Opperman, Jerry Richert, Gary Bettenhausen, Larry Dickson, Rich Vogler, Doug Wolfgang, and Brad Doty are only a few of them. World of Outlaw drivers Steve Kinser, Sammy Swindell, and Dave Blaney are probably the most familiar names currently associated with sprint car racing.

"Dutch" Baumann seated in Arthur Chevrolet's factory #2 D.O. Fronty-Ford. Baumann won 43 or 52 features in 1928 driving in big car competition. The nickname of this famous race car was the "Deuce". - Wilson Davis collection.

One of the first drivers to have a sensational season driving a dirt track big car was Charles "Dutch" Baumann as he won 43 of 52 feature races in his Fronty-Ford in 1928. Doc McKenzie bettered that mark, when he won 45 features in 1935. Hooker Hood's 56 super sprint wins in 1967 is the modern day record, although Steve Kinser came close in 1990 when he won 52 sprint car features. Kinser is probably the first driver to ever win feature races at 100 different tracks. The only two drivers who may have done it before him were Barney Oldfield and Ralph DePalma, but exact records of their accomplishments were never kept. Kinser has amassed over 350 feature wins in the World of Outlaws.

Some of the races are just as familiar as the drivers. The most prestigious sprint car race is the "Knoxville Nationals", which is held each August in Iowa. Eldora Speedway in Ohio hosts two of the nations richest sprint car races. The "Kings Royal" pays $50,000 to win, and the "The Historical Big One" pays $100,000 to win. Other prestigious sprint car events include the "National Open" at Williams Grove Speedway, Pennsylvania; the "Gold Cup" at Silver Dollar Speedway, California; and the "Dirt Cup" at Skagit Speedway in Washington.

20 *Open Wheel Race Cars*

MIDGET CARS

Most historians contend that the first real midget race was at Hughes Stadium in Sacramento, California on June 4, 1933. From there the sport springboarded across the country. The unique thing about midget car racing is that due to their small size, special tracks were not needed and they were quite adaptable to any size arena. High school running tracks, football stadiums, baseball diamonds, and even indoor halls and arenas were soon called upon to host midget racing. Some historians contend that midget racing actually began in southern California in 1913. For three years a number of amateur events were held with vehicles called cycle cars. Midget historian Crocky Wright says, "the big difference was that the midgets, when midget racing really began in 1933, were being driven by professional drivers, many who had raced big cars in the past."

Early 1930's midget racing at Loyola Stadium (CA). Bill Betteridge (car on left) and Hal Roberts race side-by-side. - Bruce Craig collection.

Here are examples of the "cycle cars" from the early 1900's. The unidentified drivers are waiting for the start of a race. - Allan E. Brown collection.

The midget craze quickly spread across the nation. The midgets quickly became the most popular form of auto racing in America. Race tracks sprung up everywhere. In 1932 there were about 350 oval tracks running in the United States. Nearly 70 percent of them were half-mile fairgrounds tracks. As midget racing caught on, an abundance of tracks became available. By the time America became involved with World War II, over 1,000 tracks had held midget races. Because these cars were better suited for smaller tracks, quite a few fairgrounds constructed special little tracks for midget racing.

Gilmore Stadium was the most famous track ever built for midget race cars. The annual "Turkey-Day Classic" started here in 1935. - Bruce Craig collection.

GILMORE STADIUM

The first track built especially for the midgets was Gilmore Stadium in Los Angeles, California. It was acknowledged as the showplace for the new sport. It opened in 1934 and continued until 1950. Ironically it closed about the same time that midget racing started losing its appeal. The annual "Thanksgiving Day Classic" for midgets started at Gilmore in 1935. The prestigious race, held each year on Thanksgiving Day, is the oldest annual race for the midgets. Since Gilmore's demise, the race has been held at various locations.

The oldest active midget track in the nation is Angell Park Speedway in Sun Prairie, Wisconsin. The first race at this dirt track was in 1938, and like Gilmore Stadium, it has never heard the noise of any other type of car in competition except for the roar of the midgets. Probably the most prestigious midget race held is the annual "Belleville Nationals" in Kansas. Drivers and fans from across the nation converge on that community each August. Another popular race is called the "Chili Bowl". It is held indoors at the Tulsa Expo Center in Oklahoma.

In the early 1930's a number of small high banked wood tracks were built for bicycle racing, but as that sport faded the midgets found their way onto some of these tracks. The small bicycle board tracks had been around for a number of years, as the first one was built in New York City in 1894. The most famous were the Nutley Velodrome in New Jersey and the Coney Island Velodrome near New York City. These 45 degree banked one-sixth mile wood tracks produced exciting racing. But the high speeds took their toll on drivers, and racing at each track only lasted a short period of time. Later other board tracks were built for midget racing inside of such famous coliseums as the Rose Bowl, the Polo Grounds, and Soldiers Field. One midget race on a board track in the Los Angeles Coliseum had 55,873 fans in attendance.

The early midgets were powered by various power plants, from motorcycle engines and outboard motorboat engines, to a scaled down version of the famous Offenhauser. These 110 cubic inch "Offies" were so powerful that they soon became the dominant engine and remained so for nearly 40 years. Another popular engine in the late 1930's was the Ford V8-60. In stock form these small engines produced 60 horsepower. The Ford V8-60 were considerably cheaper to build than the expensive Offies.

The years immediately after the war were by far the peak years for midget racing. In many areas racing was presented seven nights a week. But by mid-century the sport had faded with many factors contributing to its near demise. First, the cars had become very expensive and the car owners demanded larger purses so they could continue to afford the sport. Promoters were either forced to raise gate admissions and drive away potential customers or drop the class.

Mel Kenyon (in the car) and his brother Don (standing). Mel is one of the winningest midget drivers of all-time. - Allan E. Brown collection.

About the same time the stock car boom (jalopy, hard tops, and strictly stock) took the limelight from the midgets. The jalopies could race on the same small tracks the midgets were using and the cost was nil compared to the midgets. Also the fender bending action of the stock cars was fun to watch with plenty of action.

Immediately after the war all sports and the whole entertainment industry including baseball, football, and movie theaters enjoyed some of their best years. The servicemen had returned from the war effort with money in their pockets and entertainment was high on their list as a way to spend it. Within a few years the entertainment industry began feeling the pinch as couples married and settled down. The baby boom began and extra money was diverted from entertainment to more important household uses. Many auto racing fans could no longer afford the high priced tickets, and stock car racing was an inexpensive alternative. During the 1950's midget racing nearly disappeared. Only through the efforts of obstinate, yet courageous individuals was the sport able to continue until better times.

In the 1960's an aluminum four cylinder engine was introduced by General Motors in their Chevy IIs. It quickly took over as the poor man's powerplant for the midgets, replacing the Ford V8-60s that had been out of production for a number of years. By the 1970's the new hot setup was the air-cooled Volkswagen engine. The lightweight VW engines were first introduced in a midget by Red Caruthers in 1973. His driver, Bobby Olivero, began winning races almost immediately and soon the demand for the VWs exceeded that of the Offenhauser.

The first real safety feature to be incorporated into the midgets, since the introduction of crash helmets in 1933, was the four post roll cages in the late 1960's. At the introduction of these roll bars, the midget purists were against the addition of these protective devises, but the safety factor far outweighed any tradition and soon every sanction required the use of these extra bars. It was best said by the late George Marshman, the first promoter to mandate the roll cages at his track, "There are a lot of old race drivers around, and there are a lot of bold drivers around, but there are no old, bold drivers around."

Midget racing today enjoys a somewhat renewed interest. Gone, however, are the many weekly midget tracks. Angell Park and the Indianapolis Speedrome are the only tracks that still runs the cars on a weekly schedule. Today, most midget races are sanctioned by one of the many various traveling clubs. They include USAC, which has some of their races televised on ESPN. Three of the oldest midget groups, still in operation, are the American Racing Driver Club (A.R.D.C.), the Badger Midget Auto Racing Association (B.M.A.R.A.) and the Bay Cities Racing Association (B.C.R.A.). These organizations travel to different tracks usually as an added attraction to the track's weekly events. Although the cars are still expensive, midget racing provides competitive, exciting events.

T.Q. MIDGETS

Other variations of the midgets are T.Q. (three-quarter) midgets, half-midgets, modified-midgets, micro-sprints, and mini-sprints. These cars are similar to their larger cousins, the full midgets. But T.Q. midgets are several hundred pounds lighter, have a shorter wheelbase, and use smaller engines than the midgets. Another class of open wheel car built especially for children, ages five to 11 year old, is the quarter-midgets. They first appeared in California in July of 1954. NASCAR star Jeff Gordon was a quarter-midget graduate.

The first reported smaller midget race car was built by Stan Branowski in 1939. Bill Muth of New Jersey is considered the father of T.Q. midgets when he installed an Indian motorcycle engine in a cut down Model T chassis. He later started a club for "midget-midgets" in 1946 and built several cars, as well as parts for them. In the years immediately after World War II, T.Q. races were held in New Jersey, Connecticut (Tom Thumb Midget Association), and on Long Island. The first mention of T.Q. midget racing in California was in 1948. Probably the best known of the T.Q. midget groups is the American Three-Quarter Midget Racing Association (A.T.Q.M.R.A.). That East Coast based group was founded in 1956. A current T.Q. midget cost about $7,500 to $15,000 to build.

One of the fastest growing classes in the nation are the modified-midgets and mini-sprints. The cars are similar to full and T.Q. midgets, but the difference is the size of engines they use. The engines can range from the 125 cubic centimeter engines in some of the modified-midgets to 250 cubic centimeter engines in some of the faster mini-sprints. In the past ten years nearly 200 tracks have been built for the modified-midgets and mini-sprints.

Gary Hyland of Boise, ID poses with his Modified-midget (also called a Micro-Sprint) at Owyhee Motorcycle Club Raceway on Sept. 30, 1994. The car is powered by a 250 c.c. engine. He won the main event. - Allan E. Brown photo.

THE CHAMPIONSHIP CARS

The Championship trail, as we know it today, is the oldest form of professional auto racing in America. Perhaps the first American auto racing organization was the Automobile Club of America (ACA) which started in 1899. In March of 1902 the American Automobile Association (AAA, but generally referred to as Triple-A) was formed in Chicago as an aid to the many new motorists in the country. At that time there were about 23,000 automobiles (compared to 190 million registered vehicles in 1994). Triple-A was urged to sanction auto racing as a way to promote their new motoring club. So in 1904 Triple-A co-sanctioned, with ACA, the first "Vanderbilt Cup" race on Long Island. Triple-A went on to sanction other road course and oval track events as well, and they played an important role in shaping auto racing in America. Barney Oldfield was the 1905 AAA dirt track champion.

The AAA Contest Board was formed in 1908, and the first official National Championship race was held on June 12, 1909 in Portland, Oregon. The 102-mile finale at Portland was won by Bert Dingley. Dingley was considered AAA's first national champion by *Motor Age* in 1916, then the leading racing journal. Triple-A did not determine their National Champion by a point system until 1916. The rival ACA promoted races until 1916 before they faded out of existence.

The first cars on the circuit were basically stripped down production models, but it wasn't long before cars especially built for racing appeared. The French built Panhard is considered the forerunner of most open wheeled front engined race cars. The Panhard had the motor directly in front of the driver with the gas tank behind the driver and the radiator in front of the motor. The first race cars usually carried a riding mechanic, who would assist in monitoring the car's performance, and they helped the driver by watching for approaching competitors.

The historic race between Henry Ford and Alexander Winton at Grosse Pointe (MI) in 1902. Ford won the race and that helped him get publicity, which in turn made it possible for him to build his automotive empire. - Photo courtesy of Halifax County Historical Society.

The start of the 1949 "Indianapolis 500". The Indianapolis Motor Speedway is considered the first super speedway in America. The basic shape of the track has remained the same. Major renovations have turned the track into one of the true showplaces in all of motorsports. The grandstands in this photo have since been replaced by larger concrete and steel grandstands. - Official Indianapolis Motor Speedway photo (Allan E. Brown collection).

INDIANAPOLIS MOTOR SPEEDWAY IS BORN

During the first few years, most auto racing events were staged on city streets or country roads, along with a few oval track events that were held on dirt horse tracks. Indianapolis Motor Speedway in Indiana became the first oval track built primarily for auto racing. It opened on August 15, 1909. The two and a half mile dirt track became dusty and rutty and was difficult to race on, so later that year owner Carl Fisher decided to pave the track with bricks. The track reopened in November, but this time after three million ten-pound bricks were put in place. "The Brickyard" was born.

Another large oval dirt track was built in Atlanta, Georgia and would have preceded Indianapolis, but terrible weather delayed construction. The Atlanta Motordrome was a two-mile dirt oval, but it was short-lived as it opened on November 9, 1909 and it held its last race less than a year later on October 6, 1910. Another early dirt track was the Sioux City Speedway, which was across the St. Croix River from Sioux City, Iowa in Stevens, South Dakota. That two-mile dirt track opened in 1911, but it literally vanished by 1918. One of the more unique tracks of the period was the Twin City Motor Speedway in Minneapolis, Minnesota. The two-mile dirt track opened in 1914, but was paved with 40,000 barrels of concrete for the second race. The Twin City track was out of business by 1918. Coincidentally both sites of the Atlanta Motordrome and the Twin City Motor Speedway are now major airports.

THE FIRST INDIANAPOLIS 500

After running a number of races each year, the management at the Indianapolis Motor Speedway decided it should hold one big annual event. At first they thought about a 1000-mile race, but it was determined that it would be too long and that the spectators could not be kept interested for such a long period of time. They then agreed on a formula where they could keep the fans' attention for about six hours; thus, the distance was set at 500 miles. The first "Indianapolis 500" was run on Memorial Day, 1911. Ray Harroun in a Marmon Wasp won the first "Indy 500" in six hours and forty-two minutes.

The 21-race 1911 AAA season consisted of all road course events except for Indianapolis and an oval track race on a beach course in Jacksonville, Florida.

THE BOARD TRACKS

The first major board track was built in Playa Del Ray, California. The Los Angeles Motor Speedway was a one-mile circular track built entirely of wood. Additional information on the famous board tracks can be found in a separate chapter later in this book. The speeds that were attainable on these high banked saucers were astounding for the day. Jack Price had built a number of small wood ovals for motorcycle racing just after the turn of the century, and his designs were increased to accommodate the larger automobiles. The first board track that really caught on was the Chicago Speedway in Illinois. The track was two-miles in length. Dario Resta won the 500 mile race at Chicago on June 26, 1915. The event was a huge success as 85,000 spectators attended the first major board track race.

With the sudden success of oval track racing, there was only one road course left on the AAA National Championship schedule by 1916. In 1918 all 17 AAA races were held on board tracks, as the owners of the Indianapolis Motor Speedway opted to close during the duration of World War I.

The Baltimore-Washington Speedway in Laurel, Maryland was one of the famous board tracks. Bob McDonough (#14) and Tommy Milton (#4) get set for the start of a 1925 race. - Greg Fielden collection.

With the introduction of these high banked wood tracks the speeds increased. Advancements in technology in both chassis and engines were fantastic. Many inventions were being utilized in auto racing. The 275 cubic inch, dual-over-head cam engines in the 1914 French built Peugeots is said to have influenced the designs of future engines built by Harry Miller. Miller was one of the top chassis and engine builders during that period and his cars and the Duesenberg team cars were the only competitive American cars in the early 1920's. Miller built his first racing engine in 1915. Other inventions like the first supercharger increased horsepower substantially. Streamlining became very important as the speeds continued to rise. The famous board tracks ranged in size from one-half mile to two-miles in length.

Harry Miller built a potent four cylinder engine in 1929. He then sold this engine design to Fred Offenhauser in 1933, and Offenhauser built his first engine in 1935. The "Offy" went on to become one of the best racing engine for many decades. Offenhauser sold his company to Dale Drake and Louis Meyer in 1946, and they continued making the Drake/Meyer "Offies" for nearly 30 years.

Some of the top drivers of the teens included Harroun, Resta, Dingley, Bob Burman, Joe Dawson, Ralph DePalma, Ralph Mulford, David Bruce-Brown, Earl Cooper, Louis Chevrolet, and Eddie Rickenbacker.

The major drawback of the wood tracks was that they were exposed to the elements of nature and the wood deteriorated. After three or four years the surfaces would start to crumble and either an expensive repair job was needed or the tracks were abandoned. A couple of the board tracks were destroyed in fires. The Altoona board track in Pennsylvania, perhaps the only board track to be completely resurfaced, was the longest lasting of the wood tracks. The Altoona board track operated for eight years from 1922 until 1931.

Some of the top drivers during the peak of the board track era in the 1920's were DePalma, Tommy Milton, Jimmy Murphy, Eddie Hearne, Harry Hartz, Frank Lockhart, and Peter DePaolo, the nephew of DePalma. Many historians regard DePaolo as the best board track driver.

With the demise of board tracks after 1931, the Championship trail consisted of the "Indianapolis 500", a few dirt track events, and an occasional road course event. Even before the Great Depression had taken its toll on the nation's economy the Championship series was down to fewer than 10 races a year. The low point, not counting war years, was in 1938 when only two events counted towards the title. They were the "Indy 500" and a dirt track race in New York.

THE JUNK FORMULA ERA

New engine regulations were implemented in 1930 to eliminate the expensive supercharged engines. The cars had become very expensive, and the high powered engines had become so advanced that even though the cars only had 91.5 cubic inch engines the cars were faster than ever. The new rules called for 366 cubic inch non-supercharged engines. This six-liter engine formula was still smaller than the gigantic 600 cubic inch engines of 1911. The so-called Junk Formula era in Championship racing was instituted to encourage participation from the U.S. auto manufacturers. The American auto industry had shied away from auto racing competition since the days that the European manufacturers invaded this country with their superior racing machines. Unlike the Europeans, the American companies didn't need auto racing to sell autos. Also in 1930, the riding mechanics were utilized again. The last time riding mechanics rode along with the drivers was in 1922. The riding mechanics were part of major AAA racing again until 1937.

With the stock market crash of 1929, investment money was lost to build new tracks or race cars, and fewer people could afford the expensive sport. Indy cars were rich men's toys. Perhaps the new stock block formula came along at the right time or Championship racing might have died out completely.

The Indianapolis Motor Speedway was getting progressively rougher as the bricks were starting to deteriorate. Then in 1939 most of the track was paved with asphalt, leaving only the bricks on the front straightaway exposed. Asphalt, still used in highway construction, is assumed to have been invented by Dupont about 1930 by evaporating petroleum and then mixing it with macadam.

Championship racing, just prior to our involvement in War World II, was only a shell of what it had been during the board track era. Some of the top drivers during the 1930's included Louis Meyer, Wilbur Shaw, Rex Mays, Kelly Petillo, Mauri Rose, and Ted Horn.

Championship racing resumed with the "Indianapolis 500" in 1946, but the rest of the schedule was on one-mile dirt tracks with the exception of the Pikes Peak Hill Climb which started counting towards the championship in 1947. Horn, Rose, Mays, Bill Holland, Myron Fohr, Johnnie Parsons, Henry Banks, Tony Bettenhausen, and Jimmy Bryan were just some of the top drivers on the AAA trail right after racing was allowed to continue after World War II.

AAA QUITS

Triple-A had become sensitive to its role in racing, and decided it was time to step away from auto racing at the end of 1955. It had been sanctioning the Championship series since its beginnings, and the series consisted of the "Indy 500" and a dozen or so dirt track events each year. Although the Championship cars did run a few races at the new high banked 1.25 mile asphalt track in Darlington, South Carolina from 1950 until 1954, the majority of races were on one-mile dirt tracks.

Johnny White drove the Demler Special to a fourth place finish in the 1964 "Indianapolis 500". - Official Indianapolis Motor Speedway photo. (Michigan Motor Sports Hall of Fame collection).

The National Association for Stock Car Auto Racing (NASCAR), a stock car club based in Florida, became involved with open wheeled Championship racing in 1952 by running big cars with stock block engines in them. The series only ran seven races that year before it was abandoned.

The one-mile dirt horse track at the Wisconsin State Fair in Milwaukee, the nation's fourth oldest oval track at that time, was asphalted in 1954. Because of the sudden influx of asphalt tracks a new type of race car was introduced. It was called a Indy roadster. The driver sat offset from the engine. Instead of straddling the drive shaft in an upright position, the driver sat with his legs alongside the engine. This design created a lower center of gravity and resulted in faster cornering speeds on the paved tracks. Frank Kurtis built one of the first of these new low-slung creations, and his driver Bill Vukovich, Sr. won two straight "Indy 500" race in 1953 and 1954. Vukovich was fatally injured in a crash while leading the 1955 race in a Kurtis Kraft. These roadsters dominated the pavement races from 1953 until 1965. Heroes of the roadster era included Vukovich, Sr., Bryan, A.J. Foyt, Pat O'Connor, Rodger Ward, Jim Rathmann, Eddie Sachs, and Parnelli Jones.

USAC IS FORMED

With Triple-A gone from the picture, a new sanction had to be created to conduct Championship racing. The United States Auto Club (USAC, pronounced "Ewe-Sac") took over the reigns of the Championship Trail and continued along the same lines as before with a few events on paved oval tracks and the remaining on one-mile dirt tracks. The New Jersey State Fairgrounds in Trenton expanded their half-mile dirt track, the oldest track at that time (its first race was on September 24, 1900), into a one-mile track in 1957 and paved it. This added another track to the fold. About a dozen Championship races were being hosted each year by USAC from 1956 until 1965.

THE REAR ENGINE INVASION

Jack Brabham, from New Zealand, introduced a small rear-engined Grand Prix racer to the Championship tour at the 1961 Indianapolis 500. Although the underpowered car did not win, it showed tremendous potential. Two years later Ford Motor Company, in conjunction with Colin Chapman of the Lotus works from England, brought three cigar shaped rear-engined cars to Indianapolis. This

Dan Gurney drove this Lotus-powered-by-Ford to a seventh place finish in the 1963 "Indianapolis 500". His teammate Jimmy Clark finished second in another Lotus-Ford. These rear-engined cars changed the whole Indy car scene, for within two years the rear-engined cars had replaced the front-engined roadsters. -Robert P.Tronolone photo (Allan E. Brown collection).

Gordon Johncock (#4) leads Bobby Unser (#3) at Langhorne (PA) on June 23, 1968. Johncock won the 150 mile race. Both drivers went on to be two time winners of the "Indy 500". - Arnie deBrier photo (Allan E. Brown collection).

time with sufficient power, thank to Ford's V-8 engine, the rear-engined cars were the center of attention. Scotland's Jimmy Clark finished second in a Lotus-Ford. Clark went to Milwaukee later in the year and dominated the 200-mile race. The handwriting was on the wall, and from the middle of the 1964 season all paved track Championship races have been won in rear-engined designed cars, with the exception of a solo win by Don Branson in an A.J. Watson built roadster at Phoenix International Raceway on March 28, 1965.

Neither the rear-engined or roadster designs worked very well on the dirt tracks, and the old Panhard style cars still prevailed on dirt. Only a handful of the dirt track races now counted towards the championship. Then, in 1971, USAC separated the dirt tracks from the Championship Trail and made a separate series called the Silver Crown for the upright dirt cars. With the advent of the European influenced rear-engined cars, a few road course events came back onto the schedule in the late 1960's. From 1971 until 1977 all USAC Championship races were conducted on paved oval tracks with rear-engined cars. A number of foreign drivers started running the USAC trail because of their experience in the rear-engined machines.

Championship auto racing began to get more coverage by the media when the foreign drivers began to invade Indianapolis in the 1960's. The "Indianapolis 500" had been on national radio for a number of years, but in the late 1960's the "Indianapolis 500" mile race became available to viewers across the nation on closed circuit TV. Then the ABC Television network began broadcasting the "Indy 500" on a same day tape delay so they could edit their effort. The race is now shown in its entirety on live TV.

Some of the veterans who had grown up in front-engined cars had trouble adjusting to the completely different characteristics of the nimble rear-engined cars. But former open wheel oval track drivers like Foyt, Mario Andretti, Gordon Johncock, Jim McElreath, Johnny Rutherford, Bobby Unser, and his brother Al Unser were able to make the transition. The rear-engined era brought some new names into the sport. Mark Donohue and Dan Gurney had advanced to the Indianapolis cars from sports car racing.

CAR OWNERS TAKE CONTROL

Some of the car owners on the Championship trail had been disenchanted with the direction USAC was taking the division and decided to form their own circuit. The Championship Auto Racing Teams (CART) was incorporated and Gordon Johncock won the first CART race at Phoenix on March 11, 1979. USAC ran seven races in 1979 while CART held thirteen races. The next year USAC sanctioned only one race. CART had succeeded in taking over the Championship Trail except for the most prestigious race, the "Indianapolis 500", which remains under USAC's control, mainly because Tony Hulman, the owner of "Indy", was instrumental in forming USAC. USAC still sanctions the "Indianapolis 500" as well as its Silver Crown series and their sprint car and midget racing divisions.

CART has since incorporated more road course events than oval track events into their yearly schedule. Many of these road racing events have been held near metropolitan cities like Miami, Cleveland, Denver, Detroit, Los Angeles, and New York City in hopes of drawing national media attention to the series. Those races are held on temporary circuits either on city streets, parking lots or airport runways so they can be closer to the large cities. Championship racing has become big business with large companies sponsoring the races and the race cars. The many advantages of Madison Avenue type marketing is very important to most of the CART car owners. CART started a supplemental Indy Car series for drivers to obtain more experience. It is called the Indy Lights. This series, similar to Formula Three in Europe, has become an excellent training ground for future Championship drivers. Paul Tracy is the best known of the Indy Lights drivers to make it to the big time.

Since the inception of CART some of the top drivers to come along are Rick Mears, Michael Andretti, Bobby Rahal, and Al Unser, Jr. The series also attracts a number of foreign drivers including former Grand Prix World Champions Emerson Fittipaldi and Nigel Mansell. Car owner Roger Penske, one of the founding fathers of CART, has gone on to become the only car owner to ever win ten "Indianapolis 500" races.

A.J. Foyt was the first four time winner of the "Indianapolis 500". Foyt, known as "Super Tex", is behind the wheel of the Jim Gilmore owned Indy car in this photo. - Allan E. Brown collection.

Parnelli Jones (#98) and A.J. Foyt (#1) battle for position during a USAC Championship event at Trenton (NJ) Speedway in 1962. Both cars are the upright designed dirt cars. - Len Ashburn collection.

AIS BECOMES AN ALTERNATIVE

In the late 1980's Bill Tempero, a former Indy Car driver and car owner, formed the American IndyCar Series (AIS). He was disenchanted with CART and the fact that the cars were becoming far too expensive, with only a handful of car owners having the monetary resources to be competitive. The smaller teams couldn't afford to buy new equipment each year like the well-financed teams.

Tempero's new IndyCar concept utilized older cars with limitations on their engines. There were a number of older cars which could be purchased for considerably less than the price for which they were originally built. His idea was to give the car owners an alternative, and AIS races are held on a variety of tracks including some smaller paved oval tracks that would not have been considered for a Indy Car race previously. Tempero and Buddy Lazier are just a couple of the top AIS drivers.

INDIANAPOLIS CHALLENGES CART

Because of the steady decline in Championship racing on oval tracks, Tony Hulman's grandson, Tony George, will be at the head of a new Indy Car circuit called the Indianapolis Racing League starting in 1996. He hopes to bring the Indy Car series to more oval tracks and to break the strangle hold the car owners who make up CART (now called IndyCar) have on Championship racing. CART has succeeded in creating an American based circuit that rivals the International circuit called Formula One. In its attempt to go head to head with the Grand Prix circuit, many people feel IndyCar has lost touch with the American racing public and the type of major open wheel racing the fans are really interested in.

For many years, potential Indy car drivers climbed up the ladder starting in the open wheeled midgets and sprints, and as their experience and reputation grew they might get offered a ride in an Indy Car. This scenario is no longer true, as front-engined experience has little use in today's rear-engined cars. A person who wants to race Indy Cars now needs road racing experience in rear-engined cars. But being able to drive these high-tech and ultra-expensive race cars isn't enough. Many rides are purchased rather than earned. Multi-buck sponsorships and/or a healthy checkbook goes farther in securing a ride on the IndyCar circuit than does talent or experience.

THE BRICKYARD

The first speedway built especially for auto racing in America was the Indianapolis Motor Speedway. The race course began life in 1908 as an idea of Carl Fisher. Other people involved in what was to become the world's most famous speedway were A.C. Newby, James A. Allison, and Frank Wheeler. Plans for the track began shortly after Fisher staged a race at the Indiana State Fairgrounds. He decided that a track built for auto racing would be better suited than racing automobiles on horse tracks.

The track was designed as a 2-1/2 mile oval with a five-mile road course that would use part of the oval track. The track surface was a composite of gravel, crushed limestone, tar, and crushed stones. The track was rolled into a perfectly smooth surface. The track was rectangular in shape, with the two long straightaways being 3300 feet long, while the two shorter chutes were 660 feet long. The four corners were 1320 feet in length and were banked about 16 degrees.

The track was built to show off the Indiana automobile industry. Newby owned an automobile company called National, but he was also involved with motorcycles, and it came as no surprise that the first races were for the two-wheelers. Indianapolis Motor Speedway officially opened on August 15, 1909, but the cycle riders were scared of the huge complex, and it wasn't until the first amateur race that all-out speed was achieved by local resident, Edwin

Indianapolis Motor Speedway.
The Greatest Race Course in the World.

This early postcard shows an artist rendition of the track including the proposed five-mile road course. - Allan E. Brown collection.

And there off...the start of one of the first races at the Indianapolis Motor Speedway. It was a dirt track in the beginning. - Dick Jordan collection.

"Cannonball" Baker. He proved he wasn't "chicken", and soon the other riders put aside their fears so they would not get shown up by a "rookie." These races were the only motorcycle races ever held on the track.

The first series of auto races were scheduled for August 19. A box-seat cost $1.50, and 60,000 onlookers viewed the events. The first race was a five-mile race and Louis Schwitzer, in a Buick, flashed across the line victorious after the two-lap race. After a series of short races the day climaxed with a 250-mile event. Nine cars started the race, but the track's surface started to break up as deep ruts developed and the dust hindered the sight of the competitors. This combination created an accident that left one driver and his riding mechanic dead. Bob Burman went on to win the event. Another fatal crash two days later encouraged the track owners to consider a different type of surface.

THE BRICKYARD

It was decided to use paving bricks as the track's surface. It took workmen 63 days to lay the 3,200,000 ten-pound bricks to complete the job. The track's new nickname was "The Brickyard". The corners were now banked at nine degrees. The first race on the "bricks" was on a very cold December day in 1909. The new surface proved to be much safer and smoother.

For the next couple of years, several races were held at the track, but in 1910 it was decided to run only one big race each year. The first "Indianapolis 500" was conceived and a purse of $30,000 was set aside for the first 500 mile race on May 30, 1911. Ray Harroun won that first "Indy 500" in a Marmon Wasp.

With the introduction of the first "Indy 500", the event immediately brought national attention to the track and the annual event has since become the world's most prestigious race.

Eddie Rickenbacker (whose name was spelled Richenbacher before World War I) took over the command of the track in 1927. He was a race car driver, a World War I fighter pilot, and he built passenger cars from 1922 until 1927. He had much of the surface paved with Kentucky Rock Asphalt in 1939, as the bricks had become increasingly rough. The bricks remained on the front straight until 1961 when the rest of the track was asphalted. A small stretch of bricks, three feet wide at the start/finish line, is all that remains of the original surface.

During both World Wars racing was halted at the Indianapolis Motor Speedway. After the second World War the track lay in disarray and was in so desperate need of repair that it was doubtful that the track would ever reopen. Wilbur Shaw convinced Tony Hulman to buy the track from Rickenbacker. The Hulman family rescued the track from extinction when they purchased it in 1946. It went from ruins to a showplace in a matter of a few years. The Hulman family still own the famous track and constant improvements and upgrading have kept the track as the premier world wide race track. Nearly everything except the original shape of the track has been changed over the years, including additional seating and new concrete barriers. It is estimated that seating for over 300,000 spectators exists at the track, making it the world's largest stadium. The preliminaries to the "Indianapolis 500" are conducted during the month of May. The qualification attempts are on the two weekends prior to Memorial Day. The first day of qualification draws almost as many fans as the race itself.

The cars are heading into turn one for the first time after hearing the traditional "Gentlemen start your engines" from Tony Hulman in this 1962 photo. The lead car in the group was Rodger Ward, the eventual winner of the 1962 "Indy 500". - Len Ashburn collection.

Waiting for the start of the 1911 "Indianapolis 500". - Allan E. Brown collection.

Tommy Milton was the first person to win the Indianapolis twice (1921 and 1923). Louis Meyer was the first driver to win three "Indianapolis 500's" (1928, 1933, and 1936), and A.J. Foyt was the first four-time winner of the "Indianapolis 500" He won the race in 1961, 1964, 1967, and 1977. Other multiple winners include Wilbur Shaw (three times), Mauri Rose (three times), Bill Vukovich, Sr. (twice), Rodger Ward (twice), Bobby Unser (three times), Al Unser, Sr. (four times), Gordon Johncock (twice), Johnny Rutherford (three times), Rick Mears (four times), Al Unser, Jr. (twice), and Emerson Fittipaldi (twice).

The Hulman family added another race to the schedule in 1994 with the addition of the "Brickyard 400" for the NASCAR Winston Cup cars. The first stock car race was won by Jeff Gordon in a Chevrolet Lumina.

Jeff Gordon won the first ever "Brickyard 400" for NASCAR Winston Cup cars on August 6, 1994.

THE SUPER SPEEDWAYS

A super speedway could be best described as a large banked paved oval track. Usually only the higher banked tracks are referred to as true super speedways. By not trying to distinguish what degree of banking does a track makes a super speedway, the following list is of paved tracks three-quarter mile in length or longer. The first time any track was called a "Super Speedway" was in 1957, when New Jersey's Trenton Speedway used the phrase to describe its newly enlarged and paved track.

1907 - The initial super speedway was built in England. The famous peanut-shaped Brooklands track, a high banked 2.75 mile concrete oval, opened June 17. The track closed in August of 1939, which was about the same time World War II began escalating in Europe.

1909 - The first auto racing speedway built in America was the Indianapolis Motor Speedway in Indiana. It opened as a 2.5 mile dirt oval, but later that year it was paved with bricks. The track held the first "Indianapolis 500" in 1911. The bricks were later covered with asphalt. More details on "The Brickyard" can be found in a separate chapter.

The Indianapolis Motor Speedway. - Alden Jamison collection.

1910 - The first super speedways in America were the famous high banked board tracks. The first major wood-surfaced track was Los Angeles Motordrome in Playa del Ray, California. This circular track was one-mile long and the corners were banked 20 degrees. It was moderately successful but lasted only four seasons. Speeds in excess of 140 miles per hour were achieved at some of the board tracks. The board track era lasted from 1910 until 1931. Additional information on the famous board tracks are also found in a separate chapter.

1915 - Five new major oval tracks opened in 1915. The first really successful board track opened in Chicago, Illinois on June 26, 1915. The two-mile long Chicago Speedway lasted until 1918 when it was dismantled and a hospital for injured World War I servicemen was constructed...The new wood-surfaced Pacific Speedway in Tacoma, Washington opened on July 4. Tacoma was built as a two-mile dirt track the year before. The track went out of business in 1922...The next track built was the 1.25 mile Omaha Speedway in Nebraska. That board track opened on July 15. Only three race dates were held on the Omaha boards...Then the one-mile wood oval called Des Moines Speedway opened July 25 in Iowa, but it was shuttered in less than a year...The Twin City Speedway in Minnesota was a two-mile dirt circle when it started in 1914, but in 1915 the track was paved with concrete and ran its first race on September 5. The first race on the concrete surface was a 500 mile race won by Earl Cooper. Although the track was relatively flat, because of its huge circular size, the track was very fast. The track went out of business in 1917 and is now the site of the Minneapolis-St. Paul International Airport...The first oval track to ever hold auto racing events was the one-mile dirt track at the Narragansett Park in Cranston in 1896. But on September 18, the track, located at the Rhode Island State Fairgrounds was paved with concrete. The last race on the concrete track was held in 1923...The last big track to open that year was the Sheepshead Bay Speedway near New York City. It was a two-mile track similar to Chicago. It lasted until 1919...Another big track was under construction that year, but rumor has it that because it was too close to Sheepshead Bay, AAA would not issue it any race dates and the wood-surfaced Philadelphia Motor Speedway was abandoned before it was completed.

Sheepshead Bay (NY) was the site of one of the famous board tracks. This one lasted from 1915 until 1919. - Greg Fielden collection.

1916 - The last two board tracks to open before World War I included the Cincinnati Motor Speedway in Ohio, which opened on September 4 and Uniontown Speedway in Pennsylvania, which opened on November 27, 1916. The two-mile long Cincinatti track lasted until 1919 and the 1.125 mile Uniontown track was abandoned three years later.

1920 - Two board tracks opened shortly after the "Big War" ended. They were the Los Angeles Motor Speedway in Beverly Hills, and the Fresno Speedway, both in California. The prestigious 1.25 mile Beverly Hills oval opened on February 28. It was sold in 1924 to build the Beverly Hills-Wilshire Motel. Fresno opened on October 2. That one-mile track was located at the fairgrounds. The wood track at Fresno lasted until 1927 when the site returned to being a dirt horse track.

1921 - Two board tracks, both not far from San Francisco, California, opened this year. The first was Cotati Speedway, which opened on August 14. It was about fifty miles north of San Francisco. Its 1.25 mile wood lasted only one year. The other track, called San Francisco Speedway, was located in San Carlos, which is about thirty miles south of "Frisco". It opened on December 11. That 1.25 mile wood track was destroyed by a fire on June 19, 1922.

1922 - Kansas City Speedway opened September 17. The 1.25 mile track had turns banked at 35 degrees. It lasted but three summers. Jack Prince built this track as well as most of the other board tracks in this era.

1923 - Altoona Speedway in Pennsylvania opened on September 4. This 1.25 mile wood track lasted until 1931. It was the last of the large board tracks to close.

1924 - Charlotte Speedway in Pineville, North Carolina was the first of two new wood tracks built in 1924. It opened on October 25. The other track was Culver City Speedway in southern California. It began operation on December 15. Both tracks were 1.25 mile in length and both ceased operations in 1927.

1925 - Two more wood tracks opened in 1925...The first was the Baltimore-Washington Speedway in Laurel, Maryland. The 1.125 mile track opened on July 11 and its turns were banked at 48 degrees. It lasted only one year...Rockingham Speedway in Salem, New Hampshire was the next track built by Jack Prince. The 1.25 mile wood track opened on October 31 before 72,000 fans. The last race on the wood surface was in 1928. It was converted back to a horse track.

1926 - Two tracks opened in 1926. The highest banked of the 20 large board tracks was Miami-Fulford Speedway in Florida. The 1.25 mile track, which opened on February 22, was banked at an astronomical 50 degrees. The highest banked super speedway in the nation at the present time is Talladega Super Speedway, and its banks are only 33 degrees. Fulford also had the shortest history of any super speedway. Before the next race could be held, a massive hurricane destroyed the huge wood structure...The fastest of the board tracks opened later that year. The Atlantic City Speedway in Hammonton, New Jersey opened on May 1. Frank Lockhart turned a lap on the 1.5 mile track at an average speed of 147.7 miles per hour in 1927.

1927 - The General Motors Proving Grounds in Michigan held a 951.87 mile exhibition race on its 3.77 mile concrete oval on June 24.

1928 - Not to be outdone, the next year Packard had an exhibition race at its 2.5 mile concrete oval in Michigan. Leon Duray set a new record when he ran 148.17 miles per hour to make this the fastest oval track in America. After the stock market crash of 1929, money for investing in major speedways was non-existent.

1950 - It wasn't until after World War II that the next major track was built. The Darlington Raceway in South Carolina is generally referred to as the "granddaddy" of the super speedways. The track was built by Harold Brasington as a 1.25 mile high banked asphalt oval. It opened with the first "Southern 500" on September 4 before 25,000 spectators. The track was lengthened in 1953 to 1.375 miles. The turns are banked at 26 degrees.

1952 - The next high banked track was the Southland Speedway in North Carolina. It was a one-mile asphalt oval, but it only lasted seven years.

1954 - The one-mile oval at the Wisconsin State Fairgrounds was asphalted. The first race on this former dirt track was in 1903...The new Chrysler Proving Grounds in Chelsea, Michigan, to celebrate its opening, held an exhibition race on its 4.7 mile high banked asphalt oval. The track featured corners that were designed for very fast speeds. Jack McGrath didn't disappoint anyone as he turned the track at 179.762 mile per hour in an Indy roadster. That was a new closed course record for the United States.

1955 - The famous Autodromo di Monza circuit in Italy added a race on its new 2.666 mile high banked oval in 1955. The oval track was banked 39 degrees and was dubbed a "Speed Saucer". In both 1957 and 1958, 500 mile races were held for the USAC Championship cars. Each race consisted of three separate races adding up to 500 miles. Other Monza-style races soon became popular. The fastest average speed turned on the steep banks was 177.23 miles per hour by Ed Elision. The corners were concrete and were banked at 38 degrees. The original road course at Monza opened in 1923.

The high banked Monza oval in 1957. - Phil Harms collection.

1956 - The Ford test track in Kingman, Arizona held an exhibition race on its five mile paved oval on February 26.

1957 - Trenton Speedway in New Jersey became the newest one-mile paved oval. Originally it was a half-mile dirt oval, which saw its first auto race in 1900. The track was expanded again in 1969 when turns three and four were extended and highly banked. The new 1.5 mile track resembled Brooklands because it was peanut-shaped with a dog-leg in the back-straight. That track, located at the New Jersey State Fairgrounds, closed in 1980.

1959 - The new Daytona International Speedway, built by Bill France, opened and with it came immediate success. This success triggered construction of more high banked super speedways. Daytona became the fastest closed course speedway when Art Malone drove a modified Indy Car to a 181.561 mile per hour average. The NASCAR stock cars were running over 200 miles per hour on the track 30 years later until restrictions to slow the cars were instituted. The corners at Daytona are banked at 31 degrees. The annual "Daytona 500" is held here.

Daytona International Speedway (FL) as seen from the air. This huge 2.5 mile oval track was built in 1959. More than 150,000 fans attend the annual "Daytona 500" each year. - Official track photo.

1960 - Three new super speedways came into existence in 1960...The first major track on the West Coast, since the board track era, was built in California by Bonnie Marchbanks. The 1.3 mile paved track, better known as Hanford Motor Speedway, opened on June 12. It lasted until 1969 and was reconverted into a cotton field...Less than a week after the big track at Hanford ran its first race, Charlotte Motor Speedway in North Carolina opened. This 1.5 mile high banked asphalt track has seen constant improvements and is one of the prettiest in the nation. It is truly a showplace. The "World 600", the longest race on the NASCAR schedule, is held there each Memorial Day weekend...The next big track to open was the Atlanta Motor Speedway. The 1.5 mile track was the first oval track in Georgia that was larger than one-mile long since the two-mile dirt oval called Atlanta Speedway closed in 1910.

1963 - Goodyear's test track in San Angelo, Texas ran tire tests late in 1963. The A.J. Foyt's Indy roadster toured the high banked five-mile asphalt track at an unofficial average of 200.4 mile per hour. It was the first time speeds over 200 miles per hour were achieved on a closed course anywhere.

1964 - Phoenix International Raceway in Arizona opened. The one-mile asphalt track is quite picturesque as it sits at the bottom of a mountain. It is the scene of annual NASCAR Winston Cup and CART IndyCar events. One of the most unique events at the track is the "Copper World Classic". Four races for four different classes of cars are held each spring...Fred Lorenzen practiced at 170 miles per hour on the huge 7.7 mile Firestone Test Track in Texas.

1965 - The famous Langhorne Speedway in Pennsylvania was paved. The one-mile oval had run since 1926 as a dirt track. The track is now the site of a shopping center as it closed in 1971.

Don Branson (#4) surprised nearly everyone when he placed an up-right dirt car on the pole in a 1966 race at Langhorne (PA). Roger McCluskey (#8), who started outside of him in a rear-engined car, won the 150 mile race. Branson ended up fifth. - Allan E. Brown collection.

1968 - The Michigan International Speedway, a two-mile high banked D-shaped asphalt oval opened. The designs for the concave corners were taken from railroad drawings. This design, like some of the last board tracks, allows the track's groove to be wider. Speeds of over 230 miles per hour have been reached.

1969 - Three big tracks opened in 1969...The first was Dover Downs in Delaware. It is a unique auto and horse racing complex. The facility features a one-mile high banked paved oval for autos and a smaller dirt track inside the paved oval for parimutuel horse racing...The largest of the super speedways ever built in the United States, not for testing purposes, is the Talladega Super Speedway in Alabama. The 2.66 mile high banked track is also the highest banked of the modern day tracks. It became the fastest track when Mark Donohue toured the 33 degree banking at an average speed of 221.160 mile per hour. Talladega was built by Bill France and features two NASCAR Winston Cup races each year...The final super speedway completed in 1969 was Texas World Speedway. The track opened with a NASCAR race on December 7. The two-mile oval is a sister track to Michigan International Speedway. The USAC Indy cars also frequented the track, but it fell on hard times and the last Winston Cup race was in 1973. The track has operated only sporadically since then. It has hosted a variety of events including NASCAR Winston West, ARCA and TIDA late models.

1970 - One of the classiest tracks ever built anywhere was the beautiful Ontario Motor Speedway in southern California. The track layout was a carbon copy of the Indianapolis Motor Speedway, and the facility was ultra modern. Ontario was by far the most impressive track on the West Coast, but unfortunately the track was short-lived as it closed in 1980. Severe financial problems plagued the track, in addition to fact that the property value had escalated to a point that it was worth more to use the land other than as a race track.

1971 - The last of the modern day larger super speedways in America is the 2.5 mile track located in the Pocono Mountain resort area of Pennsylvania. A three-quarter mile track had been in operation since 1969 at Pocono, but the first race on the big track was a USAC Championship event won by Mark Donohue. The first time a NASCAR Winston Cup race was held here was in 1974. The last Indy car race was in 1989...Earlier that year the USAC Championship Trail ventured to the Autodromo de Rafaela in Argentina to run a 300 mile race. The 2.87 mile high banked asphalt oval produced a top average speed of 173.5 mile per hour. The straightaways were a full one-mile long.

1983 - Canada's largest oval track is the Sanair Super Speedway near Montreal, Quebec. The 1.33 kilometer track opened in 1983 and has hosted a couple of CART Indy car races as well as American Canadian Tour (ACT) and Stock Car Connection (SCC) late model races. The 9/10 mile track is a tri-oval.

1987 - Roger Penske purchased the former Nazareth National Speedway and renamed it Pennsylvania International Raceway. It was originally a one-mile dirt oval, and since has been asphalted. It is now called Nazareth Speedway.

1988 - Two tracks joined the ranks of super speedways. First the Calder Park Thunderdome in Australia opened. Neil Bonnett won the first major race on the 1.125 mile high banked oval on February 28. The race featured a number of NASCAR stars...Later in the summer, Richmond International Raceway in Virginia was increased from a half-mile to a three-quarter mile. The half-mile track had been in existence since 1946. The former dirt track has been the site of two NASCAR Winston Cup races each year since being paved in 1968.

1990 - The newest super speedway was built in New Hampshire on the site of the former Bryar Motorsports Park. Bob Bahre purchased the property and proceeded to construct a beautiful one-mile asphalt oval. Bahre scheduled races for the NASCAR Modifieds and NASCAR Busch North tour, and he was then able to secure an annual CART Indy car race, but to survive he knew he needed a NASCAR Winston Cup race. His dream came true in 1992 as his first Winston Cup race was a resounding success with 50,000 fans packing his New Hampshire International Speedway.

A number of other super speedways have been proposed the last few years, but mainly because of lack of funds, local opposition, or tough zoning laws, most of them have never made it past the drawing board. At the present time no fewer than four major speedways are in the planning stages.

GRAND PRIX - FORMULA ONE

Grand Prix racing is the oldest form of racing in the world and is among the most important types of auto races held. It is definitely the most prestigious series in the world. No other auto racing series has so much worldwide appeal. A person only has to search through a public library looking for auto racing books, and you will find most of the books on motorsports are on Grand Prix racing.

The word "Grand Prix" is French meaning "Big Prize." All Grand Prix Formula One races are held on road courses. They are called Formula One because they are the top division in International racing. Normally, a driver has to prove his ability in Formula Three and Formula Two before he advances to the Grand Prix circuit. Some circuits are regular courses built especially for racing, while others like Monte Carlo utilize city streets.

From the advent of the first automobiles the French became motor car conscious, and they were determined to make these self-propelled horseless carriages a main source of transportation. It's understandable that the French held the world's first auto race. It was on country roads between Paris and Rouen in 1894 and the race was about 80 miles long. The cars were either powered by steam, gasoline, or electricity. The winner was Count De Dion in a steam car. He averaged a mere 11 miles an hour.

Events started being held in other foreign countries as well. France had the only big race each year and it was called the "French Grand Prix" in 1906. The French sponsored the European Grand Prix races exclusively until 1921 when other countries began staging their own Grand Prix events, and by 1928 the "French Grand Prix" was just another race.

Ralph Mulford (#8) in a Lozier starts out in the 1911 "Vanderbilt Cup" race at Savannah (GA). Mulford won the 291 mile race. - Allan E. Brown collection.

Grand Prix - Formula One

Jimmy Murphy on his way to victory in the "French Grand Prix" at LeMans in 1921. He was driving an American-built Duesenberg. - Phil Harms collection.

JIMMY MURPHY WINS THE "FRENCH GRAND PRIX"

Only one American ever won a European Grand Prix race in the early years of the sport. Jimmy Murphy won the 1921 "French Grand Prix" in a Duesenberg. Murphy had a decided advantage as his car was the only one equipped with four wheel hydraulic brakes. America had to wait over forty years before another American car was victorious in a Grand Prix race.

Major road races started being sanctioned by the American Automobile Association (AAA) in America beginning with the first "Vanderbilt Cup" race in New York in 1904. William Vanderbilt sponsored these prestigious events. Another major road race in America was the "American Grand Prize" that was first held in Savannah, Georgia in 1908. European cars and drivers were frequent competitors in these events and usually won because of their superior equipment. It wasn't until 1908 that an American car won one of America's premier road racing events, as George Robertson drove a Locomobile to victory in the "Vanderbilt Cup" race. The last year for both races was 1916.

Major road racing ceased in America with the coming of World War I and it wasn't until 1936 that fans were able to see the world's best Grand Prix drivers in action on American soil. A special course was constructed at Roosevelt Field on Long Island, New York, and the "Vanderbilt Trophy Races" were held for two years. Both races, sanctioned by AAA, were dominated by foreign cars and drivers. Major American racing was primarily oval track in nature and none of the American cars were suited for racing on road courses.

One of the most famous Grand Prix cars of the 1920's was the Bugatti, Type 50. It was patterned after one of America's cars designed by Harry Miller. Due to the outbreak of World War II, Grand Prix racing was curtailed for obvious reasons. Racing on the European front didn't resume until 1947, and Italian and

German cars dominated the series. The current World's driving title was instituted in 1950 with Guiseppe "Nino" Farina from Italy becoming the first World Champion in the modern era. Juan Manuel Fangio from Argentina is the only five-time World Champion. He won his titles in the 1950's. The Manufacturers Championship was started by FIA in 1953.

Juan Manuel Fangio won the World Driving title in this W196 Mercedes in 1955. - Allan E. Brown collection.

Since its inception, success in Grand Prix racing has always been a matter of national prestige, and over the years, France, Italy, Germany, as well as other European countries have backed racing teams. Europe is a car seller's market and intense competition between automobile manufacturers puts the emphasis on the machines like Renault and Mercedes, and not on the drivers like in America. In recent years the trend has switched and many drivers are now national heroes.

In the late 1950's, British built Cooper-Climaxes changed the course of racing not only on the Grand Prix circuit, but eventually in the United States Auto Club's (USAC) Championship Trail as well (USAC had taken over as America's major auto racing sanction in 1955 when AAA bowed out). These small, nimble rear-engined machines with independent suspension were superior in the handling aspect of cornering. Jack Brabham from Australia won the championship for Cooper in 1959 and 1960. Brabham drove a Cooper-Climax in the 1961 Indianapolis 500 and that paved the way for other Grand Prix drivers to invade America's oval tracks. In 1957, the Automobile Competition Committee of the United States (ACCUS) was created. It is the American wing of the Federation Internationale de l'Association (FIA) which oversees auto racing internationally.

THE UNITED STATES GRAND PRIX

The first modern day "United States Grand Prix" was held at Sebring, Florida on December 12, 1959. Although Bruce McLaren from New Zealand drove a Cooper-Climax to victory, the race was a disaster financially. The next year the race was moved to California, but that race at Riverside Raceway only drew 20,000 fans to watch Sterling Moss in a rear-engined Lotus take the checkered flag. The next year the race was moved to Watkins Glen in upstate New York and everything went well. Finally the crowds were sufficient to put on such a prestigious event. It is rumored that crowds of more than 200,000 witnessed the

Grand Prix - Formula One

U.S.G.P. races at Watkins Glen in the late 1960's. This was a marvelous period of time for racing as driver interchange between the Formula One circuit and USAC was commonplace. With the introduction of rear-engined cars on the USAC Championship Trail many former and future Grand Prix champions like Jack Brabham, Denis Hulme, John Surtees, Jackie Stewart, and Jochen Rindt were frequent visitors to the United States to race the Indianapolis cars. Jimmy Clark and Graham Hill, both two time Formula One World Champions, won the prestigious, USAC sanctioned Indianapolis 500 in rear-engined cars in 1965 and 1966 respectively. American drivers including Bobby Unser and his younger brother Al, Mario Andretti, Lloyd Ruby, and A.J. Foyt were just a few of America's oval track stars who took on the world's best in Grand Prix racing. But very few American drivers felt the need to conquer the world as racing in America was both plentiful and profitable. Gordon Johncock turned down an offer to drive Formula One because he didn't want to travel.

America has had two World Champions. Phil Hill from California was the first when he drove an Italian Ferrari team car to the title in 1961. Hill's first Formula One win came at Monza, Italy the year before. He was the first American to win a Grand Prix race since Jimmy Murphy's win in France in 1921. It wasn't until 1978 that another American, Mario Andretti, would win the World Driving title. Andretti was born in Italy, but moved to Nazareth, Pennsylvania in 1955. Other Americans to win Formula One races in the 1960's include Dan Gurney and Ritchie Ginther. Gurney, who won a total of four Grand Prix races, was the first American driver to win a Grand Prix race in an American built car since 1921. Gurney's car was patriotically called an "Eagle". Dan Gurney was the only person to ever win a Formula One, an Indy Car and a NASCAR Grand National race in the same year (1967).

THE CANADIAN GRAND PRIX

The first "Canadian Grand Prix" was held on August 27, 1967 at Mosport Park near Toronto, Ontario. It was won by Jack Brabham in a car of his own design. The site of the "Canadian Grand Prix" then alternated for the next three years between Mosport and Le Circuit Mont Tremblant in Quebec until it settled in at Mosport for the next seven years (with the exception of 1975 when no "Canadian Grand Prix" was held). In 1978 the race was moved to Montreal, Quebec. The new circuit was first called Circuit de Ile Notre Dame. Canadian Gilles Villeneuve gave his countrymen something to really cheer about as he won the first "Canadian Grand Prix" at Notre Dame on October 8, 1978. The Quebec star won six Formula One races in 67 starts before he was tragically killed while practicing for the 1982 "Belgium Grand Prix". The circuit has since been renamed to Circuit Gilles Villeneuve in his honor and the annual "Canadian Grand Prix" (with the exception that there was no "Canadian Grand Prix" held in 1987) has been held at the Montreal circuit ever since.

In an unprecedented move, a second race counting towards the World Championship was awarded the United States in 1976. It was standard procedure that only one race a year was held in each participating country. Noted historian John Printz wrote, "because of huge payoffs and prize money available in the United States (after all, money talks) since 1976 we have had at least two Grand Prixes per year with the addition of Long Beach". The "U.S.G.P. West" was held on streets and highways in Long Beach, California. Clay Regazzoni in a Ferrari won that race on March 28. The regular "U.S.G.P." continued each October in Watkins Glen through 1980 when the track went into hiatus. Long Beach held Grand Prix races for seven years before they switched the race to an Indy Car race. Caesar's Palace in Las Vegas, Nevada became the newest venue for Formula One in America in 1981 when they held the first of two Grand Prixes. Then in 1982, three Formula One races in the United States were staged. Along with Long Beach and Las Vegas, the largest city in Michigan jumped on the band wagon and the "Detroit Grand Prix" was born. Detroit was a natural place to hold a world class motorsports event, as it is known as the Motor City, because the "Big Three" American automobile manufacturers (General Motors, Ford, and Chrysler) were all based there. Seven Grand Prixes were raced at Detroit, before the race was switched to the Detroit based Championship Auto Racing Teams (CART) Indy Car series (CART had taken over as the major Indy Car sanction from USAC in 1979). In 1984 an additional "U.S.G.P." was held in Dallas, Texas on park roads at the Texas State Expo. The final Formula One race at Detroit was in 1988. The next scene of a Formula One race on American soil was in Phoenix, Arizona in 1989. The three Grand Prix races at Phoenix were not financially rewarding for the city, and the March 10, 1991 race was the last Formula One race held in the United States as of the writing of this book.

The past few years a running conflict between FIA, (the organization that oversees the Grand Prix circuit) and CART (who runs the United States based IndyCar series) have kept driver interchange at a minimum. In addition the temporary demise of the "United States Grand Prix" hasn't helped the situation either. Officials of FIA and CART have both expressed their displeasure with the other circuit. CART has imitated the Formula One circuit by only allowing one race a year at each venue, by scheduling more road course events, and by initiating franchises for its car owners.

Formula One Grand Prix races are currently being held in Brazil, Japan, San Marino, Monaco, Spain, Canada, France, England, Germany, Hungary, Belgium, Italy, Portugal, Argentina, and Australia.

Other Formula One champions are Alberto Ascari (twice), Mike Hawthorne, Emerson Fittipaldi (twice), Niki Lauda (twice), James Hunt, Jody Scheckter, Alan Jones, Nelson Piquet (three times), Keke Rosberg, Alain Prost (four time champion), Ayrton Senna, and Nigel Mansell. Prost is the all-time winner on the Formula One circuit with fifty-one wins.

Niki Lauda in a Ferrari at Long Beach in 1976. - Phil Harms collection.

THE BOARD TRACKS

One of the most interesting periods in auto racing was the board track era. These large wood saucers helped bring about astounding advancements in engine designs, supercharging, metal alloys, tire development and fuel. They adequately filled the need at the time as asphalt, as we know it now, didn't exist at that time.

In the early days of oval track racing most of the tracks were dirt horse tracks. The horse track owners would not allow anything to be put on the track to keep the dust down. Tracks in recent years have taken to adding calcium-chloride to keep their dirt tracks moist. The horse track owners felt if the track surface was made harder it would cause harm to the horses that usually ran on them. Most dirt tracks after the turn of the century were dusty and often full of chuck-holes. The dust was sometimes so thick that the onlookers could not see the cars and the drivers couldn't see either. This made for very dangerous conditions.

Something had to be done. Spectators would not pay to attend a race they could not see. Plus drivers sometimes refused to drive on dusty tracks. Most car owners balked at putting their cars on tracks that developed ruts that could easily destroy their expensive machines.

Road builders tried to build paved tracks, but the liquid asphalt that was available at that time was more like a thin tar and was so poor it quickly disintegrated under the pounding of the heavy race cars. Carl Fisher at his Indianapolis Motor Speedway resorted to having his large dirt track bricked with three million ten-pound bricks. But that process was expensive and Indianapolis was the only track to ever be paved in that fashion. Twin City Motor Speedway

The banks on some of the board tracks were awesome. The banking on Altoona (PA) Speedway was 32 degrees in this 1925 photo. - Alden Jamison collection.

in Minneapolis, Minnesota paved their two-mile track with concrete, but that too was expensive.

In California an engineer by the name of Fred Moscovics had an idea. As a youth he had been a bike racing fan. He went to every bike race he could find. We have found evidence of board bicycle tracks in New York City as far back as 1894. The beautiful one-sixth mile high banked board tracks the bicycle racers used gave him an idea. Why not build an oversized version of a bike track and race cars on it? A wooden track would be dust free, smooth, fast, and quick to build.

The wood tracks were built similar to basic bridge construction. They were built from the ground up on pilings. Once the underpinnings were erected, the track surface itself was laid. These were made of either 2x4, 2x6 or 2x8 boards laid standing on edge and nailed to each other, similar to how bowling alleys are made. The board track era lasted for 21 years. There were 24 of these wood saucers built across the country. They ranged from one-half mile to two miles in length.

THE FIRST BOARD TRACK

Moscovics, along with Jack Prince, designed and built the first major wood track and the amazing board track era began. The Los Angeles Motordrome in Playa Del Ray in southern California was a circular one mile wood track that was banked at twenty degrees. According to Dick Wallen's fabulous book, *BOARD TRACK, Guts, Gold & Glory,* the press called the round track, "the pie pan". The track opened on April 8, 1910 and it was an instant success. It was really fast and better yet, the spectators could see the races clearly and go home without a layer of dust covering their clothes. The drivers found this track different from anything else on which they had ever driven, as the perfectly round track didn't require much turning of the steering wheel and the circular shape made the cars almost steer themselves.

The circular shape allowed the drivers to go flat out and although the speeds attained were impressive, the races were lackluster as the cars would spread out quickly. Perhaps the only fault with the circular shaped track was that it was too perfect. The nation's first nighttime auto races were at the Playa Del Ray track in 1911. The track was sanctioned by AAA but it never held a Triple-A national championship race. The track was destroyed by a fire in 1913.

The next board track built was in Oakland, California. Prince, who built the Oakland Motordrome, would go on to build most of the famous board tracks. The design of this circular half-mile track was a downsized version of the Playa Del Ray track. But the banking at the Oakland track was higher at forty degrees. It opened in 1911, but it was not successful and closed within a year.

Jack Prince had earlier built a number of smaller wood tracks for motorcycle racing at various places across the country including in Los Angeles (California), Chicago (Illinois) and in Springfield (Massachusetts). The first wood track that held motorcycle racing, of which we have any knowledge, was the Paterson Velodrome in New Jersey. It was a one-sixth mile high banked wood track and it ran motorcycle races in July of 1908. Some of the other wood motorcycle tracks were in Atlanta (Georgia), Detroit (Michigan), Omaha (Nebraska), South Orange (New Jersey) and in Salt Lake City (Utah). Most of these small tracks, built for motorcycle racing shortly after the turn of the century, were one-third mile in length. The Atlanta track might have been the first wood track to have an auto race car tour its banks in late 1909.

CHICAGO SPEEDWAY IS BUILT

The board track era had to wait a few years before another major track was built. Prince, figuring how to create better competition and also to provide more seating, built his next track with two straightaways rather than a round configuration. The huge two-mile Chicago Speedway in Illinois was an instant success as 85,000 spectators filed into the track to watch the inaugural 500 mile race won by Dario Resta in 1915. The Chicago track prospered until 1918 when a hospital was built on the site during World War I.

The AAA Championship cars are leaving the starting line for the first race at the new Chicago (IL) Speedway in 1915. - Greg Fielden collection.

One of the most unusual aftermaths of Chicago Speedway's success was the building of a new wood track in Tacoma, Washington. The Pacific Coast Speedway started out as a two-mile dirt oval in 1914, but the track conditions were terrible and the owners decided they would put liquid asphalt on the surface. They were aware of the problems of the liquid asphalt and how holes could develop in the track's surface. Their solution was to put a foundation of 2x4 boards running the length of the track. A three-eighth inch gap was left between the boards, which were laid flat, so the liquid asphalt could run down into the gaps and therefore, hopefully, the surface would stay intact. But with Chicago's success they decided not to pour on the asphalt and instead to race on the 2x4s. It proved to be a good idea and from 1915 until 1922 Tacoma was the only big time plank track that operated. About the only drawback of the track was that dirt and small rocks would be sucked up from between the gaps by the speeding race cars, and would then fly back into any closely following competitor.

The Chicago Speedway's instant success also encouraged Prince to build new tracks in Omaha (Nebraska) and Des Moines (Iowa). The Omaha Speedway, which opened on July 15, 1915, was a mile and a quarter track with the corners banked at 41 degrees. Only three races (one each in 1915, 1916 and 1917) were held on the Omaha track before it was abandoned. Its demise was caused when the track's surface broke up severely during the 1917 race. Actually, the downfall of most of the big wood tracks was the lack of wood preservatives. It would be interesting to see how long the tracks would have survived if the present day pressure-treated lumber had been available.

The damage from deterioration is evident to the wood surface in this photo of the Atlantic City (NJ) Speedway. - Bob Sheldon collection.

The one-mile Des Moines Speedway was a little bit smaller than the Omaha track but it lasted less than a year. It opened ten days after the Omaha track in 1915, and was owned by the Des Moines Chamber of Commerce. The turns were banked thirty degrees, and the track ran its last race on June 26, 1916.

The next board track was constructed by Blaine Miller at the location of an old horse track in the seaside resort town of Sheepshead Bay (a suburb of Brooklyn, New York). The Sheepshead Bay Speedway was a two-mile wood track with seventeen degree corners. The track was originally planned to be either bricked like Indianapolis or paved with concrete like Twin City. But with the success of the Chicago track, it was built of wood instead. The track was also an instant success, and it lasted until 1919 when the combination of mismanagement, the effects of World War I and the track's deterioration shuttered the track.

The Philadelphia Motor Speedway Association track was the next board track scheduled to be built. Construction on the two-mile long track halted when the track was only partially finished. The track, originally designed to be constructed of bricks like Indianapolis, was abandoned for a number of reasons. The reasons included the fact that Triple-A wouldn't issue them any dates. AAA thought the Philadelphia track was too close to the Sheepshead Bay track. The aborted track was near Willow Grove, Pennsylvania.

The eighth major board track was built by Harry Hake in Cincinnati in 1916. It was a carbon copy of the Chicago track and its biggest race was run on

Memorial Day in 1917 with a crowd reported at 65,000. The Indianapolis Motor Speedway usually ran its annual "Indianapolis 500" on Memorial Day, but when Indy decided not to race for the duration of World War I, it left the date open for the race at the Cincinnati Motor Speedway. The track lasted until 1919. It was reported that the track was dismantled and the wood was used to built Camp Sherman in late 1919.

The next wood track was Uniontown Speedway in Pennsylvania. It opened in 1916. Jack Prince built this 1.125 mile track with 34 degree banking. The track lasted seven years before it closed.

BEVERLY HILLS GETS A TRACK

The tenth board track was probably the most prestigious and certainly the most glamorous, not only by its appearance but by the fact that it was built in Beverly Hills, California. The Los Angeles Motor Speedway opened on February 28, 1920. Frequently movie stars would be seen at the track. The 1.25 mile track, again built by Jack Prince, cost $500,000 to build. It was one of the most successful board tracks of its era, but as property values skyrocketed in the Beverly Hills area, the track was dismantled and the property sold for development in 1924. More than 100,000 people were in attendance to watch a race on Thanksgiving Day in 1923. The site later became the location of the luxurious Beverly Hills-Wilshire Hotel.

The field gets ready for a race at the Los Angeles Motor Speedway in Beverly Hills, California. - Allan E. Brown collection.

Jack Prince and Art Pillsbury (a well known Triple-A official) then combined their efforts to build the Fresno Speedway on the fairgrounds in that central California city. Barney Oldfield had raced on the one mile dirt fairgrounds track as far back as 1904. The new track was the same size, but the corners were banked at thirty degrees. The wood track in Fresno ran from 1920 until 1927, and then the site was converted back to a horse track.

Cotati Speedway in Santa Rosa, California was the next track constructed by Prince and Pillsbury. The one and a quarter mile track only lasted a little over a year before it was torn down to build an egg farm. It seems some of the neighbors had complained about the track and the owner decided to really give them a reason to complain. Anyone who has driven by a chicken farm on a hot day will know what I mean.

Prince and Pillsbury built their next track a few miles farther south in San Francisco. The one and one quarter mile San Francisco Speedway in San Carlos was destroyed by a fire less than a year from the date it opened in 1921.

The next board track popped up in mid-America. It is rumored that the Kansas City Speedway was secretly financed by the *Kansas City Star*. It had cost $500,000 to build in 1922 by Prince and Pillsbury. But when the track was not a financial success, the daily newspaper supposedly became so disenchanted that almost all auto racing coverage disappeared from its pages. The track's last race was on July 4, 1924. The extensive stories in the *Star* prior to the track being built would certainly indicate that they were somewhat involved.

ALTOONA SPEEDWAY IS BORN

The longest lasting of the board tracks was constructed in 1923 in the central Pennsylvania town of Tipton. The Altoona Speedway was another one of the Prince and Pillsbury creations and it lasted until 1931. The one and a quarter mile track was certainly the most historic of the board tracks. The track's longevity came from being completely resurfaced with new boards. This was an expensive and time consuming job.

Board tracks, because of the high speed and the lack of safety equipment in that era, were very dangerous and numerous drivers were fatally injured driving the wood tracks. The Altoona track was one of the deadliest and had the unfortunate distinction of having three "Indianapolis 500" winners being fatally injured on its 32 degree banking. Howard Wilcox, who won the 1919 "Indy 500" crashed to his death in the track's opening race on September 4, 1923. Joe Boyer, who co-drove a Duesenburg with L.L. Corum to the 1924 "Indy 500", met his demise at Altoona less than four months after his win at Indy and Ray Keech, the 1929 "500" winner, was fatally injured in a horrendous crash less than a month after he took the checkered flag at Indy. They were not the first "Indy 500" winners to lose their lives on a board track as 1920 "Indy" winner Gaston Chevrolet was fatally injured late in that same year at the Beverly Hills track.

The first major board track located in the southeast was built by Prince in 1924 in North Carolina. The Charlotte Speedway lasted almost four years before the track's owner decided not to resurface the deteriorating surface. It looked as if an army of termites had a banquet.

The seventeenth major board track and seventh and the last to be built in California was the Culver City Speedway. The Prince and Pillsbury built track opened December 15, 1924 and was one of the highest banked board tracks at 45 degrees. The track ran its last race in 1927.

The second 1.125 mile board track was the Baltimore-Washington Speedway in Laurel, Maryland. The Prince built, 48 degree banked track was short lived as it opened in July of 1925 and held its last event in September of 1926.

The only major board track to be constructed in New England was built on the site of a mile horse track. Prince built the one and a quarter mile wood track. Peter DePaolo won the first race on Halloween Day of 1925 before 72,000 spectators at Rockingham Speedway in Salem, New Hampshire. The last race, on

56

a deteriorating track, was cut short because of a fatality to driver Fred Comer in 1928. Although the wood track was dismantled the facility still exists today as Rockingham Park and remains as a popular parimutuel horse track.

HURRICANE RUINS FISHER'S TRACK

Carl Fisher, who built the Indianapolis Motor Speedway, got into the board track business as he built the mile and a quarter Miami-Fulford Speedway in Miami Beach, Florida. He had hoped a major speedway would bring attention to this fast budding resort town. The track had the highest banking of any of the 24 board tracks. The 50 degree banked track, designed by Ray Harroun, opened on February 22, 1926. The fastest and highest banked track presently in the nation is Talladega Super Speedway in Alabama, and it is only banked at 33 degrees. A driver at Miami-Fulford had to run at least 110 miles per hour to stay on the banking. The track was a success, but before another race could be held a massive hurricane destroyed the track on September 17, 1926. No one knows just how strong the storm was as the weather instruments were carried away by gusts of winds over 150 miles per hour. The track was never rebuilt, but rather the salvageable lumber was used to rebuild the devastated resort town.

This is what is left of Miami-Fulford Speedway (FL) after a devastating hurricane made shambles of the beautiful track. - Al Powell collection.

The fastest of the board tracks was built by Prince and Pillsbury in New Jersey. The Atlantic City Speedway was banked at 45 degrees and Frank Lockhart toured the mile and a half track at an average speed of 147.727 mph. The track lasted three seasons. It opened on May 1, 1926. Harry Hartz averaged 135 miles per hour for 300 miles in the opener. Its last race was September 16, 1928. This was also the last board track to be built that was at least a mile long.

The last three major wood tracks were all one-half mile in length. The first two were built by Paul Turtin in Akron, Ohio and Bridgeville, Pennsylvania. The Akron-Cleveland Speedway opened in 1926 and held its last race in 1930. Within five years of its last race the track had completely disappeared. Times were tough during the Great Depression and the track was dismantled piece by piece by neighbors who either used the material to build housing or the wood was burned as heat for their houses.

Turtin's Pittsburgh-Bridgeville Speedway opened a year later and probably closed in 1930 as well. There is a possibility that an outlaw race was held there in May of 1931.

The twenty-fourth and final major board track to open was the half-mile Woodbridge Speedway in New Jersey. The track, built by Wilbert Paine, opened on July 21, 1928 and was at the site of a dirt track that first ran in 1926. The track was a deadly one as three drivers lost their lives in crashes at the track.

Altoona Speedway, which closed in September of 1931 had been presumed to be the last wood track, but it was not the case as Bernie Karnatz won the last ever board track race on October 18, 1931 at Woodbridge. The track was turned back into a dirt track, and it operated as such until the start of World War II.

So ended the board track era. Most of the best drivers of that time period won races on the board tracks. They include Dario Resta, Eddie Richenbacher, Ralph DePalma, Louis Chevrolet, Earl Cooper, Ralph Mulford, Tommy Milton, Eddie Hearne, Gaston Chevrolet, Jimmy Murphy, Roscoe Sarles, Harry Hartz, Bennett Hill, Harlan Fengler, Peter DePaolo, Dave Lewis, Frank Lockhart, Louis Meyer, Wilbur Shaw and Shorty Cantlon. The winningest driver on the board tracks was Ralph DePalma as he took the honors in 16 Triple-A championship events on board tracks. DePalma's nephew, Peter DePaolo is considered by many historians as the best board track driver as he had ten major board track wins.

Peter DePaolo in the Miller # 3 at Culver City (CA) Speedway in 1927. He is considered the best board track driver of all time. - Phil Harms collection.

Wilbur Shaw once told how it felt to be racing at 130 miles per hour and see a human head in the middle of the track. It was that of a carpenter repairing the track in a hole that had developed.

SMALLER BOARD TRACKS

Since the famous board track days at least seventeen smaller wood tracks have operated. Many of them were indoor tracks built in coliseums or stadiums and raced the smaller midget racers. But five of these small wood tracks were in outdoor arenas. The first two outdoor tracks, which were first constructed for bicycle racing, ran on the East Coast in the late 1930's. The Nutley Velodrome in New Jersey ran midget auto races in 1938 and 1939 on a 45 degree banked, one-seventh mile wood track. The other track was at the seaside resort of Coney Island in Brooklyn, New York. The Coney Island Velodrome was similar in size, shape and banking as Nutley and it ran the midget racers in 1939 and also in 1940. The other three outdoor small wood surfaced tracks were located in major football stadiums. A quarter mile wood track was constructed in Soldiers Field in Chicago, Illinois in 1939. It is the home of the Chicago Bears, and a series of races, called the "World Championship for Midgets", were held over an eight day period. But the most unique track was the one constructed in the Polo Grounds (the former home of the New York Giants) in New York City. The fifth mile aluminum and wood track ran two races in June of 1948 and was then disassembled and transported via the railroad across the country to Pasadena, California and reassembled in the Rose Bowl (home of the famous New Year's Day college football classic). Midget races were held on the transplanted wood track from July of 1948 until sometime in 1949.

This wood track was constructed inside of the Polo Grounds in New York City. Two races in 1948 where held on the track before it was disassembled and moved across the country by rail. It was reassembled at the Rose Bowl in Pasadena, California. - Frank Smith photo (Len Ashburn collection).

WEEKLY SHORT TRACKS

Weekly short track auto racing began to blossom in the 1930's. Before that, nearly all tracks ran only occasionally. Perhaps the first track to ever run weekly events was Legion Ascot in southern California. The track opened in 1924 and held weekly big car racing. Prior to the opening Legion Ascot, the last weekly racing may have been the final chariot races at Rome's Circus Maximus in 529 A.D. It was when the midgets came along that weekly racing really got its start.

THE MIDGETS

It was common for fairgrounds horse tracks to hold one or so races a year, many times during their annual fair on their half-mile or mile tracks. Other races at a fairgrounds, other than during the fair, were called spotters or still dates. As midget racing became popular, many tracks were built, or existing stadiums were utilized for the small cars. With their sudden popularity the races were held more often. A short time later weekly roadster races were held at a variety of venues. These larger cars, similar to sprint cars, were only popular for a brief period before weekly jalopy racing took over. Additional information on both the midgets and the roadsters can be found in the Open Wheel Race Cars chapter.

Riverview Stadium in Chicago was just one of the weekly midget tracks before World War II. - Bob Sheldon photo.

THE JALOPIES

By the late 1940's, Jalopy stock car racing had pushed midget racing from the top spot as the most popular weekly short track program. There were many factors that contributed to the sudden rise in weekly jalopy races. First, there was an abundant supply of the pre-war cars starting in 1949. Prior to that many older cars were still being used on the road. During the war, new car production was halted. Thus for a four-year period older cars had to be utilized. Maintaining a car during the war was difficult, as spare parts were hard to locate. By the time the auto industry was permitted to resume production after the treaty papers

B-K Speedway (MI) was one of the many backyard race tracks in 1951. It's hard to believe that the track has evolved over the years and is now the beautiful Kalamazoo Speedway. - Michigan Motor Sports Hall of Fame collection.

were signed, the demand for new automobiles was so great that the industry couldn't keep up. It wasn't until 1948 that new car production caught up with the demand. When that happened, it left many of these pre-war coupes and sedans to sit behind barns and garages to rust, as most had now been abandoned as far as highway use.

In the late 1940's anyone wishing to become involved with auto racing found that midget and big car racing was expensive and quite dangerous. The old jalopies were inexpensive to build and maintain and were relatively safe. It was easy to see, with an abundance of these pre-war cars and the urge for excitement, how jalopy racing blossomed.

Nearly 2,000 tracks had been built to run the jalopies by 1955. Many of them were cut out of farmers' fields, and had few if any grandstands. The spectators usually watched from an overlooking hillside. These cow pasture race tracks usually had a short life span, for as soon as a better track was built nearby, the other one would be reconverted back into pasture land. Nearly all of the tracks built in this period were made of dirt and were usually from one-quarter to one-half mile in length. About the same time, it was discovered that the jalopies were well suited to run on the same small tracks that the midgets were using. This added to the plight of the midget division. Also, many fairgrounds were in financial trouble, and it became a source of additional revenue to rent their horse tracks to stage weekly jalopy races. Like the midgets in that division's heyday, many areas saw stock car races being held seven nights a week.

The stock car boom hit its peak about 1953. Motoring down a highway, in that era, you were often reminded of the local stock car races as it seemed like every gas station or auto repair shop had a jalopy stock car parked by it.

THE MODIFIEDS

Racing people are known as very competitive and resourceful people, and the quest to win meant going faster, which meant spending more money on modifications. As the cars became more sophisticated, stock car owners were forced to quit racing as they no longer could afford it, and some tracks closed for lack of cars. These faster cars were at most times called modifieds. These modifieds, although still looking somewhat like the jalopies, were becoming finely tuned race cars with high-performance parts.

Weekly Short Tracks

THE SUPERMODIFIEDS

In the mid-1950's another type of car called a supermodified began its reign as the top weekly short track car. It was a smaller version of the regular modified car and was about the same size as a big car. It had a full roll cage, like the jalopies, and usually had an old coupe body, but the body was cut down just large enough to fit around a narrowed chassis, and just like a sprint car it was now open wheeled and only had one forward gear. The supermodifieds generally had to be pushed to be started as they did not have starters. The fleet cars quickly won race after race against the heavier modifieds, and other car owners modified their own cars in a similar fashion. At first some of these cars were called coupesters, as they were somewhat of a combination of jalopy coupes and roadsters that were popular a few years before.

New York's Nolan Swift and his "10 pins" supermodified. - Ray Rogers photo

The supermodifieds saw their peak years from the late 1950's until the mid-1960's. It wasn't long before older sprint cars were converted into supers by just adding a roll cage. The trend of cutting down the jalopies spread like wildfire across the country, but one area of the country was somewhat immune. All along the Eastern states the modifieds continued as the top division. Some other tracks couldn't afford to pay the higher purses the supermodifieds now needed to exist, and many tracks switched to post-war sedans which were now abundant.

THE LATE MODELS

In the southeast section of the country, most short track racing was patterned after the successful NASCAR Grand National circuit. NASCAR began running strictly stock automobiles in 1949. The cars on the NASCAR circuit had to be within four years of the current model. On the Southern short track circuits the cars were generally five years old or older. Some tracks still raced the old pre-war coupes, but most had switched to the passenger cars of the late 1950's and early 1960's. These newer cars were called Late Model Sportsmen, Semi-late Models, and Super Stocks. There were a few tracks in the south that ran supermodifieds (called "Skeeters" in the south), but the full bodied cars such as the Sportsmen cars were the mainstay for weekly racing in the southeast. The short track late models caught on, and during the 1970's and 1980's most areas of the country were racing the full bodied cars.

The Semi-late models were sometimes a secondary class for the modifieds or supermodifieds. It wasn't long before specialized late models started to evolve, one design for paved tracks and another design for dirt tracks. Short track late model racing had became the most popular type of weekly racing in the early 1970's. But the stock cars varied from area to area. Each locale had its own rules and different size of cars, as well as what they called the class. Some areas used the larger full-sized passenger cars, others the intermediate sized cars, and still others the compact cars. Various names have been used for the late model classes including Late Model Modifieds, Grand Americans, and Super Late Models. There were a few weekly tracks that were using the newer style bodies as far back as the early 1950's, but it wasn't until later that most areas switched from the faster and more expensive modifieds and supermodifieds to the full-fendered late models.

Dirt track and pavement racing differ drastically, and the cars were constructed to perform more efficiently on one or the other surface. Over the years a number of traveling groups have capitalized on the weekly late models. Pavement series include the American Speed Association (ASA), The NASCAR sanctioned All Pro Series, The American Canadian Tour (ACT) and the midwest based ARTGO. The most famous dirt late model circuit was the former National Dirt Racing Association (NDRA). Before its demise, NDRA equaled if not surpassed the World of Outlaws. Other current dirt track late models circuits include Short Track Auto Racing Stars (STARS), Hav-A-Tampa Dirt Racing Series (HATS), and the Midwest LateModel Racing Association (MLRA).

Ohio's Jim Dunn was one of the most popular drivers on the Midwest dirt late model circuits. He was fatally injured in a fiery accident during a NDRA late model race in Kentucky. His tragic accident brought about major changes in the dirt late model rules including eliminating the large plastic spoilers on the rear-deck. - Allan E. Brown collection.

About a quarter of America's tracks are asphalt tracks. Highway grade asphalt is a very complex mixture of high-molecular-weight hydrocarbons. These hydrocarbons contain nitrogen, oxygen, sulphur, as well as other elements in trace amounts. By the use of solvents, the hydrocarbons can be separated into asphaltenes and resins. Asphalt is one of the oldest building materials. It dates back to 3800 B.C., but only natural asphalt existed before 1900. Since then there has been controlled refining of crude petroleum (as most crude petroleum contains some asphalt). In 1870 the first asphalt road was laid in front of the city hall in Newark, New Jersey. Most early asphalt was applied as a diluted emulsion spray on a graded roadbed. It wasn't until asphalt was used as a penetrating treatment on a macadam rock base, which filled the voids and bound the stones together, that asphalt race tracks were possible. Just after the turn of the century, a few tracks tried the liquid asphalt method, but it would not hold up under the pounding of the heavy race cars. Asphalt can be applied as a hot or cold mix blended with stones, slag, sand, or gravel aggregates before it is spread on the prepared base. Perhaps the first track to use asphalt, in the form we are familiar with today, was Dupont Speedway in Denver, Colorado in 1930. The oldest asphalt track, still in existence, is Thompson Speedway in Connecticut. It was built as a paved track in 1939. The Indianapolis Motor Speedway paved over much of its original bricks with asphalt that same year.

EAST COAST MODIFIEDS

An area of the country that was somewhat immune to the supermodified invasion was the Northeast, covering New England as well as New York, New Jersey and eastern Pennsylvania. In this area the older style coupes were still predominant. Many of the short tracks in this area were NASCAR sanctioned and the coupes for that reason were retained. Except for a few paved tracks in New York and New England, and a few dirt tracks in central Pennsylvania, very few tracks in the Northeast converted to the smaller supermodifieds. Most tracks stayed with the modifieds with their older bodies. The modified followers called the supermodifieds..."Bugs", and the other fans called the modifieds..."Heavies."

Brett Bodine (#12) and Richie Evans (#61) race each other at Thompson (CT) Speedway in the early 1980's. - David Allio photo.

Two classes of Modifieds were common in the Northeast. The Modifieds and another class called Sportsmen. (not to be confused with the Late Model Sportsmen). The Sportsmen from a distance looked like a Modified, but they were not allowed as many modifications. Many times the two classes would run together. The faster modifieds would most often be handicapped by having to start in the rear of the races. The Modifieds are still the top class in the Northeast, but the old coupe bodies gave way to newer compact car body styles in the early 1970's when the older coupe bodies became scarce. In the late 1960's a split from the pavement and dirt track modifieds began. The Modifieds racing

64

on asphalt tracks were now low and sleek with the driver sitting in the same position as a production automobile. The dirt track modifieds were taller with the driver sitting in the middle of the car, straddling the drive shaft, similar to the sprint cars and midgets.

"Barefoot" Bob McCreadie of Watertown, New York is one of the top drivers on the DIRT Modified circuit. - John Grady photo.

I.M.C.A. MODIFIEDS

One of the leading sprint car organizations, the International Motor Contest Association (I.M.C.A.) went into hiatus in the late 1970's and the name was purchased by a group of four men. The I.M.C.A. races came to a halt in 1977, but the new owners, including Keith Knaack, resurrected the I.M.C.A. name with the introduction of a new low-cost class called the I.M.C.A. Modifieds a few years later. These cars look similar to the pavement Modifieds that run on the East Coast, but the cars have restrictions on the engines and tires to keep them relatively inexpensive and highly competitive. When this new economy class was introduced, skeptics said the class would not last. Car owners do not like the idea

This is what a typical I.M.C.A. modified looks like. The driver is Dave Roy of Langdon, North Dakota. - Official Grand Forks (ND) Speedway photo.

of restrictions, especially a claim on an engine. Being claimed means that if a car finishes in the top five positions, the car's engine can be claimed by one of the other finishers for $300. This has kept the high cost of racing engines from entering the class. The I.M.C.A. Modifieds not only caught on, but have replaced the now expensive late models at many tracks. Other organizations have capitalized on I.M.C.A.'s success with their own economy modified divisions. NASCAR call their low-cost modifieds Grand Americans. Another Modified group is WISSOTA, which holds most of their races in Wisconsin and Minnesota.

The I.M.C.A. modifieds have caused a resurgence of weekly racing because more people can afford to race. There are currently close to 950 oval tracks in the country. That number has increased steadily in the past ten years, in part because of the popularity of the low cost economy modifieds. During the mid-1970's, America suffered through an energy crisis and numerous tracks went out of business at that time. A number of fairgrounds horse tracks are now available for auto racing again, as horse racing is showing a decline as of late. Regular horse tracks do not want the heavy race cars excessively packing their tracks, but in the last few years horse racing, which depends on parimutuel betting to exist, is having a tough time surviving. Casinos on Indian reservations, or on floating River Boats have lured the gamblers away from many of the smaller horse tracks.

HOBBY DIVISIONS

Other divisions of cars that are common to almost all weekly short tracks are the support divisions. They can range from very low cost vehicles to expensive Sportsmen type cars. Each track is free to use any name it feels like for their support classes, and there are presently some 200 different names being used. Many of the classes could be condensed, but the tracks would rather exercise their independence. Most hobby classes are for amateur drivers. A true street stock has very few modifications, and is similar to the concept that NASCAR started with in its strictly stock division in 1949.

Weekly oval track racing has the largest spectator drawing power in North American motor sports. It is estimated that about 50 million people attend auto races each year. Over 80 percent of that figure is from the 800 weekly tracks.

A typical pure (or street) stock. Official Jennerstown Speedway (PA) photo.

DRAG RACING

Drag racing is one of the youngest forms of motor sports, but it is also one of the fastest growing sports the nation has ever seen. It especially appeals to the youth. Being an adolescent is a special time in everyone's life, and once teenagers realize their independence, one of the first things they turn to are automobiles. Drag racing, like club sports car racing, is more of a participation sport than oval track racing. If you were to go to a local drag meet, you'd notice that there are very few spectators, but rather most people are there with one of the competitors. It's common for 200 or more competitors to show up at a weekly meet. On the other end of the spectrum, some major events draw crowds in excess of 50,000.

It is said that drag racing originated from speed trials held in Southern California in the late 1930's. Young men tested their "hot-rods" at Muroc Lake. This twenty mile long dry lake was ten miles wide and proved to be an excellent playground for the hot-rodders. The dry lake was located in the Mojave Desert, and was about 100 miles northeast of Los Angeles. The area later became Edwards Air Force Base during World War II. After the war the trials were moved to the El Mirage dry lakes near Adelanto.

At first, the idea was to see how fast a person could go at the end of a measured distance. The competitors were timed individually. Soon the format switched to match races between two competitors. They would drive side by side at a slow speed, then they would accelerate to see who would be the fastest. Eventually the racers waited at a starting line, and from a dead stop they raced for the determined distance, which was usually one third of a mile. The new concept was to beat the other person to the finish line. Although raw speed draws "oohs" and "aahs", it's getting to the line faster than your competitor that counts. The winner of each run would then advance to the next round. The process was repeated until two competitors were left, and then the winner of the last race was called the "Top Eliminator".

Drag racing at the Lubbock (TX) Airport in 1955. - Len Ashburn photo.

Muroc and El Mirage weren't the only playgrounds for these "hot-rodders"; unfortunately, straight stretches of public highway were used, unbeknownst to the police, of course. Racing on the street, for obvious reasons, was illegal and downright dangerous.

Robert Peterson created a magazine for these youngsters in January of 1948. It was called *Hot Rod Magazine*. Wally Parks, the editor of *Hot Rod*, saw the importance of keeping the kids from racing on the street, and tried to find a way to improve their image, and to find them a better alternative. He had been the Executive Secretary for the Southern California Timing Association (SCTA) which started in 1937. He founded the National Hot Rod Association (NHRA) in 1951. At first, the NHRA was only interested in promoting hot-rodding, and the new club greatly impacted magazine sales. They used the motto, "Order out of Chaos." Parks also helped organize the first "Speed Weeks" at the Bonneville Salt Flats in Utah in 1949.

The first official drag race (approved by the California Highway Patrol) was on an access road to a landing field in Goleta, in April of 1949. A number of young men participated in races that day, but the primary match-up was between Tom Cobb, who owned a highly modified 1929 Ford Model A with a 1934 Ford engine. It had a Roots blower from a GMC diesel truck installed on the engine. The other driver was Fran Hernandez in his 1932 Ford, with a new Mercury V-8 engine under the hood. Hernandez won by a car length only because Cobb spun his tires on the starting line. It wasn't long before organized drag races were held at other old airstrips across the country. These decommissioned strips made perfect dragstrips for the "hot rods". They were not crowned like highways and were long enough to accelerate for a quarter mile and still had enough room to stop at the end of the runs. It was from these airstrips that the word dragstrip was invented.

C.J. "Pappy" Hart was one of the first people to see the potential of drag racing. He opened the first official dragstrip, at an old airstrip, in Santa Ana, California, on June 19, 1950.

The cars were crude at first, and many innovations were tried. After experimentation, the engines were set farther towards the rear of the car, with the driver sitting just in front of the rear axle. The cars were built as narrow as possible and their looks gained them the name of "rail."

The first NHRA sanctioned drag race was at the fairgrounds in Pomona, California in April of 1953. NHRA would go on to become the leading drag racing sanction. Their first major event was the 1955 "National Championship Drags" on concrete runways at the Great Bend Municipal Airport in Kansas, in September of 1955. Calvin Rice was the first "Nationals winner" with an elapsed time of 10.30. The "U.S. Nationals" event was moved to Indianapolis Raceway Park in 1961 and has been held there ever since. NHRA sanctioned 17 strips in California in 1956 and the next year they were sanctioning dragstrips in 25 states. A rival club called the American Hot Rod Association (AHRA) started in 1956, and when Jim Tice took command of the club it flourished. In the 1960's Larry Carrier founded the International Hot Rod Association (IHRA). The United Drag Racing Association (UDRA) was founded by Tom McEwen and Doug Kruse in the 1960's.

PROFESSIONAL DRAG RACING

Professional drag racing is broken down into three main classes, plus a number of semi-pro classes. The most recognized division is "Top Fuel." These are cars built for all-out acceleration. The word "Fuel" means a number of chemicals which make up the propellent. They can be aircraft fuel or benzine, but most often nitro-methane is the main ingredient. Nitro gives the race cars tremendous horsepower. The next class is "Funny Car", and the third professional class is the "Pro Stock." The semi-pro classes are called "Sportsmen."

TOP FUEL

The dragsters are the fastest race cars on earth. They evolved out of the first hot-rods. By stripping down the hot-rods to conserve weight the first "rails" were invented. The next developments were the slingshots and finally the rear-engined dragsters that now dominate the sport.

Mickey Thompson was one of the first to build a car that people called a "slingshot" dragster. He sat behind the rear axle, with the engine positioned directly in front of the rear axle. This combination aided in traction, which is the key element in drag racing. He was also the first person to realize that it would be advantageous if you narrowed the distance between the rear wheels. It made the back tires more closely approximate a single wide tire. Speeds in 1950 were about 120 miles per hour at the end of the quarter mile. At these kinds of speeds, parachutes are used to help slow the cars down after the run. In a few years the top speeds were mired at about 165 miles per hour, until Don Garlits turned 176.4 miles per hour at Brooksville, Florida on November 10, 1957. Californians had the hot setups for drag racing, and the Golden State youngsters wouldn't believe an "Easterner" like Don Garlits could be faster than they were, and that the times must have been fabricated. Garlits was paid to go west to run match races, and he soon proved it was no fluke. On one of his trips in California he saw a few competitors using the GMC blowers on their engines. He installed a blower and went even faster. He coined the term "Lighting the Tires". He had recently switched to the new seven inch wide M & H Racemaster drag tires, and he found he was able to leave the starting line with the tires spinning. Before that the drivers eased out of "the hole," trying not to spin.

"Big Daddy" Don Garlits in one of the first "Swamp Rats". Garlits is regarded as the most familiar name in drag racing. The Tampa, Florida driver was the first person to exceed 175 miles per hour in the quarter-mile driving this car. Photo courtesy of the Don Garlits Museum of Drag Racing.

NHRA banned fuel mixtures in 1957 and went back to pump gas for all of its classes. The top speeds in NHRA's top division dropped dramatically, but all the while the fuel-burning cars were still setting new records at AHRA, IHRA and independent meets. With fuel banned in NHRA, other innovations were tried like airplane engines or multiple engines to regain the power that was lost. A number of twin-engined dragsters were built and many were successful. Tommy Ivo went so far as to have Kent Fuller build him a four wheel drive dragster with four Buick engines. It was quite the sight to see him "smoke" all four wheels when leaving the line, and although the horsepower was impressive on Ivo's car, the extra weight hindered the performance. Reduced weight was the way to go, and the car builders dropped the extra horse-powered multiple-engined cars for lighter single-engined cars. NHRA brought back the Top Fuel cars in late 1963. Actually they made two divisions at that time. One was called "Top Fuel" and the other "Top Gas".

Records differ as to who was the first driver to break the 200 mile per hour barrier. It was either Chris Karamesines or Don Garlits in 1964 (depending on which sanction you recognize). Garlits was first person to top 250 miles per hour in 1975 in his slingshot dragster. Kenny Bernstein became the first driver to run 300 miles per hour on March 20, 1992 at the "GatorNationals" in Gainesville, Florida. Garlits had a disastrous run in his slingshot at Lion's Drag Strip in California on March 8, 1970. The transmission exploded, and the car split in half. He spent six weeks in the hospital from leg injuries. While recuperating, he decided to build a rear-engined dragster. He reasoned that the rear-engine design was safer, because if the engine blew, the shrapnel would fly behind the driver. When Garlits debuted his new rear-engined car in late 1970, after slight modifications, it went fast. He did not invent the rear-engined design, but he was certainly the first to perfect it. Within a year, most of his competitors switched to the rear-engined rails as well. For stability the wheel bases of a Top Fuel car are about 260 inches long.

Some of the other best Top Fuel drivers over the years include Don Prudhomme, Shirley Muldowney, Connie Kalitta, Gary Beck, and Joe Amato. In a surprise move, IHRA dropped the Top Fuel class when interest started to falter in 1984. IHRA ran with the Funny Cars as their top division for three years before bringing the Top Fuel cars back. AHRA's last major event was in 1988.

FUNNY CARS

Funny cars, sometimes referred to as "floppers", started out as Factory Experimentals (F/X) in the early 1960's. The American auto manufacturers saw a way of promoting new car sales to the younger generation by selling high performance street cars. These factory-built beasts were known as "Muscle Cars". Some of the fastest street-legal cars ever built came out of Detroit in the 1960's. The "Big Three" were shrewd when they started taking to the dragstrips with variations of these high-powered creations. A transformation was taking place, and the cars, although looking stock, were actually expertly crafted race cars. By 1967 the cars were altered even more, and the new class became "Super Factory Experimentals" (S/FX). Jack Chrisman made a successful debut with a 1964 Mercury Comet powered by a blown, fuel-burning 427 cubic inch engine. The first F/X cars that were tabbed "Funny Cars" were the Chrysler team cars in 1965

Don Nicholson in his Comet Cyclone at U.S. 131 Dragway (MI). These Factory Experimentals evolved into the modern day funny car. - John Lacko photo.

when they moved the bodies back on the chassis. This gave the car more weight on the rear tires. These cars had the front tires 10 inches farther forward, and the rear tires were 15 inches farther forward than their original showroom position. At first glance, there was something funny about them. Hence the term "Funny Car" was born.

Bruce Larson in 1965 took the S/FX class one step farther when he debuted a car with a lightweight one-piece fiberglass body. To get into his Chevrolet, the body was hinged at the rear of the car, with the body flipping up. These cars were first called "Flip Tops", and soon were called "Floppers". The current Funny Cars barely resemble passenger cars, but watching them is impressive. Their times and speeds are only a tick behind the "rails". IHRA dropped the Funny Cars in 1991. Some of the most successful Funny Car drivers include Bernstein, Prudhomme, Raymond Beadle, Ed McCulloch, Mike Dunn, and John Force.

Mike Dunn at the wheel of Roland Long's Hawaiian Punch sponsored funny car. - Photo courtesy of the Hawaiian Punch racing team.

PRO STOCKS

The newest professional class is the Pro Stocks. These street-legal looking cars are capable of speeds nearing 200 miles an hour in the quarter mile. The class made its debut in 1970 and has been very popular. The NHRA cars have enormous 500 cubic inch engines under the hoods. IHRA has gone even farther and many of their competitors have "Mountain Motors" with upwards of 800 cubic inches. Pro stock driver Bob Glidden has won more NHRA major events than any driver in all of the three pro series. Other top Pro Stock drivers include Warren Johnson and Darrell Alderman.

SPORTSMEN RACING

Sportsmen racing, also known as class racing, is one of the oldest forms of drag racing. It was unfair to put a high-powered hot-rod against a street-legal car, so different classes were devised. A complex set of rules was drawn up to determine what class each car should be put in. Classes like "C Stock", "D Stock", "E Stock", etc. were determined by a weight-to-horsepower ratio. Other classes were added such as "Altered" for cars that were modified. By the late 1950's many of the classes were separated between standard transmission and automatic transmission. The classes now reflected "M Stock", "M Stock Automatic", etc. Each driver would then compete with the other drivers in their class. Each winner would eliminate his competition and then would race another person until there was only one winner for each class. The last run in each class was called a "Trophy Run", as the winner was usually awarded a trophy. Then by using some sort of handicapping system, the class winners would advance on to race the winners in the other classes until an overall winner was determined. Each car

Sportsman racer Dan Van Koevering leaves the line at Brainerd (MN) at the NorthStar Nationals in 1991. He races his 4,020 pound 1978 Oldsmobile in the M/SA class. The car has a 403 cubic inch engine under the hood and it was originally listed from the factory at 275 horse power. Sportsman racing is an intricate part of the national events. - Dan Van Koevering collection.

72

was labeled with its class and a corresponding number, usually put on a side window with white shoe polish. Once a person lost, the shoe polish was rubbed off. Each class winner was allowed to keep his number on, and it was prestigious for someone to drive his car all week with this class number left on the car. It let everyone know that he had won his class at the local dragstrip.

For unknown reasons, each sanction uses different names for their sportsmen classes. NHRA's current sportsmen classes are called Alcohol Dragster, Alcohol Funny Car, Competition, Super Stock, Stock, Super Comp and Super Gas. These semi-pro cars can cost into the tens of thousands of dollars. Many of these classes have an index, or determined elapsed time, at which they should be shooting. IHRA also has a sportsmen program. The names are Top Dragster, Hot Rod, Modified, Top Sportsmen, Super Stock, Stock, Quick Rod, and Super Rod.

E.T. BRACKET RACING

Robert Leonard, IHRA's competition director, said, "If it wasn't for bracket racing, there wouldn't be any (drag) racing." Elapsed Time (E.T.) Bracket racing is the main entry level division in drag racing. It is estimated that 80 to 90 percent of drag racers compete in bracket racing. There may be over 100,000 competitors in this division. The neat thing is that a person can have a highly-tuned, made for drag racing car, or he can use a street car in bracket racing. It is believed that E.T. Bracket racing was originated by Alex Theofilos at Sunset Dragstrip in western Pennsylvania in 1962. The concept is simple. A racer determines how long it will take him to get from the starting line to the finish line. He then writes that time somewhere on the car where it can be seen by the officials (this is called dialing in your time). Then two cars are matched side-by-side with their separate times logged into a computer and the difference is then transferred to the electronic starting light, known as a "Christmas Tree". If one racer says his car will do the measured time at 12.00 seconds and the other thinks he can run it in 10.50 seconds, the first racer then gets a 1.5 second head-start, meaning the first driver will get the green light 1.5 seconds before the other driver does. Theoretically, both racers should hit the finish line at the same time, but here is where another factor is introduced. It is called reaction time. A perfect reaction time is .500 for bracket and most sportsmen classes, while a .400 reaction time is perfect in the pro ranks and some of the faster sportsman classes. If a bracket racer leaves the line one-half of a second after the last yellow light appears his reaction time is a perfect .500, but if his competitor has a reaction time of .900, and both of them are right on their dial-in times, the competitor with the .500 reaction time will win. Some other factors come into play in E.T. Brackets which can make for even more interesting twists. First, if a driver leaves the line before his green light appears, a red light appears on the "Tree". This means he has "red-lighted", and thus he is disqualified. The other factor occurs when a person gets to the finish line faster than he dialed in, then he is disqualified as well. This is called breaking-out. If both competitors red-light, then the one who left first loses. If both drivers break-out, the one who was farthest from the dial-in time is the loser. This is known as first or worst.

E.T. brackets makes a great handicapping system, because it allows the dragstrips to pit fast cars against slow cars, and both have an equal chance to win. Many of the bracket tracks have shortened their tracks from one-quarter of a mile to one-eight of a mile to give the competitors a longer slow down area.

MOTORCYCLES

Many of the top speeds in 1950 were set by motorcycles. Al Keys set the speed record when he went 121.62 miles per hour on a Harley-Davidson. The lightweight bikes could leave the starting line faster, and it was no surprise when Lloyd Grant became the first person to go the quarter-mile in under eleven seconds in 1953. It was also the last time a bike set the all-time record. In IHRA competition, Elmer Trett from Georgia made a run in 1994 at 231.24 miles per hour with an E.T. of 6.457 in the quarter mile. He was riding a 1327 cc Kawasaki in the Pro Stock motorcycle division.

OTHER DRAG RACING

Other forms of drag racing exist, including jet dragsters, sand drags, monster trucks, and tractor and truck pulls. Art Malone drove the first jet-powered dragster at Lion's Dragstrip on August 6, 1960. These ultra-powerful cars are not allowed to race side by side because it would be too dangerous, but they put on amazing exhibition runs. The jet-powered cars were the first to unofficially travel over 300 miles per hour in the quarter mile. It is an awesome sight to see one of these monsters light up the night with their after-burner.

The jet-powered "Super Mario" funny car leaves the line trailing flames and smoke. - Photo courtesy of Mario Carranca.

In sand drags the cars race side by side, but on sand instead of asphalt or concrete. Rather than race for an eighth mile or a quarter mile, the cars only travel 300 feet, but when the cars leave the line they shoot a rooster-tail of sand into the air from their huge tires that have tread that looks more like a paddle wheel on a river boat.

Monster trucks are another popular type of drag racing. These pick-up trucks have been highly modified. The bodies have been lifted several feet off the ground with huge tires added. They can race side by side, but they go over obstacles (like old automobiles) on the way to the finish line.

Tractor and truck pulls have probably been around longer than regular drag racing. Originally two tractors were hooked up back to back, and the object was to pull the opponent backwards. Soon the competitors were made to pull a wagon full of weight instead. Additional weights were then added until only one person had the power to pull it anymore. Now a contraption called a "Sled" was invented. This device shifts more weight to the pulling vehicle as the tractor or truck is in motion. The person who can pull the full distance, or the longest distance, then is the winner.

LATE MODELS

Late model racing is one of the most popular types of racing in North America, with the NASCAR Winston Cup Series as the most prestigious series in all of American auto racing. Late model stock car racing started becoming popular in the late 1930's. The late models are many times referred to as stock cars. Although it is said that the first stock car race was held in 1907 or thereabouts, little is recorded about the early years of this form of racing as the open wheeled race cars dominated headlines. Perhaps the first major stock car race was the "Long Island Stock Car Classic" on the 22.75 mile circuit utilizing city streets of Long Island on September 29, 1909. Ralph DePalma won a 100 mile stock car race on the wood-surfaced Chicago Speedway on August 7, 1915. Stock car racing continued, but at a very low keyed level until Oakland Speedway in California ran a 250 mile stock car race in 1934. Louis Meyer won the event in a 1934 Ford.

Then a couple of years later a race was scheduled for production automobiles on a special course in Daytona Beach. The track consisted of heading north on the beach (the sand at the surf's edge packs hard enough to support automobiles with little problem), and then the cars went through an opening in the sand dunes and out onto the pavement of Highway A-1-A. The cars then continued down the highway until they came to another opening in the sand dunes about two miles to the south and then it was back out to the beach. The scheduled 250 mile race, which was held on March 8, 1936, was sanctioned by the American Automobile Association (AAA) and was won by Milt Marion in a Ford at an average speed of 48 miles an hour for the shortened 200 mile race (the corners had become rutty and treacherous).

Triple-A was the major sanctioning body in North America at that time and had been sanctioning races as far back as 1904 with its premier event the prestigious "Indianapolis 500" for the open wheeled championship cars. If a driver was racing in Triple-A, it meant that driver had reached the pinnacle in auto racing. Triple-A also sanctioned sprint car racing at that time. Bill France, Sr. was an entrant and wound up finishing the race in fifth place. He was a successful stock car driver as he had won a 300 mile event in Fort Wayne, Indiana in 1940. He would go on to become the key person behind stock car racing in future years.

On the West Coast, a 500 mile race on the high banked Oakland Speedway was held in 1938. Bud Rose won the race as fourteen of the 33 starters finished the grueling event. Bill France, Sr. took over the promotions of the annual Daytona beach/road circuit that same year. Besides the Daytona events, other major stock car events were held at Langhorne Speedway in Pennsylvania and Lakewood Speedway in Georgia. Auto racing in the United States was halted for the duration of World War II.

Ed Barnett in a Chrysler leads at the 1947 Livermore (CA) strictly stock race. Dana photo (Rod Eschenburg collection).

NASCAR IS BORN

When the treaty papers were signed at the end of World War II auto racing started up again. A strictly stock car race was held on the runways at the Livermore Naval Air Station in California on July 27, 1947. Frank Phillips won the 500 mile race on a 1.5 mile D-shaped track.

Bill France, Sr. became the director of the National Championship Stock Car Circuit (N.C.S.C.C.) in 1947, but stock car racing wasn't progressing fast enough for France and so on December 14, 1947, he along with Red Vogt, Ed Otto, Bill Tuthill and 31 other auto racing enthusiasts formed the National Association for Stock Car Auto Racing. The sanction is referred to as NASCAR (pronounced "Nas-Car"). The organization was incorporated on February 20, 1948 with France being elected as president and Cannonball Baker becoming NASCAR's first commissioner. Three divisions were proposed for the young sanction, those being strictly stocks (later to be called Grand National and currently known as the Winston Cup Series), modifieds, and roadsters. But because of a shortage of new model cars following World War II, as the automobile manufacturers weren't up to full production yet, there were no NASCAR strictly stock races in 1948.

The first NASCAR races were for the modified cars, which were the older style cars (generally the widely available 1930's automobiles) with hopped up motors. NASCAR's third division was the roadsters, which were open wheeled stock cars that looked more like sprint cars than stock cars. That division was short lived and replaced a few years later with a stock block open wheeled championship division, which too was short lived.

The Central States Racing Association (C.S.R.A.), which was primarily sanctioning open wheeled racing (Big Cars and Midgets), began running some Stock Car events in 1948 but little is known about their races.

Then on February 20, 1949, NASCAR tried an experimental race. Along with the 100 mile roadster race on the two-mile circular oval at Broward Speedway in Florida, they held a short race for strictly stock late model sedans.

The cars were for the most part new models or built since World War II ended. The concept was to hold races incorporating newer family sedans thus generating interest from the new car buying public. Benny Georgeson won the ten mile strictly stock race in a Buick. NASCAR had started when the nation was entering a buyer's market. The race was successful enough to pave the way for NASCAR's first official race for strictly stock cars to be held a few months later.

IMCA SANCTIONS ITS FIRST STOCK CAR EVENT

The idea of completely strictly stock car racing caught on quickly and the International Motor Contest Association, the number two open wheeled sanction in America held their first strictly stock car race at the Topeka Fairgrounds in Kansas on May 30, 1949. Bob McKim of Salina, Kansas in a 1949 Oldsmobile 88 won the 200 lap race on the half-mile dirt track in front of 9,000 spectators. There were 27 entries for the race. McKim finished 12 laps ahead of Ray Putnam, who finished second in a Chevrolet. Frank Winkley, who finished fourth in a Kaiser, was an IMCA promoter (Auto Racing, Inc.). IMCA (which is properly pronounced as the letters in the acronym imply - "Eye-Em-Cee-Aye"), which began in 1915, ran at least eleven more stock car events (and maybe as many as fifteen) in 1949. The complete results from that year may be lost forever as only a portion of the official records from that year's Stock Car Division still exists.

There was no point championship that first year, but by 1956 IMCA was claiming in their yearbook that Eddie Anderson was the 1949 Stock Car champion. Had points been counted, Anderson would have surely been the champion as he won at least four of the IMCA stock car events in 1949. IMCA continued sanctioning stock car events up to the point the sanction went into hiatus at the end of 1977. Herschel Buchanon became the first official IMCA champion in 1950. Other IMCA champions over the years included Shorty Perlick, Ernie Derr (a twelve-time champion and the winner of over 350 IMCA stock car events), Don White, Johnny Beauchamp, Dick Hutcherson, Irv Janey, Gordon Blankenship, Bill Schwader, and Ferris Collier. Kent Tucker was the final IMCA stock car champion in 1977. IMCA resurfaced and is the leader in economy racing.

Ernie Derr of Keokuk, Iowa won over 350 I.M.C.A. stock car events in his career. This is the most wins any one driver has ever amassed in a major late model circuit. Richard Petty in comparison has 200 wins on the NASCAR circuit. - Clair Schreiber photo (courtesy of I.M.C.A.).

KANSAS BECOMES A HOME FOR THE STRICTLY STOCKS

Besides the earlier mentioned IMCA race in Topeka, other strictly stock events were held on a variety of Kansas airports. On May 30, 1949 a race was held at the Great Bend Municipal Airport on a makeshift three-mile tri-oval utilizing three runways. Bill Robinson won the 160 mile race in a 1949 Packard sponsored by the Argonne American Legion Post. Marion Smith finished second in an Oldsmobile 88. Other strictly stocks events were held at the Hutchinson Airport on June 29, 1949 and the Dodge City Airport on July 24, 1949. At least three more Kansas airports held strictly stock races in 1950. They were the Liberal Airport, the Herington Airport, and the Pratt Airport.

NASCAR'S FIRST OFFICIAL STRICTLY STOCK RACE

The first major NASCAR strictly stock race was held at the old Charlotte Speedway in North Carolina on June 19, 1949. The 200 lap race on the three-quarter mile dirt track was won by Glenn Dunnaway in a 1947 Ford, but he was later disqualified for having "altered rear springs". The cars were supposed to be strictly stock with the only modification allowed being a reinforced steel plate on the right front wheel to prevent the lug nuts from pulling through the rims, thus the win was then given to Jim Roper, who had finished second, but had only completed 197 laps in his 1949 Lincoln. Roper was a veteran midget and stock car driver from Halsted, Kansas. A crowd of 13,000 witnessed the first official NASCAR strictly stock car race. Incidently, Roper had finished dead last (tenth) at the race three weeks before at Great Bend when his transmission failed. Seven more NASCAR strictly stock events were held in 1949 with Red Byron being named their first strictly stock point champion.

Lee Petty hustles down Highway A-1-A on the old Daytona Beach (FL) road/beach track in his Oldsmobile during the 1958 race. He was the first three-time NASCAR Grand National champion. - Len Ashburn photo

The NASCAR strictly stocks received an official sounding name when they began being called the Grand National (GN) Division in 1950. They were also sometimes referred to as Late Model Stock Cars. Over the years some of the NASCAR champions included Herb Thomas, Tim Flock, Lee Petty (the first three time champion), Buck Baker, Ned Jarrett, Joe Weatherly, Richard Petty (son of Lee, and the first seven-time champion), David Pearson, Benny Parsons, Cale Yarborough, Dale Earnhardt (a seven-time champion), Darrell Waltrip, Bobby Allison, Terry Labonte, Bill Elliott, Rusty Wallace and Alan Kulwicki.

AAA ENTERS THE STOCK CAR BUSINESS

Although the NASCAR Grand National events were quickly becoming a popular attraction, the major auto racing sanctioning body in the country was still AAA. Triple-A started sanctioning stock car races in 1950 mainly to keep NASCAR from getting established in the Indiana, Ohio and Illinois area, where Triple-A was the dominant sanctioning body. Jay Frank became AAA's first Stock Car champion. Being an open wheel sanction their efforts were never 100 percent behind the stock cars, and although that division continued even after Triple-A departed racing in 1955, and the United States Auto Club (USAC, pronounced "Ewe-Sac") was formed to take over as the nation's top auto racing sanction, the stock car division was treated to a half-hearted effort by the sanction's hierarchy. The division was never allowed to reach its full potential. The peak for the USAC stock car division was in the 1960's when factory support from the automobile companies helped generate interest. When the factory teams pulled out, USAC's stock car division eventually faded out of existence. Before USAC dropped the stock cars it went through a major change in 1985 when it dropped the NASCAR style new cars and ran the short track dirt, late model cars instead. Over the thirty plus years that the combination of Triple-A and USAC held stock car events such notable drivers were crowned AAA stock car champions including Rodger Ward, Marshall Teague, Fred Lorenzen, Norm Nelson, Paul Goldsmith, Don White, Parnelli Jones, A.J. Foyt, Roger McCluskey, Butch Hartman (who won the USAC Stock Car championship an unprecedented five times), Ramo Stott, Joe Ruttman, and Dean Roper. Charlie Sentman and Billy Moyer, Jr. won the title during the short track period.

Marshall Teague posed for a photographer at a NASCAR Grand National race at the Grand Rapids (MI) Speedrome in the early 1950's. Teague was the AAA stock car champion in 1952 and 1954. He helped make the Hudson Hornets famous on the NASCAR circuit. - Dick Lee collection.

The impressive Charlotte (NC) Motor Speedway. It is the one of the nicest stock car tracks in the world. - Nancy Brown photo.

THE SUPER SPEEDWAYS

One of the first super speedways (paved tracks over three-quarter mile in length) to be built since the famous board track era was Darlington Raceway in South Carolina. Harold Brasington, who built the massive 1.25 mile track, acquired a C.S.R.A. sanction for his first "Southern 500", but when entries were slow coming in, he asked Bill France, Sr. to co-sanction the stock car event. On September 4, 1950 the race was held with 75 cars starting the grueling 400 lap race. Many of the NASCAR GN drivers had never run on an asphalt track before and the mechanics had no idea that the high banked asphalt corners would literally eat up tires. Red Byron blew out 24 tires on the way to finishing third in the race. Johnny Mantz, who had run a number of Triple-A championship races on paved tracks, was the only driver to realize how hard the track would be on tires, and, unbeknownst to the other competitors, he fitted his 1950 Plymouth with hard compound truck tires. Although he was the slowest qualifier for the race, from his 43rd starting spot he took the lead on lap fifty and rode off into the sunset while the other drivers were having tire problems. By pacing himself at about 75 miles per hour, he was nine laps ahead of second place finisher Fireball Roberts at the end of the 500 mile race.

With the increased popularity of the NASCAR GN circuit a number of other super speedways were built. Southern Speedway in Raleigh, North Carolina first opened with an Indy Car race in 1952, but the track ran NASCAR GN races from then on, up until it closed in 1958. Also in 1958 the first NASCAR GN race was held at the New Jersey State Fairgrounds in Trenton. The one-mile paved track used to be a half-mile dirt track. It was lengthened and paved in 1957. The track was lengthened again in 1969 to 1.5 miles, but the track has since been razed with the last racing there in 1980.

In 1959 Bill France, Sr. opened up his new venue, the Daytona International Speedway in Florida. This track was built to replace racing on the beach/road circuit. The most prestigious stock car race, the "Daytona 500" is held here each February. Charlotte Motor Speedway and Atlanta Motor Speedway both opened in 1960 with NASCAR GN events. Constant upgrading and improvements have made Charlotte Motor Speedway one of the showplaces of auto racing. Phoenix International Speedway in Arizona opened in 1964 for the Indy cars, but it wasn't until 1988 that the first NASCAR Winston Cup race was held on that one-mile

80

oval. The next super speedway built was the one-mile North Carolina Motor Speedway in Rockingham in 1965. In 1968 the two-mile Michigan International Speedway opened with the first GN race being held there the following year.

Three new super speedways were finished in 1969. The first was the high banked one-mile track of Dover Downs Speedway in Delaware. A second super speedway built by the France family opened in September. It was the Alabama International Speedway (now called Talladega Super Speedway) and is the fastest track as well as the longest track (2.66 miles) at which the NASCAR Winston Cup Series races. Texas World Speedway in College Station (a sister track to Michigan International Speedway and a track that set idle for a while) opened late in the year. The last Winston Cup race at Texas World Speedway was in 1973.

In 1970 Ontario Motor Speedway in Southern California opened. It was a magnificent facility and a carbon copy of the Indianapolis Motor Speedway, but unfortunately escalating property value put it out of business in 1980.

The 2.5 mile Pocono International Raceway was built in 1971 with the first NASCAR Winston Cup race there in 1974.

With a sudden over saturation of big tracks, many super speedways were proposed, but none made it to the final construction stages until Bob Bahre opened his New Hampshire International Speedway in 1990. The first Winston Cup race on the one-mile New Hampshire International Speedway was in 1993.

One of the more unusual tracks on which the NASCAR Grand National circuit ever raced was the Montgomery Air Force Base in New York. Although 1.9 miles in length, it doesn't qualify as a super speedway because the race there in 1960 was on a tri-oval track consisting of three runways.

OTHER STOCK CAR CLUBS

Over the years a number of stock car clubs have come and gone. Clubs like the National Stock Car Racing Association (NSCRA), the United Stock Car Racing Association (USCRA), the National Auto Racing League (NARL) and the American Stock Car Racing Association (ASCRA) were early clubs that have gone by the wayside.

Gary Bettenhausen (#55) in a Dodge leads the Fords of Mario Andretti (#11) and Jack Bowsher (#21) through a corner of the road course at Indianapolis (IN) Raceway Park during a USAC stock car event. - Len Ashburn photo.

ARCA COMES INTO EXISTENCE

In 1953 Toledo, Ohio's John Marcum started a stock car organization called Midwest Auto Racing Club (MARC). James Romine was crowned the first MARC champion. The club, running in the Great Lakes area, changed its name to the Automobile Racing Club of America (ARCA, pronounced "Are-Cah") in the 1960's when it had outgrown its name. Marcum aligned with Bill France, Sr. and he was asked to run an annual race at Daytona International Speedway starting in 1964. ARCA, which uses basically the same type of cars and rules as the NASCAR Winston Cup circuit is still going strong and some of their races are run as preliminary events for Winston Cup events at such tracks as Atlanta, Talladega, Michigan, Pocono and of course Daytona. Over the years some of the MARC/ARCA champions included Iggy Katona (a former midget car driver who turned to stock car racing, and the only six-time champion), Nelson Stacy, Jack Bowsher, Benny Parsons, Ramo Stott, Ron Hutcherson, Dave Dayton, Moose Myers, Bob Dotter, and Bobby Bowsher (the son of former champion, Jack).

NAME CHANGED TO WINSTON CUP

In the beginning NASCAR ran an exhausting number of Grand National races each year, with an average of 51 races each year from 1955 to 1971, with the most being 62 races counting towards the 1964 championship. Sometimes events were held at two different tracks on the same day.

Things changed in 1971 as R.J. Reynolds became the major sponsor for the series with its backing of the Winston cigarette brand. The name was changed from Grand National to the Winston Cup Series. Along with the Winston sponsorship came a reduced number of races as R.J.R. only wanted major events of at least 250 miles to count towards the championship. The 1972 schedule was cut to 31 races. The condensed series now consisted of twenty races at eleven different super speedways, two races on the road course at Riverside, California and the remainder on half-mile paved short tracks. Dirt tracks, where NASCAR's

Richard Petty is NASCAR's first seven-time Winston Cup Champion. He also holds the all-time win record with 200. Petty retired from active competition at the end of the 1992 season. - David Allio photo.

Late Models

I.M.C.A. late model action. Three Chevy's battle it out at Hawkeye Downs in Iowa. Bud Burdick is in the number 8. - photo courtesy of I.M.C.A.

roots began, had become a thing of the past for the Winston Cup Series. Richard Petty won the last ever NASCAR GN dirt track race on September 30, 1970, at the half-mile dirt track at the North Carolina State Fairgrounds in Raleigh.

Bill France, Sr. retired in 1972 and stepped down, and his son Bill France, Jr. took over the reigns of NASCAR. Bill, Jr., along with help from R.J. Reynolds, has taken the NASCAR Winston Cup Series straight to the top in American motor sports. The 30 race schedule in 1993 saw over four million fans file through the turnstiles, which is an average of 127,000 per event according to Goodyear Tire's annual survey. Starting in the late 1960's the "Daytona 500" became available to viewers on closed circuit TV.

NASCAR moved up another rung on the ladder and into the national spotlight when the 1979 "Daytona 500" became the first flag-to-flag nationally televised Winston Cup race. Since then the series has grown enormously and every race is now televised live by one of the television networks. The fan appeal for the Winston Cup races rivals any of the other major sports in the country.

Interest in the Winston Cup Series increased again when a new race was added to the circuit in 1994. The "Brickyard 400" was the first ever stock car race to be held at the Indianapolis Motor Speedway. The race drew nearly 300,000 fans and would have out-drawn the annual "Indianapolis 500" had it not been for restrictions in the number of tickets sold by the track. When the tickets went on sale for the "Brickyard 400", three times the number of ticket requests were received than the speedway's seats could hold. Young 23 year old sensation Jeff Gordon won the rich "Brickyard 400" on August 6, 1994, and took home over $600,000 in prize money. That was more prize money for one race than champion Richard Petty won in the complete 1979 season.

The complete history of the NASCAR Winston Cup Series can be found in the excellent series set of books by Greg Fielden, entitled *Forty Years of Stock Car Racing.*

UNITED STATES TRACKS

ALABAMA

Ace Speedway - see: Del Edd Raceway

Alabama Int'l Dragway - Steele - 1/8 mile paved dragstrip (March, 1994 - present)

Alabama Int'l Motor Speedway - see: Talladega Super Speedway

Alabama State Fairgrounds - see: Fairgrounds Speedway

Alamiss Speedway - Wilmer - 1/4 mile dirt oval (6/03/83 - 1986)
(aka: Stateline Speedway)

Albertville Speedway - Albertville - 1/4 mile dirt oval (years unknown)

Andalusia Fairgrounds - Andalusia / located at the Covington County Fairgrounds
1/2 mile dirt oval (1921 & 1922)

Andalusia Speedway - Andalusia - 1/2 mile dirt oval (c.1951)

Anniston - dirt oval (1937)

Anniston Speedway - Anniston - 3/8 mile dirt oval (c.10/13/51 - c.1972) now the
site of a commercial building

Athens Fairgrounds - Athens / located at the Limestone County Fairgrounds
1/2 mile dirt oval (early 1950's)

Bobby Allison accepts the checkered flag after a win at Montgomery Motor Speedway. - Len Heyden collection.

Atmore Dragway - Atmore - 1/8 mile paved dragstrip (1972 - present)

Auburn-Opelika Oval - Opelika - 1/2 mile dirt oval (10/31/54 - c.1955)
(aka: Midway Speedway) / Sam McQuagg started his driving career here
now the site of the Midway Shopping Center on US 29

Baileyton Good Time Drag Strip - Baileyton - 1/8 mile dragstrip (1966 - present)

Baldwin County Raceway - Summerdale - 3/8 mile dirt oval (1989 - 1992)

Bama Dragway - Jasper (Sumiton) - 1/8 mile paved dragstrip (1991 - present)

Bama Speedway - Kimbrough - 1/2 mile dirt oval (c.1974 - 1976)

Bill's Speedway - see: Hanceville Speedway

Birmingham Dragway - see: Lassiter Mountain Dragway

Birmingham Int'l (Super) Speedway - see: Fairgrounds Raceway

Birmingham - also see: Iron Bowl, Legion Field Stadium

Brooklyn Speedway - Brooklyn - 3/8 mile dirt oval (c.1973 - 1975)

Capital City Dragway - Montgomery / (aka: Montgomery Int'l Dragway)
1/8 & 1/4 mile paved dragstrips (c.1984 - present)
located next to Montgomery Motor Speedway

Chatom Int'l Raceway - Chatom - 1/8 mile paved dragstrip (1989 - present)

Chattahoochee Valley Speedway - Halesburg - 3/8 mile dirt oval (1971)
the track was located southeast of Abbeville

Childersburg - dirt oval (years unknown)

Chisholm Speedway - Montgomery - 1/2 mile dirt oval (c.1951 - c.9/09/56)

Citronelle Motor Speedway - Citronelle - 1/4 mile dirt oval (c.1979 - 1981)

Competition Dragway - Helena - 1/8 mile paved dragstrip (c.1964)

Courtland Airport - Courtland - paved road course (1955 - c.1963)
1/4 mile paved dragstrip (c.1969 - c.1972)

Crossville Speedway - Crossville - 1/4 mile dirt oval (1971 - 1980)

Crystal Springs Speedway - Gadsden / the track was located on US 431
1/2 mile dirt oval (c.1953 - c.1957)

Cullman Speedway - Cullman / (aka: Lidy's Speedway)
3/8 mile dirt oval (c.1955 - 1976)

Dale County Dragway - Newton - 1/8 mile paved dragstrip (c.1986 - c.1989)

Dallas County Dragway - Selma / (aka: Selma Dragway)
1/8 mile paved dragstrip (c.1981 - 1989) (1993 - present)
(aka: Lakeside Dragway) / (aka: Selma Lakeside Dragway)
the track was flooded from 1990 - 1992 when the lake was raised

Decatur Speedway - Decatur - 3/8 mile dirt oval (early 1950's)

Deep South Speedway - Grove Hill - 3/8 mile dirt oval (years unknown)

Del Edd Raceway - Attalla - 1/4 mile dirt oval (1952) (c.1962 - 1973)
(aka: Ace Speedway)

Dixie Race Track - Tuscaloosa - dirt oval (1950)

Dixie Speedway - Midfield - 1/4 mile paved oval (1958 - 1974)
(aka: Midfield Speedway)

Dixie Speedway - Sayre - see: Heart O' Dixie Speedway

Dothan Dragway - Dothan - 1/4 mile paved dragstrip (c.1970)

Dothan Fairgrounds - Dothan / located at the Tri-State Fairgrounds
1/2 mile dirt oval (1920's) (c.1953 - c.1956)
3/8 mile dirt oval (c.1971 - 1975) / (aka: Dothan Motor Speedway)

Dothan - also see: Napier Field, Rocket Motor Speedway

East Alabama Motor Speedway - Phenix City / built by Jimmy Thomas
3/8 mile dirt oval (3/18/73 - present) / Bud Lunsford won the first race
the track held the first ever NDRA late model race here on 8/05/78, the race
was won by Bobby Thomas, the son of the promoter

Fairgrounds Raceway - Birmingham / located at the Alabama State Fairgrounds
1.0 mile dirt oval (c.1906 - c.1917) / originally built as a horse track
1/2 mile dirt oval (c.1933 - 1942) (10/01/46 - 1961)/ new stands built in 1928
ran a number of NASCAR Grand National races starting on 9/07/58
1/4 mile dirt oval (1958 - 1961) / 1958 promoter was Bob Harmon
5/8 mile paved oval (6/28/62 - present) / 1975 promoter was Bobby Allison
(aka: Birmingham Super Speedway) / (aka: Birmingham Super Raceway)
(aka: Birmingham Int'l Raceway) / (aka: Birmingham Int'l Speedway)

Federal Motor Speedway - Federal - 1/2 mile dirt oval (c.1983 - 1987)

*The hillside seating of the nice East Alabama Motor Speedway. Jimmy Thomas
built the track in 1973. - Official track photo.*

86

Flomaton Speedway - Flomaton - 1/4 mile dirt oval (c.1975 - c.1993)

Gadsden Raceway - Gadsden - 1/2 mile dirt oval (4/28/73 - c.1981)
3/8 mile dirt oval (1983 - present)

Gadsden Speedway - Gadsden - dirt oval (1953)

Grannie's Raceway - Piedmont - 1/4 mile dirt oval (c.1980 - 1982)
an arsonist burned all of the track's buildings to the ground

Green Valley Dragway - Gadsden (Glencoe) / next to Green Valley Speedway
1/8 mile paved dragstrip (c.1977 - present) / (aka: Green Valley Dragstrip)

Green Valley Speedway - Gadsden (Glencoe) / (aka: Green Valley Short Track)
3/8 mile dirt oval (1972 - 1984) (1988 - present)
(aka: Green Valley Raceway) / located next to Green Valley Dragway

Guin Speedway - Guin - 3/10 mile dirt oval (c.1972 - 1975)

Guntersville Speedway - Guntersville - 1/4 mile dirt oval (c.5/03/53 - c.1953)

Hanceville Speedway - Hanceville - 3/8 mile dirt oval (c.1989 - present)
(aka: Bill's Speedway)

Heart O' Dixie Speedway - Sayre - 1/4 mile paved oval (1960 - present)
(aka: Sayre Speedway) (aka: Dixie Speedway) (aka: Sayre's Dixie Speedway)

Holiday Raceway - Woodstock - 1/8 mile paved dragstrip (1968 - present)

Hollis Crossroads Speedway - Hollis - 1/4 mile dirt oval (1979 - c.1984)

Huntsville - 1/4 mile dirt oval (c.1950 - c.9/25/52) / maybe at a fairgrounds

Huntsville Airport - Huntsville - 2.2 mile paved road course (late 1960's)

Huntsville Dragway - Huntsville - 1/8 mile paved dragstrip (c.1981 - present)
(aka: Madison County Dragway)

Huntsville Fairgrounds - Huntsville / located at the Madison County Fairgrounds
1/2 mile dirt oval (1928) (1947) (1949)

Huntsville Motor Speedway - Huntsville - 1/4 mile dirt oval (1960)
1/4 mile paved oval (c.1961 - present) / (aka: Huntsville Speedway)
(aka: Huntsville Int'l Speedway) / (aka: Huntsville Int'l Raceway)

I-20 Speedway - Pell City - 3/8 mile dirt oval (c.1979 - 1983)
(aka: Winston Speedway)

Idle Hour Speedway - Phenix City - 1/4 mile dirt oval (c.5/16/47 - c.1948)

Iron Bowl - Birmingham - 3/8 mile dirt circle (c.1939 - 1942) (1946 - 1952)

Jake's Dragway - see: Moulton Dragway

Jasper Speedway - see: Super Eight Speedway

Kennedy Raceway - Kennedy - 1/4 mile dirt oval (4/12/86 - present)

L.A. Raceway - Loxley - 3/8 mile dirt oval (Sept., 1987 - present)
(aka: Lower Alabama Raceway) / L.A. is short for Lower Alabama

Lake View Estates - Mobile / (aka: New Mobile Speedway)
6/10 mile dirt oval (c.1948 - c.1953)
ran a NASCAR Grand National race on 4/08/51 won by Tim Flock

Lakeside Dragway - see: Dallas County Dragway

Lakeside Speedway - Wilsonville - 1/4 mile dirt oval (1992 - present)

Lassiter Mountain Dragway - Birmingham / (aka: Birmingham Dragway)
1/4 mile paved dragstrip (1969 - present)

Lee County Int'l Raceway - Phenix City / (aka: Tri-County Raceway)
3/8 mile dirt oval (c.1971 - 1981) / later became a Motocross track

Legion Field Stadium - Birmingham - 1/5 mile dirt oval (6/05/40 - 1941)

Lidy's Speedway - see: Cullman Speedway

Little Winston - see: I-20 Speedway

Lower Alabama Raceway - see: L.A. Raceway

Madison County Dragway - see: Huntsville Dragway

Marbury Dirt Track - Marbury - 1/4 mile dirt oval (c.1994 - present)

Midfield Speedway - see: Dixie Speedway - Midfield

Midway Speedway - see: Auburn-Opelika Oval

Mobile Dirt Track - Mobile - 1/4 mile dirt oval (1984 & 1985)

Mobile Fairgrounds - Mobile / located at the Gulf Coast Fairgrounds
1/2 mile dirt oval (c.1921 - c.1935)

Mobile Int'l Raceway - Irvington - 1/2 mile paved oval (1965 - present)
1/8 mile paved dragstrip (c.1981 - present) / (aka: Mobile Int'l Speedway)

Mobile - also see: Lake View Estates

Montgomery Fairgrounds - Montgomery - 1/2 mile dirt oval (1920's - c.7/15/34)

Montgomery Int'l Dragway - see: Capital City Dragway

Montgomery Midget Speedway - Montgomery - 1/8 mile dirt oval (1980's)

Jack Martin (#712) and Red Farmer (#F97). - Len Heyden photo.

The half-mile, Montgomery Motor Speedway. - Len Heyden collection.

Montgomery Motor Speedway - Montgomery - 1/2 mile paved oval (1955 - present)
   Bob Harmon was promoter 1958 - 1973 / next to Capital City Dragway
   ran a number of NASCAR GN races / first one 4/17/55 / last one 12/08/68
   held first ever All-Pro sanctioned race on 9/07/80
   (aka: Montgomery Int'l Raceway) / (aka: Montgomery Int'l Speedway)

Montgomery - paved road course (1970's)

Montgomery - also see: Capital City, Chisholm, Sunbelt

Moulton Dragway - Moulton - 1/8 mile paved dragstrip (c.1989 - present)
   (aka: Jake's Dragway) / located next to Moulton Speedway

Moulton Speedway - Moulton - 1/4 mile dirt oval (c.1975 - 1982) (1984 - present)
   located next to Moulton Dragway

Muscle Shoals - 1/4 mile dirt oval (c.1959 - c.1968)

Napier Field - Dothan - paved road course (late 1950's)

New Hope Dragway - New Hope - 1/4 mile paved dragstrip (c.1965)

New Site Speedway - New Site - 3/8 mile dirt oval (c.1975 - c.1977)

North Alabama Speedway - Tuscumbia / (aka: North Alabama Dragway)
   3/8 mile dirt oval (1977 - 1987) (1990 - present)
   1/8 mile paved dragstrip (c.1981 -   present)

Off Road Westover Alabama - Westover - 1/4 mile dirt oval (April, 1993 - present)

Onycha Raceway - Opp - 3/8 mile dirt oval (August, 1993 - present)

Opelika Fairgrounds - Opelika / located at the Lee County Fairgrounds
   1/2 mile dirt oval (1920's)

Opp - see: Onycha Raceway, South Alabama Motor Speedway

Penton Raceway - Penton - 1/4 mile dirt oval (years unknown) / probably 1950's

Penton Raceway - Penton - 3/10 mile dirt oval (1980 - 1984)
   1/4 mile dirt oval (1985 - present) / (aka: Penton Speedway)

Phenix Dragstrip - Phenix City / (aka: Phenix Dragway)
   1/8 mile paved dragstrip (1963 - c.1979) (c.1982 - present)

Piedmont Speedway - Piedmont - dirt oval (late 1950's)

Ragland - 1.0 mile dirt oval (1961) / located north of Pell City
   Jerry Massey won the only auto race held on this track

Rocket Motor Speedway - Dothan / (aka: Rocket Speedway)
   3/8 mile paved oval (c.1973 - 1986) / (aka: Westgrove Speedway)

Sand Mountain Dragway - Section / (aka: Sand Mountain Raceway Park)
   1/8 mile paved dragstrip (c.1981 - present)

Sayre Speedway - see: Heart O' Dixie Speedway

Scottsboro Speedway - Scottsboro - dirt oval (1952 & 1953)

Selma - 1/8 mile dirt oval (1958) / ran micro-midgets

Selma Dragway - see: Dallas County Dragway

Selma Speedway - Selma - 1/6 mile dirt oval (c.1982 - c.1983) / ran Mini-Sprints

Shelby County Speedway - Alabaster - dirt oval (c.1978 - 1979)

Skypark Speedway - Florence - 1/2 mile dirt oval (c.4/10/51 - c.1951)

South Alabama Motor Speedway - Opp / (aka: Twin City Speedway)
   4/10 mile paved oval (June, 1973 - present) / home of annual "Rattlesnake 100"

Stateline Speedway - see: Alamiss Speedway

Sumiton Speedway - Sumiton - 1/2 mile dirt oval (1939) / located in a cow pasture

Sunbelt Championship Dragway - Montgomery
   1/8 mile paved dragstrip (1994 - present)

Super Eight Speedway - Jasper / (aka: Jasper Speedway)
   1/4 mile paved oval (1968) (1991 - present)

Super Six Speedway - Winfield - 1/4 mile dirt oval (9/04/93 - present)

Red Farmer (F97), Friday Hassler (#15), Donnie Allison (#88), and Bob Burcham (#1) at Montgomery Motor Speedway - Len Heyden photo.

Sylacauga Dragway - Sylacauga / (aka: Sylacauga Int'l Dragway)
1/8 mile paved dragstrip (c.1981 - 1991) (1994 - present)

Talladega Grand Prix Raceway - Talladega
1.3 mile paved road course (1986 - present)

Talladega Short Track is one of the south's premier weekly tracks. The track races every Saturday night. - Official track photo.

Talladega Short Track - Talladega - 1/3 mile dirt oval (4/29/77 - present)
1/8 mile dirt oval (1989 - present) / (aka: Little Talladega Raceway)
the tracks are located 1/2 mile east of Talladega Super Speedway

Talladega Super Speedway - Talladega / (aka: Alabama Int'l Motor Speedway)
2.66 mile paved oval (9/12/69 - present) / turns banked 33 degrees
4.0 mile paved road course (11/09/69 - 1983) / proposed in January of 1967
Tiny Lund fatally injured in a crash here on 8/17/75
became U.S.'s fastest closed course track when Mark Donohue toured the
oval track at 221.160 mph in the Sunoco Porsche on 8/09/75

Tallassee - 1/2 mile dirt oval (early 1950's)

Thunder Mountain Speedway - Fyffe - 3/8 mile dirt oval (October, 1992 - present)
the track is located near Rainsville

Thunder Valley Speedway - Choccolocco - 1/3 mile dirt oval (1989 - c.1992)
an arsonist burned all of the track's buildings to the ground in 1993

Tri-Cities Speedway - Gadsden - 4/10 mile dirt oval (c.1951 - 1955)

Tri-County Raceway - see: Lee County Int'l Raceway

Tuskegee - paved road course (late 1950's)

Twin City Speedway - see: South Alabama Motor Speedway

W.W. Speedway - Hanceville - 1/4 mile dirt oval (1986 - 1989)

Warrior Auto Raceway - Fultondale - 1/4 mile paved oval (c.1962 - 1967) (1983)

Westgrove Speedway - see: Rocket Motor Speedway

Winston County Dragway - Lynn - 1/8 mile paved dragstrip (c.1969 - present)

ALASKA

Action Raceway - see: Twin City Raceway

Alaska Speedway - see: Turnagain Speedway

Anchorage - road course (1964 - c.1978) / sports car races held on city streets
  the races were run each January during the "Fur Rendezvous Days"

Big Valley Raceway - see: Polar Raceway Park

Capitol Speedway - Willow - 3/8 mile dirt oval (1978 - present)

Fairbank Racing Lions - Fairbanks - 1/4 mile paved dragstrip (c.1991 - present)
  the police close off an industrial highway for organized drag racing

Fairbanks - dirt oval (late 1930's or early 1940's)

Fairbanks Fairgrounds - Fairbanks - dirt oval (1966)
  located at the Tanana Valley State Fairgrounds / the fair started in 1924

Golden Nugget Speedway - Anchorage - dirt oval (c.1954)

Greater Fairbanks Raceway - see: Robert Mitchell Memorial Speedway

Ice Palace Race Track - Eagle River - 3/8 mile dirt oval (c.1973 - c.1974)

Kenai Peninsula Raceway - see: Twin City Raceway

Kodiak Island Raceway - Kodiak / located at a fairgrounds (rodeo grounds)
  3/8 mile dirt oval (1976 - 1991) (1993 - present)
  (aka: Kodiak Island Speedway)

Mitchell Memorial Raceway - see: Robert Mitchell Memorial Speedway

North Pole Speedway - North Pole - 3/8 mile dirt oval (5/30/68 - 1983)

North Star Speedway - Fairbanks - dirt oval (1950)
  the location is now the Joy School

Polar Raceway Park - Palmer - 1/4 mile paved dragstrip (1963 - present)
  1/4 mile dirt oval (c.1980 - 1986) / (aka: Big Valley Raceway)
  (aka: Valley Raceway) / (aka: Thunder Valley Raceway)

Rendezvous Speedway - Fairbanks - 1/4 mile paved oval (c.1953 - c.1955)
  located north of town on Steese Highway

Robert Mitchell Mem. Raceway - Fairbanks - 1/4 mile dirt oval (1979 - present)
  (aka: Greater Fairbanks Raceway) / (aka: Mitchell Memorial Raceway)
  the track was built by volunteer help

Snow Bowl - Anchorage - 1/5 mile dirt (ice) oval (2/26/56)
  ran a modified race on an ice covered ball park / temperature was 5 degrees
  the total purse was only $400 as a dog sled race was being run nearby

Tanana Valley Speedway (Fairgrounds) - see: Fairbanks Fairgrounds

Turnagain Speedway - Anchorage - 1/4 mile paved oval (c.1957 - c.1966)
(aka: Alaska Speedway)

Twin City Raceway - Kenai - 3/8 mile dirt oval (c.1970 - 1982) (1987 - present)
(aka: Action Raceway) / (aka: Kenai Peninsula Raceway)

Valley Raceway - see: Polar Raceway Park

ARIZONA

Adobe Bowl - see: Tucson Speedway

Arizona State Fairgrounds - Phoenix / located at McDowell & 19th
1.0 mile dirt oval (11/11/10 - 1941) (1946 - 1963)
held last AAA championship race on 11/06/55 (on the mile track)
1/2 mile dirt oval (November, 1934 - 1937)
5/8 mile dirt oval (3/20/38 - 1940) / Phoenix Suns Coliseum now on site
5/8 mile paved oval (1941) (c.1946 - c.1956)
1/8 mile dirt oval (1/27/85 - present)
ran a number of NASCAR GN races on the 1.0 mile track in 1950's & 1960's

Arrowhead Raceway - Glendale - dirt oval (years unknown) / probably 1950's

Beeline Dragway - Scottsdale - 1/4 mile paved dragstrip (c.1961 - c.1982)

Bennett Speedway - Phoenix - 1/4 mile dirt oval (October, 1937 - c.1/23/38)

Biltmore Speedway - Phoenix - 1/5 mile dirt oval (1/20/35 - c.1935)

Bisbee Speedway - Bisbee - 1/4 mile dirt oval (1973)

Camelback Speedway - Phoenix - dirt oval (years unknown)
located at 24th & Camelback

Camp Grant Speedway - see: Channell's Midwestern Speedway

Jimmy Bryan in his last ride. He was fatally injured the day this photo was taken at Langhorne (PA). - Mike Ringo photo (Len Ashburn collection).

Canyon Raceway - Phoenix - 3/8 mile dirt oval (c.1981 - present)
  located 25 miles north of Phoenix / held Slick 50 TV Series 1993/1994

Casa Grande Fairgrounds - see: Central Arizona Raceway

Central Arizona Raceway - Casa Grande (11 Mile Corner)
  5/8 mile dirt oval (1939) / located at the Pina County Fairgrounds
  1/5 mile dirt oval (1/14/40) / (aka: Sun Valley Speedway)
  1/4 & 1/2 mile dirt oval (1973 - 1981)
  3/8 mile dirt oval (1982 - 1986) (1988) (1990) (1992 - present)

Central Speedway - see: Coolidge Speedway

Chandler - 1/4 mile paved dragstrip (1959)

Channell's Midwestern Speedway - Winkelman / (aka: Camp Grant Speedway)
  1/2 mile dirt oval (c.1971 - c.1982)

Coolidge Speedway - Coolidge - 1/4 mile dirt oval (c.1954 - c.1957)
  (aka: Central Speedway)

Copper Bowl Speedway - see: Globe-Miami Speedway

Corona Speedway - see: Tuscon Raceway Park

D.A.V. Speedway - see: Northern Raceway

Davis-Monthan Air Force Base - Tucson - 1/4 mile paved dragstrip (1957)

Douglas - 1/5 mile dirt oval (1935) / ran midgets

Douglas - dirt oval (1952)

Downtown Airport Speedway - Tucson - 1/8 mile dirt oval (11/07/54) / Micros

Eloy - 1/4 mile dirt oval (early 1950's)

Eloy Airport Dragway - Eloy - 1/4 mile paved dragstrip (1970's)

Eloy Grand Prix - Eloy / held an annual sports car race on the city streets
  1.3 mile city street paved road course (c.1979 - 1990)

FasTrack Int'l Speedway - see: Phoenix Int'l Raceway

Flagstaff D.A.V. Speedway - see: Northern Raceway

Firebird Int'l Raceway - Chandler - 1/4 mile paved dragstrip (1983 - present)
  3/8 mile dirt oval (8/09/83 - 1984) (1987 - 1989)
  1.1, 1.25 & 1.6 mile paved road courses (1983 - present) / SCCA TA in 1985

Flagstaff - 1/2 mile dirt oval (c.1929 - 1939)

Flagstaff - also see: Northern Raceway

Ford Test Track - Kingman - 5.0 mile paved oval (2/26/56) / ran exhibition race

Gilpin Speedway - Tucson - dirt oval (c.1950) / on the Northwest side of town

Globe-Miami Speedway - Globe / (aka: Copper Bowl Speedway)
  1/4 mile dirt oval (1952 - present)

Jerome - paved road course (c.1962)

Jordan Speedway - Phoenix - 1/4 mile dirt oval (1935 - 1937) / ran midgets

Kingsley Ranch - Tucson - dirt oval (3/07/48) / located on Nogales Highway

Luke Air Force Base - Phoenix - 2.5 mile paved road course (5/03/53)

Manzanita Speedway - Phoenix / located at West Broadway & 35th Ave.
    1/4 mile dirt oval (c.8/29/51 - 8/18/85) / formerly a dog racing track
    1/2 mile dirt oval (11/21/54 - present) / held the Slick 50 TV Series in 1992
    1/3 mile dirt oval (5/24/85 - present)

Mesa Fairgrounds - Mesa - 5/8 mile dirt oval (3/15/48)

Mohave Valley Raceway - Bullhead City - 1/3 mile dirt oval (4/10/93 - present)

Northern Raceway - Flagstaff - dirt oval (1954) (aka: D.A.V. Speedway)
    was a NASCAR sanctioned track / (aka: Flagstaff D.A.V. Speedway)

Papago Park - Scottsdale - 1/4 mile dirt oval (1946) / near prisoner of war camp

Perryville Air Strip - near Phoenix - 1/4 mile paved dragstrip (c.1955 - c.1961)

Phoenix Fairgrounds - see: Arizona State Fairgrounds

Phoenix Grand Prix - Phoenix / races were the US Grand Prix for Formula One
    2.36 mile paved city street road course (6/04/89) (3/10/90) (3/11/90)
    2.34 mile paved city street road course (3/10/91)

Phoenix Int'l Raceway - Phoenix / (aka: FasTrack Int'l Speedway)
    1.0 mile paved oval (3/22/64 - present)
    first race was a USAC Indy car race / 1st NASCAR WC race was on 11/06/88
    Bobby Marshman crashed in practice in 11/27/64 / he died on 12/04/64
    2.75 mile paved road course (April, 1964 - 1990)
    1.51 mile paved road course (1991 - present)

Supermodifieds at Phoenix for the 1992 "Copper World". - Nate Mecha photo.

Phoenix Midget Speedway - Phoenix / located at 17th & Garfield
1/5 mile dirt oval (12/03/39 - c.1941) (c.1946 - c.1948)

Phoenix Raceway Park - Phoenix - 1/4 mile paved dragstrip (1963 - present)
1/8 mile dirt oval (c.1983 - 1989) / (oval aka: Sidewinder Speedway)
(aka: Phoenix Dragway) / trying to build a 3/8 mile paved oval

Phoenix Rodeo Grounds - Phoenix - 1/4 mile dirt oval (1942)

Phoenix - also see: Arizona State, Arrowhead, Beeline, Bennett, Biltmore,
Camelback, Canyon, Firebird, Jordan, Luke AFB, Manzanita, Papago,
Perryville, Riverside, South Mountain, Sportsland, Thomas Road

Pima County Fairgrounds - see: Tucson Fairgrounds

Pinal County Fairgrounds - see: Central Arizona Speedway

Prescott Rodeo Grounds - Prescott - dirt oval (c.1935 - 1942) (1946 - c.1947)

Quechan Speedway - see: California section

Raven Raceway - see: Tucson Raceway Park

Riverside Speedway - Phoenix - 1/5 mile dirt oval (c.7/24/36 - c.7/09/37)

Roosevelt Speedway - Roosevelt - 1/10 mile dirt oval (10/20/38 - 2/05/39)

Safford - 1/4 mile dirt oval (7/04/39) (1952)

Sara Park Raceway - Lake Havusa - 1/4 mile dirt oval (1987 - present)
(aka: Sara Park Speedway)

Scottsdale - 1.0 mile dirt oval (years unknown)

Sidewinder Speedway - see: Phoenix Raceway Park

Smith City Speedway - Smith City - 1/4 mile dirt oval (1981)

South Mountain Speedway - Phoenix - 1/4 mile dirt oval (7/30/49 - 4/02/55)
1/2 mile dirt oval (c.1955 - c.1957) / located south of town
1/4 mile paved oval (c.1956 - c.1957)

Sportsland Raceway - Phoenix - 1.5 mile paved road course (1967)

Sun Valley Speedway - see: Central Arizona Raceway

Thomas Road Speedway - Phoenix - dirt oval (years unknown) / probably 1950's

Tri-City Speedway - Safford - 1/4 mile dirt oval (1990 - present)

Tucson - 1/4 mile dirt oval (5/18/46) / maybe Tucson Speedway or the fairgrounds

Tucson Dragway - Tucson - 1/4 mile paved dragstrip (c.1981 - c.1989)

Tucson Fairgrounds - Tucson - 1.0 mile dirt oval (10/06/35- c.1941) (1946- c.1954)
1/2 mile dirt oval (1/16/55 - c.1956) / at the Pima County Fairgrounds
1/4 mile dirt oval (10/05/35) (1970's) / (aka: Tucson Speedway)
(NOTE: reportedly there was no racing in Tucson from 1917 until 1935)
Roger McCluskey & Bill Cheesbourg careers started here

Tucson Municipal Airport - 1.8 mile paved road course (c.1959 - c.12/03/61)

Tucson Raceway Park - Tucson / (aka: Corona Speedway) / (aka: Raven Raceway)
1/4 & 1/2 mile dirt ovals (4/12/69 - 1985) (1987 - 1992)
3/8 mile paved oval (1993 - present) / (aka: Tucson Int'l Speedway)

Tucson Rodeo Grounds - Tucson - 1/4 mile dirt oval (c.6/19/53 - 1955)
5/8 mile dirt oval (November, 1939 - c.1941) (c.1946 - c.5/15/55)
ran a NASCAR GN race here on 5/15/55 won by Danny Letner

Tucson Speedway - Tucson / (Aka: Adobe Bowl) / (aka: Tucson Motor Speedway)
1/4 mile dirt oval (c.1950 - 1968) / promoters Bob Huff and Dudley Froy

Tucson - also see: Davis-Monthan AFB, Downtown Airport, Gilpin, Kingsley

Willcox - paved road course (5/06/56)

Winkelman - dragstrip (years unknown) / probably 1950's or 1960's

Winslow Dragstrip - Winslow - 1/4 mile paved dragstrip (1959 - 1990)
located at an airport

Yuma - 1/4 mile dirt oval (1950's) / located at 16th and Arizona Ave.

Yuma Speedway - Yuma - 1/4 mile dirt oval (1968 - 1978) (1986 - 1987)
3/8 mile dirt oval (1989 - present) / (aka: Yuma Int'l Speedway)

ARKANSAS

Airport Speedway - see: Beaver Lake Speedway

Arkansas Raceway Park - see: Lake Ouachita Speedway

Arkansas Speedway - Redfield / (aka: Redfield Speedway)
1/4 mile dirt oval (1963 - 1968)

Arkansas State Fairgrounds - Little Rock / the fairgrounds was built in 1921
1/2 mile dirt oval (c.5/16/25 - c.1937)

Ashdown Speedway - see: Thunder Road Speedbowl

B & M Speedway - see: Pocahontas Speedway & Squaw Valley Speedway

Batesville Speedway - Locust Grove / same site as Independence County Raceway
3/8 mile dirt oval (8/16/91 - present) / track built by Larry Shaw

Bear Creek Speedway - Marshall - 1/4 mile dirt oval (May, 1992 - present)

Beaver Lake Speedway - Rogers - 1/4 mile dirt oval (c.1971 - 1987) (1989)
(aka: Airport Speedway)

Bee Branch Motorsports Park - see: Chuck Wagon Race Track

Beebe Speedway - Beebe - 1/4 mile dirt oval (1982 - present)

Benton Speedbowl - Benton - 1/4 mile dirt oval (c.1955 - c.1967)

Bismarck Speedway - Bismarck - 1/4 mile dirt oval (c.1975 - c.1977)

Blytheville Fairgrounds - Blytheville - 1/2 mile dirt oval (c.1938 - 9/28/41)
    1/5 mile dirt oval (7/04/39 - 1/11/39) / at the Mississippi Co. Fairgrounds

Blytheville Speedway - Blytheville - 1/4 mile dirt oval (c.1966 - c.1970)

Burns Park - Little Rock - paved road course (4/24/60) / on park roads

Carlisle Drag-O-Way - Carlisle - 1/4 mile paved dragstrip (c.1960 - 1989)
    (aka: Carlisle Dragway) / property was owned by the city / now an airstrip

Centerville Dragway - Centerville - 1/4 mile paved dragstrip (1975 - present)

Centerville Speedway - Centerville - 1/4 mile dirt oval (1968 - 1993)

Chuck Wagon Race Track - Bee Branch / (aka: Bee Branch Motorsports Park)
    1/4 mile dirt oval (10/02/92 - late 1992)
    irate neighbor's had a court injunction and was able to close track

Clearview Speedway - see: Pocahontas Speedway

Cleburne County Speedway - Heber Springs - 1/4 mile dirt oval (c.1973 - c.1975)

Conway - 1/4 mile dirt oval (1950's)

Cottonwood Speedway - (location unknown) - dirt oval (c.1966)

Crawford County Speedway - Van Buren / now owned by Don Schoenfeld
    3/8 mile dirt oval (1967 - 1985) (1987) (1990 - present)

Crowley's Ridge Raceway - Paragould - 1/4 mile dirt oval (1987 - present)

Des Ark Raceway - Des Arc - 1/4 mile dirt oval (1972 - 1975)

El Paso Raceway - El Paso - 1/2 mile dirt oval (1986 - c.1990)

Fayetteville Fairgrounds - Fayetteville - 1/2 mile dirt oval (11/06/32)

Fayetteville Motor Speedway - see: Razorback Speedway

*Crowley's Ridge Raceway near Paragould, Arkansas. The one-quarter mile
track opened in 1987. - Official track photo.*

Flippin Speedway - Flippin - dirt oval (c.1969 - 1970)

Flying Saucer Speedway - Fort Smith - 1/4 mile dirt oval (c.1949)

Fort Smith Fairgrounds - Fort Smith - 1/2 mile dirt oval (7/13/47 - c.1952)

George Ray Dragstrip - Paragould - 1/8 mile paved dragstrip (10/29/61 - present)
(aka: George Ray Hot Rod Dragstrip)

Gooberstown Raceway - see: Jonesboro Speedway

Grand Prairie Grand Prix - see: Stuttgart Airfield

Green Forest Speedway - Green Forest - 1/4 mile dirt oval (c.1973 - 1975)

Harden Speedway - see: Midway Racing Center

Harrisburg Speedway - Harrisburg - 1/4 mile dirt oval (1991 - present)

Hilltop Speedway - Eureka Springs - 3/8 mile dirt oval (c.1974 - c.1977)

Hope Raceway - Hope - 1.75 mile paved road course (1960's)

Howard County Speedway - Nashville - dirt oval (1970's)

I-30 Speedway - Little Rock (Bryant) - 1/4 mile dirt oval (3/29/68 - present)
1/8 mile paved dragstrip (c.1977) / (aka: Interstate 30 Speedway)
(aka: New Benton Speedbowl)

Independence County Raceway - Locust Grove / (aka: Locust Grove Speedway)
1/2 mile dirt oval (c.1971 - 1977) / converted into a catfish pond
also see: Batesville Speedway

Interstate 30 Speedway - see: I-30 Speedway

Jacksonville - 1/4 mile dirt oval (c.1957)

Jacksonville - 1/4 mile dirt oval (early 1950's)

I-30 Speedway as seen from the air in 1992. - Official track photo.

Jennylind Speedway - (location unknown) - 1/4 mile dirt oval (c.1959 - 1963)

Jonesboro Fairgrounds - Jonesboro - 1/2 mile dirt oval (10/02/18) (1930's)

Jonesboro Raceway - Jonesboro - 3/8 mile dirt oval (1980) / only year it ran

Jonesboro Speedbowl - Jonesboro - paved oval (c.1968 - c.1970)

Jonesboro Speedway - Brookland - 3/8 mile dirt oval (5/14/88 - 1988)
    (aka: Gooberstown Raceway)

Konmack Park - Bentonville - dirt oval (c.1950)

Lake Ouachita Speedway - Mount Ida - 3/8 mile dirt oval (Sept., 1990 - present)
    (aka: Arkansas Raceway Park) / never held a race under the Arkansas name

Little Rock - 1/4 mile dirt oval (late 1940's) / located on Mayville Road

Little Rock Fairgrounds - see: Arkansas State Fairgrounds

Little Rock Speedway - Little Rock - 1/6 mile dirt oval (c.1936 - 1940)

Little Rock - also see: Burns Park, I-30, Ozark Mountain, Rodeo Arena, Round-Up

Locust Grove Speedway - see: Independence County Raceway

Memphis-Ark Speedway - Lehi - 1.5 mile dirt oval (10/09/54 - 1957)
    1/4 mile dirt oval (5/07/55 - 1957) / was 14 miles west of Memphis on US 70
    only Arkansas track to ever hold NASCAR Grand National events

Midway Racing Center - Sheridan (Junet) / (aka: Harden Speedway)
    1/4 mile dirt oval (c.1981 - 1988) (1990 - present)

Bill "Maverick" Golden in his famous "Little Red Wagon". He is the original exhibition wheel stander. The "Little Red Wagon" was acclaimed by Hot Rod Magazine as America's most famous race vehicle. - Bill Golden collection.

100

Midway Speedway - Paragould - 1/4 mile dirt oval / built in 1989 / no grandstands track and cement walls around track were built / but never held a race

Mount Clair Road Speedway - Cove - 3/8 mile dirt oval (April, 1990 - present) (aka: Play Fair Oval Track)

Nash Speedway - see: Thunder Road Speedbowl

New Benton Speedbowl - see: I-30 Speedway

Newport Optimist Dragway - Newport / (aka: Newport Optimist Dragstrip) 1/8 mile concrete dragstrip (c.1964 - present) / on old airport runways

North Arkansas Speedway - Yellville - 5/16 mile dirt oval (9/08/89 - present) located between Yellville and Flippin

Northwest Arkansas Speedway - Pea Ridge - 1/4 mile dirt oval (5/02/92 - present)

Oak Grove Speedway - Glenwood (Caddo Gap) - 1/4 mile dirt oval (1990 - present)

Oppelo Speedway - Oppelo / (aka: Petit Jean Valley Raceway) 3/8 mile dirt oval (c.1970 - c.1977)

Orchard Park Speedway - Murfreesboro - 1/4 mile dirt oval (1992 - present)

Osceola Speedway - Osceola - 1/4 mile dirt oval (c.1968)

Ozark Mountain Speedway - North Little Rock - dirt oval (1950's) (1980)

Petit Jean Valley Speedway - see: Oppelo Speedway

Pike County Speedway - Kirby - 1/4 mile dirt oval (c.1975 - c.1977)

Play Fair Oval Speedway - see: Mount Clair Road Speedway

Plumerville Speedway - Plumerville - 1/4 mile dirt oval (July, 1992 - present)

Pocahontas Speedway - Pocahontas - 3/8 mile dirt oval (1984 - present) (aka: B & M Speedway) / (aka: Clearview Speedway)

Polk County Speedway - Mena - 1/4 mile dirt oval (c.1974 - c.1977)

Prescott Raceway - Prescott / (aka: Prescott Raceway Park) 1/4 mile paved dragstrip (c.1981 - present)

Razorback Speedway - Fort Smith - 1/4 mile paved dragstrip (1963 - 1974) 3/8 mile dirt oval (c.1965 - 1974)

Razorback Speedway - see: Thunder Valley Speedway

Rector Speedway - Rector - 1/4 & 1/2 mile dirt ovals (c.1968 - c.1971)

Redfield Speedway - see: Arkansas Speedway

Riverside Speedway - West Memphis / (aka: West Memphis Speedway) 1/4 mile dirt oval (5/06/50 - present) / (aka: Riverside Int'l Speedway)

Rodeo Arena Speedway - North Little Rock- 1/5 mile dirt oval (6/01/41 - c.6/15/41)

Round-Up Midget Race Track - North Little Rock / promoter was Doc Sosebee 1/4 mile dirt oval (7/11/47 - c.1948) / (aka: Crow Mountain)

Russellville Speedbowl - Russellville - 1/4 mile dirt oval (c.1975)

Searcy Speedway - Searcy / (aka: White County Speedway)
    1/4 mile dirt oval (c.1969 - c.1973)

South Arkansas Speedway - Smackover - 1/4 mile dirt oval (c.1975 - 1980)

Spring River Speedway - Ravenden - 1/4 mile dirt oval (1978 - 1985)

Squaw Valley Speedway - Pocahontas - 1/4 mile dirt oval (1980) (1987)
    located north of town on Highway 115

Stateline Speedway - Texarkana - 1/4 mile dirt oval (1980 - present)

Stuttgart Airfield - Stuttgart / (aka: Grand Prairie Grand Prix)
    2.6 mile paved road course (1959 - c.1972)
    1/4 mile paved dragstrip (c.1970 - c.1972) / (aka: Stuttgart Dragway)

Stuttgart Speedway - Stuttgart - 3/8 mile paved oval (1972 - 1975)

Texarkana Fairgrounds - Texarkana - dirt oval (10/03/47 - 10/05/47)

Thunder Road Speedbowl - Ashdown / (aka: Ashdown Speedway)
    1/4 mile dirt oval (1975 - 1976) / (aka: Nash Speedway)

Thunder Valley Speedway - Fayetteville / (aka: Fayetteville Motor Speedway)
    3/8 mile dirt oval (1970 - c.1983) (c.1987 - 1990) (1992 - present)
    (aka: Razorback Speedway)

Thunderbird Dragway - Walnut Ridge - 1/4 mile paved dragstrip (c.1963)

Tri-State Speedway - Fort Smith - see: Oklahoma chapter

Twin Lake Speedway - Mountain Home - 1/4 mile dirt oval (1988 - c.1991)

Valley Springs Speedway - Harrison - dirt oval (1960's)

Warren Speedway - Warren - 1/4 mile dirt oval (1978 - 1983)

West Memphis Speedway - see: Riverside Int'l Speedway

White County Speedway - see: Searcy Speedway

Whittington Park Speedway - Hot Springs National Park
    1/4 mile paved oval (5/30/47 - 7/12/47)
    1/4 mile dirt oval (7/24/47 - c.1953)

Wynne Stadium - Heber Springs - 1/2 mile dirt oval (c.1977 - c.1980)

Chuck Wagon Race Track operated in 1992. - Allan E. Brown photo.

CALIFORNIA

101 Speedway - Eureka - dirt oval (years unknown) / this was not Redwoods Acres

5-H Ranch Speedway - Roscoe (Sun Valley) - 1/4 mile dirt oval (1/11/48 - c.1948)
    located at 8358 San Fernando Road

Agoura Park - Agoura - 2.0 mile dirt road course (1953) / ran CRA roadsters

Agricultural Park - Los Angeles - dirt oval (c.1908 - 1920's)
    1/3 mile wood oval (early 1910's) / ran motorcycles on wood track
    the track was torn down to build the Los Angeles Coliseum

Airport Speedway - Fresno - 1/5 mile dirt oval (8/04/35 - c.10/20/35)

Airport Speedway - see: Kearney Bowl

Alisal Speedway - Salinas - 3/8 mile paved oval (3/28/48 - c.1952) (1954)
    1/3 mile dirt oval (1952 & 1953) / Pat Flaherty won race on 3/28/48
    (aka: Salinas Speedway) / (aka: Salinas Valley Stadium)
    the grandstands burned down in 1955

All-American Speedway - Roseville / (aka: Roseville Speedway)
    1/4 mile dirt oval (c.1955 - 1970) / (aka: All-American Raceway)
    1/4 mile paved oval (1970 - present) / 1st called All-American in 1971
    located at the Placer County Fairgrounds

Allemand Speedway - Gilroy - 1/2 mile dirt oval (Feb., 1946 - Sept., 1947)
    built and promoted by Henry Allemand on his farm
    track was located six miles east of Highway 101 on Gilroy Hot Springs Road
    Allemand closed track until further notice citing crop harvest
      but actually it closed because of a fatality on the track and the
      recent re-opening of Palm Beach Speedway in nearby Watsonville

Altamont Speedway - Livermore / (aka: Bernal Memorial Raceway)
    1/2 mile dirt oval (1965) / 1st pavement feature won by Billy Vukovich Jr.
    1/4 & 1/2 mile paved ovals (7/22/66 - 1969) (1973 - 1974) (Sept., 1976 - 1978)
    (1980 - 7/12/83) (4/11/91 - 1991)
    track held a Rolling Stone concert and drew 250,000 people, but the
    track was nearly destroyed by an ensuing riot. The concert was
    featured in the film "Gimme Shelter" / called Bernal in 1982 and 1983

Alturas Rodeo Grounds - Alturas - dirt oval (5/22/55 - c.1957)
    first attempt at racing on 5/15/55 was snowed out

Alturas Speedway - Alturas / (aka: Modoc Speedway 41)
    1/4 mile dirt oval (c.1971 - c.1980) / (aka: Modoc Speedway)

Alviso Speedway - San Jose (Alviso) / located north of State Street
    1/4 mile dirt oval (7/26/35 - c.1936) (c.8/11/56 - c.1964) / former dog track

Anaheim Convention Center - Anaheim - indoor concrete oval (1968)

Anderson Speedway - see: Shasta Speedway

Angels Camp Fairgrounds - Angels Camp / located at Calaveras Co. Fairgrounds
    1/5 & 1/2 mile dirt ovals (May, 1947 - c.1951)

Antelope Valley Fairgrounds - see: Lancaster Fairgrounds

Antelope Valley Raceway - see: Los Angeles County Raceway

Antioch Fairgrounds Speedway - Antioch - 1/2 mile dirt oval (c.4/30/50 - c.1950)
    1/4 mile dirt oval (1951 - present) / (aka: Contra Costa District Fair)
    the smaller track was built by John Soares

Arcata Airport - Arcata - 2.1 mile paved road course (8/19/56)
    William "Pete" Snell was fatally injured when his sports car flipped
    the "Snell Foundation" to test helmets was started in his memory

Arco Arena - Sacramento - 1/10 mile indoor concrete oval (2/27/88 - 1990)

Ascot Gold Cup Race - Los Angles (Alhambra) - 5.0 mile road course (11/27/24)
    ran was held on Thanksgiving Day / won by Frank Lockhart

Ascot - Los Angeles (Florence) / now the site of a Goodyear Tire Plant
    1.0 mile dirt oval (1912 - c.4/15/16) / at the Los Angeles County Fairgrounds
    1.0 mile oiled dirt oval (c.11/30/16 - 1/11/20)
    Joe Boyer won last auto race on 11/27/19 / last race was a motorcycle race
    ran midget races in April of 1914 & 3/21/15

*The original Ascot in America was this one mile dirt oval in southern
California. - Phil Harms collection.*

Ascot Motor Speedway - see: Legion Ascot Speedway

Ascot Park - Los Angeles (Gardena) / (aka: Bill McKay's Los Angeles Speedway)
    1/2 mile dirt oval (May, 1957 - 1990) / (aka: New Ascot Stadium)
    ran their first NASCAR GN race on 5/30/59, won by Parnelli Jones
    1/4 mile dirt oval (1963 - 1990) / 1st called Ascot on 9/18/59
    3/4 mile dirt road course (9/22/59) / located on South Vermont Street
    Don Branson & Dick Atkins were fatally injured here on 11/12/66
    the late J.C. Agajanian was the 1977 RPM Promoter of the Year
    after J.C.'s death his sons Cary (1986 RPM Promoter of Year), Chris
      and J.C., Jr. ran the track / now an industrial area

Ascot Speedway - Los Angeles (Venice) / located on Washington Blvd.
1/7 mile dirt oval (1952) / ran TQ midgets / (aka: New Ascot Speedway)

Ash Can Derby - Highland - 1/4 mile dirt oval (1945 - c.1947)
(aka: Gate City Speedway) / located on East 3rd St. east of San Bernadino
(aka: Paradise Valley Speedway)
Troy Ruttman started his driving career here when he was 14 years old

Atascadero Speedway - Atascadero - 1/5 mile dirt oval (9/06/53 - 9/22/73)
lady racer Stevi Cederstom won the last race / now a housing development
located at Mt. Carmel & Santa Clara / backstraight had 100 foot drop off

Athletic Bowl - see: Dinuba Legion Bowl

Atlantic Speedway - Los Angeles (Commerce) / (aka: Atlantic Blvd. Speedway)
Bill Betteridge fatally injured in a crash here on 6/10/37
3/8 mile dirt figure eight course (1/24/36) had a tunnel & bridge
1/2 mile dirt road course (1936) / used part of the track and parking lot
1/4 mile D-shaped dirt oval (4/16/37 - 10/04/38)
1/4 mile paved oval (3/05/39 - 7/30/42) / was located near Compton
located at Atlantic Blvd. & Olive St. / site is now the Long Beach Expressway

Auburn Fairgrounds - Auburn / located at the Gold Country Fairgrounds
1/4 mile dirt oval (c.9/02/56 - c.5/21/74) / (aka: Auburn Speedway)
the 5/21/74 race was delayed when a mortar shell was found on backstretch

Bakersfield - 11.15 mile road course (7/04/11 - 1915) / ran AAA champ cars

Bakersfield Fairgrounds - Bakersfield / located at the old Kern Co. Fairgrounds
1.0 mile dirt oval (4/27/13 - c.1918) (5/10/25 - 10/10/25)(1930 - 1/03/32)
1/2 mile dirt oval (1931 - 1932) (10/14/45) / north of town on Chester Ave
track was built in 1913 / Barney Oldfield set a world's record here in 1913
(aka: Bakersfield Speedway) / mgr: Paul Derkum / (aka: Derkum Dirt Track)
AAA races were held on 4/27/13, 5/10/25, 10/10/25, 3/01/31 & 1/03/32
the last race was a AMA motorcycle race in late 1945

Bakersfield Raceway - Famoso - 1/4 mile paved dragstrip (1952 - present)
(aka: Smokers Dragstrip) / (aka: Famoso Dragstrip)

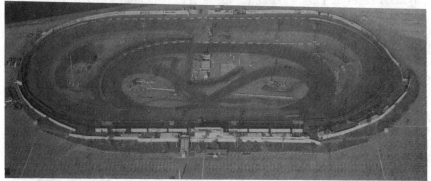

The famous Ascot Park in Gardena, California. The multi-purpose track closed in 1990. - Jim Peterson photo.

Bakersfield Rodeo Arena - Bakersfield / at the new Kern County Fairgrounds
1/10 mile dirt oval (3/12/89) / located on the southeast side of town

Bakersfield Speedway - Bakersfield (Oildale) / (aka: Oildale Speedway)
1/4 mile dirt oval (5/05/46 - Nov., 1958) / (aka: Bakersfield Speedbowl)
Bill Vukovich, Sr. won the first race on 5/05/46
1/2 mile dirt oval (c.1955) / (aka: Bakersfield Thunderbowl)
1/4 mile paved oval (5/30/59 - 1979) / located north of Bakersfield
1/4 mile dirt oval (1980 - 1991) / (aka Oilbowl Speedway)
1/3 mile dirt oval (March, 1992 - present) / Rick & Roger Mears raced here

Bakersfield Speedway - located on Highway 99 - see: Sportsman Park

Bakersfield - also see: Mesa Marin Speedway, Minter Field

Balboa Stadium - San Diego (Ocean Beach) / (aka: San Diego Stadium)
1/4 mile dirt oval (1937 - 7/25/42) (9/19/45 - 7/04/61)
(aka: Balboa Park Stadium) / the track was torn out when San Diego
  Chargers football team moved here from Los Angeles

Banning - 1/2 mile dirt oval (c.7/05/26 - c.1929) / now a housing development
Ted Horn's driving career started here / maybe 1.0 mile before 1926

Barona Speedway - Ramona - 1/6 mile dirt oval (c.4/16/94 - present)

Barstow - 1/4 mile paved oval (10/05/52 - c.1959)
located .5 mile east of town on U.S. 66 / maybe dirt oval at first

Barstow Speedway - Barstow - 1/3 mile dirt oval (10/01/61 - 1969)
located on Riverside Drive / now Rotary Bicycle Motocross course

Baxter Stadium - Stockton / located at a college baseball diamond
1/4 mile dirt oval (6/18/33 - 1933) / (aka: College of the Pacific)
1/5 mile dirt oval (c.9/19/40 - 8/30/41) / (aka: Stockton Ball Diamond)

Bay Meadows Race Track - San Mateo / still a famous horse track
1.0 mile dirt oval (11/26/50 - c.9/02/56) / Tony Bettenhausen won 1st race
ran NASCAR GN races on 8/22/54, 7/31/55 & 8/19/56

Baylands Raceway Park - Fremont / bleachers from Ontario Motor Speedway
1/4 mile paved dragstrip (1959 - 1988) / home of the "Golden Gate Nat'ls"
1/4 mile dirt oval (1974 - 1980) / appx. site of old Frank Yuill Field
3/8 mile dirt oval (August, 1981 - Nov., 1988) / (aka: Fremont Raceway)
1/4 mile dirt oval (1984)

Bayshore Stadium - San Francisco (Daly City) / formerly a dog track
1/4 mile dirt oval (11/04/45 - 1962) / located next to Cow Palace

Bean Bowl - Oceanside - 1/5 mile dirt oval (10/23/38 - c.1941) (August, 1946)

Belmont City - paved road course (1953)

Belmont Speedway - Belmont / (aka: Belmont City Stadium)
1/4 mile dirt oval (7/23/47 - 9/25/59) / ran motorcycles and midgets
Joe Leonard was a star here on motorcycles when he was in his teens
now the site of industrial buildings

Bernal Memorial Raceway - see: Altamont Speedway

106

Beverly Hills Speedway (board track) - see: Los Angeles Motor Speedway

Bishop Dragstrip - Bishop - 1/4 mile paved dragstrip (1963 - 1964)

Bishop Fairgrounds - Bishop - 1/10 mile dirt oval (1976) / ran TQ midgets
   located at the Tri-County Fairgrounds

Blackstone Bowl - Fresno - 5/8 mile high banked oiled dirt oval (1947 - c.1952)
   turns banked 38 degrees / site is now the Montgomery Wards shopping plaza

Blythe Speedway - Blythe - 1/4 mile dirt oval (c.1983 - 1989)
   1/4 mile paved oval (1992 - present) / at the Colorado Country Fairgrounds

Bolado Park - Hollister - 1/8 mile dirt oval (1988 - present)
   ran Modified-midgets up until 1993 / now only motorcycle races

Bonelli Ranch Stadium - see: Saugus Speedway

Boonville Fairgrounds - Boonville - 1/2 mile dirt oval (1953)

Brotherhood Dragway - Los Angeles (Log Beach) / located on Terminal Island
   500 foot paved dragstrip (11/20/93 - 1993)
   1/4 mile paved dragstrip (1974 - 1984) (1994 - present)

Buchanan Field - Concord - 2.3 mile paved road course (8/21/55 - c.7/01/56)

Buellton Speedway - Buellton - dirt oval (c.1952 - c.1953)

Burbank - see: Jeffrey's, Jeffries

Cabrillo Speedway - San Diego - 1/4 mile dirt oval (1/01/50 - 1951)
   1/10 mile dirt oval (8/13/50) / located just off Highway 101

Cajon Speedway - El Cajon - 1/4 mile dirt oval (1961 - 1963)
   3/8 mile dirt oval (4/11/64 - 1965)
   3/8 mile paved oval (April, 1966 - present)

Cajon Speedway near San Diego, California as seen from the air. The figure-eight track runs through the middle of the oval track. The facility opened as a dirt track in 1961. It was paved with asphalt in 1966. - Official track photo.

The old California State Fairgrounds in Sacramento. The one-mile track surrounds a half-mile track used for horse racing. - Allan E. Brown collection.

Cal Expo - Sacramento - 1.0 mile dirt oval (1978 - present)
    built to replace the old California State Fairgrounds
    holds an annual AMA Nat'l motorcycle race
    first auto race was a USAC Silver Crown race in 1989

California Mid-State Fairgrounds - see: Paso Robles Fairgrounds

California Mid-Winter Fairgrounds - see: Imperial Speedway

California State Fairgrounds - Sacramento / built as a horse track in 1906
    1.0 mile dirt oval (1912) (9/02/46 - 10/25/70)
    2.1 mile road course (1956 - 1969) / site is now a shopping center
    ran a number of NASCAR GN races in 1950's & 1960's

California State Fairgrounds (new) - see: Cal Expo

Calistoga Speedway - Calistoga / located at the Napa County Fairgrounds
    1/2 mile dirt oval (10/23/38 - c.1941) (c.1946 - present)
    1/3 mile dirt oval (c.1953) / built as a horse track
    Gary Patterson fatally injured here on 5/29/83

Would you believe this is Calistoga Speedway? It was a bit primitive in this 1953 ARA sprint car photo. - Rod Eschenburg photo (courtesy of Don Radbruch).

108   *California*

Candlestick Park - San Francisco - 1.9 mile paved road course (1963 - 8/11/65)
   ran sports car events in the parking lot of the ball diamond

Capital Speedway - see: West Capital Speedway

Carlsbad Speedway - Carlsbad - 1/4 mile paved dragstrip (1963 - present)
   1/8 mile dirt oval (1985 - present) / (aka: Carlsbad Raceway)

Carnegie Speedway - Tracy - 1/12 mile dirt oval (1977 - 1985) / ran micro-midgets

Carpinteria Thunderbowl - Carpinteria / the track was actually in Rincon Point
   1/4 mile dirt oval (8/04/47 - 1956) / ran midgets, jalopies & roadsters

Carrell Speedway - Los Angeles (Gardena) / (aka: Gardena Bowl)
   1/2 mile dirt oval (1940 - 1942) (7/31/46 - Oct. 1948)
   1/2 mile paved oval (10/24/48 - c.1954) / owner: Emmett J. Malloy
   Bobby Ball crashed here in 1952, he died on 2/27/54 of the injuries
   held first CRA (roadster) race here on 9/02/46 / in movie "Big Wheel"
   1.0 mile dirt road course (1949) (9/10/50) (9/17/50 roadsters) (10/08/50)
   located at 174th & Vermont / located one mile north of Ascot Park
   the promoter was J.C. Agajanian / the track torn down for Artesia Blvd.
   named after Judge Carrell who owned the property

Castle Air Force Base - Merced - paved road course (1953)

Cedarville Speedway - Cedarville / located at the Modoc District Fairgrounds
   1/2 mile dirt oval (c.1949 - c.1951)
   5/16 mile dirt oval (c.1974 - 1989) (1991 - present)

Champion Speedway - San Francisco (Brisbane) / near Daly City
   1/4 & 1/2 mile dirt oval (9/09/63 - 1966) (actually was .436 mile)
   1/8 mile paved dragstrip (c.1970) / across from Candlestick Park

Chico Speedway - Chico - 1/4 mile dirt oval (1953 - 1962)
   located on East Eighth Street

Chico Fairgrounds - see: Silver Dollar Speedway

Chico - also see: Cycleland, Hahn Field, Highway 99 Speedway

Chowchilla Fairgrounds - Chowchilla - 1/5 mile dirt oval (5/15/93) / USAC TQ race

Chowchilla Speedway - Chowchilla / George Robson started his career in 1930
   1.0 mile dirt oval (c.1927 - c.1941) (c.1947 - c.1955)

Chris Beck Arena - Santa Rosa / ran BCRA midgets on a rodeo grounds
   1/8 mile dirt oval (1980) / located at the Sonoma County Fairgrounds

Chula Vista - see: Paradise Mesa, South Bay, Speedway 117

Clovis - dirt oval (5/16/37) (1940)

Clovis Speedway - Clovis / (aka: Clovis Rodeo Grounds)
   1/2 mile dirt oval (c.11/12/50 - 10/30/76)
   1/5 mile dirt oval (5/27/51 - c.1951)

Colorado River Country Fairgrounds - see: Blythe Speedway

Colton - see: Inter-City, Morrow Field, Orange Empire, Tri-City Speedway

Compton Motor Speedway - Compton - oval (1956)

Compton - also see: Moto Speedway

Contra Costa Grand Prix - Pittsburg - 2.1 mile paved road course (1965)
   located at Camp Stoneman near Pittsburg

Contra Costa Stadium - Walnut Creek (Pacheco) / site is now I-680 expressway
   1/5 mile dirt oval (6/15/46 - 1960) / located four miles north of town

Converey - (location unknown) - dirt oval (years unknown)

Corona Fairgrounds - Corona / (aka: Corona Speedway)
   1/2 mile dirt oval (2/02/47 - c.1953) / located 4 miles NW on River Road

Corona Raceway - Corona - 1/4 & 1/2 mile dirt ovals (1/10/71 - Oct., 1984)
   Danny Caruthers was seriously injured here 10/30/71, he died 11/04/71

Corona Road Race - Corona - 2.76895 mile oiled dirt city street oval (9/09/13)
   2.76895 mile paved city street (circular) oval (11/26/14 & 4/08/16)
   track was Grand Avenue Blvd., a road that circled the town of Corona
   the first race was for a celebration called the "California's Admission Day"
   Bob Burman fatally injured in a crash here on 4/08/16

Costa Mesa Fairgrounds - Costa Mesa / located at the Orange County Fairgrounds
   2.0 mile paved road course (12/14/57)
   1/8 mile dirt oval (1956) (1970) (1992) / small oval for speedway motorcycles
      ran TQ midgets on special events in 1956, 1970 & 1992 on oval track

Cotati Dragstrip - Cotati - 1/4 mile paved dragstrip (c.1958 - c.1964)

Ready for the start of the 1916 Corona Road Race. - Bob Sheldon collection.

110

Cotati - Santa Rosa (Cotati) - 2.2 mile paved road course (5/26/57 - 1959)
1.9 mile paved road course (4/23/60 - 1971)

Cotati Speedway - Santa Rosa (Cotati) / (aka: North Bay Speedway)
1.25 mile wood oval (8/14/21 - 10/20/22) / turns were banked 38 degrees
built by Jack Prince and Art Pillsbury / torn down to build an egg farm
practice and qualifying were held on 7/31/21 / 30,000 fans at first race
ran a stock car race in May of 1922 / now site of housing development

Cow Palace - San Francisco (Daly City) / ran midgets and speedway cycles
1/7 mile dirt indoor oval (3/15/52 - c.2/14/59)
1/7 mile concrete indoor oval (c.1970 - 1975)

Crescent City Fairgrounds - Crescent City - 1/2 mile dirt oval (c.6/23/51)
located at the Del Norte County Fairgrounds

Crows Landing Naval Air Station - Crows Landing / located south of Modesto
3.0 mile paved road course (1967) (1992 - 1993) / ran SCCA TA in 1967

Culver City / (aka: Junior Vanderbilt Cup Race) / held the first midget auto race
8 block dirt square (1913 & 3/24/14) / the races were 10 laps long
Stuart Morrison who invented the midget racer and also the first Hot Rod
in 1908 was an entrant in the races

Culver City Legion Bowl - Culver City - 1/5 mile dirt oval (3 races in 1933)
1/4 mile dirt oval (8/20/41 - 9/17/41) / located near Venice

Culver City Speedway - Culver City - 1/2 mile dirt oval (10/30/32 - 1933)
1/5 mile dirt oval (8/26/34 & 9/02/34)

Culver City Speedway - Culver City / different location than C.C. Legion Bowl
1/4 mile high banked paved oval (3/30/47 - 10/04/54) / a former dog track
1/2 mile dirt/paved road course (10/19/47 & 10/26/47) < used part of oval
1/2 mile paved road course (2/27/49 & 3/20/49) / used the parking lot only
1/4 mile dirt oval (1951) (1956) / located at Washington & Lincoln Blvd
torn down in 1954 / sold to Douglas Aircraft / now the site of warehouses
featured in the movie "Big Wheel" staring Mickey Rooney

Culver City Speedway - Culver City / site later became movie studios
1.0 mile dirt oval (c.1923 - 1924) (1927) / raced inside wood track 1927
1.25 mile wood track (12/14/24 - 3/06/27) / turns were banked 45 degrees
the wood track was built by Jack Prince and Art Pillsbury
the track wasn't ready for the first scheduled race on 11/27/24
the cars started practicing on 11/30/24 / (aka: New Ascot Motor Speedway
Red Cariens fatally injured on 11/29/25 / later used for exhibition runs
1.25 mile dirt oval (c.1928 - c.1929)

Cycleland - Chico - 1/8 mile dirt oval (c.1985 - present) / see: Highway 99 Spwy
a motorcycle track / also ran mini-sprints 1985 to 1988

De Anza Park Speedway - see: Riverside Fairgrounds

DeCarlo Speedway - Gilroy - 1/10 mile dirt oval (July, 1979 - Sept., 1979)
located behind DeCarlo's Feed Store / ran Micro-Midgets

Del Mar Road Course - see: Grand Prix of San Diego - Del Mar

Del Mar Speedway - Del Mar / built by Bing Crosby in 1937
　　1.0 mile dirt oval (10/16/49 & 11/06/49) (1994) / was a horse track
　　ran autos in 1949, ran an AMA motorcycle event in 1994
　　Rex Mays fatally injured on 11/06/49 / Bing Crosby owned track in 1949
　　1.5 mile paved parking lot road course (1959) / now a fairgrounds
　　also see: Grand Prix of Greater San Diego

Delta Speedway - Stockton - 1/8 mile dirt oval (1985 - present) / runs mini-sprints

Denver - (location unknown) - 1/2 mile dirt oval (c.1933)

Derkum Dirt Speedway - see: Bakersfield Fairgrounds

Devil's Bowl - Salinas - 3/8 mile dirt road course (1945 - 1947) / ran jalopies

Dinuba Legion Bowl - Fresno / (aka: Athletic Bowl) / (aka: Dinuba Speedway)
　　1/5 mile dirt oval (c.6/26/35 - c.12/10/39) (c.6/14/51 - c.1951)

Dixon May Fairgrounds - Dixon - 3/8 mile dirt oval (c.1966 - c.1982)

Dixon Speedway - Dixon - 1/4 mile dirt oval (1950's - early 1960's)
　　1/4 mile paved dragstrip (1950's - early 1960's)

Dodger Stadium - Los Angeles - 1.3 mile paved parking lot road course (1963)

Don-Mar Speedway - see: Firestone Blvd. Speedway

Eastside Speedway - San Jose - 1/2 mile dirt oval (12/09/34)
　　owner J.R. Wilson / destroyed in a fire in 1939 / (aka: Eastside Flat Track)

El Cajon - 1/5 mile dirt oval (10/01/38 - 10/09/38)

El Cajon Valley Speedway - El Cajon - 1/4 mile banked dirt oval (5/28/50 - 1951)
　　located two miles east of city limits on Highway 80 (now Main St.)

El Cajon - also see: Cajon Speedway

El Camino Speedway - Oceanside - 1/5 mile dirt oval (1958) / (aka: Bean Bowl)

El Centro Fairgrounds - see: Imperial Raceway

El Mirage - (near Adelanto) desert dragstrip (1937 - c.1939) (1946 - c.1950)
　　held speed trials on the desert sand

El Monte American Legion Stadium - El Monte / ran micro midgets
　　1/12 mile indoor wood oval (1962) / it was a stadium with a wood floor

El Monte - also see: Lakeland Stadium

El Toro Raceway - Costa Mesa / (aka: Orange County Speedway)
　　1/8 & 1/5 mile dirt ovals (May, 1956 - 1978) / ran TQ midgets & full midgets

Elmhurst (board track) - see: Oakland Motordrome

Elsinore Raceway - Elsinore - 1/5 mile dirt oval (1968 & 1969)
　　(aka: Munz Speedway) / located at 29400 Riverside Drive

Emeryville Speedway - Emeryville / formerly a dog track & speedway cycle track
　　1/4 mile dirt oval (1912 - 11/04/37) / first auto race on was 10/18/34
　　ran motorcycles from 1912 - 1937

112

Empire Speedway - see: Orange Empire Speedway

Ernie Purssell Memorial Speedway - Grass Valley
1/4 mile dirt oval (c.5/30/58 - present) / at the Nevada County Fairgrounds
dedicated to Ernie Purssell, a local driver who was fatally injured in
the last race at the old Sacramento Fairgrounds in 1970
1st called Ernie Purssell Memorial in 1971 / (aka: Grass Valley Speedway)
the track configuration has changed from D-shaped to an oval
built in 1951 as a baseball diamond / (aka: Muhcahy Field)

Escondido - 1/5 mile dirt oval (9/09/38 - 9/17/38)

Eureka - 1/5 mile dirt oval (late 1930's) / ran midgets

Eureka Drag Strip - see: Samoa Airport

Eureka - also see: 101 Speedway, Redwood Acres

Exhibition Park - Los Angeles / located at 35th & Figeroa
1.0 mile dirt oval (1912 - 1913)

Fairmont Park - see: Riverside Fairgrounds

Famoso Dragstrip - see: Bakersfield Raceway

Fawn Speedway - Weed - oval (c.1953) / located between Mt. Shasta & Weed

Feather River Speedway - Oroville / behind the airport on Oroville-Gridley Road
5/8 mile dirt tri-oval (7/04/53) / ARA big car race won by Ernie Koch
5/16 mile dirt oval (7/24/53 - 8/06/54) / track closed when equipment sold
(aka: Oroville Speedway)

Ferndale Fairgrounds - Ferndale / located at the Humboldt County Fairgrounds
1/2 mile dirt oval (c.8/24/47 - 8/24/58)

Firestone Blvd Speedway - Norwalk (Downey) / (aka: Firestone Blvd Motordrome)
1/4 mile dirt oval (c.8/24/47 - 1950) / (aka: Don-Mar Speedway)
1/8 mile dirt oval (1/11/48) / (aka: Don-Mar Stadium)

Folsom Road Speedway - Gilroy - dirt oval (1947) / ran roadsters

Fontana Int'l Dragway - Fontana - 1/4 mile paved dragstrip (1952 - 1969)
(aka: Fontana Drag City) / located near San Bernadino

Fort Ord - paved road course (11/10/57)

Fort Ord Speedway - Fort Ord - 1/8 mile dirt oval (2/19/50 - 1950)
dirt oval (1951) / ran stock cars / (aka: Ord Speedway)

Fortuna - dirt oval (1949) / ran two BCRA midget races / maybe at Rohner Park

Forum - Los Angles (Inglewood) - 1/10 mile indoor paved oval (1/25/68 & 2/01/68)
where the L.A. Lakers play basketball / racing was halted after two midget
events when the rubber left on the floor after the two midget races caused
problems for freezing for ice hockey

Frank Chance Field - Fresno - 1/5 mile dirt oval (c.5/26/39 - c.6/19/39)

Fremont Raceway - see: Baylands Raceway Park

Fresno Dragways - Fresno - 1/4 mile paved dragstrip (1964 - c.1972) / on Hwy 41

Fresno Entertainment Park Speedway - Fresno - 1/4 mile dirt oval (1955 - c.1956)
   (aka: Fresno Recreation Speedway)

Fresno - road course (1912 - 1916) / held during Raisen Day Celebration

Fresno Speedway - Fresno - 1.0 mile dirt oval (c.10/13/04 - c.10/02/15) (1932)
   1.0 mile wood oval (10/02/20 - c.10/02/27) / (aka: Fresno District Fair)
   the wood track was built by Jack Prince and Art Pillsbury
   Jimmy Murphy won 1st race on wood track / turns were banked 30 degrees
   the wood track had a 1/2 mile horse track in the middle
   Alton Soules fatally injured on 10/01/21 / (aka: Raisen Day Speedway)
   one race was held after 10/02/27 on the board track for dirt track cars
   1/2 mile dirt oval (10/01/27) (9/03/51) / (aka: Mercer Co. Fairgrounds)
   Duane Carter, Sr. started his career on the dirt track in 1932

Fresno State College Stadium - Fresno / (aka: C.J. Stadium)
   1/4 mile dirt oval (8/06/37 - 8/28/37) / (aka: Hughes Stadium)

Fresno - also see: Airport, Blackstone, Dinuba, Frank Chance, Hammer, Hughes,
   Radcliff, Selland, Valley

Galt Fairgrounds - Galt - 1/2 mile dirt oval (c.7/19/52)
   located at the Sacramento County Fairgrounds / built as a horse track 1935

Gardena - 1/4 mile dirt oval (1924) / only ran a couple of races

Gardena Speedway - Los Angeles - 1/5 mile dirt oval (12/12/54 - 11/28/57)
   1/4 mile dirt oval (1/01/58 - c.2/23/58) / (aka: Western Speedway)
   1/3 mile dirt oval (3/09/58 - c.1967) / located at 139th & Western
   promoter: J.C. Agajanian / (aka: Gardena Stadium)

The board track at the Fresno Fairgrounds in 1926. The wood-surfaced one mile oval lasted from 1920 until 1927. The turns were banked at 30 degrees. The track was reconverted into a horse track. - Bob Sheldon collection.

Gilmore Stadium - Los Angeles (Hollywood) / owned by A.F. Gilmore
  1/5 mile dirt oval (5/28/34 - 5/28/36) / first race was a motorcycle race
  Curly Mills won the first auto race on 5/31/34 / torn down in 1951
  1/4 mile dirt oval (7/30/36 - 6/07/42) (11/20/45 - 11/23/50)
  Chet Mortemore was fatally injured here 10/25/35 (first midget fatality)
  located at Fairfax & Beverly Blvd. / now part of CBS Television City

Glandimis Fairgrounds - (location unknown) - dirt oval (years unknown)

Glen Helen OHV Park - San Bernadino / runs Speedway cycles & Micro-Midgets
  1/8 mile dirt oval (1988 - 1990) (1994 - present)
  300 foot sand drags (1993 - present)

Glendale Road Race - Glendale - 1.9 mile road course (c.1914 - 2/03/15)
  ran an AAA race in 1915 / called Tropica Road

Golden Gate Fields - Albany - 1.0 mile dirt oval (1939) / ran motorcycles

Golden Gate Park - San Francisco
  3.1 mile paved city street road course (1952 & 1953)

Golden State Int'l Raceway - see: Sears Point Raceway

Golden State Raceway - see: Santa Maria Dragstrip

Goleta - 3/10 mile paved (road) dragstrip (April, 1949 - c.1950)
  the first legalized dragstrip (approved by the California Highway Patrol)
  the track was an access road to an airport

Goleta Airport - see: Santa Barbara Municipal Airport

Goshen Speedway - Goshen - 5/8 mile dirt oval (1931) (6/10/34 - 10/24/37) (1940)
  located at the Visalia Fairgrounds / (aka: San Joaquin Valley Track)

Grand Central Airport - Glendale - 2.3 mile paved road course (10/15/50 - 1955)

Grand Prix of Greater San Diego - Del Mar / located at the Del Mar Fairgrounds
  1.62 mile paved parking lot road course (10/16/87 - 1992)
  also see: Del Mar Speedway / ran IMSA GT races

Grand Prix of Long Beach - Long Beach / (aka: Toyota Grand Prix of Long Beach)
  2.02 mile city street road course (9/28/75 - 3/30/80)
  held U.S. Grand Prix (Formula One) here 1976 - 1982
  2.13 mile paved city street road course (3/15/81 - 1985)
  1.67 mile paved city street road course (1986 - 1993)
  1.59 mile paved city street road course (1994 - present)

Grape Bowl - see: Lodi Stadium

Grass Valley Fairgrounds - see: Ernie Purssell Memorial Speedway

Greater San Francisco Speedway (board track) - see: San Francisco Speedway

Greenwich Village - Girand - 1.0 mile dirt road course (8/05/34)
  ran a 75 mile midget race which was won by Bill Betteridge

Grenfell Speedway - Crescent City - 1/4 mile dirt oval (c.8/14/54)
  1/4 mile paved oval (6/12/54 - c.1962) / located five miles north of town

Gridley Fairgrounds - Gridley - 1/3 mile dirt oval (8/22/52)
3/8 mile dirt oval (c.1964 - c.1979) / at the Butte County Fairgrounds

Half Moon Bay Dragway - Redwood City - 1/4 mile paved dragstrip (1957 - 1965)

Hammer Field - Fresno - 1/4 mile paved dragstrip (1952)

Hanford Fairgrounds - see: Kings Speedway

Hanford Motor Speedway - Hanford / (aka: Marchbanks Stadium Speedway)
5/8 mile paved/dirt oval (c.10/28/51 - 1965) / owner: Bonnie Marchbanks
5/8 mile track had asphalt straightaways and dirt corners
1.8 & 2.5 mile paved road courses (late 1950's - c.1965)
1/3 mile paved oval (1959) / complex torn down in April, 1984
3/4 mile paved oval (1965 - 1967) / site is now cotton fields
1.3 mile paved oval (6/12/60 - 1968) / ran NASCAR GN & USAC Indy Cars
1.5 mile paved oval (4/13/69) possibly 1.3 & 1.5 were same track
    or the track was rebuilt a little larger

Hangtown Speedway - see: Placerville Speedway

Hahn Field Speedway - Chico - 1/4 mile dirt oval (5/29/52 - c.8/28/52)
located at the former home of the Chico Dons (semi-pro baseball team)
track was egg-shaped / located at 5th & Oak / the promoter was John Giebe

Hansen Dam Park - Pacoima - 1.3 mile paved road course (6/19/55)

Hawthorne Bowl - Hawthorne / located at 190th St. & Hawthorne Ave.
1/5 mile dirt oval (February, 1956) / ran TQ midgets

Hayward Motorcycle Speedway - Hayward / (aka: Hayward Depot Speedway)
dirt kidney shaped track (1960's - 1974) / located on Depot Road
ran motorcycles and Micro-midgets

Hell's Half Acre - Los Angles (Hollywood) - 5/8 mile dirt road course (1938 - 1939)

Hellesburg - (location unknown) - 1/4 mile dirt oval (1950's)

Hemet Fairgrounds - Hemet - 1/7 mile dirt oval (6/14/52 - 1955) / ran TQ midgets
in the 1970's a 1/10 mile speedway motorcycle track was erected on site

Herlong - oval (c.5/27/54 - c.1955)

High Desert Raceway - Victorville - 1/4 mile paved dragstrip (c.1977)

High Desert Speedway - see: Independent Motorsports Park

High Desert Speedway - Susanville - 5/8 mile dirt oval (1952)
1/4 mile dirt oval (c.1954 - c.1982) (1993 - present)
(aka: Susanville Speedway) / located at the Lassen County Fairgrounds

Highway 99 Speedway - Chico - 1/8 mile dirt oval (1993) / next to Cycleland

Hills Ferry Speedway - Newman - 1/8 mile dirt oval (1980 - 1985)(1992 - present)

Holtville Aerodrome Int'l Raceway - Holtville / at an old WWII Navy Air Station
1.4 & 1.9 mile paved road courses (c.1961 - present)
1/4 mile paved dragstrip (1963 - c.1986) / (aka: Holtville Raceway)
(aka: Holtville Aerodrome Dragstrip) / (aka: Aerodrome Int'l Raceway)

Holtville Int'l Raceway - Holtville - oval (years unknown)

Hourglass Field - San Diego - 1.0 mile paved road course (c.7/10/55 - c.9/28/58)
  1.7 mile paved road course (10/19/57) / ran CRA sprints in 1956
  located near Miramar / at an old airport shaped like an hourglass

Hughes Stadium - Sacramento / (aka: Sacramento Junior College) / built in 1928
  1/4 mile dirt oval (6/04/33 - c.1941) (c.1946 - 1967) / at 3835 Freeport Blvd.
  first modern day midget race held here on 6/04/33 / won by Dave Oliver
  (aka: Sacramento Stadium) / (aka: Charles C. Hughes Memorial Stadium)
  John Soares won the first ever "Gold Cup" here on 9/03/51

Hughes Stadium - Fresno - see: Fresno State College

Humboldt County Speedway - see: Indianola Speedway

Huntington Beach - 1/2 mile dirt oval (1932)

Huntington Beach Legion Speedway - Huntington Beach / (aka: Talbert Stadium)
  1/5 mile dirt oval (12/08/46 - 12/15/46) (3/20/49 - 1952)
  1/4 mile paved oval (1947 - c.1957) / located neat Beach Blvd. & Atlanta
  1/8 mile dirt oval (7/12/48 - 10/24/48)

Imperial Raceway - El Centro (Imperial) / at California Mid-Winter Fairgrounds
  1.125 mile dirt oval (February, 1913 - 1940) / Barney Oldfield won first race
  1/5 mile dirt oval (3/16/35 & 3/17/35) / Ernie Triplett died here 3/04/34
  1/4 mile dirt oval (2/07/37 - c.1942) / (aka: Imperial Fairgrounds)
  1/2 mile dirt oval (10/21/45 - 1983) / (aka: Imperial Speedway)
  3/8 mile dirt oval (1984 - present)

Imperial Valley Micro-Midget Speedway - Brawley / located north of Imperial
  1/8 mile dirt oval (c.7/09/51 - c.1951)

Independent Motorsports Park - Pearsonville / (aka: High Desert Speedway)
  1/4 mile dirt oval (1974 - present) / (aka: Pearson Speedway)

Indian Dunes Park - Valencia
  1/6, 1/5 & 3/8 mile dirt ovalS (c.1975 - c.1985)

Indianola Speedway - Indianola / (aka: Humboldt County Speedway)
  1/4 mile dirt oval (6/19/55 - 1955) / built as a motorcycle track
  the first auto race here was held on 8/25/55
  1/5 mile dirt oval (6/23/57 - c.6/22/58) / near Mid-Way Drive-In off Hwy 101

Indio Drag Strip - Indio - 1/4 mile paved dragstrip (c.1970)

Indio Fairgrounds - Indio / located at the Cowchilla Valley Fairgrounds
  1/4 mile sand oval (4/15/51 - c.1951) / ran TQ midget races

Ingleside - San Francisco - 1.0 mile dirt oval (11/04/03 - 11/08/04)
  race scheduled for 1906 canceled because of the San Francisco earthquake

Inter-City Speedway - Colton - 1/2 mile concrete oval (c.1926 - 1934)
  built by Colton Cement Company

Inyokern Dragstrip - Inyokern - 1/4 mile dragstrip (10/24/54 - present)
  one of the oldest continual strips and has been operated since the track's
  beginning by the Dust Devil's Auto Club / at an old Navy air base

Irwindale Raceway - Irwindale - 1/4 mile paved dragstrip (1957 - 1961)
1/10 mile paved oval (3/15/61) / ran TQ midgets on oval track
(aka: Irwindale Speedway) / location is now a Miller Brewing Plant

Jeffrey's Oval - Burbank - 5/8 mile dirt oval (1962) / possibly Jeffries Ranch

Jeffries Ranch - Burbank - 1/2 mile dirt oval (c.1931 - c.1935)
built by Jim Jeffries (who was a heavy weight boxing champion)

Joe Allen Ranch - Gilroy - 1/10 mile dirt oval (1978 - July, 1979)
located in a walnut grove off New Ave. / ran Micro-Midgets

Kearney Bowl - Fresno (aka: Italian Amusement Park) / (aka: Fresno Speedway)
1/5 mile dirt oval (5/17/36 - 7/26/42) (1945 - 1959)
1/5 mile paved oval (4/08/60 - Sept., 1970) / torn down in Nov., 1970
(aka: Airport Speedway) / across the street from the old Airport Speedway
Bill Vukovich, Sr. & Bill Vukovich, Jr. both started here
proposed 1.0 mile paved oval track in 1967

Kenilworth Park - Petaluma - 1.0 mile dirt oval (1928) (1936)
site of current Petaluma Fair Speedway and Keniworth Junior High School

Kern County Speedway - Rosamond - 1/4 mile paved oval (11/27/93 - present)
located next to Willow Springs Raceway

King City - dirt oval (1948)

Kingdon Airport Road Race - Lodi - paved road course (c.1958 - c.1960)

Kingdon Dragstrip - Lodi - 1/4 mile paved dragstrip (11/11/51 - c.1977)
the first promoter was Bob Cress / same site as Kingdom Airport

Kings Speedway - Hanford - 1.0 mile dirt oval (c.9/25/17 - c.1925)
1/2 mile dirt oval (1951) (8/29/59) / located at Kings County Fairgrounds
1/3 mile dirt oval (6/11/83 - present)
1/8 mile dirt oval (4/04/86 - 1991) < inside of 1/3 mile track
1/8 mile dirt oval (1992 - present) < located in pit area of 1/3 mile track

Kingsburg Race Circuit - Stateline / located near Lake Tahoe, Nevada
1.9 mile paved road course (10/01/67)

LaGrange Speedway - LaGrange - 1/2 mile dirt oval (c.1958)

Laguna Seca Raceway - Monterey - 1.92 mile paved road course (11/10/57 - 1988)
2.214 mile paved road course (Sept., 1988 - present)

Lake Perris Speedway - Lake Perris / opened in 1987 for speedway motorcycles
1/10 mile dirt oval (1987 - present) / first auto race was on 10/11/92

Lakeland Stadium - El Monte - 1/4 mile dirt oval (7/11/48 - 1949)

Lakeport Speedway - Lakeport - 1/3 mile dirt oval (1949 - c.1954)
1/4 mile paved oval (c.1971 - present) / at the Lake County Fairgrounds

Lakeside Arena - San Diego (Lakeside) / (aka: Lakeside Rodeo Grounds)
1/5 mile dirt oval (2/06/38) / (aka: Lakeside Speedway)
1/4 mile dirt oval (10/20/46 - c.1951)

Lancaster Fairgrounds - Lancaster - 3/8 mile dirt oval (c.1954 - c.1955)
   1/5 mile dirt oval (9/27/63 - 9/02/76) / the Antelope Valley Fairgrounds
   1/8 mile dirt oval (1980) (8/31/84 - 1987) (1992 - 1993)

Lassen View Speedway - Redding - 1/4 mile dirt oval (9/01/52 - c.1952)
   1/2 mile dirt oval (4/12/53 - c.1953) / five miles southeast on Highway 44

Lazy J Speedway - Stockton - 1/4 mile dirt oval (1947 & 1948)
   1/4 mile paved oval (1950's) / located at Del Paso Road & 16th

Legion Ascot Speedway - Los Angeles (Alhambra) / (aka: Ascot Motor Speedway)
   5/8 mile oiled dirt oval (1/20/24 - 1/26/36) / (aka: Legion Speedway)
   3.5 mile dirt road course (11/27/24) / located at Valley Blvd. & Soto
   the race on the road course was called the Targo Florio in 1924
   1.385 mile dirt oval course (4/23/34) / began night racing in 1929
   1/2 mile dirt oval (7/11/34 - 1936) / ran a 250 mile race in 1935
   Bob Carey fatality injured 4/13/33 / Al Gordon fatality injured 1/26/36
   Ronnie Householder started his career here / grandstand burned 1936
   site became housing in August of 1940

Legion Ascot Speedway in 1930 as seen from the air. The track was one of the most popular tracks in the country. - Bob Sheldon collection.

Lemoore Midget Speedway - Lemoore / (aka: Lemoore Jet Bowl)
   1/10 mile dirt oval (1947 - 1993) / first auto race was in 1959
   1/8 mile dirt oval (1994) / built as a motorcycle track

Lettuce Bowl - El Centro - dirt oval (c.1958 - c.1960) / located at 4th & Euclid
   (aka: Swarthout Speedway) / (aka: Micro Midget Speedway)

Lincoln Park Stadium - Los Angeles - 1/7 mile dirt oval (1946 - 1947)
   1/4 mile dirt oval (2/06/49 - 1952) / ran exhibition TQ race 10/01/49
   the very first track to ever hold races for TQ midgets
   1/5 mile dirt oval (5/06/52 - 1952) / ran TQ midgets on 1/5 mile track

Connie Kalitta in his slingshot dragster called the "Bounty Hunter" at Lions Dragstrip in the late 1960's. - Mike Lahr photo (Allan E. Brown collection).

Lions Dragstrip - Wilmington - 1/4 mile paved dragstrip (9/15/55 - 1972)
    (aka: Long Beach Dragstrip) / often referred to as "The Beach"
    Mickey Thompson was the promoter in the 1950's / C.J. Hart after that

Live Oak Speedway - Live Oak - 1/4 mile dirt oval (5/30/67 - 1971)
    (aka: Live Oak Stadium) / (aka: Live Oak Memorial Stadium)

Livermore Naval Air Station - Livermore / was an abandoned Navy Airfield
    1.5 mile paved D-shaped oval (7/27/47)
    ran a 500 mile late model stock car race - won by Frank Phillips

Lodi - also see: Kingdon

Lodi Cycle Track - Lodi - small dirt oval (1976) / ran micro-midgets

Lodi Stadium - Lodi - 1/4 mile dirt oval (1 race in 1942) (9/22/45 - 1946)
    1/3 mile dirt oval (c.1954 - c.8/10/56) / (aka: Grape Bowl)

Lompoc Speedway - Lompoc - oval (c.1953)

Lone Pine Park - Lone Pine - 1/5 mile dirt oval (c.9/01/35) / at a city park

Long Beach - 1.9 mile road course (February, 1934)

Long Beach - 1/4 mile paved dragstrip (1955 - c.1971) / maybe Brotherhood

Long Beach Grand Prix - see: Grand Prix of Long Beach

Long Beach Stadium - Long Beach / (aka: Veterans Stadium)
    1/4 mile dirt oval (1930's) (1948)

Long Beach - also see: Brotherhood Dragway, Moto Speedway

Los Angeles - 1.0 mile dirt oval (11/22/03) (1905)

Los Angeles - 1/3 mile wood oval (1909) / built by John Prince
    ran motorcycles only

Los Angeles Coliseum - Los Angeles / site of 1932 & 1984 Olympics
    1/4 mile dirt oval (1938 - 1942) / also site of first Super Bowl in 1967
    same site as the old Agricultural Park
    1/4 mile paved oval (8/11/45 - 3/16/48) / the Coliseum was built 1923
    1/4 mile wood oval (7/10/48 - 8/13/48) (held 6 races on the wood track)
    one of the races on the wood track had 55,873 spectators in attendance
    the Coliseum received extensive damage in the 1994 Earthquake
    some of 1980's Supercross motorcycle events had over 60,000 fans

Los Angeles County Fairgrounds - see: Pomona Raceway & Ascot (Florence)

Los Angeles County Raceway - Palmdale / (aka: Antelope Valley Raceway)
    1/4 mile paved dragstrip (1980 - present)

Los Angeles Dragstrip - see: Pomona Raceway

Los Angeles Grand Prix - see: Palasades Del Ray

Los Angeles Junk Yard Derby - see: Hell's Half Acre

Los Angeles Motor Speedway - Beverly Hills / located on Wilshire Blvd.
    1.25 mile wood oval (2/28/20 - 2/24/24) / turns were banked 35 degrees
    Mgr: A.M. Young / built by Jack Prince / (aka: Los Angeles Speedway)
    Joe Boyer ran 110 mph in exhibition run on 2/05/20 / $500,000 to build
    first race set for 2/22/20 was rained out / (aka: Beverly Hill Speedway)
    Gaston Chevrolet & Eddie O'Donnell fatally injured on 11/25/20
    over 100,000 fans came to watch a 150 mile race on 11/29/23
    one of the more successful, and finest tracks, sold because the property
        became too valuable / became site of the Beverly Hills-Wilshire Hotel

Work has begun on the famous board track called the Los Angeles Motor Speedway in Beverly Hills. The construction process and the 35 degree banking can easily be seen in this 1919 photograph. - Bob Sheldon collection.

The nation's first major board track was the Los Angeles Motordrome in Play Del Ray, California. Phil Harms collection.

Los Angeles Motordrome - Playa Del Ray / 1st wood track built for auto racing
  1.0 mile wood perfect circle (4/08/10 - 1/12/13) / turns banked 20 degrees
  designed and owned by Frederick E. Moscoviks / built by Jack Prince
  promoter was Walter Hempel, who was also the promoter at the Ascot mile
  held night racing c.1911 / board track destroyed by fire in 1913
  ran AAA races, but never a AAA National Championship race
  (according to the book *Board Track, Guts, Gold and Glory* the press
  called the round-shaped track, "the pie pan")

Los Angeles Municipal Airport - see: Mines Field

Los Angeles - small dirt oval (1910) / sand lot ball diamond
  Alex Pabst raced a midget race car he built

Los Angeles Speedway - Los Angeles / (aka: New Los Angeles Speedway)
  1.0 mile B-shaped dirt oval (10/25/36 & 11/29/36)
  Rajo Jack won a 200 mile stock car race / promoter was Frank C. Hulbert
  the site was the same location as Mines Field / located in Inglewood
  now the site of the Los Angeles Int'l Airport

Los Angeles Stadium - Los Angeles - 1/3 mile wood oval (1912) / ran motorcycles

Los Angeles - also see: Agricultural Park, Ascot, Atlantic, Carrell, Dodge Stadium,
  Exhibition Park, Forum, Gardena, Gilmore, Hell's Half Acre, Legion Park,
  Lincoln Park, Loyola, Mines Field, Rose Bowl, Sawyers, Tournament Park,
  Venice, Victor McLaglen, White Sox

Los Banos Fairgrounds - Los Banos - 1/2 mile dirt oval (c.1927 - c.1932)
  1/10 mile dirt oval (May, 1978) / ran two Micro-Midget races in 1978

Loyalton - oval (5/23/54 - c.1954)

Loyola High School Stadium - Los Angeles / located on Venice Avenue
  1/5 mile dirt oval (8/10/33 - 2/01/34) / promoter was Dominic Distrace
  site later became St. Vincent College, and later Loyola College

122

Madera Airport - Madera - 2.6 mile paved road course (1951 - 1953) (1959)
1/4 mile paved dragstrip (1954 - 1965) / (aka: Madera Airport Dragway)
tracks were located on runways at the airport / (aka: Madera Road Race)

Madera Speedway - Madera - 1/2 mile dirt oval (3/10/40) / was a horse track
1/4 mile dirt oval (2/23/47)   /   1/4 mile paved oval (3/30/47 - c.1954)

Madera Speedway - Madera - 1/2 mile dirt oval (c.1958 - c.1959)
1/3 mile paved oval (6/25/72 - present) / replaced old Madera Speedway
located at the Madera District Fairgrounds

March Air Force Base - Riverside - 3.5 mile paved road course (11/08/53, 11/07/54)

Marchbanks Stadium - see: Hanford Motor Speedway

Mariposa County Fairgrounds - Mariposa - 1/2 mile dirt oval (c.11/02/24)
1/4 mile dirt oval (c.1952 - 1965) (1979 - c.1984)

Marysville - 1/2 mile dirt oval (c.1937 - 5/05/40)

Marysville Dragstrip - Yuba City - 1/4 mile paved dragstrip (c.1970)

Marysville - also see: Peachbowl, Sierra Mesa, Twin Cities

McLaglen Stadium - see: Victor McLaglen Stadium

Merced Fairgrounds Speedway - Merced - 1/5 mile dirt oval (c.1946 - c.1956)
1/2 mile dirt oval (6/03/56) NASCAR GN race on the 1/2 mile track
1/4 mile dirt oval (c.1961 - present)

Merced - also see: Castle Air Force Base

Mesa Marin Raceway - Bakersfield / located east of town
1/2 mile high banked paved oval (4/16/77 - present)
Billy Vukovich III fatality injured here on 11/25/90

Metcalf Raceway Park - Metcalf - 1/8 mile dirt oval (5/11/85 - 1988)

Micro Park - Redondo Beach - 1/10 mile dirt oval (4/05/56 - c.1956) / TQ midgets

Milpitas - 1/4 mile dirt oval (early 1950's)

Mines Field - Los Angeles (Inglewood) - 1.9 mile dirt road course (1932- 1935)
ran a stock car race on 2/18/34 / was the first airport road course
1.56 mile dirt road course (12/23/34) / ran AAA champ car race
now the site of the Los Angeles Int'l Airport
also see: Los Angeles Speedway

Minter Field - Bakersfield - 3.2 mile paved road course (1955 - c.6/02/57)

Modesto 99 Stadium - Modesto - 1/4 mile dirt oval (7/04/47 - c.1953)
Bill Vukovich, Sr won the first feature race / ran midgets & roadsters
1/4 mile paved oval (c.1954 - 9/29/56) / (aka: Modesto 99 Speedway)
located at Highway 99 and Hatch Road / now the site county road yard
Johnny Brazil started his driving career here

Modesto High School Track - Modesto - 1/4 mile cinder oval (1933)

Modoc Speedway - see: Alturas Speedway

Moffett Naval Air Station - San Jose (Sunnyvale) - paved road course (1953)

Monterey Bay - Monterey - 1/4 mile paved dragstrip (1951)

Monterey County Fairgrounds - Monterey - dirt oval (early 1950's)
    1/8 mile dirt oval (1992) / running Go-Karts since 1986

Montgomery Field - San Diego - paved road course (7/21/56 & 7/22/56) / an airport

Moose Field - Vallejo - 1/6 mile dirt oval (12/05/37) / was a baseball park

Morrow Field - Colton - 1/4 mile paved dragstrip (c.1956 - c.1960)

Moto Speedway - Long Beach (Compton) / at Long Beach Blvd. & Artesia Blvd.
    1/5 mile dirt oval (12/12/33 - 9/27/35) (1950's) / now mobile home park

Munz Speedway - see: Elsinore Raceway

Muroc Dry Lake - dirt oval (1931 - c.5/06/34) / located in the Mojave Desert
    sand dragstrip (1931 - 1940) / the first organized drag races were held here
    site of land speed record attempts / Southern California Timing Association
    Tommy Milton ran 151.3 mph on 4/14/24 / Frank Lockhart ran 1964 mph
    the site became Edwards Air Force Base during World War II

Navy Field - San Diego - dirt oval (1935) / ran midgets

Neil's Sportsman Park - San Diego - 5/8 mile dirt oval (11/24/32 - 1933)
    1/5 mile dirt oval (c.9/16/34 - c.10/07/34)

Neptune Beach Speedway - Alameda - 1/5 mile dirt oval (6/06/35 - 11/14/39)
    at a ballpark next to Neptune Amusement Park / (aka: Neptune Speedway)

New Ascot Motor Speedway (board track) - see: Culver City Speedway

Al Pompo at San Jose Speedway. - Allan E. Brown collection.

New Jerusalem - 1/4 mile paved dragstrip (1951)

New Stockton Stadium - see: Stockton 99 Speedway

Newhall - dirt oval (late 1930's)

Newman - 1/2 mile dirt oval (1934 - c.1/05/36)

North Bay Speedway (board track) - see: Cotati Speedway

Northern California Speedway - Yreka / (aka: Siskiyou Golden Speedway)
1/4 mile dirt oval (5/17/52 - c.1984) (4/16/92 - present)
(aka: Yreka Speedway) / (aka: Siskiyou Speedway)

Oakdale - 1/2 mile dirt oval (1955) / only ran one race

Oakland Airport - Oakland - paved road course (1962)

Oakland Baseball Park - Emeryville - 1/4 mile paved oval (9/20/53 - late 1953)

Oakland - dirt oval (1950's) / located in Elmhurst district

Oakland Exhibition Building - Oakland - 1/10 mile paved oval (1/08/49 - c.1966)
Bob Barkhimer was the promoter / Bob Sweikert was the 1st track champion

Oakland Motordrome - Oakland (Elmhurst) / built by Jack Prince
1/2 mile wood perfect circle (4/23/11 - 4/21/12) / turns banked 40 degrees
downsized copy of Playa Del Ray, CA (which was a one mile wood track)
races scheduled for 1/28/11 and 2/04/11 were rained out
ran AAA races, but never a AAA National Championship race
the town name of Elmhurst no longer exist (consolidated into Oakland)

The Oakland Motordrome from 1911. The cars in this photo include Louis Disbrow, Howdy Wilcox, Dave Lewis and Bert Dingley. - Phil Harm collection.

Action from one of the 500-mile stock car races on the high-banked Oakland Stadium. The turns were banked 45 degrees, but there was little passing as the preferred groove was right up next to the wall. - Bruce Crowley collection.

Oakland Speedway - San Leandro / also see: Oakland Stadium
    1.0 mile high banked dirt oval (10/18/31) / located on East 14th St.
    1.0 mile high banked oiled dirt oval (11/11/31 - 1941)
    1/2 mile flat dirt oval (5/26/35 - 1941) inside larger track
    Fred Agabashian started his driving career here in 1931
    held a couple of 500 mile stock cars races / torn down during WWII
      (also had a road course, but when a driver died in a preliminary event
        the feature race was held on the oval instead)

Oakland Stadium - San Leandro / built by Charles Colyer
    same location as Oakland Speedway, but track was opposite direction
    5/8 mile high banked paved egg shaped oval (6/29/46 - c.1953)
    Troy Ruttman set the track record of 116 mph on 5/02/50 / turns 45 degrees
    1/4 mile paved oval (7/03/46 - 1955) / held 500 lap sprint car race 1952
    Eli Vukovich won a 500 lap race the same day his brother Bill won 1953 Indy
    5/8 mile paved/dirt oval (11/08/53 - 1955) / this track had dirt corners
    ran a couple of NASCAR GN races on 10/14/51 & 8/01/54
    Bob Sweikert's career started here / now site of Bay Fair Shopping Center

Oakland - also see: Portola Road Course

Oceanside Recreation Park - Oceanside - 1/5 mile dirt oval (11/10/45 - c.5/08/48)
    built as a motorcycle track / first confirmed auto race was on 7/10/47
    located one mile east of town on Mission Road

Oil Bowl Speedway - see: Bakersfield Speedway

Oildale Speedway - see: Bakersfield Speedway

Ontario Motor Speedway - Ontario / first proposed in 1956 by Kermit Pollack
　　2.5 mile paved oval (9/06/70 - 12/16/80) / 180,000 fans at first race
　　patterned after the Indianapolis Motor Speedway / ground broke 11/01/66
　　3.19 mile paved road course (3/27/71 - 1980)
　　1/4 mile paved dragstrip (1970 - 1980)
　　torn down when property value continued to escalate
　　(was to originally been called Los Angeles Int'l Motor Speedway)
　　Don Garlits had first ever 250 mph (250.69) run here on 10/11/75
　　Don Prudhomme 1st ever 5 second (5.98) run in a Funny Car on 10/12/75
　　Jim McElreath won the first event
　　first track to have sensors in pavement for scoring purposes

Ontario - road course (5/19/19) / located on Euclid Avenue

Orange Co. Int'l Raceway - East Irvine - 1/4 mile paved dragstrip (1967 -11/06/83)
　　2.0 mile paved road course (June, 1967 - 1968)

Orange Empire Speedway - Colton - 1/5 mile paved oval (1938 - 7/01/42)

Orange Show Speedway - San Bernadino / located as the Orange Show
　　1/4 mile dirt oval (5/01/47 - February, 1964)
　　1/4 mile paved oval (April, 1964 - present)

Orcutt - dirt oval (1950's)

Ord Park Speedway - San Ysidro / (aka: San Ysidro Speedway)
　　1/4 mile dirt oval (1951 - 1953)

Orland Fairgrounds - see: Glenn County Fairgrounds

Orland Speedway - Orland - 1/2 mile dirt oval (c.1951 - 1973)
　　1/4 mile dirt oval (1989 - 1992) / located at the Glenn County Fairgrounds

Oro Dam Raceway - Oroville - 1/4 mile paved dragstrip (1963 - 1989)

Oroville Speedway - see: Feather River Speedway

Owensmouth - (location unknown) - dirt oval (1913)

Oxnard Speedway - Oxnard - 1/4 mile dirt oval (1950 & 1951) (7/28/57)
　　located at north end of Ventura Road / track was in a river bottom

Palasades Del Ray - Los Angeles / (aka: Los Angeles Grand Prix)
　　road course (2/13/27) race was rained out

Palm Beach Speedway - Watsonville / ran roadsters on sand dunes ovals
　　1/2 mile D-shaped dirt oval (late 1930's) (8/10/47 - 1948) (9/01/57)
　　1/4 mile dirt oval (7/04/48 - c.1948) / west of town on Beach Road

Palm Springs - 1/10 mile dirt oval (10/16/54) / ran TQ midgets

Palm Springs Airport - Palm Springs - 2.9 mile paved road course (4/16/50 - 1952)
　　2.0 mile paved road course (3/21/53)
　　2.6 mile paved road course (3/22/53 - 1955)
　　2.2 mile concrete/asphalt road course (12/03/56 - c.1/24/60)
　　1.1 mile paved road course (1989) ran Super Vees / still runs vintage cars

Palmdale - 1/4 mile paved dragstrip (c.1964)

Ralph DePalma in a Mercedes roars away from the starting line for the 1915 "Vanderbilt Cup" at the Panama-Pacific Expo. Dario Resta (the #9 on the left of the photo) won the race in a Peugeot. - Bruce Craig collection.

Panama-Pacific Expo Road Race - San Francisco / (aka: San Francisco Expo)
    3.8489 mile paved road course (1909 - 11/27/15) (1940)
    Dario Resta won the 1915 Vanderbilt Cup race here on 3/06/15
    the main straightaway were board (wood) planks for the 1915 race
    (aka: San Francisco World's Fair) / ran midgets here in 1915

Paradise Mesa - Chula Vista - 1/4 mile paved dragstrip (March, 1951 - c.1952)
    promoter was Fred Davies / track was located at an old Navy airstrip
    1/2 mile dirt/paved oval (1952) / ran jalopies on the oval
    (aka: Paradise Valley Airport)

Paramount Ranch - Agoura - 2.0 mile paved road course (8/18/56 - c.1961)
    1/10 mile paved oval (1961) / different location as Agoura Park

Paso Robles Fairgrounds - Paso Robles / located at San Luis Obispo Fairgrounds
    1/2 mile dirt oval (c.1919 - c.1941) (c.1947 - c.1952)
    Frank Lockhart started his driving career here
    Babe Stapp started his driving career here on 6/04/23
    1/4 mile dirt oval (1952) / (aka: California Mid-State Fairgrounds)
    1/8 mile dirt oval (8/19/84 - 1989) (1992 - 1993)

Peach Bowl - Marysville - 1/5 mile dirt oval (1948 - 1952)
    1/4 mile dirt oval (5/12/53 - 1959)

Pearson Speedway - see: Independent Motorsports Park

Pebble Beach - 2.1 paved city street road course (c.11/12/50 - c.1956)
    races were held on the Seventeen Mile Road between Carmel & Monterey

Perris Valley Speedway - Perris - oval (years unknown) / (aka: Perris Raceway)

Pershing Park Speedway - Santa Barbara - 1/5 mile dirt oval (8/24/34 - 11/13/34)

Petaluma Fairgrounds Speedway - Petaluma - 1/4 mile dirt oval (1954 - c.1975)
3/8 mile dirt oval (c.1965 - present) / same site as Kenilworth Park

Pismo Beach - dirt oval (1919)

Pittsburg - 1/6 mile dirt oval (1939) / located at an old baseball diamond

Placerville Speedway - Placerville / (aka: Hangtown Speedway)
1/7 mile dirt oval (5/20/51 - c.1951) / Bill Vukovich Sr. first winner
1/4 mile dirt oval (1965 - present) / at the El Dorado Co. Fairgrounds

Playa Del Rey Motordrome (board track) - see: Los Angeles Motordrome

Plaza Park Raceway - Visalia - 1/7 mile dirt oval (5/10/87 - 1991)
1/5 mile dirt oval (1992 - present) / (aka: Visalia Plaza Park)

Pleasanton Fairgrounds - Pleasanton / located at the Alameda County Fairgrounds
1/2 mile dirt oval (c.9/27/14)

Pleasanton Fairgrounds - Pleasanton / located at the Alameda County Fairgrounds
1/2 mile dirt oval (7/18/65 - 1970) / now site of a golf course
paved road course (1960's) / different site than old fairgrounds of 1914
1/4 mile paved dragstrip (1960's)

Pleasanton - also see: Neptune Beach Speedway

Plumas County Fairgrounds - see: Quincy Speedway

Point Loma Road Race - San Diego - 5.982 mile road course (3/02/13 - 1916)

Pomona Raceway - Pomona - 1/4 mile paved dragstrip (1951 - present)
1/2 mile dirt oval (c.8/23/34 - 10/03/37)(4/16/50 - 1958)(1991 - present)
ran a NASCAR GN event on 6/08/57 won by Eddie Pagan on 1/2 mile track
held the first ever NHRA sanctioned event here in April of 1953
2.0 mile paved road course (1953 - 1962) / road course in parking lot
located at the Los Angeles Co. Fairgrounds / (aka: Los Angeles Dragstrip)
oval track runs AMA Nat'l motorcycle events / last auto race was c.1958
home of NHRA drag racing's "Winternationals" and "Winston Finals"

Port of Stockton - Stockton - paved road course (1960 - c.6/05/66)

Porterville Drag Strip - Porterville - 1/4 mile paved dragstrip (c.1970)

Porterville Speedway - see: Rocky Hill Speedway

Porterville - also see: Spinner Airport Speedway

Portola Road Course - Oakland (San Leandro)
21.5 mile road course (1906 - 1910) / ran a AAA champ race on 10/24/09
10.923 mile road course (2/22/11)

Prairie City SVRA Raceway Park - Folsom - 1/8 mile dirt oval (5/25/92 - present)
located on public land

Quechan Speedway - Winterhaven - 3/8 mile dirt oval (2/24/80 - 1988)

Quincy Speedway - Quincy - 1/4 mile dirt oval (1933)
1/2 mile dirt oval (8/14/48 - c.1970) / at the Plumas County Fairgrounds
3/8 mile dirt oval (1979 - present)

California   **129**

Radcliff Speedrome - Fresno - 1/5 mile dirt oval (1930's) / ran Speedway bikes

Raisen Day Speedway (board track) - see: Fresno Speedway

Ramona - 1/4 mile paved dragstrip (1949) / ran unofficial drag races

Reche Canyon - San Bernadino - dirt road course (1955) / ran midgets

Red Bluff Fairgrounds - see: Sun Country Fairgrounds

Redding - dirt oval (c.8/05/56)

Redding Raceway - Redding - 1/4 mile paved dragstrip (1953 - present)
(aka: Redding Air Station) / (aka: Redding Dragstrip)
located at the Redding Municipal Airport

Redlands - dirt oval (1930's) / probably located at a fairgrounds

Redwood Acres Raceway - Eureka - 3/8 mile dirt oval (1947 - 1987)
5/8 mile dirt oval (5/30/56 & 5/30/57) / ran NASCAR GN races on 5/8 mile
3/8 mile paved oval (1988 - present) / at the Redwood Acres Fairgrounds
(aka: Redwood Acres Speedway)

Redwood Empire Raceway - see: Ukiah Speedway

Reeves Air Force Base - (location unknown)
2.6 mile paved road course (10/03/53 & 10/04/53)

Riverglade (Dragway) Speedway - see: Speedway 605

Riverside Fairgrounds - Riverside / located at the Riverside County Fairgrounds
1/2 mile dirt oval (1923 - c.1941) (c.1946 - 1960's)
Mel Hanson's career started here in 1930 / (aka: De Anza Park Speedway)
Rex May's career started here on 9/07/31 / (aka: Fairmont Park)
(aka: Riverside Speedway) / last auto race in c.1958 / ran cycles after that

Action from the November 20, 1960 "United States Grand Prix" at Riverside International Raceway. This photo was looking from turn seven of the popular road course. - Len Ashburn photo.

130

Riverside Int'l Raceway - Riverside / (aka: Riverside Int'l Motor Speedway)
2.5, 2.47, 2.62 & 3.275 mile paved road courses (9/22/57 - 1988)
first race won by Ritchie Ginther / ran U.S. Grand Prix here in 1960
the 1st NASCAR GN race was a 500 mile race on 6/01/58 won by Eddie Gray
Joe Weatherly, reigning NASCAR champion, was fatally injured here 1/19/64
1/2 mile paved oval (6/25/60 - c.1966) / ran NASCAR WC 1963 until 1988
1/4 mile paved dragstrip (c.1959 - c.1970) (1983 - 1986)
other fatalities on the road course included Billy Foster, Bill Spence
Sonny Easley & Tim Williamson

Riverside Speedway - see: Riverside Fairgrounds

Riverside - also see: March Air Force Base

Rocky Hill Speedway - Porterville / (aka: Porterville Speedway)
1/4 mile dirt oval (c.1939 - c.1941) (1946 - present)
1/8 mile dirt oval (12/11/49) / (aka: Porterville Speedbowl)
(aka: Porterville Rocky Hill Speedway) / originally a baseball diamond

Rohner Park Speedway - Fortuna - 1/5 mile dirt oval (5/05/57 - c.1957)

Roscoe - see: 5-H Ranch Speedway

Rose Bowl - Los Angeles (Pasadena) / stadium where famous football game is held
1/5 mile dirt oval (8/13/46 - 10/29/46) / Sam Hanks was promoter in 1946
1/5 mile paved oval (6/03/47 - 10/05/47) / ran midget and roadster races
1/5 mile wood oval (7/27/48 - 1949)
the wood track was the same one used in the Polo Grounds in New York

Roseville Fairgrounds - see: All-American Speedway

Sacramento - 1/4 mile dirt oval (1936 & 1937)
located at Fruitridge & Stockton / site is now a shopping plaza

Sacramento Fairgrounds - see: California State Fairgrounds

Sacramento Raceway Park - Sacramento - 1/4 mile dragstrip (5/10/64 - present)
1/4 mile dirt oval (1990)
1/4 mile dirt oval (1994 - present) < different location than other oval

Sacramento Stadium - see: Hughes Memorial Stadium - Sacramento

Sacramento Speedway - see: West Capital Speedway

Sacramento - also see: Arco, Cal Expo, Hughes Stadium, Thunder Park

Salinas - 1/2 mile dirt oval (1920's)

Salinas Dragstrip - Salinas - 1/4 mile paved dragstrip (1950 - 1965)
(aka: Salinas Municipal Airport)

Salinas Speedway - see: Alisal Speedway

Salinas - also see: Devil's Bowl

Samoa Airport Dragstrip - Eureka - 1/4 mile paved dragstrip (c.1953 - present)
(aka: Eureka Drag Strip)

San Bernadino - dirt oval (1912)

California   **131**

San Bernadino County Sports Stadium - San Bernadino
1/4 mile paved oval (4/09/39 - 10/22/39)
1/2 mile dirt/paved oval (3/10/40 - c.4/07/40)
half of the larger track was dirt and the other half was asphalt

San Bernadino Int'l Airport - San Bernadino / formerly Norton Air Force Base
1/8 mile paved dragstrip (9/10/94 & 9/17/94)

San Bernadino Speedway - San Bernadino - 1/2 mile dirt oval (1945) / no stands

San Bernadino - also see: Glen Helen, Orange Show, Reche, Swing

San Carlos (board track) - see: San Francisco Speedway

San Carlos Stadium - San Carlos - 1/4 mile dirt oval (1947)

San Diego - 1.0 mile dirt oval (3/31/12 & 1/01/13) / on a beach

San Diego - 91.7 mile city street road course (1/01/13) / ran AAA champ cars
probably Point Luma Road Race

San Diego Dragway - Ramona - 1/4 mile paved dragstrip (c.1963 - 1964)

San Diego Speedway - San Diego - 1.0 mile dirt circle (1/05/47)
the promoter was Kelly Petillo / 13 sprint cars and 2 hot rods ran in race

San Diego Stadium - San Diego (Mission Valley) - paved road course (1970's)
in the parking lot of the San Diego Chargers Stadium
different location than Balboa Stadium

San Diego Stadium - see: Balboa Stadium

San Diego World's Fair Expo - San Diego - road course (March, 1916)

San Diego - also see: Cabrillo, Hourglass, Lakeside Arena, Montgomery Field,
Navy Field, Neil's, Point Loma, Silvergate, Sport's Field

San Fernando Raceway - San Fernando - 1/4 mile paved dragstrip (1955 - 1969)
referred to as "The Pond"

San Francisco Motordrome - San Francisco / (aka: San Francisco Coliseum)
1/5 mile dirt oval (5/12/35 - 10/08/40) / (aka: San Francisco Stadium)
originally built for speedway motorcycles

The San Francisco Motordrome - Ted Wilson photo (Erwin Eszlinger collection).

132

San Francisco Speedway - San Carlos / (aka: Greater San Francisco Speedway)
   1.25 mile wood oval (12/11/21 - 6/14/22) / turns banked 38 degrees
   built by Jack Prince & Art Pillsbury / 40,000 fans were at the 1st race
   destroyed by fire on 6/19/22 / now the site of an airport

San Francisco World's Fair Expo - see: Panama-Pacific Expo Road Race

San Francisco - also see: Bayshore, Candlestick, Champion, Cow Palace,
   Golden Gate, Ingleside, Seals, Tanforan

San Gabriel Valley Dragstrip - San Gabriel / located at Live Oark & Riverglade
   1/4 mile paved dragstrip (1956 - c.1958) (1961 - c.1963)

San Gabriel Valley Speedway - see: Speedway 605

San Joaquin Valley Track - see: Goshen Speedway

San Jose - 1.0 mile dirt oval (4/14/12)

San Jose Fairgrounds Coliseum - San Jose
   1/10 mile indoor concrete oval (c.1968 - c.1970)

San Jose Motordrome - San Jose / (aka: Asahi Park)
   1/5 mile dirt oval (9/28/41 - c.10/19/41)

San Jose Speedway - San Jose - 1/4 mile dirt oval (5/19/46 & 5/26/46)
   1/4 mile paved oval (6/02/46 - 11/09/47) / located on Tully Road
   1/2 mile dirt oval (7/31/48)
   1/3 mile dirt oval (1948) / Bob Barkhimer was a promoter here
   1/3 mile paved oval (4/24/49 - 9/03/77) / now site of a mobile home park

San Jose Speedway - San Jose / located at King Road & Alum Rock Avenue
   5/8 mile dirt oval (1923 - 8/06/39) / ran semi-stocks in 1933
   Ted Horn started his driving career here in 1926
   grandstands burned 8/06/39 / sold for housing development March, 1940

San Jose Speedway - San Jose / located at the Santa Clara County Fairgrounds
   1/2 mile dirt oval (1948 - 1958) (1967 - c.1990) / NASCAR GN race 9/15/57
   1.0 mile dirt oval (10/21/51 - c.1955) (1957 & 1958) (1972 - 4/25/93)
   Joe James crashed here on 11/02/52 and he died of injuries 3 days later
   dirt road course (1954) / AMA Nat'l motorcycle events were held on mile
      track 1957-1993, and also on the 1/2 mile from 1967 to 1971 (no autos)
   1/4 mile dirt oval (1977 - c.1990) / (aka: San Jose Fair Speedway)
   started running weekly races in 1977 after San Jose Speedway closed
   1/3 mile dirt oval (c.1991 - present)

San Jose - also see: Alviso Speedway, Eastside Speedway, Moffitt Air Force Base

San Leandro road race - see: Portola Road Course

San Luis Obispo Fairgrounds - see: Paso Robles Fairgrounds

San Ysidro Speedway - see: Ord Park Speedway

Sand Hill Speedway - Brentwood / a motorcycle track / first race autos in 1992
   1/5 mile dirt oval (1973 - present)

Santa Ana Airport - Santa Ana - 1/4 mile paved dragstrip (6/19/50 - c.1959)
the manager was C.J. "Pappy" Hart / the nations first official dragstrip
the track closed when the airport traffic became too busy
(aka: Orange County Airport)

Santa Ana Municipal Bowl - Santa Ana - 1/5 mile dirt oval (1933 - Sept. 1934)

Santa Ana Naval Air Station - Santa Ana - 2.0 mile paved road course (6/25/50)
maybe the same location as the Santa Ana Airport

Santa Barbara - 1/4 mile dirt oval (8/09/47) / located close to ocean

Santa Barbara Municipal Airport - Goleta / (aka: Goleta Airport)
2.2 mile concrete/asphalt road course (1939) (c.1952 - 1967)

Santa Barbara - also see: Pershing Park Speedway

Santa Cruz - 1/5 mile dirt oval (1933 & 1934)

Santa Cruz - also see: Skyway Park Airport

Santa Maria Dragstrip - Santa Maria - 1/4 mile paved dragstrip (c.1963 - c.1976)
(aka: Golden State Raceway)

Santa Maria Fairgrounds - Santa Maria / at the Santa Barbara Fairgrounds
1/2 mile dirt oval (c.1919 - c.1941) (9/16/45 - c.1961)
1/5 mile dirt oval (7/25/37)

Santa Maria Speedway - Santa Maria - 1/3 mile dirt oval (May, 1964 - present)
built by and still operated by Doug Fort

*Doug Fort's beautiful Santa Maria Speedway. The hillside grandstands offers
a great view of the races. - Official track photo.*

The line-up for a "Vanderbilt Cup" at Santa Monica. - Bruce Craig collection.

Santa Monica - 8.401 city street road course (1907 - 3/15/19)
   Ralph DePalma won the 1914 Vanderbilt Cup race here on 2/26/14
   Dario Resta won the 1916 Vanderbilt Cup race here on 11/16/16

Santa Monica Fairgrounds - Santa Monica - 1/4 mile dirt oval (July 1937)(1953)

Santa Monica Municipal Stadium - Santa Monica
   1/4 mile dirt oval (5/31/36 - 10/28/38)

Santa Rosa - 1/4 mile paved dragstrip (c.1956)

Santa Rosa Fairgrounds Coliseum - Santa Rosa / at the Sonoma Co. Fairgrounds
   1/12 mile concrete indoor oval (c.1968 - 2/28/76)

Santa Rosa Fairgrounds - Santa Rosa / located at the Sonoma County Fairgrounds
   1.125 mile dirt oval (8/22/08 & 8/23/08) (1927 & 1928) (1970's)
   still is a horse track / ran motorcycles here in 1970's

Santa Rosa Rodeo Grounds - see: Chris Bech Arena

Santa Rosa Speedway - Santa Rosa / located at the Sonoma County Fairgrounds
   1/4 mile dirt oval (1939) (c.8/17/41 - c.10/12/41) (6/16/46 - c.1962)

Santa Rosa - also see: Cotati, Sonoma County

Saugus - 1/4 mile paved dragstrip (1951 - c.1957)
   (aka: Six-S Ranch Air Park) / the track manager was Lou Baney

Saugus Speedway - Saugus (Santa Charita) / built in 1924 for rodeos
   (aka: Hoot Gibson Rodeo Grounds) / (aka: Bonelli Ranch Stadium)
   1/4 mile dirt oval (1939) (9/19/45 - c.7/17/48) / 1939 owner: Bill Bonelli
   1/3 mile dirt oval (6/06/54 - 6/20/54) / Ray Lavely ran track in 1945
   1/3 mile paved oval (6/27/54 - present)
   Ray Wilkins was the 1990 RPM Promoter of the Year

Saugus Speedway in 1945. - Steve Larson collection (courtesy of Don Radbruch).

Sawyers - Los Angeles - dirt oval (c.1947) / ran hot rods

Schellville Speedway - Schellville / located at the Sonoma Valley Airport
1/8 mile dirt oval (c.1978 - c.1983) / ran Micro-Midgets

Seals Stadium - San Francisco / home of the San Francisco Seals (baseball)
1/4 mile paved oval (12/01/45 - 12/09/45) / built around ball diamond
may have ran in October of 1945 / the pavement was on top of board base

Sears Point Raceway - Sonoma / (aka: Golden State Int'l Raceway)
1.7 & 2.52 mile paved road course (1968 - present)
1/4 mile paved dragstrip (March, 1969 - present)
ran first NASCAR Winston Cup race on 6/11/89
(aka: Sears Point Int'l Raceway)

Seaside Park Speedway - Ventura - 1/5 mile dirt oval (11/11/34)

Selland Arena - Fresno - 1/10 mile indoor concrete oval (2/15/87 & 2/14/88)

Selma Rodeo Grounds - Selma / (aka: Selma Speedway)
1/5 mile dirt oval (c.6/09/51 - 1964)

Shasta Speedway - Anderson / located at the Shasta Fairgrounds
3/8 mile dirt oval (1952 - 1958) (1960 - 1969)
1/4 mile dirt oval (1970 - 1972) / (aka: Anderson Speedway)
1/3 mile paved oval (1973 - present)

Sheriff Posse Grounds Speedway - Redding - 1/5 mile dirt oval (5/24/51 - 1951)
3/8 mile dirt oval (5/20/52 - c.1952) / at the East end of Butte St.

Shiloh Grange Track - Modesto - dirt oval (5/24/36)

Sierra Mesa Nat'l Raceway - Marysville (Browns Valley)
3/8 mile dirt oval (c.1970 - c.1971) / located nine miles east of Marysville
1/2 mile paved oval (c.5/01/72 - c.10/14/73)

Brad Doty was one most popular competitors on the World of Outlaws tour. He won the prestigious "Pacific Coast Classic" at Ascot Park in 1986. A horrifying crash at Eldora left him paralyzed. - Allan Brown collection.

Silver Dollar Speedway - Chico / located at the Butte County Fairgrounds
    1/4 mile dirt oval (March, 1935 - c.1941) / Duane Carter was first winner
    1/5 mile dirt oval (March, 1935) / the second race was on a shorter track
    1/2 mile dirt oval (5/22/49 - 1951)   / (aka: Third District Fair)
    1/4 mile dirt oval (1962 - present) / new 1/4 mile track constructed
    the home of the annual "Gold Cup" since 1980

Silvergate Speedway - San Diego (Mission Bay) / now the site of Sea World
    5/8 mile dirt oval (Nov., 1932 - 3/29/36) / just north of the San Diego River

Siskiyou Golden Speedway - see: Northern California Speedway

Six-S Ranch Air Park - see: Saugus

Skyway Park Airport - Santa Cruz - 1/4 mile paved dragstrip (10/08/50 - c.1951)
    1/4 mile dirt dragstrip (early 1950's) / dirt drags ran at least one time

Smokers Dragstrip - see: Bakersfield Raceway

Sonoma Co. Airport - Santa Rosa - 3.9 mile paved road course (1956 & 6/26/57)

South Bay Speedway - Chula Vista / located two miles from Speedway 117
    1/5 mile 'D' shaped oval (1951 - 1952)
    1/4 mile dirt oval (5/04/52 - 1953)

South Bay Speedway - see: Speedway 117

South Gate Speedway - see: Trojan Speedway

Southern Speedway - South Gate / located at Atlantic & Tweedy
1/2 mile oiled dirt oval (6/07/36 - 4/25/37)
George Robson won the first race in a roadster
1/2 mile paved oval (5/09/37 - 4/26/42) / O.D. Lavely was a manager
(aka: Southern Ascot Speedway) / ran under this name from 1/23/38 on
3/5 mile B-shaped dirt track (8/21/38)
torn down in 1942 / now site of residential housing

Speedbowl - see: Bakersfield Speedway

Speedway 117 - Chula Vista / built as a motorcycle track in 1966 as a TT track
1/2 mile dirt oval (1967 - Oct., 1983) / (aka: South Bay Speedway)
(aka: Mesa Speedway) / called Mesa when it was a motorcycle track
tracks name changed in 1971 / Don Basile bought track in 1973
1/4 mile egg-shaped dirt oval (1971 - 1983) / renamed 117 in 1980
the track was located less than one mile from the Mexico border
Scott Bloomquist started his career here at age 17

Speedway 605 - Irwindale / oval track grandstands were from Whiteman Stadium
1/4 & 1/2 mile paved ovals (1966 - 1977) / Art Atkison was the promoter
1/4 mile paved dragstrip (1966 - 1977) / (aka: Riverglade Dragway)
Vince Giamformaggio won a $10,000 to win Late Model race here in 1975
(aka: San Gabriel Valley Speedway) / (aka: Riverglade Speedway)
located on Riverglade Road / now the site of an industrial park
(aka: Irwindale Raceway)

Spinners Airport Speedway - Porterville - 3/8 mile dirt oval (1988)

Sportland Park - Bakersfield / located on Highway 99
1/4 mile dirt oval (1933 - 7/31/42) / (aka: Bakersfield Speedway)
first auto (midget) race was on 11/20/38 / ran motorcycles before

Sports Field Stadium - San Diego - 1/5 mile dirt oval (1933 - c.9/22/34)

Stockton 99 Speedway - Stockton - 1/4 mile dirt oval (5/22/47 - c.1949)
1/4 mile paved oval (c.1950 - present)
(aka: New Stockton Stadium) / (aka: Stockton Stadium)

Stockton Air Field - Stockton - 2.6 mile paved road course (6/09/56 - 1959)

Stockton Ball Diamond - see: Baxter Stadium

Stockton Fairgrounds - Stockton - 1.0 mile dirt oval (1920's - c.1938) (1952)
1/2 mile dirt oval (1/06/46 - c.1950) / at the San Joaquin Fairgrounds
small dirt oval (1976) / ran micro-sprints on small track

Stockton Stadium - see: Stockton 99 Speedway

Stockton - also see: Delta, Lazy J, Port of Stockton

Sun Country Fairgrounds - Red Bluff - 1/2 mile dirt oval (5/06/51)
1/6 mile dirt oval (8/25/90 - present) / at the Red Bluff Fairgrounds

Sunrise Valley Raceway - Adelanto - 1/4 mile dirt oval (1994 - present)

Susanville Speedway - see: High Desert Speedway

Swarthout Speedway - see: Lettuce Bowl

138   *California*

Swing Auditorium - San Bernadino / (aka: Orange Show Auditorium)
1/10 mile indoor concrete oval (1964)

Taft - dirt oval (11/10/40)

Tanforan Horse Track - San Mateo / located near San Francisco
1.0 mile dirt oval (9/20/08) (11/16/24) (3/22/25) / one more race in 1925

Temecula Motorsports Park - Temecula - 1/4 mile dirt oval (c.1994 - present)

Thunder Park Speedway - Sacramento - 1/2 mile dirt oval (10/09/80)
located across from Sacramento Raceway Park

Thunderbowl Raceway - Tulare / located at the Tulare County Fairgrounds
1/2 mile dirt oval (c.9/28/40 - c.1941) (c.1946 - c.1953)
1/3 mile dirt oval (1980) (1988 - present) / ran motorcycles in 1980
(aka: Tulare Thunderbowl)

Thunderhill Park - Willows - 1.85 mile paved road course (10/29/93 - present)
built by contribution by the members of the SCCA San Francisco region

Thunderhill Park is the nations newest permanent road course. The track opened
in 1993 and was funded by contributions. - Official track photo.

Torrey Pines - LaJolla - 2.7 mile paved road course (July, 1952 - 1/25/56)
Dan Gurney started here in 1955 / now the site of a golf course

Tournament Park - Los Angeles (Pasadena) - 1.0 mile dirt oval (1913)

Tracy High School - Tracy - 1/4 mile cinder oval (6/25/33) / ran midgets

Tracy Municipal Airport - Tracy - 2.7 mile paved road course (1958) (8/23/59)

Travis Air Force Base - Fairfield - paved road course (1954)

Tri-City Speedway - Colton - 5/8 mile dirt oval (1933 - c.2/17/35) (1945)

Triple M Speedway - see: Twin Cities Speedway

Trojan Speedway - South Gate / (aka: South Gate Speedway)
1/10 mile paved oval (1963) / Johnny Parsons, Jr. started his career here
1/5 mile dirt oval (1963 - c.1973)

Tulare High School - Tulare - 1/4 mile cinder oval (1933)

Tulare Thunderbowl - see: Thunderbowl Raceway

Tulare Thunderbowl - Tulare / the track was actually in Octol
    1/5 mile dirt oval (1946 - 1953) / (aka: Murphy's Thunderbowl)

Tustin - 1/4 mile paved dragstrip (1950) / (aka: Lighter-Than-Air Base)
    located on a military base runway

Twin Cities Speedway - Marysville - 1/4 mile dirt oval (1968 - present)
    1/8 mile dirt oval (1986) / (aka: Triple M Speedway)
    may have ran Modified-Midgets in 1967

Ukiah Speedway - Ukiah - 1/4 mile dirt oval (1951 - c.1960)
    1/4 mile paved oval (c.1964 - present) / (aka: Redwood Empire Raceway)
    located at the Redwood Empire Fairgrounds

Vaca Valley Raceway - Vacaville - 2.1 mile paved road course (7/05/58 - 1972)
    1/4 mile paved dragstrip (1956 - 1970) / (aka: Vaca Valley Speedway)
    1.25 mile paved oval (1959 & 1960)

Vallejo Recreation Center - Vallejo - 1/5 mile paved oval (1933)
    1/5 mile dirt oval (5/12/38 - c.9/01/38)

Vallejo Speedway - Vallejo - 1/4 mile dirt oval (c.1961 - 1979)

Vallejo Speedway - Vallejo - 1/6 mile dirt oval (5/16/41 - 7/16/42)
    1/5 mile dirt oval (7/23/42) (9/02/45) / (aka: New Vallejo Speedway)
    located next to the Vallejo Recreation Center track

Vallejo Speedway - see: West Coast Speedway

Valley Speedway - Fresno - 5/8 mile high banked dirt oval (c.4/11/48 - c.1948)

Venice Speedway - (Los Angeles) Venice - 3.23 mile road course (c.1910 - 1916)
    corners were made of wood boards / ran midgets in 1914

True champions are always winners...Sonny Easley waves the checkered flag. He
was fatally injured in a freak accident at Riverside (CA). - Dan Mahony photo.

140   *California*

Ventura - 1/2 mile dirt oval (c.7/28/24 - c.1927)

Ventura County Drag Strip - Oxnard - 1/4 mile paved dragstrip (1972)
  located at the Oxnard Air Force Base

Ventura Speedway - Ventura / located at the Ventura County Fairgrounds
  1/5 mile dirt oval (1978 - present)

Ventura Stadium - Agoura - 1/8 mile dirt oval (1957) / located on Ventura Avenue
  the track was located near the old Agoura Park

Ventura - also see: Seaside

Vernalis Raceways - Modesto - 1/4 mile paved dragstrip (c.1970)

Victor McLaglen Stadium - Los Angeles / destroyed by a flood in 1938
  1/5 mile dirt oval (6/17/36 - 7/29/36)
  located at Glendale Blvd. near the Los Angeles River / site is now I-5

Victorville Fairgrounds - Victorville / at the San Bernadino County Fairgrounds
  1/4 mile dirt oval (1982) (1992)

Vina Raceway - Vina - 1.125 mile paved road course (6/02/68) / airstrip runways

Visalia - 3.125 mile road course (1914) (1915) (7/04/17) / ran AAA races

Visalia Airport Dragstrip - Visalia - 1/4 mile paved dragstrip (1960's)

Visalia Fairgrounds - see: Goshen Speedway

Visalia Plaza Park - see: Plaza Park

Visalia Speedway - Visalia / the track was actually in Goshen / maybe fairgrounds
  1/5 mile dirt oval (c.7/04/34 - c.1941) (c.1946 - 1953)

Vista - 1/6 mile dirt oval (8/27/38)

Watsonville Speedway - Watsonville - 1/4 mile dirt oval (5/27/60 - present)
  1/2 mile dirt oval (1971) / one race on 1/2 mile track only
  1/8 mile dirt oval (7/22/84 - 1985) / at the Santa Cruz County Fairgrounds
  (aka: Watsonville Fair Speedway)

Watsonville - also see: Palm Beach Speedway

Weed - 1/5 mile dirt oval (1936 - c.7/04/38) / located at a ballpark

Weed Fairgrounds - Weed - 1/2 mile dirt oval (c.1952) / ran ARA sprints

West Capital Raceway - Sacramento / (aka: Capital Speedway) < first name
  1/4 mile dirt oval (5/25/47 - 5/31/80) / John Soares won the first race
  1/2 mile dirt oval (1954 - 1972) / (aka: Sacramento Speedway)
  (aka: West Capital Speedway) / first called West Capital in 1972
  located at 4200 West Capital Avenue / home of the "Gold Cup" 1955 to 1979

West Coast Speedway - Vallejo - 1/4 mile dirt oval (c.8/16/50 - c.1952) (4/15/56)
  5/8 mile dirt oval (c.1953 - c.1959) / (aka: Vallejo Speedway)
  Walt Faulkner fatally injured on 4/22/56 / (first USAC Late Model fatality)

Western Speedway - see: Gardena Speedway

White Sox Park - Los Angeles - 1/4 mile dirt oval (1936)
   located in black section of city / mostly black drivers

Whiteman Stadium - Pacoima / owned by Marv Whiteman
   1/3 mile paved oval (1966 - 1969) / two turns high banked / two flat

Willits Speedway - Willits - 1/2 mile dirt oval (1936 & 1937)
   1/4 mile paved oval (c.9/23/56 - c.1975) / (aka: Willits Rodeo Grounds)

Willow Springs Motorsports Park - Rosamond / also see: Kern County Speedway
   2.0 mile oiled dirt road course (11/22/53 - 1958) (1962)
   2.5 mile oiled dirt road course (1955 & 1956)
   ran NASCAR GN races on the oiled dirt road course on 11/20/55 & 11/11/56
   ran night races under Arc-lights in 1958 / Dave McDonald started here
   2.5 mile paved road course (1962 - present)
   1/4 mile paved dragstrip (1962) / (aka: Willow Springs Int'l Raceway)
   3/8 mile dirt oval (4/12/87 - present)

Willows Speedway - Willows - 1/4 mile dirt oval (5/17/52 - c.1960)
   (aka: Willows Horsemen's Speedway) / at the Willows Riding Grounds

Winterhaven Speedway - Winterhaven - 1/4 mile dirt oval (c.1968)

Winters Airport - Winters - paved road course (1958)

Yreka (Fairgrounds) Speedway - see: Northern California Speedway

This is Willow Springs Motorsports Park. The 2.5 mile road course and both of the oval tracks are visible in this photo. - Official track photo.

COLORADO

Adams County Road Course - Denver - paved road course (1970's)

Adams County Speedway - see: Littleton Fairgrounds

Akron Fairgrounds - Akron - 1/5 mile dirt oval (c.1937)
1/2 mile dirt oval (early 1950's) / at the Washington County Fairgrounds

Alamosa - dirt oval (1936)

Arapahoe County Speedway - see: Littleton Fairgrounds

Arkansas Valley Raceway - Penrose - 1/3 mile dirt oval (1970)

Aspen Sports Car Club - Aspen - 1.2 mile paved road course (1963 - present)
(aka: Woody Creek Raceway) / (aka: Aspen Int'l Raceway)

Bandimere Speedway - Denver - 1/4 mile paved dragstrip (April, 1960 - present)
home of the NHRA sanctioned Mile High Nationals

Bandimere Speedway. Notice the mountainside seating. - Track photo.

Beacon Hill Speedway - Pueblo - 1/5 mile paved oval (1963 - present)
(aka: Pickard's Beacon Hill Speedway)

Brighton Speedway - Brighton - 1/2 mile dirt oval (9/01/46 - early 1950's)

Brush - 1/2 mile dirt oval (7/04/53) / AAA race won by Harry Stockman

Buckley Field - Denver - paved road course (7/12/59)

Cactus Park Speedway - see: Grand Junction Nat'l Speedway

Calhan - dirt oval (1961)

CDR Tech Track - see: Continental Divide Raceway

Centennial Park - Denver - 1.0 mile dirt oval (9/23/51) (9/28/52)
was a horse track / ran two AAA champ cars

Century 21 Speedway - Denver (Aurora) - 1/3 mile paved oval (7/04/71 - 1973)
1/4 mile paved dragstrip (1971 - 1973) / proposed 1.2 mile paved oval
paved road course (1971 - 1973)

Colorado National Speedway is one of the finest short tracks in the country. The track was asphalted in 1989. - Official track photo.

Colorado Nat'l Speedway - Erie - 3/8 mile dirt oval (Sept., 1965 - 1972)
  1/2 mile dirt oval (1973 - 1988) / build by Gene Heffley
  1.0 mile dirt oval (5/01/73 - 1973) / ran four races on the mile track
  3/8 mile paved oval (5/06/89 - present) / promoter: George Butland 1973-1988

Colorado School of Mines Stadium - Golden - 1/5 mile dirt oval (8/21/38 & 8/22/38)

Colorado Springs - 1/2 mile dirt oval (1934) / located at the rodeo grounds

Colorado Springs - 1/4 mile paved dragstrip (1952)

Colorado Springs Int'l Speedway - Colorado Springs
  1/4 mile paved oval (1976 - Sept. 1985) / now an industrial park
  1/8 mile paved dragstrip (1976 - 1985) / located east of town on SR 94

Colorado Springs - also see: Colorado Turk, Pikes Peak, Sportsman Park

Colorado State Fairgrounds - Pueblo - 1/4 mile dirt oval (8/23/37)
  1/2 mile dirt oval (6/15/15 - c.1928) (6/26/32 - c.1941)(8/31/46 - c.1965)
  ran a motorcycle race on 6/15/15 / first auto race was on 9/21/16

Colorado Turf Club Speedway - Colorado Springs / located 15 miles south
  1/3 mile paved oval (6/08/74) / Larry Phillips won the only auto race

Continental Divide Raceway - Castle Rock / ran USAC Indy cars in 1968 & 1970
  2.8 mile paved road course (8/08/58 - 1972) / (aka: CDR Tech Track)
  1/4 mile paved dragstrip (7/19/59 - 1972) / promoter was Nick Colbert
  1/2 mile paved oval (1960) / Ray Lavely was the tracks first manager
  2.66 mile paved road course (1982 - c.1983) / torn down in 1985

Cortez - 1/2 mile dirt oval (1926) / probably at a fairgrounds

Cortez Fairgrounds - see: Fairgrounds Speedway

Cortez Race Track - Cortez - 1/4 mile dirt oval (1955 & 1956)
  located 2 miles east of town on SR 160 / near current Fairgrounds Speedway

Cortez - also see: Thunderbird Speedway

Craig Speedway - Craig - 1/4 mile dirt oval (c.1974 - 1977)

Delta - 1/4 mile dirt oval (8/08/48 - 1949) / built by Paul Campbell

Delta Speedway - Delta - 1/4 mile dirt oval (1969 - 1983) (1986)

Denver - 1/5 mile dirt oval (1936) / located near Higley Airport

Denver - 14.5 mile city street road course (7/05/09) / ran AAA champ cars

Denver Coliseum - Denver - 1/10 mile concrete indoor oval (1/29/54 & 2/16/54)

Denver Fairgrounds - Denver - 5/8 mile dirt oval (1946 - 1947)
  located on the top of South Table Top Mountain, southwest of Denver
  located at the Jefferson County Fairgrounds

Denver Fairgrounds - Denver - 5/8 mile dirt oval (late 1960's)
  (aka: Adams County Fairgrounds) / located northeast of Denver

Denver Grand Prix - Denver / ran CART IndyCars & SCCA TA downtown Denver
  1.9 mile city street paved road course (8/25/90 - 8/25/91)

Denver Int'l Raceway - see: Mile High Dragway

Denver - also see: Adams County, Bandimere, Buckley, Centennial Park,
  Century 21, Dupont, Englewood, Lakeside, Lowery Field, Merchants Park,
  Mile High, Overland Park, Rocky Mountain, Second Creek

Dupont Speedway - Denver - 1/2 mile dirt oval (c.1932) / new grandstands in 1932
  5/8 mile high banked paved oval (8/01/32 - 1941) / owner: Ray Bradbury
  nations first asphalt track / held first IMCA big car paved track races
  located five miles northeast of downtown Denver on Brighton Road

Durango Fairgrounds - Durango - 1/2 mile dirt oval (c.1947 - c.1955)

Durango - also see: Grandview Raceway, Triple-A Speedway

Englewood Speedway - Denver (Sheridan) - 1/3 mile dirt oval (6/08/47 - c.1959)
  1/3 mile paved oval (c.1960 - 1979) / built by Charley Codner
  track was torn down because Charley's son Richard Codner thought he
  would be selling it for a shopping center, when the deal fell through he
  tried to rebuild the track but the city rejected his request

Fairgrounds Raceway - Cortez - 1/3 mile dirt oval (1986 - present) / east of town
  built to replace Thunderbird Speedway

Fort Collins Speedway Park - Fort Collins / maybe dirt the first year
  1/5 mile paved oval (8/10/46 - c.6/11/50)

Fort Morgan - see: I-76 Speedway

Glenwood Springs - 1/5 mile dirt oval (6/18/37 & 6/19/37) / ran midgets

Grand Junction Nat'l Speedway - Grand Junction / (aka: Cactus Park Speedway)
  1/4 mile dirt oval (1969 - c.1985) / (aka: Grand Valley Nat'l Speedway)

Grand Speedway - Grand Junction - 1/4 mile dirt oval (5/28/50 - c.1959)

Grand Junction - also see: Two Rivers, Land's End

Grand View Raceway - Durango - 1/4 mile dirt oval (1969-1971)
  located five 5 miles southwest of   town

Hayden Speedway - Hayden - 1/4 mile dirt oval (1975 - present)
  (aka: Yampa Valley Raceway)

Holyoke Speedway - Holyoke / (aka: Phillips County Raceway)
1/2 mile dirt oval (c.1954) (1956 - 1966) (c.1985 - 1989)
located at the Phillips County Fairgrounds

Hotchkiss Fairgrounds - Hotchkiss / (aka: Delta County Fairgrounds)
1/2 mile dirt oval (1930's)

Hugo - dirt oval (1930's)

I-76 Speedway - Fort Morgan - 1/4 mile dirt oval (c.1968 - present)
(aka: Morgan County Raceway)

Island Grove Park - Greeley - 1/4 mile dirt oval (1938 - c.1941) (c.1946 - 1965)
1/2 mile dirt oval (1961) / Bill Hill promoted a race on the 1/2 mile

Julesburg Dragway - Julesburg - 1/4 mile paved dragstrip (c.1961 - present)
(aka: Platte Valley Dragway)

Julesburg Fairgrounds - Julesburg - dirt oval (1954) / ran weekly NASCAR stocks

Kit Carson County Speedway - Burlington - 3/8 mile dirt oval (1988 - 1993)
located at the Kit Carson County Fairgrounds

Kremmling - 1/4 mile dirt oval (c.1957)

La Junta Raceway - La Junta - 2.0 mile paved road course (5/26/57 - 1961)
the races were held on active airport runways until the FAA found out
1.6 mile paved road course on old taxiways & runways (1974 - present)

*Keith Andrews in a roadster at Brighton (CO) from the late 1930's. The
Studebaker engine reportedly was one that ran in the "Indianapolis 500." - Frank
Brennfoeder collection (courtesy of Don Radbruch).*

146

La Junta Speedway - see: Melon Bowl Speedway

Lakeside Speedway - Denver - 1/5 mile dirt oval (4/24/38 - 8/28/38)
Lloyd Axel won the first race on dirt / Roy Sherman won first on asphalt
1/5 mile paved oval (5/14/39 - 7/29/42) (5/22/46 - 1988)
Jimmy Malloy's career started here in 1955 / (aka: Lakeside Ballpark)
track closed after a race car hit the catch fence and killed a spectator
located at the Lakeside Amusement Park / the manager was Ray Koch

Lakeside Speedway (new) - see: Second Creek Raceway

Lamar - 1/2 mile dirt oval (April, 1950)

Lamar Speedway - Lamar - 1/3 mile dirt oval (1986 - present)

Land's End Auto Race - Grand Junction / (aka: Land's End Auto Hill Climb)
dirt hill climb (7/04/40 & 7/04/41) (1982 - present)

Limon - dirt oval (1941)

Littleton Fairgrounds - Littleton - 1/2 mile dirt oval (c.1947 - c.1958)
1/4 mile dirt oval (c.1955) / located at the Arapahoe County Fairgrounds
(aka: Arapahoe County Speedway)

Lowery Field - Denver - 1/4 mile paved dragstrip (1951 - c.1955)

May Valley Speedway - Lamar - 1/4 mile dirt oval (5/05/84 - present)

Melon Bowl Speedway - La Junta - 1/5 mile paved oval (8/05/47 - 7/10/50)
(aka: La Junta Speedway)

Merchants Park - Denver - 1/5 mile dirt oval (5/09/37 - 9/13/39)
site is now the Merchants Park Shopping Center / a former ball park

Midway Dragstrip - see: Two Rivers Raceway

Mile High Dragway - Denver - 1/4 mile paved dragstrip (1964 - c.1977)
(aka: Tower Road Dragway) / (aka: Rocky Mountain Dragways)
(aka: Denver Int'l Dragway) / now the site of Second Creek Raceway
built by Al Brawncucci / site is next to current Rocky Mountain Speedway
(aka: Thunder Road Dragway)

Monte Vista - 1/4 mile dirt oval (1953)

Morgan County Raceway - see: I-76 Speedway

Mountain View Motor Sports Park - Mead / located north of Denver on I-25
1.8 mile paved road course (c.1986 - present)

Overland Park - Denver - 1.0 mile dirt oval (1909 - 1931) / site is still a park
Ralph DePalma won a AAA race on 7/19/25

Penrose Fairgrounds - Penrose / probably at the Fremont County Fairgrounds
1/2 mile dirt oval (c.5/04/58)

Phillips County Raceway - see: Holyoke Speedway

Pikes Peak Auto Hill Climb - Colorado Springs (Cascade)
12.42 mile dirt road course hill climb (8/12/16 - 1941) (1946 - present)

Pikes Peak Speedway - Colorado Springs - 1/5 mile paved oval (8/16/46 - 1977)
located at the north end of the Colorado Springs Int'l Airport

Platte Valley Dragway - see: Julesburg Dragway

Pueblo - 1/4 mile paved dragstrip (1956)

Pueblo - 1/5 mile cinder oval (1937) / ran midgets on a high school running track

Pueblo Fairgrounds - see: Colorado State Fairgrounds

Pueblo Motorsports Park - Pueblo - 1/4 mile paved dragstrip (1976 - present)
2.2 mile paved road course (1976 - present) / trying to build 1/3 mile dirt oval

Pueblo Speedway - Pueblo - 1/5 mile paved oval (8/08/47 - c.1964)

Pueblo - also see: Beacon Hill

Raceland - see: Rocky Mountain Speedway

Rifle Fairgrounds - Rifle - 1/2 mile dirt oval (early 1950's)
located at the Garfield County Fairgrounds and Rodeo Grounds

Rocky Ford Fairgrounds - Rocky Ford - 1/5 & 1/2 mile dirt ovals (1960's)
mostly ran only motorcycles / located at the Otero County Fairgrounds

Rocky Mountain Dragways - see: Mile High Dragway

Rocky Mountain Speedway - Denver / same site as old Mile High Dragway
1/2 mile dirt oval (1982 - 1984) (April, 1989 - present) / (aka: Raceland)
reopened in 1989 when Colorado Nat'l Speedway in Erie was asphalted

Royal Gorge Speedway - Canon City - 1/2 mile dirt oval (c.8/22/52 - c.5/03/59)

Roadster action at the Littleton (CO) Fairgrounds in 1949. Don Padia (#73) races with Frank Crater (#88). - Leroy Byers photo (Don Radbruch collection).

148

Second Creek Raceway - Denver - 1.7 mile paved road course (9/09/83 - present)
   located northeast of downtown Denver / next to Rocky Mountain Speedway
   1/5 mile paved oval (c.7/04/94 - present) / (aka: Lakeside Speedway)
   same site as Mile High Dragway

Sportsman Park - Colorado Springs - 1/4 mile dirt oval (c.1961)
   1/4 mile paved oval (c.7/03/62 - c.1968) / promoter Roy Sportsman
   1/4 mile dirt oval (c.1969 - c.1973) / (aka: Colorado Springs Raceway Park)
   located across from Pikes Peak Speedway

Steamboat Springs / runs annual motorcycles and vintage sports car races
   1.7 & 2.3 mile city street paved road courses (c.1985 - present)

Steamboat Springs - 1/4 mile dirt oval (1968 - 1969)

Sterling Fairgrounds - Sterling / located at the Logan County Fairgrounds
   1/2 mile dirt oval (7/03/36 - c.1941) (c.1946 - c.7/05/54) (1961)

Table Top Mountain - see: Jefferson County Fairgrounds

Thunder Mountain Speedway - Olathe - 1/3 mile dirt oval (1994 - present)

Thunder Road Dragway - see: Mile High Dragway

Thunderbird Speedway - Cortez - 3/8 mile dirt oval (1972 - 1985)
   the track was located northwest of town

Tower Road Dragway - see: Mile High Dragway

Trinidad - 1/5 mile dirt oval (1937) / ran midgets

Triple-A Speedway - Durango - 1/4 mile dirt oval (1954 - c.1957)

Two Rivers Raceway - Grand Junction / (aka: White Water Hill Raceway Park)
   1/4 mile paved dragstrip (1964 - present) / (aka: Midway Dragstrip)
   (aka: Two Rivers Raceway) / the name was changed from Two Rivers when
   the promoter kept receiving telephone calls about boat racing

White Water Hill Raceway Park - see: Two Rivers Raceway

Woody Creek Raceway - see: Aspen Sport Car Club

Yampa Valley Raceway - see: Hayden Speedway

Yuma County Fairgrounds - Yuma - 5/8 mile dirt oval (early 1950's)

CONNECTICUT

Bulkeley Stadium - Hartford - 1/5 mile dirt oval (1936) / motorcycles only

Branford Park - New Haven - 1/2 mile dirt oval (7/25/1899 - c.7/25/1900)

Bridgeport Speedway - Bridgeport - located on Route 1-A near River Street
   1/5 mile paved oval (6/30/47 - 1954) / possibly ran in 1955
   1/10 mile dirt oval (6/03/51) / ran T.Q. midgets on small track
   (aka: Candlelite Stadium) / sold in February, 1955 for a Drive-In Theater

Bristol Fairgrounds - Bristol - 1/2 mile dirt oval (1933 - 10/21/34)

Candlelite Stadium - see: Bridgeport Speedway

Charter Oak Park - Hartford - 1.0 mile dirt oval (6/16/05 - 1920)
  1/2 mile dirt oval (1923) (1927) (1929)

Cherry Park Speedway - Avon - 1/2 mile dirt oval (1933 - 1939)
  1/5 mile paved oval (7/28/46 - 1951) (1954) / torn down in 1959

Connecticut Int'l Raceway - Colchester - 1/4 mile dragstrip (c.1961 - c.1986)
  (aka: Connecticut Dragway)

Connecticut Speedway - Derby - 3/4 mile dirt oval (6/24/34) (9/02/34) (1937)
  (aka: Island Park Speedway)

Danbury (CT) Speedway from the air. You can seen the remnants of the half-mile track in this photo. - Joe Saleem collection.

Danbury Fair Racearena - Danbury / the grandstands burned down on 8/08/22
  1/2 mile dirt oval (10/06/08 - 10/07/39) / (aka: Danbury Fair Race Track)
  1/5 mile paved oval (6/01/40 - 5/10/42) (Sept., 1945 - 1955) / inside 1/2 mile
  1/4 mile paved oval (5/31/47 - 9/30/51) / (aka: Danbury Fair Speedways)
  1/3 mile dirt oval (10/05/51 - 6/07/58) / 1/2 mile oval shortened in 1951
  1/3 mile paved oval (6/14/58 - 9/19/81) / (aka: Danbury Speedway)
  held boat racing in a water filled moat outside of the track in August of 1948
  the site is now a shopping mall

Donovan Field - see: West Haven Speedway

Huntington Speedway - Shelton - 1/2 mile dirt oval (c.1933 - c.1939)

Island Park Speedway - see: Connecticut Speedway

Legion Speedway - Meriden - dirt oval (years unknown)

Lime Rock Park - Lime Rock - 1.53 mile paved road course (4/18/57 - present)
  1/4 mile paved dragstrip (1958) / track proposed for 3.0 mile road course
  also a proposed 1.5 mile paved oval in 1959

150

New Haven Arena - New Haven - 1/10 mile indoor wood oval (1936 - 3/24/37)

New Haven Velodrome - New Haven - dirt oval (c.1940 - c.1941)

New Haven Veteran Coliseum - New Haven - 1/10 mile indoor oval (1993-present)

New London - dirt oval (1920's)

New London-Waterford Speedbowl - see: Waterford Speedbowl

Newfield Park - Bridgeport - 1/5 mile dirt oval (5/14/35 - 9/18/40)
    Bill Holmes was the first winner / formerly a trotter horse track

North Haven Speedway - New Haven - 1/5 mile dirt oval (c.1937) / motorcycles

Norwich Fairgrounds - Norwich - 1/2 mile dirt oval (7/04/33)

Plainville Stadium - Plainville - 1/4 mile dirt oval (4/10/49)
    1/4 mile paved oval (4/17/49 - 1980)

Bob Ellis at Danbury (CT) in 1964 - Joe Saleem collection.

Plymouth Speedway - Plymouth - dirt oval (1965) / (aka: Valley Park Speedway)

Rockville Driving Park - Rockville - 1/2 mile dirt oval (late 1930's)

Sage Park Speedway - Windsor - 1/2 mile dirt oval (8/12/34 - 8/19/34)

Savin Rock - see: West Haven Speedway

Stafford Motor Speedway - Stafford Springs / formerly a horse track built in 1892
    1/2 mile dirt oval (1948 - 10/03/66) / covered grandstands burned in 1957
    1/5 mile paved oval (5/28/48 - c.1952) (1994 - present) / Stafford Fairgrounds
    1/2 mile paved oval (1967 - present) / home of the annual "Spring Sizzler"

Stratford - dirt oval (1958) ran micro-midgets

Suffield - 1/4 mile dirt oval (late 1940's - early 1950's)

Thompson Int'l Speedway - Thompson / (aka: Thompson Speedway)
    5/8 mile paved oval (5/26/40 - 10/19/41) (10/14/45 - present)
    listed as a 1/2 mile in the beginning / NASCAR lists it as a .542 mile
    Freddie DeSarro died in a modified crash here on 12/01/78
    1.56 mile paved road course (8/17/52 - early 1970's)
    1/4 mile paved oval (1949 - c.1965) / (aka: New Thompson Speedway)
    1/4 mile paved dragstrip (1958 - c.1959)
    also has a 1/4 midget track called Little T Speedway

Valley Park Speedway - see: Plymouth Speedway

Waterford Speedbowl - Waterford - 1/3 mile dirt oval (4/15/51 - 4/29/51)
    1/3 mile paved oval (5/19/51 - present)
    (aka: New London-Waterford Speedbowl) / ran an exhibition race on 4/09/51

West Haven Speedway - West Haven - 1/5 mile dirt oval (7/07/35 - 10/27/35)
    1/5 mile paved oval (5/28/36 - 9/11/41) (8/30/45 - c.1961)
    (aka: West Haven Motordrome) / (aka: Savin Rock Amusement Park)
    (aka: Donovan Field) / Al Herman died here in a crash on 6/18/60
    dedicated to "Wild Bill" Donovan, former manager of the New York Yankees

Westport - paved road course (c.1966)

DELAWARE

Airport Speedway - New Castle - 1/10 mile dirt oval (1980 - 1988)
    1/8 mile dirt oval (1989 - present) / runs modified-midgets

Augustine Beach Speedway - Port Penn - 1/2 mile dirt oval (1930's)

Blackbird Speedway - Blackbird - 1/10 mile dirt oval (c.1964 - 11/05/78)

Blue Hen Speedway - Harrington - dirt oval (1960) / ran micro-midgets

Bowers Beach - dirt oval (1950's) / now the site of Heartbreak Hotel

Capital Speedway - Dover / located five miles north of Dover
    1/2 mile dirt oval (c.7/19/52) / (aka: Dover Speedway)
    1/4 mile dirt oval (4/24/54 - c.10/12/57)

Dara Speedway - Harrington - oval (years unknown)

Delaware Int'l Speedway - Delmar / same site as old Delmar Speedway
    1/2 mile dirt oval (9/06/65 - present) / (aka: Delmar Speedway)
    located next to U.S. 13 Dragway / (aka: U.S. 13 Super Speedway)

Delaware Motorsports Park - Seaford - 1/10 mile dirt oval (c.1983 - present)
    1/6 mile dirt oval (1989 - present) / (aka: Middleford Speedway)
    (aka: Seaford Speedway)

Delaware Speedway - see: Sea Coast Speedway

Delaware Sports Center - Wilmington - 1/5 mile dirt oval (5/30/35 - 1936)
  located seven miles south of town

Delaware State Fairgrounds - Elsmere / (aka: Elsmere Fairgrounds)
  1/2 mile dirt oval (c.1930 - c.1939)

Delaware State Fairgrounds - Harrington / at the Kent-Sussex Co. Fairgrounds
  1/2 mile dirt oval (1921 - c.1941) (c.1946 - present)
  became the Delaware State Fairgrounds in 1962

Delmar Speedway - Delmar - 1/2 mile dirt oval (1949 - 1953) (c.9/28/58 - c.1958)
  1/4 mile dirt oval (3/22/53 - c.5/17/53) (aka: Delmar Raceway)
  1/2 mile paved oval (6/07/53 - 1958) / also see: Delaware Int'l Speedway

Dover Downs Int'l Speedway - Dover / track was proposed in September of 1967
  1.0 mile paved oval (7/06/69 - present) / turns banked 24 degrees
  first race was a NASCAR Winston Cup race won by Richard Petty

Dover Speedway - see: Capital Speedway

Elsmere Fairgrounds - see: Delaware State Fairgrounds - Elsmere

Georgetown Speedway - Georgetown - dirt oval (1950's)

Georgetown Speedway - see: Sea Coast Speedway

Hares Corners - New Castle - 1/2 mile dirt oval (1930's)

Harrington Fairgrounds - see: Delaware State Fairgrounds

Harrington - also see: DARA Speedway, Blue Hen Speedway

Little Haven - dirt oval (years unknown) / located in a farmer's field

Little Lincoln Speedway - Lincoln - 1/4 mile dirt oval (5/27/67 - c.1975)

Loves Speedway - see: Volunteer Speedway

Meyers Speedway - Bridgeville - 1/2 mile dirt oval (4/10/50 - c.1950)

"Dyno Don" Nicholson in his "Eliminator" Cougar. - Allan E. Brown collection.

Middleford Speedway - see: Delaware Motorsports Park

Milford Speedway - Milford / (aka: New Milford Speedway)
  1/2 mile dirt oval (c.1934 - c.1941) (c.1946 - c.1950)

Nanticoke Speedway - Bridgeville - 1/2 mile dirt oval (c.3/26/50 - c.1950)

Pacer Park - (location unknown) - 1/10 mile dirt oval (1979 - 1980)

Redden Micro Midget Speedway - Redden - 1/8 mile dirt oval (4/21/85 - 1985)

Rehoboth Speedway - see: Volunteer Speedway

Seacoast Speedway - Georgetown / (aka: Georgetown Speedway)
  1/2 mile dirt oval (3/18/50 - 1963) (1971 - 1990) (1992 - present)
  1/4 mile dirt oval (1971 - 1982) (1984 - c.1985) / (aka: Stokley Speedway)
  1/4 mile paved dragstrip (c.1956 - c.1957) / (aka: Delaware Speedway)

Seaford Speedway - see: Delaware Motorsports Park

Stokley Speedway - see: Sea Coast Speedway

U.S. 13 Dragway - Delmar - 1/4 mile paved dragstrip (8/28/63 - present)
  located next to Delaware Int'l Speedway

U.S. 13 Super Speedway - see: Delaware Int'l Speedway

Volunteer Speedway - Rehoboth Beach / (aka: Rehoboth Speedway)
  1/2 mile dirt oval (1936- c.1941) (1946 - c.1951) / (aka: Loves Speedway)
  1/4 mile dirt oval (6/30/51 - c.1951)

Wildcat Recreation Park - Dover - dirt oval (1980's)

Willow Grove - 2/5 mile dirt oval (1950 - 1951)

Willow Grove - dirt oval (1969) / only 1.25 miles from Willow Grove Speedway

Willow Grove Speedway - Willow Grove - 1/3 mile dirt oval (c.1969 - c.1970)

Wilmington Speedway - New Castle / located south of New Castle on US 13
  1/3 mile paved oval (6/15/52 - 8/13/55) (5/18/58 - c.1958) / torn down

Wilmington Speedway - Wilmington - dirt oval (c.5/14/50 - c.1950)

DISTRICT OF COLUMBIA

Benning Speedway - 1/2 mile dirt oval (9/06/15) (6/05/37 - c.1937)

Capitol Speedway / the track was located at Montana & New York Avenue
  1/5 mile dirt oval (7/25/39 - 10/17/39) / first race won by Duke Nalon

Robert F. Kennedy Stadium - 1/4 mile dirt oval (5/06/73)

Uline Arena - 1/11 mile indoor concrete oval (1948) (11/20/50) (11/21/50)

Washington Stadium - 1/10 mile indoor concrete oval (1939) / ran midgets

FLORIDA

Amelia Earhart Field - see: Masters Field

Auburndale Speedway - Winter Haven (Auburndale) / (aka: Tri-Cities Speedway)
1/4 mile paved oval (11/16/74 - present)
site is near the location of the former Lake Region Raceway
(aka: Auburndale Speedway Park) / (aka: Winter Haven Speedway)

Barberville Speedway - see: Volusia County Speedway

Bay County Speedway - Youngstown / (aka: Boss Hogg Int'l Speedway)
1/4 mile dirt oval (c.1982 - 1985) / (aka: Youngstown Speedway)
1/3 mile dirt oval (1986 - present)

Beaches Speedway - Panama City - 3/8 mile paved oval (1973 - 1979)
1/4 mile paved dragstrip (early 1970's)

Ben White Raceway - Orlando - 5/8 mile dirt oval (c.5/02/48 - 1950's) a horse track

Boca Raton Airfield - Boca Raton - 3.0 mile paved road course (3/09/57 - 3/08/59)
location is currently the site of Florida Atlantic University

Boss Hogg Int'l Speedway - see: Bay County Speedway

Boynton Beach Speedway - Boynton Beach - 1/8 mile paved oval (c.1958 - c.1962)

Bradley Field - Fort Lauderdale - 1/4 mile paved oval (January, 1953 - 1955)

Emil Reutimann gives a wave after a win. This photo was given to Bill Seith by Emil in the early 1950's. Buzzie and Wayne Reutimann are Emil's sons.

Bradley Horse Track - Fort Lauderdale - 1/2 mile dirt oval (January, 1929)

Brevard County Speedway - see: Melbourne Speedway

Bronson Motor Speedway - Bronson / (aka: Bronson Speedway)
1/3 mile paved oval (c.1976 - 1985) (1987 - present)
patterned after its sister track Monadnock Speedway in New Hampshire

Brooksville Airport - Tampa / Don Garlits set a record of 176.4 mph on 11/10/57
1/4 mile concrete dragstrip (c.1955 - c.1958)

Broward Motor Speedway - see: Miami-Hollywood Speedway

Broward Speedway - Fort Lauderdale / (aka: Forman Field)
2.0 mile paved circle (1/23/49 - 2/27/49)
ran NASCAR modifieds and sports cars on 1/23/49 on a circular taxiway
ran sports cars on 2/20/49 / (aka: Broward Bowl)
ran NASCAR modifieds, sports cars & strictly stocks on 2/27/49
the facility was an old airfield shaped like a spoked wheel / the spokes
were the runways and outside circle were the taxiway
the strictly stock races were the predecessors of NASCAR Grand Nationals
also see: Fort Lauderdale-Davie Speedway

Bryant Stadium - Lakeland - 1/4 mile dirt oval (12/02/46 - c.1946)

Buccaneer Dragway - Fernandina Beach - 1/4 mile paved dragstrip (1966)

Camp Foster - Jacksonville - 1.0 mile brick & dirt oval (9/03/34 - c.5/19/39)
the races were held on parallel roads, a brick road and the other of dirt
1.25 mile brick & dirt oval (11/27/38 - 1/29/39)
originally an Army base / the site is now the Jacksonville Navy base

Central Florida Dragway - see: Orlando Speed World

Central Florida Speedway - see: Orlando Speedway

Charlotte County Speedway - North Fort Myers - see: Sun Coast Speedway

Charlotte Co. Speedway - Punta Gorda - 3/8 mile paved oval (12/15/90 - present)
tried to build in 1988 but was stopped by the city for permit infractions

Citrus County Speedway - Inverness - 1/4 mile dirt oval (1954 - 1960)
1/4 mile paved oval (11/10/60 - present) / (aka: Inverness Speedway)
located at the Citrus County Fairgrounds

City Park - Daytona Beach - 1/5 mile dirt oval (1950's) / still a baseball field

Cocoa Airport - see: Titusville-Cocoa Speedway

Cocoa Beach - 1/2 mile dirt oval (1948)

Collier County Speedway - Naples / (aka: Gator Motor Speedway)
1/4 mile paved oval (1971 - 1985)

Columbia County Speedway - see: Columbia Motorsports Park

Columbia Motorsports Park - Ellisville - 1/2 mile dirt oval (1974 - 1987)
1/2 mile paved oval (1988) (1990 - present) / (aka: North Florida Raceway)
(aka: Gateway Nat'l Raceway Park) / (aka: Columbia County Speedway)

156

Corry Field - Pensacola (Warrington) / located at a old Naval Air Station
3.0 mile concrete road course (c.1953 - 1966)
(aka: Pensacola Fiesta of Five Flags Sports Car Racing Course)

Country Boy Speedway - Boynton Beach - 3/8 mile dirt oval (1979 - 1980)
the track was located in a field

County Line Speedway - Clewiston / (aka: Hendry County Speedway)
1/4 mile dirt oval (c.1977 - 1980) / (aka: Clewiston Speedway)

Dade City Speedway - Dade City - 1/2 mile dirt oval (c.1/13/51 - c.1951)
located at the Pasco County Fairgrounds

Davie - see: Fort Lauderdale-Davie

Daytona Beach - 3.2 mile beach/paved oval (3/08/36 - 8/24/41) (4/14/46 - c.8/17/47)
the track used part of State Highway A-1-A and the Atlantic Ocean beach
first race was a 200 mile AAA stock car race won by Milt Marion
located farther north than the beach track used in the 1950's

Daytona Beach - 2.2 mile beach/paved oval (2/15/48 - c.1957)
the new tracks were farther south of beach/paved street oval track of 1930's
4.15 mile beach/paved street oval (2/15/48 - 3/16/60)
Paul Goldsmith won last auto race (NASCAR GN race) on 2/23/58
track was replaced by the Daytona Int'l Speedway / promoter: Bill France
they continued to race motorcycles on the track until 3/13/60

*This unique shot of the pace lap of the 1952 Daytona Beach classic was taken
by Len Ashburn. Pat Kirkwood (#99) and Lloyd Moore (#59) in Chryslers lead
the rest of the field down Highway A-1-A. Kirkwood finished third behind the
Hudson's of Marshall Teague (from 11th) and Herb Thomas (who started 4th).*

Daytona Beach Memorial Stadium - Daytona Beach / ran midgets for Speedweeks
1/5 mile coral oval (c.2/16/54 - 1975) (1978) / at the Daytona Beach College
1/5 mile paved oval (1976 & 1977) / ran modifieds & midgets 1976 & 1977

Daytona Beach Mem. Stadium - Daytona Beach / located west of town
1/4 mile dirt oval (1989 - present) replaced college stadium west of town
opened with motorcycle racing / the first auto race in 1992

Cale Yarborough in the Hardees Thunderbird leads a group of cars off of the banking at Daytona Int'l Speedway. - Dave Franks photo.

Daytona Int'l Speedway - Daytona Beach / Bill France, Sr. built / proposed in 1953
    2.5 mile paved tri-oval (2/01/59 - present) / turns banked 31 degrees
    Marshall Teague was fatally injured in an accident on 2/11/59 (Indy car)
    Lee Petty won the first "Daytona 500" on 2/22/59 in a photo finish
    Jim Rathmann won the only USAC Indy car race held here on 4/04/59
    1.6, 3.1 & 3.81 mile paved road courses (4/05/59 - 2/03/84)
    1/4 mile paved dragstrip (1961) / used back straightaway
    3.3 mile paved road course (7/03/84 - present)
    Kyle Petty started his driving career here with a win in 1979

Daytona Raceway - see: New Smyrna Speedway

Daytona Beach - also see: City Park, Spruce Creek

Deland Drive-In Raceway Park - Deland - 3/8 mile dirt oval (3/06/66 - 1973)
    two miles south on McGregor Road / closed for not having building permits

Deland Fairgrounds - see: Volusia County Fairgrounds

Deland Int'l Raceway - Deland - 1/4 mile paved dragstrip (1966 - c.1970)
    located at the Deland Airport

Deland Midgets Speedway - Deland - dirt oval (1937) / ran midgets

DeSoto Dragstrip - Bradenton / located next to DeSoto Speedway (oval track)
    1/4 mile paved dragstrip (June, 1973 - present)
    home of the annual "Snowbird Nationals"

DeSoto Speedway - Bradenton / (aka: Tom Stimus' DeSoto Speedway)
    3/8 mile paved oval (1978 - present) / (aka: DeSoto Memorial Speedway)

Dixie Speedway - Cross City - 1/4 mile dirt oval (1975 & 1976)

Dixie Speedway - Fort Myers - 1/4 mile paved oval (years unknown)

Dunnellon Airport - Tampa - paved road course (1/17/60 - 1963)

East Bay Raceway near Tampa. The one-third-mile track is one of the fastest tracks for its size in the country. - Official track photo.

East Bay Raceway - Gibsonton - 1/3 mile dirt oval (2/05/77 - present)
    (aka: Florida Nat'l Speedway) / home of "East Bay National" for sprint cars

Eau Gallie Speedway - see: Melbourne Speedway

Everglades Speedway - Davie - 1/2 mile paved oval (7/04/50) / at a rodeo grounds

Fernandina Beach - 1/2 mile beach oval (1964 - 1967) / located near a marsh

Fernandina Beach - 2.0 mile beach oval (c.10/27/35 - 11/27/38)
    1.0 mile beach oval (1940 - 1941) (1948) / located north of Jacksonville
    the races were around barrels set out on the beach of the Atlantic Ocean

Fernandina Beach Airport - Fernandina Beach / races on airport runways
    2.8 mile paved road course (early 1960's - early 1970's)
    sometimes referred to as "Little Sebring"

Festival Park Speedway - Zephyrhills - 1/2 mile dirt oval (c.1986 - present)
    runs vintage race cars only

One of Curtis Turner's hairy slides on the sands of Daytona Beach. Len Ashburn, who took this photo, said, "Turner would start getting sideways one-quarter mile before entering the north turn."

The line-up for the 1982 "Snowball Derby" at Five Flags. - Don Grassman photo

Five Flags Speedway - Pensacola - 1/2 mile dirt oval (5/31/53)
    1/2 mile paved oval (6/13/53 - present)
    Herb Thomas won NASCAR GN 6/14/53 / home of annual "Snowball Derby"
    1/4 mile paved oval (1970's) / track was patterned after Darlington Raceway
    the very first race on 5/31/53 ended on the first lap with a 17 car pileup
    the track was built by Bud Williamson, Sr. / it cost $90,000 to build

Flagler County Airport - Flagler Beach - 1/4 mile paved dragstrip (1957 - 1958)

Flagler Speedway Park - Miami - 1/4 mile paved oval (6/25/39 - 3/29/42)
    located on West Flagler St. & 72nd / (aka: Princess Park)
    Ralph DePalma was the promoter in 1940

Florida City Speedway - Florida City - 1/10 mile paved oval (1961 - 1975)
    (aka: South Florida Speedway) / ran T.Q. midgets and mini-stocks
    Gary Smith was fatally injured here on 5/24/69 / very first T.Q. fatality

Florida Int'l Speedway - see: Lakeland Interstate Speedway

Florida Nat'l Speedway - see: East Bay Raceway

Florida Sports Park - Naples - 1/3 mile dirt oval (1992 - present)
    located next to the Swamp Buggy track in a dried up bog
    the 1/3 mile track has run Karts since c.1986

Florida State Fairgrounds - Jacksonville - see: Jacksonville Fairgrounds

Florida State Fairgrounds Speedway - Tampa / east of town at I-4 & US 301
    1/2 mile dirt oval (4/11/79 - 2/08/89) / replaced Plant Field
    also see: Tampa Int'l Speedway

Florida State Fairgrounds - Tampa (downtown) - see: Plant Field

Florida Suncoast Dome - Saint Petersburg - 1/4 mile dirt oval (2/07/92 & 2/08/92)
    ran World of Outlaw sprints inside dome / promoter went broke / indoor oval

Fort Lauderdale - also see: Bradley, Broward

Fort Lauderdale-Davie Speedway - Fort Lauderdale / also see: Broward Speedway
    1/4 mile flat paved oval (11/07/48 - c.1953) / located at 1400 NW 19th St.
    1/8 mile dirt oval (10/24/53 - c.1953) / ran T.Q. midgets on dirt track
    the tracks were on a hanger pad at Forman Field / next to the runways

Fort Myers Dragstrip - Fort Myers - 1/4 mile paved dragstrip (c.1963 - c.1965)

Fort Myers Speedway - see: Sun Coast Speedway

Fort Pierce Airport - Fort Pierce / (aka: Saint Lucie County Airport)
3.0 mile paved road course (December, 1954 - 11/17/57)

Fort Pierce Speedway - Fort Pierce - 1/4 mile paved oval (c.5/19/56 - c.1959)
built by Doug Mullins / the track was located on Orange Avenue
closed because Gold Coast Speedway was built by rival car owner

Fort Walton Beach Speedway - Fort Walton Beach - 1/4 mile dirt oval (c.1952)

Fulford-Miami Speedway (board track) - see: Miami-Fulford Speedway

Funland Park - Miami - 1/4 mile dirt oval (1/17/39 - 2/17/39)
(aka: Miami Speedway) / (aka: Ruty's Playland Park) / on NW 7th Ave

Gainesville Airport - Gainesville - paved road course (1956 - 1959)

Gainesville Fairgrounds - Gainesville - 1/2 mile dirt oval (1925)
located at the Alachua County Fairgrounds

Gainesville Raceway - Gainesville - 1/4 mile paved dragstrip (c.1969 - present)
1.6 mile paved road course (c.1977 - c.1984) / (aka: Gainesville Dragway)
Kenny Bernstein turned first ever 300 mph run (301.7) here on 3/20/92
home of the annual "NHRA GatorNationals"

Gainesville Speedway - Gainesville - 3/8 mile dirt oval (1965)

Richard Hutchins leaves the line in his "Chevy Rebellion" wheel-standing pick-up. The wheel-standers are a popular exhibition at dragstrips across the country. - Richard Hutchins collection.

Gateway Nat'l Raceway Park - see: Columbia Motorsports Park

Gateway Speedway - Milton / (aka: Santa Rosa Speedway)
  3/8 mile dirt oval (1983 - c.1989) / located close to Southern Speedway

Gator Motor Speedway - Naples - see: Collier County Speedway

Gator Speedway - Jacksonville - see: JAX Raceways

Geneva Dragstrip - see: Osceola Airport Dragstrip

Gold Coast Speedway - see: Fort Pierce Speedway

Gold Coast Speedway - see: Treasure Coast Speedway

Golden Gate Speedway - Tampa / located on the NE side of town on Fowler Ave.
  1/3 mile paved oval (May, 1962 - 9/16/78) (1981 - 1984)
  Richard Petty won a NASCAR Grand Nat'l race here on 11/11/62
  grandstands were sold to Citrus Co. Speedway, FL and Lee Speedway, NH

An aerial view of Golden Gate Speedway. The track was located just east of Busch Gardens in Tampa. - Alden Jamison collection.

Golden Triangle Strip - Oldsmar - 1/4 mile paved dragstrip (1961)

Goodall - (location unknown) - beach oval (1907)

Grand Prix of Miami - Miami / located at Bicentennial Park in downtown Miami
  1.85 mile paved city street road course (2/27/83 - 1985) / runs IMSA GT
  1.873 mile paved city street road course (1986 - present)
  (aka: Miami Grand Prix) / (aka: Toyota Grand Prix of Miami)

Grand Prix of Palm Beach - West Palm Beach / (aka: South Florida Fairgrounds)
  1.9 mile paved road course (1988 - 1991) / replaced downtown races

Grand Prix of Palm Beach - West Palm Beach / raced on downtown city streets
  1.62 mile paved road course (6/21/86 - 1987)

Gulf Coast Speedway - Lynn Haven - oval (early 1970's)

Gulf County Speedway - Wewahitchka - 5/8 mile dirt oval (1992 - present)
  (aka: Wewa Motor Speedway)

Haines City Speedway - Haines City - dirt oval (c.3/02/52 - 1953)

Hallandale Speedway - see: Hollywood Speedway

Havana Speedway - Havana - 3/8 mile dirt oval (late 1950's)

Henderson Field - Tampa / former World War II Air Force fighter base
1/4 mile paved dragstrip (late 1950's) / site is now part of Busch Gardens

Hendry County Speedway - see: County Line Speedway

Hialeah Speedway - Hialeah - 1/3 mile paved oval (7/18/54 - present)
Bobby Allison, Donnie Allison, Red Farmer & Gary Balough all started here

Hollywood Int'l Speedway - see: Miami-Hollywood Speedway

Hollywood Speedway - Hallandale / location Pembroke Rd & Farmers Market Rd
1/4 mile paved oval (1/15/55 - c.1969) / (aka: Hallandale Speedway)
1/8 mile paved oval (c.6/25/58 - c.1958)

Immokalee Dragway - Naples - 1/4 mile paved dragstrip (1970's)

Inverness Speedway - see: Citrus County Speedway

Jacksonville - also see: Camp Foster, Onslow, Pablo, Speedway Park, Tropical

Jacksonville Beach - 1/2 mile dirt oval (11/11/37) / race won by Joie Chitwood

Jacksonville Fairgrounds - Jacksonville / (aka: Florida State Fairgrounds)
1/2 mile dirt oval (c.1924 - c.1934) / (aka: Flagler Fairgrounds)

Jacksonville Municipal Stadium - Jacksonville - 1/4 mile dirt oval (4/19/42 - 1942)

Jacksonville Speedway - Jacksonville / LeeRoy Yarbrough started here in 1952
1/2 mile dirt oval (3/16/47 - 5/26/73) / (aka: Speedway Park)
1/4 mile dirt oval (11/16/48 - c.1948) (4/16/54 - c.1955)
(aka: JAX Speedway) / referred to as JAX in 1950 / site is now apartments
ran four NASCAR GN races on 11/04/51, 3/06/52, 2/13/55 & 12/01/63
Wendell Scott won the NASCAR Grand National race on 12/01/63

JAX Raceways - Jacksonville - 1/4 mile paved oval (6/09/68 - 1972) / north of town
(aka: Gator Speedway) first name / (aka: New Jacksonville Speedway)
1/8 mile paved dragstrip (c.1969 - present) / (aka: JAX Dragstrip)
1/2 mile dirt oval (1973 - present) / Julian Klein, owner of Jacksonville
Speedway converted the paved oval into a dirt track and opened it
shortly before he had to close his other track on the west side of town

Journalista Speedway - Cocoa Beach - 1/2 mile dirt oval (1926)

Kissimmee Airport - Kissimmee - paved road course (1/22/61) / races on runways
1/4 mile paved dragstrip (c.1957 - 1960's)

Kissimmee Stadium - Kissimmee - 1/5 mile dirt oval (1/17/41 - 1942)
the stadium was and still is a Rodeo arena

Lake City - 1/4 mile paved dragstrip (1955)

Lake City Speedway - see: South Ridge Speedway

Lake Region Raceway - Winter Haven (Auburndale) / (aka: Polk Co. Speedway)
   1/4 mile dirt oval (c.11/15/52 - 6/28/58) / (aka: Winter Haven Raceway)
   1/4 mile paved oval (7/19/58 - 9/18/71)
   (aka: Winter Haven Motor Speedway)
   in 1974 Tri-Cities Speedway was built on the same site
Lake Wales - 1/4 mile paved dragstrip (1953) / Don Garlits started his career here

Lakeland - also see: Bryant, Silver Dollar

Lakeland Interstate Speedway - Lakeland / (aka: Florida Int'l Raceway)
   1/4 mile paved dragstrip (February, 1971 - 1977) (1992 - present)
   1/4 mile paved oval (1971 - 1977) (1987 - present)
   5/8 mile paved oval (4/16/71 - 1977) / (aka: Lakeland Interstate Raceway)
   1.8 mile paved road course (C.1972 - 1974) / (aka: Lakeland Drag Strip)

Lakeland - paved road course (late 1950's)
   the course was in the parking lot of the Detroit Tigers training field

Lakeland Speedway - Lakeland - 3/8 mile high banked paved oval (1/01/56 - 1957)
   located 1/2 mile from Silver Dollar Speedway / site now a mobile home park

Legion Field Stadium - Pensacola - 1/4 mile paved oval (11/22/40 - 1941)

Lehigh Acres - paved road course (1963) / east of Fort Myers

Lightning Speedway - see: Ocala Speedway

Lion's Speedway - Largo - 1/8 mile dirt oval (early 1960's) / ran Micro-midgets

Longwood - 1/2 mile dirt oval (c.1927)

MacDill Air Force Base - Tampa / ran sports cars on air base runways
   4.2 mile concrete road course (2/21/53 & 1/31/54)

Marianna - dirt oval (8/12/51)

Marion County Speedway - see: Ocala Raceway

Martin County Midget Speedway - Stuart - dirt oval (early 1960's)

Masters Field - Miami - 1/4 mile paved dragstrip (c.1956 - 1961) (1963 - 1964)
   3.5 mile paved road course (1/12/58 - 1959) / on an air force base runways
   didn't run in 1962 because of military build-up during the Cuban crisis
   located on NW 27 Avenue, actually located next to Amelia Earhart Field
   (aka: Orange Bowl Grand Prix) / often referred to as Amelia Earhart Field

Medley Stadium - Palmetto - 1/4 mile paved oval (c.1950 - 1953)
   1/3 mile paved oval (1/28/52 - 1964) / promoters: Jenin Bros. in 1950's
   (aka: Palmetto Speedway) < called Palmetto 1960 - 1964
   located at 74th and Milan Dairy Road / track built by Leon Dodd

Melbourne - dirt oval (1948)

Melbourne Speedway - Melbourne - 1/4 mile paved oval (3/16/57 - 1977)
   (aka: Brevard County Speedway) / (aka: Spinning Wheel Speedway)
   (aka: Eau Gallie Speedway) / town of Eau Gallie was absorbed by Melbourne

Miami - 1/2 mile dirt oval (7/04/15) / ran motorcycles

164

Miami Grand Prix - see: Grand Prix of Miami

Miami Motor Speedway - Miami - 1/4 mile paved oval (1/12/36 - 2/05/36)

Miami Speedway - Miami - 1/4 mile dirt oval (11/11/34 - 1/06/35)

Miami Speedway - see: Funland Park

Miami-Fulford Speedway - Miami Beach (Biscayne Bay) / turns banked 50 degrees
  1.25 mile wood oval (2/22/26) / (aka: Fulford-Miami Speedway)
  designed by Ray Harroun / built by Carl F. Fisher who built Indianapolis
  Pete DePaolo won a 300 mile race / Tommy Milton had fast time 142.93 mph
  destroyed by a massive hurricane on 9/17/26 / only one race held
  the wood and material were used to rebuild the town of Miami Beach

Miami-Hollywood Speedway - Hollywood (Pembroke Pines) / 8 miles west of town
  1/4 mile paved dragstrip (March, 1966 - 12/12/92)
  1/3 mile paved oval (6/13/66 - 1977) (1984)
  1.6 mile paved road course (1967 - c.1979) / (aka: Broward Motor Speedway)
  (aka: Miami-Hollywood Speedway Park) / (aka: Hollywood Int'l Speedway)

Miami - also see: Flagler, Masters Field, Opa-Locka, Orange Bowl, South Airport,
  Tamiami, University of Miami

Million Dollar Speedway - see: Silver Dollar Speedway

Moroso Motorsports Park - West Palm Beach / (aka: Palm Beach Int'l Raceway)
  2.25 mile paved road course (1965 - present) / ran SCCA TA race in 1983
  1/4 mile paved dragstrip (1965 - present) / currently owned by Dick Moroso
  the 12 hours of Sebring was to move here in 1967, the deal fell through

Myakka City - small dirt oval (1986) / ran T.Q. midgets

New Jacksonville Speedway - see: JAX Raceways

New Orlando Speedway - see: Orlando Speedway

New Smyrna Beach - 1.0 mile beach oval (7/17/38) / 1/2 mile beach oval (4/06/53)

New Smyrna Beach Airport - New Smyrna Beach / ran sports cars on runways
  2.4 mile paved road course (2/10/57 & 2/16/58)

The oval track at the Orlando Speedworld. Barely visible in the top left-hand of the photo is the dragstrip. - Official track photo.

New Smyrna Speedway. - Official track photo.

New Smyrna Speedway - New Smyrna Beach (Samsula) / (aka: Daytona Raceway)
1/2 mile dirt oval (1965) / dirt track built by Benny Corbin
1/2 mile paved oval (1966 - present) / home of "World Series of Racing"

North Florida Raceway - see: Columbia Motorsports Park

North Okaloosa County Raceway - Baker - 1/4 mile dirt oval (March, 1986 - 1987)
3/8 mile dirt oval (1988 - present)

Oakfield Speedway - Pensacola - 1/4 mile dirt oval (1964 & 1965)
located at Marlane and Cerny Roads

Ocala Speedway - Ocala (Zuber) - 1/4 mile dirt oval (November, 1952 - 1963)
3/8 mile dirt oval (1964 - 1989) / 3/8 track built by Benny Corbin
1/2 mile dirt oval (1990 - present) / (aka: Lightning Speedway)
(aka: Ocala Raceway) / located six miles north of Ocala on old US 441
(aka: Marion County Speedway) / the oldest active oval track in Florida

Ocean Speedway - see: Ormond Beach

Okaloosa Dragway - Crestview - 1/4 mile dragstrip (c.1981 - c.1982)

Onslow Speedway - Jacksonville - dirt oval (c.1952)

Opa-Locka Optimist Speedway - Miami - 1/3 mile paved oval (c.1948 - c.1952)
1/2 mile dirt oval (11/13/49 - c.1952) / located north of Miami
closed because track was on military property and Korean conflict began

Orange Bowl - Miami - dirt oval (1934) / ran motorcycles

Orange County Raceway - Orlando (Bithlo) - 1/8 mile dirt oval (1988 - present)
located next to Orlando Speed World

Orlando - 1/2 mile dirt oval (1930's)

Orlando Speed World - Orlando (Bithlo) - 3/8 mile paved oval (8/18/74 - present)
1/4 mile paved dragstrip (1966 - present) / located east of town
(aka: Central Florida Dragway)

Orlando Speedway - Orlando (Taft) - 1/4 mile paved oval (2/01/48 - 1971)
(aka: New Orlando Raceway) / (aka: Orlando Midget Speedway)
(aka: Central Florida Speedway) / located south of Orlando

Orlando - also see: Ben White, Orange County, Sunbrock, Tangerine Bowl

166

Ormond Beach - 12.5 mile beach course (1904 - 1908) / raced around barrels
    15.0 mile beach road course (1/25/07) / road course had seven turns
    1.0 mile beach oval (3/14/37) / raced around barrels
    Ormond Beach was the site of the famous speed trials on the beach
    The first year a car raced on the beach was 1902 / (aka: Ocean Speedway)
    Sig Haugdahl was first person to exceed 180 mph in   1923
    Frank Lockhart was fatality injured in a speed trial crash on 4/25/28

Sig Haugdahl drove this Wisconsin Special to a record run of 180 miles per hour at Ormond Beach in 1923. You will not find the record in most books as AAA would not recognize it. Haugdahl and his car owner J. Alex Sloan were with the rival I.M.C.A. sanction. - Photo courtesy of I.M.C.A.

Osceola Airport - Osceola - 2.3 mile paved road course (early 1970's)
    1/4 mile paved dragstrip (1965) / (aka: Osceola Dragstrip)
    (aka: Geneva Dragstrip)

Pablo Beach - Jacksonville Beach - 5.0 mile beach oval (3/28/11 - 11/31/11)

Palatka Speedway - see: Putnam County Raceway

Palm Beach Int'l Raceway - see: Moroso Motorsports Park

Palm Beach Shores - 2.1 mile paved road course (1/02/50 - 12/09/51)

Palm Beach Speedway - see: South Florida Fairgrounds Speedway

Palmetto Speedway - see: Medley Stadium

Paxon Field - see: Tropical Raceway

Pensacola - 1/4 mile paved dragstrip (1970's)

Pensacola Motor Speedway - Pensacola - 1/4 mile dirt oval (4/28/46 - 1949)
    1/4 mile paved oval (3/10/50 - c.1954) (c.5/17/57 - 1957)
    the site is now the Westwood Mall

Pensacola - also see: Corry Field, Five Flags, Legion Field, Oakfield

Phillips Field - Tampa - 1/4 mile dirt oval (11/29/39)
  1/4 mile paved oval (12/10/39 - c.1941) (c.12/04/46 - c.1964)
  (aka: University of Tampa Stadium)

Plant Field - Tampa / (aka: Florida State Fairgrounds) / located downtown Tampa
  1/2 mile dirt oval (2/03/21 - 2/14/42) (2/05/46 - c.1980)
  Charlie Roe was first winner / (aka: South Florida Fairgrounds) < 1st name
  J. Alex Sloan was the first promoter / mostly ran IMCA sprints during fair
  (aka: Tampa Speedway) / closed shortly after fair moved to east of town
  site is now the Tampa University Athletic Field / uses racetrack grandstands

Polk County Speedway - see: Lake Region Raceway

Pompano Beach Speedway - Pompano Beach / (aka: Pompano Park) / horse track
  1.0 mile dirt oval (July, 1927) (1929) (10/09/49 - 1/15/50)
  Jim Frankland promoted an IMCA sprint car show on 1/15/50

Powerhouse Dragway - Panama City - 1/8 mile paved dragstrip (1991 - present)

Princess Park - see: Flagler Speedway Park

Punta Gorda Speedway - Punta Gorda - 1/5 mile paved oval (1960's)
  (aka: Charlotte County Speedway)

Putnam County Raceway - Satsuma / (aka: Satsuma Race-Way)
  3/8 mile dirt oval (4/09/67 - present) / (aka: Putnam County Speedway)
  (aka: Palatka Speedway)

Rocket Speedway - see: Sunbrock Speedway

Rodeo Grounds - Homestead - dirt oval (years unknown)

Ruty's Playland Park - see: Funland Park

Saint Augustine Beach - beach oval (1920's) (1946) / raced around barrels

A Ferrari enters a turn at Sebring in 1958. - Len Ashburn photo.

168

An aerial view of the new Saint Augustine Speedway. - Official track photo.

Saint Augustine Speedway - St. Augustine - 5/8 mile dirt oval (3/20/93 - present)
  (aka: Saint Johns County Motorsports Complex) / three miles north of town

Saint Augustine Speedway - Saint Augustine / (aka: Saint Augustine Raceway)
  1/4 mile paved oval (May, 1966 - 1970) / one mile south of town on US 1

Saint Johns County Motorsports Complex - see: Saint Augustine Speedway

Saint Petersburg - also see: Florida Suncoast, Sunshine, Tri-City Sportsman

Saint Petersburg Grand Prix - Saint Petersburg / ran on downtown city streets
  2.0 mile city street paved road course (11/03/85) / won by Willy T. Ribbs
  2.0 mile city street paved road course (1986 - 1990)
  the circuit in 1985 ran "over water" to the pier / ran SCCA TA races

Santa Rosa Speedway - see: Gateway Speedway

Sara Mana Speedway - Sarasota - 1/4 mile paved oval (2/03/52 - 1971)
  (aka: Sarasota-Bradenton Speedway) / (aka: Sara Mana Speedbowl)
  the site became a trailer park

Sarasota County Fairgrounds - Sarasota - dirt oval (1954 - July, 1954)

Sarasota-Bradenton Speedway - see: Sara Mana Speedway

Satsuma Race-Way - see: Putnam County Raceway

Sebring Int'l Raceway - Sebring / partially on the runways of Hendrick Field
  3.5 mile asphalt & concrete road course (12/31/50)
  5.2 mile asphalt & concrete road course (3/15/52 - 1986)
  1.4 mile paved road course (1970's - present) / ran U.S. Grand Prix 12/12/59
  4.86 mile paved road course (3/22/84 - 1986) / formerly a B-17 bomber base
  4.11 mile paved road course (1987 - 1990) / home of "12 Hours of Sebring"
  3.7 mile paved road course (1991 - present) / (aka: Sebring Int'l Dragway)
  1/4 mile paved dragstrip (1956) (6/17/92 - present)
  held first ever SCCA TA races here on 3/25/66 won by Jochen Rindt

Seminole Speedway - Casselberry - 1/4 mile dirt oval (April, 1946 - c.1954)
1.0 mile dirt oval (February, 1946 - c.1948)

Silver Dollar Speedway - Lakeland / (aka: Million Dollar Speedway)
3/8 mile dirt oval (c.1955 - c.1958) / located on US Highway 92
track was located across from the Silver Dollar Drive-In Theatre
the site is now a trailer park

Soldiers Field - see: Tropical Raceway

South Airport Speedway - Miami - dirt oval (c.10/13/40 - 1940)

South Florida Fairgrounds Speedway - West Palm Beach
1/2 mile dirt oval (12/31/49 - c.4/03/55) / (aka: Palm Beach Speedway)
ran NASCAR Grand National races on 1/20/52, 2/01/53 & 2/07/54
1/3 mile dirt oval (c.5/06/55 - 1955) / (aka: Southland Speedway)
1/2 mile paved oval (10/16/55 - 12/10/83) / oval track torn out 5/15/84
(aka: Palm Beach County Fairgrounds) / also see: Grand Prix of Palm Beach

South Florida Speedway - see: Florida City Speedway

South Ridge Speedway - Lake City / (aka: Lake City Speedway)
4/10 mile dirt oval (c.12/18/55 - 1978) (1987 - present)

Southern Raceway - Milton - 3/8 mile dirt oval (9/03/88 - present)
located closed to Gateway Speedway / (aka: Southern Speedway)

Southland Speedway - see: South Florida Fairgrounds Speedway

Speedway Park - Jacksonville - 1/2 mile dirt oval (10/25/53 - c.1953)
probably a different track than Jacksonville Speedway

Speedway Park - Jacksonville - see: Jacksonville Speedway

Speedway Park - Tampa - 1/2 mile dirt oval (11/14/48 - c.1/24/54)
1/4 mile dirt oval (7/04/50 - 9/04/54) / Jim Hurtubise started here in 1952
located one mile west of Dale Mabry Highway on West Hillsborough Ave.
the site later became a lumber company, which has since closed

Speedway Park in Tampa, Florida - Bill & Susie Seith collection.

Spinning Wheel Speedway - see: Melbourne Speedway

Spruce Creek Dragway - Daytona Beach - 1/4 mile paved dragstrip (2/21/59- 1965)
   paved road course (late 1960's) / located at the Spruce Creek Airport
   (aka: Spruce Creek Raceway) / the promoter was Ed Otto

Stock Island Speedway - Key West - 1/3 mile paved oval (c.10/06/55 - c.1970)

Stuart Fairgrounds - Stuart - dirt oval (1955) / at the Martin County Fairgrounds

Sun Coast Speedway - North Fort Myers - 1/5 mile paved oval (c.1968 - c.1975)
   (aka: Fort Myers Speedway) / (aka: Charlotte County Speedway)
   located three miles north of the Lee County line on US 41

Sunbrock Speedway - Orlando - 1/4 mile paved oval (c.1949 - c.1957)
   (aka: Rocket Speedway) / the promoter was Larry Sunbrock

Sunshine Drag Strip - Saint Petersburg - 1/8 mile paved oval (c.1966 - present)
   (aka: Sunshine Dragway) / built by Leo Musgrave and Al Lamphier
   Emory Cook drove to the first 200 mph run here in a Funny Car on 10/14/66

Sunshine Speedway - Saint Petersburg - 1/4 mile paved oval (1/23/60 - present)
   built by Leo Musgrave and Al Lamphier / next to Sunshine Drag Strip

Tallahassee - 1/2 mile dirt oval (early 1950's) / located in an old ammo dump

Tallahassee - 1/4 mile paved dragstrip (1960's & 1970's) / west of town on Rt 20

Tallahassee - 3/8 mile dirt oval (early 1950's)

Tamiami Park Raceway - Miami - 1.742 mile paved park road course (11/10/85)
   1.784 mile paved county park road course (11/09/86 - 1988)
   (aka: Nissan Indy Challenge) / CART Indy cars / promoter: Ralph Sanchez
   (aka: Greater Miami Indy Challenge) / (aka: Beatrice Indy Challenge)
   ran SCCA TA race in 1986

Tamiami Stadium - Miami / located at 82nd & Tamiami Trail
   1/10 mile paved oval (11/23/52 - 1/31/53) / ran T.Q. midgets

Tampa Dragway - Tampa / located east of town near where I-4 is now
   1/4 mile paved dragstrip (1950's - c.1970)

Tampa Fairgrounds - see: Florida State Fairgrounds

Tampa Int'l Speedway - Tampa / located at the new Florida State Fairgrounds
   1.87 mile paved road course (11/25/88) / ran IMSA GT
   1.92 mile paved road course (1989 - 1990) / ran next to oval track
   (aka: World Challenge of Tampa)

Tampa Speedway - see: Plant Field

Tampa - also see: Brooksville, Dunnellon, Golden Gate, Henderson, MacDill,
   Phillips, Plant Field, Speedway Park, The Shore, Twin City

Tangerine Bowl - Orlando - dirt oval (1947) / ran midgets / now called Citrus Bowl
   located west of town near the East-West Expressway

The Shore - Tampa (Oldsmar) - 1/2 mile dirt oval (1/24/37) at an Army base
soldiers raced jeeps / site is now Florida Downs Horse Track
1.0 mile dirt oval (1/26/46) / stock car race won by Bill France, Sr.

Thompson Bowl - Ocala - 1/10 mile dirt oval (c.12/03/55 - c.1955) / Micro-Midgets

Thunderbolt Raceway - Jacksonville Beach - 1/4 mile paved dragstrip (1953-c.1970)

Titusville-Cocoa Speedway - Titusville - 1.6 mile paved road course (12/30/56)
Fireball Roberts won a 100 mile NASCAR Grand Nat'l race in 1956
3.5 mile paved road course (7/20/58) / tracks were on airport runways

Tom Stimus' DeSoto Speedway - see: DeSoto Memorial Speedway

Treasure Coast Speedway - Fort Pierce / (aka: Gold Coast Speedway)
1/4 mile paved oval (1959 - 4/30/74) / built by Hardy Sloan
located on Angle Road about three miles from Fort Pierce Speedway

Tri-Cities Speedway - see: Auburndale Speedway

Tri-City Sportsman Park - Saint Petersburg - 1/4 mile dirt oval (5/31/52 - 7/05/52)
1/4 mile paved oval (7/25/52 - c.1955) / site is now an industrial park

Tropical Raceway - Jacksonville - 1/2 mile dirt oval (1/31/37 - c.5/05/41)
1/6 mile dirt oval (12/04/38 - c.12/31/39) / (aka: Tropical Park Speedway)
(aka: Soldiers Field) / (aka: Paxon Field)

Twin City Dragway - Tampa - 1/4 mile paved dragstrip (1965)

University of Miami (South Campus) - South Miami (Pine Woods)
2.5 mile paved road course (2/13/55) / formerly was Richmond Naval Base

Valkaria Dragway - Vero Beach (Sebastian) - 1/4 mile paved dragstrip (1962-1965)
dragstrip opened when Masters Field became unavailable during the military
build-up of the Cuban crisis / (aka: Sebastian Airport)
2.23 mile paved road course (c.7/19/64 - early 1970's)
located at an old World War II airfield / (aka: Valkaria Airport)

Venice Airport - Venice - 2.9 mile paved road course (1958 & 1959)

Vero Beach Airport - Vero Beach - 3.25 mile paved road course (3/08/52 - 1/10/53)

Vero Beach - oval (1951)

Vero Beach Raceway - Vero Beach - 1/3 mile paved oval (c.1971 - 1977)

Volusia County Fairgrounds - Deland / became a plant for WWII war project
1/2 mile dirt oval (c.1924 - 1940) (c.1/21/51 - c.1953)

Volusia County Speedway - Barberville - 1/4 mile dirt oval (1968 - 1969)
3/8 mile dirt oval (August, 1969 - 1971) / originally built by Benny Corbin
1/2 mile dirt oval (2/11/72 - 1989) / (aka: Barberville Speedway)
1/2 mile paved oval (1989 - present)
3/8 mile dirt oval (2/10/93 - present) / new dirt track next to paved one

West Palm Beach - 1/10 mile paved oval (1960's) / ran T.Q. midgets

West Palm Beach - also see: Grand Prix of Palm Beach, Medley, Moroso

West Palm Beach - beach oval (1905)

West Palm Beach Fairgrounds - see: South Florida Fairgrounds Speedway

West Palm Beach High School Stadium - W. Palm Beach - dirt oval (1934) midgets

Wewa Motor Speedway - see: Gulf County Speedway

Winter Haven Motor Speedway - see: Lake Region Raceway

Winter Haven Speedway - see: Auburndale Speedway & Lake Region Raceway

Winter Haven Speedway - see: Lake Region Raceway

Youngstown Speedway - see: Bay County Speedway

Zephyrhills Airport - Zephyrhills - 1/4 mile paved dragstrip (1950 - c.1955)

GEORGIA

441 Speedway - see: Four-Forty-One Speedway

Albany Dragway - see: U.S. 19 Dragway

Albany Fairgrounds - Albany - 1/2 mile dirt oval (c.1920) (1950)
3/8 mile dirt oval (late 1950's) / (aka: Albany Speedway) / west of town

Albany Speedway - Albany - 1/2 mile dirt oval (1961 - c.1985)
located six miles from U.S. 19 Dragway

Albany - also see: Suicide, Turner Air Force Base, U.S. 19

Arrow Speedway - Monroe - oval (years unknown) / maybe Campton or Kart track

Ashburn Speedway - Ashburn - 3/8 mile dirt oval (late 1950's)

Athens Speedway - Athens - 1/4 mile dirt oval (November, 1959 - c.1972)
1/3 mile dirt oval (c.1973 - 1990) / now the site of an industrial park

Atlanta - 1/3 mile wood oval (c.1909 - c.1912) / ran motorcycles
had an exhibition run by a race car in 1910

Atlanta Dragway - Commerce - 1/4 mile paved dragstrip (3/25/70 - present)
(aka: Atlanta International Dragstrip)

Atlanta Fairgrounds - see: Lakewood Speedway

Atlanta International Raceway - see: Atlanta Motor Speedway

Atlanta Midget Speedway - see: Atlanta Speedway

Atlanta Motor Speedway - Hampton / (aka: Atlanta International Raceway)
1.522 mile paved oval (7/31/60 - present) turns banked 24 degrees
was to open on 11/22/59 but rain delayed construction
first race was a NASCAR Grand National race (Winston Cup)
2.5 mile paved road course (1991 - present)
a NASCAR Winston Cup race scheduled for 3/14/93 was snowed out

Atlanta Motordrome - Atlanta (Hapeville) / the president was Asa G. Candler, Jr.
   2.0 mile dirt oval (11/09/09 - 10/06/10) / (aka: Atlanta Speedway)
   Ray Harroun won the last race / now the site of Atlanta Int'l Airport
   a race scheduled for 10/08/10 was rained out / (aka: Candler Field)

Atlanta Speed Shop Dragway - Covington / (aka: Newton County Dragstrip)
   1/4 mile paved dragstrip (1959 - 1992) / (aka: Newton Dragstrip)

Atlanta Speedway - Atlanta / (aka: Chattahoochee Speedway)
   1/2 mile dirt oval (c.1920 - c.1921) / (aka: Dixie Speedways)
   (aka: Hamilton Speedway) / built by George Hamilton
   1/2 mile high banked dirt oval (12/14/29 - 7/04/30)
   track had worlds record at 23.3 seconds on 35 degrees banked track in 1930
   located at Pace's Ferry Road & the Chattahoochee River

Atlanta Speedway - Atlanta / east of downtown on Fair St. & Memorial Drive
   1/5 mile dirt oval (5/21/40 - 1942) / located at the Warren Athletic Field
   formerly the site of the Sports Arena / (aka: Atlanta Midget Speedway)

Atlanta - also see: Lakewood Park, New Atlanta, Peach Bowl

Atomic Age Speedway - see: Pulaski County Speedway

Augusta Fairgrounds - see: Lakeside Fairgrounds Speedway

Augusta International Speedway - Augusta - 1/2 mile dirt oval (1961 - c.1963)
   Joe Weatherly won a NASCAR Grand Nat'l race on 1/2 mile track on 6/19/62
   1/4 mile paved dragstrip (1962) / located on Windsor Springs Road
   3.0 mile paved road course (10/17/63 - 1969) / (aka: Augusta Speedway)
   Fireball Roberts won a NASCAR Grand Nat'l race on road course 10/17/63
   other winners on road course included Dave McDonald & Ken Miles
   1/2 mile paved oval (9/13/64 - 10/19/69) / NASCAR GN races on paved track

Augusta Speedway - see: Augusta International Speedway & Hayloft Speedway

Augusta - also see: Dan Bowles, Duffie Sandpit, Garden City, Gordon Park

Bainbridge - see: Dixie Raceways

Banks County Speedway - Homer - 1/3 mile dirt oval (c.5/25/56 - 1964)
   1/3 mile paved oval (1965)

Baxley Speedway - Baxley - 1/2 mile D-shaped dirt oval (c.1961)

Blue Ridge Speedway - see: Sugar Creek Raceway

Bower's Speedway - see: Speedway Park - Martinez

Boyd's Speedway - see: Chattanooga Raceway Park

Brainerd Optimist Dragstrip - Ringgold - 1/8 mile dragstrip (1961 - present)

Braselton Speedway - Gainesville (Braselton) - dirt oval (1940's or 1950's)

Brunswick Speedway - Brunswick - dirt oval (1949 or 1950)

Butler Speedway - Butler - dirt oval (probably 1950's)

Calhoun Speedway - Calhoun - dirt oval (1951)

Calhoun - also see: Paradise Dragstrip, Skyway Speedway

Campton Speedway - Campton - dirt oval (late 1940's - early 1950's)

Candler Field - see: Atlanta Motordrome

Canton Int'l Speedway - Canton - 1/3 mile dirt oval (1968)
1/3 mile paved oval (c.1969 - c.1971) / north of town near the airport

Canton Speedway - Canton (Hickory Flats) / four miles south of town on Hwy 140
1/4 mile dirt oval (May, 1953 - 1957) (1959) / located on Hickory Flats Road
Bud Lunsford started his driving career here

Canton - also see: Cherokee Motor Speedway

Carmichael Speedway - see: Hayloft Speedway

Carrollton - dirt oval (1950)

Cedartown Fair Speedway - Cedartown - dirt oval (1947 - 1955)
located at the Polk County Fairgrounds / promoted by Jack Smith

Cee-Jay Speedway - see: Swainsboro Raceway

Centennial Stadium - Macon / (aka: Macon Stadium Speedway)
1/4 mile dirt oval (7/25/41 - 1942)

Central City Park Speedway - Macon / located at the Georgia State Fairgrounds
1.0 mile dirt oval (1920's - 11/27/38) / first ran stock cars on 11/27/38
1/2 mile dirt oval (July, 1947 - c.5/06/56) / (aka: Macon Speedway)
(aka: Macon Fairgrounds Speedway) / fairgrounds established in 1851
ran a NASCAR GN race on 9/09/51

Central Georgia Speedway - see: New Cochran Speedway

Charlie's Raceway - see: New Lavonia Speedway

Chattahoochee Speedway - see: Atlanta Speedway

Rusty Wallace is one of the top drivers in the nation. He has won nearly one-third of the NASCAR Winston Cup races in the past two years aboard a Roger Penske owned car. He enters the track as he is ready to go out for a practice session at the Indianapolis Motor Speedway in 1993. - Nancy Brown photo.

Chattanooga Raceway Park - Ringgold / built by E.A. Boyd
    1/3 mile dirt oval (1952 - c.1961) (1977 - present)
    1/3 mile paved oval (c.1962 - 1976) / (aka: Boyd's Speedway)
    located just south of the Tennessee/Georgia line
    the facility also has a 1/6 mile dirt track for Karts that is in Tennessee
    (aka: Chattanooga International Raceway)

Cherokee Motor Speedway - Canton (Waleska) - 1/4 mile dirt oval (1967 - 1969)
    located north of Canton on SR 5

Chickamauga Raceway - Chickamauga - 1/3 mile dirt oval (years unknown)

Chulio Speedway - Rome - 1/4 mile dirt oval (3/13/55 - c.1956)

Classic South Speedway - see: Gordon Park Speedway

Columbus - 1/5 mile dirt oval (8/09/41 - 1942)

Columbus Fairgrounds - Columbus / at the Chattahoochee Valley Fairgrounds
    1/2 mile dirt oval (10/25/17)

Columbus Speedway - Columbus - 1/2 mile dirt oval (c.7/25/48 - c.1953)

Columbus Super Speedway - Columbus - 1/4 mile paved oval (c.1949 - c.9/02/57)
    1/2 mile paved oval (c.1949 - c.1955) / Jimmy Thomas was the promoter
    (aka: Rocket Speedway)

Cordele Motor Speedway - Cordele - 3/8 mile dirt oval (1982 - present)
    (aka: Cordele Speedway) / (aka: Interstate Raceway)

Cordele Municipal Airport - Cordele - paved runway road course (5/14/60-5/15/60)

Cordele Speedway - Cordele - dirt oval (1950's)

Coweta Raceway Park - Newnan / (aka: Coweta County Speedway)
    1/4 mile dirt oval (1959 - 1979) (1981 - 1989) (c.1993 - present)

Crazy 8 Speedway - see: International City Speedway

CSRA Timing Assn. Dragstrip - Waynesboro - 1/4 mile paved dragstrip (1950's)

Cummings Speedway - Forsyth - dirt oval (early 1970's)
    this track was not Forsyth County Speedway

Dahlonega Speedway - Dahlonega - dirt oval (1960's)

Dallas Speed Bowl - Dallas - 3/8 mile dirt oval (7/04/54 - 1963)
    (aka: Dallas Speedway) / held races New Years Day 1955,1956,1957,1958,1959

Dallas - also see: Southeastern Int'l Dragway

Dalton - 3/4 mile dirt oval (late 1940's)

Dalton Speedway - Dalton - 1/3 mile dirt oval (c.1961)

Dan Bowles Speedway - Augusta - dirt oval (1930's) / was a horse track

Dawsonville Speedway - see: Thunder Lake Speedway

176

Dixie Raceways - Bainbridge - paved road course (1965) / maybe at an airport
    1/4 mile paved dragstrip (c.1960)

Dixie Speedway - Atlanta - see: Atlanta Speedway

Dixie Speedway - Jasper - 1/4 mile dirt oval (7/04/53 - 1954)
    located five miles south of town on SR 143

Dixie Speedway - Ringgold - see: Lake Winnepansaukie Speedway

Dixie Speedway - Woodstock - 1/3 mile dirt tri-oval (5/07/69 - 1973)
    1/3 mile paved tri-oval (1974 - 1976) / track was built by Bud Lunsford
    3/8 mile dirt tri-oval (3/26/77 - present) / (aka: Dixie Tri-Oval Speedway)
    Hal Hamrick was promoter in 1974-1976 / Mike Swims promoter since 1977
    Bill Elliott started his driving career here in 1974

Dodge County Speedway - see: Eastman Speedway

Donalsonville Road Course - Donalsonville - paved road course (years unknown)

Double H Drag Strip - Blue Ridge - 1/4 mile paved dragstrip (1965)

Douglas County Speedway - see: Seven Flags Speedway

Douglasville Fairgrounds - Douglasville - 1/2 mile dirt oval (years unknown)
    located at the Douglas County Fairgrounds

Douglasville - also see: Seven Flags Speedway

Duffie Sandpit Speedway - Augusta - dirt oval (1970) / off of Milledgeville Road

Eastman Fairgrounds - Eastman / located at the American Legion Fairgrounds
    1/2 mile dirt oval (11/12/39) (1951) (1955) (1958)
    (aka: Dodge County Speedway) / (aka: Eastman Speedway)

Elberton Airport Dragstrip - Elberton - 1/4 mile paved dragstrip (1960's & 1970's)

Ellijay Speedway - Ellijay - 1/3 mile dirt oval (years unknown)
    (aka: Gilmer County Speedway)

Fairburn Dragway (Road Course) - see: Skyport Speedway

Flower Bowl Speedway - Summerville - dirt oval (c.1948)

Forsyth County Dragway - Cumming - 1/4 mile paved dragstrip (5/05/63 - c.1963)
    located four miles west of Cumming on Highway 20 / next to oval track

Forsyth County Speedway - Cumming - 4/10 mile dirt oval (1968 - 1976)
    the located was next to the Forsyth County Dragway

Fort Oglethorpe Speedway - Fort Oglethorpe - dirt oval (early 1950's)

Four-Forty-One Speedway - Dublin / (aka: 441 Speedway)
    1/2 mile dirt oval (1960 - 1982) (1985 - 1989) (1991 - present)

Fulton County Dragway - see: Skyport Speedway

Gainesville Fairgrounds - Gainesville / at the Northeast Georgia Fairgrounds
    1/2 mile dirt oval (1946 - 1947) (1949) / (aka: Gainesville Speedway)
    a horse track located in downtown Gainesville / promoted by Max Looper

Gainesville Municipal Airport - Gainesville - paved dragstrip (c.8/28/55 - c.1958)
paved road course (5/25/57 - 1959) / (aka: Gainesville Speedway Drag Strip)

Gainesville Speedway - Gainesville / promoted by Max Looper
1/2 mile dirt oval (1949 - 1956) / actually closer to a 5/8 mile
the track was located four miles north of Gainesville on US 129
the site is now part of Lake Sidney Lanier / lake filled in winter of 1956

Gainesville Speedway - see: Max Looper Speedway

Gainesville - also see: Braselton, Hall County, Lanier, Max Looper, Road Atlanta

Garden City Speedway - Augusta - 1/2 mile dirt oval (c.1948 - c.1954)
the track was located at Kissinger and White Road

Georgia Int'l Speedway - see: Peach State Speedway

Georgia Speedway - Macon - dirt oval (1948) / maybe Central City Park Speedway

Georgia State Fairgrounds - see: Central City Park Speedwy

Gilmer County Speedway - see: Ellijay Speedway

Gold Star Speedway - Savannah / on White Bluff Road / (aka: Ranch Park)
1/5 mile dirt oval (12/08/40 - c.11/23/41) / (aka: Savannah Speedway)

Golden Isles Speedway - Waynesville - 1/2 mile dirt oval (11/30/70 - present)
built by S.O. Jenkins

The half-mile dirt track of Golden Isles Speedway. Jesse Guy has owned and operated this track since 1989. - Official track photo.

Gordon Park Speedway - Augusta (Grovetown) / same site as Hayloft Speedway
1/2 mile dirt oval (c.1979 - present) / (aka: Classic South Raceway)

Greensboro Dragstrip - Greensboro - 1/4 mile paved dragstrip (1960's)

Griffin Speedway - Griffin - dirt oval (c.1947)

Habersham Speedway - Toccoa - 1/2 mile dirt oval (1946 - 1948)

Hall County Speedway - Gainesville - 1/4 mile dirt oval (1957 - 1959) (1962 - 1970)

Hamilton Speedway - see: Atlanta Speedway

Hampton Downs Race Track - Hampton - 1/2 mile dirt oval (10/29/67)
    ran a AMA motorcycle race / located next to Atlanta Int'l Raceway

Hartwell Motor Speedway - Hartwell / (aka: Hartwell Speedway)
    3/8 mile dirt oval (c.1972 - c.1977) (1985 - present) / (aka: Hartwell Raceway)

Hartwell - paved dragstrip (1950's or 1960's)

Hawkinsville Fairgrounds (Speedway) - see: Pulaski County Speedway

Hayloft Speedway - Augusta (Grovetown) / built by H.G. Carmichael
    3/8 mile dirt oval (3/29/48 - 1955) / (aka: Carmichael Speedway)
    Gober Sosebee won a NASCAR Grand National race here on 6/01/52
    located near Camp Gordon (now called Fort Gordon)
    (aka: Augusta Speedway) / now the site of Gordon Park Speedway

Head Hunters Putt Putt Bush Track - Eatonton / run by the Head Hunters Club
    1/8 mile paved dragstrip (c.1987 - 1992) / new track aside of old track
    1/8 mile paved dragstrip (1993 - present) / grandstands now on old strip

Hiawassee Speedway - Hiawassee - dirt oval (years unknown)

Holiday Downs Speedway - Fairburn (Palmetto) / formerly a horse track
    1/3 mile dirt oval (1968 - 1970) / located next to the Skyport Speedway

Hollywood Speedway - Hollywood - 1/4 mile dirt oval (1956) / ran only two races
    the neighbors didn't like the track so the owner built chicken coops
    the track was located just north of Toccoa

Homer G. Walker Speedway - Macon - dirt oval (1940's & 1950's)

Houston County Dragway - see: Warner Robins Dragway

Houston County Speedway - see: International City Speedway

Hunter Army Air Field - Savannah - 3.5 & 5.0 mile paved road courses (3/14/54)

Huston Brothers Dragstrip - see: Skyport Speedway

I-16 Dragway - see: Twiggs County Dragway

I-75 Speedway - Valdosta - 1/2 mile dirt oval (April, 1962 - 1966)
    located south of Valdosta off of I-75 / (aka: Valdosta 75 Speedway)
    ran NASCAR GN races on 8/25/62, 6/23/64 & 6/25/65

International City Speedway - Warner Robins / (aka: Crazy 8 Speedway)
    1/4 mile dirt oval (c.1964 - 1981) / (aka: Houston County Speedway)

Interstate Raceway - see: Cordele Motor Speedway

J & J Speedway - see: New Cochran Speedway

Jackson County Speedway - Jefferson - 1/2 mile dirt oval (5/16/48)

Jefco Speedway - see: Peach State Speedway

Jessup - dirt oval (1950)

Jones County Speedway - see: Modified Sportsman Speedway

Keysville Speedway - see: Tye Harden Speedway

LaGrange Speedway - see: Troup County Speedway

Lake Winnepansaukie Speedway - Ringgold / (aka: Dixie Speedway)
    1/4 mile dirt oval (c.1946 - c.1949) / located near Chattanooga, Tennessee

Lakeside Fairgrounds Speedway - Augusta / located at the Augusta Fairgrounds
    1/2 mile dirt oval (c.1914 - c.1929) / Eddie Hearne won in 1914
    located near Lake Olmstead on Washington Road

Lakewood Speedway - Atlanta / located at the Southeastern Fairgrounds
    1.0 mile dirt oval (1915 - 10/02/41) (9/02/45 - 9/03/79)
    the fairgrounds was built in 1915 / ran motorcycles only in 1915 & 1916
    first auto races were on 7/28/17 (Ralph DePalma & Barney Oldfield winners)
    the first stock car race at Lakewood was held on 11/12/38
    Frank Mundy started his racing career here in 1939
    George Robson & George Barringer fatally injured in a crash on 9/02/46
    1/4 mile dirt oval (7/11/46 - 1948) (1951) (5/28/66)
    ran 11 NASCAR GN races from 11/11/51 to 6/14/59 / (aka: Little Lakewood)
    Frank Luptow fatally injured here in a AAA stock car crash on 9/21/52
    1/4 mile dirt dragstrip (4/25/54 - c.1957) / first official GA drag races
    the promoters in the 1940's & 1950's was Ted Edwards
    Bob Flock teamed up with Ted Edwards as promoters of the dragstrip
    also held motorboat races on the lake inside of the oval track

Looking at the first turn of Lakewood Speedway. Occasionally drivers would end up in the lake after an accident. - Joe Cawley photo.

Lanier Raceway - Gainesville (Braselton) - 3/8 mile dirt oval (1982 - 1986)
3/8 mile paved oval (1987 - present) / built by Bud Lunsford
track is located across from Road Atlanta (road course)
track owner Bud Lunsford was the 1987 RPM Promoter of the Year

Lavonia Speedway - Lavonia - 4/10 mile dirt oval (6/16/56 - July, 1956)

Lavonia Speedway - see: New Lavonia Speedway

Lithonia Speedway - Lithonia / (aka: Lithonia-DeKalb Speedway)
1/2 mile dirt oval (9/15/48 - c.1951) / located on SR 124
1/4 mile dirt oval (c.1960 - 1967)
ran by Dixie Stock Car Racing Club (blacks) / also ran races for whites

Lloyd's Drag Strip - Blairsville - 1/5 mile paved/dirt dragstrip (5/05/63 - c.1964)
1/5 mile paved dragstrip (1965 - 1967) / race schedule 4/28/63 rained out
built by Lloyd, Grace and Donald Young

Lyons Fairgrounds - see: Vidalia Airport

Mableton Speedway - Mableton - dirt oval (8/21/48 - 1949)
located 10 miles west of Atlanta at Bankhead Highway & Gordon Road

Macon Fairgrounds (Speedway) - see: Central City Park Speedway

Macon Raceway - Bryon / (aka: Middle Georgia Raceway)
1/2 (.5479) mile paved oval (5/10/66 - 8/28/82) (10/14/84 - 11/18/84)
a still was found under the track by revenuers in Sept. of 1967
ran a number of NASCAR GN races / first one 9/08/51 / last one 11/07/71
track was located at the Peach State Fairgrounds

Macon Stadium Speedway - see: Centennial Stadium

*Jody Ridley from Chatsworth, GA is one of the nation's best pavement short
track drivers. He is a champion on the NASCAR sanctioned All-Pro Series.
This picture is from the Birmingham Fairgrounds. - Rolland Rickard photo.*

Macon - also see: Centennial, Central City, Georgia Speedway, Homer Walker

Max Looper Speedway - Gainesville / (aka: Gainesville Speedway)
5/8 mile dirt oval (6/05/48 - c.11/14/48) (1952 - 1956)
promoted by Max Looper / Goober Sosebee won the first race
site was covered by water when Lake Lanier was filled in winter of 1956

McRae - dirt oval (1950)

McRae Speedway - McRae / (aka: Telfair County Speedway)
1/2 mile dirt oval (early 1960's - 1972) (1981 - 1982)

Middle Georgia Dirt Track - see: New Cochran Speedway

Middle Georgia Raceway - see: Macon Speedway

Modified Sportsman Speedway - Gray / (aka: Jones County Speedway)
1/4 mile dirt oval (1960's)

Montezuma Speedway - Montezuma - dirt oval (years unknown)

Morris Station Speedway - see: New Atlanta Speedway

Morrow Speedway - Morrow - 3/4 mile dirt oval (c.1952 - c.1955)

New Atlanta Speedway - Atlanta - 5/8 mile dirt oval (1947 - 1952)
built by Ted Edwards in 1946 / Bob Flock bought the track in 1946
south of town on Jonesboro Road / (aka: Morris Station Speedway)

New Cochran Speedway - Cochran / (aka: J & J Speedway)
3/8 mile dirt oval (1981 - c.1984) (c.1987 - 1989) (1992 - present)
(aka: Middle Georgia Dirt Track) / (aka: Central Georgia Speedway)
called 4/10 mile at one time / (aka: Cochran Motor Speedway)

New Lavonia Speedway - Lavonia - 3/8 mile dirt oval (1971 - 1989)
3/8 mile paved oval (3/23/90 - present) / (aka: Lavonia Speedway)
(aka: Charlie's Speedway) / Charlie Mize was the promoter

New Senoia Speedway - see: Senoia Speedway

Newton (County) Dragstrip - see: Atlanta Speed Shop Dragway

North Georgia Speedway - Chatsworth / (aka: North Georgia Raceway)
1/4 mile dirt oval (1973 - c.1979) (1984 - present)

North Valdosta Race Track - see: Thunderbowl Speedway

Ocilla Speedway - Ocilla - dirt oval (1938)

Oglethorpe Speedway - Savannah - 1/2 mile dirt oval (5/06/51 - present)
ran NASCAR Grand Nat'ls races on 3/28/54 & 3/06/55

Okefenokee Speedway - see: Waycross Motor Speedway

Overnite Speedway - Martinez - 1/4 mile dirt oval (1956) / off Davis Road
the track was built overnight by Harold Lonegan in his clay pit with the use
of a borrowed county road grader that was left on his property

Palmer Speedway - Warner Robins - 1/4 mile dirt oval (c.1954 - c.1958)

Paradise Dragstrip - Calhoun - 1/8 & 1/4 mile paved dragstrips (1961 - present)
Richard Petty ran the 43jr funny car here on 4/25/65

Patten Speedway - Thomasville (Patten) / (aka: Pavo Speedway)
1/2 mile dirt oval (1963 - 1964)

Pavo Speedway - see: Patten Speedway

Peach Bowl Speedway - Atlanta - 1/4 mile dirt oval (5/28/49 - 9/17/50)
1/4 mile paved oval (9/30/50 - 1971) / built by Roy Shoemaker
1/5 mile dirt oval (c.4/16/55 - c.1955) / inside paved oval
track was located at 1040 Brady Ave. in northwest Atlanta

*"Tootle" Estes (with foot on nerf bar) celebrates after a win at the Peach Bowl
in the early 1960's. His son Rocky is behind the front wheel. The man at the
right is James Bradberry. The middle person is unknown. - Mike Bell
collection.*

Peach State Speedway - Jefferson / ran NASCAR GN races 11/03/68 & 11/02/69
1/2 mile paved oval (7/30/67 - c.1971) (7/11/81 - 1988) (1990 - present)
1/8 mile paved dragstrip (late 1960's) / (aka: Georgia Int'l Speedway)
(aka: Jefco Speedway)

Ponce De Leon Ave. Speedway - Decatur - dirt oval (years unknown)

Pulaski County Speedway - Hawkinsville / located at the Pulaski Co. Fairgrounds
1/2 mile dirt oval (c.1953 - c.1966) / (aka: Hawkinsville Speedway)
(aka: VFW Race Track) / (aka: Atomic Age Speedway)

Ranch Park - see: Gold Star Speedway

Red's Drag Strip - see: Southeastern Int'l Dragway

Ringgold - see: Brainerd, Chattanooga, Lake Winnepansaukie

Road Atlanta - Gainesville (Braselton) / home of annual National Runoffs
2.52 mile paved road course (9/13/70 - present)

Rocket Speedway - see: Columbus Super Speedway

Roebling Road Raceway - Savannah - 2.05 mile paved road course (1954 - present)
(aka: Savannah International Raceway) / built by Robert Roebling

Rome - dirt oval (1950)

Rome Speedway - Rome - 3/8 mile dirt oval (c.1957 - c.1967)
1/2 mile dirt oval (c.1967 - present) / (aka: Rome International Speedway)

Rome - also see: Chulio Speedway, Turkey Mountain Speedway

Saint Simons Island - paved road course (6/15/57) (6/16/57) (6/14/59)
held sports car races on the runways of the Malcolm B. McKinnon Airport

Sand Mountain Speedway - Trenton - dirt oval (mid-1970's)

Savannah - 1.0 mile dirt oval (2/23/04)

Savannah - 1/4 mile paved dragstrip (1961)

Savannah Dragstrip - Savannah - 1/8 mile paved dragstrip (1965 - present)
located on US 17, next to Savannah Speedway

Savannah Fair Speedway - Savannah / located at the Chatham Co. Fairgrounds
1/2 mile dirt oval (c.1924) (1931) (9/15/35 - 11/26/39) / maybe 1940 too

Savannah Int'l Speedway - see: Roebling Road

Savannah Speedway - Savannah - 1/2 (.479) mile dirt oval (1962 - c.8/25/67) (1981)
LeeRoy Yarbrough won his first NASCAR GN race here on 6/01/64
also ran NASCAR GN races on 4/30/67, 8/25/67, 10/17/69, & 3/15/70
1/2 mile paved oval (c.10/17/69 - 1981) / (aka: New Savannah Speedway)
located on US 17, next to Savannah Dragway
the oval track was purchased in 1981 by the promoter of Oglethorpe
Speedway, so no one else could run this track opposite his other track

Savannah Speedway - Savannah - 1/4 mile paved oval (12/01/40)

Savannah Speedway - Savannah - dirt oval (1948)

Savannah Speedway - see: Gold Star Speedway

Savannah Vanderbilt Cup Grand Prix - Savannah
(aka: Savannah-Effingham Raceway) / ran prestigious American Grand Prize
17.14 mile city street road course (3/18/08 & 3/19/08)
9.8 mile city street road course (11/25/08)
25.13 mile city street road course (11/26/08)
17.3 mile city street road course (11/11/10 & 11/12/10)
17.1 mile city street road course (11/27/11 - 11/30/11)
Ralph Mulford won the 1911 Vanderbilt Cup race here on 11/27/11

Savannah-Effingham Motorway - Savannah - paved road course (1965)

Savannah-Effingham Raceway - see: Savannah Vanderbilt Cup Grand Prix

Savannah - also see: Gold Star, Hunter, Oglethorpe, Roebling Road, Sea Island

Sea Island Beach - Savannah - dirt oval (8/02/36) / located near St. Simons Island

Senoia Speedway - Senoia - 3/8 mile dirt oval (1967 - 1988)
3/8 mile paved oval (3/12/89 - present) / (aka: Senoia Raceway)
(aka: New Senoia Raceway)

Sessions Lake - Dublin - 1/5 mile dirt oval (8/17/41 - 1942)

Seven Flags Speedway - Douglasville / (aka: West Atlanta Speedway)
3/8 mile dirt oval (1968 - 1983) (1987 - present)
(aka: Douglas County Speedway) / (aka: Douglasville Speedway)
was to become a 1/2 mile paved oval and called Warren Speedway in 1984

Silver Dollar Raceway - Reynolds - 1/8 mile paved dragstrip (c.6/05/94 - present)

Skyport Speedway - Fairburn - 1/4 mile paved dragstrip (1954 - 1970's)
1/4 mile dirt oval (April, 1959 - c.1959) / the promoter was Ted Edwards
2.0 mile paved/dirt road course (3/18/56) / (aka: Fulton County Dragway)
the road course main straight was a paved runway, the rest was dirt
(aka: Fairburn Dragway) / (aka: Skyway Speedway) / (aka: Skyway Airport)
(aka: Fairburn Road Course) / (aka: Skyway Airport Race Track)
tracks were located four miles south of town at the old Fairburn Airport
turned back into an airport in the 1980's / (aka: Huston Brothers Dragstrip)

Skyway Airport - see: Skyport Speedway

Skyway Speedway - Calhoun - 1/2 mile dirt oval (1947 - 1948) / ran midgets

Southeastern Int'l Dragway - Dallas - 1/4 mile dirt dragstrip (c.1956)
1/4 mile paved dragstrip (1956 - present) / aka: Red's Drag Strip)
Richard Petty crashed his 43jr. funny car on the dragstrip in 1965
the dragstrip was completely redone in 1988 / it is now a 1/8 mile strip

The drivers at Toccoa Speedway in 1956 pose for a group picture. Note the lack
of driving uniforms and variety of racing helmets, including what looks like a
football helmet on one driver in the middle. - Mike Bell collection.

Southeastern Speedway - Covington / (aka: Sugar Bowl Speedway) / near Conyers
1/4 mile paved oval (7/13/62 - c.1968) / called Sugar Bowl in 1962 & 1963

Southern Dragway - Douglas - 1/8 mile paved dragstrip (1988 - present)

Speedway Park - Martinez - 1/4 mile dirt oval (1949 - c.8/01/53) / on Highway 28
1/4 mile paved oval (8/2/53 - 1964) / (aka: Bower's Speedway)

Speedway Park - Swainsboro - 1/4 mile dirt oval (1969 - early 1970's)
3/8 mile dirt oval (9/14/92 - present)

Stockbridge - 1/2 mile dirt oval (late 1930's) / moonshiners raced their cars
Bob & Fonty Flock started here / the track was in a cow pasture

Sugar Bowl Speedway - see: Southeastern Speedway

Sugar Creek Raceway - Blue Ridge - 1/2 mile dirt oval (1968 - c.1971)
1/3 mile dirt oval (1985 - present) / (aka: Blue Ridge Speedway)

*Sugar Creek Raceway from the air. The three-eighths-mile red-clay oval runs
their weekly program on Friday nights. - Official track photo.*

Suicide Circle - Albany - 1/2 mile dirt oval (late 1950's) / southeast side of town

Swainsboro Raceway - Swainsboro / (aka: Swainsboro Motor Speedway)
1/2 mile dirt oval (c.1964 - c.1975) (1980 - present)
(aka: Cee-Jay Speedway)

Swainsboro - also see: Speedway Park

Telfair County Speedway - see: McRae Speedway

Theresa Speedway - Douglas - 1/2 mile dirt oval (late 1970's)

Thomaston Super Speedway - Thomaston - 1/2 mile dirt oval (9/08/46 - 1955)
promoted by Jack Smith / (aka: Thomaston Speedway)

Thomasville - 1/2 mile dirt oval (early 1930's) / ran motorcycles

Thomson Airport Dragstrip - Thomson - 1/4 mile paved dragstrip (1950's)

Thunder Lake Speedway - Dawsonville - 1/2 mile dirt oval (late 1950's)
(aka: Dawson County Speedway) / (aka: Dawsonville Speedway) / Go-Karts?

Thunderbowl Speedway - Valdosta - 3/8 mile dirt oval (1957- 1962)(1968 - present)
1/8 mile paved dragstrip (c.1983) / (aka: North Valdosta Race Track)

Tifton Speedway - Tifton - 1/2 mile dirt oval (1949 - 1950) / maybe a fairgrounds

Toccoa Speedway - Toccoa - 1/4 mile dirt oval (5/07/55 - 1972)
3/8 mile dirt oval (1973 - present) / built by Garland Sheriff

Troup County Speedway - La Grange - 1/3 mile dirt oval (1953 - 1959)
1/2 mile dirt oval (c.4/03/55 - c.1955) / (aka: LaGrange Speedway)
3/8 mile dirt oval (c.1965 - c.1969) / located on Highway 219 near US 27

Turkey Mountain Speedway - Rome - dirt oval (mid-1960's)

Turner Air Force Base - Albany / (aka: Sowega Airport)
4.5 mile paved road course (10/26/52)
5.0 mile paved road course (10/25/53 - 10/24/54)

Twiggs County Dragway - Jeffersonville / (aka: I-16 Dragway)
1/8 mile paved dragstrip (c.1981- present)

Twin Lakes Raceway - Elberton - 1/4 mile dirt oval (July, 1957 - 1960)
Charlie Mize was the last promoter

Tye Harden Speedway - Keysville - 1/4 mile dirt oval (1980)
(aka: Keysville Speedway) / built by Herbert Reese

U.S. 19 Dragway - Albany / (aka: Albany Dragway)
1/8 mile paved dragstrip (c.1969 - present)

Valdosta 75 Speedway - see: I-75 Speedway

Valdosta - also see: Thunderbowl Speedway

VFW Raceway Track - see: Pulaski County Speedway

Vidalia Airport - Vidalia - 1/2 mile dirt oval (1949 - 1951) / next to runways
paved road course on runways (1950's or 1960's) / (aka: Lyons Fairgrounds)
1/8 mile paved dragstrip (c.1964 - 1986) / (aka: Vidalia Dragstrip)

Ware Speedway - see: Waycross Motor Speedway

Warner Robins Dragway - Warner Robins / (aka: Houston County Dragway)
1/4 & 1/8 mile dragstrips (1965 - present) / located on Highway 96

Warner Robins - also see: International City Speedway, Palmer Speedway

Waycross Motor Speedway - Waycross - 1/2 mile dirt oval (1959 - present)
(aka: Okefenokee Speedway) / (aka: Ware Speedway)

West Atlanta Speedway - see: Seven Flags Speedway

Winder-Barrow Speedway - Winder
1/4 mile dirt oval (1963 - 1984) (c.1992 - present)

Wrightsville - 1/4 mile paved dragstrip (9/18/55 - c.1955)

Yellow River Dragstrip - Covington - 1/4 mile paved dragstrip (c.1963 - c.1969)
11 spectators were killed in a crash here in 1969 / not Atlanta Speed Shop
promoter: Buck Campbell / site is now a mobile home park next to I-20

Zebulon 8 Raceway - Zebulon - 3/8 mile dirt oval (1968 - 1973)

HAWAII

Civic Auditorium - Honolulu (Oahu) - 300 foot concrete oval (2/01/57) / ran Micros

Dillingham Field - Mokuleia (Oahu)
3.0 mile paved road course (4/21/57) (5/11/58) (7/07/59)

Hawaii Raceway Park - Ewa Beach (Oahu) - 1/4 mile dirt oval (1/01/62 - present)
1/4 mile paved dragstrip (c.1964 - present)
2.0 mile paved road course (c.1973 - c.1975)
1.3 mile paved road course (1992 - present)

Hawaii Speedway - Honolulu (Oahu) - dirt oval (3/15/35 - c.5/04/41)
(aka: Honolulu Speedway) / ran midgets

Hilo Dragstrip - Hilo (Hawaii) - 1/4 mile paved dragstrip (c.1981 - present)

Hilo (Hawaii) - dirt oval (1953)

Honolulu (Oahu) - dirt oval (1924) ran big cars

Honolulu Speedway - see: Hawaii Speedway

Honolulu Stadium - Honolulu (Oahu) - dirt oval (1951 - 1957)
located at a baseball stadium / NASCAR sanctioned track

Kahului Fairgrounds - Kahului (Maui) - 1.0 mile dirt oval (1952 - 1953)
(aka: Kahului Stadium) / NASCAR sanctioned track

Kauai County Fairgrounds - Kauai - dirt oval (c.1952) / NASCAR sanctioned track

Kauai Raceway Park - Mana (Kauai) - 1/4 mile paved dragstrip (1973 - present)

Kuhuka Field - Oaka (location unknown) - paved airport road course (early 1960's)

Maui Raceway Park - Puunene (Maui) - 1/4 mile paved dragstrip (1963 - present)

Olympic Park - Waikiki (Oahu) - 1/4 mile dirt oval (c.4/25/36 - 1941) / ran midgets

Pearl City (Oahu) - 1/4 mile dirt oval (early 1950's)

IDAHO

Airport Speedway - see: Pocatello Super Speedway

Allen - dirt oval (late 1920's)

Blackfoot Fairgrounds - Blackfoot - 1/2 mile dirt oval (c.9/12/52 - c.1953)
  located at the Eastern Idaho State Fairgrounds

Boise - 1/4 mile paved dragstrip (c.1956)

Boise Fairgrounds - Boise / located at the Western Idaho State Fairgrounds
  1/2 mile dirt oval (7/04/15) (c.10/02/20 - c.1940) (c.1947 - c.1951)
  (aka: Intermountain Fairgrounds) / ran motorcycle race in 1915

Boise - paved road course (1950's)

Caldwell Rodeo Arena - Caldwell - 1/10 mile indoor paved oval (c.1992 - present)

Cambridge Fairgrounds - Cambridge - 3/8 mile dirt oval (early 1950's)
  located at the Washington County Fairgrounds

Colburn Raceways - Sandpoint - 1/2 mile dirt oval (was to have run on 7/06/68)
  also proposed was a 2.75 mile paved road course & 1/4 mile paved dragstrip
  have not confirmed that the facility was ever finished

Dragway City Raceway - Pocatello / formerly a WWII Air Base
  1/4 & 1/8 mile paved dragstrips (1958 - present) / (aka: Pocatello Dragway)
  (aka: Pocatello Dragstrip) / (aka: Pocatello Raceway Park)
  (aka: Intermountain Raceway Park)

Empire Raceway - Post Falls (Stateline) - 1/8 mile dirt oval (1994 - present)
  located behind current Stateline Stadium / located near Coeur d'Alene

Firebird Raceway - Emmett - 1/4 mile paved dragstrip (1967 - present)
  3/8 mile paved oval (1971 - c.1986) (c.1990) / (aka: Super Oval Speedway)
  (aka: Firebird Dragway)

This pretty asphalt track is Magic Valley Speedway in Twin Falls, Idaho. The NASCAR sanctioned track was built in 1986. - Official track photo.

Freedom Bird Raceway - see: Noise Park Raceway

Hillside Speedway - Moscow - dirt oval (c.1961 - c.1962)

Idaho State Fairgrounds - see: Blackfoot Fairgrounds, Boise Fairgrounds

Intermountain Raceway Park - see: Drag City Raceway

Lehmi County Motorsports - Salmon / located at the Lehmi County Fairgrounds
1/4 mile dirt oval (May, 1994 - present)

Lewiston Fairgrounds - Lewiston - 1/2 mile dirt oval (10/12/12)
located at the Interstate Fairgrounds

Lewiston Rodeo Grounds - Lewiston - dirt oval (c.1951 - c.1955)
located at the Lewiston Roundup Grounds

Lewiston Speedway - Lewiston - 1/4 mile paved oval (c.1962 - 1976)
located in North Lewiston area / later became a junkyard

Magic Valley Speedway - Rupert - 3/8 mile paved oval (1971 - 1982)

Magic Valley Speedway - Twin Falls - 3/8 mile dirt oval (5/17/86 - 1987)
3/8 mile paved oval (1988 - present) / built to replace track in Rupert

Meridian Speedway - Meridian - 1/4 mile dirt oval (1949 - c.1954)
1/4 mile paved oval (c.1954 - present)
track was outside of a high school football field at one time

Noise Park Raceway - Idaho Falls - 1/3 mile dirt oval (1980 - 1993)
(aka: Russet Lions Noise Park) / (aka: Freedom Bird Raceway)

Northwest Speedway - see: Stateline Speedway

Owyhee Motorcycle Club Raceway - Boise - 1/8 mile dirt oval (1987 - present)
started running auto in 1987 / a motorcycle racing complex open since 1943

Panhandle Speedway - Sandpoint - 1/2 mile dirt oval (1974 - 1981)

Pocatello Dragway - see: Dragway City Raceway

Pocatello Speedway - Pocatello - 1/4 mile paved oval (1956 - present)
(aka: Airport Speedway) / (aka: Pocatello Super Speedway)

Owyhee Motorcycle Club Raceway is a typical one-eighth mile Modified-Midget track. Sharing the card this night were Modified-Midgets, Motorcycles, and Go-Karts. - Allan E. Brown photo.

190

Riverside Speedway - Potlatch - 1/4 mile dirt oval (c.1959 - 1964)

Russet Lions Noise Park - see: Noise Park Raceway

Skyline Speedway - Idaho Falls - paved oval (c.1962 - 1966)

Sportsman Speedway - Blackfoot - 1/4 mile paved oval (c.5/22/65 - c.8/29/70)

Stateline Stadium & Speedway - Post Falls (Stateline) / near Couer d'Alene
1/4 mile paved oval (1972 - present) / 1/2 mile from old Stateline Spwy
Track's buildings were destroyed during a riot at a rock concert in 1976
(aka: Northwest Speedway) / (aka: State Line Speedway)
sister track is Ephrata Speedway in Washington / next to Empire Raceway

Stateline Speedway - Stateline - 1/5 mile dirt oval (early 1960's)
1/5 mile paved oval (c.1963 - 9/07/64) / burned to ground in Aug. of 1984
located 1/2 mile south of current State Line Speedway

Super Oval Speedway - see: Firebird Dragway

Thunder Bluff Raceway - Twin Falls - 3/8 mile dirt oval (1976 - 1985)

Tumbleweed Raceway - Mountain Home - 1/4 mile paved dragstrip (c.1981-c.1986)

Wilkins Speedway - Caldwell - dirt oval (c.1949 - c.1950)

ILLINOIS

124th Field Artillery Armory - see: Chicago Armory

3-I Ball Park - Springfield - 1/5 mile dirt oval (1935 - 1937)
the track surrounded the playing field of a ball diamond

87th Street Speedway - Chicago / at 1111 East 87th St. / (aka: Gill Stadium)
1/4 mile dirt oval (c.8/29/48 - 1949) (4/20/52 - 5/03/53)
1/4 mile paved oval (5/10/53 - c.8/16/56) / was a former softball park
site is now the vacant Community Discount Department Store
Red Duvall won the last race on dirt and the first race on pavement

The cars are practicing at 87th Street Speedway in 1955. - Bob Sheldon photo.

Admiral Stadium - Des Plaines - 1/10 mile dirt oval (6/14/51 - 8/30/51) TQ midgets
the site was sold to an electric company for a new sub station

Albion Fairgrounds - Albion - 1/2 mile dirt oval (1950's)
1/8 mile dirt oval (1992) / located at the Edwards County Fairgrounds
ran stocks in 1950's / ran Modified-midgets in 1992 - rained out in 1993

Aledo Fairgrounds - see: Mercer County Speedway

Alton Drag Raceway - Alton - 1/4 mile paved dragstrip (c.1961 - c.1971)

Alton Speedway - see: Godfrey Speedway

Amboy - 1/2 mile dirt oval (1929 & 1930) / probably at the Lee Co. Fairgrounds

American Giants Ball Park - Chicago / located at 39th & Wentworth
1/5 mile dirt oval (9/24/39) / raced around baseball diamond
the stadium was a Negro league ball diamond / drivers were all blacks

The American Giants Ball Park in 1939. - Bob Sheldon collection.

American Legion Speedway - see: Legion Speedway

Anna Fairgrounds - Anna - 1/2 mile dirt oval (9/01/34) / at Union Co. Fairgrounds

Arcola Speedway - Arcola - 1/8 mile dirt oval (c.1987 - 1989)

Atomic Speedway - Knoxville - 1/5 mile dirt oval (1950)

Augusta Fairgrounds - Augusta - 1/6 mile dirt oval (1977) / ran T.Q. midgets
located at the Hancock County Fairgrounds

Aurora Downs - North Aurora (Chicago) - 1.0 mile dirt oval (7/03/27 - c.1930)
1/2 mile dirt oval (5/30/47 - 6/13/54) (7/22/60 - 1962) / a horse track
later became Fox Fields / torn down in the late 1980's

Avon Fairgrounds - Avon / located at the Fat Steer Show fairgrounds
1/8 mile dirt oval (1982 & 1983) / ran T.Q. midgets during the fair

Baldwin Park - Quincy / probably located at the Adams County Fairgrounds
1/2 mile dirt oval (c.8/12/28 - c.1935) (7/21/40)

Baty's Barn - Peoria - 1/10 mile indoor dirt oval (3/18/56 - 1956)
1/8 mile (outdoor) dirt oval (6/17/56 - c.1956) / ran Micro-midgets

Belle-Clair Speedway - Belleville / located at the St. Clair County Fairgrounds
1/2 mile dirt oval (1946) / Arnie Knepper started driving here in 1948
1/5 mile dirt oval (6/15/48 - present)

Belleville Athletic Field - Belleville - 1/5 mile dirt oval (c.8/02/36 - 1939)

Belmont Fairgrounds - Belmont / located at the Wabash County Fairgrounds
1/2 mile dirt oval (c.8/17/58 - c.1964) / replaced fairgrounds in Mt. Carmel

Belvidere Fairgrounds - Belvidere / located at the Boone County Fairgrounds
1/2 mile dirt oval (9/09/18) (1946 & 1947)

Bennett Raceway - Utica - paved road course (c.1984 - present) / Go-Kart track
(aka: Utica Raceway) / ocassionally local sports car clubs use this track

Benton Fairgrounds - Benton / located at the Franklin County Fairgrounds
1/2 mile dirt oval (5/13/28 - 1929) (4/13/47 - c.1949)

Benton Raceway - Benton - 1/4 mile dirt oval (1971 - 1973)

Blackhawk Farms Raceway - Rockton - 1.8 mile paved road course (c.1970 - 1990)
1.95 mile paved road course (1991 - present)

Bloomington Fairgrounds - Bloomington - dirt oval (1920's)
located at the McLean County Fairgrounds

Bob-Jo Speedway - see: Sycamore Speedway

Bond County Fairgrounds - Sherman - 1/4 mile dirt oval (1994 - present)

Bourbon Fairgrounds - Bourbon / probably located at the Douglas County
Fairgrounds 1/2 mile dirt oval (early 1950's)

Breese - 1/2 mile dirt oval (10/09/27)

Broken Springs Speedway - Dupo - dirt oval (1950) / (aka: Valley Park Speedway)

Browning Field - East Moline - 1/4 mile cinder oval (c.1934 - late 1935)

Brownstown Fairgrounds - see: Fayette County Speedway

Bureau County Speedway - Princeton / located at the Bureau County Fairgrounds
1/2 mile dirt oval (c.1951 - c.1973) / (aka: Princeton Raceway)
1/4 mile dirt oval (1981 - present)

Bushnell Speedway - Bushnell - 1/2 mile dirt oval (1937)
1/5 mile dirt oval (c.1950 - 1952)

Byron Dragway - Rockford / (aka: Rockford Dragway)
1/4 mile paved dragstrip (7/04/64 - 1987) (1994 - present)

Cahokia Dragstrip - Cahokia - 1/4 mile paved dragstrip (c.1954 - c.1960)

Cahokia Midget Speedway - Cahokia - 1/4 mile dirt oval (c.8/13/38 - 6/14/42)
Jimmy Snyder fatally injured here in a crash on 6/29/39 / located on SR 3
grandstands burned down in 1945 / (aka: Snyder Memorial Speedway)

Cairo - see: Cotter Field Speedway

Calumet Speed Bowl - Calumet City (Chicago) / at Torrence & 169th in (Lansing)
   built as a dog racing track (Calumet Kennel Club), but never used as such
   1/2 mile square dirt oval (late 1920's - 10/28/34)
   1/5 mile dirt oval (7/18/36 - 9/16/36) / (aka: Torrence Midget Speedway)
   the track permitted parimutuel betting at the race on 9/16/36 race and then
   held a party afterwards and the grandstands were mysteriously destroyed by
   a fire on the morning of 9/17/36 / (aka: Torrence Speedway)

Cambridge Fairgrounds - Cambridge / at the Greater Henry Co. Fairgrounds
   1/2 mile dirt oval (1950's)

Camp Ellis Air Force Base - Ipava - 1/4 mile paved dragstrip (1955 - 1956)

Camptown Acres - East Dubuque - 3/8 mile dirt oval (early 1950's)
   site is now a supper club

Canton Fairgrounds - Canton - dirt oval (early 1950's) / maybe the Lewistown Fair

Canton - also see: Spoon River Speedway

Carlinsville Fairgrounds - Carlinsville / located at the Macoupin Co. Fairgrounds
   1/2 mile dirt oval (1965)

Carmi Fairgrounds - Carmi / located at the White County Fairgrounds
   1/2 mile dirt oval (late 1940's & early 1950's) (1973)
   1/8 mile dirt oval (1973) / ran T.Q. midgets on the small track

Carpenterville - see: Meadowdale International Raceway

Carrollton Fairgrounds - Carrollton / located at the Greene County Fairgrounds
   1/2 mile dirt oval (1960's)

Carsonville - (located unknown) - dirt oval (1937)

Carthage Fairgrounds - Carthage - 1/2 mile dirt oval (1930's) / at Hancock Co Fair

Gary Bettenhausen was a two-time (1969 & 1971) USAC sprint car champion.
In this picture he glides the Willie Davis Chevy through a turn at Terre Haute
on August 11, 1968. - John Mahoney photo.

194

Bobby Grim won more than 150 sprint car features after World War II in I.M.C.A. competition. - Allan E. Brown collection.

Casner - dirt oval (1937 - c.9/19/37) / ran Hobos (jalopies) and sprint cars

Central Stadium - see: Municipal Athletic Field

Centralia - 1/4 mile paved oval (c.7/23/54)

Centralia - also see: Marion County Speedway

Champaign Airport - Champaign - 1.0 mile dirt oval (May, 1938 - c.7/04/38)

Champaign County Fairgrounds - Urbana / (aka: Champaign-Urbana Speedway)
    1/2 mile dirt oval (c.1925 - 5/30/42) (c.5/18/52 - c.1985)
    1/5 mile dirt oval (1925) / (aka: Urbana Speedway)
    1/4 mile dirt oval (5/12/40 - 6/23/42) (6/04/47 - 7/02/47) (6/03/49 - c.1951)
    (aka: Twin City Speedway) < called Twin-City from 1940 to 1942
    1/4 mile paved oval (8/27/47 - c.1948)
    grandstands burned down in 1928, and were not replaced until 1939
    (the new grandstands came from the old Kankakee Fairgrounds)

Champaign Motor Speedway - Champaign / torn down in the Spring of 1980
    1/4 & 1/2 mile dirt ovals (9/23/73 - 4/14/79) / (aka: Twin City Speedway)

Champaign - also see: Urbana, Wilson Park Speedway

Chanute Air Force Base - Rantoul - 2.875 mile paved road course (6/14/53 - 1954)

Charleston - 1/4 mile paved dragstrip (1957) / not Coles County Dragway USA

Charleston Fairgrounds - Charleston - 1/2 mile dirt oval (c.1926 - 8/18/40)
    1/4 mile dirt oval (5/09/47 - 1964) / at the Coles County Fairgrounds

Charleston Speedway - Charleston - 3/8 mile dirt oval (c.1972 - present)

Charleston - also see: Coles County Dragway USA, Humphries Speedway

Chester Speedway - Chester - 1/2 mile dirt oval (10/06/34) / at Randolph Co. Fair
    1/5 mile dirt oval (early 1950's - 1958) / (aka: Randolph County Speedway)
    the site is now a golf course

Building the wood track inside of the Chicago Armory in 1938. Only one race was held on the track. - Bob Sheldon collection.

Chicago Armory - Chicago / located at 52nd & Cottage Grove
　1/10 mile indoor dirt oval (11/18/34) / first indoor midget race
　1/5 mile indoor dirt oval (11/29/34 - 11/08/40)
　1035 foot indoor wood oval (11/13/38) / Paul Russo won on wood track
　(aka: 124 Field Artillery Armory) / now the Nat'l Guard Armory

Chicago Auditorium - Chicago - indoor paved oval (1935)

Chicago Coliseum - Chicago / located at 15th & Wabash / since torn down
　1/10 mile indoor paved oval (10/02/35) (1947 & 1948)

Chicago Fairgrounds - see: Cook County Fairgrounds

Chicago International Amphitheatre - see: International Amphitheatre

Chicago Motor Speedway - see: Evanston Speedway

Chicago Riding Club - Chicago / located at 333 East Erie (downtown)
　1/8 mile indoor dirt oval (2/24/35 - 2/12/36)
　site is now the location of the CBS TV and Radio Stadio

Chicago Speedway - Chicago (Maywood) - 2.0 mile wood oval (6/26/15 - 7/28/18)
　built by Jack Prince / turns banked 17 degrees / (aka: Speedway Park)
　Dario Resta won 500 mile AAA race on the opening day before 85,000 fans
　also held a 300 mile motorcycle race on 10/12/15
　located at 9th Ave. & 12th St. / the Hines Memorial Hospital was built
　on the site for wounded soldiers during World War I
　site is now the Loyala Medical Center Complex (NW side of Chicago)

Chicago Stadium - Chicago / home of Chicago Black Hawks (NHL hockey team)
　1/5 mile dirt indoor oval (5/08/35) / located at 1800 West Madison

Chicago Times-Herald Contest - Chicago to Evanston and then back to Chicago
105 mile road course (November 28, 1895) / this was the first scheduled auto
race in the United States / eight cars started the race, J. Frank Duryea
won at a 6.66 mph average / (the race was originally scheduled for 7/04/95
but when no cars were ready, it was held on Thanksgiving Day instead.)

Chicago-Waukegan-Chicago / two cars started the race but only one finished
92 mile road course (11/02/1895) / the event started at 55th & Halsted

Chicago - also see: 87th Street, American Giant's, Aurora Downs, Calumet Speed
Bowl, DePaul Stadium, Evanston, Expo Park, Gano Field, Half Day, Hanson
Park, Harlem, Hawthorne, Int'l Amphitheatre, Lansing, Lezi Park,
Libertyville, Mance Park, North Shore, O'Hare Stadium, Playland Park,
Raceway Park, Riverview, Rosemont Horizon, Santa Fe, Shrewbridge,
Soldiers Field, Sparta Stadium, Washington Park, White City

Clark County Speedway - see: Marshall Fairgrounds

Clearview Speedway - Paris - 1/2 mile dirt oval (5/20/28 - c.1940)
1/5 mile dirt oval (5/11/41 - 1942) / built by Frank Davis / north of town

Clinton - dirt oval (1920's & 1930's) (1941)
probably at the old DeWitt County Fairgrounds

Coles County Dragway USA - Charleston / (aka: Rolling Thunder Dragway)
1/8 mile paved dragstrip (1970 -   present)

Coles County Speedway - Mattoon / the track may have been paved at one time
1/8 mile dirt oval (1956 - c.1957) (c.1986 - present)

Cook County Fairgrounds - Chicago / located at 1600 North & 1st Ave.
1/2 mile dirt oval (8/19/34 - 1940) / (aka: Stockham's Fairgrounds)
1/4 mile dirt oval (1935) / site is now Maywood Park Horse Track

Cordova Dragstrip - Cordova - 1/4 mile paved dragstrip (Fall of 1956 - present)
(aka: Quad City Dragway) / (aka: Quad City Drag Strip)

*This view of the first turn at the board track at the Chicago Speedway shows the
17 degree banking. - Bob Sheldon collection.*

Cottage Hills - 1/4 mile paved dragstrip (c.1969)

Cotter Field Speedway - Cairo - dirt oval (1938 - 11/11/39)

Crawford County Speedway - Stoy / (aka: Robinson Speedway)
   1/4 mile dirt oval (5/08/55 - 1977) / (aka: Sportsman Park)
   located at the Illinois-Indiana Expo

Danville Fairgrounds - Danville / located at the Eastern Illinois Fair & Expo
   1/2 mile dirt oval (1917 - 1931) (7/22/34 - 6/28/42) (c.1946 - c.8/02/53)
   1/5 mile dirt oval (5/21/41 - 7/28/41) / fire destroyed grandstands 1952
   1/4 mile dirt oval (1942) (5/12/46) (6/24/56) (1962 - 1964)
   (aka: Fair Park) / replaced with the Vermilion County Speedway

The covered grandstands at the old Danville Fairgrounds. Sprint cars are on the track in this 1947 photo. - Bob Sheldon photo.

Danville Speedbowl - Danville / located at I-74 & Bowman Ave.
   1/4 mile dirt oval (c.1964 - 1972)

Decatur Fairgrounds - Decatur / located at the Macon County Fairgrounds
   1/2 mile dirt oval (c.7/04/27 - 9/07/36) / fairgrounds built in 1923

Decatur Speedway - Decatur / located at the Decatur-Macon County Fairgrounds
   1/10 mile dirt oval (c.8/17/56 - 1970) / maybe new fairgrounds in 1949

Decatur - also see: Hoff Speedway

DeKalb Fairgrounds - DeKalb / (aka: Prather Field)
   1/2 mile dirt oval (5/15/49 - 1950)

DePaul Stadium - Chicago - 1/5 mile dirt oval (1935) / at Sheffield & Webster St

Devil's Bowl Speedway - Fountain Green - 1/5 mile dirt oval (1985 - 1986)

Dixie Speedbowl - Kankakee - 1/2 mile dirt oval (11/11/27) / at SR 1 & SR 17
   (aka: Dixie Speedway)

Dixie Speedway - Canton - see: Spoon River Speedway

Dupo Race Track - Dupo - 1/5 mile dirt oval (1940's & 1950's) / at Legion Park
   maybe Broken Springs Speedway

The start of the 100-mile AAA Championship race at DuQuoin State Fairgrounds in 1953. - Bob Sheldon photo.

DuQuoin State Fairgrounds - DuQuoin - 1/2 mile dirt oval (9/12/36 - 9/12/40)
    the 1/2 mile track is now a training horse track just west of mile track
    1.0 mile dirt oval (9/06/41) (8/31/46 - present)
    Ted Horn was fatally injured here in a crash on 10/10/48

East 33rd Street Speedway - see: Streator Speedway

East Moline - 1/2 mile dirt oval (1920's) / ran motorcycles

East Moline Speedway - East Moline / located at the Rock Island Co. Fairgrounds
    1/4 mile dirt oval (6/25/50 - present) / (aka: Quad City Raceway)

East Moline - also see: Browning Field, Quad City Speedway

Eastern Illinois Raceway - see: Vermilion County Speedway

Eighty-Eight Dragway - Rockford - 1/8 mile paved dragstrip (early 1950's)

Chuck Amati with his sprint car in the 1970's. - Allan E. Brown collection.

El Paso - 1/2 mile dirt oval (1925 - c.9/03/27)

Elgin Road Race - Elgin / the races were sponsored by the Elgin Watch Company
    8.4733 mile road course (8/26/10 - 8/21/15) (8/23/19 - 8/28/20) (1932 - 8/25/33)
    famous road race held on city streets

Elgin Speedbowl - Elgin - dirt oval (1939 & 1940)

Empire Speedway - Mount Carmel - 1/5 mile dirt oval (c.1947 - 1952)
    1/2 mile dirt oval (1951) / located at the Wabash County Fairgrounds

Evanston Speedway - Evanston (Chicago) / at Lincoln & Devon
    1/2 mile dirt oval (1931 - 8/09/36) / (aka: Lincolnwood Motor Speedway)
    1/4 mile dirt oval (6/12/35 - c.7/26/36) / (aka: Chicago Motor Speedway)
    (aka: Chicago Midget Speedway) / Jimmy Snyder, Emil Andres, Paul Russo
    & Cowboy O'Rourke started their careers here / torn down in June 1937

*Emil Andres is on the pole and Cowboy O'Rourke is outside in this 1932
picture of Evanston Speedway from 1932. - Bob Sheldon collection.*

Evansville Speedway - Evansville - 1/5 mile dirt oval (early 1950's)

Expo Gardens - see: Peoria Fairgrounds

Expo Park Speedway - Aurora (Chicago) - 1/5 mile dirt oval (7/09/35 - 9/10/39)

Fairbury Fairgrounds - see: American Legion Speedway

Fairfield Fairgrounds - Fairfield / located at the Wayne County Fairgrounds
    1/4 & 1/2 mile dirt ovals (4/18/48 - c.1973)

Farmer City Fairgrounds - Farmer City - 1/2 mile dirt oval (1938 - 1940)
    1/10 mile dirt oval (1938) / (aka: Farmer City Midget Oval)
    1/5 mile dirt oval (8/10/39 - 9/28/39)
    1/6 mile oval (6/06/40 - 9/26/40) / moved in 1941 to new site
    located at the Farmer City/DeWitt County Fairgrounds

Farmer City Raceway - Farmer City / located three blocks from old fairgrounds
    1/4 mile dirt oval (5/30/41 - 7/23/42) (9/03/45 - present)
    located at the Farmer City/DeWitt County Fairgrounds

Farrow Chicks Park - Peoria / located south of town
    dirt oval (5/06/40 - c.6/03/40) / (aka: Farrows Speedway)

Fayette County Speedway - Brownstown / (aka: Brownstown Speedway)
 1/4 mile dirt oval (4/27/41)(1946)(c.1967 - c.1977)(1983)(1987 - present)
 located at the Fayette County Fairgrounds

Freeport Raceway Park - Freeport / located next to Stephenson Co. Fairgrounds
 1/2 mile dirt oval (c.1937 - c.1941) (c.1946 - 1987) (1989 - present)
 Mel Kenyon started his career here in 1955 / (aka: Freeport Raceway)
 (aka; Stephenson County Speedway) / (aka: Freeport Super Raceway)
 1/4 mile dirt oval (late 1970's - 1987)

Galesburg District Fairgrounds - Galesburg / ran AAA championship cars
 1.0 mile dirt oval (8/29/14, 10/14/14, 11/22/14, 6/09/15, 6/22/16) (1921)

Gano Field - Chicago / located west of Halsted on 115th
 1/5 mile dirt oval (8/25/35 - 9/15/35)

Gateway Int'l Speedway - East Saint Louis / (aka: Saint Louis Int'l Raceway)
 1/4 mile paved dragstrip (6/16/67 - present) / (aka: Gateway Int'l Raceway)
 2.28 mile paved road course (6/09/85 - present) / ran SCCA TA in 1985
 .965 mile paved oval (5/18/86) / ran ARCA late models on oval track

Gem City Speedway - Quincy - 1/4 mile dirt oval (1949 - c.1957)

Gill Stadium - see: 87th Street Speedway

Godfrey Motor Speedway - Alton (Godfrey) / (aka: Godfrey Speedway)
 1/4 mile dirt oval (1950 - present) / (aka: Alton Speedway)

Godfrey Speedway - Godfrey (Melville) / (aka: Alton Speedway)
 1/5 mile dirt oval (5/15/35 - c.6/09/36)

Greenup Fairgrounds - Greenup / located at the Cumberland County Fairgrounds
 1/2 mile dirt oval (c.1925 - 8/10/39)
 1/4 mile dirt oval (c.1940 - 7/03/41) (c.1946 - 1953)

Greenville Fairgrounds - Greenville / dirt oval (1960's) / old Bond Co. Fairgrounds

Griggsville Fairgrounds - Griggsville / located at the Pike County Fairgrounds
 1/2 mile dirt oval (August, 1934 - c.1939) / may have ran before 1934
 the fairgrounds is now called the Western Illinois Fairgrounds

Grundy County Fairgrounds - see: Mazon Speed Bowl

Grundy County Speedway - Morris / located at the Grundy County Fairgrounds
 1/3 mile paved oval (5/30/71 - present) / Ray Freeman won the 1st feature
 new fairgrounds built to replace one torn down in 1970 at Mazon Speed Bowl
 home of the "Wayne Carter Classic"

Half Day Speedway - Chicago - 1/4 mile paved dragstrip (1951 - 1953)

Hanson Park - Chicago - 1/4 mile dirt oval (5/30/47 - 1948)
 located at a high school football field on Central, south of Fullerton

Harlem Race Track - Chicago / located at 59th & Harlem
 1.0 mile dirt oval (c.10/03/04 - 7/13/07) / (aka: Harlem Speedway)
 Ray Harroun started his driving career here in 1905

Harrisburg Speedway - Harrisburg / located at the Saline County Fairgrounds
1/2 mile dirt oval (c.7/22/50 - c.1968)

Harvard - oval (1930's)

Harvard Speedway - Harvard - 1/5 & 1/2 mile dirt ovals (6/05/47 - 1954)
track closed shortly after the owner, A. Damato passed away in July, 1954

Havana Speedway - see: Lascelles Speedway

Hawthorne Horse Track - Chicago / located at Cicero & 36th St.
1.0 mile dirt oval (5/30/1905 - 10/31/26) (1954) / held AAA & IMCA races
the site is now a 1/2 mile training track for Sportsman Park (horse track)
Carl Marchese started his driving career here in 1923

Henry Fairgrounds - Henry / located at the Marshall-Putnam Fairgrounds
1/4 mile dirt oval (c.1939 - 1942) / (aka: Marshall-Putnam Speedway)
1/2 mile dirt oval (6/28/42)

Highland Speedway - Highland / located at the Madison County Fairgrounds
1/4 mile dirt oval (7/22/54 - present)

Hofer's Death Valley Speedway - East Peoria
1/5 mile dirt oval (1950) / the track had a hill in the backstretch

Hoff Speedway - Decatur - 1/5 mile dirt oval (c.6/30/40)

Hollywood Park - Danville - dirt oval (years unknown)

Hull Speedway - Hull - dirt oval (years unknown)

Humphries Speedway - Charleston - 1/4 mile dirt oval (1965)

I-57 Raceway Park - see: Interstate 57 Dragway

I-74 Speedway - Knoxville / located at the Knox County Fairgrounds
1/2 mile dirt oval (c.1932 - 5/10/42) (7/17/55 - present)

Illiana Speedway - see Indiana chapter

Illinois State Fairgrounds - Springfield / original track ran east and west
1.0 mile dirt oval (c.1910 - 8/17/29) / grandstands faced south
a new $450,000 grandstands was built and opened on 8/20/27
1.0 mile dirt oval (8/24/34 - 8/16/41) (8/17/46 - present)
the track was rebuilt so the fans were not facing the afternoon sun
the current grandstands face east and the track runs north and south

Independence Motorcycle Track - (location unknown)
1/4 mile dirt oval (c.5/09/56 - 1956) / ran Micro-midgets

International Amphitheatre - Chicago / (aka: Chicago Int'l Amphitheatre)
1/8 mile indoor dirt oval (1/03/35) (11/10/40 - 4/26/42) (11/03/46 - 1948)
Jimmy Snyder won the race on 1/03/35 / it was the first AAA midget race
1/8 mile indoor paved oval (1/13/51 - 1/16/54) (1958 - 1964) (1/06/90)
1.0 mile paved indoor road course (3/09/58) / the road course threaded
through the three buildings that make up the Amphitheatre complex
400 foot indoor paved dragstrip (1962 - 1964)
(aka: Stockyards Amphitheatre) / located at Halsted & 43rd

Interstate 57 Dragway - West Frankfort - 1/4 mile dirt oval (5/01/76 - 1985)
1/4 mile paved dragstrip (Aug., 1972 - present) / (aka: I-57 Raceway Park)

Iuka - 1/2 mile dirt oval (7/06/41)

Jacksonville Raceway - Jacksonville / located at the Morgan County Fairgrounds
1/2 mile dirt oval (1946 - 1959) / (aka: Jacksonville Speedway)
1/4 mile dirt oval (c.1965 - present)

Jim Fitzpatrick Stadium - Springfield / located at 2700 South 4th St.
1/5 mile dirt oval (8/18/47 - early 1950's) / (aka: Fitzpatrick Stadium)

Joliet - 1/2 mile dirt oval (10/18/01)

Joliet Memorial Stadium - Joliet - 1/4 mile dirt oval (6/07/52 - 1963)
1/4 mile paved oval (6/06/64 - 1986) / Ray Elliott won feature 6/06/64

Joliet Park - Joliet - 1/2 mile dirt oval (1927 - 1930's)

Joliet - Singer's Midget Speedway, Saint Joseph Baseball Park

Joslin Fairgrounds - Joslin / located at the Rock Island County Fairgrounds
1/2 mile dirt oval (1910's) / ran motorcycles

K & L Raceway - Mount Vernon - 1/8 mile dirt oval (c.1988 - 1991)
located on the southeast side of town

K & L Raceway - Mount Vernon / (aka: I-57 Raceway) / southwest side of town
1/4 mile dirt oval (6/11/88 - present) / (aka: Mount Vernon I-57 Speedway)

Kankakee - Dixie Speedbowl, Lightning Midget, McNeil, Sugar Island

Kankakee Fairgrounds - Kankakee / located at the Kankakee County Fairgrounds
1/2 mile dirt oval (8/31/18 - c.1937) / (aka: Interstate Fairgrounds)
Charles "Dutch" Baumann was fatally injured here on 8/28/30

The midgets pack the track at the new Kankakee Fairgrounds in 1981. See the next page for the track's listings. - Bob Sheldon Photo.

Kankakee Speedway - Kankakee / located at the Kankakee County Fairgrounds
1/2 mile dirt oval (c.1940 - c.1941) (c.1946 - c.1949)
1/4 mile dirt oval (5/13/49 - 1957) (1967 - present)
dirt road course (5/30/49) / replaced old fairgrounds in 1930's

Kewanee Fairgrounds - Kewanee - 1.0 mile dirt oval (c.1925 - c.9/03/28)

Kewanee Speedbowl - Kewanee - 1/10 mile indoor paved oval (12/30/60 - 1961)

Kickapoo Playland Park - Heyworth - 1/10 mile dirt oval (7/13/58 - c.1958)
located six miles from Bloomington

King City Motor Speedway - Mount Vernon - 1/4 mile dirt oval (8/20/47 - 1949)

Knoxville Fairgrounds - see: I-74 Speedway

Knoxville - also see: Atomic Speedway

Lake Benton Speedway - Benton - 1/4 mile dirt oval (early 1950's)

Lansing (Chicago) - 1/5 mile dirt oval (1939 & 1940)

LaPlace - 1/4 mile dirt oval (years unknown) / located near Cerro Gordo

LaSalle Speedway - LaSalle - 1/4 mile dirt oval (1986 - 1990) (1992 - present)
site was a former Drive-In theater / currently owned by Tony Izzo
the former site of Tri-City Speedway in the 1940's

Lascelles Speedway - Havana / (aka: Havana Speedway)
1/5 mile dirt oval (1939 & 1940)

Lawrenceville Airport - Lawrenceville - 1/4 mile paved dragstrip (c.1953 - 1955)
1.7 mile paved road course (1954 - 1962) / Lawrenceville Municipal Airport
Lloyd Scott turned the first ever 150 mph speed at a dragstrip in 1955

Lawrenceville Co. Speedway - Lawrenceville - 1/4 mile dirt oval (c.6/15/47- c.1955)

Legion Speedway - Fairbury / located at the Fairbury Fairgrounds
1/2 mile dirt oval (c.1926 - 1933) (7/13/35) (9/25/38)
1/4 mile dirt oval (1939 - 9/41/41) (5/22/46 - present)
also referred to as American Legion Speedway
a program from the track in 1982 stated the 1/4 mile track was built 1945

Lenzi Park Speedway - Chicago (Hodgkins) / in a ballpark at US 66 & East Ave
1/8 & 1/6 mile dirt ovals (5/30/52 - 1953) / (aka: Cole Lenzi Field)

LeRoy - 1/2 mile dirt oval (1920's or 1930's)

Lewistown Fairgrounds - Lewistown / located at the Fulton County Fairgrounds
1/2 mile dirt oval (c.1935 - 5/21/39) (9/01/46 - c.1954)
1/6 mile dirt oval (1977)

Lexington Motor Speedway - Lexington
1/2 mile dirt oval (c.8/22/27 - 1931) (6/24/34) (late 1930's)

Libertyville Horse Track - Chicago (Libertyville)
1/2 mile dirt oval (8/09/13) / built as a harness track in 1903
torn down in 1918 / site is now a housing development

204   *Illinois*

Lightning Midget Speedway - Kankakee - dirt oval (1938)

Lightning Speedway - Watseka / located at the Iroquois County Fairgrounds
    1/2 mile dirt oval (c.7/25/26 - c.1938) / (aka: McCullough Speedway)

Lincoln Fairgrounds - Lincoln / located at the Logan County Fairgrounds
    1/2 mile dirt oval (9/15/46 - early 1950's)

Lincoln Speedway - Lincoln - 1/5 mile dirt oval (5/05/40 - c.1941) (c.1946 - 1967)
    located on Garfield Ave. south of Route 176

Lincolnwood Motor Speedway - see: Evanston Speedway

Litchfield Sports Arena - Litchfield / (aka: Litchfield Speedway)
    1/4 mile dirt oval (c.9/04/50 - c.1950)

Little Springfield - see: Springfield Speedway

Loda Motor Speedway - Loda - 1/2 mile dirt oval (1920's)

Lovington - dirt oval (1937) / ran jalopies

Macomb - 1/4 mile dirt oval (1960) / probably at the fairgrounds

Macomb Fairgrounds - Macomb - 1/2 mile dirt oval (1928) (7/28/46)
    1/4 mile dirt oval (9/01/49) / located at the McDonough County Fairgrounds

Macomb Speedway - Macomb / (aka: Spring Creek Speedway)
    1/5 mile dirt oval (1968 - present) / runs T.Q. midgets & Mini-stocks

Macon Speedway - Macon - 1/8 mile dirt oval (4/03/46 - c.9/21/46)
    Don Branson started his driving career here in 1946
    1/5 mile dirt oval (5/31/47 - present) / (aka: Macon County Speedway)
    Wayne Webb was the promoter for many years
    held first ever NAMAR midget race here on 7/08/72

Mance Park Speedway - Chicago (Hodgkins) - 1/5 mile dirt oval (5/03/53-c.9/26/54)
    1/5 mile paved oval (c.6/05/55 - 1960) / at 6300 SE Ave. & LaGrange Ave
    owners were Harold & Bill Mance / Bryant Tucker last stock car champion

Manteno - dirt oval (years unknown)

Marion - 1/2 mile dirt oval (1920's or 1930's)

Marion County Speedway - Centralia - 1/5 mile dirt oval (c.1968 - 1977)

Marion County Speedway - see: Southern Illinois Speedway

Marion Fairgrounds - see: Williamson County Speedway

Marion - also see: Southern Illinois, Turnpike Speedway, Williamson Co Speedway

Marshall Fairgrounds - Marshall / located at the Clark County Fairgrounds
    1/5 mile dirt oval (8/09/46 - c.9/06/47) / (aka: Clark County Speedway)
    1/2 mile dirt oval (6/15/47 - early 1950's)

Marshall-Putnam Speedway - see: Henry Fairgrounds

Martinsville Fairgrounds - Martinsville - 1/2 mile dirt oval (early 1950's)

Mason County Dragway - Havana - 1/8 mile paved dragstrip (1968 - present)
(aka: Mid-State Dragway)

Mattoon Fairgrounds - Mattoon - 1/2 mile dirt oval (early 1920's) (1938)

Mattoon - also see: Coles County Speedway

Maywood - see: Chicago Speedway

Mazon Speed Bowl - Mazon - 1/2 mile dirt oval (1917 - 9/01/35)
1/5 mile oiled dirt oval (9/15/36 - 9/01/41)
1/4 mile dirt oval (1946) / located at the Grundy County Fairgrounds
1/4 mile paved oval (8/30/47 - 1970) / torn down in 1970

McCullough Speedway - see: Lightning Speedway

McNeil Speedway - Kankakee - 1/5 mile dirt oval (8/08/37 - 7/04/38)
located next to the fairgrounds at the Civic Airport

Meadowdale International Raceway - Carpenterville / at SR 31 & Huntley Road
3.27 & 4.2 mile paved road courses (9/14/58 - 1969)
(aka: Illinois International Raceway) / races included USAC late models
2.5 mile paved road course (7/14/64 ran ARCA late models)
ran a SCCA TA race here in 1968 won by Mark Donohue

Mendota Fairgrounds - see: Tri-County Speedway

Mercer County Speedway - Aledo / located at the Mercer County Fairgrounds
1/2 mile dirt oval (c.7/04/28 - 5/30/42) (7/04/46 - c.1959)
1/5 mile dirt oval (1963) / ran T.Q. midgets in 1963
1/4 mile dirt oval (1991 - present) / (aka: Aledo Speedway)

Metrocentre - Rockford - 1/10 mile indoor concrete oval (1/10/87) / USAC midgets

Metropolis Speedway - Metropolis / located at the Massac County Fairgrounds
1/2 mile dirt oval (c.1953 - c.1970)

Mid-State Dragway - see: Mason County Raceway

Midstate Raceway - Mount Olive - 1/2 mile dirt oval (c.1984 - 1989)
formerly a motorcycle track / first auto race was on 1/19/85

Milledgeville Fairgrounds - Milledgeville / located at the Carroll Co. Fairgrounds
1/5 mile dirt oval (c.1960 - c.1973) / new fairgrounds opened in 1953

Mineral Springs Park - Rock Falls - 1/2 mile dirt oval (1910's - 10/09/20)

Mitchell - 3/8 mile dirt oval (years unknown)

Monee District - Monee - 1/2 mile dirt oval (c.1927 - c.1939)
1/4 mile dirt oval (7/04/40) (9/08/40)

Monmouth Fairgrounds - Monmouth / located at the Warren County Fairgrounds
1/8 mile dirt oval (c.1982 - c.1984) / ran T.Q. midgets

Monticello Fairgrounds - Monticello / located near Cerro Gordo
1/5 mile dirt oval (6/14/40 - 7/25/41) (c.1946 - c.1955)
1/4 mile dirt oval (July, 1956 - c.1958)

Morris Fairgrounds - see: Grundy County Speedway

Morrison Fairgrounds - Morrison / located at the Whiteside County Fairgrounds
1/2 mile dirt oval (c.1915 - c.1937) / ran motorcycles c.1915 to c.1919
first auto races were in 1920's

Motion Raceway - Moweaqua - 1/4 mile paved dragstrip (c.1977 - c.1984)

Mount Carmel Fairgrounds - see: Empire Speedway

Mount Carroll Fairgrounds - Mount Carroll / located at the Carroll Co Fairgrounds
1/2 mile dirt oval (1930's or 1940's) / ran motorcycles only

Mount Hawley Speedway - Peoria / built by Frank Dixon
1/4 mile dirt oval (c.5/21/49 - 1954) / (aka: Peoria Midget Speedway)
located at Highway 88 & Highway 174 next to the Mount Hawley Airport

Mount Sterling Fairgrounds - Mt. Sterling - 1/2 mile dirt oval (4/23/39 - 5/14/39)
1/6 mile dirt oval (1977) / located at the Brown County Fairgrounds

Mount Vernon Fairgrounds - Mt. Vernon / at the Jefferson Co Fairgrounds
1/2 mile dirt oval (c.10/14/28 - c.1941) (5/03/53 - c.1969) (8/22/75)
1/4 mile dirt oval (May, 1940 - 9/16/40) / (aka: Fairgrounds Raceway)

Mount Vernon I-57 Speedway - see: K & L Raceway

Mount Vernon - also see: K & L Raceway, King City Motor Speedway

Municipal Athletic Field - Peoria / (aka: Central Stadium)
1/4 mile dirt oval (6/05/38 - c.8/07/38)

Murphysboro Speedway - Murphysboro - 1/5 mile dirt oval (1948)

Nashville - 1/4 mile paved dragstrip (1963 - 1965)

Nashville Speedway - Nashville - dirt oval (years unknown)

New Berlin Fairgrounds - New Berlin / located at the Sangamon Co. Fairgrounds
1/4 mile dirt oval (1980)

New Berlin Rodeo Grounds - New Berlin - 1/5 mile dirt oval (5/08/40 - 7/03/40)

New Lake Speedway - Springfield - 1/4 mile dirt oval (c.8/06/36 - c.8/13/36)

North Shore Polo Grounds - Chicago - 1/2 mile dirt oval (7/06/24)

O & W Speedway - see: Thawville Speedway

O'Hare Stadium - Chicago (Schiller Park) / at Mannheim & Irving Park Rd
1/4 mile paved oval (6/17/56 - Sept., 1968) / torn down in 1968
Fred Lorenzen was the late model track champion in 1958
1/8 mile dirt oval (6/13/58 - c.1958)
the equipment for the track came from CeMar Acres in Iowa
the site is now an industrial park located south of O'Hare Int'l Airport

Olney City Park - Olney / located at the Richland County Fairgrounds
1/4 & 1/2 mile dirt oval (c.8/07/53 - c.1955) (1982 - 1984)
1/8 mile dirt oval (7/09/94 - present)

Olney - also see: White Squirrel Speedway

Oregon Fairgrounds - Oregon - 1/2 mile dirt oval (early 1950's)
1/8 mile dirt oval (1966) / located at the Ogle County Fairgrounds

Oswego Drag Raceway - Oswego - 1/4 mile paved dragstrip (c.1955 - 1972)

Ottawa Fairgrounds - Ottawa / located at the LaSalle County Fairgrounds
1/5 mile dirt oval (8/22/36 & 8/23/36) (1940's)

Palatine - dirt oval (7/10/27 & 7/08/28) / located northwest of Chicago

Palisades Raceway - Dunlop - 1/6 mile dirt indoor oval (1953) (c.1/02/55 - c.1955)

Pana Tri-County Fairgrounds - Pana - 1/2 mile dirt oval (early 1950's)(1961)(1965)
Wayne Webb promoted motorcycle races here in the 1980's

Paris Speedway - Paris / located at the Edgar County Fairgrounds
1/2 mile dirt oval (1922 - 1941) (Sept., 1945 - c.1972)

Pecatonia Fairgrounds - Pecatonia / located at the Winnebago County Fairgrounds
1/2 mile dirt oval (1930's) (c.6/30/40 - 8/10/41) (c.1946 - c.1977) (1983) (1987)

Pekin Speedway - Pekin - 1/4 mile dirt oval (c.1955)

Peoria - Baty's Barn, Farrows Chicks Park, Hofer's Death Valley Speedway,
Mount Hawley Speedway, Municipal Athletic Field

Peoria Civic Center - Peoria - 1/10 mile indoor paved oval (Dec., 1987 & 1988)

Peoria Fairgrounds - Peoria - 1.0 mile dirt oval (August, 1905 - May, 1933)

Peoria Fairgrounds - Peoria / possibly this new fairgrounds was built in 1945
1/2 mile dirt oval (10/05/49 - 1958) / (aka: Expo Gardens)
1/4 mile dirt oval (1950) / located at the Heart of Illinois Fairgrounds
paved road course (7/04/53) / (aka: National Implement & Vehicle Show)
1/8 mile dirt oval (1950's or 1960's) / ran Micro midgets on smaller track

Peoria Midget Speedway - see: Mount Hawley Speedway

Peoria Speedway - Peoria / located west of town / built by Frank Dixon
1/4 mile dirt oval (c.7/21/65 - present)
the track was 20 foot under water during the flood of 1993

Peotone Speedway - Peotone - 1/2 mile dirt oval (c.5/27/34 - c.1940)
1/5 mile dirt oval (5/12/48 - 1953) / at the Will County Fairgrounds
1/4 mile dirt oval (1958) (1961) - 1979) (1983)

Petersburg - 1/2 mile dirt oval (7/16/39) / probably at the Menard Co. Fairgrounds
small dirt oval (1966) / ran T.Q. midgets on small track

Pinckneyville Fairgrounds - Pinckneyville - dirt oval (c.1957 - c.1958)
located at the Perry County Fairgrounds

Pingree Grove - 1/2 mile dirt oval (1926) / located near Elgin

Pittsfield Speedway - Detroit - 1/3 mile dirt oval (c.1961 - 1973)

Playland Park - Chicago (Justice) / located at 79th & LaGrange Ave.
   1/5 mile dirt oval (1953 & 1954)

Prairie Capital Convention Center - Springfield / located downtown / ran midgets
   1/10 mile concrete indoor oval (3/05/83 - 1984) (1986) (1988)

Prather Field - see: DeKalb Fairgrounds

Princeton Fairgrounds - see: Bureau County Speedway

Quad City Dragway - see: Cordova Dragway

Quad City Raceway - see: East Moline Speedway

Quad City Speedway - East Moline - 1/4 mile dirt oval (late 1940's - c.1953)
   the site is now I-80

Quincy Raceway - Quincy - 1/4 mile dirt oval (1975 - present)

Quincy - also see: Baldwin Park, Gem City Speedway

Raceway Park - Blue Island (Chicago) / Harry McQuinn 1st winner
   1/5 mile dirt oval (9/24/38 - 7/28/42) (8/25/45 - 4/08/51)
   1/5 mile paved oval (4/22/51 - present) / (aka: Raceway Park Motordrome)
   probably ran first race in the U.S. after World War II ended (8/25/45)
   billed as world's busiest track / held 80 meets in 1951 (4 nights a week)
   held weekly dog racing (non-parimutuel) in 1953 / located at 130th & Ashland
   Bud Koehler won 490 feature events at Raceway Park in his career
   held a 136 car enduro race in October of 1992

Raceway Park looking from over the pit area in 1953. The track was one of the
busiest tracks in the nation as it held over 80 races in 1951. The Chicago track
was a very popular facility. - Bob Sheldon photo.

Raceway Park (board track) - see: Chicago Speedway

Randolph County Speedway - see: Chester Fairground

Riverside Speedway - Pittsfield - 1/8 mile dirt oval (1990 - 1992) (1994 - present)
the track, located next to the Illinois River, was under water in 1993

Riverview - Chicago - 1/3 mile wood oval (1910 - 1912) / ran motorcycles only
another wood track built by Jack Prince / probably at the amusement park

Riverview Stadium - Chicago / located next to the old Riverview Amusement Park
1/5 mile dirt oval (6/04/36 - 7/29/42) / located at 2600 West Addison

Riverview Stadium from 1938. - Bob Sheldon photo.

Robinson Speedway - see: Crawford County Speedway

Roby Speedway - see Indiana chapter

Rochelle - 1.0 mile dirt oval (1910's & 1920's)

Rochester - 1/4 mile dirt oval (1960's)

Rockford Dragway - see: Byron Dragway

Rockford Speedway - Rockford - 1/4 mile paved oval (5/26/48 - present)
Johnny McDowell was the 1st winner / home of annual "Short Track Nat'ls"
the late Hugh Deery was the 1976 & 1984 RPM Promoter of the Year

Rockford - also see: Eighty-Eight Dragway, Metrocentre

Rolling Thunder Raceway - see: Coles County Dragway USA

Ropp Midget Speedway - Wilmington / built by Freeman Ropp
1/4 mile dirt oval (8/11/41 - 9/15/41)

Rose City Speedway - Pana - dirt oval (1946 & 1947)

Rosemont Horizon - Chicago (Rosemont) / located northeast of O'Hare Field
1/10 mile indoor concrete oval (12/13/86) (3/19/88) (12/10/88) (1/05/91)

210

Rushville Fairgrounds - Rushville / located at the Schuyler County Fairgrounds
    dirt oval (1977)

Saint Elroy Track - Silvis - 1/2 mile dirt oval (early 1920's)

Saint Joseph Baseball Park - Joliet - 1/5 mile dirt oval (10/19/41) / ran midgets

Saint Louis Int'l Raceway - see: Gateway Int'l Speedway

Salem - dirt oval (years unknown) / possibly at the Marion County Fairgrounds

Sandoval - 1/4 mile dirt oval (years unknown)

Sandwich Fairgrounds - Sandwich - 1/2 mile dirt oval (6/29/41 - 9/05/41) (8/11/46)

Santa Fe Park - Chicago (Willow Springs) / located at 91st & South Wolf Road
    1/2 mile dirt oval (1920's) (ran horses in 1986) / park was built in 1892
    Tornado destroyed grandstands in the late 1920's
    same site of current Santa Fe Speedway / track in different location

Santa Fe Speedway - Chicago (Willow Springs) / located at 91st & South Wolf Rd
    7/16 mile dirt oval (5/31/53 - present) / located at a picnic grove
    1/4 mile dirt oval (1953 - present)
    the late Howard Tiedt was the 1982 RPM Promoter of the Year
    same location of Santa Fe Park, tracks were in different spots on property
    ran NASCAR Grand Nat'l race on 7/10/54, Dick Rathmann won in a Hudson

Seneca - 1/4 mile paved dragstrip (1955 - 1956)

Shelbyville Fairgrounds - Shelbyville - 1/2 mile dirt oval (8/03/35)
    1/4 mile dirt oval (9/07/41 - c.1941) (July, 1946 - c.1949)
    located at the Shelby County Fairgrounds

Shrewbridge Ball Park - Chicago / located at 74th & Morgan
    1/5 mile dirt oval (5/15/35) / midget race won by Ronney Householder

Sidney - dirt oval (1938)

Singer's Midget Speedway - Joliet / located west of town in a field
    1/5 mile dirt oval (6/04/39 - 1941) / built by Corky Singer

Snyder Memorial Speedway - see: Cahokia Midget Speedway

Santa Fe Speedway as it looked in 1953. - Bob Sheldon photo.

The board track that was constructed inside of Soldiers Field. A series of races called the "World Series for Midgets" was held on the wood track in 1939. Bob Sheldon photo.

Soldier Field - Chicago / located at 14th St. & Lake Shore Drive
    1/4 mile cinder oval (5/19/35) / stadium was built in 1926
    1/4 mile banked wood oval (6/18/39 - 6/25/39) / (aka: Grants Park Stadium)
    held the World Championship for midgets on the wood track
    1/4 mile dirt oval (5/04/42 - 5/31/42) / home of the NFL Chicago Bears
    1/4 mile paved oval (6/16/46 - 1958) / had 68,000 fans at race in 1953
    1/2 mile paved oval (c.7/21/56 - 1967) / ran NASCAR GN race on 7/21/56
    3/8 mile paved oval (1967 - June, 1968) / track torn out in 1970
    closed by hippies who protested the city financing of auto racing

Soldiers Field drew enormous crowds for its weekly "Hardtop" races in the 1950's, as evident in this 1952 picture. - Bob Sheldon photo.

Southern Illinois Speedway - Marion / (aka: Marion County Speedway)
1/8 mile dirt oval (1989 - present)

Sparta Fairgrounds - Sparta - 1/2 mile dirt oval (10/28/34)(1969) (7/11/73-7/11/75)

Sparta Stadium - Chicago - dirt oval (6/24/35 - 9/20/35)
located at Cermak & Kostner

Speedbowl Park - Springfield - 1/4 mile dirt oval (1930's)
also referred to as Dreamland

Speedbowl Park - Sterling / Billy Arnold won the race on 7/04/26
3/4 mile D-shaped dirt oval (7/04/26 - 10/04/36) (6/08/41)
1/5 mile dirt oval (7/29/36 - c.6/05/38) / (aka: Sterling Speedbowl)
1/3 mile dirt oval (c.5/18/58 - 1969)

Spoon River Speedway - Canton / (aka: Dixie Speedway)
3/8 mile dirt oval (4/30/83 - present)

Sportsman Park - see: Crawford County Speedway

Spring Creek Speedway - see: Macomb Speedway

Springfield - 1/2 mile dirt oval (1928 - mid 1930's) / torn down in 1938
located north of the Illinois State Fairgrounds on 8th St.

Springfield Fairgrounds - see: Illinois State Fairgrounds

Springfield Speedway - Springfield / (referred to as Little Springfield)
1/5 mile dirt oval (c.7/19/48 - 1981) / Joe Shaheen builder & promoter
1/4 mile dirt oval (1982 - 1987)

Springfield - also see: 3-I Ball Park, Jim Fitzpatrick Stadium, New Lake
Speedway, Prairie Capital Convention Center, Speedbowl Park

Starved Rock - Utica - 1/2 mile dirt oval (7/22/40 - 9/29/40)

Stephenson County Speedway - see: Freeport Raceway Park

Stockholm's Fairgrounds - see: Cook County Fairgrounds

Streator - dirt oval (7/15/14)

Streator Speedway - Streator / (aka: East 33rd Street Speedway)
1/4 mile dirt oval (c.1947 - c.1949) (c.9/27/53)

A look at Streator Speedway from 1948. - Bob Sheldon photo.

Stronghurst Fairgrounds - Stronghurst / at the Henderson County Fairgrounds
1/8 mile dirt oval (1982 - 1986) / ran T.Q. midgets during the fair

Stubblefield Auto Race Track - Tampico - 1/2 mile dirt oval (11/20/32) / ran stocks

Sugar Island - Kankakee - 1/4 mile dirt oval (c.1959 - c.1966)

Sullivan - dirt oval (1937 & 1938) / ran Hobos (jalopies)

Sycamore Speedway - Sycamore - 1/3 mile dirt oval (1963 - present)
1/4 mile dirt oval (1969 - present) / (aka: Bob-Jo Speedway)
started as a Go-Kart track in 1960 / first called Sycamore Speedway in 1970

Taylorville Speedway - Taylorville - 1/2 mile dirt oval (c.9/03/27 - 1930)
1/4 mile dirt oval (6/08/41 - 1942) / located at Christian Co. Fairgrounds
1/5 mile dirt oval (c.1981 - 1983)
1/3 mile dirt oval (7/21/83 - c.1984) (1988 - c.1990)

Thawville Speedway - Thawville / the promoter was Rudy Nichols
1/5 mile dirt oval (5/30/40 - 5/27/41)
(aka: O & W Speedway) / the owners were Olson & Woodward

Torrence Speedway - see: Calumet Speed Bowl

Torrence Speedway in 1936. - Bob Sheldon collection.

Towanda Raceway - Towanda - 1/8 mile dirt oval (c.6/08/58 -1958) / ran
Micro-midgets

Tri-City Speedway - Granite City - 1/2 mile dirt oval (5/30/61 - present)
1/4 mile dirt oval (1961 - present)

Tri-City Speedway - LaSalle - 1/5 mile dirt oval (1947 - 1948)
same location as the current LaSalle Speedway

Tri-County Speedway - Mendota - 1/2 mile dirt oval (1942) (6/16/46 - c.1955)
1/4 mile dirt oval (1952) / located at the Mendota Tri-County Fairgrounds
1/3 mile dirt oval (c.1985 - 1987)

Turnpike Speedway - Marion - 1/4 mile dirt oval (1950's - early 1960's)
track was located south of the town of Energy

Tuscola - dirt oval (1937 & 1938) ran hobos (jalopies)

Twin City Speedway - see: Champaign Motor Speedway

Urbana (Champaign) - 1/2 mile dirt oval (late 1920's - 1933)
the grandstands burned down in 1933

Urbana Fairgrounds - see: Champaign County Fairgrounds

Utica Raceway - see: Bennett Raceway

Valley Park Speedway - see: Broken Springs Speedway

Vermilion County Speedway - Danville / at the Vermilion County Fairgrounds
1/4 mile dirt oval (1967 - present) / (aka: Eastern Illinois Raceway)
the track at the new Danville fairgrounds was built in 1963

Vienna Fairgrounds - Vienna / located at the Johnson County Fairgrounds
1/2 mile dirt oval (early 1950's)

Warren Fairgrounds - Warren - 1/2 mile dirt oval (1941)
1.7 mile dirt oval (1964 - 8/15/65) / ran T.Q. midgets on smaller track

Wasco Speedway - Saint Charles - 3/8 mile egg shaped dirt oval (1932 - 9/06/36)

Washington Park - Chicago / located at 51st & Cottage Grove
1.0 mile dirt oval (1899) / formerly a horse track

Watseka Fairgrounds - see: Lightning Speedway

Waukegan - 1/2 mile dirt oval (c.1930 - 11/06/32) / on the west side of town

Waukegan Speedway - Waukegan / site is now an industrial park & trailer park
1/4 mile dirt oval (9/04/49 - 1968) (May, 1979 - 9/15/79)
1/4 mile paved oval (1969 - 1978) / (aka: Waukegan Speedway Park)
rained out after heats races on 9/04/49 / first feature on 9/11/49

Wayne City Speedway - Wayne City - 1/8 mile dirt oval (1993 - present)

White City Speedway - Chicago - dirt oval (1935)
located at the White City Amusement Park at 66th & South Park

White Rose Speedway - Belleville - dirt oval (c.7/12/40 - 1940)

White Squirrel Speedway - Olney / now the site of a cement plant
1/4 mile dirt oval (1956 - 1977)

Williamson County Speedway - Marion - 1/8 mile dirt oval (1985 - 1988)

Williamson County Speedway - Marion / at the Williamson County Fairgrounds
3/8 mile dirt oval (c.1964 - c.1977)

Willowbowl Speedway - Sibley - 1/8 mile dirt oval (c.1988 - 1991)

Wilmot Hills - paved road course (1955)

Wilson Park Speedway - Champaign - 1/2 mile dirt oval (5/22/38 - 8/11/38)

Winnebago County Fairgrounds - see: Pecatonia Fairgrounds

Wyoming - 1/10 mile dirt oval (c.6/30/58 - c.1958) / ran Micro-midgets

INDIANA

16th Street Speedway - see: West 16th Street Speedway

25th Street Speedway - see: Fastrack

Action Track Dragway - Terre Haute / located at Vigo County Fairgrounds
1/8 mile paved dragstrip (7/04/57 c.1984) (5/30/87 - present)
also see: Terre Haute Action Track

Alexandria Motor Speedway - Alexandria - dirt oval (1940)
located 3/4 mile from Armscamp Speedway

Alexandria Speedway - see: Armscamp Speedway

Alexandria - also see: Hilltop Speedway

Allen County Expo Center - Fort Wayne / new home of the Fort Wayne Komets
1/10 mile indoor concrete oval (1990) (1994) / Mini-Sprints & Karts 1990
located next to the Allen County Memorial Coliseum / Dwarf Cars 1994

Allen County Memorial Coliseum - Fort Wayne / old home of Fort Wayne Komets
1/10 mile indoor concrete oval (1/09/53 - 1989) / next to new Expo Center
held last AAA race here on 12/27/55 / Don Branson was the winner
also held first USAC race here on 1/08/56 / Gene Hartley was the winner

Anderson Speedway - Anderson / (aka: Sun Valley Speedway)
1/4 mile paved oval (7/05/48 - present) / built by Joe Helpling
Mel Hansen was the first winner / home of the annual "Little 500"

Andrews Speedway - Andrews - 1/8 mile dirt oval (1963 - c.1964)

Angola Motor Speedway - Angola / (aka: Steuben County Speedway)
3/8 mile dirt oval (c.1969 - 1970) / (aka: Lakeview Raceway)
3/8 mile paved oval (1971 - present)

An aerial view of Angola Motor Speedway (better known as Steuben County Speedway). - Jack Brown photo.

Armscamp Speedway - Alexandria / located on the G.J. Armstrong's farm
1/4 mile paved oval (7/27/41 - 7/12/42) (4/14/46 - 1948)
1/4 mile dirt oval (1948 - 1959) / (aka: Alexandria Speedway)
built by Joe Armstrong & Frank Scampmore / closed when stands burned

Art Zipp's Speedway - see: Indianapolis Speedrome

Avilla Motor Speedway - Avilla - 3/8 mile dirt oval (1965 - 1969) (1982 - 1988)
3/8 mile paved oval (1970 - present) / (aka: Avilla Raceways)
1/4 mile paved dragstrip (May, 1967 - 1981) (1989 - present)
the oval track grandstands are from South Anthony Speedway
the tracks were built by Howard Bice

*Avilla Speedway and Avilla Dragway (behind turn one of the oval track).
Official track photo.*

Baer Field Raceway - Fort Wayne / located southwest of town next to the airport
1/2 mile paved oval (5/24/64 - 1975) (1977 - present)
(aka: Fort Wayne Raceways) / built by John Weisenhauer
site of a Go-Kart track built in 1961 / Kart track is now the pit area
part of the grandstands collapsed during an event in the early 1980's
3/8 mile paved oval (1994 - present)

Bartholomew County 4-H Fairgrounds - see: Columbus Fairgrounds

Bass Lake Speedway - Bass Lake - 1/5 mile paved oval (1952 - c.1957)

Beanblossom Dragway - see: Brown Co. Dragway

Bedford - 1/2 mile dirt oval (c.6/17/28 - c.1938) / maybe at Bedford Fairgrounds

Bedford Fairgrounds - Bedford - dirt oval (1971) / at Lawrence Co. Fairgrounds

Bedford - also see: Eureka Speedway, Williams Speedway

Belmont Stadium - Indianapolis - 1/5 mile dirt oval (7/30/38 - c.8/06/38)

Benton County Speedway - Oxford - 3/8 mile dirt oval (1967 - 1976)
3/8 mile paved oval (1977 - present) / (aka: Henry's Speedway)
(aka: Chase Raceway) / ran for many years by Avery Henry

Bicknell Fairgrounds - Bicknell / located at the Knox County Farm Fairgrounds
1/5 mile dirt oval (c.1968 - 1980)

Indiana **217**

Fourteen-time World of Outlaw champion Steve Kinser at Ascot Park (CA) in 1987. - Phil Dullinger photo.

Bitterlings Family Speedway - Winamac - 1/4 mile dirt oval (1992)
    the track is setting idle waiting for the local governmental to OK it to run

Black Demon Speedway - Saint Marys of the Woods / located NW of Terre Haute
    1.0 mile dirt oval (c.7/30/27 - 8/26/28)

Bloomington Motor Speedway - Bloomington - 5/8 mile dirt oval (c.10/26/47-c.1956)
    1/4 mile dirt oval (5/17/50 - c.1956) / at the old Monroe County Fairgrounds

Bloomington Speedway - Bloomington / (aka: Mitchell's Motor Speedway)
    5/8 mile dirt oval (1923 - 1941) (c.1946) / located south of town
    1/4 mile dirt oval (5/10/63 - 1978) (1982 - present)

Bloutcher - Vernon - 1/4 mile dirt oval (1960's) / maybe Twin Cities Raceway Park

Bluffton - 1/10 mile dirt oval (1953) / ran T.Q. midgets

Bolens Speedway - Martinsville - 1/5 mile dirt oval (years unknown)
    located five miles south of town

Boone County Fairgrounds - see: Lebanon Fairgrounds

Boonville Fairgrounds - Boonville / located at the Warrick County Fairgrounds
    1/2 mile dirt oval (c.1951 - c.1954) (1985)

Brandywine Speedway - see: Greenfield Midgetdrome or Greenfield Speedbowl

Brazil Speedway - Brazil / built to replace Black Demon Speedway
    1/2 mile oiled dirt oval (7/29/28 - c.1930) / surface was liquid asphalt
    located one mile east of town on National Road (now called U.S. 40)

Broadway Speedway - see: Southlake Speedway

218

Brookville Fairgrounds - Brookville / located at the Franklin County Fairgrounds
1/6 mile dirt oval (1988) / (aka: Franklin County Park Speedway)

Brown County Dragway - Nashville (Beanblossom) / (aka: Beanblossom Dragway)
1/8 mile paved dragstrip (1968 - present)

Brownstown Speedway - Brownstown / located at the Jackson County Fairgrounds
1/2 mile dirt oval (1952 - c.1963)
1/10 mile dirt oval (1960) / ran T.Q. midgets on small oval
1/4 mile dirt oval (c.1963 - present) / home of the "Jackson 100" for LMs

Bunker Hill Dragstrip - Bunker Hill / located ten miles north of Kokomo
1/8 mile paved dragstrip (8/22/56 - present)
3/8 mile paved oval (1967 - 1982) / (aka: Bunker Hill Speedway)
3/8 mile dirt oval (1983 - 1984) / (aka: Bunker Hill Motor Speedway)

Burlington Fairgrounds - Burlington - 1/2 mile dirt oval (1916)

Butler University Bowl - Indianapolis / located at the university football field
1/4 mile dirt oval (5/15/35 & 5/29/35) / promoted by Howdy Wilcox II

Camden Raceway - Camden - 1/8 mile dirt oval (1988 - present) / ran Karts 1987

Camp Atterbury Air Force Base - Columbus
3.73 mile paved road course (5/30/54)   Phil Cole helped organize this race

Capitol Speedway - Plymouth - 3/8 mile paved oval (c.8/22/52 - present)
(aka: Plymouth Speedway) / (aka: Capitol Speedway of Plymouth)

Carey Ranch - Indianapolis - 1/2 mile dirt oval (5/07/39 - 1941) / in farmers field
1/4 mile dirt oval (5/21/39 - c.1939) / located at 8000 S. Meridian St.

Carlisle - 1/4 mile dirt oval (c.1949 - mid-1950's)

Caruthers - (location unknown) - 1/4 mile dirt oval (1968) / ran for two months

Castleton - 1.0 mile dirt oval (early 1930's)

Cayuga Fairgrounds - Cayuga / located at the Vermilion County Fairgrounds
1/2 mile dirt oval (8/23/46) / ran a midget race

Centlivre Park Speedway - Fort Wayne / (aka: Centlivre Speedway)
1/2 mile dirt oval (9/19/14 - 1926) (1928 - 7/08/28) (1941) (1948)
owned by the C.L. Centlivre Brewing Company

Chandler Raceway - Chandler / (aka: Greater Evansville Raceway)
3/8 mile dirt oval (5/28/71 - 1985) (1991 - present)
located next to Greater Evansville Raceway / (aka: Chandler Raceway Park)
(aka: Owen Hills Raceway) / (aka: Mid-America Raceway)

Charlestown Speedway - Charlestown - 1/3 mile dirt oval (1980 - 1982)
1/3 mile paved oval (4/15/83 - present) / built by Clark Nuckles
(aka: Charlestown Motor Speedway)

Charlottesville Speedrome - Charlottesville - 1/5 mile dirt oval (6/15/41 - 1941)

Chase Raceway - see: Benton County Speedway

Chesterfield - see: Riverview Park, Skyview Track

Circus City Speedway - see: Miami County Speedway

Clark Speedway - Vincennes / (aka: George Rogers Clark Speedway)
    1/2 mile dirt/sand oval (c.7/02/27 - c.1932)
    located three miles west of town on Lawrenceville Road

Clems Lake Speedway - Decatur - 1/4 mile dirt oval (c.5/10/52 - c.1953)

Clermont Lions Club Raceway - Clermont - 1/10 mile dirt oval (years unknown)
    ran T.Q. midgets / probably on the grounds of Indianapolis Raceway Park

Clifton Hill - Columbus / (aka: The Hole in the Wall)
    1/4 mile dirt oval (1946 - 1948) (1950 - c.1960)

Clintonville - (location unknown) - 1/2 mile dirt oval (early 1930's) / maybe Clinton

Fred Leill on the "pole" and Harry McQuinn outside in the 1930's photo from Clintonville. - Allan E. Brown collection.

Columbia City Speedway - see: Lake View Speedway

Columbus Fairgrounds - Columbus / at the Bartholomew County 4-H Fairgrounds
    1/5 mile dirt oval (c.1976 - 1991) (1993 - present)
    located south of Columbus on U.S. 31-A

Columbus Speedway - Columbus / located at the old Bartholomew County
    1/2 mile dirt oval (c.4/25/37 - c.1941) (1946 - c.1973) / near downtown
    1/4 mile dirt oval (7/28/49 - c.1955) / (aka: Columbus Motor Speedway)

Columbus - also see: Camp Atterbury Air Force Base, Clifton Hill Fairgrounds

Connersville - 1/5 mile dirt oval (10/23/38) / the first race was rained out

Converse Speedway - Converse / located at the Converse Fairgrounds
    1/2 mile dirt oval (c.1922 - c.1941) (1946 - 1950)
    Bob Carey started his driving career here in 1922
    Howdy Wilcox II was fatally injured here while flagging a race on 10/14/46

Corydon Pike Speedway - New Albany - 1/6 mile dirt oval (8/17/38 - 1939)

County Line Raceway - Brazil (Harmony) - 1/5 mile dirt oval (c.1991 - present)
    Kart track that opened in 1990 / started running Modified-Midgets 1991

Covington Fairgrounds - Covington - 1/2 mile dirt oval (1920's)

Crawfordsville Fairgrounds - Crawfordsville / at Montgomery Co. Fairgrounds
    1/2 mile dirt oval (c.7/15/28 - early 1930's)

Crawfordsville Speedway - Crawfordsville - 1/4 mile dirt oval (c.1947 - c.1950)

Crown Point - 23.274 mile city street road course (6/18/09 & 6/19/09)
    the races were known as the famous "Cope Trophy Race"

Crown Point Fair Raceway - Crown Point / at the Lake County Fairgrounds
    1/2 mile dirt oval (1919 - 1930) (7/22/34 - 8/17/41) (5/05/46 - c.8/23/53)
    ran motorcycle races in 1919 / ran first auto races in 1920
    1/5 mile dirt oval (6/14/47 - 1953) / (aka: Crown Point Midget Track)

Dation - (location unknown) - dirt oval (c.5/28/49) / maybe Dayton

Derby City Dragway - see: Harrison Co. Dragway

Dixie Speedway - Sullivan / located two miles north of town on Dixie B Highway
    1/2 mile dirt oval (5/06/28 - 9/30/28) / (aka: Hal Richarts Speedway)

Dugger - see: Sullivan Speedway

Eastside Speedway - see: Indianapolis Speedrome

Elkhart Motor Speedway - see: New Elkhart Speedway

Elnora Fairgrounds - Elnora / located at the Daviess County Fairgrounds
    1/5 mile dirt oval (c.1963 - 1977) (1980) / (aka: Elnora Speedway)

Eureka Speedway - Bedford - 1/4 mile dirt oval (1960's)
    maybe the same track as Williams Speedway

Evansville Fairgrounds - Evansville / at the Vanderburgh County Fairgrounds
    1/2 mile dirt oval (1917 - 1919)

Evansville Midget Velodrome - Evansville / located east of town
    1/4 mile dirt oval (7/21/40)

Evansville Speedrome - Evansville - 1/5 mile dirt oval (c.8/31/47 - 1959)
    the site is now a miniature golf course, go-kart rental complex

Evansville - also see: Pride Speedway, Saint Joe Speedway, Tri-State Speedway

Fairgrounds Speedway - see: Princeton Fairgrounds

Fairmount Park - Fairmount - 1/2 mile dirt oval (1910) (c.9/16/34 - c.8/02/36)

Fastrack - Terre Haute / located at 25th & Fort Harrison
    1/5 mile paved oval (8/08/46 - 1948) / (aka: 25th Street Speedway)
    1/5 mile dirt oval (1949 - c.1958) / promoters: Earl Unversaw & Charlie Shine

Fort Wayne - 1/5 mile dirt oval (6/19/36) / located at a dog track
    maybe located at Fort Wayne Raceway

Fort Wayne Driving Park - Fort Wayne / located at State Street & Anthony Blvd
1.0 mile dirt oval (10/02/02 - 9/21/13) / built for horse in 1890
the site is now a housing development

Fort Wayne Raceways - see: Baer Field Raceway

Fort Wayne Speedway - Fort Wayne / located north of town on Coliseum Road
5/8 mile high banked dirt oval (8/10/30 - 1936)
5/8 mile high banked paved oval (1937 - 1942) (6/09/46 - 7/26/64)
1/2 mile dirt oval (6/25/46 - 1964) / dirt track inside of paved oval
built by Dutch McKinley / other promoters include John Diehna
(aka: Allen County Fairgrounds & Exhibition Grounds)
torn down in 1965 and property was sold to Ford & General Motors

Fort Wayne - also see: Allen County, Centlivre Park, League Park, South Anthony

Frankfort Speedway - Frankfort / located at the Clinton County Fairgrounds
1/2 mile dirt oval (c.1932 - 10/10/37)

Franklin Speedway - Franklin / located at the Johnson County Fairgrounds
1/2 mile dirt oval (c.9/04/38 - 9/17/41) (9/16/46 - early 1950's)
1/10 mile dirt oval (1967) / ran T.Q. midgets on small track

Freedom New Hope Raceway - see: Speed's Dragway

Frenchtown - dirt oval (1958)

Funk's Lake - see: Winchester Speedway

Gas City Speedway - Gas City - 1/4 mile dirt oval (1987 - 1988)
(aka: I-69 Speedway) / closed when city wanted them to hook up to sewer

George Rogers Clark Speedway - see: Clark Speedway

Rich Vogler at Eldora (OH) on July 3, 1981. Vogler was a two-time USAC sprint car champion. - John Mahoney photo.

Goshen Fairgrounds - Goshen / located at the Elkhart County Fairgrounds
3/8 mile paved oval (5/19/50 - 1951) (5/08/53 - c.9/27/53) (1963)
(aka: New Goshen Speedway) / fire destroyed the grandstands on 10/04/51
(aka: American Legion Speedway) / (aka: Fairgrounds Speedway)

Greater Evansville Raceway - Chandler / (aka: Chandler Raceway Park)
1/8 mile paved dragstrip (1964 - present) / next to Chandler Raceway

Greene County Speedway - Owensburg - 7/16 mile dirt oval (1992 - present)

Greenfield Fairgrounds - Greenfield - 1/2 mile dirt oval (1922) (4/28/40 - 1941)
1/5 mile dirt oval (8/08/40 or 8/15/40) / at the Hancock Co. Fairgrounds

Greenfield Midgetdrome - Greenfield / (aka: Greenfield Stadium)
1/5 mile dirt oval (1938 - 7/25/42) (1946 - c.1948)
located on Highway 40 / site is near where K-Mart is now located
maybe called Brandywine Speedway at one time

Greenfield Speedbowl - Greenfield - 1/2 mile dirt oval (6/01/47 - c.1949)
(aka: Leary's Speedway) / located three miles south of town
maybe called Brandywine Speedway at one time

Greensburg - 1/4 mile dirt oval (c.1958 - c.1959)
maybe Greensburg Fairgrounds or New Cedar Lake Speedway

Greensburg Fairgrounds - Greensburg - 1/10 mile dirt oval (c.1953 - c.1959)
1/5 mile dirt oval (1964 - 1992) / at the Decatur County Fairgrounds

Greentown Fairgrounds - Greentown / located at the Howard County Fairgrounds
1/8 mile dirt oval (1990)

Greenwood - dirt oval (late 1940's)

Hal Richarts Speedway - see: Dixie Speedway

Hammond Raceway - Hammond - 5/8 mile dirt oval (9/12/37- 7/12/42) (1946- 1947)
became the site of the Hammond Outdoor Theater and a mobile home park
(aka: New Hammond Raceway) / located at U.S. 41 & Sheffield

Hammond - also see: Roby, Wolf Lake

Harrison Co. Dragway - Elizabeth - 1/8 mile paved dragstrip (1970's - 1985)
(aka: Derby City Dragway)

Henry's Speedway - see: Benton County Speedway

Hi-Bank Speedway - see: Salem Speedway

Hillsboro - small dirt oval (1967) / ran T.Q. midgets

Hilltop Speedway - Alexandria / located 1/4 mile west of Hwy 9 on Hwy 28
1/4 mile dirt oval (7/09/50 - c.1951)

Hobart - 3/4 mile dirt oval (7/03/21 - 1922)

Hole in the Wall - see: Clifton Hill

Hoosier Dome - Indianapolis / located downtown where the Indianapolis Colts play
1/6 mile paved indoor oval (1/19/85 - 1986) (1988 - present)

Hoosier Motor Speedway - Indianapolis / located at 38th & Pendleton Pike
    1/2 mile dirt oval (11/11/22 - c.9/01/24) / ran a 100 mile race 9/03/23
    Howdy Wilcox II started his driving career here in 1922

Hoosier Speedbowl - see: Richmond Midget Speedway

Huntington Fairgrounds - Huntington / at the Huntington County Fairgrounds
    1/2 mile dirt oval (c.10/20/15 - c.1918)

Huntington Motor Speedway - Huntington / built by Frank Funk
    5/8 mile dirt oval (8/26/28 - c.1938)

Hutton's Park - see: the old Scottsburg Fairgrounds

I-65 Motor Speedway - see: Scott County Speedway

I-69 Speedway - see: Gas City Speedway

Illiana Motor Speedway - Schererville / built for motorcycles by Harry Molenaar
    1/2 mile dirt oval (1945 - 1961) / first auto race was on 6/26/49
    1/4 mile dirt oval (c.8/27/50 - 1961) / (aka: Schererville Speedway)
    1/2 mile paved oval (5/13/62 - present) / first called Illiana in 1952
    the first race on pavement was won by Johnny Rutherford (IMCA Sprints)
    Jack Nichols (7/21/68) & Whitey Gerken (10/08/73) were fatally injured here

Indiana State Fairgrounds Arena - Indianapolis / located on East 38th St.
    1/10 mile concrete indoor oval (3/11/73 - c.1982) / built in 1939
    1/8 mile dirt indoor oval (1989) / (aka: Indiana State Fair Coliseum)

Indiana State Fairgrounds Coliseum - Indianapolis / located on East 38th St.
    1/6 mile concrete indoor oval (3/20/35 - c.3/24/37) / became horse barn 1958

*A.J. Foyt lets it all hang out in the "Hoosier 100" for USAC Championship cars
at the Indiana State Fairgrounds on September 6, 1969. - John Mahoney photo.*

Indiana State Fairgrounds - Indianapolis / located on East 38th St.
  1.0 mile dirt oval (6/19/1903 - 1916) (c.7/04/28 - 1941) (9/15/46 - present)
  Barney Oldfield turned 60.4 mph on 6/20/1903 in Fords Red Devil
  built as a horse track in 1892 / the first grandstands cost $19,990 to build
  located on property called the Voss Farm / replaced downtown fairgrounds
  races rained out on 5/30/03, 6/01/03 & 6/18/03 / held practice on 6/18/03
  a new concrete grandstands was built for $225,000 in 1931
  the property was used as Army Air Corp storage during WWII

Indianapolis Midget Speedway - Indianapolis / located at 9200 South Meridian St.
  1/6 mile dirt oval (5/26/40 - c.6/09/40)

Indianapolis Motor Speedway - Indianapolis (Speedway)
  2.5 mile dirt oval (8/15/1909 - 8/21/1909) / located at 4700 West 16th St.
  the first race was a motorcycle event won by Cannonball Baker
  the first auto race was on 8/19/1909, won by Louis Switzer
  originally a 5.0 mile road course was planned using the infield & oval
  2.5 mile brick oval (12/18/1909 - 9/16/16) (1919 - 5/30/38)
  2.5 mile paved oval (1939 - 5/30/41) (1946 - present)
  the first "Indianapolis 500" was held on 5/30/11, won by Ray Harroun
  the backstretch and corners were asphalted in 1939 / the rest in 1961
  (aka: Indianapolis Speedway Park) / the town is now called Speedway
  Jeff Gordon won the first NASCAR WC "Brickyard 400" race on 8/06/94
  over 50 drivers have been fatally injured at Indianapolis Motor Speedway
  including Floyd Roberts (5/30/39) who won the 1938 "Indy 500" and
  Bill Vukuvich, Sr. (5/30/55) who won the 1953 and 1954 "Indy 500s"
  other famous drivers fatally injured at Indianapolis include Tony
  Bettenhausen, Sr. (5/12/61),   Eddie Sachs and Dave MacDonald (5/30/64)

The start of the 1973 "Indianapolis 500". - Official track photo.

The Indianapolis Raceway Park complex. The oval track is on the right, and the dragstrip on the left. Official track photo.

Indianapolis Raceway Park - Clermont / located west of Indianapolis
    1/4 mile paved dragstrip (1960 - present) / home of "U.S. Nationals"
    5/8 mile dirt oval (5/28/61 & 5/29/61) / A.J. Foyt won a USAC sprint car
    race on 5/28/61 and Don White won a USAC stock car race the next day
    1.875 & 2.5 mile paved road courses (6/24/61 - present)
    5/8 (.686) mile paved oval (7/14/61 - present)
    Gary Bettenhausen started his driving career here in 1963
    site of many of the "Thursday or Saturday Night Thunder" races on ESPN
    the first ever Nationally televised drag race was here in 1961 on ABC TV
    1980's promoter, Bob Daniels, was the 1988 RPM Promoter of the Year

Indianapolis Speedrome - Indianapolis / at Kitley & US 52 (SE side of town)
    1/5 mile concrete oval (9/09/41 - 7/31/42) (11/18/44)
    Ted Hartley won inaugural race / built by the Sexton brothers
    ran in 1944 when the U.S. Government briefly lifted the ban on auto racing
    during World War II, the race was won by Duke Nalon
    1/5 mile paved oval (9/01/45 - 9/05/48) (1950 - present)
    1/5 mile dirt oval (9/12/48 - 1949) / pavement covered over with dirt
    (aka: Art Zipp's Speedway) / (aka: Eastside Speedway)
    also has a figure 8 track which has been running since 8/07/54

Indianapolis - also see: Belmont, Butler, Carey, Hoosier, Stout, Walnut Gardens

Jefferson County Fairgrounds - see: Madison Fairgrounds

Jungle Park - Rockville / 9 miles north of town near Turkey Run State Park
    1/2 mile dirt/paved oval (7/05/26 - 7/26/42) (9/23/45 - c.1957) (1960)
    built by Earl A. Parker, who was killed by a race car during time trials,
    when he was trying to fix a rut in the track on 8/14/27
    the corners were dirt and the straights were crushed rock and pavement
    1/4 mile dirt oval (mid-1950's) / Frank Funk later owned the track
    Bobby Grim started his career here in 1947 / now the site of the Turkey
    Run Canoe Trip Rental (currently owned by Charlie Sentman's dad)

The famous Jungle Park near Turkey Run State Park in Rockville, Indiana.
Bob Sheldon photo.

Kendallville Fairgrounds - Kendallville / located at the Noble County Fairgrounds
    1/4 mile dirt oval (7/04/27) (7/15/53 - 1963) (aka: Kendallville Speedway)

Kentland - dirt oval (1961)

Knob Hill Race Track - West Point - 1/5 mile dirt oval (5/11/47 - 7/27/47)

Kokomo Driving Park - Kokomo - 1/2 mile dirt oval (8/18/03) / horse track

Kokomo Speedway - Kokomo - 1/2 mile dirt oval (c.7/04/25)

Kokomo Speedway - Kokomo - 1/4 mile dirt oval (7/06/47 - present)
    this track is a different location than the Kokomo Speedway in 1925

Lafayette - 1/4 mile paved oval (1940) / located four miles northeast on Hwy 25

Lafayette Fairgrounds - Lafayette / Wilbur Shaw started his career here in 1921
    1/2 mile dirt oval (c.1916 - c.1922) / at the Tippecanoe County Fairgrounds

Lafayette Speedway - Lafayette - 1/2 mile dirt oval (1945 - c.1948)
    1/2 mile paved oval (1948) / located 1/2 mile south of town on U.S. 52

Lafayette Stadium Speedway - Lafayette / located southeast of town on Hwy 38
    1/5 mile paved oval (c.7/20/47 - c.9/27/57) / turned into a pasture in 1958

Lake Placid - Hartford City - 1/4 mile dirt oval (c.1937 - 1939)

Lake View Speedway - Churubusco / (aka: Columbia City Speedway)
1/4 mile dirt oval (1950 - c.1953)

Lakeview Raceway - see: Steuben County Speedway

Lawrence County Speedway - (location unknown) - 1/4 mile dirt oval (1947)

Lawrenceburg Speedway - Lawrenceburg / at the Dearborn Co. Fairgrounds
1/2 mile dirt oval (1910 - c.1937) (6/26/49 - c.5/14/50) (1957 or 1958)
1/4 mile dirt oval (1946 - present)

League Park - Fort Wayne / located at a minor league baseball stadium
1/5 mile dirt oval (6/01/35 - 6/19/36)

Leary's Concrete Midget Speedway - see: Riley Park

Leary's Speedway - see: Greenfield Speedbowl

Lebanon Fairgrounds - Lebanon / located at the Boone County Fairgrounds
1/8 mile dirt oval (1993 - present)

Lincoln Park Speedway - Putnamville / in downtown Putnamville on U.S. 40
1/4 mile dirt oval (7/11/69 - 1981) / built by Buck Arnold
5/16 mile dirt oval (1982 - present)

Linton - 1/4 mile dirt oval (early 1950's - 1959) / ran T.Q. midgets

Linton Race Track - Linton - 1/2 mile dirt oval (7/10/27 & 7/10/28)

Lion's Delaware County Fairgrounds - Muncie
1/2 mile dirt oval (9/13/21) (c.10/01/38 - 1941) (1946 - early 1950's)
1/6 mile dirt oval (c.1963 - c.1982) (1992 - present)

Littell Park - Greensburg - 1/2 mile dirt oval (10/05/30) / ran jalopies

Logansport Fairgrounds - Logansport - 1/2 mile dirt oval (5/07/39 - 6/29/41) (1961)

*Audie Swartz in his supermodified in 1961. Audie is the father of late model
star Charlie Swartz. - Allan E. Brown collection.*

228

Logansport Speedway - Logansport - 1/2 mile dirt oval (9/15/46 - 1948)

Logansport Speedway - see: U.S. 24 Speedway

Loogootee Fairgrounds - see: Martin County Fair Speedway

Madison Fairgrounds - Madison / located at the Jefferson County Fairgrounds
1/5 mile dirt oval (c.1963 - present) / runs T.Q. midgets

Marengo Speedway - Marengo - 1/4 mile dirt oval (years unknown)

Marion Fairgrounds - Marion / located at the Grant County Fairgrounds
1/2 mile dirt oval (c.1931 - c.7/14/36) / ran sprint cars
1/8 mile dirt oval (1992 - present) / runs Modified-Midgets during fair

Marion - road course (1919) / ran motorcycles only

Marion Speedway - Marion - 1/5 mile dirt oval (6/03/49)

Martin County Fair Speedway - Loogootee / at the Martin County Fairgrounds
1/4 mile dirt oval (1973 - 1978) (1990 - present)

Martinsville Fairgrounds - Martinsville / at the Morgan County Fairgrounds
1/4 mile dirt oval (6/17/55 - c.1959)
1/7 mile dirt oval (c.1963 - c.1985) (1988 - 1989) (1991 - present)

Mellott Speedway - Mellott - 1/4 mile dirt oval (c.1948 - c.1956)

Memorial Stadium - Terre Haute - 1/5 mile dirt oval (8/26/35 - 9/14/36)

Miami County Speedway - Peru / located at the Miami County Fairgrounds
1/8 mile dirt oval (1985 - 1991) (1994 - present)
(aka: Circus City Speedway)

Mid-America Raceway - see: Greater Evansville Raceway, Chandler Raceway

Mishawaka - 1/4 mile dirt oval (c.7/13/56 - c.1956)

Mishawaka - also see: Playland Park

Mitchell Speedrome - Mitchell / (aka: Mitchell Speedway)
1/2 mile dirt oval (c.9/29/46 - c.1957)
1/4 mile dirt oval (1963) / the track had a lake in the middle

Mitchell's Motor Speedway - see: Bloomington Speedway

Monticello Fairgrounds - Monticello - 1/4 mile dirt oval (1939 - 1941) (1946 - 1950)
probably at the White County Fairgrounds

Monticello Speedway - Monticello / (aka: New Monticello Speedway)
1/4 mile dirt oval (7/26/50 - c.1956) / Jack McGrath was first winner
1/2 mile dirt oval (1956) / located south of town on Highway 39
the site is now a church and a housing development

Montpelier Lions Speedway - Montpelier / located at the Montpelier Fairgrounds
1/4 mile dirt oval (4/28/40 - c.1941) (8/25/46 - c.1955) (1985 - present)

Morgan County Fairgrounds - see: Martinsville Fairgrounds

The egg-shaped Mount Lawn Speedway was built around a baseball diamond in 1935. - Official track photo.

Mount Lawn Speedway - New Castle / built by Les Brown
   3/10 mile egg-shaped paved oval (9/15/35 - 1942) (Sept. 1945 - present)
   1/2 mile dirt oval (1935 - 7/26/42) (9/07/46 - 1949)
   located at the Mount Lawn Park / site of the old New Castle Fairgrounds
   the 3/10 mile track had a baseball diamond in the infield

Mountain Raceway - Stinesville - 1/8 mile dirt oval (1985) / off SR 46

Muncie Dragway - Muncie - 1/4 mile paved dragstrip (1959 - present)
   (aka: Muncie Int'l Raceway, Muncie Raceway & Muncie Int'l Dragway)

Muncie Fairgrounds - see: Lion's Delaware County Fairgrounds

Muncie Motor Speedway - Muncie / 1/4 mile paved oval (1964 - 1973) (1985-1990)
   closed by the EPA because it was a toxic dump site

Muncie Velodrome - Muncie - 1/5 mile paved oval (6/14/40-6/26/42) (4/19/46-1946)

Nashville Fairgrounds - Nashville / located at the Brown County Fairgrounds
   1/8 mile dirt oval (1986 - 1987) / ran T.Q. midgets

New Albany Speedway - New Albany - 1/5 mile dirt oval (6/25/39 - 9/24/39)
   this track was not the Corydon Pike Speedway

New Castle Fairgrounds - see: Mount Lawn Speedway

New Castle Speedway - New Castle - 1/4 mile dirt oval (7/27/46 - c.1946)
   1/4 mile paved oval (August, 1946 - c.1946) / (aka: Sullivan's Track)
   promoted by Dan Sheek / located on the northeast edge of New Castle

New Cedar Lake Speedway - Greensburg - 1/4 mile dirt oval (7/01/51)

New Elkhart Speedway - Elkhart / (aka: Uncle Joe's Speedway)
   1/4 mile paved oval (c.7/05/51 - c.1953) / (aka: Elkhart Motor Speedway)
   located at 21st Street and Hively Ave. / ran by Joe Hamsher

New Goshen Speedway - see: Goshen Fairgrounds

230

New Harmony Fairgrounds - New Harmony / at the Posey County Fairgrounds
1/2 mile dirt oval (8/16/31) (1939)

New Paris Speedway - New Paris - 1/4 mile dirt oval (June, 1947 - 8/22/48)
built by Joe Hamsher / (aka: Old Hickory Ridge) / (aka: Hamsher Bowl)
1/4 mile paved oval (9/05/48 - present)

North Manchester Fairgrounds - North Manchester / maybe at Wabash Co. Fair
1/2 mile dirt oval (c.9/27/19 - c.10/02/26)

Oak Park Race Track - Montezuma - dirt oval (7/22/28)

Oakland City Speedway - Oakland City / (aka: Oakland City Speedrome)
1/5 mile high banked dirt oval (8/18/49 - c.1951)
the first feature race was rained out and made up on 8/25/49

Odon Oval - Odon - 1/4 mile dirt oval (7/04/46 - 1947)

Osceola Dragway - Osceola - 1/4 mile paved dragstrip (1982 - present)

Osceola Motor Speedway - Osceola - 1/4 mile dirt oval (c.6/04/50 - c.1955)
(aka: Virg George's Hot Rod Speedway)

Osgood Fairgrounds - see: Ripley County Fairgrounds

Outlaw Speedway - Fortville - 1/5 mile dirt oval (c.1980 - 1982)
located just off of U.S. 67 / torn down in 1983

Owen Hills Speedway - see: Mid-America Raceway

Paoli - dirt oval (1972)

Paoli Speedway - Paoli - 1.0 mile dirt oval (1930's)

Paragon Speedway - Paragon - 3/8 mile dirt oval (c.6/02/57 - present)
built by Harry Redkey / Mike & Sue Johnson were promoters in 1980's

Parkersburg - 1/2 mile dirt oval (1970's)

Pendleton - dirt oval (1950's)

Perry County Speedway - Leopold / located at the Tell City Fairgrounds
1/4 mile dirt oval (c.1969 - c.1980) / (aka: Tell City Speedway)

Peru Fairgrounds - see: Miami County Speedway

Parnelli Jones at Williams Grove Speedway (PA). - Larry Jendras collection.

Playland Park in Mishawaka from 1952. - Bob Sheldon photo.

Playland Park - Mishawaka - 1/2 mile dirt oval (1919 - 7/19/42) (9/16/45 - c.1956)
    1/5 mile dirt oval (8/01/36 - 1942) (1945 - 1952) / NASCAR race 7/20/52
    1/5 mile paved oval (1953 - c.1957) / the promoter was Ed Wegner
    located at the Springbrook Park / the site is now a golf course

Pleasant Hill - Union City - 1/4 mile dirt oval (c.1953 - c.1958)

Pleasant Lake Speedway - Pleasant Lake / located four miles south of Angola
    1/4 mile dirt oval (c.1964) / built by Howard Bice
    closed by the town because Bice didn't get any permits

Plymouth Speedway - see: Capitol Speedway of Plymouth

Porter Speedway - Porter (Chesterton) / (aka: Mineral Springs Race Track)
    1.0 mile dirt oval (7/05/20 - 1937)
    1.125 mile dirt oval (1922) / Jack Leech was the promoter

Portland Fairgrounds - Portland / located at the Jay County Fairgrounds
    1/2 mile dirt oval (c.1924 - c.9/05/27) (1930) (early 1950's)
    1/5 mile dirt oval (c.1981 - 1982) / ran T.Q. midgets on the small track

Pride Speedway - Evansville - 1/2 mile dirt oval (late 1920's - c.11/06/32)

Princeton Fairgrounds - Princeton / located at the Gibson County Fairgrounds
    1/2 mile dirt oval (c.1941) (1946 - c.1977) / (aka: Fairgrounds Speedway)
    1/4 mile dirt oval (c.1952 - c.1957)

Putnam Park Road Course - Mount Meridian / located south of town
    1.8 mile paved road course (1992 - present)

Raceland Speedway - McCordsville / located between Fortville & McCordsville
    1/5 mile paved oval (5/31/42 - 7/19/42) (Sept., 1945 - 1949)
    built as a dog track but never used as such / (aka: the Dog Track)
    the track had a covered grandstands with theater seats
    the floor of the grandstand was glazed tile / site is now a farmer's field

Raceway Park - Chesterfield - 1/4 mile paved oval (years unknown)

Rags Mitchell's 16th Street Speedway - see: West 16th Street Speedway

Rensselaer Raceway - Rensselaer / located at the Jasper County Fairgrounds
    1/2 mile dirt oval (1952 - 1956) / (aka: Rensselaer Speedway)
    3/8 mile dirt circle (1957 - 1987) / Ted Knorr was the last promoter

Richmond Fairgrounds - Richmond / located at the Wayne County Fairgrounds
    1.0 mile dirt oval (early 1900's) / (aka: Single G Oval)
    1/2 mile dirt oval (9/03/28 - c.1932) / located near Centerville

Richmond Midget Stadium - Richmond / located west of town on US 40
    1/4 mile paved oval (9/07/41 - 7/23/42) (1946 - c.1963)

Riley Park - Greenfield / (aka: Leary's Concrete Midget Speedway)
    1/5 mile concrete oval (c.8/17/40 - 1942)
    after the ban on auto racing during World War II, the track was flooded
       with water, and boat races were held

Ripley County Fairgrounds - Osgood - 1/2 mile dirt oval (late 1920's - c.1931)
    1/5 mile dirt oval (c.1979 - 1984) (1986 - 1990) (1992 - present)

Roanoke Fairgrounds Coliseum - Roanoke - indoor oval (6/03/37)

Roby Speedway - Hammond / on the south side of Indianapolis Blvd & 107th
    1.0 mile oiled dirt oval (1920 - 9/20/36) / (aka: New Roby Speedway)
    built in 1920 for motorcycle racing / first auto race was in 1922
    Billy Arnold started his career here
    various promoters include: B. Ward Beam, Jack Leech & Carl Stockholm
    the grandstands were condemned in 1937 / site is now an industrial area
    the Chicago Skyway expressway now runs down the backstretch

One of Indiana's most famous tracks was Roby Speedway in Hammond. The one-mile dirt track ran from 1920 to 1936. - Bob Sheldon collection.

Rochester Fairgrounds - Rochester - 1/2 mile dirt oval (1922) / at Fulton Co. Fair
1/4 mile dirt oval (9/03/90 - 1991) / Ira Hall started here in 1922

Rochester Speedway - Rochester - 1/2 mile dirt oval (7/04/27 - 9/09/34)
Ted Hartley won the inaugural race in a sprint car

Rockford - 1/2 mile dirt oval (1926)

Rushville Fairgrounds - Rushville - 1/10 mile dirt oval (1954) (9/07/57)
1/6 mile dirt oval (c.1959 - 1985) (1988 - present)
located at the Rush County Fairgrounds

Rushville Motor Speedway - Rushville - 1/2 mile dirt oval (c.7/29/27- early 1930's)

Saint Joe Race Track - Evansville / south of Evansville on Saint Joe Street
1/5 & 1.2 mile dirt ovals (1939 - 9/07/41) (c.1946 - 1953)
(aka: Saint Joe Speedway)

Salem - 1/2 mile dirt oval (1921 - 1931) / located on the east edge of town
ran by the American Legion / the property was sold in 1934

Salem Fairgrounds - see: Thunder Valley Raceway

Salem Speedway - Salem / located west of town / (aka: Salem Super Speedway)
1/2 mile oiled dirt oval (6/22/47) / (aka: Greater Salem Super Speedway)
1/2 mile paved oval (7/24/47 - 4/26/81) (1987 - present)
Bob Sweikert fatally injured here on 6/17/56 / (aka: Hi-Bank Speedway)
Rich Vogler fatally injured here on 7/26/90 / on the west side of town

Savage Speedway - Gary / located on 4th Ave. (Industrial Highway)
1/4 mile dirt oval (c.1946 - 1955) / the site is now a junk yard

*This 13 year old kid is none other than Jeff Gordon in his first sprint car ride
at East Bay Raceway in Tampa, Florida. Gordon successfully competed in
sprints cars and midgets before moving on to the NASCAR Winston Cup series.
Bill Morrow photo.*

234

Indiana

Schererville Speedway - see: Illiana Speedway

Scott County Speedway - Scottsburg / south of town at Scott Co. Fairgrounds
1/4 mile dirt oval (c.1963 - c.1971) / ran T.Q. midgets on smaller track
3/8 mile dirt oval (1982 - 1985) (1990 - 1991) (1993 - present)
(aka: I-65 Motor Speedway) / (aka: I-65 Speedway)

Scottsburg Fairgrounds - Scottsburg / located at the old Scott County Fairgrounds
1/2 mile dirt oval (1930's) (1947 - c.1948) (6/24/51)
the track was located near downtown Scottsburg / (aka: Hutton's Park)

Scottsburg Fairgrounds - see: Scott County Speedway

Seelyville Speedway - Seelyville - 1/2 mile dirt oval (5/15/27)
probably was Sunflower Speedway

Shady Hill Raceway - Medaryville - 1/4 mile dirt oval (1971 - present)
ran motorcycles at the beginning / the first auto race was on 7/02/83

Shelbyville Fairgrounds - Shelbyville / located at the Shelby County Fairgrounds
1/8 mile dirt oval (late 1930's) (1955) (1983 - 1987)

Sixteenth Street Speedway - see: West 16th Street Speedway

Skyview Track - Chesterfield - 1/2 mile high banked dirt oval (1948) maybe 1950

South Anthony Speedway - Fort Wayne - 3/10 mile dirt oval (5/20/51 - 1952)
3/8 mile paved oval (5/02/53 - 7/24/64) / south of town on Anthony Blvd.
(aka: Walter-McCulloch Speedway) / the site is a housing development

South Bend Fairgrounds - South Bend - 1/2 mile dirt oval (1921)

South Bend Motor Speedway - South Bend - 1/4 mile paved oval (8/23/46-present)

Southlake Speedway - Crown Point - 1/4 mile dirt oval (1957 - 1980)
1/3 mile dirt oval (1981 - present) / (aka: Broadway Speedway)

Speed's Dragway - Freedom - 1/8 mile paved dragstrip (1967 - present)
1/4 mile dirt oval (1980 - 1981) / (aka: Freedom New Hope Raceway)

Spencer Park - Logansport - 1/2 mile dirt oval (c.1916 - c.1929)
maybe at the Logansport Fairgrounds

Spice Valley Speedway - Mitchell - dirt oval (unknown) / maybe Mitchell Spdrme

Sportsdrome Speedway - Jeffersonville - 1/4 mile paved oval (8/28/47 - present)

Springbrook Park - see: Playland Park

Steeple Chase - Muncie - 3/4 mile dirt road course (1930's)

Steuben County Speedway - see: Angola Motor Speedway

Stout Field - Indianapolis / located south of town on South Holt Road
1.6 mile paved road course on runways (9/27/53) (10/20/57)
1/4 mile concrete dragstrip (1950's)

Sullivan Speedway - Sullivan - 1/2 mile dirt oval (7/25/27 - c.6/24/28)
located on the north side of town

Sullivan Speedway - Sullivan (Dugger) - 1/4 mile dirt oval (c.1950 - 1960)
now the site of a sewage pond

Sullivan Speedway - Sullivan / located south of town on old US 41
1/6 mile dirt oval (1950's) (c.1986 - 1988) (c.1991 - present)

Sun Valley Speedway - see: Anderson Speedway

Sunflower Park - Brazil (Seelyville) / located 8 miles east of Terre Haute
1/2 mile dirt oval (c.1924 - c.5/03/31) / ran a 6 hour jalopy race in 1926
located near Coverland on National Road (now called U.S. 40)

Sweet Owen Speedway - Spencer - 1/4 mile dirt oval (c.1969 - 1983) (1987)

Syracuse - 1/8 mile dirt oval (7/09/50 - c.1950)

Taylorsville - 1/4 mile dirt oval (early 1950's) / located in a cow pasture

Tell City Fairgrounds (Speedway) - see: Perry County Speedway

Johnny Parsons at Terre Haute in 1991. - Randy Jones photo.

Terre Haute Action Track - Terre Haute / built in 1949 / (aka: The Action Track)
1/2 mile dirt oval (6/15/52 - 1987) (1990 - present) / at Vigo Co. Fairgrounds
Joe James was the first winner / located next to Action Track Dragway

Terre Haute Fairgrounds - Terre Haute / ran motorcycles in 1911
1.0 mile dirt oval (1911) (c.5/23/14 - 6/30/28)

Terre Haute - also see: Black Demon, Fastrack, Memorial Stadium, Sunflower

Thunder Valley Raceway - Salem / located at the Washington County Fairgrounds
1/2 mile dirt oval (1915 - c.1920) (c.1940 - c.1941) (c.1946)
1/5 mile dirt oval (c.1963 - c.1983) (1986 - present) / south side of town

Thunderdrome Speedway - Fairview - 1/4 mile dirt oval (c.7/13/41 - c.5/10/42)

Tipton Fairgrounds - Tipton - 1/2 mile dirt oval (7/22/34 - c.5/23/37)

Tri-Lakes Speedway - Merriam - 1/10 mile dirt oval (1953 - 1960) / T.Q. midgets

Tri-State Speedway - Haubstadt / builder: Ed Helfrich, now owned by his son Tom
1/4 mile dirt oval (1957 - present) / located north of Evansville

Twin Cities Raceway Park - Vernon - 1/10 mile dirt oval (c.7/17/57 - c.1957)
1/4 mile dirt oval (c.1963 - present) / (aka: Twin Cities Speedway)

U.S. 20 Speedway - Plato - 1/4 mile dirt oval (1960)

U.S. 24 Speedway - Logansport - 1/10 mile dirt oval (1960 - c.1961)
1/8 mile paved oval (1962 - 1990) / located west of town in U.S. 24
1/8 mile dirt oval (1991 - present) / (aka: Logansport Speedway)

U.S. 30 Dragway - Merrillville - 1/4 mile paved dragstrip (1957 - 1985)

U.S. 41 Int'l Speedway - Morocco - 1/4 mile paved dragstrip (May, 1993 - present)

Uncle Joe's Speedway - see: New Elkhart Speedway

Union County Speedway - Liberty / (aka: Whitewater Valley Speedway)
3/8 mile high banked dirt oval (1970 - 1982)
3/8 mile semi-banked dirt oval (1983 - present)

Unionport - dirt oval (1955)

Upland Raceway - Upland - 1/8 mile dirt oval (c.1989 - 1990)

Valparaiso Raceway - Valparaiso - dirt oval (7/01/34 - 8/26/34) / horse track

Vevay Fairgrounds - Vevay / located at the Switzerland County Fairgrounds
1/6 mile dirt oval (1976) (1980) / ran T.Q. midget races

Vincennes - 1/4 mile dirt oval (1934) (1941) / located near the O'Neal Airport

Vincennes Fairgrounds - Vincennes / located at the old Knox County Fairgrounds
1/2 mile dirt oval (1914 - 8/31/18) / ran motorcycles 1914 to 1918
the only auto race was held on 8/31/18

Vincennes Speedway - Vincennes / located 3/4 mile north of town
1/2 mile dirt oval (7/15/28 - c.7/22/28) / this was not Clark Speedway

Virg George's Hot Rod Speedway - see: Osceola Motor Speedway

Wabash Fairgrounds - Wabash / located at the Wabash County Fairgrounds
1/2 mile dirt oval (c.1927 - c.1929)

Walnut Gardens Speedway - Indianapolis (Camby) / south of town on Hwy 37
1/2 mile dirt oval (7/05/29 - c.1934)

Walter-McCulloch Speedway - see: South Anthony Speedway

Warren Fairgrounds - Warren - 1/2 mile dirt oval (9/07/14 - 1930)

Warsaw Speedway - Warsaw / located at the Kosciusko County Fairgrounds
1/4 mile dirt oval (c.6/18/49 - 1986) / (aka: Warsaw Motor Speedway)
3/8 mile dirt oval (1987 - 8/11/90) / Larry Moore started here in 1960
closed by nine influential neighbors that lived on Winona Lake
ran a figure eight race during the fair in 1993

Waveland - dirt oval (late 1940's) / located in a cornfield

The pace lap at West 16th Street Speedway - Len Ashburn photo.

West 16th Street Speedway - Indianapolis / across from Indianapolis Motor Spdwy
(aka: 16th Street Speedway) / (aka: Indianapolis Midget Speedway)
1/4 mile paved oval (5/29/46 - 1958) / (aka: Speedbowl Park)
(aka: Rags Mitchell's West 16th Street Speedway) / now a shopping plaza

Whitewater Valley Speedway - see: Union County Speedway

Williams Speedway - Bedford - 1/4 mile dirt oval (late 1950's - early 1960's)
maybe the same track as Eureka Speedway

Winamac Speedway - Winamac / located at the Pulaski County Fairgrounds
1/4 & 1/2 mile dirt ovals (late 1940's - early 1950's)

Winchester Speedway - Winchester / built in a cornfield by Frank Funk
1/2 mile flat oiled dirt oval (1914 - 1921) / (aka: Funk's Lake)
1/2 mile banked dirt oval (1922 - 1929) / (aka: Funk's Motor Speedway)
1/2 mile high-banked oiled dirt oval (9/01/29 - 5/30/42)(9/03/45 - c.1950)
ran a NASCAR Grand National race here on 10/15/50, won by Lloyd Moore
1/2 mile high-banked asphalt oval (c.1951 - present)
promoters: Frank Funk (1914 - 3/30/63) / Pete Wales (1963-1970)
                    Roger Holdeman (1971 - present)

Winchester Speedway in 1939 - Bob Sheldon photo.

Wolf Lake Midget Speedway - Hammond - 1/5 mile dirt oval (6/09/35 - c.8/23/35)
1/5 mile paved oval (6/12/36 - c.1937) / this was not Hammond Raceway

Wolf Lake Speedway - Hammond / on a man-made island in middle of Wolf Lake
1.0 mile dirt (sand) oval (7/16/33 - 1934)

Zipp's Speedway - see: Indianapolis Speedrome

IOWA

34 Raceway - see: Thirty-Four (34) Raceway

Adams County Speedway - Corning / located at the Adams County Fairgrounds
1/2 mile dirt oval (1940) (c.8/14/58 - present)

Adel - 1/4 mile dirt oval (early 1950's) / possibly at the Dallas Co. Fairgrounds

Afton Fairgrounds - Afton - dirt figure eight (1993) / at the Union Co. Fairgrounds

Air View Speedway - Monticello - 1/4 mile dirt oval (late 1950's) / near the river

Airport Speedway - see: South Dakota chapter

Algona Fairgrounds - see: Kossuth County Raceway

Allison Fairgrounds - Allison / located at the Butler County Fairgrounds
1/2 mile dirt oval (early 1950's)

Alta Fairgrounds - see: Buena Vista County Raceway

Alta Speedbowl - Alta - dirt oval (1961)

Anamosa - 1/2 mile dirt oval (1910's) (c.1925 - c.1928)

Arnolds Park Speedway - Arnolds Park - 1/5 mile dirt oval (1936) (early 1950's)

Atlantic Fairgrounds - Atlantic / located at the Cass County Fairgrounds
1/2 mile dirt oval (1910) (1929) (9/02/35 & 7/04/36)

Audubon County Speedway - Audubon / located at the Audubon Co. Fairgrounds
4/10 mile dirt oval (c.1967 - 6/01/76) (1988 - present)
the original track built by Johnny Beauchamp / revamped in 1988

Avoca Fairgrounds - Avoca / located at the Pottawattamie County Fairgrounds
dirt oval (c.1958 - 1965)

Bedford Fairgrounds - Bedford / located at the Taylor County Fairgrounds
1/2 mile dirt oval (c.1917 - c.1919) (1926) (8/10/40 - 8/09/41)(c.1946 - 1950's)

Belmond Fairgrounds - see: Clarion Fairgrounds

Benton County Speedway - Vinton / located at the Benton County Fairgrounds
1/2 mile dirt oval (8/08/41) (8/03/46 - c.1955)
1/4 mile dirt oval (c.1973 - 1983) (1985) (1987 - present)
(aka: Vinton Speedway)

Big Four Speedway - Nashua - 1/4 mile dirt oval (c.1971 - 1973)
possibly at the Big Four Fairgrounds

Blackhawk Speedway - Keosauqua - dirt oval (1968) / ran T.Q. midgets

Bloomfield Speedway - Bloomfield / located at the Davis County Fairgrounds
1/2 mile dirt oval (c.1934 - 8/13/41) (8/16/46 - c.1954) (1967)
3/8 mile dirt oval (1968 - 1975) (1992 - present)

Boone Speedway - Boone - 1/3 mile dirt oval (1967 - present)
track operator Bob Lawton was 1992 RPM Promoter of the Year
home of the annual "IMCA Nationals"

Boone - also see: North Side Driving Park

Buena Vista Raceway - Alta / at the Buena Vista County Fairgrounds
1/2 mile dirt oval (c.1915 - 1921) (5/30/46 & 8/13/46)
1/5 mile dirt oval (9/22/46 - 1946) / the fair started in 1904
3/8 mile dirt oval (8/11/55 - 1983) (1987 - present)
(aka: Buena Vista County Raceway)

Burlington Fairgrounds - Burlington / located at the Des Moines Co. Fairgrounds
1/2 mile dirt oval (7/09/15 - 1942) (7/14/46 - c.1960)
the first race on 7/09/15 was a AAA sanctioned champ race
1/4 mile dirt oval (7/04/40) (c.1946 - c.1965) / the fair started in 1904
(aka: Hawkeye Fairgrounds) / (aka: Tri-State Fairgrounds)

Burlington - also see: Thirty-Four (34) Raceway

Bushnell T.Q. Speedway - (location unknown) - 1/10 mile dirt oval (1956)
T.Q. midgets / possibly in Illinois instead / or Bussard Track

Bussard Track - Fort Dodge - 1/10 mile dirt oval (6/03/56 - c.1956) / Micro-midgets

Calhoun County Fairgrounds - Rockwell City / track under water in flood of 1993
1/2 mile dirt oval (1938) (9/16/51) (early 1960's) / ran one heat on 9/16/51
and had a fatality, the rest of the program was cancelled
1/4 mile dirt oval (1993 - present) / ran figure eight races in late 1980's
located at the Rockwell City Park / (aka: Calhoun County Exposition)

Multi-time I.M.C.A. champion Emory Collins in his 318 cubic inch "Offy". This was one of Collins' favorite pictures. - Bob Stolze photo.

240

Ce Mar Acres - Cedar Rapids / located between Cedar Rapids & Marion
   1/5 mile dirt oval (8/18/46 - c.1954) / (aka: Cedar Rapids Speed Bowl)
   located at the Ce Mar Acres Amusement Park

Cedar Falls Fairgrounds - Cedar Falls / located at the Cedar Valley Fairgrounds
   1/2 mile dirt oval (c.9/24/15 - c.1930)

Cedar Falls Raceway - Cedar Falls / (aka: Neita Dragway)
   1/4 mile paved dragstrip (1965 - present) / (aka; Cedar Falls Dragway)

Cedar Rapids (Fairgrounds) Speedway - see: Hawkeye Downs Raceway

Cedar Rapids Speed Bowl - see: Ce Mar Acres

Centerville Fairgrounds - Centerville / at the Appanoose County Fairgrounds
   1/4 mile dirt oval (c.1947 - c.1951)

Central City Fairgrounds - Central City / located at the Linn County Fairgrounds
   1/2 mile dirt oval (1910's) (1928) / only held horse races since 1928

Chariton Speed Bowl - Chariton / located at the Lucas County Fairgrounds
   1/2 mile dirt oval (1948 - c.1963) / (aka: Chariton Raceway)
   1/4 mile dirt oval (1964) / (aka: Southern Iowa Community Park)

Cherokee Fairgrounds - Cherokee / located at the Cherokee County Fairgrounds
   1/4 mile dirt oval (late 1950's)

Churchill Downs - see: Midway Downs

Clarinda Fairgrounds - Clarinda / located at the Page County Fairgrounds
   1/2 mile dirt oval (1934 & 1935)

Clarion Fairgrounds - Clarion - 1/2 mile dirt oval (1918)
   located at the Wright County Fairgrounds

Clarmond Raceway - see: Wright County Speedway

Clay County Fairgrounds - Spencer / the fairgrounds opened in 1918
   1/2 mile dirt oval (c.9/11/34 - c.1941) (9/03/46 - 1980) (1985 - present)

The I.M.C.A. sprint cars wait to be pushed off at the Spencer Fairgrounds in 1948. Identified drivers are Billy Snyder (#13), Ernie Johnson (#5), and Emory Collins (#7). - Bob Stolze photo.

Clinton Fairgrounds - Clinton / the fairgrounds was built in 1881
   1/2 mile dirt oval (1911) (1920's) (1950's)

Clinton Speedway - Clinton - 1/4 mile dirt oval (1960's) / possibly at fairgrounds

Collins Field - LeMars - 3/8 mile dirt oval (c.1969 - 1973)
   the track was dedicated to Emory Collins

Columbus Junction Fairgrounds - see: Louisa County Fairgrounds

Community Track - see: Dayton Rodeo Grounds

Coon River Fairgrounds - Coon River / located at the Carroll County Fairgrounds
   dirt figure eight track (1993)

Cordes Speedway - see: Tunis Speedway

Corning Fairgrounds - see: Adams County Speedway

Corydon Fairgrounds - Corydon / located at the Wayne County Fairgrounds
   1/2 mile dirt oval (early 1950's)

Council Bluff Fairgrounds - Council Bluffs / dirt oval (1950's)
   at West Pottawattamie County Fairgrounds
   also ran figure eight races during the fair in 1984

Council Bluffs - 1/5 mile dirt oval (9/03/38 - 1938)

Council Bluffs - dirt oval (1910) / probably a horse track or a fairgrounds

Council Bluffs - also see: Playland Park

Crawford County Speedway - Denison / located at the Crawford Co. Fairgrounds
   1/2 mile dirt oval (c.8/14/51 - present)

Cresco Speedway - Cresco / located at the Howard County Fairgrounds
   1/2 mile dirt oval (c.9/01/36 - 8/29/41) (8/26/46 - 1963)
   3/8 mile dirt oval (1964 - present)

Davenport Baseball Stadium - Davenport - 1/5 mile dirt oval (7/14/35 - c.1935)

Davenport Fairgrounds - Davenport / located at the old Scott County Fairgrounds
   1.0 mile dirt oval (1904 - c.8/16/16) / different site from new fair

Davenport Speedway - Davenport / located at the Mississippi Valley Fairgrounds
   1/2 mile dirt oval (8/20/20 - 7/14/42) (c.8/24/45 - 1984) (1987 - present)
   Herb Thomas won a NASCAR GN race here on 8/02/53 (only Iowa GN race)
   1/4 mile dirt oval (9/23/45 - c.1964) (1982 - c.1986)
   John Gerber was the promoter in the late 1940's to the mid 1950's
   the 1/4 mile track was torn out in the mid 1960's and put back in 1982

Dayton Rodeo Grounds - Dayton / (aka: Dayton Speedway)
   1/5 mile dirt oval (c.1962 - 1967) / (aka: Community Speedway)
   (aka: Community Track)

Decatur County Speedway - Decatur City - 1/4 mile dirt oval (1972 - 1982)
   located off of Highway 2 / this track was not at a fairgrounds

Decorah Fairgrounds - see: Nordic Speedway

242

Denison Fairgrounds - see: Crawford County Fairgrounds

Derby Speedway - Derby - 1/10 mile dirt oval (1984 - c.1986) / off Hwy 65

Des Moines - 1/5 mile dirt oval (5/01/40 - 9/06/41) / at East 21st & Dean

Des Moines Fairgrounds - see: Iowa State Fairgrounds

Des Moines Grand Prix - Des Moines / run a downtown city streets
    1.8 mile paved city street road course (1989 - 1991)
    2.1 mile paved city street road course (1992) (1994 - present)
    the race was cancelled in 1993 because of the great flood of 1993
    (aka: Ruan Greater Des Moines Grand Prix) / SCCA Trans-Am

Des Moines Speedway - Des Moines / (aka: Western League Ball Park)
    1/5 mile dirt oval (1938)

Des Moines Speedway - Valley Junction - 1.0 mile wood oval (7/25/15 - 6/26/16)
    owned by the Des Moines Chamber of Commerce / built by Jack Prince
    turns were banked 30 degrees / Joe Cooper fatally injured on 8/07/15
    site is now a cornfield just west of the current Penn-Dixie Cement Plant
    the town of Valley Junction is now called West Des Moines

Des Moines - also see: Greater Des Moines, Pioneer, Vandalia, Veterans Arena

DeWitt Fairgrounds - DeWitt / located at the Clinton County Fairgrounds
    1/2 mile dirt oval (c.1911 - 1928)

DeWitt High School - DeWitt - 1/10 mile dirt oval (1965) / ran T.Q. midgets

Donnellson Fairgrounds - see: Lee County All-Star Speedway

Dubuque Fairgrounds Speedway - Dubuque / at the Dubuque Co. Fairgrounds
    3/8 mile dirt oval (1969 - present) / (aka: Dubuque Speedway)

Dubuque Speed Bowl - see: Sportsbowl

Johnny White (#1) in the Sid Weinberger Homes Chevy leads Pete Folse in
Hector Honore's (#2) Offy at Des Moines in 1963. - Bob Stolze collection.

Dubuque - also see: Municipal Athletic Field, Sportsbowl

Eddyville Dragway - Eddyville - 1/8 & 1/4 mile paved dragstrips (1964 - present)
1/4 mile paved oval (1994 - present)

Eldon Raceway - Eldon / located at the Wapello County Fairgrounds
1/2 mile dirt oval (c.1934 - 8/21/41) (8/22/46 - 1982) (1984 - present)
1/5 mile dirt oval (early 1950's)

Eldora Fairgrounds - see: Greenbelt Speedway

Emerson Speedway - Emerson - 1/8 mile dirt oval (1967)

Essex - dirt oval (early 1950's) / Bob Kosiski used to run here

Expo Park - Fort Dodge / located at the Webster County Fairgrounds
1/2 mile dirt oval (c.1928 - c.7/04/36)
1/4 mile dirt oval (1949 - early 1950's)

Fair Street Speedway - see: Kossuth County Raceway

Fairfield Fairgrounds - Fairfield / located at the Jefferson County Fairgrounds
1/4 mile dirt oval (c.1984 - 1993)

Farley Speedway - Farley - 3/8 mile dirt oval (c.5/15/49 - c.1953)

Farley Speedway - Farley / (aka: New Farley Speedway) / high banked track
1/2 mile clay oval (1970 - 1977) (1982 - 1985) (1987) (1989 - present)

Fayette County Raceway - West Union / at the Fayette County Fairgrounds
5/8 mile dirt oval (1947 - 1952) / (aka: Fayette County Fair Raceway)
1/4 mile dirt oval (1959 - 1992) / new grandstands in 1947
3/8 mile dirt oval (1993 - present)

Fort Dodge Fairgrounds - see: Expo Park

Fort Dodge Midget Speedway - Fort Dodge - 1/5 mile dirt oval (Oct,1941-10/19/41)

Fort Dodge - also see: Bussard Track, Sportsman Park

Fort Madison Speedway - Fort Madison - 1/4 mile dirt oval (c.1964 - c.1967)

Frontier Park - see: Hawkeye Downs Speedway

Glenwood Fireman's Field - Glenwood - 1/4 mile dirt oval (10/20/46)

Golden Hawk Speedway - see: I-35 Speedway

Great Jones County Fairgrounds - Monticello
1/2 mile dirt oval (c.1954 - c.1989) (1991 - present)

Greater Des Moines Dragway - Des Moines / located west of Des Moines
1/4 mile paved dragstrip (c.1958-c.1963)
Bob Trostle started his racing career prior to his oval track racing

Greenbelt Speedway - Eldora / located at the Hardin County Fairgrounds
1/2 mile dirt oval (1929) (8/06/40) (8/08/41) (8/16/46 - c.1958)
(6/27/87 - 1990) (1992 - present) / (aka: Harconia Raceway)

244   *Iowa*

Greene County Speedway - Jefferson / located at the Greene County Fairgrounds
  1/2 mile dirt oval (early 1920's) (early 1950's - c.1956)
  Gus Schrader started his driving career here in the early 1920's
  1/4 mile dirt oval (1970 - c.7/07/80) (1983 - present)
  (aka: Jefferson Speedway)

Greenfield Fairgrounds - Greenfield - dirt oval (1949) / at Adair Co. Fairgrounds

Greenwood Roadway - Indianola - 3.1 mile paved road course (c.1963 - 1965)

Guthrie Center Fairgrounds - Guthrie Center - dirt figure eight (1993)
  located at the Guthrie County Fairgrounds

Hamilton County Speedway - Webster City / at the Hamilton Co. Fairgrounds
  1/4 mile dirt oval (1938 - 9/03/41) (6/09/46 - 5/25/47)
  1/2 mile dirt oval (6/08/47 - present)

Hampton Fairgrounds - Hampton / located at the Franklin County Fairgrounds
  1/2 mile dirt oval (8/24/16)

Harconia Raceway - see: Greenbelt Speedway

Harlan Fairgrounds - see: Shelby County Speedway

Harvey Bowl - see: Midway Downs

*Emory Collins (#7) and Ben Musick (#1) race side by side at Hawkeye Downs
in 1947. - Bob Stolze collection.*

Hawkeye Downs Speedway - Cedar Rapids / located at the All Iowa Fairgrounds
  1/2 mile dirt oval (9/07/25 - 8/15/41) (5/30/46 - 1988)
  Gus Schrader won the first feature race on 9/07/25 / (aka: Frontier Park)
  1/4 mile dirt oval (c.1950 - c.1964) / (aka: Cedar Rapids Speedway)
  1/2 mile paved oval (5/05/89 - present) / (aka: Hawkeye Downs)

Hawkeye Raceway - Blue Grass - 1/4 mile dirt oval (1963 - 1980)
  3/8 mile dirt oval (1982 - present)

Howard County Fairgrounds - see: Cresco Speedway

Humboldt County Dragway - Dakota City
1/8 mile paved dragstrip (1962 - present)

Humboldt Fairgrounds - Humboldt / located at the Humboldt County Fairgrounds
1/2 mile dirt oval (early 1950's)

I-29 Speedway - Sidney - 1/2 mile dirt oval (c.1971 - 1973) (1976 - c.1977)
(aka: Whitehead Speedway) / the track was located west of I-29 on Hwy 2
the grandstands were setting in the middle of a corn field after it closed
(usually referred to as Nebraska City, NE even through track was in Iowa)

I-35 Speedway - Mason City / located at the Northern Iowa Fairgrounds
1/2 mile dirt oval (c.1963 - present) / (aka: Cerro Gordo Fairgrounds)
1/4 mile dirt oval (1984) / (aka: Golden Hawk Speedway)
(aka: Mohawk Speedway)(aka: Mason City Speedway) / located west of town

Independence Motor Speedway - Independence / at the Buchanon Co. Fairgrounds
1/2 mile dirt oval (c.1934 - 1941) (c.1946 - c.1948)
1/3 mile dirt oval (c.8/14/53 - 1974) / 3/8 mile dirt oval (1975 - present)

Indianola Fairgrounds - Indianola - 1/2 mile dirt oval (7/04/17 - 8/07/41)
1/4 mile dirt oval (1948 - 1950) (1989 - 1993) / at Warren County Fairgrounds
neighbors complained and forced the track to close at the end of 1993

Interstate Speedway - see: South Dakota chapter

Iowa City Fairgrounds - Iowa City / located at the Johnson County Fairgrounds
dirt oval (1922) / ran motorcycles

Iowa City Road Course - Iowa City - paved road course (5/02/54)

Iowa State Fairgrounds Pavilion - Des Moines / located east of town
1/10 mile indoor concrete oval (11/15/36 & 11/19/36) / ran midgets

Iowa State Fairgrounds Speedway - Des Moines / located east of town on 30th
1/2 mile dirt oval (8/14/1907 - 6/14/42) (7/04/46 - 1986) (1989 - present)
the fairgrounds opened in 1886 / ran IMCA sprints from 1915 - 1977

*Tom Bigelow heads the pack out of turn No. 4 and down the chute at the Iowa
State Fair in Des Moines. - Photo courtesy of I.M.C.A.*

Jackson County Speedway - Maquoketa / at the Jackson County Fairgrounds
  1/2 mile dirt oval (1910's) (c.1934) (c.1950 - early 1960's)
  1/4 mile dirt oval (1946 - 1952) / (aka: Jackson County Fair Speedway)
  3/8 mile dirt oval (c.1971 - 1982) (1991 - present)
  (aka: Maquoketa Speedway)

Jefferson Fairgrounds - see: Greene County Speedway

Keokuk Fairgrounds - Keokuk - 1/2 mile dirt oval (1910's - c.1924)

Keokuk - also see: Lee County Raceway Park, Sportsman Park

Keosauqua Fairgrounds - Keosauqua - 1/2 mile dirt oval (8/06/41)
  located at the Van Buren County Fairgrounds

Kessell Speedway - see: Pioneer Speedway

Knoxville Raceway - Knoxville / located at the Marion County Fairgrounds
  1/2 mile dirt oval (c.1910 - 9/16/14) (1930's - c.9/26/41) (1949 - present)
  started running weekly in 1954 / home of the annual "Knoxville Nationals"

*An aerial view of Knoxville Raceway. The white building in the top left-hand
corner is the National Sprint Car Hall of Fame. - Official track photo.*

Kossuth County Raceway - Algona / located at the Kossuth County Fairgrounds
  1/2 mile dirt oval (c.1935 - 8/21/41) (9/02/46 - c.5/30/47)
  1/4 mile dirt oval (c.1951 - 1981) (1986) (1989)
  4/10 mile dirt oval (1990 - present) / (aka: Kossuth County Speedway)
  (aka: Fair Street Speedway)

Kossuth County Speedway - see: Fair Street Speedway

Lakeside Speedway - (location unknown) - 1/8 mile dirt oval (1972 - 1980)
  located near Carter Lake

Lee County Raceway Park - Keokuk / (aka: Tri-State Dragway)
  1/4 mile dirt oval (c.1966 - c.1977) / (aka: Lee County Dragway)
  1/8 mile paved dragstrip (c.1977 - 1987)

Lee County Speedway - Donnellson / located at the Lee County Fairgrounds
   1/2 mile dirt oval (c.5/30/18 - 5/17/42) (c.1946 - 7/24/54) (1956 - 1985)
   3/8 mile dirt oval (6/13/86 - present) / (aka: Lee County Raceway)
   (aka: Donnellson Dirt Track) / (aka: Lee County All-Star Raceway)

Little Indianapolis Speedway - Cedar Rapids - dirt oval (1939 - 9/29/40)

Louisa County Fairgrounds - Columbus Junction / (aka: Twin River Raceways)
   1/4 mile dirt oval (c.1949 - c.8/30/49) / (aka: Columbus Junction Race Oval)
   1/2 mile dirt oval (c.1956 - 1976) (1980) (1985) (1988 - present)
   the track was under water in 1993 when the Iowa River flooded

Mahoneys Park - Davenport - 1/4 mile dirt oval (c.5/07/50 - 1950)
   the site is now a resort on a lake

Malvern Fairgrounds - Malvern - 1/5 & 1/2 mile dirt oval (early 1950's)
   located at the Mills County Fairgrounds

Manchester Fairgrounds - Manchester - 1/2 mile dirt oval (8/09/51)
   located at the Delaware County Fairgrounds

Manson Fairgrounds - Manson - 1/2 mile dirt oval (8/27/18 (1929) (5/16/48)

Maquoketa Fairgrounds - see: Jackson County Speedway

Marcus Community Fairgrounds - Marcus - dirt oval (years unknown)

Marengo Fairgrounds - Marengo / located at the Iowa County Fairgrounds
   1/2 mile dirt oval (1920's & 1930's) (1970 - 11/02/72)
   (aka: Marengo Raceway)

Marion County Fairgrounds - see: Knoxville Raceway

Marion Fairgrounds - Marion / located at the Interstate Fairgrounds
   1/2 mile dirt oval (1910)

Marshalltown - dirt oval (1950's) / located southeast of town on Highway 37

Marshalltown Fairgrounds - Marshalltown / closer to downtown than current fair
   1/2 mile dirt oval (c.1934 - 1941) (c.7/27/47 - c.1964)
   1/4 mile dirt oval (1940)

Marshalltown Speedway - Marshalltown / located at the Central Iowa Fairgrounds
   1/4 mile dirt oval (c.1965 - present) / located on southeast side of town
   (aka: Marshall County Fairgrounds)

Mason City Fairgrounds - Mason City / close to downtown than new fairgrounds
   1/2 mile dirt oval (c.1914 - 8/31/41) (5/19/46 - c.1955)
   1/4 mile dirt oval (1950) / (aka: Mohawk Speedrome)
   located at the Cerro Gordo County Fairgrounds

Mason City - also see: Raceway Park, Short Circuit Midget Speedway

Midway Downs - Charles City - 5/8 mile dirt oval (c.7/06/52 - 1955)
   1/4 mile dirt oval (c.1954 - 1969) (1976 - 1977) / torn down in 1979
   (aka: Churchill Bowl) / (aka: Harvey Bowl) / (aka: Harvey Race Bowl)

Milford - 1/4 mile dirt oval (mid 1950's)

Mississippi Valley Fairgrounds - see: Davenport Speedway

Missouri Valley Fairgrounds - Missouri Valley / at the Harrison Co. Fairgrounds
1/2 mile dirt oval (1934) (early 1950's)

Mohawk Speedrome - see: Mason City Fairgrounds

Monticello Fairgrounds - see: Great Jones County Fairgrounds

Mount Pleasant Fairgrounds - Mount Pleasant - 1/2 mile dirt oval (c.1951 - 1983)
located at the Henry County Fairgrounds

Mount Vernon - 1/2 mile dirt oval (1928) (9/10/37)

Moville Fairgrounds - Moville / located at the Woodbury County Fairgrounds
1/2 mile dirt oval (9/05/39) / ran a figure eight race in 1984

Municipal Athletic Field - Dubuque - 1/5 mile dirt oval (9/01/40)

Muscatine Speedway - Muscatine - 1/5 mile dirt oval (1939 - 1941)

Nashua Fairgrounds - Nashua / located at the Chickasaw County Fairgrounds
1/2 mile dirt oval (7/04/42) (1946 - 1948)

Nat'l Cattle Congress Hippodrome - Waterloo / at the Nat'l Cattle Congress Expo
1/10 mile indoor concrete oval (11/16/36) (11/22/58) / ran midgets

Neita Dragway - see: Cedar Falls Dragway

New Farley Speedway - see: Farley Speedway

Newton Fairgrounds - Newton / located at the Jasper County Fairgrounds
1/2 mile dirt oval (1934)

Newton Speedway - Newton - 1/5 mile dirt oval (1947)
1/4 mile dirt oval (1948 - 1973) / site is now a little league park

Nordic Speedway - Decorah / located at the Winneshiek County Fairgrounds
1/2 mile dirt oval (8/17/15 - 7/05/42) (8/17/47 - c.8/15/58)
1/4 mile dirt oval (c.1959 - 1977) (1983 - present)
(aka: Decorah Speedway)

North Iowa Speedway - see: I-35 Speedway

North Side Driving Park - Boone / located at 22nd & Linn
1/2 mile dirt oval (1912 - c.1917)

Ocheyedan - dirt oval (c.1927 - c.1929)

Onawa Fairgrounds - Onawa / located at the Monona County Fairgrounds
dirt oval (early 1950's) / ran figure eights 1983 & 1984

Orange City - 1/4 mile dirt oval (7/05/37 - c.1938)

Osage Fairgrounds - Osage - 1.0 mile dirt oval (9/27/12)
1/2 mile dirt oval (6/30/46 - 6/03/51)
1/4 mile dirt oval (Aug., 1957 - c.1966) / at the Mitchell Co. Fairgrounds

Oskaloosa Fairgrounds - see: Southern Iowa Speedway

Osky Speedway - see: Southern Iowa Fairgrounds

Ottumwa Aces Speedway - Ottumwa - 1/4 mile dirt oval (5/21/50 - 1952) (1954)
    located west of town just off on US 34

Ottumwa - dirt oval (1940)

Ottumwa Sports Arena - Ottumwa - 1/4 mile dirt oval (5/04/52 & 1953) (1955)
    located north of town on US 63 on Francis Kelsey's farm

Perry Fairgrounds - Perry - 1/2 mile dirt oval (9/29/35)

Perry Speedway - Perry - 1/4 mile dirt oval (1954) / maybe at the fairgrounds

Pioneer Speedway - Des Moines / located at Southeast 14th & Hartford
    1/4 mile dirt oval (c.8/15/51 - c.1958) / (aka: Kessell Speedway)
    now the site of the Pioneer Drive-In Theater / called Kessell in 1951 only

Playland Park - Council Bluffs / (aka: L & G Playland Park) / torn down in 1977
    1/4 mile dirt oval (6/07/47 - c.1954) / Tiny Lund started his career here
    1/4 mile paved oval (c.1955 - 1977)

Raah Speedway - Oskaloosa - 1/5 mile dirt oval (1988 - 1992)
    opened as a Go-Kart track in 1986 / ran Mini-sprints 1988 to 1992

Raceway Park - Mason City - dirt oval (1961)

Rapid Raceway - Rock Rapids / located at the Lyons County Fairgrounds
    1/2 mile dirt oval (c.1929 - c.1941) (c.1946 - 1960's)
    3/8 mile dirt oval (early 1970's - present)

Danny Lasoski of Dover, MO is the reigning Knoxville Raceway champion. He is one of the nation's top sprint car drivers. - Jeff Jones photo.

Red Oak Fairgrounds - Red Oak / located at the Montgomery County Fairgrounds
 1/2 mile dirt oval (c.1908 - c.1910)
 Eddie Richenbacher started his driving career here in 1910
 1/8 mile dirt oval (1961 - 1966) (7/18/91 - present)

Richland 77 Speedway - Richland - dirt oval (1977) / maybe Go-Karts only

Ringgold County Speedway - Mount Ayr - 1/2 mile dirt oval (c.1975 - c.1977)
 probably located at the Ringgold County Fairgrounds

Riverview Speedway was on the same site as the Sioux City Fairground tracks. Located at an amusement park the "Thriller" roller-coaster is in the background. - Bob Stolze collection.

Riverview Speedway - Sioux City / same property as old Sioux City Fairgrounds
 1/5 mile dirt oval (6/30/36 - 10/11/36) (1946 - 1955) (1957)
 1/5 mile paved oval (6/13/37 - 6/13/42) (7/04/45)
 the 7/04/45 race was run with the permission of the D.O.T.

Rock Rapids - 1/6 mile wood oval (1940's)

Rock Rapids Fairgrounds - see: Rapids Speedway

Ruan Greater Des Moines Grand Prix - see: Des Moines Grand Prix

Sac City Fairgrounds - Sac City / located at the Sac County Fairgrounds
 1/2 mile dirt oval (c.1929 - 1941) (8/13/46 - c.1956) (1972)

Shelby County Speedway - Harlan / located at the Shelby County Fairgrounds
 1/2 mile dirt oval (c.1917 - c.1929) (c.1931 - 1941) (c.1946 - 1983)
 4/10 mile dirt oval (1988 - present)

Shenandoah - dirt oval (9/17/17) (7/10/18) (1920's)

Short Circuit Midget Speedway - Mason City - dirt oval (c.6/07/42 - 1942)

Sigourney - 1/8 mile dirt oval (c.1981 - c.1991)

Sioux City Dragway - Sioux City - 1/4 mile paved dragstrip (c.1969 - c.1972)

Sioux City Fairgrounds - Sioux City - 1.0 mile dirt oval (1907 - 1908)
     also had a 1/2 mile dirt oval only used for horse racing until 1910
     track torn out in 1910 / was the same property of the next listing
     (aka: Interstate Fairgrounds) / the fair started in 1894

*The Interstate Fairgrounds in Sioux City in 1927. The historic site had three
different tracks on the property. - Bob Stolze collection.*

Sioux City Fairgrounds - Sioux City / same site as other Sioux City Fairgrounds
     1/2 mile dirt oval (9/17/16 & 9/18/16) (1925) (1933 - 1935)
     the track was torn out in 1935 / became Riverview Speedway in 1936
     site of the track later became the Midway Grounds and Exhibition Building

Sioux City Speedway - see: South Dakota chapter

Soo Speedbowl - Cherokee - 1/5 mile dirt oval (1949 - 1952)

Soos Speedway - Sioux City - 1/4 mile dirt oval (6/01/63) / located at a ballpark

Southern Iowa Fairgrounds - Oskaloosa / at the Southern Iowa Fairgrounds
     1/2 mile dirt oval (c.1931 - 8/05/41) (8/09/46 - present)
     (aka: Osky Speedway) / (aka: Mahaska County Fairgrounds)

Spencer Fairgrounds - see: Clay County Fairgrounds

Sportsbowl - Dubuque - 1/4 mile dirt oval (1953 - c.1965) / site is now city dump
     (aka: Dubuque Speed Bowl)

Sportsman Park - Fort Dodge / located on the east edge of town on Highway 20
     1/5 mile dirt oval (c.1948 - c.1954)

Sportsman Park - Keokuk - dirt oval (1962)

Stuart Speedway - Stuart / (aka: Stuart Raceway)
     1/4 mile dirt oval (1962 - present)

Thirty-Four (34) Raceway - Burlington - 3/8 mile dirt oval (4/16/66 - present)

Thompson - dirt oval (years unknown) / maybe at Winnebago County Fairgrounds

Tipton - 1/2 mile dirt oval (8/30/46 - c.1950) / possibly at the fairgrounds

Tipton Int'l Speedway - Tipton / located at the Cedar County Fairgrounds
1/2 mile dirt oval (1920's) (1948 - 1954) / (aka: Cedar County Raceway)
1/4 mile dirt oval (c.1954 - 1978) (1981 - present) / ran motorcycles 1920's

Tri-State Dragway - see: Lee County Raceway Park

Tunis Speedway - Waterloo - 1/4 mile dirt oval (1947 - early 1950's)
1/2 mile dirt oval (early 1950's) / (aka: Cordes Speedway)
3/8 mile dirt oval (mid 1950's - c.1983) / first called Cordes in 1966

Vandalia Speedway - Des Moines - 1/4 mile dirt oval (1968)

Veterans Arena - Des Moines - 1/10 mile indoor concrete oval (11/04/89 - 12/30/89)

Vinton Fairgrounds - see: Benton County Speedway

Wapello Fairgrounds - Wapello - 1/5 mile dirt oval (7/17/65) / located east of town

Wapello Speedway - Wapello - 3/8 mile dirt oval (1993 - present) / south of town

Waterloo - 1/4 mile dirt oval (1940 - c.6/18/41)

Waterloo Auditorium - Waterloo - 1/10 mile indoor oval (1/23/54 - c.1960) / T.Q.s

Waterloo Fairgrounds - Waterloo / located at the Black Hawk County Fairgrounds
1.0 mile dirt oval (1920's)

Waterloo Raceway - Waterloo - 1/8 mile paved oval (April, 1958 - c.1960)
ran T.Q. and Micro-Midgets

Waterloo - also see: National Cattle Congress, Tunis Speedway

Waukon Fairgrounds - Waukon / located at the Allamakee County Fairgrounds
1/4 mile dirt oval (c.1964 - 1978) (1980) / (aka: Waukon Speedway)

Waverly Fairgrounds - Waverly / located at the Bremer County Fairgrounds
1/2 mile dirt oval (9/08/16) (8/20/35)

Webster City Fairgrounds - see: Hamilton County Speedway

West Liberty Raceway - West Liberty / at the Muscatine County Fairgrounds
1/2 mile dirt oval (1930's) (7/06/58 - present)
(aka: West Liberty Speedway)

West Union Fairgrounds - see: Fayette County Fair Raceway

What Cheer Fairgrounds - What Cheer / at the Keokuk County Fairgrounds
1/2 mile dirt oval (1934) / the track is still in existence

Whitehead Speedway - see: I-29 Speedway

Williamsburg - 1/2 mile dirt oval (1920's)

Woodland Park - see: Sioux City Speedway (South Dakota chapter)

Wright County Speedway - Clarion (Belmond) / (aka: Clarmond Raceway)
1/5 mile dirt oval (9/14/52 - c.1969) (1984 & 1985) (1990 - present)
the track was partially under water during the big flood of 1993

KANSAS

77 Speedway - see: Seventy-Seven Speedway

81 Speedway - see: Eighty-One Speedway

Abilene Fairgrounds - Abilene - 1/2 mile dirt oval (c.1924 - 1931) (1949 & 1950)
    1/5 mile dirt oval (8/20/40 - 8/22/41) / at the Central Kansas Fairgrounds

Agricultural Hall - Salina - 1/10 mile dirt indoor oval (9/20/39-11/20/40)(10/18/47)

Air Capital Speedway - see: Frontier Raceway

Airport Midget Speedway - Hutchinson - 1/5 mile dirt oval (8/11/40) (8/18/40)

Airport Park - Salina / located on airport runways of the old Salina Airport
    1.4 & 1.7 mile concrete road courses (1967 - c.1984)
    now running solo events / (aka: East Crawford Recreation Area)

Alaskan Ice Palace - Wichita / located at an ice hockey arena
    1/10 mile indoor concrete oval (10/09/40 - 10/27/40)
    later became a housing development

Anthony Fairgrounds - Anthony / located at the Harper County Fairgrounds
    1/2 mile dirt oval (c.7/21/35 - 7/19/41)

Arkansas City - 1/2 mile dirt oval (early 1930's) / maybe Seventy-Seven Speedway

Arkansas City Dragway - Arkansas City - 1/4 mile paved dragstrip (c.1973- c.1975)
    this track was replaced by Mid-America Dragway in 1984

Arkansas City - also see: Mid-America Dragway, Seventy-Seven Speedway

Atchison Speedway - Atchison - 1/4 mile dirt oval (c.1957)

Avalon Speedway - Salina - 1/4 mile dirt oval (8/13/39 - 1939)
    1/5 mile dirt oval (1940 - c.5/18/41)

Badlands Raceway - see: Yates Center Raceway

Belleville High Banks - Belleville - 1/2 mile flat dirt oval (1911 - 1932)
    1/2 mile high-banked dirt oval (1932 - 8/28/41) (8/29/46 - present)
    the banks were 18 foot high in the 1950's / they were lower a little since
    1/4 mile dirt oval (8/25/41 - 8/29/41) / ran midgets on 1/4 mile track
    1/8 mile dirt oval (1984 - 1991) / T.Q. midgets run on small tracks
    1/4 mile dirt oval (1992 - present) / at the North Central Kansas Fairgrounds

Beloit Fairgrounds - Beloit - 1/8 mile dirt oval (9/09/41) (9/13/41)
    1/2 mile dirt oval (c.1947 - c.1958) / at the Mitchell County Fairgrounds
    1/8 mile dirt oval (c.1990 - present) / runs T.Q. midgets on small track

Beverly Track - Salina - 1/5 mile dirt oval (9/10/38 - c.7/07/39)

Bo Stearns Speedway - Wichita - 1/2 mile dirt oval (c.1928 - c.8/06/38)
    1/5 mile dirt oval (c.1937 - 1939) / formerly a horse track
    the site was three miles north of present day 81 Speedway / now a ranch

254

Boot Hill Speedway - see: Dodge City Speedway

Burden Fairgrounds - Burden / located at the Eastern Cowley County Fairgrounds
1/8 mile dirt oval (late 1950's) / ran T.Q. midgets

Burlington - 1/2 mile dirt oval (11/13/49)

Caney Valley Speedway - Caney / (aka: Caney Speedway)
1/4 mile dirt oval (1971 - present)

CeJay Stadium - Wichita / located at George Washington Blvd. & Oliver Street
1/5 & 3/10 mile dirt ovals (8/26/45 - 1955) / (aka: CeJay Speedway)
Bill Mears (Rick & Roger's father) was a jalopy champion here
the promoter was Carl Johnson / equipment was from West Side Speedway
the site is now an activity center for Cessna Aircraft employees

Chase Speedway - Chase - 3/8 mile dirt oval (1973) (1975) / didn't run in 1974

Cheyenne Speedway - Hoisington - dirt oval (1953)

Clay Center Fairgrounds - Clay Center - 1/2 mile dirt oval (1940)(c.10/23/49- 1953)
1/8 mile dirt oval (1993 - present) / located at the Clay County Fairgrounds

Coffeyville Airport - Coffeyville - paved road course (5/22/55)

Coffeyville Fairgrounds - Coffeyville / located at the Montgomery Co. Fairgrounds
1/2 mile dirt oval (c.1934 - 8/19/38) (1946 - 1959)
the fairgrounds was also known as the Inter-State Fairgrounds

Coffeyville Speedway - see: Hobbs Speedway

Coffeyville - also see: State Line, Mid-America (Oklahoma chapter)

Colby Fairgrounds - see: Thomas County Speedway

Coldwater - 1/2 mile dirt oval (early 1930's)

Coldwater - 1/2 mile dirt oval (early 1930's) / different located

Frank Luptow, a three-time I.M.C.A. champion. - Allan E. Brown collection.

Concordia Fairgrounds - Concordia - 1/5 mile dirt oval (9/11/38 - c.9/25/38)
  1/2 mile dirt oval (c.6/10/51 - c.1954) / at the Cloud County Fairgrounds
  1/8 mile dirt oval (c.1987 - present) / runs T.Q. midgets on small track

Cottonwood Falls - 1/2 mile dirt oval (1936 & 1937) (9/03/49 - c.1951)

Council Grove - 1/2 mile dirt oval (c.1924 - early 1930's)

Cowley County Dragway - see: Mid-America Dragway

D & D Speedway - see: Humboldt Speedway

Delphos Fairgrounds - Delphos - 1/2 mile dirt oval (early 1930's - c.1941)
  1/5 mile dirt oval (8/23/39) (8/25/41) / at the Ottawa County Fairgrounds

Dighton Fairgrounds - see: Lane County Raceway

Dighton Fairway - Dighton - 1/2 mile dirt oval (1930's) / at Lane Co. Fairgrounds
  1/4 mile dirt oval (8/01/40) (c.1986 - 1992) / (aka: Lane County Raceway)

Dirtona Raceway - Hugoton - 3/8 mile dirt oval (c.1993 - present)

Dodge City - 2.0 mile dirt oval (7/04/14) (7/04/15) (7/04/16) (7/04/20) (7/04/21)
  ran national motorcycle events in 1914, 1915, 1916, & 1920
  located north of town / the only auto races were in 1921

Dodge City Airport - Dodge City - 2.5 mile paved oval (7/24/49) (4/29/56)
  3.0 mile paved road course (4/29/56) / races were on airport runways
  ran strictly stocks in 1949 / sports car in 1956 (used both size tracks)

Dodge City - road course (1912 & 1913)

Dodge City Speedway - Dodge City / located at the Ford County Fairgrounds
  1/2 mile dirt oval (c.1934 - c.1941) (c.1951 - c.1952)
  1/4 mile dirt oval (c.1953 - 1964) / (aka: Boot Hill Speedway)
  3/8 mile dirt oval (1966 - present) / no racing in 1965 because of a flood
  (aka: Wright Stadium) / (aka: McCarthy Speedway)

East Crawford Recreation Area - see: Airport Park

Eighty-One Speedway - Wichita - 1/4 mile dirt oval (7/19/53 - c.1956)
  1/2 mile dirt oval (5/31/54 - 1979) / built by Jim Robbins
  3/8 mile flat dirt oval (c.5/31/58)
  3/8 mile banked dirt oval (1980 - present) / (aka: Robbins Speedway)

Eisenhower Park - Abilene - 1/2 mile dirt oval (1952 - 1953) / maybe a fairgrounds

Elmwood Park Speedway - Norton / located at Norton County Fairgrounds
  1/2 mile dirt oval (c.8/14/51 - present) / (aka: Norton Speedway)
  (aka: Norton Fairgrounds Speedway)

Emporia Fairgrounds - Emporia - 1/5 mile dirt oval (9/18/38)
  1/2 mile dirt oval (6/27/48) (1963) / located at the Lyon Co. Fairgrounds

Fairgrounds Speedway - Liberal / located at the Five State Fairgrounds
  1/2 mile dirt oval (9/01/54) / (aka: Fairgrounds Speedway)
  3/8 mile dirt oval (c.7/04/56 - present) / (aka: Liberal Speedway)
  a minor league baseball team plays in the infield of the race track

Fifty-Four Speedway - see: Yates Center Raceway

Five State Dragway - see: Sundown Dragway

Five State Fairgrounds - see: Fairgrounds Speedway

Fort Dodge - road course (1915) / ran motorcycles only / east of Dodge City

Fort Scott - 1/4 mile dirt oval (1950's - late 1960's)

Frontier Raceway - Wichita / located west of town on US 54 / former horse track
3/8 mile dirt oval (1963 - 1965) / the concrete grandstands are still there
1/2 mile dirt oval (4/10/66 - Sept., 1966) / (aka: Air Capital Speedway)

Fun Valley Speedway - see: Hutchinson Raceway Park

Garden City - 1/2 mile dirt oval (1951)

Garden City Dragstrip - Garden City - 1/4 mile paved dragstrip (1963 - 1965)

Garden Raceway - see: Wallbanger Speedway

Golden Belt Speedway - see: Great Bend Motorplex

Goodland - dirt oval (6/11/50) (1970's) / probably at the Goodland Fairgrounds

Goodland Fairgrounds - see: Sherman County Speedway

Great Bend - 1/2 mile dirt oval (c.1924 - 1930's)

Great Bend - 1/4 mile dirt oval (7/04/40 - c.1940)

Great Bend - dirt oval (1930's) / at a different location

Ernie Derr (#3) jumps into an early lead over Ramo Stott (#0) and the rest of the I.M.C.A. stock cars at the Topeka Fairgrounds in 1965. The track hosted the very first I.M.C.A. late model race on May 30, 1949. The track closed in 1981 and the site is now the Topeka Expo Center. - Photo courtesy of I.M.C.A.

Great Bend Motorplex - Great Bend / (aka: Great Bend Municipal Airport)
  1/4 mile paved dragstrip (1954 - 1968) (c.1977 - present)
  1/4 mile dirt oval (c.1963 - 1986) / (aka: Great Bend Raceway)
  (aka: Golden Belt Speedway) / (aka: Great Bend Speedway)
  held the very first NHRA Nat'l event here in late September of 1955
  Lloyd Scott turned the first ever 150 mph run (151.00) here in 1955
    also see: the Great Bend Municipal Airport

Great Bend Municipal Airport - Great Bend / strictly stocks on airport runways
  3.0 mile paved tri-oval (5/30/49 - 1951) / 9,000 fans for first race
  the track consisted of three runways at a former Army Air Base
  the first race was sponsored by the Argonne American Legion Post, and the
    160 mile race won by Bill Robinson / also see: Great Bend Motorplex

Greentop - (location unknown) - dirt oval (1954)

Hardtner Fairgrounds - Hardtner - 1/4 mile dirt oval (c.1950 - c.1951)

Heartland Park - Topeka - 1/4 mile paved dragstrip (1989 - present)
  1.8 & 2.5 mile paved road courses (1989 - present) / south of town
  Chuck Etchells drove to the first 4 second run in a Funny Car (10/03/93)
  Jim Epler drove to the 1st ever 300 mph run here in a Funny Car (10/03/93)
  ran a SCCA TA race here on the road course in 1989

Herington Airport - Herington / ran strictly stocks on runways / dirt corners
  1.0 mile paved/dirt oval (10/09/49 - 1950) / the straights were runways

Hiawatha - 1/2 mile dirt oval (c.9/03/24 - c.1924)

Hiawatha Speedway - Hiawatha - 1/4 mile dirt oval (1957)

Higley Field - see: Smith Center Raceway

Hill City Fairgrounds - Hill City / located at the Graham County Fairgrounds
  1/4 mile dirt oval (c.1959 - 1960)

Hobbs Speedway - Coffeyville - 1/8 mile paved oval (1961 - c.1984)
  1/4 mile dirt oval (c.1985 - 1986) / (aka: Coffeyville Speedway)

Humboldt Speedway - Humboldt / (aka: M & M Speedway) (aka: D&D Speedway)
  1/4 mile dirt oval (c.1973 - 1987) (1990 - present) / (aka: Wayside Speedway)

Hutchinson Airport - Hutchinson / located at a former Naval Air Base
  2.9 mile paved road course (6/29/49) (1960's - early 1970's)

Hutchinson Fairgrounds - see: Kansas State Fairgrounds

Hutchinson Raceway Park - Hutchinson / located west of town
  1/4 mile dirt oval (c.1970 - 1979) / (aka: Salt City Speedway)
  3/8 mile dirt oval (1980 - present) / (aka: Fun Valley Speedway)
  same site as Salt Hawk Speedway but track now faces a different direction

Hutchinson - also see: Airport Midget, Mohawk, Salt Hawk, Sunflower

Independence Airport - Independence - paved road course (late 1950's)

Iola Fairgrounds - Iola / located at the Allen County Fairgrounds
  1/2 mile dirt oval (9/01/49 - c.1951)

258

Jayhawk Hot Rod Track - Wichita - 1/2 mile dirt oval (1948)

Jayhawk Speedway - Newton / (aka: Jayhawk Stadium)
   1/3 mile dirt oval (c.9/26/48 - c.8/17/56)

Jehu (pronounced Yeh-Hoo) (located unknown) - 1/4 mile dirt oval (c.1964- c.1970)

Junction City - dirt oval (1940)

Junction City Raceway - see: Flint Hill Speedway

Kansas City - 1/12 mile indoor oval (1986) / promoted by Bob Baker

Kansas Expocenter - Topeka / located at the Topeka Fairgrounds
   1/10 mile indoor concrete oval (1987 - 1988) / promoted by Bob Baker
   exact same site as the former Topeka Fairgrounds 1/2 mile dirt track
   (aka: International Wheat Show) / (aka: Topeka Expo Center)

Kansas State Fairgrounds - Hutchinson / the track was built in 1912
   1/2 mile dirt oval (c.9/18/14 - 9/19/41) (September, 1945 - present)
   1/5 mile dirt oval (7/02/39 - 1941)

Kansas City - also see: Lakeside, Overland Park & Missouri chapter

Kenwood Park - Salina - 1/2 mile dirt oval (6/30/40 - 1940)

Kingman Fairgrounds - Kingman / located at the Kingman County Fairgrounds
   1/5 mile dirt oval (10/13/38 & 10/14/38)

Lake Afton Grand Prix - Wichita / southwest of Wichita on roads around a lake
   1.8 mile paved city street road course (1964 - 1991)

Lake Garnett Grand Prix - Garnett / ran on roads circling Lake Garnett
   2.84 mile paved road course (7/04/59 - c.1972)

Lakeside Speedway - Kansas City - 1/2 mile dirt oval (4/17/55 - 1956)(1961 - 1988)
   Pat O'Connor won on 4/17/55 / located at Leavenworth and 92nd
   1/4 mile dirt oval (5/26/56 - c.1960) / (aka: Lakeside Stadium)
   the site was converted to the Woodland dog track

Lakeside Speedway - Kansas City - 1/2 mile paved oval (7/21/89 - present)
   built to replace the old Lakeside Speedway / (aka: New Lakeside Speedway)
   Doug Wolfgang was seriously injured in practice accident in 1992
   the track was 26 foot under flood water in 1993 because of the great flood
   located northwest of Kansas City near the Missouri River

Larned - 1/4 mile dirt oval (c.7/15/56 - c.1958)

Lawrence - 1/2 mile dirt oval (1920's) / probably at the Douglas Co. Fairgrounds

Lawrence - 1/4 mile dirt oval (c.1953 - c.1967)

Lawrence Dragway - Lawrence - 1/8 mile paved dragstrip (c.1981 - 1987)

Liberal Airport - Liberal - 2.3 mile paved oval (5/14/50) / ran strictly stocks

Liberal Fairgrounds - see: Fairgrounds Speedway

Linn County Speedway - Pleasanton - 3/8 mile dirt oval (6/13/86 - present)

Little Apple Raceway - see: Midwest Raceway

Little Estes Park - Scandia - 1/5 mile dirt oval (1947 & 1948)

M & M Speedway - see: Humboldt Speedway

M & N Raceways - see: Wichita Int'l Raceway

Marval Park - Parsons - 1/5 mile dirt oval (9/26/48) (7/04/49) / ran midgets

McCarthy Speedway - see: Dodge City Speedway

McConnell Air Force Base - Wichita - 1/4 mile paved dragstrip (8/24/58)

Meade - dirt oval (1938)

Meridian Speedway - Wichita - 1.5 mile dirt oval (c.7/04/16 - c.9/04/22)
    (aka: Speedway Park) / ran motorcycles and automobiles

Meridian Track - Wichita - 1/5 mile dirt oval (8/13/39 - c.8/27/39)

Mid-America Dragway - Arkansas City / (aka: Cowley County Dragway)
    1/4 mile paved dragstrip (1984 - present)

Mid-America Fairgrounds - see: Topeka Fairgrounds

Midwest Raceway - Manhattan - 1/8 mile paved dragstrip (1983 - present)
    (aka: Little Apple Raceway)

Mohawk Speedway - Hutchinson - 1/4 mile dirt oval (June, 1955 - 1963)
    the track was located west of town

Molden - (location unknown) - dirt oval (years unknown)

Mound City Fairgrounds - Mound City / located at the Linn County Fairgrounds
    1/8 & 1/2 mile dirt ovals (1950's)

National Speedway - Topeka - 1/4 mile dirt oval (1939 - c.7/04/41)

Neosho Falls - dirt oval (1960's)

New Lakeside Speedway - see: Lakeside Speedway

Newton - see: Jayhawk Speedway

Norton Fairgrounds (Speedway) - see: Elwood Park Speedway

Oakley Fairgrounds - Oakley - 1/2 mile dirt oval (c.6/04/50 - 1952)
    located at the Logan County Fairgrounds

Oberlin Fairgrounds - Oberlin / located at the Decatur County Fairgrounds
    1/2 mile dirt oval (c.1951 - c.1982) / (aka: Oberlin Race Track)
    1/8 mile dirt oval (c.1993 - present)

Olathe - dirt oval (years unknown)

Olathe Naval Air Station - Olathe - paved road course (c.1968 - c.1971)

Osborne Speedway - Osborne / located at the Osborne County Fairgrounds
    1/2 mile dirt oval (c.1954 - present)

Ottawa - 1/4 mile dirt oval (1960)

Ottawa Fairgrounds - Ottawa / located at the Franklin County Fairgrounds
1/2 mile dirt oval (10/16/16)

Overland Park Speedway - Kansas City - 1/2 mile dirt oval (8/27/39)
located five miles south of town on US 69

Paolo - 1/4 mile dirt oval (1960)

Plaza Speedway - Junction City - 1/4 mile dirt oval (1956 - 1965)

Plaza Speedway - Junction City / (aka: Flint Hills Speedway)
3/8 mile dirt oval (c.1981 - 1992) (1994 - present)
(aka: Junction City Raceway) / under water during the great flood of 1993

Plaza Speedway (new) - see: Flint Hill Speedway

Pony Express Speedway - Highland - dirt oval (years unknown)

Pratt Airport - Pratt - 1.6 mile paved oval (6/18/50) / ran strictly stocks

Quibbs - (location unknown) - dirt oval (1935)

Robbins Speedway - see: Eighty-One Speedway

Rock Road Raceway - Wichita - 1/4 mile paved dragstrip (1960's)

Rooks County Speedway - Stockton / located at the Rook County Fairgrounds
1/2 mile dirt oval (c.1933 - c.1941) (c.1946 - c.1952) (c.8/20/58 - present)
(aka: Stockton Race Track)

*This classy limestone block grandstands is located at the Rooks County
Fairgrounds in Stockton, Kansas. - Allan E. Brown photo.*

Rush Center Fairgrounds - Rush Center / located at the Rush County Fairgrounds
1/2 mile dirt oval (1930's) (8/17/40)

Russell - 1/2 mile dirt oval (c.6/10/50 - c.1954)

Salina - 1/2 mile dirt oval (1946)

Salina - 1/2 mile dirt oval (c.10/19/15 - 1933) / possibly at Tri-Rivers Fairgrounds

Salina Raceway - Salina / (aka: Tri-Rivers Speedway) / (aka: Salina Speedway)
3/8 mile dirt oval (1970 - present) / (aka: Saline County Speedway)

Salina - also see: Agricultural Hall, Airport Park, Avalon, Beverly, Kenwood Park

Salt Hawk Speedway - Hutchinson / same site as Hutchinson Raceway Park
1/4 mile dirt oval (c.1955 - 1963)

Sam's Stadium - Emporia - 1/4 mile dirt oval (4/23/50 - c.1950)

Scott City - 1/2 mile dirt oval (1921 only)

Scott City Speedway - Scott City / located at the Scott County Fairgrounds
1/2 mile dirt oval (c.6/18/50 - c.1954)

Seventy-Seven Speedway - Arkansas City - 1/3 mile dirt oval (May, 1956 - 1960)
the site is now a rodeo grounds

Shawnee County Speedway - see: Topeka Raceway

Shawnee Lake - (located unknown) - paved road course (years unknown)

Sherman County Speedway - Goodland / at the Sherman County Fairgrounds
1/5 mile dirt oval (8/27/36) (8/28/36) / (aka: N.W. Kansas Fairgrounds)
1/2 mile dirt oval (8/27/36) (8/26/37)
3/8 mile dirt oval (June, 1985 - present)

Sixty-Nine (69) Speedway - Pittsburg - 1/4 mile dirt oval (5/24/53 - 1954)
the site is now a shopping center / located on US 69

Skyline Speedway - Topeka - 1/4 mile dirt oval (1960's)

Smith Center - 1/2 mile dirt oval (early 1930's)

Smith Center Raceway - Smith Center / (aka: Higley Field)
3/8 mile dirt oval (c.1971 - c.1980)

Speedbowl - Wichita - 1/8 mile dirt oval (7/08/50 - 1950) / ran T.Q. midgets

Speedway Park - see: Meridian Speedway

State Line Speedway - Coffeyville - 1/4 mile dirt oval (September, 1992 - present)

Sundown Dragway - Liberal / (aka: Five State Raceway)
1/4 mile paved dragstrip (1970 - present)

*Darrell Dake (#44) leads Doc Narber (#43), Bob Kosiske (#35), and Newt
Bartholomew (#2) at the Topeka Fairgrounds. - Photo courtesy of I.M.C.A.*

262

Sunflower Aerodrome - Yoder / maybe same site as Hutchinson Airport
    2.6 mile paved road course (c.1971 - 1990) (1992 - 1993)

Sunflower State Expo - see: Topeka Fairgrounds

Thomas County Speedway - Colby / located at the Thomas County Fairgrounds
    1/2 mile dirt oval (8/20/37 - 1940) (1969)
    3/8 mile dirt oval (1983 - present) / (aka: Colby Fairgrounds Speedway)

Thunder Hill Speedway - Mayetta - 3/8 mile dirt oval (4/15/94 - present)

Topeka - 1/4 mile paved dragstrip (1952)

Topeka - 1/5 mile dirt oval (c.18/12/34 - c.1934)

Topeka Fairgrounds - Topeka / located at the Mid-America Fairgrounds
    1/2 mile dirt oval (1902 - 9/12/41) (9/10/46 - 1981)
    1/5 mile dirt oval (5/19/39 - c.6/24/39) / 1/2 mile track torn out in 1983
    (aka: Topeka Racing Association Fairgrounds) / horse track built in 1878
    (aka: Kansas State Free Fairgrounds) / (aka: Sunflower State Expo)
    ran the first ever I.M.C.A. stock car race here on 5/30/49
    also see: Topeka Expo Center

Topeka Raceway Park - Topeka / (aka: Shawnee Co. Speedway) / east of town
    1/4 mile dirt oval (c.6/21/57 - 1982) (1984 - 1993)
    1/8 mile dirt oval (late 1980's - 1993) / (aka: Topeka Raceway)

Topeka - also see: Heartland Park, National Speedway, Skyline Speedway

Tri-Rivers Speedway - see: Salina Speedway

WaKeeney Speedway - WaKeeney / located at the Trego County Fairgrounds
    1/2 mile dirt oval (c.8/28/36 - c.1941) (c.1946 - 1978) (1985 - 1990)
    3/8 mile dirt oval (1991 - present) / horse racing only from 1979 to 1984

Walker Dragstrip - Russell - 1/4 mile paved dragstrip (1960's)

Wallbanger Speedway - Garden City - 1/8 mile dirt oval (1969 - present)
    (aka: Garden Raceway)

Washington Fairgrounds - Washington / at the Washington County Fairgrounds
    1/8 mile dirt oval (1980 - 1993) / runs T.Q. midgets on small track

Wayside Speedway - see: Humboldt Speedway

West Side Midget Speedway - Wichita / (aka: West Side Athletic Field)
    1/8 mile dirt oval (5/25/41 - 1941) / Guy McHenry won first race
    1/5 mile dirt oval (1942 - 7/31/42) / (aka: West Side Ball Park)

Wichita Coliseum - Wichita - indoor oval (3/31/79 & 4/01/79) / ran Micro-midgets

Wichita - dirt oval (1943) / ran illegally during the ban of racing during WWII
    the track was located in a farmer's field

Wichita Int'l Raceway - Wichita - 1/4 mile paved dragstrip (1963 - present)
    (aka: M & N Raceways)

Wichita - paved road course on city streets (years unknown)

Wichita - also see: Alaskan Ice, Bo Stearns, CeJay, Eighty-One, Frontier, Jayhawk Hot Rod, Lake Afton, McConnell Air Force Base, Meridian, Rock Road, Speedbowl, West Side

Winfield Fairgrounds - Winfield / located at the Cowley County Fairgrounds
  1/2 mile dirt oval (7/14/35) (7/27/35) (May, 1956) (1967 - 1971)
  Joie Chitwood started his race car driving career here in 1935

Woodson County Speedway - see: Yates Center Raceway

Wright Stadium - see: Dodge City Speedway

Yates Center Raceway - Yates Center / (aka: Fifty-Four Speedway)
  3/8 mile dirt oval (c.1968 - 1977) (1984 - 1988) (1992 - present)
  (aka: Woodson County Speedway) / (aka: Badlands Raceway)
  (aka: Yates Center Speedway)

KENTUCKY

201 Speedway - Paintsville - 1/4 mile dirt oval (7/01/83- 1985)(1989)(1991- present)
  (aka: Highland Raceway Park) / (aka: Paintsville Speedway)

Ashland - see: Checkered Flag, Raceland, River Cities

Barren County Speedway - Glasgow / located at the Barren County Fairgrounds
  3/8 mile dirt oval (1974 - present)

Beech Bend Raceway - Bowling Green - 1/8 mile paved dragstrip (c.1963 - present)
  1/3 mile paved oval (c.1948 - c.1980) (1986 - present)
  (aka: Bowling Green Int'l Speedway) / (aka: Bowling Green Int'l Raceway)

Benton - 1/2 mile dirt oval (8/25/40)

Big Three Raceway - Vanceburg - 1/4 mile dirt oval (1967 - 1975)

Blue Grass Dragway - Lexington - 1/4 mile paved dragstrip (c.1970 - c.1972)

Bluegrass Dragway - see: Bluestone Speedway

Bluestone Speedway - Morehead - 1/8 mile paved dragstrip (c.1965 - c.1973)
  1/2 mile dirt oval (1960's - c.9/22/74) / (aka: Bluegrass Dragway)
  site is now office buildings / (aka: Morehead Motor Speedway)
  located near Nicholasville

Bonnieville - dirt oval (early 1960's)

Burnside Speedway - see: Lake Cumberland Speedway

C H K Raceway - see: Paducah Int'l Raceway

Campbellsville Fairgrounds - see: Taylor County Speedway

Carrollton Fairgrounds - Carrollton / located at the Carroll County Fairgrounds
  3/8 mile dirt oval (c.8/22/53 - c.1959)

Carrollton Speedway - Carrollton - 1/4 mile dirt oval (1960's) / on Sixth St.

Carter Co. Showtime Speedway - Olive Hill - 3/8 mile dirt oval (4/23/93- present) (aka: Thunder Hill)

Cave City Speedway - Cave City - 1/4 mile dirt oval (July, 1993 - present)

Cedar Grove Raceway - Morgantown - 1/3 mile dirt oval (1989 - present)

Central City - 8/10 mile dirt oval (c.6/30/40 - 1940)

Central City Fairgrounds - see: Central Park Speedway - Central City

Central Park Raceway - Central City / located at the Muhlenberg Co. Fairgrounds 1/4 mile dirt oval (c.1968 - 1976)

Central Park Raceway - McHenry - 1/2 mile dirt oval (1987 - present)

Checker Flag Raceway - Ashland - 3/8 mile dirt oval (1980 - 1989) / now junk yard

Clay City Speedway - Clay City / (aka: Clay City Raceway) 1/2 mile dirt oval (c.1964 - 1978) (1984) (1987 - 1993) located next to Mountain Parkway Motorplex (dragstrip)

Columbia Fairgrounds - Columbia / located at the Adair County Fairgrounds 1/2 mile dirt oval (years unknown)

Corbin Speedway - Corbin - 1/2 mile dirt oval (1953 - c.8/29/54) (1960's) only Kentucky track to hold NASCAR GN race, won by Lee Petty on 8/29/54 located at the Whitley County Fairgrounds / site was nearer town

A "Slingshot" dragster blasts the front wheels off the ground in this action shot at Beech Bend Raceway. - Official track photo.

Corbin Speedway - Corbin / (aka: Corbin Motor Speedway)
   1/4 mile paved oval (1973 - 1986) (1989 - present) / located SW of town

Creeks Run - Vanceburg - 1/4 mile dirt oval (early 1970's)

Danville Sportsdrome Speedway - Danville - 1/4 mile paved oval (c.1961 - 1970)
   1/4 mile dirt oval (c.7/26/58 - c.1960) (1970 - c.1973)

Dawson Speedway - Dawson Springs - 1/4 mile dirt oval (c.1948 - c.1950)

Dayton-Tacoma Speedway - Dayton / (aka: Tacoma Park Speedway)
   1/5 mile dirt oval (7/24/40 - 8/10/40) / located northeast of Covington

Death Valley Speedway - (location unknown) - dirt oval (c.1947 - c.1948)

Ellis Park - Henderson - 1.0 mile dirt oval (c.1948 - c.1952) / a horse track
   (aka: Henderson Speedrome) / (aka: Henderson Speedway)

Ellis Speedway - Owensboro (Reed) - 1/4 mile dirt oval (1966)
   1/4 mile paved oval (1966 - 1971) / site was 12 miles west of Owensboro

Fairgrounds Speedway - Louisville / located on Kentucky State Fair property
   1/3 mile paved oval (June, 1961 - 1980) / southside of town
   various promoters included Bob Hall, Milt Hartlauf & Steve Stubbs

Falmouth Fairgrounds - Falmouth / located at the Pendleton County Fairgrounds
   1/2 mile dirt oval (9/13/54) (1955)

Fleming County Raceway - Goddard - 1/4 mile dirt oval (1988 - present)

Florence Speedway - Florence / (aka: Northern Kentucky Speedway)
   3/8 mile paved oval (1955 - 1961) / (aka: Northern Kentucky Speedbowl)
   1/4 & 3/8 mile dirt ovals (1962) / (aka: Northern Kentucky Race Bowl)
   1/2 mile dirt oval (1962 - present) / (aka: Northern Motor Speedway)
   the covered grandstands were destroyed by arson on 8/28/84

Fox Valley Raceway - Flemingsburg - 1/4 mile dirt oval (1976 & 1977)

Frankfort Speedway - Frankfort / (aka: Interstate Speedway)
   1/4 mile dirt oval (1971 - 1982) / (aka: Franklin County Speedway)

Franklin County Speedway - see: Frankfort Speedway

Freedom Hall - see: Kentucky Fair Expo Center Arena

Fulton - 1/2 mile dirt oval (early 1920's) (1939) / was an old horse track

Glasgow Fairgrounds - see: Barren County Speedway

GLV Raceway - see: Windy Hollow Speedway

Greensburg Fairgrounds - Greensburg / located at the Green County Fairgrounds
   1/4 mile dirt oval (late 1940's - early 1950's)

Hartford Fairgrounds - Hartford / located at the Ohio County Fairgrounds
   1/2 mile dirt oval (1924) (10/08/38 & c.5/28/39) (c.1948 - c.1957)
   (aka: Kentucky Speedway) / the track was lined with trees

Henderson Speedrome (Speedway) - see: Ellis Park

266

Highland Raceway Park - see: 201 Speedway

Hilltop Speedway - Kenton - 3/8 mile dirt oval (9/20/55 - c.1956)

Hilltop Speedway - Middlesboro - dirt oval (1948) / ran midgets

Hodgenville - 1/2 mile dirt oval (10/20/40)

Hook's Park - Paducah - 1/5 mile dirt oval (10/13/40 - c.1941)

Hopkinsville Speedway - Hopkinsville - 1/2 mile dirt oval (early 1970's)

Horse Cave - dirt oval (1951) / ran 9 races in 1951

Howe Valley Speedway - Howe Valley - 5/8 mile dirt oval (c.1972 - c.1977)

Ideal Ball Park - Falmouth - 1/5 mile dirt oval (10/18/36)

Interstate Speedway - see: Frankfort Speedway

Jefferson County Armory - Louisville / (aka: Louisville Armory)
    1/10 mile concrete indoor oval (11/07/52 - 1953) / ran Mini-stocks
    the building is now called the Louisville Gardens

Keeling Raceway - see: Paducah Int'l Raceway

Kentucky Fair Expo Center Arena - Louisville / at the new State Fairgrounds
    1/10 mile indoor concrete oval (12/31/60) / (aka: Freedom Hall)

Kentucky Int'l Raceway - see: Latonia Horse Track

Kentucky Motor Speedway - Louisville / track located on 18th Street Road
    1/2 mile dirt oval (7/06/26) (1929 - 10/09/32) / promoted by Don Zeiter
    (aka: Kentucky Speedway)

Kentucky Motor Speedway - Whitesville - 1/4 mile paved oval (1960 - present)
    Darrell Waltrip started his driving career here in 1965 / near Owensboro

Kentucky Speedway - see: Hartford Fairgrounds

Kentucky State Fair Pavilion - Louisville / (aka: Louisville Coliseum)
    1/10 mile indoor concrete oval (5/17/35 - 1941) (1946 - c.1/01/48)
    1/8 mile indoor dirt oval (10/18/52) / (aka: Horse Show Pavilion)
    located at the old Kentucky State Fairgrounds west of town

Kentucky State Fairgrounds - Louisville / at new fairgrounds south of town
    1.8 mile paved road course (5/04/57) (4/27/58) (6/14/59)
    ran sports cars in paved parking lots next to Fairgrounds Motor Speedway

Kentucky State Fairgrounds - Louisville / located west of town / torn down 1950's
    1/2 mile dirt oval (c.9/14/18 - 1932) (1941) (1946 - c.1951)

Lake Cumberland Speedway - Somerset - 3/8 mile dirt oval (8/12/83 - present)
    located six miles south of Somerset on US 27 / (aka: Burnside Speedway)

Lake Cumberland Sports Drome - Somerset / (aka: Somerset Motor Speedway)
    1/4 mile dirt oval (c.1970 - 1973) / located three miles north on US 27

Latonia Horse Track - Covington / (aka: Kentucky Int'l Raceway)
  1.0 mile dirt oval (5/14/11) / 1911 race won by Barney Oldfield in the same car
    that Ray Harroun drove to victory in first Indy 500 two weeks later
  1/4 mile dirt oval (1937) / ran midgets on small track
  5/8 mile dirt oval (5/28/67 - 10/01/72) / 5/8's was a former trotter track

Lawrenceburg Fairgrounds - Lawrenceburg / at the Anderson County Fairgrounds
  1/4 mile dirt oval (5/25/41) (1954) (1965)

Lebanon Fairgrounds - Lebanon / located at the Marion County Fairgrounds
  1/2 mile dirt oval (mid-1930's - c.1941) (c.1946 - c.1954)

Legion Speedway - Russellville - 1/4 mile dirt oval (c.1954)

Leitchfield Fairgrounds - Leitchfield / located at the Grayson County Fairgrounds
  1/5 mile dirt oval (1963 - 1973) (1987)

Lexington Fairgrounds - Lexington / located at the Blue Grass Fair & Exhibition
  1.0 mile dirt oval (5/23/06) (1929) / reported 36,000 fans saw the 1906 race
  (aka: Kentucky Trotting Horse Breeder Association Track)
  Barney Oldfield and Bill Pickens promoted the 1906 race

Lonnie's Speedway - Cumberland - 3/8 mile dirt oval (c.1971 - 1977)

Lost Creek Speedway - Jackson (Lost Creek) / site is now a housing development
  1/3 mile paved oval (5/06/72 - 1975) (1984)
  Bobby Olivero won a USAC midget race here on 6/16/73, this was the first
    win in the midget Division with a Volkswagen engine

Louisville - 1.0 mile dirt oval (c.1909 - c.9/29/29) / a horse track

Louisville Coliseum - see: Kentucky State Fair Pavilion

Louisville Downs - Louisville - 1/2 mile dirt oval (10/01/67 - 1991)
  ran ARCA LMs & USAC midgets 1967 & 1968 / AMA motorcycles 1967-1991

Louisville Fairgrounds - see: Kentucky State Fair & Fairgrounds Motor Speedway

Louisville Motor Speedway as it looked in 1993. The back straightaway was pushed out in 1994 to make a 7/16 mile track as well. - Official track photo.

Louisville Motor Speedway - Louisville / built to replace Fairgrounds Speedway
3/8 mile paved oval (4/22/88 - present)
7/16 (.438) mile paved oval (5/15/94 - present)

Louisville - also see: Kentucky Fair Expo, Kentucky Motor Speedway - Louisville

Ludlow - 1/3 mile wood oval (1910's) / ran motorcycles

Mac's Speedway - Vanceburg - 1/4 mile dirt oval (late 1960's)
located near the Foodland Grocery Store / (aka: Vanceburg Auto Race Track)

Madisonville Motor Speedway - Madisonville - 1/8 mile dirt oval (7/11/92 - 1993)
1/4 mile dirt oval (1994 - present)

Mayfield Fairgrounds - Mayfield / located at the Graves County Fairgrounds
1/2 mile dirt oval (c.8/23/58 - 1964) / (aka: Purchase District Fairgrounds)

McCracken County Drag Strip - see: West Kentucky Dragway

Middlesboro Speedway - Middlesboro - dirt oval (1954) / maybe Hilltop Speedway

Monticello - 1/4 mile dirt oval (1960's)

Morehead Motor Speedway - see: Bluestone Speedway

Morehead - also see: Rowan Sports Arena

Morgantown Fairgrounds - Morgantown / located at the Butler Co. Fairgrounds
1/2 mile dirt oval (years unknown)

Mount Olivet Speedway - Mount Olivet - 1/4 mile dirt oval (late 1950's)

Mount Sterling Fairgrounds - Mount Sterling / at Montgomery Co. Fairgrounds
1/4 mile dirt oval (years unknown)

Mountain Motor Speedway - Whitesburg - 3/8 mile dirt oval (May, 1969 - present)
1/12 mile paved dragstrip (October, 1990 - present)
(aka: Mountain Motor Dragway)

*The dragstrip at the Mountain Motor Speedway is between the grandstands
and the oval track. - Official track photo.*

Mountain Parkway Motorplex - Clay City / located next to Clay City Speedway
1/4 mile paved dragstrip (c.1963 - present)

Mud Lick Valley Raceway - Tollesboro - 3/8 mile dirt oval (8/07/93 - present)

Murray State University Center - Murray - 1/10 mile indoor paved oval (2/19/83)

Northern Kentucky Speedway - see: Florence Speedway

Ohio County Park - Hartford - 1/8 mile dirt oval (1986 - 1991) / ran Mini-sprints

Ohio Valley Raceway - West Point - 1/8 mile paved dragstrip (c.1966 - present)

Onion Speedway - (location unknown) - dirt oval (c.1947 - c.1948)

Owensboro Dragstrip (Raceway Park) - see: Windy Hollow Speedway

Owensboro Fairgrounds - Owensboro / located at the Daviess County Fairgrounds
1/5 mile dirt oval (6/04/48) / (aka: Tri-State Fairgrounds)
1/4 & 1/2 mile dirt ovals (7/03/48 - c.1955) / (aka: Legion Park)
1/7 mile dirt oval (1990 & 1991) / possibly a new fairgrounds for 1990

Owensboro (Maceo) - 1/2 mile dirt oval (late 1940's - c.1960) / northeast of town

Owensboro - also see: Ellis Speedway - Owensboro, Kentucky Motor - Whitesville

Paducah Fairgrounds - Paducah / located at the McCracken County Fairgrounds
1/2 mile dirt oval (1963) (1983) / (aka: West Kentucky Fairgrounds)

Paducah Int'l Raceway - Paducah / (aka: C H K Raceway)
3/8 mile dirt oval (1970 - 9/04/87) / (aka: Keeling Raceway)
Jim Dunn fatally injured during a NDRA race here on 5/07/83

Paducah Speedway - Paducah / (aka: Reidland Raceway)
dirt oval (c.1964 - c.1974) / site is now a housing development

Paducah Speedway - see: Smith Speedway

Paducah - also see: Hook's Park, West Kentucky Dragway

Paintsville Speedway - see: 201 Speedway

Paris - 1/4 mile dirt oval (1950's)

Pennyrile Raceway Park - Mortons Gap - 1/2 mile dirt oval (May, 1991 - present)

Perry County Speedway - Hazard / the track was built in an old coal strip mine
1/2 mile dirt oval (7/03/83 - 1988) (1990 - present)

Pine Knot Speedway - Pine Knot - 1/4 mile dirt oval (1979 - 1981)

Ponderosa Speedway - Junction City - 3/8 mile dirt oval (9/15/72 - present)

Raceland - Ashland - 1.0 mile dirt oval (1927 & 1928)

Radcliff - 1/4 mile dirt oval (1950's)

Reidland Raceway - see: Paducah Speedway

Richmond Raceway - Richmond - 3/10 mile dirt oval (May, 1966 - present)

Richmond - also see: Sports Arena Speedway

River Cities Raceway Park - Ashland - 1/8 mile dragstrip (c.1986 - present)

Riverview Speedway - Milton - 1/4 mile dirt oval (c.1963 - 1973)

Rock Castle Raceway - Mount Vernon / (aka: Rock Castle County Speedway)
   1/3 mile dirt oval (July, 1981 - 1988) (1990) (1992 - present)

Rooster Lake Speedway - Paris - dirt oval (c.1987)

Rowan Sports Arena - Morehead - 1/3 mile dirt oval (c.1949 - c.1954)

Russell Springs Fairgrounds - Russell Springs / at the Russell County Fairgrounds
   3/8 mile dirt oval (c.1963 - c.1970)

Sandy Valley Speedway - Allen / (aka: Sandy Valley Sports Arena)
   dirt oval (c.1953 - c.1955) / located near Prestonburg

Saylersville Speedway - Saylersville - 3/8 mile dirt oval (c.1971 - 1972)

Saylersville Speedway - Saylersville - 3/8 mile dirt oval (c.1985 - present)

Shepherdsville - 1/2 mile dirt oval (1941)

Smith Speedway - Paducah - 1/4 mile dirt oval (7/04/49 - 1954)
   (aka: Paducah Speedway)

Somerset Motor Speedway - see: Lake Cumberland Sports Drome

Sports Arena Speedway - Richmond - 1/4 mile dirt oval (c.8/24/51 - c.1964)

Sturgis Drag Strip - Sturgis - 1/4 mile paved dragstrip (c.1956 - c.1972)

Tacoma Park Speedway - see: Dayton-Tacoma Speedway

Taylor County Speedway - Campbellsville / located at the Taylor Co. Fairgrounds
   3/8 mile dirt oval (c.1952 - 1982) (1984 - present)

Thorn Hill Dragstrip - Kenton - 1/8 & 1/4 mile paved dragstrips (1957 - present)

Thunder Mountain Speedway - (location unknown) / was in eastern Kentucky
   3/8 mile dirt oval (years unknown)

Thunder Ridge - Prestonsburg - 3/8 mile dirt oval (7/16/94 - present)
   the track is located inside of a harness horse track

Trenton - dirt oval (c.1954)

Trenton Speedway - Trenton / (aka: US 41 Speedway) / (aka: 41-E Speedway)
   1/4 mile dirt oval (c.1976 - c.1980) (1985 - 1989) (1991)

Tri-City Dragstrip - (location unknown) - 1/8 mile paved dragstrip (1970's)
   maybe Bluestone Speedway

U.S. 60 Dragway - Hardinsburg - 1/8 mile paved dragstrip (c.1964 - present)

US 41 Speedway - see: Trenton Speedway

Vanceburg Auto Race Track - Vanceburg - dirt oval (years unknown)
possibly was Big 3 or Creeks Run

Vanceburg - also see: Big Three, Creeks Run

West Kentucky Dragway - Paducah - 1/4 mile paved dragstrip (c.1970 - c.1978)
(aka: McCracken County Drag Strip)

Windsor Fairgrounds - Windsor - 1/2 mile dirt oval (early 1950's)

Windy Hollow Speedway - Owensboro / (aka: Owensboro Raceway Park)
1/4 mile dirt oval (c.1975 - 1981) (1986 - present) / (aka: GLV Raceway)
1/8 mile paved dragstrip (4/02/71 - present) / (aka: Owensboro Dragstrip)

LOUISIANA

167 Evangeline Speedway - see: One-Sixty-Seven Daredevil Speedway

171 Speedway - see: One-Seven-One Speedway

Amelia Road - see: Louisiana 500 Speedway

B & D Speedway - see: Hickory Speedway

Bastrop - dirt oval (1973)

Baton Rouge - 1/2 mile dirt oval (1941)

Baton Rouge Dragway - see: State Capitol Dragway

Baton Rouge Int'l Speedway - Prairieville / David Pearson first winner
5/8 mile paved oval (12/10/66 - 1978) / first race was a NASCAR GN race
(aka: Louisiana Int'l Speedway) / (aka: Pelican Int'l Raceway)
built by Ed Grady (a teamster union head) / site is now housing

Baton Rouge Raceway - Baton Rouge (Baker) / (aka: Carroll's Raceway Park)
3/8 mile dirt oval (1974 - present)

Doug Ingalls at Boothill Speedway near Shreveport. - Rolland Rickard photo.

Bayou Raceway - Minden - 1/4 mile dirt oval (1970 - 1984) (1988)
    (aka: Hilltop Racing Bowl) / (aka: Bayou Gatorbowl Raceway)

Boothill Speedway - Shreveport / (aka: I-20 Raceway) / located west of town
    1/4 mile dirt oval (c.1973 - present)

*Flat track motorcycle races are a popular attractions at fairgrounds. This
picture is from the Ionia County Fairgrounds (MI). - Tom DeVette photo.*

Bullet Speedway - Bastrop - 1/4 mile dirt oval (1987 - 1991)

Cajun Raceway - Sterlington - 1/2 mile dirt oval (1970's)

Calcasieu Int'l Speedway - Lake Charles - 1/2 mile dirt oval (c.1971)
    (aka: Horseman's Park) / (aka: Lake Charles Speedway)

Calhoun Speedway - see: I-20 Motor Speedway

Carroll's Raceway Park - see: Baton Rouge Raceway

Cenla Raceway - Forest Hill - 1/4 mile paved dragstrip (c.1970)

Cenla Raceways - Alexandria - 1/4 mile paved dragstrip (c.1977)

Chennault Air Force Base - Lake Charles
    3.0 mile paved road course (c.1967 - 1986)

Covington - 1/2 mile dirt oval (1941)

Crowley Dragstrip - Crowley - 1/4 mile paved dragstrip (c.1964 - c.1965)

Dare Devil Raceway - Glendora - 1/4 mile dirt oval (1971)

DeSoto Airport - see: Mansfield Airport

Dixie Speedway - Farmerville - 1/4 mile dirt oval (1990 - present)

Dixieland Speedway - Saint Rose - 5/8 mile paved oval (1960's)

Forest Hill Speedway - Forest Hill - 1/4 mile dirt oval (Sept., 1968 - present)

Franklinton Speedway - Franklinton - 1/4 mile dirt oval (1979 - 1981)

Gonzales - 1/2 mile dirt oval (early 1930's)

Grand Prix Du Mardi Gras - New Orleans / downtown New Orleans city streets
1.5 mile paved road course (6/16/91 & 1992)

Grant Speedway - Bentley - 3/8 mile dirt oval (1983 - 1985)

Great Southern Speedway - Angie - 1/4 mile dirt oval (1979 - c.1983)

Hammond - dirt oval (1922)

Hammond - paved road course (late 1950's)

Harmon Airport Dragstrip - Monroe - 1/4 mile paved dragstrip (c.1963 - c.1965)
(aka: Bob Harmon Memorial Speedway)

Haynesville Dragway - Haynesville - 1/4 mile paved dragstrip (c.1970 - 1979)

Hickory Speedway - Hickory (LaCombe) / (aka: Tammany Speedway)
1/4 mile dirt oval (c.1969 - c.1977) (4/13/91 - present)
(aka: B & D Speedway) / (aka: St. Tammany Speedway)

Hilltop Racing Bowl - see: Bayou Raceway

Horseman's Park - see: Calcasieu Int'l Speedway

I-20 Motor Speedway - Calhoun / (aka: Calhoun Speedway)
1/4 mile dirt oval (c.1987 - 1989) (1992 - present)

Jefferson Park - Plaucheville - dirt oval (c.1921) / located near Camp Plaucheville

Jefferson Speedway - New Orleans - 1/4 mile dirt oval (10/20/91 - present)

Lafayette Fairgrounds - Lafayette - 1/2 mile dirt oval (1950's)

Lake Charles Dragway - Lake Charles - 1/4 mile paved dragstrip (c.1981 - c.1989)

Lake Charles Raceway - see: Calcasieu Int'l Speedway

LaPlace Dragway - LaPlace - 1/4 mile paved dragway (May, 1962 - 1980)
built by Thirl Biggins / later became an oval mud track

Loranger Speedway - see: Spillway Speedway

Louisiana 500 Speedway - Kenner - 1/4 mile dirt oval (1964) (1966 - 1967)
1/4 mile paved oval (1965) / (aka: Amelia Road) / now a junkyard

Louisiana Hilltop Raceway - Shreveport (Bossier City)
2.0 mile paved road course (9/03/60 - 1965) / (aka: "Top O' the Hill")
formerly Gidden's Castle Resort / converted into a Baptist Summer Camp

Louisiana Int'l Speedway - Denham Springs - 1/2 mile dirt oval (1965)
built by Bill Evans

Louisiana Int'l Speedway - see: Baton Rouge Int'l Speedway

Louisiana Raceway Park - Eunice - 1/4 mile paved dragstrip (1986 - present)

Louisiana Speedway - see: Louisiana State Fair Speedway

The I.M.C.A. stock cars in front of the grandstands of the Louisiana State Fairgrounds in Shreveport from 1967. - Photo courtesy of I.M.C.A.

Louisiana State Fair Speedway - Shreveport / built as horse track in 1905
    1.0 mile dirt oval (11/10/10 - 1936) / Barney Oldfield won the first race
    1/2 mile dirt oval (c.1931 - 11/22/41) (10/19/46 - 1969)
    Lee Petty won only NASCAR GN race ever held in Louisiana here on 6/07/53
    1/2 mile paved oval (10/18/69 - 1980) / (aka: Louisiana Speedway)
    Gus Schrader was fatally injured here on 10/22/41

Mansfield Airport - Mansfield / (aka: DeSoto Parish Airport)
    2.4 mile paved road course (c.8/04/56 - 7/06/59) / ran on the runways

Mardi Gras Grand Prix - see: Grand Prix Du Mardi Gras

Mardi Gras Track - New Orleans - 1.0 mile dirt oval (2/21/09 - 1918) (May, 1921)

Monroe - see: Harmon Airport, River City, Twin City

New Orleans - 1/5 mile dirt oval (1941) / formerly Saint Bernard Dog Track

New Orleans - also see: Grand Prix du Mardi Gras, Jefferson, Mardi Gras

New Orleans Motor Speedway - New Orleans
    1/4 mile paved oval (10/20/46 - c.1947)

New Orleans - paved road course (11/29/59)

One-Seven-One Speedway - Leesville - 1/4 mile dirt oval (c.1952 - 1985)

One-Sixty-Seven Daredevil Speedway - Sunset / (aka: 167 Evangeline Speedway)
    1/4 mile dirt oval (c.1975 - c.1977)

Pelican Int'l Raceway - see: Baton Rouge Int'l Speedway

Pelican State Dragstrip - Opelousas - 1/4 mile paved dragstrip (1954 - c.1969)
    possibly State Capitol Dragway

Pollock Dragway - Pollock - 1/4 mile paved dragstrip (c.1970)

Rebel Speedway - Amite - 1/4 mile dirt oval (late 1960's - early 1970's)

River City Raceway - Monroe - 1/4 mile dirt oval (1981) (1987)
(aka: River City Speedway)

Rosepine Raceway - DeRidder - 1/4 mile dirt oval (c.1973 - 1975)

Saint Tammany Speedway - see: Hickory Speedway

Shreveport - 1/4 mile dirt oval (8/20/39)

Shreveport Dragway - Shreveport - 1/4 mile paved dragstrip (c.1964 - c.1978)

Shreveport Fairgrounds - see: Louisiana State Fair Speedway

Shreveport - also see: Boothill & Louisiana Hilltop

South Park Speedway - Alexandria - 3/8 mile dirt oval (early 1970's)

Southland Raceway - Houma - 1/4 mile paved dragstrip (c.1970 - c.1976)

Spillway Speedway - Loranger - 1/4 mile dirt oval (1973 - 1987) (1989 - present)
(aka: Loranger Speedway)

State Capitol Dragway - Baton Rouge / (aka: Baton Rouge Dragway)
1/4 mile paved dragstrip (c.1970 - 1989) (1991 - present)
Don Prudhomme had first ever 250.0 mph run in a Funny Car on 5/23/82

Super Bee Speedway - Chatham - 1/4 mile dirt oval (1988 - present)
(aka: Chatham Speedway)

Tallulah Fairgrounds - Tallulah / located at the Louisiana Delta Fairgrounds
1/2 mile dirt oval (10/17/48) (10/16/49)

Tammany Speedway - see: Hickory Speedway

Thibodaux Speedway - Thibodaux - 1/2 mile dirt oval (c.1954 - c.1959)

Top O' the Hill - see: Louisiana Hilltop Raceway

Twin City Drags - Monroe - 1/4 mile paved dragstrip (c.1965 - present)
(aka: Twin City Dragway) / same location at Cajun Speedway's oval track

Webster Speedway - Haughton - 1/4 mile dirt oval (6/05/93 - present)

MAINE

A & A Dragway - see: Winterport Dragway

Andover Fairgrounds - Andover - dirt oval (years unknown)

Aroostock County Int'l Speedway - see: Spud Speedway

Arundel Speedway - Kennebunkport / built by Clifford Parker
1/3 mile paved oval (5/17/63 - 1964) (1967) (1971)

Bangor Fairgrounds - Bangor - dirt oval (8/26/50) / (aka: Bass Park)

Beech Ridge Motor Speedway - West Scarborough / built by Jim McConnell
  1/3 mile oiled dirt oval (5/30/49 - 1986)
  1/3 mile paved oval (1987 - present)

Belfast Fairgrounds - Belfast / (aka: Belfast Speedway)
  1/2 mile dirt oval (9/03/50 - c.1952)

Biddeford Speedway - Biddeford - 1/3 mile dirt oval (1966 & 1967)

Brewer Fairgrounds - Brewer / (aka: Brewer Speedway)
  1/2 mile dirt oval (9/09/50 - c.1952)

Challenger Int'l Raceway - see: Spud Speedway

Cherryfield Speedway - Cherryfield - 1/3 mile dirt oval (1950 - 1971)
  (aka: Washington County Speedway)

Ellsworth Speedway - Ellsworth - 4/10 mile dirt oval (1960's)
  4/10 mile paved oval (late 1960's)

Exeter Fairgrounds - Exeter - 1/2 mile dirt oval (c.1952 - early 1960's)

Haleysville Speedway - Rangeley - 1/4 mile dirt oval (1979)

Hermon Speedway - see: Speedway 95

Kennebunk - 1/2 mile dirt oval (1936) / possibly at a fairgrounds

Lewiston Fairgrounds - see: Maine State Fairgrounds

Lincoln County Speedway - see: Wiscasset Speedway

Maine State Fairgrounds - Lewiston - 1/2 mile dirt oval (1941) (c.1946 - c.1953)

New Glouchester Track - N. Glouchester - 1/2 mile dirt oval (8/06/39) (mid 1950's)

Norridgewock Airport - Norridgewock / run by the Cumberland Motor Club
  1.1 mile paved road course (1958 - 1968) / on airport runways

Norridgewock Fairgrounds - Norridgewock / (aka: Norridgewock Race Track)
  1/2 mile dirt oval (6/06/51)

Norway Fairgrounds - Norway / located at the Oxford County Fairgrounds
  1/2 mile dirt oval (1950 - c.1951)

Old Orchard Beach - 1.125 mile peanut shaped dirt oval (c.1937)

Old Orchard Beach - beach oval (c.9/04/11 - c.1916)

Oxford Plains Speedway - Oxford / home of the annual "Oxford 250"
  1/2 mile dirt oval (5/27/50 - 1953) (1955) (1957 - 1960)
  1/3 mile paved oval (6/04/61 - present) /
  1/8 mile paved dragstrip (c.1976 - present)
  held three NASCAR Grand Nat'l races (1966, 1967, 1968) on oval track

Queen City Speedway - see: Speedway 95

Sanford Dragway - Sanford - 1/4 mile paved dragstrip (c.1959 - 1960's)

Sanford Speedway - Sanford - 1/3 mile dirt oval (c.1952 - c.1956)

Leo Clary (#41) dominated the All Star League race at Albany-Saratoga Speedway (NY) on July 30, 1968. Here he laps fifth place runner "Bugs" Stevens in the number 3. - Allan E. Brown collection.

Skowhegan Fairgrounds - Skowhegan - 1/2 mile dirt oval (1946 - c.1951)
(aka: Skowhegan State Fairgrounds)

Speedway 95 - Bangor (Hermon) - 1/3 mile paved oval (1966 - present)
(aka: Hermon Speedway) / (aka: Queen City Speedway)
(aka: Thunder Speedway) / (aka: Queen City Raceway)

Springfield Speedway - Springfield - 1/3 mile dirt oval (c.1957 - c.1965)

Spud Speedway - Caribou / (aka: Challenger Int'l Raceway)
1/4 mile paved oval (1964 - 1988) (1991 - present)
(aka: Aroostock County Int'l Speedway) / built by Wayne Souses

Superior Speedway - see: Wiscasset Speedway

Thunder Speedway - see: Speedway 95

Topsham Fairgrounds - Topsham (Brunswick) - 1/2 mile dirt oval (10/27/35)

Unity Raceway - Unity / located on the Unity Fairgrounds / formerly a horse track
1/2 mile dirt oval (10/22/49 - 1956) / the first feature was rained out
the first full program was completed on 6/17/50
1/3 mile dirt oval (6/09/57 - 1961)
1/3 mile paved oval (6/17/62 - 1979) (1981 - present)

Unity Raceway - Unity - 1/2 mile dirt oval (10/22/49 - 1956) / a former horse track
the 1st feature was rained out / the 1st full complete program was on 6/17/50
1/3 mile dirt oval (6/09/57 - 1961) / located on the Unity Fairgrounds
1/3 mile paved oval (6/17/62 - 1979) (1981 - present)

Washington County Speedway - see: Cherryfield Speedway

Waterville-Oakland Race Track - Oakland - 1/2 mile dirt oval (9/17/50 - 1951)
the grandstands collapsed 1/2 hour before the first race was to be held

Windsor Fairgrounds - Windsor - 1/2 mile dirt oval (10/01/50 - 1951) / horse track

Winterport Dragway - Winterport - 1/8 mile paved dragstrip (c.1957 - present)
(aka: A & A Dragway) / formerly an old airfield

Wiscasset Motor Speedway - Wiscasset / (aka: Lincoln County Speedway)
1/3 mile paved oval (c.1971 - 1988) (1991 - present)
(aka: Superior Speedway)

278

MARYLAND

75-80 Dragway - Monrovia - 1/4 mile paved dragstrip (c.1960 - present)
(aka: 75-80 Drag-A-Way) / located next to Monrovia Speedway

Andrews Air Force Base - Camp Springs / located east of Washington D.C.
4.25 mile paved road course on runways (5/02/54)

Aquasco Speedway - Aquasco - 1/4 mile concrete dragstrip (c.1957 - c.1972)
oval (late 1950's or early 1960's) / maybe NASCAR sanctioned

B & J Speedway - Salisbury - 1/4 mile dirt oval (c.5/27/50 - c.1950)

Baltimore Coliseum - Baltimore - dirt oval (1900) / motorcycles / on Harford Ave.

Baltimore Memorial Stadium - Baltimore / located at 33rd & Ellerslie
1/4 mile dirt oval (9/20/39 & 9/28/39) / also had four rain outs

Baltimore-Washington Speedway - Laurel / built by Jack Prince
1.125 mile wood oval (7/11/25 - 9/25/26) turns were banked 48 degrees
Bob McDonough was awarded win in the first event, rechecking the scoring
charts later revealed that Peter DePaolo had won instead

Baltimore-Washington Speedway - see: Beltsville Speedway

Baltimore - also see: Electric Park, Pimlico, Prospect Park, Westport

Bel Air - 1/2 mile dirt oval (c.1933)

Beltsville Speedway - Beltsville / (aka: Baltimore-Washington Speedway)
1/2 mile paved oval (7/21/65 - 1979) / first called Beltsville in 1966
built by Tom Lillis / Wayne Kindness was a promoter here in the 1970's

*Al Daily (#41) and Danny Collins (#45) race in front of the "Beltsville Wall".
The twenty foot high wall had to be constructed because neighbors complained
about the noise. - Fred Seim photo (Larry Jendras, Jr. collection).*

Braddock Heights - 1/4 mile dirt oval (1953 - 1957)

Budds Creek - see: Maryland Int'l Raceway & Potomac Speedway

Cambridge - 1/2 mile dirt oval (c.1929 - early 1930's)

Capital Raceway - Crofton - 1/4 mile paved dragstrip (September, 1961 - present)
(aka: Capital Raceway Park) / (aka: Capital Dragway)

Cecil County Dragway - Bayview - 1/4 mile paved dragstrip (c.1963 - present)
Jim Thornton drove to first 8 second Funny Car run here on 8/07/65
(aka: Cecil County Dragoway)

Clear Spring - 1/2 mile dirt oval (c.1949)

Condon Speedway - Sykesville - 1/3 mile dirt oval (c.7/23/54 - 1960)

Conococheagua Speedway - see: Hagerstown Speedway

Croom - dirt oval (1958) / ran motorcycles only

Cumberland Airport - Cumberland / (aka: Maryland Municipal Airport)
1.6 mile paved road course on runways (5/20/52 - 1971)

Cumberland Speedway - Cumberland / located at the Cumberland Fairgrounds
1/2 mile dirt oval (c.1924 - c.1940) (6/19/66 - 9/05/83) (1991 - present)
(aka: Greater Cumberland Raceway)

Dara Speedway - Whitesburg - dirt oval (1970 & 1971)

Deep Creek Lake Speedway - McHenry - 3/8 mile dirt oval (1952 - 1955)

Denton - dirt oval (1950's)

Dorsey Speedway - Dorsey - 1/5 mile dirt oval (1950) / only ran one race
built by Jack Coburn, Dave Wawse & Ken Whitaker

Dorsey Speedway - Dorsey - 1/4 mile dirt oval (c.9/03/51 - 1985)
a new track built close to the above track

The driver of this number 22 is Elmo Langley. The year was 1953. Harry Clifton photo (Larry Jendras, Jr. collection).

280

Electric Park - Baltimore - 1/2 mile dirt oval (11/22/1900)

Fairchild Road Race Course - see: Hagerstown Municipal Airport

Frederick Airport - Frederick - 1/4 mile paved dragstrip (1956 - c.1957)

Frederick Fairgrounds - Frederick - 1/2 mile dirt oval (1910's - 1922)
1/2 mile dirt oval (5/30/38 - 5/21/39) (7/05/48 - c.1955) (1975 - present)
runs an annual motorcycle race each year / last auto race was in 1977

Gentleman's Driving Park - (location unknown) - dirt oval (1916)

Greater Cumberland Raceway - see: Cumberland Raceway

Hagerstown Fairgrounds - Hagerstown - 1/2 mile dirt oval (1920's) near downtown

Hagerstown Municipal Airport - Hagerstown / (aka: Fairchild Road Race Course)
2.4 mile paved road course on runways (10/09/55 & 10/16/55)

Hagerstown Speedway - Hagerstown / located five miles west of town
1/2 mile dirt oval (Aug., 1948 - present) / built by Stanley Schetrompf
covered grandstand torn down in 1967 / (aka: Conococheagua Speedway)
ran first ever $50,000 to win race on a dirt track on 6/11/83

Lanham Speedway - Lanham / (aka: West Lanham Speedway)
1/5 mile high banked paved oval (6/24/41 - 5/15/42) (1945 - 1954)
Johnny Roberts (NASCAR modified champion) started his career here 1950

Laurel - 1/5 mile dirt oval (8/13/39)

Laurel (board track) - see: Baltimore-Washington Speedway

Laureldale - (location unknown) - 1/2 mile dirt oval (c.1934 - c.1935)

Legion Speedway - Pocomoke City - dirt oval (May, 1950)

Marine Speedway - see: Saint Mary's Speedway

Marlboro Motor Raceway - Upper Marlboro - 1/3 mile dirt oval (c.8/17/52- 8/23/53)
4/10 mile dirt oval (9/13/53 - 1953)
1/3 mile paved oval (3/24/54 - 1969)
0.9 mile & 1.7 mile paved road courses (5/22/55 - 1969)
2.4 mile paved road course (5/12/57) / ran SCCA Trans-Am 1967 & 1968

*Late models at Marlboro Raceway. The cars in this picture include a Nash,
Studebaker and three Fords. - Larry Jendras, Jr. collection.*

Maryland Airport Speedway - Pomonkey - 1/2 mile dirt oval (c.1950 - c.1953)

Maryland Int'l Raceway - Budds Creek - 1/4 mile paved dragstrip (c.1964- present)
(aka: Budds Creek Dragway) / (aka: St. Mary's Drag-O-Way)

Mason-Dixon Dragway - Hagerstown - 1/4 mile paved dragstrip (c.1963 - present)

Mason-Dixon Speedway - see: Pennsylvania chapter

Milford Mills Speedway - see: Pikesville Speedway

Monrovia Speedway - Monrovia - 1/8 mile dirt oval (c.1993 - present)

Ocean Downs Raceway - Ocean City - 1/2 mile dirt oval (late 1970's) / horse track

Pikesville Speedway - Pikesville - 5/8 mile dirt oval (1927 - c.1935)
Bill France, Sr. started his driving career here in 1929
(aka: Milford Mills Speedway)

The big cars were the top attraction at Milford Mill Speedway in the 1930's.
Larry Jendras, Jr. collection.

Pimlico Track - Baltimore - 1.0 mile dirt oval (5/30/08) (7/04/08) (1930's)
famous horse track where the Preakness is held each year

Potomac Speedway - Budds Creek - 3/8 mile dirt oval (1974 - present)
located next to Maryland Int'l Raceway (dragstrip)

Prospect Park - Baltimore - dirt oval (8/02/24)

Ritchie Raceway - Brooklyn (Glen Burnie) - 1/2 mile dirt oval (c.9/25/26 - c.1929)
located two miles south of Brooklyn on Governor Ritchie Highway
(aka: Governor Ritchie Speedway) / maybe same location as 1948 track

Ritchie Raceway - Brooklyn (Glen Burnie) / sold for housing development in 1955
3/8 mile dirt oval (8/08/48 - 1948) (5/13/53 - 1954)
Wally Campbell won on 8/08/48 in a modified / (aka: Ritchie Speedway)
located two miles south of Brooklyn on Annapolis Blvd.
converted to a somewhat successful harness track in late 1948

Rockville Fairgrounds - Rockville - 1/2 mile dirt oval (1927 - 1929)

Salisbury - 1/2 mile dirt oval (1929)

Saint Mary's Speedway - Lexington Park / located at the Patuxent Naval Base
    4/10 mile dirt oval (5/24/52 - c.1958) / (aka: Marine Speedway)

Taneytown Fairgrounds - Taneytown - 1/2 mile dirt oval (mid 1950's)

Vista Raceway - Lanham - 1/2 mile dirt oval (c.1957 - early 1960's)
    located on Vista-Lottsford Road, between Rts 450 & 704
    owned and operated by the Lanham Land & Sea Club (blacks)

Westport Stadium - Baltimore - 1/5 mile dirt oval (5/05/51 - 8/10/63)
    built around a baseball diamond / the promoter was Bill Heiserman

Wicomico Civic Center - Salisbury - 1/10 mile indoor concrete oval (1/11/86)

MASSACHUSETTS

Alumni Field - Lowell - 1/5 mile dirt oval (6/20/38 - 9/29/41) / on Rogers St.

Athol Fairgrounds - Athol - 1/2 mile dirt oval (c.1937 - 7/04/41) (1947)

Attleboro Speedway - see: Interstate Speedway Park

Baylies Stadium - New Bedford - 1/3 mile paved oval (6/05/40 - 9/10/41)
    1/5 mile dirt oval (1948 - 4/18/49) / motorcycles 1948 / (aka: Cawley Stadium)
    on Coggeshill St. / torn down in December 1949 / site is now part of I-195

Bellingham - 1/5 mile dirt oval (1949) / the track was dirt for the first race
    1/5 mile paved oval (1949 - 1951) (1953) / site became an ice cream parlor

Beverly Airport - Danvers - 2.6 mile paved road course (7/05/55 & 1956)

Bigberry Stadium - see: Fall River Speedway

This is how Roscoe "Pappy" Hough toured the country. The photo was taken at Hersey (PA) on May 9, 1940. "Pappy" has the distinction of being the first person to ever get to 500 different tracks, either as a driver or as a car owner. Phil Harms collection.

Boston Gardens - Boston - 1/10 mile indoor dirt oval (12/10/36 - 12/17/36)
    1/10 mile indoor dirt oval (12/10/36 - 12/17/36) (2/04/37 - 2/25/37)
    1/10 mile flat indoor wood oval (1/14/37) / possibly outdoor track
    1/10 mile banked indoor wood oval (11/11/37 - 1/27/38)

Boston - also see: Lincoln Park, Readville, West Roxbury

Bridgwater Grange Park - Bridgewater - 1/2 mile dirt oval (7/04/36)

Brockton Fairgrounds - Brockton / located west of town on State Route 123
    1/2 mile dirt oval (early 1920's) (1927 - c.9/13/41)
    1/5 mile dirt oval (late 1940's) / the tracks were torn out in 1973
    the grandstands was destroyed by fire in 1936 / ran IMCA sprints in 1920's
    reportedly had 94,000 fans for a AAA big car race here in 1934

Cambridge Fairgrounds - Cambridge - 1/2 mile dirt oval (c.1935 - 8/19/39)

Cambridge - also see: Charles River Park .

Camp Joe Hooker - see: Lakeville Speedway

Cawley Stadium - see: Baylies Stadium

Century Stadium - see: West Springfield Speedway

Charles River Park - Cambridge - 1/3 mile dirt oval (November, 1898)
    the race was won by a Stanley Steamer

Chatham Speedway - Chatham - 1/5 mile dirt oval (mid-1970's)
    1/5 mile paved oval (1977)

Country Club of Brookline - Brookline - dirt oval (6/15/01)

Crescent Oval - Springfield - oval (1940) / maybe West Springfield Speedway

Dracut Speedway - Dracut - 1/4 mile paved oval (6/03/46 - 1955)
    the track was built and promoted by Alex Beloit

Eastern State Expo Coliseum - West Springfield / at the Eastern States Expo
    1/10 mile indoor dirt oval (3/04/94) (3/05/94) / ran Mini-sprints

Eastern State Expo Speedway - West Springfield / at the Eastern States Expo
    1/2 mile dirt oval (c.1917 - c.9/20/41) / ran IMCA big cars in 1920's
    ran AAA big cars in 1930's   /   U.S. Army used site during World War II
    5/8 mile dirt oval (9/19/47 - 9/20/52) / the fair started in 1912
    5/8 mile paved oval (9/25/53 - 1968 / the track partially torn out in 1968

Evergreen Speedway - New Bedford - 1/2 mile dirt oval (c.5/30/39 - c.1940)
    the site is now the New Bedford Airport

Fall River Speedway - Fall River / (aka: Bigberry Stadium)
    1/4 mile dirt oval (6/09/39 - 7/24/42) / the site later became a playground

Golden Cove Race Track - Chelmsford - 1/2 mile dirt oval (9/21/35) / one race only

Golden Spur Speedway - see: Lakeville Speedway

Great Barrington - 1/2 mile dirt oval (c.10/03/36 - c.1941) (9/22/46) / horse track

Horace Mann Speedway - Franklin / (aka: New Franklin Speedway)
   1/2 mile dirt oval (7/04/40 - c.10/12/40) (9/02/46)
   1/5 mile paved oval (5/30/41 - 7/30/42) / formerly a horse track
   the site is now a shopping plaza on Rte 140

Hyannis Port - 1.0 mile dirt (sand) road course (5/12/35) / raced on sand dunes

Interstate Speedway Park - South Attleboro
   1/2 mile dirt oval (1922 - c.1924) (c.1933 - Sept., 1936) (4/19/38)
   (aka: Attleboro Speedway) / the site is now a shopping center

Lakeville Speedway - Lakeville / probably was Massachusetts' last dirt track
   1/2 mile dirt oval (late 1920's) (1938) (10/19/41 - 11/11/41) (c.1946) (c.1964- 1975)
   (aka: Camp Joe Hooker) / (aka: Middleboro Fairgrounds)
   named after Gen. Joe Hooker when it was a horse training Army camp
   (aka: Golden Spur Speedway) / located near Middleboro

Lawson Speedway - Scituate - dirt oval (1920's)

Lincoln Park - Boston - 1/5 mile dirt oval (8/10/35)
   New England's first midget races were held here

Lowell - 10.6 mile city street road course (1907 - 9/08/09) (Sept. 1912)
   (aka: Merrimack Valley Course) / ran AAA champ cars

Lynn - dirt oval (1932)

Marlborough - 1/2 mile dirt oval (1934 - 11/11/35)

Marshfield Fairgrounds - Marshfield - 1/2 mile dirt oval (1933 - 8/25/34) (7/04/36)

Marstons Mills - paved city street road course (6/29/35)

Medford Bowl - Medford - 1/4 mile paved oval (9/07/46 - 1954)
   located on Revere Beach Parkway / (aka: Mystic Valley Speedway)
   the site was to become a drive-in theater, but was turned down by council

Medford - also see: Radio Bowl, Riverside Park.

Two racer head down the straightaway at the Readville track in 1909. This is one of the earliest tracks in New England. - Bruce Craig collection.

Middleboro Fairgrounds - see: Lakeville Speedway

Mohawk Stadium - Lunenburg - oval (c.6/25/48 - c.1949)
   the site later became a drive-in theater

Mystic Valley Speedway - see: Medford Bowl

New Bedford - 1/4 mile paved dragstrip (c.1957) / located at the airport

New Bedford - also see: Baylies Stadium, Evergreen Speedway.

New Franklin Speedway - see: Horace Mann Speedway

New Springfield Speedway - see: West Springfield Speedway

Northampton Fairgrounds - Northampton / located at the Three Co. Fairgrounds
   1/2 mile dirt oval (1933 - 9/07/41) / (aka: Driving Park) / a horse track

Norwood Arena - Norwood - 1/4 mile paved oval (6/14/48 - 1972)
   Johnny Bernardi was 1st winner / races on 5/31/48 & 6/07/48 were rain outs
   Ralph Moody & Pete Hamilton started their careers here
   Dave Dion was the last Late Model champion / site now an industrial park

Red Cummings at Norwood Arena in 1950. - Howard White photo.

Orange Dragstrip - Orange (Fitchburg) - 1/4 mile paved dragstrip (1954 - c.1970)

Oxford Fairgrounds - Oxford - 1/2 mile dirt oval (1930's) (Sept., 1946)
   maybe located at the Sturbridge Fair

Pines Speedway - see: The Pines Speedway

Pynchon Park - Springfield - 1/5 mile dirt oval (5/22/37)

Radio Bowl - Medford - 1/3 mile paved oval (8/17/41 - c.8/31/41)
   1/4 mile paved oval (6/10/41 - 9/23/41)

Readville - Boston (Hyde Park) - 1.0 mile dirt oval (1902 - 5/31/37)
  Ralph DePalma won his first ever race here in 1908 / ran IMCA in 1915
  also ran AAA big cars / originally built as a horse track
  used by the government as a landing strip during World War II
  destroyed by a hurricane in 1938 / actually located near Hyde Park

Rhythm Inn Speedway - Millers Falls - 1/3 mile dirt oval (5/25/51 - c.1959)

Riverside Park - Medford - 1/5 mile dirt oval (1937)
  1/4 mile dirt oval (6/22/38 - 9/21/39) / ran midgets

Riverside Park Speedway - Agawam - 1/5 mile paved oval (6/02/48 - 1972)
  1/4 mile paved oval (1972 - 1985) / at the Riverside Park amusement park
  1/4 mile high-banked paved oval (1986 - present)

Rockdale Park - Peabody - 1/2 mile dirt oval (7/03/30 & 9/01/30)
  was a harness track that opened in 1925 / site is now housing development

Rockland Speedway - Rockland - 1/4 mile dirt oval (1939)
  1/4 mile paved oval (c.7/13/40 - c.7/20/40)

Round the Houses - Edgertown (Martha's Vineyard) - street road course (1935)

Saugus - 1.25 mile dirt oval (1931) / ran one AAA race

Saugus - 1/4 mile dirt oval (1946 - c.1958)

Seekonk Speedway - Seekonk - 1/4 mile paved oval (5/30/46 - 1979)
  first race was a Bay State Midget Racing Association won by Oscar Ridlon
  held the first NEMA midget race here on 5/30/53 / also modifieds here
  1/3 mile paved oval (1980 - present) / (aka: the Cement Palace)
  owned and promoted by D. Anthony Venditti / still run by his family
  D. Anthony was the 1978 RPM Promoter of the Year

Affectionately known as the "Cement Palace", Seekonk Speedway is only one of
two weekly tracks left in Massachusetts. - Official track photo.

Springfield - 1/3 mile wood oval (October, 1909) / built by Jack Prince
the corners were banked 48 degrees / ran motorcycles only

Springfield Fairgrounds - see: Eastern State Expo

Springfield - also see: Crescent Oval, Pynchon Park, Westover Air Force Base.

Sturbridge Fairgrounds - Sturbridge - 1/2 mile dirt oval (c.9/05/36 - c.5/30/40)

The Pines Speedway - Groveland / located at an old amusement park
1/5 mile dirt oval (8/29/40 - 10/09/41) (August, 1946 - c.1946)
1/4 mile paved oval (c.1947 - 1971) / (aka: The Pines Midget Speedway)

Topsfield Fairgrounds - Topsfield - 1/5 mile dirt oval (7/29/37 - 9/10/41)
1/2 mile dirt oval (9/10/33 - 7/04/41) (5/30/46 - 1950's)

Wayland Circuit - Wayland - 1.0 mile dirt road course (10/07/34 - 11/17/35)

Warr Park - Wareham - 1/2 mile dirt oval (c.1926)

West Peabody Speedway - West Peabody / site is now a high school running track
1/4 mile paved oval (1946 - c.1963)

West Roxbury Speedway - Boston (West Roxbury) - 1/2 mile dirt oval (1936)

West Springfield Speedway - West Springfield / former dog track on Memorial Ave
1/4 mile paved oval (7/21/39 - 5/16/42) (4/27/46 - 1958)
a fire destroyed the grandstands on 1/05/47 / (aka: Century Stadium)
(aka: New Springfield Speedway) / now site Century Center Shopping Plaza

Westboro Speedway - Westborough - 1/4 mile paved oval (8/05/47 - 9/14/85)
the property is now the site of the Speedway Mall

Westborough - 1/4 mile paved dragstrip (c.1957) / possibly didn't run

Westover Air Force Base - Springfield - paved road course on runways (2/03/54)

Weymouth Fairgrounds - Weymouth - 1/2 mile dirt oval (c.5/30/36 - 10/13/41)

Whitney Lake - 1/3 mile ice oval (2/07/54 - c.1954)

Worcester Fairgrounds - Worcester / located at the New England Fairgrounds
1/2 mile dirt oval (c.1920 - c.10/12/35)

MICHIGAN

4-H Speedbowl - see: Greenville Speedway

Adrian Speedway - Adrian / located at the Lenawee County Fairgrounds
1/2 mile dirt oval (c.1928) (c.1947) / (aka: Maple City Speedway)
1/4 mile dirt oval (7/08/47 - c.5/26/55) (1976) (1981 - 1982)

Adventure Mountain Speedway - Greenland / at the Ontonagon Co. Fairgrounds
1/3 mile dirt oval (1987 - present) / (aka: Venture Raceway)

Air Park Speedway - Douglas - 3/8 mile dirt oval (c.1952 - c.1953) (1958 - c.1963)
located two miles south of Saugatuck / (aka: Cloverleaf Stadium)

Albion Speedway - Albion - 1/4 mile dirt oval (1952 - c.1953)
    built for midget race cars by Owen Granger, Sr.

Algonac - dirt oval (1941) ran hobos (jalopies)

Allegan Fairgrounds - Allegan / located at the Allegan County Fairgrounds
    1/2 mile dirt oval (1938) (c.9/14/47 - c.1953)

Allen Speedway - Gladwin - 1/4 mile dirt oval (1950's) / promoter was Ray Allen

Alpena Fairgrounds - Alpena / located at the Alpena County Fairgrounds
    1/2 mile dirt oval (c.1952 - c.1953) (1978)

American Legion Speedway - see: West Branch Speedway

Ann Arbor Fairgrounds - Ann Arbor / located at the Washtenaw Co. Fairgrounds
    1/2 mile dirt oval (1929 - 1933)

Auburn Speedway - see: Tri-City Motor Speedway

Auto City Speedway - Flint - 1/4 mile dirt oval (4/16/55 - 1987)
    7/16 mile dirt oval (1959 - 1987)
    1/8 mile dirt dragstrip (1972)
    1/4 & 7/16 mile paved ovals (c.5/09/87 - present)

B-K Speedway - see: Kalamazoo Speedway

Bad Ax Fairgrounds - Bad Ax - 1/2 mile dirt oval (9/07/47 - c.1951)
    located at the Huron County Fairgrounds

Bay City Fairgrounds - Bay City / located at the Bay County Fairgrounds
    1/2 mile dirt oval (6/06/15 - c.8/18/35) (1970's)
    Henry Banks started his driving career here in 1932

Belleaire - dirt oval (1950's)

Benton Harbor - dirt oval (7/04/17) ran a AAA race

Bob Senneker in front of the old covered grandstands at Berlin Raceway. This photo was taken by Ray Rogers in 1969.

Berlin Raceway from the air. Chet Mysliwiec has been the promoter of the track since 1951. - Jason Vogel photo (courtesy of Dick Lee).

Berlin Raceway - Grand Rapids (Marne) / located at the Berlin Fairgrounds
  1/2 mile dirt oval (9/20/47 -1947) (1951 - 1965)
  1/5 mile dirt oval (4/28/51 - c.1960) (aka: Marne Speedway)
  5/8 mile dirt road course (c.1961) / located 7 miles west of Grand Rapids
  7/16 mile paved oval (1966 - present) / the fair started in 1856
  covered grandstands burned to ground by an arsonist in July of 1973

Big Rapids Fairgrounds - Big Rapids / located at the Mecosta County Fairgrounds
  1/2 mile dirt oval (1950) (9/06/53) (1960's) (1981 & 1982)

Bigelow Field - Grand Rapids / located at 39th St. & South Division
  1/4 mile dirt oval (5/03/38 - 1941) (10/08/47 - c.1952)
  built around a baseball diamond / (aka: Zeiters Midget Speedway)
  Ralph Reel & Ralph Feist were both fatally injured in accidents here
  the ball field is now the site of a McDonald's and a laundromat

Birchwood Speedway - see: Thunderbird Raceway

Birmingham - dirt oval (1938 & 1939)

Bob's Picnic Grounds - see: M-59 Speedway

Bristol Road Speedway - see: Flint Midget Speedway

Brohman Raceway - Brohman - dirt oval (late 1950's)

Bronson - 1/2 mile dirt oval (6/12/27 & 7/10/27)

Butler Motor Speedway - Quincy (Butler) - 1/4 mile dirt oval (1952 - 1955)
  3/8 mile oiled dirt oval (1956 - present)

Cadillac Fairgrounds - Cadillac / located at the Northern District Fairgrounds
  1/2 mile dirt oval (7/27/35) (9/16/38 & 9/17/38)
  3/8 mile dirt oval (c.7/04/50 - c.1968) / (aka: Cadillac Speedway)

Capital City Speedway - Lansing - 1/2 mile dirt oval (c.1949)
1/4 mile dirt oval (c.7/04/51 - c.1964) / located near the airport

Caro Fairgrounds - Caro / located at the Tuscola County Fairgrounds
1/2 mile dirt oval (c.8/24/51 - c.1956)

Cass City Raceway Park - see: Thunder Road Speedway

Cassopolis Fairgrounds - Cassopolis / located at the Cass County Fairgrounds
1/2 mile dirt oval (late 1920's) / (aka: New Cassopolis Speedway)
1/4 mile dirt oval (1948) (6/15/52 - c.1954)

Center Raceway - Grawn - 1/4 mile dirt oval (5/30/68 - 1976)

Central Michigan Dragway - see: Mid Michigan Motorplex

Central Michigan Speedway - see: Saint Alma Speedway

Central Missouri Speedway - see: Triple-M Speedway

Charlotte Fairgrounds - Charlotte / located at the Eaton County Fairgrounds
1/2 mile dirt oval (1946) (5/21/50 & 7/04/50)

Cheboygan Fairgrounds - Cheboygan / at the Northern Michigan Fairgrounds
1/2 mile dirt oval (1961) (1985) / now called Cheboygan Co. Fairgrounds

Chief Pontiac Speedway - Pontiac / located on Lake Angeles Road
3/8 mile dirt oval (9/17/50 - c.1955) / (aka: Gay Day Speedway)
3/8 mile paved oval (5/15/55 - c.1957) / (aka: Lake Angeles Speedway)
4/10 mile dirt oval (c.1957)

Christiana Lake Speedway - (location unknown) / located in southwest Michigan
1/2 mile dirt oval (years unknown)

Chrysler Proving Grounds - Chelsea - 4.7 mile paved oval (6/16/54) (6/30/54)
Jack McGrath turned a lap of 179.762 mph on 6/16/54 in an exhibition race
Sam Hanks turned 182.554 mph on 6/30/54 in Chrysler powered Indy car

Clarke's Motor Speedway - see: I-96 Speedway

Clinton Speedway - Clinton - 1/10 mile dirt oval (1957 & 1958)
ran by the Clinton Jr. Chamber of Commerce

Cloverleaf Stadium - see: Air Park Speedway

Cobo Hall - Detroit - 1/15 mile indoor concrete oval (1/04/86 & 1/05/86)

Coleman - 3/8 mile dirt oval (1950 & 1951)

Croswell Fairgrounds - Croswell - 1/2 mile dirt oval (early 1950's)

Crystal Raceway - Crystal - 1/4 mile paved oval (1948 - 1952)
3/8 mile dirt oval (7/04/53 - 1959) (1964 - present)

Davison Fairgrounds - Davison / located at the Genesee County Fairgrounds
1/2 mile dirt oval (c.1926 - c.9/30/34) (5/23/37 - c.6/22/41)
the fairgrounds opened in 1903 / (aka: Rosemoor Park)
the site is now the Rosemoor housing subdivision

Delaney Speedway - Grand Rapids (Standale) / located at M-45 & 8th Ave.
   1/2 mile dirt oval (1946 & 1947) / in a cow pasture

Detroit - 1/5 mile dirt oval (1934) / located at Adair & East Jefferson

Detroit Coliseum - see: Michigan State Fairgrounds Coliseum

Detroit Dragway - Detroit - 1/4 mile paved dragstrip (1959 - present)
   one of the first constructed dragstrips / built by Gil Kohn
   held the 1959 and 1960 N.H.R.A. U.S. National here

Detroit Driving Club - see: Grosse Pointe

Detroit Fairgrounds - see: Michigan State Fairgrounds

Detroit Grand Prix - Detroit (Belle Isle) / located on the island of Belle Isle
   2.1 mile paved city street road course (1992 - present) / CART IndyCars

Detroit Grand Prix - Detroit / located on city streets in downtown Detroit
   2.59 mile paved city street road course (6/04/82 - 1987)
   2.493 mile paved city street road course (1988 - 1991) / ran SCCA TA
   U.S. Grand Prix for Formula One in 1982, 1983 / CART IndyCars 1986-1991

Detroit (Highland Park) - dirt oval (1905) / located at John R & 6 Mile Road

Detroit Motordrome - Detroit - wood oval (1910's) / probably ran motorcycles only

*A look at one of the banked corners of the wood-surfaced Detroit Motordrome.
Little is known about this track, but it is believed if was a motorcycle track in
the early 1900's. - George Koyt collection.*

Detroit - also see: Cobo Hall, Flat Rock, Grosse Point, Joe's, Motor City, New
   Midget, New Pilgrim, Northville, Partington's Pastures, Roesink,
   Sand Lotters, University of Detroit

Dickinson County Speedway - see: Norway Speedway

Dixie Motor Speedway - Birch Run - 1/4 mile dirt oval (8/05/51 - 1958)
   1/3 mile paved oval (1959 - present)
   carved out a 1/2 mile track, but it was never finished

Don Pike Speedway - Pontiac (Berkley) - dirt oval (1955)

Dorr Raceway - Dorr - 1.0 mile paved road course (1965)

East Jordan Fairgrounds - East Jordan - dirt oval (1950's)
    located at the Charleviox County Fairgrounds

East Lansing Fairgrounds - East Lansing / located near Coral Gables
    1/2 mile dirt oval (c.1926 - c.7/12/36)

Eastern Michigan Speedway - Imlay City / (aka: Central Michigan Speedway)
    3/8 mile oval (1965) / turns concrete, straights dirt / (aka: Moffatt's Corners)

Escanaba Int'l Speedway - Escanaba / 1/2 mile dirt oval (1928 - 1941)(1946 - 1952)
    at the Upper Peninsula State Fairgrounds / (aka: Superior Speedway)
    1/4 mile dirt oval (1953 - 1977)   /   3/8 mile paved oval (1978 - 1986)
    converted into a 1/2 mile horse track in 1987, horse track now defunct

Eureka Speedway - see: Glennie Int'l Speedway

Federation Ball Park - Port Huron - 1/5 mile dirt oval (c.8/15/39 - c.8/22/39)
    located at 24th & LaPeer Avenue

Flat Rock Speedway - Detroit (Flat Rock) / ARCA (MARC) sanctioned since 1962
    1/4 mile paved oval (8/14/53 - present) / NASCAR sanctioned in 1955
    it was the first track built with rubberized asphalt
    Benny Parsons started his driving career here in 1962 in a figure 8 car

Flint Motor Speedway - Flint / (aka: Bristol Road Speedway)
    1/5 mile dirt oval (9/30/39 - c.6/06/42) / (aka: Flint Midget Speedway)
    the promoters were Don & Carson Zeiter

Flint - also see: Auto City Speedway, Lakeside Park, Playland Park

Fowlerville Fairgrounds - Fowlerville - 1/2 mile dirt oval (1926) (c.6/05/49 - c.1956)
    ran motorcycles in 1926 / Ralph Hepburn started racing cycles here in 1926

Frederic Speedway - Frederic - 1/4 mile dirt oval (7/24/55 - c.1968)

Fruitport Midget Speedway - Nunica (Fruitport) / between the towns on US 16
    1/4 mile paved oval (1947 - c.1952) / (aka: Western Michigan Speedway)

Galesburg Speedway - Galesburg - 1/4 mile dirt oval (6/13/48 - 1950)
    3/8 mile paved oval (1951 - present) / the track was built by Paul Beebe

Gay Day Speedway - see: Chief Pontiac Speedway

General Motors Proving Grounds - Milford / ran 950 mile exhibition race
    3.77 mile concrete oval (6/24/27)

Glennie International Speedway - Glennie / located on Highway 65
    1/4 mile dirt oval (early 1950's) / (aka: Eureka Speedway)

Gogebic County Speedway - see: Ironwood Fairgrounds

Grand Haven River Road Jalopy Track - Grand Haven - dirt oval (1947)

Grand Rapids - dirt oval (1930's) / located on East Paris Ave.

Grand Rapids Motor Speedway - Grand Rapids / located at 36th & Eastern Ave.
    1/4 mile dirt oval (5/30/40 - c.5/19/42) / (aka: Kamp's Speedway)

The Grand Rapids Speedrome. - Mich. Motor Sports Hall of Fame collection.

Grand Rapids Speedrome - Grand Rapids (Comstock Park) / located north of town
  1.125 mile dirt oval (9/26/1903 - 1937) / (aka: West Michigan State Fair)
  1/4 mile dirt oval (6/13/50 - 1956) / (aka: Kent County Fairgrounds)
  1/2 mile dirt oval (6/13/50 - 1956) / (aka: Comstock Park Fairgrounds)
  1/4 mile paved oval (1957 - 1963) / (aka: Grand River Speedway)
  1/2 mile paved oval (6/13/64 - 7/30/66) / closed for new US 131 Expressway
  John Benson, Sr. & Bob Senneker both started their driving careers here

Grand Rapids Stadium - Grand Rapids / north of town on West River Drive
  1/10 mile indoor concrete oval (2/27/52 - 2/22/56) / ran midgets & Crosleys
  was a ice hockey arena, later became a department store, and then went
  back to a hockey rink again / now used for flea markets

Grand Rapids - also see: Berlin, Bigelow, Delaney, Kent County, Welsh

Grattan Raceway Park - Grattan - 1/4 mile paved dragstrip (1965 - c.1967)
  2.0 mile paved road course (June, 1965 - present) / (aka: Grattan Raceway)

Grayling Airfield - Grayling / located at the National Guard airfield
  2.0 mile paved road course (late 1950's - c.1962)

Greenville Fairgrounds - Greenville - 1/2 mile dirt oval (8/03/29)
  located at the Montcalm County Fairgrounds

Greenville Raceway - see: Harvard Speedway

Greenville Speedway - Greenville - dirt oval (c.1952 - c.1954)
  located 2 miles north on SR 91 / (aka: 4-H Speedbowl)

Grosse Pointe (Detroit) - 1.0 mile dirt oval (10/10/01 - c.1915) / built in 1893
  Henry Ford won the first race (his only race as a driver)
  Barney Oldfield won his first race here in 1902 / (aka: Detroit Driving Club)
  located at Jefferson & Connors / became the site of a Hudson auto plant
  ran a 1000 mile race on 8/08/1904 / exclusive homes now occupy the site

Harrison Fairgrounds - Harrison / located at the Clare County Fairgrounds
  1/2 mile dirt oval (1983 & 1984)

Hart Fairgrounds - Hart / located at the Oceana County Fairgrounds
3/8 mile dirt oval (1947) (1961) (1965) (1969)

Hartford Motor Speedway - Hartford - 1/2 mile dirt oval (5/30/51 - 1970)
1/2 mile paved oval (1971 - 1981) / Bob Senneker promoted for one year
1/2 mile dirt oval (1983) / the pavement was removed in 1983
at the Hartford Fairgrounds / first home of Dick Beebe's "Dealer's Choice"

Harvard Speedway - Harvard / on Lapple St. / (aka: Greenville Raceway)
3/8 mile dirt oval (1946 - c.1954) / (aka: WARE's Speed Bowl)

Hastings Fairgrounds - Hastings / located at the Barry County Fairgrounds
1/2 mile dirt oval (c.4/25/48 - c.1951) / located just west of downtown

Hastings Motor Speedway - Hastings - 1/4 mile dirt oval (c.1947 - early 1950's)
1/4 mile paved oval (c.1953 - 1965) / (aka: Hasting's Old M-37 Raceway)
Gordon Johncock (1955) & Sammy Sessions (1958) started their careers here
(aka: Hasting's Drive-In Speedway)

High Point Speedway - Kalkaska - 3/8 mile dirt oval (c.1967 - c.1975)

Holland - dirt oval (1940)

Hornes Speedbowl - Reed City - 1/4 mile dirt oval (1950's or 1960's)

Houghton Lake - 1/4 mile dirt oval (1951 & 1952)

Howell Fairgrounds - Howell - dirt oval (1938)

Hudsonville Fairgrounds - Hudsonville / at Hudsonville Community Fairgrounds
1/4 mile dirt oval (mid-1970's) / ran Mini-champs

I-96 Speedway - Lake Odessa - 1/2 mile dirt oval (8/27/71 - present)
1/4 mile dirt oval (c.1980 - present) / (aka: Ionia County Speedway)
built by Steve Clarke / (aka: Clarke's Motor Speedway) / (aka: I-96 Raceway)

Imlay City Fairgrounds - Imlay City / located at the Eastern Michigan Fairgrounds
1/2 mile dirt oval (early 1950's)

Imlay City Speedway - Imlay City / north of town on Clear Lake Road
1/4 mile paved oval (early 1970's) / also see: Eastern Michigan Speedway

Ionia County Speedway - see: I-96 Speedway

Ionia - dirt oval (early 1950's) / located in a sand pit west of town

Ionia Fairgrounds - Ionia / located at the Ionia County Free Fairgrounds
1/2 mile dirt oval (c.8/17/35 - 8/23/41) (8/10/46 - c.1982)
the fairgrounds was built in 1868 / ran a 500 lap jalopy race on 8/26/51

Iron Mountain Fairgrounds - Iron Mountain
1/2 mile dirt oval (7/04/41) (c.8/10/46 - 1950)

Ironwood Fairgrounds - Ironwood - 1/2 mile dirt oval (c.1950)
1/4 mile dirt oval (late 1960's) / located at the Gogebic County Fairgrounds
1/3 mile dirt oval (1978 - 1981) / (aka: Gogebic County Speedway)

Ishpeming Speedway - Ishpeming - dirt oval (years unknown)

Ithaca - dirt oval (7/04/38)

Jackson Legion Fairgrounds - Jackson / located at the Jackson Co. Fairgrounds
  1/2 mile dirt oval (c.1913 - 1937) (1941 - 6/28/42) (9/08/46 - 1953)
  1/4 mile dirt oval (5/12/35 - c.1937) / (aka: Legion Motor Speedway)
  1/4 mile paved oval (920/47 - c.1953) / currently a horse track

Jackson Midget Speedway - Jackson / located 1/2 mile west on US 12
  1/5 mile oiled dirt oval (6/04/39 - c.1939)

Jackson Motor Speedway - Jackson - 1/4 & 1/2 mile dirt ovals (10/03/48 - c.1955)
  Carl Scarborough won first race in 1948 / located north of town off of US 27
  3/8 mile dirt oval (c.9/06/54 - 1958)   /   3/8 mile paved oval (1959 - 1974)

An aerial view of Jackson Motor Speedway. The track was a popular track in the 1960's. - Michigan Motor Sports Hall of Fame collection.

Jeddo - 1/2 mile dirt oval (c.1951 - c.9/23/51)

Joe's Race Track - Detroit - dirt oval (years unknown)

Joe's Speedway - Farwell (Clare) - 1/4 mile dirt oval (early 1950's - c.1956)

Jones Speedway - Allegan - 1/4 mile dirt oval (late 1940's - mid-1950's)

Kalamazoo Fairgrounds - Kalamazoo / located at the Kalamazoo Co. Fairgrounds
  1.0 mile dirt oval (9/26/14 - 8/03/35) / (aka: Recreation Park)
  1/5 mile dirt oval (5/10/39 - 8/09/39)
  1/2 mile dirt oval (c.1972 - c.1986) (1993 - present) / motorcycles since 1993

Kalamazoo Speedway - Kalamazoo / (aka: B-K Speedway)
  3/8 mile paved oval (7/30/50 - present) / (aka: Kalamazoo Motor Speedway)

Kamp's Speedway - see: Grand Rapids Motor Speedway

Kendall Speedway - Kendall - dirt oval (1950's)

Kent County Airport - Grand Rapids / the site is now an industrial park
  paved road course (5/01/64 & 5/02/64) / ran on runways when airport closed

Kezer Midget Speedway - see: Roesink Stadium

Lake Angeles Speedway - see: Chief Pontiac Speedway

Lake Odessa Fairgrounds - Lake Odessa - 1/2 mile dirt oval (1982 - 1983)

Lakeside Park - Flint - 1/6 mile dirt oval (6/07/35 - 6/28/35)

296

Lansing Speedway - see: Spartan Speedway

Lansing - also see: Capital City Speedway, East Lansing Fairgrounds

Lapeer Int'l Dragway - Lapeer - 1/4 mile paved dragstrip (7/04/68 - present)

Legion Motor Speedway - see: Jackson Legion Fairgrounds

Livonia - 1/4 mile paved dragstrip (1950) / on industrial road beside Echo Road

Ludington Fairgrounds - Ludington / located at the Mason County Fairgrounds
1/2 mile dirt oval (late 1930's) (c.1947 - c.1953)
1/4 mile dirt oval (c.1961 - 1983) / (aka: U.S. 10 Raceway)

M-113 Raceway - Fife Lake - 1/4 mile dirt oval (12/09/79 - present)

M-37 Dragway - Brohman - 1/8 mile paved dragstrip (1960's - c.1972)

M-59 Speedway - Pontiac - 3/8 mile dirt oval (1955)
3/8 mile paved oval (c.1957) / (aka: Bob's Picnic Grounds)

Mancelona - dirt oval (1950's)

Manchester Speedway - Manchester - 3/8 mile dirt oval (c.1965 - 1977)

Manistee County Dragway - see: Northern Michigan Dragway

Manistee County Fairgrounds - Onekema / runs midgets Labor Day weekend
1/2 mile dirt oval (1961 - 1986) (1993 - present)

Maple City Speedway - see: Adrian Fairgrounds

Maple Island Speedway - see: Whiskey Ridge Raceway

Marion Fairgrounds - Marion - 1/2 mile dirt oval (years unknown)

Marne Speedway - see: Berlin Raceway

Marshall Fairgrounds - Marshall / located at the Calhoun County Fairgrounds
1/4 & 1/2 mile dirt ovals (c.1946 - c.1954)

An unidentified driver in this picture from the Grand Haven River Road Jalopy Track from 1947. - Michigan Motor Sports Hall of Fame collection.

Merritt Speedway near Houghton Lake, Michigan. Official track photo.

Mason Fairgrounds - Mason / located at the Ingham County Fairgrounds
    1/2 mile dirt oval (c.1933 - c.1941) (c.1946 - early 1950's)
    1/4 mile dirt oval (8/29/37) / ran midgets on small track

Memorial Speedway - Garden City - 1/10 mile dirt oval (c.9/28/52 - 1954) (1957)
    the track ran T.Q. midgets

Merritt Speedway - Lake City (Merritt) - 1/4 mile dirt oval (1968 - present)

Michigan Ideal Speedway - Springport - 3/8 mile paved oval (10/07/89 - present)

Michigan Int'l Speedway - Brooklyn / built by Larry LaPatin
    2.0 mile paved oval (10/13/68 - present) turns banked 18 degrees
    first race was for USAC Indy cars, won by Ronnie Bucknum
    first NASCAR Grand National (Winston Cup) race was on 6/15/69
    originally proposed in 1966 as Michigan Motor Speedway in Detroit
    3.0 mile paved road course (5/11/69 - 5/0/73)
    1.9 mile paved road course (1984)

Michigan Ideal Speedway. - Official track photo.

The start of one of the supermodified races at the Michigan State Fairgrounds. Ken Coles photo (Michigan Motor Sports Hall of Fame collection).

Michigan State Fairgrounds Coliseum - Detroit
   2/13 mile indoor dirt oval (3/15/35 - 5/08/37) (11/25/39 - 4/18/42)
   (aka: Detroit Coliseum) / located at 8 Mile Road & Woodward

Michigan State Fairgrounds - Detroit / located at 8 Mile Road & Woodward
   1.0 mile dirt oval (1899 - c.1941) (1946 - 1966) / ran weekly in 1965
   1/4 & 1/2 mile dirt oval (1966) / tracks are now parking lots for fair
   Paul Goldsmith started his driving career here
   the track ran the first ever I.M.C.A. race here on 5/30/15

Mid Michigan Motorplex - Stanton - 1/4 mile dirt dragstrip (1954)
   1/4 mile paved dragstrip (c.1955 - present) / at an old airport
   (aka: Central Michigan Dragway) / Dick LaHaie started here in 1958

Mid-City Speedway - see: Standish Asphalt Speedway

Mid-Michigan Raceway - Muir / built by Ross & Nanette Ferguson
   1/3 mile dirt circle (2/26/89 - 1991)

Milan Int'l Dragway - Milan - 1/4 mile paved dragstrip (April, 1963 - present)
   (aka: Milan Dragway) / built by Clifton Riley

Milburg Speedway - Milburg - 3/8 mile dirt oval (c.1946 - 1952)
   1/4 mile paved oval (6/21/53 - c.1960) / at the Milburg Fairgrounds

Milford Speedway - Milford / located at the Oakland County Fairgrounds
   1/2 mile dirt oval (4/20/39 - 9/15/40) (c.9/22/46 - c.1949)

Millington - dirt oval (1940)

Monroe Speedway - Monroe - 1/2 mile dirt oval (7/24/49 - 1949)
1/4 mile dirt oval (c.7/16/50 - c.1954) / (aka: Fairgrounds Speedway)
located at the Monroe County Fairgrounds

Motor City Dragway - Marine City - 1/4 mile paved dragstrip (c.1958 - c.1976)
located 30 miles north of Detroit at 26 Mile & Meldrum near Mt. Clemens

Motor City Speedway - Detroit / located at 13801 8 Mile Road (near Schoenherr)
1/2 mile oiled dirt oval (10/02/32 - c.10/09/38) / Bob Carey won 1st race
1/4 mile dirt oval (5/31/36 - 7/30/42) (6/03/46 - 5/11/53)
1/4 mile cold paved oval (7/11/40 - late 1940) / called V.F.W first
1/4 mile paved oval (5/13/53 - c.9/20/58) / (aka: V.F.W. Speedway)
started being called Motor City in 1939 / (aka: Zeiter's Motor Speedway)
built by Don & Carson Zeiter / (aka: New Detroit Motor Speedway)
(aka: Eight Mile Road Speedway) / (aka: Zeiter's Midget Speedway)
the located in now the site of a shopping center

*Race cars line up for the pace lap at V.F.W. Speedway in 1932. The track was
also known as Motor City Speedway. - Bob Sheldon collection.*

Mottville Speedway - Mottville - 1/4 mile dirt oval (7/04/50 - 1966)
1/4 mile paved oval (c.1967 - present) (aka: South West Michigan Speedway)

Mount Clemens Race Track - Mount Clemens / formerly a horse track
1/2 mile dirt oval (1920) (1936) (9/02/51 - 1972) (aka: Sunshine Speedway)
1/4 mile dirt oval (1951 - 1972) / (aka: Mount Clemens Raceway Park)
1/4 & 1/2 mile paved ovals (5/12/73 - 9/07/85) (aka: Old Race Track Park)
called New Detroit Metropolitan Speedway in 1958 / now an industrial park

Mount Pleasant Speedway - Mount Pleasant
1/4 mile dirt oval (1955 - 1983) (1988 - present)
(aka: New Mount Pleasant Speedway)

Muskegon - see: Thunderbird Raceway, Whiskey Ridge Raceway

New Baltimore - pear-shaped oiled dirt oval (8/20/39 - c.1939) (7/24/49)

New Cassopolis Speedway - see: Cassopolis Fairgrounds

New Detroit Metropolitan Speedway - see: Mount Clemens Race Track

New Midget Speedway - Detroit / located on Joseph Campau
  1/4 mile dirt oval (5/08/38 - c.7/13/38) / Wally Zale first winner

New Pilgrim Speedway - Detroit / located at 12 Mile Road & Dequindre
  1/4 mile dirt oval (6/23/40 - 10/27/40) / promoted by Jess Partington

New Pontiac Speedway - Pontiac - 1/4 mile dirt oval (c.5/25/52 - c.1952)

Newago County Speedway - see: Whiskey Ridge Raceway

North Branch - 1/2 mile dirt oval (5/15/49)

Northern Michigan Dragway - Kaleva / (aka: Manistee County Dragway)
  1/8 mile paved dragstrip (c.1968 - c.1984) (1988 - present)

Northern Michigan Raceway - Elmira - 1/4 mile dirt oval (1970 - 1980)
  1/4 mile paved oval (1981 - 1986) (1994 - present)
  closed in 1986 when nearby Onaway Speedway opened

Northville Downs - Detroit (Northville) / (aka: Northville Speedway)
  1/2 mile dirt oval (1939) (7/04/57) (1980's) / currently a horse track
  Mel Larson was the promoter in 1957 / ran motorcycles in 1980's

Norway Speedway - Norway / located at the Dickinson County Fairgrounds
  1/4 mile dirt oval (1967 - 1978) / (aka: Vulcan Speedway)
  1/4 mile paved oval (1979 - present) / (aka: Dickinson County Speedway)

Nunica Speedway - Nunica - 1/4 mile dirt oval (1950's) / near golf course

Onaway Speedway - Onaway - 1/4 mile paved oval (7/04/83 - present)

Onekema Fairgrounds - see: Manistee County Fairgrounds

Onondaga Dragway - Onondaga - 1/4 mile paved dragstrip (c.1965 - c.1971)

Owendale Speedway - Owendale - 1/4 mile dirt oval (1950 - 1984) (1986 - present)

*Dick Carter was one of the best dirt track drivers to come out of Michigan.
Allan E. Brown collection.*

*The start of a big race at Owosso Speedway in the early 1950's. - Michigan
Motor Sports Hall of Fame collection.*

Owosso Speedway - Owosso (Ovid) / Perry Grim was the first winner on 9/12/41
　　1/4 mile dirt oval (9/12/41 - 1942) (c.8/28/46 - 1953) / built by Lyle May
　　the site was used as a concentration camp during World War II
　　1/2 mile dirt oval (9/16/46 - 1972) / (aka: Rocket Motor Speedway)
　　1/4 mile paved oval (1953 - 1983) / (aka: Gale's Sports Arena)
　　1/2 mile paved oval (1972 - 1982) / Rich Senneker fatally injured 1973
　　1/2 mile dirt oval ((5/19/83 - July, 1988) / (aka: M-21 Speedway)
　　1/4 mile dirt oval (1984 - 1988) / Al Stockton removed pavement in 1983
　　3/8 mile paved oval (7/31/88 - present)

Packard Proving Grounds - Utica - 2.5 mile concrete oval (6/14/28)
　　ran an exhibition race / Leon Duray turned a lap of 148.17 mph

Paka Plaza - Jackson - 1/3 mile paved road course (8/26/84)
　　ran Mini-Champs in a shopping center parking lot

Partington's Pastures - Detroit / located at 14-1/2 mile Road & Ryan
　　1/4 mile dirt oval (8/22/41 - 1942) (9/16/45 - 1952) / (aka: Ryan Speedway)
　　built and promoted by Jess Partington / (aka: New Ryan Speedway)
　　(aka: The New Speedway) / site is now housing

Pat n Bill Speedway - Battle Creek - 1/4 mile dirt oval (c.5/22/40 - 5/28/41)

Petoskey Fairgrounds - Petoskey - 1/4 mile dirt oval (c.1961)
　　located at the Emmet County Fairgrounds

Petoskey Motor Court Speedway - Petoskey - dirt oval (1950's or 1960's)

Pickford Fairgrounds - Pickford - 1/2 mile dirt oval (early 1950's)

Plat Field - Ann Arbor - dirt oval (late 1940's)

Playland Park - Flint - dirt oval (years unknown)

Pontiac - paved road course on city streets (1974)

Pontiac Silverdome - Pontiac / home of the Detroit Lions (NFL football team)
1/5 mile indoor paved oval (12/06/80) (2/26/83) (2/27/83) (1/14/84)
1/5 mile indoor dirt oval (1/30/82) (3/06/82)

Pontiac - also see: Chief Pontiac, Don Pike, M-59, New Pontiac

Port Huron Fairgrounds - Port Huron / located at the Saint Clair Co. Fairgrounds
1/2 mile dirt oval (6/04/15) / ran IMCA big cars

Port Huron - also see: Federation Ball Park, Sunset Speedway

Prairie River Speedway - Centreville - 1/4 mile dirt oval (9/03/51 - 1956)

Raceland Speedway - Oscoda / (aka: Wilber Speedway)
1/4 mile dirt oval (1972 - c.1977)

Recreation Park - see: Kalamazoo Fairgrounds

Redford - (location unknown) - dirt oval (1938 or 1939)

Rendezvous Bowl - Sister Lakes / the track had a glass dance floor in the infield
1/4 mile paved oval (6/19/47 - c.1949) / may have ran in 1952 as well

Richmond Fairgrounds - Richmond / located at the Macomb County Fairgrounds
1/2 mile dirt oval (9/03/51)

Roanoke Speedway - Fruitport - 3/8 mile dirt oval (1953)

Rochester Fairgrounds - Rochester - 1/2 mile dirt oval (c.1928)

Rocket Motor Speedway - see: Owosso Speedway

Roesink Stadium - Hamtramck (Detroit) / (aka: Kezer Midget Speedway)
1/5 mile dirt oval (1933 - c.8/31/34) / torn down in 1941

Rolling Hills - Suttons Bay - 1/4 mile dirt oval (1950 - 1957)

Romeo - 1/4 mile dirt oval (1930's - c.1941) (1946) / at Minot St. & W. St. Clair
now the site of a high school running track

Rose City - dirt oval (1950's)

Rosebud Speedway - Buchanan - dirt oval (years unknown)

Rosemoor Park - see: Davison Fairgrounds

Ryan Speedway - see: Partington's Pastures

Saginaw Fairgrounds - Saginaw / (aka: Spencer Speedway)
1/2 mile dirt oval (c.5/30/18 - c.1941) (c.1947 - 1954) (1956 & 1957)
Pete Spencer was the promoter in 1950's / became a parking lot in 1957

Saint Alma Speedway - Saint Louis / 1.5 miles south of Saint Louis on US 27
1/5 mile dirt oval (5/26/56 - c.1961) / (aka: Central Michigan Speedway)

Saint Johns Fairgrounds - Saint Johns / located at the Clinton Co. Fairgrounds
1/2 mile dirt oval (early 1920's - 1930's)

Saline Road Course - Saline - paved road course (c.1985 - c.1986) / Mini-Champs

Sand Lotters Park - Detroit - 1/3 mile dirt oval (7/09/35 - c.7/23/35) / midgets

Sands Speedway - Marquette / (aka: Thunder Valley Raceway)
1/4 mile paved oval (1970 - 1984) / (aka: Superior Speedway)

Saranac Speedway - Saranac / located southeast of town
3/8 mile dirt oval (c.1951 - late 1950's) / (aka: Saranac Speedbowl)

Scottville - dirt oval (c.1947)

Singer Speedway - Wyandotte - 1/2 mile dirt oval (c.1915) / a horse track

South West Michigan Speedway - see: Mottville Speedway

Spartan Speedway - Lansing / located south of town on Cedar St.
1/4 mile paved oval (7/20/56 - present) / (aka: Lansing Speedway)
(aka: Spartan Motor Speedway) / first called Spartan in 1964

Spencer Speedway - see: Saginaw Fairgrounds

Standish Asphalt Speedway - Standish - 1/2 mile dirt oval (1967 - 1971)
1/4 mile dirt oval (1972 - 1984) / (aka: Mid-City Speedway)
1/4 mile paved oval (1990 - present) / (aka: Standish Speedway)

Standish - dirt oval (c.1946)

Sunset Speedway - Port Huron / located five miles west of town
1/4 mile dirt oval (c.1948 - c.1958)

Sunshine Speedway - see: Mount Clemens Race Track

Superior Speedway - see: Sands Speedway

Tecumseh Airport - Tecumseh - 1/4 mile paved dragstrip (1957)

Three Rivers - city street road course (c.1910 - c.1911)

Thunder Road Speedway - Cass City / (aka: Cass City Raceway Park)
3/8 mile dirt oval (1960's - 1980)

Thunder Valley Raceway - see: Sands Speedway

Thunderbird Raceway - Muskegon - 3/8 mile dirt oval (6/28/58 - present)
1/4 mile paved dragstrip (1960's - c.1982) / (aka: Birchwood Speedway)

*Tom Maier drove Ed Howe's green hornet called "GoIng" to many wins in the
early 1970's. - Tom DeVette photo.*

304

Traverse City Fairgrounds - Traverse City / the site is now a park
1/2 mile dirt oval (9/25/15) (c.1932) (c.1952 - c.1961)
located at the Northwestern Michigan Fairgrounds

Tri-City Dragway - Midland - 1/4 mile paved dragstrip (c.1961 - c.1976)
(aka: Saginaw's Tri-City Dragway)

An early 1960's photo of a drag race. Dick LaHaie is on the left in his Oldsmobile. - Michigan Motor Sports Hall of Fame collection.

Tri-City Motor Speedway - Auburn - 1/4 mile dirt oval (8/11/47 - 1960)
1/4 & 1/2 mile paved oval (1963 - present) / (aka: Auburn Speedway)

Tunnel Park Speedway - Holland - dirt oval (1 race in late 1940's)
the track was dismantled the next day and no trace of a track was left

Ubly Dragway - Ubly - 1/4 mile paved dragstrip (May, 1962 - present)

Union City - 1/2 mile dirt oval (1920's)

Union Park - Saginaw - dirt oval (1905)

University of Detroit Stadium - Detroit / the promoter was Don Zeiter
1/4 mile cinder oval (5/25/35 - 9/05/35) / ran on the running track

US 10 Raceway - see: Ludington Fairgrounds

US 131 Raceway Park - Martin - 1/4 mile paved dragstrip (1962 - present)
1/2 mile high banked dirt oval (5/20/79 - 1984) (1987)
Don Nicholson drove the first Funny Car to a 7 second run here on 9/17/66

USA Speedway - Stanton - 1/3 mile dirt oval (7/08/90 - 9/16/90)
site was and is still currently a motocross track

V.F.W. Speedway - see: Motor City Speedway

Venture Raceway - see: Adventure Mountain Speedway

Vermontville High School - Vermontville - 1/4 mile cinder oval (c.1928)

Vulcan Speedway - see: Norway Speedway

WARE's Speed Bowl - see: Harvard Speedway

Waterford Hills - Waterford - 1.5 mile paved road course (1958 - present)

Welsh Civic Auditorium - Grand Rapids / at the downtown convention center
1/10 mile indoor concrete oval (1/05/90) / (aka: Welsh Auditorium)
ran dwarf cars and motorcycles in conjunction with a monster truck show

West Branch - 1/4 mile dirt oval (c.1952 - c.1958) / not West Branch Speedway

West Branch Speedway - West Branch - 1/4 mile dirt oval (1956 - 1965)
1/4 mile paved oval (1966 - 1977) / (aka: American Legion Speedway)

Western Michigan Speedway - see: Fruitport Midget Speedway

Whiskey Ridge Raceway - Muskegon / northeast of town on Maple Island Road
3/8 mile dirt oval (1948 - 1960) (c.1972 - 1976)
(aka: Maple Island Speedway) / (aka: Newago County Speedway)

Whiskey Run - Gobles - 1/4 mile dirt oval (late 1940's)

Whittemore Speedway - Whittemore - 1/2 mile dirt oval (1948 - late 1950's)
1/4 mile dirt oval (early 1960's - 1987) / 1/4 mile paved oval (1988 - present)

Wilber Speedway - see: Raceland Speedway

Wings Stadium - Kalamazoo - 1/12 mile indoor concrete oval (12/10/78)
ran Mini-Champs on the concrete floor of the ice arena

Winston Speedway - Rothbury / located on Winston Road west of Rothbury
1/3 mile dirt oval (1980 - 1987) (1989) (1992 - present)

Yale - 1/4 mile dirt oval (1936)

Zeiters Midget Speedway - Detroit - see: Motor City Speedway

Zeiters Midget Speedway - Grand Rapids - see: Bigelow Field

Zilwaukee Speedway - Zilwaukee / the promoter was Ken Culbert
1/5 mile dirt oval (1954 - 1960)

*David Carlson suffered minor injuries in his trip over the bank at Whiskey
Ridge Raceway in an early roadster race. - Bob Sheldon collection.*

306

MINNESOTA

212 Speedway - see: Renville Speedway

Ada Raceway - Ada - 1/2 mile dirt oval (late 1930's - 1941) / horse track built 1895
3/8 mile dirt oval (c.1950 - c.6/26/53) (8/02/75) (7/05/82 - 1987) (1991)
(1993 - present) / located at the Norman County Fairgrounds

Aitkins Raceway - Aitkins - 1/2 mile dirt oval (early 1950's)
1/4 mile dirt oval (1987 - present) / at the Aitkins County Fairgrounds

Albert Lea Fairgrounds - Albert Lea / located at the Freeborn County Fairgrounds
1/2 mile dirt oval (1942) (8/19/46 - 8/04/73) / track torn out

Alexandria Fairgrounds - see: Viking Speedway

Anoka County Fairgrounds - Anoka - 1/2 mile dirt oval (1950's)

Appleton Fairgrounds - Appleton - 1/2 mile dirt oval (c.1954 - c.1958)
located on an Indian Reservation at the Swift County Fairgrounds

Arlington Raceway - Arlington - 1/2 mile dirt oval (c.1953 - present)
located at the Sibley County Fairgrounds / (aka: Arlington Motor Speedway)

Arrowhead Speedway - see: Proctor Speedway

Atwater Speedway - Atwater - 1/2 mile dirt oval (1956 - c.1958)

Austin Fairgrounds - Austin - 1/2 mile dirt oval (1929 - 1941) (6/02/46 - c.1977)
1/5 mile dirt oval (6/27/41 - 7/18/41) / at the Mower County Fairgrounds
ran first ever IMCA old-timers meet here in 1984

Back 40 Speedway - Staples - 1/4 mile dirt oval (1993 - present)

Barnesville Fairgrounds - Barnesville - dirt oval (1968) / at Clay Co. Fairgrounds

Bearcat Expos Speedway - see: Crystal Speedway

*Modifieds race on the new pavement at the Minnesota State Fairgrounds.
Alden Jamison photo.*

Bemidji Fairgrounds - Bemidji - 1/2 mile dirt oval (7/10/38) (c.1947 - c.1954)
located at the Beltrami County Fairgrounds

Bemidji Raceway - Bemidji - 1/4 mile dirt oval (early 1980's - present)

Bird Island Fairgrounds - see: Island Speedway

Blaine - see: North Starr International Motor Speedway

Bloomington Municipal Stadium - Bloomington - paved road course (c.1959-c.1963)
sports cars raced in the parking lot of the Metropolitan Stadium

Blue Earth Fairgrounds - Blue Earth / located at the Faribault Co. Fairgrounds
1/2 mile dirt oval (6/01/47 - c.1954)

Boyd Karting Track - Boyd - 1/6 mile dirt oval (1980 - c.1984)

Brainerd International Raceway - Brainerd / (aka: Donnybrook Int'l Speedway)
3.0 mile paved road course (8/11/68 - present) / many SCCA TA races
1/4 mile paved dragstrip (1968 - present)

Brainerd International Raceway. - Official track photo.

Brooten Speedway - Brooten - 1/5 mile dirt oval (c.1977 - c.1984)

Buffalo River Speedway - Glyndon - 3/8 mile dirt oval (1953)
3/8 mile paved oval (1954-1967) / (aka: Glyndon Speedway)
3/8 mile dirt oval (1968 - present) / (aka: Fargo-Morehead Speedway)
(aka: F & M Speedway)

Cambridge Speedway - Cambridge - 1/8 mile dirt oval (8/06/89 - 1989)
located at the Isanti County Fairgrounds

Camden Speedway - Lynd (Russell) - 1/4 mile dirt oval (c.1958 - c.1960)

Canby Fairgrounds - see: Yellow Medicine County Fairgrounds

Cannon Falls Fairgrounds - Cannon Falls - 1/2 mile dirt oval (1960's)
located at the Cannon Valley Fairgrounds

Cannon River Speedway - Morristown - 3/8 mile dirt oval (early 1950's - 1980)

Chateau Speedway - Lansing - 3/8 mile dirt oval (1960's - 1983) (1985 - present)

Clinton Fairgrounds - Clinton / located at the Big Stone County Fairgrounds
5/8 mile dirt oval (c.1948 - c.1959)

Concrete Speedway - see: Twin City Motor Speedway (Fort Snelling)

Crookston Fairgrounds - Crookston - 1/2 mile dirt oval (7/16/16) (1950's)

Crystal Speedway - Robbinsdale / located at the Bearcat Legion Expo Grounds
1/2 mile dirt oval (c.7/18/47 - 1949) / built by Don Vogt
(aka: Bearcat Expos Speedway) / now the site of a cemetery

Detroit Lake Fairgrounds - Detroit Lake - 1/2 mile dirt oval c.1950)
located at the Becker County Fairgrounds

Dodge County Speedway - Kasson - 1/2 mile dirt oval (8/19/41) (c.1946 - c.1951)
3/8 mile dirt oval (1955 - present) / (aka: Kasson Speedway)
located at the Dodge County Fairgrounds

Donnybrook Int'l Speedway - see: Brainerd Int'l Raceway

Duluth - see: Proctor Speedway, West Duluth Speedway

Elko Speedway - Elko - 1/4 mile dirt oval (1/02/66 - March, 1966)
3/8 mile paved oval (4/01/66 - present) / (aka: Minnesota Nat'l Speedway)

F & M Speedway - see: Buffalo River Speedway

Fairmont Int'l Raceway - Fairmont / at the Martin County Fairgrounds
1/2 mile dirt oval (c.1932 - c.1941) (c.1946 - present)
(aka: Fairmont Speedway)

Fargo-Morehead Speedway - see: Buffalo River Speedway

Faribault Fairgrounds - Faribault / located at the Rice County Fairgrounds
1/2 mile dirt oval (1936 - 1941) (1945 - 1984) (1986 - present)

Farmington Speedway - Farmington / located at the Dakota County Fairgrounds
5/8 mile dirt oval (5/25/47 - c.8/19/51) / held first roadster race in MN

Fergus Falls Fairgrounds - Fergus Falls / at the Ottertail County Fairgrounds
1/2 mile dirt oval (8/20/52) (6/06/52) (7/24/53)

Fertile Fairgrounds - Fertile - 1/2 mile dirt oval (7/20/46)
located at the Polk County Fairgrounds

Fiesta City Speedway - Montevideo / located at the Chippewa County Fairgrounds
1/2 mile dirt oval (1933) (1948) (1957) (1959 - c.1963)
3/8 mile dirt oval (1982 - 1983) (1988 - present)

Fort Snelling - see: Twin City Motor Speedway - Minneapolis (Fort Snelling)

French Lake Speedbowl - French Lake - 1/4 mile dirt oval (c.1957 - c.1959)

Gary Speedway - Gary - 1/4 mile dirt oval (1960's)

Glenville Fairgrounds - Glenville - 1/2 mile dirt oval (early 1950's - c.1969)

Glenwood Fairgrounds - Glenwood - 1/2 mile dirt oval (9/12/41)
    located at the Pope County Fairgrounds

Glyndon Speedway - see: Buffalo River Speedway

Golden Spike Speedway - Sauk Rapids / (aka: Saint Cloud Motor Speedway)
    3/8 mile dirt oval (5/28/61 - July, 1982) (7/12/86 - present)

Golden Spike Speedway near St. Cloud, Minnesota. - Official track photo.

Goodview Speedway - Winona - 1/2 mile dirt oval (1950 - 1951)

Grand Rapids Motor Speedway - Grand Rapids / at the Itasca County Fairgrounds
    1/4 mile dirt oval (c.1948 - present) / (aka: Grand Rapids Speedway)

Grant County Raceway - see: Herman Fairgrounds

Greenbush Race Park - Greenbush - 3/8 mile dirt oval (6/26/91 - present)

Grove Creek Park - Grove City / (aka: Grove Creek Park Speedway)
    3/8 mile dirt oval (1979 - 1991) (1993 - present)
    1/8 mile paved dragstrip (Sept, 1987 - present) (aka: Grove Creek Speedway)

Hallock Speedway - see: Kittson County Speedway

Hamline - see: Minnesota State Fairgrounds Speedway

Herman Fairgrounds - Herman / located at the Grant County Fairgrounds
    1/2 mile dirt oval (c.1959 - 1981) / (aka: Grant County Fairgrounds)

Hiawatha Speedway - Cloquet - dirt oval (early 1950's)

Hiawatha Speedway - Red Wing - 1/4 mile dirt oval (1951 - 1974)

Hibbing Raceway - Hibbing / located at the Saint Louis County Fairgrounds
    1/2 mile dirt oval (c.7/18/15 - c.1919) (1926 - 8/10/41)
    3/8 mile dirt oval (c.1946 - 1956) (1959 - present)

Highland Park Stadium - Minneapolis - 1/5 mile dirt oval (6/09/37 - c.7/21/37)

Hopkins Fairgrounds - Hopkins - 1/4 mile dirt oval (c.7/28/56 - c.7/29/56)
    located at the Hennepin County Fairgrounds

310

Howard Lake Fairgrounds - Howard Lake / located at the Wright Co. Fairgrounds
1/2 mile dirt oval (c.1946 - 1947) (1982) (1992 - present)
runs motorcycle races and vintage cars on special events

Huntsville Speedway - East Grand Forks - 1/4 mile dirt oval (1950's)

Hutchinson Fairgrounds - Hutchinson / located at the McLeod County Fairgrounds
1/2 mile dirt oval (c.1941) (c.6/16/46 - c.8/17/75)

I-94 Int'l Speedway - Fergus Falls - 3/8 mile dirt oval (6/05/93 - 6/25/94)
3/8 mile paved oval (7/04/94 - present)
built by Don Engebretson / similiar to other I-94 Speedway in Sauk Centre

I-94 Speedway - Sauk Centre - 3/8 mile dirt oval (5/17/91 - 1993)
3/8 mile paved oval (5/20/94 - present) / built by Don Engebretson
similar to other I-94 Speedway (Fergus Falls)

Int'l Speedway - Int'l Falls - 1/2 mile dirt oval (c.1977)

A couple of Mopar competitors at Interstate Dragway. - Allan E. Brown photo.

Interstate Dragways - Morehead (Glyndon) - 1/4 mile dragstrip (5/01/59 - present)

Island Speedway - Bird Island / located at the Renville County Fairgrounds
1/4 mile dirt oval (c.1952 - 1974) (1987 - present)

Jackson Speedway - Jackson / (aka: Jackson V.F.W. Speedway)
1/2 mile dirt oval (9/23/34 - 1941) (1946 - present)
(aka: V.F.W. Speedway) / located at the Jackson County Fairgrounds

Jordan Fairgrounds - Jordan / located at the Scott County Fairgrounds
3/8 mile dirt oval (1989 - c.1990) / ran motorcycles during the fair 1990

Kandi Raceways - Willmar / located at the Kandiyohi County Fairgrounds
1/2 mile dirt oval (c.7/01/51 - 1978) (1991)
3/8 mile dirt oval (1992 - present) / (aka: Willmar Raceway)

Kittson County Speedway - Hallock - 1/2 mile dirt oval (c.1953)
1/4 mile dirt oval (c.1973 - c.1977) (1988 - 1993)
located at the Kittson County Fairgrounds

Luverne Fairgrounds - see: Rock County Fairgrounds

Madison Speedway - Madison -1/2 mile dirt oval (9/13/41) (c.9/09/51 - 1977)
3/8 mile dirt oval (1978 - present) / at the Lac Qui Parle Co. Fairgrounds

Mahnomen Raceway - Mahnomen / located at the Mahnomen County Fairgrounds
3/8 mile dirt oval (July, 1980 - 1985) (1987)

Mankato Fairgrounds - Mankato / located at the Blue Earth County Fairgrounds
1/2 mile dirt oval (c.8/04/35 - c.1941) (c.1947 - 1954)

Mankato Speedbowl - Mankato - 1/4 mile dirt oval (c.1953 - c.1954)

Marshall Fairgrounds - Marshall / located at the Lyon County Fairgrounds
1/2 mile dirt oval (1950's - c.1969)

Metro Speedrome - Minneapolis (Saint Anthony) / the manager was Stew Reamer
1/4 mile paved oval (7/09/60 - 1960)

Minneapolis Armory - Minneapolis - indoor concrete oval (c.1/01/54 - c.1961)

Minnesota Dragway - Minneapolis - 1/4 mile dragstrip (c.1963 - c.1976) / Hwy 242

Minnesota National Speedway - see: Elko Speedway

Minnesota State Fair Speedway - Saint Paul (Hamline) (Minneapolis)
1.0 mile dirt oval (8/18/04 - 9/04/39) / built as a horse track
held a 24 hour enduro race on 6/28/07 / town was called Hamline
1/2 mile dirt oval (8/31/40 - 8/31/41) (8/24/46 - 1963)
1/2 mile paved oval (8/29/64 - present)

*The new asphalt surface at the Minnesota State Fairgrounds is being finished
in 1964. - Alden Jamison photo.*

Minneapolis - also see: Highland Park, Metro, Minnesota Drag, Twin City Motor

Montevideo Fairgrounds - see: Fiesta City Fairgrounds

Montgomery Speedway - Montgomery - 1/5 mile dirt oval (c.1989 - 1993)
started out as a motorcycle track / first auto races in 1991

Mora Fairgrounds - Mora - 1/8 mile dirt (1990) / at the Kanabec Co. Fairgrounds

Morris Fairgrounds - Morris - dirt oval (c.1980) / at Stevens County Fairgrounds
(aka: Stevens County Raceway)

Murray County Raceway - Slayton / located at the Murray County Fairgrounds
1/2 mile dirt oval (c.1958 - c.1957) / (aka: Murray Country JC's Speedway)
3/8 mile dirt oval (c.8/16/58 - 1984) (1988 - present)
(aka: Slayton V.F.W. Speedway) / (aka: Slayton Speedway)

New Brighton - see: North Starr International Motor Speedway

New Ulm Fairgrounds - New Ulm / located at the Brown County Fairgrounds
1/2 mile dirt oval (1930's) (8/16/41) (6/30/46 - early 1960's)
1/4 mile dirt oval (1963) (1987 - 1992)

Nobles County Fairgrounds - see: Worthington Fairgrounds

North Central Motor Speedway - Brainerd / (aka: Brainerd Raceway)
1/3 mile dirt oval (1969 - present) / (aka: North Central Speedway)

North Starr International Motor Speedway - New Brighton (Blaine)
1/2 mile dirt oval (7/21/50 - 1979) / (aka: North Starr Speedway)
1/4 mile paved dragstrip (c.1958 - 1960's) / now an industrial park
1/4 mile dirt oval (c.6/27/55 - 1968) / (aka: Twin City Speedway)
1/4 mile paved oval (1969) / original name was Twin City Speedway
the 1/2 mile oval track was tri-oval shaped for a short time
Frank Winkley was an occasional promoter in the early 1950's

Oklee Speedway - Oklee - dirt oval (c.1971 - 1972)

Olmstead Co. Fairgrounds - Rochester - 1/2 mile dirt oval (1942) (c.1946 - c.1960)
1/4 mile semi-banked dirt oval (1954 - 1956) (1958 - 1985) (1987 - present)
1/4 mile high banked dirt oval (1957)

Owatonna Fairgrounds - see: Steele County Fairgrounds

Paynesville - 1/4 mile dirt oval (late 1950's - early 1960's)

Pine City Fairgrounds - Pine City - 1/2 mile dirt oval (early 1950's)
located at the Pine County Fairgrounds

Pipestone County Fairgrounds - Pipestone - 1/2 mile dirt oval (1950's)
1/6 mile dirt oval (1983 - present) / runs annual Enduro race on small track

Preston Fairgrounds - dirt oval (8/22/41) / at the Fillmore County Fairgrounds

Princeton Speedway - Princeton / located at the Mille Lacs County Fairgrounds
1/4 mile dirt oval (1957 - present)

Proctor Speedway - Proctor / located at the South Saint Louis Co. Fairgrounds
1/2 mile dirt oval (1948 - early 1950's) / (aka: Arrowhead Speedway)
3/8 mile dirt (early 1950's - present)

Raceway Park - Shakopee - 1/4 mile dirt oval (1956 - 1957)

Raceway Park - Shakopee - 1/4 mile paved oval (June, 1958 - present)
different location than other Raceway Park / Jerry Hansen started here

Dust flies from the stock car races at the Redwood Falls Speedbowl.
Jack Rebstock photo (Allan E. Brown collection).

Redwood Falls Speedbowl - Redwood Falls - 1/3 mile dirt oval (Sept., 1952 - 1956)
   one mile north of town in a valley, just west of old North Redwood Road

Redwood Speedway - Redwood Falls / located at the Redwood County Fairgrounds
   1/2 mile dirt oval (7/04/41) (1960) (1968 - present)
   1/5 mile dirt oval (1989 - present)

Renville Speedway - Renville / (aka: 212 Speedway)
   1/2 mile dirt oval (c.1954 - c.1960)

Rex Speedway - Saint Paul - 1/2 mile dirt oval (c.7/10/49 - c.1954)
   Tony Rechtzigel built for his nephew Jerry Richert, Sr. to learn on

Rochester Auditorium - Rochester / (aka: Mayo-Clinic Auditorium)
   1/10 mile indoor concrete oval (c.1/02/54 - 1/16/55) ran T.Q. midgets

Rochester Fairgrounds - see: Olmstead County Fairgrounds

Rock County Fairgrounds - Luverne - 1/2 mile dirt oval (1938 - 1940)
   1/4 mile dirt oval (c.8/13/39) (10/02/47 - c.1969)
   1/8 mile dirt oval (1982 - present)

Roseau County Fairgrounds - Roseau - 1/2 mile dirt oval (early 1950's)

Rum River Raceway - Isanti - 1/2 mile dirt oval (c.1973 - 1974)

Rush City - 1/4 mile dirt oval (mid 1950's)

Saint Charles Fairgrounds - see: Winona County Speedway

Saint Cloud Fairgrounds - Saint Cloud
   1/2 mile dirt oval (c.1915) (7/11/37) (late 1940's - 1950's)

Saint Cloud Motor Speedway - see: Golden Spike Speedway

Saint Cloud Speedway - Saint Cloud - 1/4 mile dirt oval (1950's) / south of town

Saint James Fairgrounds - Saint James / at the Watonwan County Fairgrounds
   dirt oval (early 1950's)

314

Saint Paul Auditorium - Saint Paul
1/10 mile indoor oval (c.1935 - c.1941) (c.1946 - c.1/03/54)

Saint Paul Civic Center - Saint Paul
1/5 mile indoor concrete oval (12/12/85 - 1985) (1988)

Saint Paul Fairgrounds - see: Minnesota State Fair Speedway

Saint Paul Hippodrome - Saint Paul - indoor paved oval (1935)

Saint Paul - also see: Rex Speedway

Saint Peters Fairgrounds - Saint Peters - 1/2 mile dirt oval (early 1950's)
located at the Nicollet County Fairgrounds

Saint Peters Speedway - Saint Peters / located on Highway 169
1/4 mile dirt oval (c.1957 - c.1977)

Sauk Centre Speedway - Sauk Centre / located at the Stearns Co. Fairgrounds
1/2 mile dirt oval (c.1915) (c.1975)

Sauk Rapids Fairgrounds - Sauk Rapids / located at the Benton Co. Fairgrounds
dirt oval (c.1937)

Slayton Fairgrounds - see: Murray County Speedway

Southport Field - (location unknown) - 1.4 mile paved road course (1967)

Steele County Fairgrounds - Owatonna / home of the "Gopher 50"
1/2 mile dirt oval (c.1932 - 8/17/41) (6/23/46 - present)

Stevens County Raceway - see: Morris Fairgrounds

Stillwater Speedway - Lake Elmo - 1/4 mile dirt oval (1953 - 1978)
(aka: Stillwater Speedbowl) / located at the Washington County Fairgrounds

Sunbird Speedway - Winona - 1/4 mile dirt oval (c.1955 - c.1960)

Sunbury Speedway - Sunbury - 1/2 mile dirt oval (c.1957 - 1959)

The Wheel - Mound - 1/4 mile dirt oval (1960's)

Thief River Falls Fairgrounds - Thief River Falls / at Pennington Co. Fairgrounds
1/2 mile dirt oval (c.1938 - c.1941) (c.1946 - c.1952)

Twin City Motor Speedway - Minneapolis (Fort Snelling)
2.0 mile dirt circle (10/24/14)
2.0 mile concrete circle (9/05/15 - 7/14/17) / 40,000 barrels of cement
Earl Cooper won $20,000 on 9/05/15 for a 500 mile AAA race
Ira Vail won last race on 7/14/17 / (aka: Concrete Speedway)
became the Wold-Chamberlain Airfield in 1923
now the site of the Minneapolis-Saint Paul Int'l Airport

Twin City Speedway - New Brighton (Blaine) - see: North Starr Int'l Speedway

Viking Speedway - Alexandria / located at the Douglas County Fairgrounds
1/2 mile dirt oval (7/04/28) (1941 - 1942) (8/20/46) (c.1964 - present)
maybe a new track built in 1964

Virginia/Eveleth - paved road course (late 1950's)

Wadena County Fairgrounds - Wadena - 5/8 mile dirt oval (8/01/51 - 1972)

Warren Fairgrounds - Warren / located at the Marshall County Fairgrounds
 1/2 mile dirt oval (7/13/46) (c.1968 - c.1970) (1973) (7/11/92 - present)

Waseca County Fairgrounds - Waseca - 1/4 mile dirt oval (1986 & 1987)
 1/2 mile dirt oval (6/16/35 - c.1941) (c.1947 - c.1952)

Wee Town Outlaw Speedway - Fergus Falls (aka: West Central Speedway)
 1/2 mile dirt oval (c.1962 - 1986) (1988 - present)

West Central Speedway - see: Wee Town Outlaw Speedway

West Duluth Speedway - Duluth - 3/8 mile dirt oval (1954 - 1956)
 located at 75th and Grand St.

Wheaton Fairgrounds - Wheaton / located at the Traverse County Fairgrounds
 1/2 mile dirt oval (9/05/41)

Whitewater Speedway - see: Winona County Speedway

Windom Fairgrounds - Windom / located at the Cottonwood County Fairgrounds
 1/2 mile dirt oval (c.8/28/35 - c.1938)

Winona County Speedway - Saint Charles / located at the Winona Co. Fairgrounds
 1/4 mile dirt oval (1950's) (1982 - 1987) (1990 - present)
 (aka: Whitewater Raceway)

Worthington Speedway - Worthington / located at the Nobles County Fairgrounds
 3/8 mile dirt oval (c.8/06/55 - 1985) (1987 - 1989) (1991) (1994 - present)
 (aka: Worthington Raceway) / (aka: Noble County Speedway)

Yellow Medicine County Fairgrounds - Canby
 1/2 mile dirt oval (c.6/03/48- c.1966)(1974- 1979)(1982 - 1986)(1988 - present)

MISSISSIPPI

67 Checker Flag Speedway - see: Gulf Coast Checkered Flag Speedway

Attalla Speedway - Kosciusko - 1/4 mile dirt oval (c.1973 - 1978) (1985 - present)

Blue Mountain Dragway - Ripley - 1/8 mile paved dragstrip (c.1981 - 1989)

Biloxi / Gulfport / Long Beach - also see: Economy, Gulf Coast, North Biloxi,
 Sun Coast, Twin Oaks

Bo-Breaze Speedway - Philadelphia - 1/8 mile dirt oval (1984 - 1988)

Booneville Speedbowl - Booneville - 1/4 mile dirt oval (c.1972 - 1979)

Byhalia Raceway - Byhalia - 1/8 mile paved dragstrip (3/01/85 - present)
 3/8 mile dirt oval (1986 - 1990) / (aka: Cotton Boll Speedway)
 (aka: Dixieland Speedway) / (Byhalia Raceway Park)

Chickasaw Speedway - Okolona - 3/8 mile dirt oval (1991 - present)

Columbus Speedway - Columbus - 1/4 mile dirt oval (c.1971 - present)
(aka: Columbus Speedbowl)

Corinth Midget Raceway - Corinth - 1/10 mile dirt oval (1977 - 1983)

Corinth Speedway - Corinth - dirt oval (late 1960's)

Cottage Lane Speedway - Calhoun City - 1/4 mile dirt oval (c.1977)

Cotton Boll Speedway - see: Byhalia Raceway Park

County Line Speedway - Columbia - 1/4 mile dirt oval (c.1977 - c.1980)

Dixie Auto Raceway - Jackson (Pearl) - 3/8 mile dirt oval (1980)

Dixie Speedway - see: Hub City Motor Speedway

Dixieland Speedway - see: Byhalia Raceway Park

Economy Raceway - Gulfport - dirt oval (years unknown)

Forest Fairgrounds - Forest / located at the Scott County Fairgrounds
dirt oval (early 1950's)

Fulton Dragway - Fulton - 1/8 mile paved dragstrip (1981 - present)

Greenville Dragway - Greenville / same location as Greenville Speedway
1/4 mile paved dragstrip (c.1958 - 1991) (1993 - present)

Greenville Speedway - Greenville - 1/4 mile dirt oval (c.1952- 1985)(1987- present)

Greenwood Speedway - Greenwood - dirt oval (years unknown)

Gulf Coast Checkered Flag Speedway - Biloxi
1/4 mile dirt oval (3/18/83 - 1992) / (aka: 67 Checkered Flag Speedway)

Gulf Coast Dragstrip - Biloxi - 1/4 mile paved dragstrip (c.1960 - c.1964)

*The late Gene Chupp during hot laps at Duck River Speedway. He won his
last feature this day. - Jimmy R. Mathis photo.*

Gulf Coast Motor Speedway - see: North Biloxi Speedway

Gulf Coast Speedway - Biloxi / (aka: Gulfport Speedway)
    1/4 mile dirt oval (c.1952 - c.1957)

Gulfport Dragway - Gulfport - 1/4 mile paved dragstrip (c.1972 - present)

Halls Speedway - Centerville - 1/4 mile dirt oval (1993 - present)

Hattiesburg - 1/5 mile dirt oval (Sept., 1941) / ran midgets

Hattiesburg Int'l Dragway - see: Hub City Dragway

Hattiesburg Raceway - Hattiesburg / (aka: Rawl Springs Speedway)
    1/4 mile dirt oval (c.1974 - 1975) / located six miles north of town

Hattiesburg Speedway - see: Hub City Motor Speedway

Holly Springs Speedway - Holly Springs - 1/8 mile dragstrip (c.1989 - 1992)

Hub City Dragway - Hattiesburg / (aka: Hattiesburg Int'l Dragway)
    1/4 mile paved dragstrip (1964 - 1988) (1990 - present)
    tower burned down in 1989 (possibly arson) / used to be an airport

Hub City Motor Speedway - Hattiesburg / (aka: Hattiesburg Motor Speedway)
    3/8 mile dirt oval (1980 - present) / (aka: Dixie Speedway)
    (aka: Hattiesburg Speedway)

Jackson - dirt oval (c.1947 - c.1959)

Jackson Dragway - Jackson (Pearl) - 1/4 mile paved dragstrip (c.1981 - 1984)

Jackson Fairgrounds - see: Mississippi State Fairgrounds

Jackson Int'l Speedway - Jackson (Clinton) - 1/2 mile paved oval (7/14/68 - 1985)
    Armond Holley (supermodified) & Freddy Fryar (late model) were 1st winners

Jackson - also see: Dixie Auto, Little Dixie, Mississippi Coliseum

Jax Trax - Jackson - 1/4 mile dirt oval (9/14/91 - present)

Joyner's Motorama Speedway - Meridian (Causeyville) - dirt oval (3/17/73 - 1973)
    located six miles southeast of Meridian / it wasn't Whynot Raceway

Kilgore's Speedway - Tupelo - 1/4 mile dirt oval (1990) / didn't have grandstands

Laurel Fairgrounds - Laurel / located at the South Mississippi Fairgrounds
    1/2 mile dirt oval (c.1927 - c.1941) (c.1947 - c.1952)
    1/2 mile paved oval (c.1966 - c.1970)

Little Dixie Speedway - Jackson - 1/8 mile dirt oval (1983 & 1984)

Little Yazoo Dirt Track - Yazoo City / (aka: Little Yazoo Speedway)
    1/4 mile dirt oval (1979 - 1985)

Magnolia State Speedway - see: Spencer Speedway

Meridian Fairgrounds - Meridian / at the Mississippi-Alabama State Fairgrounds
    1/2 mile dirt oval (c.1917 - c.9/30/37) (10/06/51)

318

Midway Speedway - Yazoo City - 1/4 mile dirt oval (1981 & 1982)

Mississippi Coliseum - Jackson - indoor oval (years unknown)

Mississippi State Fairgrounds - Jackson - 1/2 mile dirt oval (7/18/03 - c.1937)

Mississippi-Alabama Speedway - see: Whynot Raceway

Myrtle Dragway - see: U.S. 78 Dragway

North Biloxi Speedway - Biloxi / (aka: Gulf Coast Motor Speedway)
1/4 mile dirt oval (c.1973 - c.1977)

North Mississippi Motor Park - Corinth - 1/4 mile dirt oval (1993 - present)

Northeast Mississippi Motorsports - Aberdeen
1/8 mile paved dragstrip (9/01/92 - present)

Pearl River Speedway - Picayune - 1/4 mile dirt oval (1965 - c.1966)

Pearson Nat'l Speedway - Louisville - 1/2 mile dirt oval (1977 - 1984)

Pike County Speedway - Magnolia - 3/8 mile dirt oval (9/15/92 - present)

Pine Ridge Speedway - Baldwyn - 1/4 mile dirt oval (1992 - present)

Preston Raceway - Preston - 1/8 mile paved dragstrip (1987 - present)

Rawls Springs Speedway - see: Hattiesburg Raceway

Shannon Speedway - Shannon - 3/8 mile dirt oval (April, 1992 - present)

Simpson Co. Motorsports Park - Mendenhall - 1/4 mile dirt oval (1990 - present)

Sonic Speedway - Carson - 1/4 mile dirt oval (1977)

Speedbowl - Boyle - dirt oval (years unknown)

This cut-down coupe, with a Ford flat-head engine under the hood, ran at the Jackson dirt track in 1959. - Jimmy R. Mathis photo.

Spencer Speedway - Tupelo (Verona) / (aka: Magnolia State Speedway)
3/8 mile dirt oval (1979 - 1986) (1989)

State Line Raceway - Columbus - 1/8 mile dirt oval (c.1988 - 1989)

Sun Coast Speedway - Gulfport - 1/4 mile dirt oval (3/28/92 - present)

Tunica Road Course - Tunica - 1.0 mile paved road course (c.1994 - present)

Tupelo - also see: Kilgore's Speedway, Spencer Speedway

Tupelo Fairgrounds - Tupelo / located at the Mississippi-Alabama Fairgrounds
1/2 mile dirt oval (1927) (1930's) (1954)

Twin Oaks Speedway - Long Beach - 1/4 mile dirt oval (c.1974 - c.1977)

U.S. 78 Dragway - Myrtle - 1/8 mile concrete dragstrip (c.1981 - 1989)
(aka: Myrtle Dragway)

Vicksburg Speedway - Vicksburg - dirt oval (years unknown)

Whynot Raceway - Meridian (Whynot) / (aka: Mississippi-Alabama Speedway)
3/8 mile dirt oval (1967 - 1985) (1988 - present) / (aka: Whynot Speedway)

Williamson & Sons Speedway - Louisville - 3/8 mile dirt oval (1977 - c.1979)

Wren Speedway - Amory - 1/2 mile dirt oval (c.1977 - c.1980)

MISSOURI

142 Speedway - Thayer - 1/4 mile dirt oval (1977 - 1979) / on SR 142

65 Dragway - Sedalia - 1/4 mile paved dragstrip (1960's & 1970's)
timing tower was converted to a massage parlor

65 Raceway Park - Branson - see: Ozark Mountain Raceway

65 Speedway - Chillicothe / (aka: Kline's Speedway) / located on US 65
1/4 mile dirt oval (c.1971 - c.1973)

65 Speedway - Sedalia - 1/8 mile dirt oval (1983 - 10/09/88) / promoter: Bill Utz

71 Speedway - Neosho - 3/8 mile dirt oval (c.1965 - c.1974)

71 Speedway - Savannah - see: Savannah Speedway

Acme Speedway - Lebanon - 1/5 mile dirt oval (c.5/09/54)

Adrian Speedway - Adrian - 1/4 mile dirt oval (7/15/84 - present)

Airport Speedway - Springfield - 1/4 & 1/8 mile dirt ovals (May, 1991 - present)

Airport Speedway - Springfield / (aka: MS-CA Speedway)
1/4 mile dirt oval (c.1966 - c.1975) / maybe current Airport Speedway

Amazonia - dirt oval (1977 - 1980)

American Legion Memorial Park - see: Savannah Speedway

American Legion Speedway - see: Cape Girardeau Fairgrounds

American Royal Coliseum - Kansas City
  1/12 mile indoor dirt oval (10/30/38 - 2/18/40) (2/28/87 - 3/01/87)

Ball Park Speedway - see: Saint Louis Speedway

Bates County Speedway - see: Butler Fairgrounds

Bentley - (located unknown) - 1/2 mile dirt oval (c.1931) / maybe Berkeley

Bethany Speedway - Bethany / the Northwest Missouri State Fairgrounds
  1/2 mile dirt oval (c.1934 - c.1941) (c.9/07/47 - c.1985)
  1/4 mile dirt oval (1990 - present)

Beverly Speedway - Beverly - 1/4 mile dirt oval (c.1955 - c.6/05/59)
  28 spectators were injured when a race car went into the stands on 6/05/59
  possibly Flying Saucer Speedway

Birdsong Speedway - Poplar Bluff - 1/4 mile dirt oval (late 1960's - c.1977)

Bismarck Fairgrounds - Bismarck - 1/4 mile dirt oval (late 1950's - c.1963)

Blytheville Speedway - Caruthersville - dirt oval (c.1968) / maybe in Arkansas

Bolivar - 1/2 mile dirt oval (7/25/48)

Bolivar Speedway - Bolivar - 3/8 mile dirt oval (c.1967 - 1986) (1988)
  the track is now the pit area of Speedway U.S.A.

Boonville Fairgrounds - Boonville / located at the Cooper County Fairgrounds
  dirt oval (1954 - 1955)

Brookfield - dirt oval (1918) / possibly at the Linn County Fairgrounds

Brookfield - dirt oval (c.1956) / possibly at the Linn County Fairgrounds

Butler Speedway - Butler / located at the Bates County Fairgrounds
  1/4 mile dirt oval (7/15/55 - c.1960) / (aka: Bates County Speedway)

Larry Phillips of Springfield, Missouri is a two-time NASCAR Winston Racing Series champion. He is a frequent visitor to victory lane, having won nearly 500 features in his career. - Official Winston Racing photo.

Cabool - dirt oval (years unknown)

Cape Girardeau Fairgrounds - Cape Girardeau / (aka: American Legion Speedway)
1/2 mile dirt oval (5/31/42) (1948) (9/09/52) / (aka: Arena Park Speedway)
Everett Saylor fatally injured on 5/31/42 / Joie Chitwood won the race
located at the Southeast Missouri District Fairgrounds
maybe ran a race in 1992 or 1993

Capital Speedway - Elston - 1/5 mile dirt oval (1951 - 1953)

Capital Speedway - Holts Summit - 3/8 mile dirt oval (1967 - present)

Capital Speedway - see: Jefferson City Fairgrounds

Carthage Fairgrounds - Carthage / located at the Jasper County Fairgrounds
1/2 mile dirt oval (10/06/15 - c.1932)

Cartwell Speedway - (location unknown) - 1/5 mile dirt oval (1951 - 1954)

Caruthersville - dirt oval (early 1950's)

Caruthersville Speedway - Caruthersville - 3/8 mile dirt oval (7/15/88 - present)

Central Missouri Speedway - Warrensburg - 1/8 mile dirt oval (1984 - present)
(aka: Tri-M Speedway)

Charleah Speedway - Rolla - paved oval (1968) / not Rolla Speedway

*The driver posing with his sprint car is none other than NASCAR Winston
Cup star Ken Schrader. The photo was taken at I-70 Speedway in 1984.
Schrader is a true "goodwill" ambassador of racing as he races at about 60
different tracks each year. - James Wilson photo.*

Charleston JayCee Speedway - Charleston - 3/8 mile dirt oval (1965 - 1970)
 the property was owned by Governor Warren Hearns

Chillicothe - 1/5 mile dirt oval (9/28/46) / maybe at the Livingston Co Fairgrounds

Clinton - see: Golden Valley Speedway

Columbia - 1/4 mile dirt oval (1950's)

Creve Coeur Lake Speedway - Saint Louis (Creve Coeur) / promoter: Don Zeiter
 1/2 mile dirt oval (c.1929 - c.7/14/35) / (aka: Motor Speedway)
 the track closed when the grandstands blew down

Crossroads Speedway - Joplin / located two miles west of Main St. on 7th
 1/4 mile dirt oval (4/23/39 - c.1940)

D & F Speedway - see: DeSoto Speedway

Delmar Track - Saint Louis - dirt oval (5/07/05)

Desloge - 1/4 mile dirt oval (1950's) / maybe Elvins Speedway

DeSoto Speedway - DeSoto / (aka: D & F Speedway)
 1/4 mile dirt oval (c.1974 - c.1978)

Devil's Bowl - Springfield - 1/4 mile dirt oval (1953 & 1954)
 this track is reportedly close to the current site of Airport Speedway

Double Nickel Raceway - see: Sikeston Int'l Raceway

Double X Speedway - California / (aka: Woody's Speedway)
 1/4 mile dirt oval (1964 - 1971) (1975 - present)
 the track was removed and replaced with a rodeo grounds in 1972
 the track was rebuilt in the same spot in 1975

Eastside Speedway - see: Grundy County Raceway

El Dorado Springs - 1/4 mile dirt oval (1953 & 1954) / east of town on US 54

Electric Park - Kansas City - dirt oval (years unknown)

Elm Ridge Track - Kansas City - 1.0 mile dirt oval (10/03/06 - c.1910)

Elsberry Speedway - Elsberry - 3/10 mile dirt oval (c.1974 - 1978)

Elvins Speedway - Elvins - 1/5 mile dirt oval (c.1952 - c.1955) / near Flat River
 maybe called Leadbelt Speedway at one time

Empire Speedway - see: Saint Francois County Raceway

Excelsior Speedway - Excelsior / (aka: JayCee Speedway)
 1/4 mile dirt oval (c.1954)

Fairgrounds Coliseum - Springfield - 1/10 mile indoor concrete oval (1971)
 located at the Ozark Empire Fairgrounds

Fairgrounds Speedway - see: Springfield Fairgrounds

Fort Wood Speedway - Waynesville - paved oval (c.1968)

Fredericktown Speedway - Fredericktown - 1/4 mile dirt oval (early 1950's)

Golden Valley Speedway - Clinton - 1/5 mile dirt oval (1953 - 1957)

Goldman Stadium - Kansas City - 1/5 mile dirt oval (c.9/16/38 - c.1938)

Gray's Stadium - Kansas City / located at Saint John & Belmont
1/5 mile dirt oval (c.1939)

Greyhound Speed Lanes - Moberly / located three miles east of town on US 24
1/4 mile dirt oval (6/12/57 - c.1958)

The Greyhound Speed Lanes in Moberly, Missouri. - Allan E. Brown collection.

Grundy County Raceway - see: Trenton Fairgrounds

Hamilton - 1/2 mile dirt oval (7/04/46 - c.6/26/49) / maybe Caldwell Co Fairgrounds

Hannibal - 1/4 mile dirt oval (c.1959 - c.1961)

Hannibal Motor Speedway - Hannibal - dirt oval (late 1960's)

Heart of America Speedway - Kansas City / on US 40 next to the Big Blue River
1/3 mile dirt oval (10/03/48 - c.1951)
the site would be about 1 mile west of the current Truman Sports Complex

Higginsville - 1/2 mile dirt oval (early 1930's) / maybe Lafayette Co. Fairgrounds

Hillsboro Race Track - Hillsboro - 1/4 mile dirt oval (1964 - 1966)

Holmes Road Speedway - Kansas City / located south of town
1/4 mile dirt oval (1963 - 1969) / (aka: West Line Speedway)

Hopkins - Hopkins - 1/3 mile dirt oval (c.7/04/48 - 1949)

Houston - dirt oval (1950's or 1960's)

Humansville City Park - Humansville / located at a football field
1/5 mile dirt oval (c.1965 - c.1984)

I-44 Speedway - see: Lebanon I-44 Speedway

I-55 Raceways - Pevely - 1/3 mile dirt oval (1974 - present)
1/8 mile paved dragstrip (c.1980 - present) / (aka: I-55 Speedway)
the dragstrip was completely under water in the big flood of 1993

I-70 Speedway - Odessa - 1/2 mile paved oval (8/08/69 - 1980)
Jay Woodside won the first race / track was called .540 mile at one time
1/2 mile dirt oval (1981 - 1987) / Greg Weld covered the asphalt with dirt
1/2 mile paved oval (7/31/88 - present) / (aka: I-70 National Speedway)
home of the "World Cup 400" late model race

Independence - 1.0 mile dirt oval (c.6/17/16 - c.1922)

Interstate Speedway - Springfield - 1/8 mile dirt oval (1985 - 1986)
maybe Airport Speedway

Jackson County Speedway - Independence - 1/2 mile dirt oval (1925 - c.1933)

Jamesport Speedway - Jamesport - 1/4 mile dirt oval (1987 - present)

JayCee Speedway - see: Excelsior Speedway

Jefferson City Fairgrounds - Jefferson City / at the Cole County Fairgrounds
1/4 mile dirt oval (1954 - c.1958) / (aka: Capital Speedway)

Jefferson City - 1/2 mile dirt oval (c.5/06/34) / maybe at Cole Co. Fairgrounds

Jefferson City - also see: Capital Speedway - Jefferson City

Joplin 66 Speedway - Joplin / located west of town at Blackcat Road & 13th
3/8 mile dirt oval (c.7/24/93 - present)

*The modern Joplin 66 Speedway has grandstands on both sides of the track
and is one of the nicest new tracks. - Official track photo.*

Joplin Speedway - Joplin / located at Alt. US 71 & 20th / now an industrial park
1/5 mile dirt oval (1939 - c.1941) (c.1946 - 1977) / (aka: Ozark Speedway)

Joplin - also see: Cross Road, M & K Speedway, North Fork

Kahoka - 1/2 mile dirt oval (6/02/46) / maybe at the Clark County Fairgrounds

Kahoka Dragway - Kahoka - 1/8 mile paved dragstrip (late 1950's - early 1960's)

Kansas City - 1/4 mile dragstrip (1956)

Kansas City Int'l Raceway - Independence - 1/4 mile dragstrip (c.1962 - present)
paved road course (1960's) / located south of town on Noland Road
3/16 mile dirt oval (1984 - 1987) / ran mini-sprints on the oval track

Kansas City Road Course - Kansas City - 1.5 mile city street road course (1986)
    races were through Penn Valley Park

Kansas City Speedway - Kansas City - 1.125 mile dirt oval (7/22/16)
    only race won by Ralph DePalma / located at 85th St. & Indiana
    track closed when grandstands burned down on 12/05/16

Kansas City Speedway - Kansas City - 1.25 mile wood oval (9/17/22 - 7/04/24)
    built by Jack Prince & Art Pillsbury / turns banked 35 degrees
    located south of K.C. at 95th and Holmes Road / 9/16/22 race rained out
    it cost $500,000 to build / Roscoe Sarles was fatally injured on 9/17/22
    (rumor has it the track was secretly financed by the Kansas City Star,
    and when the track failed, the Star stopped its coverage of auto racing)
    The site became a Pratt and Whitney airplane engine plant during World
       War II / the site later became a factory of the Bendix Co.
    (aka: Million Dollar Speedway)

Kansas City - also see: American Royal, Electric Park, Elm Ridge, Goldman,
    Gray's, Heart of America, Holmes, Jackson Co., Olympic, Pla-Mor, Riverside

The cars line up for a start of a race at the Kansas City Speedway. It was one of the famous board tracks. - Bob Sheldon photo.

Kirksville Fairgrounds - Kirksville / located at the Adair County Fairgrounds
    1/2 mile dirt oval (c.5/16/48 - c.1962) / (aka: Kirksville Speedway)
    1/4 mile dirt oval (c.1967 - 1987) / (aka: Northeast Missouri Fairgrounds)

Kline's Speedway - see: 65 Speedway - Chillicothe

Lake Hill Int'l Raceway - Saint Louis - 1/5 mile dirt oval (6/29/48 - 1966)
1/3 mile paved oval (1967 - 1978) / located in the town of Valley Park
Rusty Wallace started his driving career here in 1972

Lake of the Ozarks Speedway - Osage Beach - 1/5 mile dirt oval (c.7/08/50- c.1952)

Lake Ozark Speedway - Camdenton - 1/3 mile dirt oval (April, 1980 - 1985)

Lakeside Speedway - Saint Joseph - 1/2 mile dirt oval (c.9/19/48 - 1948)

Lebanon I-44 Speedway - Lebanon - 3/8 mile dirt oval (1983 - 1988)
3/8 mile paved oval (1989 - present)

Legion Speedway - see: Savannah Fairgrounds

Lewistown Fairgrounds - Lewistown / located at the Lewis County Fairgrounds
1/4 mile dirt oval (1993 - present) / runs Modified-midgets

M & K Speedway - Joplin / located west of town near the Missouri/Kansas border
1/5 mile dirt oval (c.1967)

Macon Fairgrounds - Macon / located at the Macon County Fairgrounds
1/2 mile dirt oval (c.1935) (8/18/46 - c.1959)

Malden Jaycee Speedway - Malden - 1/4 mile dirt oval (1960's)

Maryville Fairgrounds - Maryville / located at the Nodaway County Fairgrounds
1/4 mile dirt oval (6/11/49 - 1949) (c.1961 - 1965)
the property is now the site of the Nodaway County Recreation Complex

Maxwellton Track - see: Saint Louis World's Fair

Maysville Fairgrounds - Maysville / located at the DeKalb County Fairgrounds
1/5 mile dirt oval (1949 & 5/04/50)

Memphis Fairgrounds - Memphis / located at the Scotland County Fairgrounds
1/2 mile dirt oval (1950 - 1956) (6/05/60 - c.1983)

Mexico Fairgrounds - Mexico / located at the Audrain County Fairgrounds
1/2 mile dirt oval (7/04/37 - 8/16/41) (c.1957)

Mid-America Raceways - Wentzville - 1/4 mile paved dragstrip (c.1964 - present)
2.86 mile paved road course (c.1964 - 1985) / ran SCCA TA races in 1966

Middletown - 1/2 mile dirt oval (8/31/38 - 7/13/41)

Million Dollar Speedway - see: Kansas City Speedway (board track)

Missouri Int'l Race Park - Benton - 3/8 mile dirt oval (5/11/91 - present)
1/8 mile paved dragstrip (1991 - present)

Missouri State Fairgrounds - see: State Fair Speedway

Mo-Ark Raceway - see: West Plains Speedway

Mo-Kan Dragway - Asbury - 1/4 mile paved dragstrip (1962 - present)

Moberly Race Track - Moberly - 1/4 mile dirt oval (c.1948)

The steep grandstands at Moberly Speedway give the fans an unobstructed view of the races. - Terry Ford photo.

Moberly Speedway - Moberly / located four miles west of town on US 24
    3/8 mile dirt oval (7/28/89 - present) / Steve Kinser won the first event
    (aka: Moberly Motorsports Complex)

Moberly - also see: Greyhound Speed Lanes

Monett Speedway - Monett - 1/4 mile dirt oval (1969 - c.1972)
    3/8 mile dirt oval (c.1973 - present)

Motor Speedway - see: Creve Coeur Lake Speedway

Mound City - 1/4 mile paved dragstrip (1951)

Mountain View - dirt oval (1950's or 1960's)

MS-CA Speedway - see: Airport Speedway

Nevada - dirt oval (early 1930's)

Nevada Speedway - Nevada - 1/4 mile dirt oval (c.1965 - present)

North Fork Speedway - Joplin - 3/8 mile dirt oval (1994 - present)

Northwest Missouri State Fairgrounds - see: Bethany Speedway

Oakland Stadium - see: Walsh Stadium

Olympic Stadium - Kansas City / the promoter was Dutch Miller
    1/5 mile flat dirt oval (6/02/35 - 10/23/38)
    1/5 mile banked dirt oval (5/14/39 - 7/26/42) (8/26/45 - 1951)
    1/4 mile banked dirt oval (1952 - 1974) / located on Harry S. Truman Road
    A.J. Foyt won his first USAC race here in a midget on 5/12/57

Osage Beach - 1/4 mile dirt oval (7/08/50) / maybe Lake of the Ozarks Speedway

Ozark Empire Fairgrounds - see: Springfield Fairgrounds

Ozark Int'l Raceway - Rogersville - 1/4 mile paved dragstrip (1979 - present)
    (aka: Sho-Me Dragway)

Ozark Mountain Raceway - Branson / (aka: 65 Raceway Park)
    3/8 mile dirt oval (1980 - 1984)

Ozark Speedway - see: Joplin Speedway

328

Parkside Speedway in Sweet Springs, Missouri. - Allan E. Brown photo.

Pacific - 1/4 mile paved dragstrip (1960's)

Parkside Raceway - Sweet Springs - 1/8 mile dirt oval (1983 - present)
    same site as the old Sweet Spring Memorial Park

Pevely Speedway - Pevely - 1/4 mile dirt oval (1956) / at Highway Z & US 67

Pla-Mor Park - Kansas City - dirt oval (c.9/12/37 - late 1937)

Plantation Speedway - see: Sikeston Speedway

Platte City Fairgrounds - Platte City / located at the Platte County Fairgrounds
    1/2 mile dirt oval (c.5/01/49 - c.1957) / located near Tracy
    1/3 mile dirt oval (c.1950 - c.1953) / (aka: Flying Saucer Speedway)
    (aka: Platte County Speedway)

Platte County Speedway - see: Flying Saucer Speedway

Pony Express Speedway - Saint Joseph - dirt oval (c.1956 - c.1959)

Poplar Bluff - 1/2 mile dirt oval (c.9/29/18 - 1930's)
    probably at the Butler County Fairgrounds

Poplar Bluff - dirt oval (1950 - c.1951) / probably at the Butler Co. Fairgrounds

Potosi Speedway - Potosi - 1/4 mile dirt oval (1960's) / maybe Washington Co Fair

Princeton Fairgrounds - Princeton - 1/2 mile dirt oval (1950's)
    located at the Mercer County Fairgrounds

Ramona Park Speedway - St. Louis (Berkley) - 5/16 mile dirt oval (1933- c.5/31/36)
    located on Carson Rd, north of Natural Bridge Road near Ramona Lake Park

Reeds Spring - dirt oval (1950's or 1960's)

Richmond Speedway - Richmond - dirt oval (c.1953 - c.1954)
    maybe at the Ray County Fairgrounds

Riverdale Speedway - Saint Louis / located at Telegraph Road & Meramac
    1/4 mile dirt oval (6/09/46 - c.1947)

Riverside Stadium - Kansas City - 1/5 mile dirt oval (5/30/39 - c.8/25/39)
    1/2 mile dirt oval (6/08/39) (6/03/51 - c.1954) / formerly a horse track
    1/4 mile dirt oval (5/31/52 - 1988) / located in the town of Riverside

The start of the "Missouri 200" at I-70 Speedway. - Photo courtesy I.M.C.A.

Rolla - 1/4 mile dirt oval (1954 & 1955)

Rolla Fairgrounds - Rolla / located at the Central Missouri Regional Fairgrounds
    1/2 mile dirt oval (7/04/69 - 1970) / (aka: Rolla Speedway)
    1/2 mile paved oval (7/03/71 - 6/29/74) / the last race was the "USA 300"
    Tom Maier won the last race, but the promoter took off with the purse

Rosecran Airfield - Saint Joseph - paved road course (7/31/55)

Saint Charles Speedway - Saint Charles - 1/4 mile dirt oval (Aug., 1956 - present)

Saint Francois County Raceway - Farmington - 1/4 mile dirt oval (1970 - 1982)
    located at the Saint Francois Co. Fairgrounds / (aka: Empire Speedway)
    3/8 mile dirt oval (1983 - present)

Saint Joseph Fairgrounds - Saint Joseph / at the Buchanan County Fairgrounds
    1/2 mile dirt oval (c.8/23/14 - c.1935) / John Gerber started here in 1921

Saint Joseph - also see: Lakeside, Pony Express, Rosecran Airfield, Thames

Saint Louis Arena - Saint Louis
    1/10 mile indoor concrete oval (1/15/35 - 10/27/36) (11/11/41)

Saint Louis Speedway - Saint Louis / located on South Broadway
    1/5 mile dirt oval (1934 - 1937) / (aka: Ball Park Speedway)

Saint Louis World's Fair - Saint Louis / (aka: Maxwellton Track)
    1.0 mile circular dirt oval (1903 - 7/04/07) (8/09/14 - 11/22/22)
    maybe ran in May of 1923 as well

Saint Louis - also see: Creve Coeur, Delmar, Lake Hill, Ramona Park, Riverdale,
    Smartt Field, Sylvan Beach, Walsh Stadium, Wellston

Saint Marys - 1/4 mile dirt oval (1950's)

Saint Marys - 1/4 mile dirt oval (1960's) different site than other St. Marys track

Saline County Speedway closed in 1983. - Terry Ford photo.

Saline County Speedway - Marshall - 1/2 mile dirt oval (c.1921 - early 1930's)
    1/4 mile dirt oval (c.5/06/54 - 1983) / (aka: Sportsman Speedway)
    the site is now a soybean field

Savannah Speedway - Savannah / located at the Andrews County Fairgrounds
    1/2 mile dirt oval (c.7/16/50 - c.1956) / (aka: Legion Speedway)
    1/4 mile dirt oval (c.6/28/57 - present) / (aka: 71 Speedway)
    also known as the American Legion Memorial Park

Sedalia - dirt figure eight course (1951 & 1952) / located at 28th & Ingram

Sedalia Fairgrounds - see: State Fair Speedway

Sedalia - also see: 65 Dragway, 65 Speedway, Thunderbowl Speedway

Semo Dragstrip - Malden - 1/4 mile paved dragstrip (c.1965)

Senath Fairgrounds - Senath / located at the Dunklin County Fairgrounds
    dirt oval (early 1950's) / promoted by the Senath American Legion

Sho-Me Dragway - see: Ozark Int'l Raceway

Sikeston Drag Strip - Sikeston - 1/8 mile paved dragstrip (5/10/69 - present)

Sikeston Int'l Raceway - Sikeston - 3/10 mile dirt oval (1978 - 7/18/87)
    a fist fight broke out between the promoter & the drivers at the last race
    (aka: Double Nickel Raceway) / located north of town

Sikeston Speedway - Sikeston (Miner) / (aka: Plantation Speedway)
    1/4 mile dirt oval (c.1972 - c.1979) / located southeast of town

Smartt Field - Saint Louis - paved road course (5/04/57 - c.10/11/59)

Smithville Fairgrounds - Smithville - 1/2 mile dirt oval (c.7/01/28 - c.1936)
    1/3 mile dirt oval (4/25/48 - 9/10/48) / located north of Kansas City

Southern Missouri Raceway - West Plains / located Northwest of town on SR 14
    1/4 mile dirt oval (1988 - 1991) (1993 - present)

Speedway U.S.A. - Bolivar - 3/8 mile paved oval (1989 - present)
the pit area is located where the old Bolivar Speedway was

Sportsman Speedway - see: Saline County Speedway

Springfield Fairgrounds - Springfield / located at the Ozark Empire Fairgrounds
1/2 mile dirt oval (10/13/37 - 9/07/41) (5/26/46 - c.8/09/72)
1/5 mile dirt oval (9/17/48)
1/5 mile paved oval (c.5/21/54 - c.1964)
1/4 mile paved oval (c.1965 - 1974) / (aka: Fairgrounds Speedway)
1/4 mile dirt oval (c.8/08/75 - c.1987)
1/2 mile paved oval (4/01/73 - c.1987) / Dean Roper won on 4/01/73

Springfield Int'l Dragway - Springfield - 1/4 mile paved dragstrip (c.1965 - c.1970)

Springfield - also see: Airport Speedway, Devil's Bowl, Interstate Speedway

The I.M.C.A. stock cars on the pace lap for the 100 mile race at the Missouri State Fairgrounds in 1971. Ernie Derr won the race. - courtesy of I.M.C.A.

State Fair Speedway - Sedalia / located at the Missouri State Fairgrounds
1.0 mile dirt oval (10/02/15 - 8/23/41) (8/18/46 - 1985) (1989 - present)
Lou Disbrow won the first race (an IMCA big car race) / horse track
1/2 mile dirt oval (8/27/49 - 1985) (1989 - present) / built in 1901
Bobby Grim won the first race on the 1/2 mile track built in 1936
ran parimutuel horse races only from 1986 to 1988

Swanterville - (location unknown) - dirt oval (early 1950's)

Sweet Springs Memorial City Park - Sweet Springs
1/2 mile dirt oval (7/04/52 - c.1952)
1/4 mile dirt oval (c.1953 - 1955) / site is now Parkside Raceway

Sylvan Beach Speedway - Saint Louis (Kirkwood) / at US 66 & Meramac Road
1/4 mile dirt oval (c.9/07/36 - c.9/05/37)

Syracuse - 3/4 mile dirt figure eight course (May, 1950 - c.1951)

Thames Stadium - Saint Joseph - 1/5 mile dirt oval (5/02/39 - c.7/19/40)

Thunderbowl Speedway - Sedalia / four miles southwest of town on Highway B
1/3 mile dirt oval (1958 - c.1964)

Trenton - dirt oval (7/18/18) / possibly at the Trenton Fairgrounds

Trenton Fairgrounds - Trenton / at the North Central Missouri Fairgrounds
1/4 mile dirt oval (October, 1950 - c.1973) / (aka: Eastside Speedway)
(aka: Grundy County Raceway)

Tri-M Speedway - see: Central Missouri Speedway

Tri-State Speedway - Portageville - dirt oval (1960)

U.S. 36 Raceway - Cameron - 1/8 mile paved dragstrip (8/15/90 - present)

Versailles - 1/4 mile egg shaped dirt oval (1951) / at a baseball field

Vine Hill Speedway - Bowling Green - 1/4 mile dirt oval (c.1971 - c.1977)

Walsh Stadium - Saint Louis / located at the Saint Louis University
1/5 mile dirt oval (5/30/35 - 7/29/42) (5/21/46 - c.1956)
(aka: Oakland Stadium) / torn down in April, 1957

Wappapella - dirt oval (c.1970 - c.1971)

Warrensburg - 1/4 mile dirt oval (1955 & 1956)
located on Highway 50, just east of the Sky Haven Motel

Waynesville - dirt oval (years unknown)/ maybe Fort Wood Speedway

Wellston - 1/2 mile dirt oval (1918) / a western suburb of Saint Louis

Wentzville - dirt oval (early 1950's)

West Line Speedway - see: Holmes Road Speedway

West Plains Speedway. - Official track photo.

West Plains - 1/2 mile dirt oval (1950's) / located north of town

West Plains - 1/4 mile dirt oval (years unknown) / located on Highway K

West Plains - 1/4 mile paved oval (late 1950's - 1960's)
    located five miles north of town on US 63

West Plains Speedway - West Plains - 3/8 mile dirt oval (c.1973 - 1985)
    1/3 mile dirt oval (1986) / (aka: Mo-Ark Raceway)

West Plains Speedway - West Plains - 3/8 mile dirt oval (6/24/89 - present)

West Plains - also see: Southern Missouri Speedway

Woody's Speedway - see: Double X Speedway

MONTANA

Anaconda - dirt oval (7/22/17) / ran a AAA race / probably at a fairgrounds

Belaro Speedway - see: Magic City Speedway

Big Sky Speedway - Kalispell / (aka: Tri-City Speedway) / across from the airport
    1/4 mile paved oval (1971 - 1990) / located northeast of town

Billings Fairgrounds - Billings / located at the Yellowstone Expo
    1/2 mile dirt oval (c.8/05/17 - c.1924) / now called Montana Fairgrounds

Billings - also see: Flying Oval, Golden Rod, Magic City

Bozeman Dragway - Bozeman - 1/4 mile paved dragstrip (c.1963 - c.1965)

Bozeman Fairgrounds - Bozeman / located at the Gallatin County Fairgrounds
    1/2 mile dirt oval (c.1952 - c.1956)

Butana Speedway - see: Mining City Speedway

Butte - 1/5 mile dirt oval (8/21/37) (8/22/37) (8/23/37) / ran midgets

Butte Shrine Int'l Raceway - Butte - 1/4 mile dirt oval (1977 - 1984)

Capital City Speedway - Helena / (aka: Thunder Road Speedway)
    1/4 mile dirt oval (1977 - present)

Deer Lodge Fairgrounds - Deer Lodge - 1/2 mile dirt oval (c.1927)
    located at the Tri-County Fairgrounds / the fair started in 1912

Deer Lodge Speedway - Deer Lodge / (aka: Sunset Speedway)
    1/2 mile dirt oval (c.1983 - 1985) (1987 - 1988)

Duck Creek Speedway - Fort Peck - 1/4 mile dirt oval (1974 - c.1977)

Electric City Speedway - Great Falls (Black Eagle) / (aka: Great Falls Speedway)
    3/10 mile dirt oval (1953 - present) / (aka: Electric City Raceway)

Farwest Speedway - Libby - 1/4 mile dirt oval (c.1977)

Flying Oval - Billings - 1/4 mile paved oval (1960's)

334

Forsyth Fairgrounds - Forsyth / located at the Rosebud-Treasure Co. Fairgrounds
4/10 mile dirt oval (1992 - present) / run only during the fair with a
class of cars called Bump & Run (similar to a Demo Derby)

Garden City Speedway - see: Miller Creek Race Track

Glendive Fairgrounds - see: Hustlers Dragway

Golden Rods Raceway - Billings - 1/4 mile paved dragstrip (c.1965)

Great Falls - dirt oval (1960's) / not at the fairgrounds

Great Falls Dragway - Great Falls - 1/4 mile paved dragstrip (c.1970)

Great Falls Fairgrounds - Great Falls / at the Northwest Montana Fairgrounds
1/2 mile dirt oval (7/29/17) (1934 - c.1937) (c.6/22/52 - c.1962)
NOTE: Reportedly there was no racing in Montana in 1932 or 1933.

Great Falls Speedway - see: Electric City Speedway

Harve Fairgrounds - Harve / located at the Hill County Fairgrounds
1/2 mile dirt oval (c.1960) / (aka: Hill County Speedway)

Helena - 1/4 mile dirt oval (1960's)

Helena Fairgrounds - see: Montana State Fairgrounds

Hill County Speedway - see: Harve Fairgrounds

Hub of the Valley Speedway - Bozeman - 1/4 mile dirt oval (1967 - present)

Hustlers Dragway - Glendive - 1/4 mile paved dragstrip (c.1970 - c.1982)
dirt oval (1953) / located at the Dawson County Fairgrounds

Kalispell - dirt oval (c.1953)

Kalispell - also see: Big Sky, LaSalle, Raceway Park

King Dam Dragway - see: Lewistown Raceway

Electric City Speedway in the early 1960's. - Len Ashburn photo.

LaSalle Speedway - Kalispell - 1/4 mile paved oval (1960's) / next to the airport

Lewistown Raceway - Lewistown - 1/4 mile paved dragstrip (c.1964 - present)
(aka: King Dam Dragway)

Livingston Fairgrounds - Livingston / located at the Park County Fairgrounds
1/4 mile dirt oval (c.1953 - c.1955)

Lost Creek Raceway - Anaconda - 1/8 mile paved dragstrip (5/10/87 - present)

Magic City Speedway - Billings - 1/4 mile dirt oval (c.1974 - present)
(aka: Belaro Speedway) / (aka: Yellowstone Speedway)

Miles City Fairgrounds - Miles City / located at the Eastern Montana Fairgrounds
1/2 mile dirt oval (7/04/37) (c.6/18/52 - c.1953) (1957)

Miller Creek Race Track - Missoula / (aka: Garden City Speedway)
1/4 mile dirt oval (1967 - 1977) / site is now a housing development

Mining City Speedway - Missoula / (aka: Butana Speedway)
1/4 mile dirt oval (1952 - 1981)

Mission Valley Speedway - Polson - 1/4 mile paved oval (1971-1980) (1983-present)

Missoula - dirt oval (1970) / only year the track ran

Missoula Fairgrounds - Missoula - 1.0 mile dirt oval (c.1916 - c.1924)

Missoula - also see: Miller Creek, Mining City

Montana State Fairgrounds - Helena - 1.0 mile dirt oval (9/21/15 - 1924)

Plentywood Fairgrounds - Plentywood / located at the Sheridan Co. Fairgrounds
1/4 mile dirt oval (c.1953 - c.1954)

Raceway Park - Kalispell - 1/4 mile paved oval (5/08/91 - present)
located north of town on US Highway 93

*The Old Time Racers Association visited the new Raceway Park in Kalispell,
Montana on June 29, 1991. - Robert G. Hunter photo.*

Scobey Raceway - Scobey - 1/4 mile dirt oval (c.1977)

Sidney - 1/2 mile dirt oval (7/04/37) (7/05/37) (1953) / maybe at a fairgrounds

Spike Naranche Memorial Dragway - Anaconda - 1/4 mile paved dragstrip (c.1970)

Sunset Speedway - see: Deer Lodge Speedway

Three Forks - 1/4 mile dirt oval (c.1967)

Thunder Road Speedway - see: Capital City Speedway

Tri-City Speedway - see: Big Sky Speedway

Tuscor Speedway - Trout Creek - 1/4 mile dirt oval (9/17/94 - present)

Yellowstone Speedway - see: Magic City Speedway

NEBRASKA

Ak-Sar-Ben Speedway - Omaha / located near Pacific St. & 60th St.
1.0 mile dirt oval (1910) (7/04/31) (1950's) / Nebraska spelled backwards
now the site of the Ak-Sar-Ben Race Track (horse track)

Albion Fairgrounds (Speedway) - see: Boone County Raceway

Alliance Speedway - Alliance - 1/4 mile paved oval (1958 - 1974) (1987 - present)

Arlington Speedway - Arlington - 1/3 mile dirt oval (c.1954 - 1959)

Auburn - 1/2 mile dirt oval (1950's)

Auburn - dirt oval (July, 1927)

Aurora Fairgrounds - Aurora - dirt oval (1937) / at Hamilton Co. Fairgrounds

Bartlett Fairgrounds - Bartlett / located at the Wheeler County Fairgrounds
3/10 mile dirt oval (early 1950's)

Bassett Fairgrounds - Bassett / located at the Rock County Fairgrounds
1/2 mile dirt oval (early 1950's)

Beatrice Fairgrounds - Beatrice / located at the old Gage County Fairgrounds
1/2 mile dirt oval (c.1924 - c.1941) (1946 - c.1948) / near the river

Beatrice Speedway - Beatrice - 1/2 mile dirt oval (c.6/24/51 - c.1951)
3/8 mile dirt oval (c.1952 - present) / at the new Gage County Fairgrounds

Benkelman Fairgrounds - Benkelman - 1/4 mile dirt oval (mid 1950's)
3/8 mile paved oval (c.1958 - mid 1960's) (1982 - 1985) (1988 - 1989)
3/8 mile dirt oval (1990 - c.1992) / located at the Dundy Co. Fairgrounds

Boone County Raceway - Albion / located at the Boone County Fairgrounds
1/2 mile dirt oval (c.1949 - c.1974) / (aka: Albion Speedway)
3/8 mile dirt oval (c.1975 - present)

Bristol - 1/4 mile dirt oval (1955)

Broken Bow Fairgrounds - Broken Bow / located at the Custer Co. Fairgrounds
1/2 mile dirt oval (c.1953 - c.1954)

Buffalo County Expo Center - Kearney - 1/10 mile indoor oval (1/18/91)

Butte - dirt oval (1938)

Capitol Beach Amusement Park - see: Lincoln Speedway

Cedar County Raceway - Hartington / located at the Cedar County Fairgrounds
1/2 mile dirt oval (1947) (1949) / (aka: Eastside Speedway)
1/4 mile dirt oval (9/06/38) (c.1954 - c.1957) (c.1974 - 1977) (1991 - present)
the site used to have a 1.0 mile horse track back in the late 1800's

Challengers Dragstrip - Ainsworth - 1/4 mile paved dragstrip (c.1965)

Clay Center Fairgrounds - Clay Center / located at the Clay County Fairgrounds
1/2 mile dirt oval (1941) (7/08/51 - c.1951)

Clearwater - 1/4 mile dirt oval (1971 - 1973)

Columbus Fairgrounds - Columbus / located at the Platte County Fairgrounds
1/2 mile dirt oval (9/01/50) (8/30/51)

Columbus - also see: Rebel Raceway, U.S. 30 Speedway

Cornhuskers Raceway Park - Omaha - 1/4 mile paved dragstrip (c.1969 - c.1972)

Cornhuskers Raceway Park - Waverly - 1/10 mile dirt oval (1982 - 1988)
1/8 mile dirt oval (1989 - present) / (aka: K & P Raceway) / NE of Lincoln
started out as Kart track / added Modified-midgets & Mini-sprints in 1986

Crofton - 1/4 mile dirt oval (1964 - 1967)

David City Fairgrounds - David City / located at the Butler County Fairgrounds
1/2 mile dirt oval (early 1950's) / maybe running again

David City Speedway - David City - 1/4 mile dirt oval (1980 - 1989)
site is now a rodeo arena

Dawson County Speedway - Lexington / located at the Dawson Co. Fairgrounds
1/2 mile dirt oval (c.1925 - c.1933) (early 1950's - c.1956)
3/8 mile dirt oval (c.1953 - present) / (aka: Platte Valley Speedway)

A look at the track and grandstands of Eagle Raceway. - Allan Brown photo.

338

Deshler Fairgrounds - Deshler / located at the Thayer County Fairgrounds
   1/2 mile dirt oval (8/20/35 - 8/23/35) (6/18/50 - c.1970)
   1/4 mile dirt oval (c.1984 - present)
   had ran T.Q. midgets in late 1980's, but now only runs Enduros

Eagle Raceway - Eagle - 1/3 mile dirt oval (1963 - present) / east of Lincoln
   home of annual "Eagle National's"

Eastside Speedway - see: Cedar County Raceway

Fairbury - 1/10 mile dirt oval (1940) / ran midgets

Fairbury Fairgrounds - Fairbury / located at the Jefferson County Fairgrounds
   1/2 mile dirt oval (c.1949 - c.1967) / (aka: Fairbury Speedway)
   3/8 mile dirt oval (c.1983 - 1987) (1989 - present)
   only ran Figure 8 racing from 1990 to 1993 during the annual fair

Franklin Fairgrounds - Franklin / located at the Franklin County Fairgrounds
   1/2 mile dirt oval (7/05/25) (early 1950's)

Franklin Speedway - Franklin - 3/8 mile dirt oval (c.1953 - 1977)

Gage County Speedway - see: Beatrice Speedway

Grand Island - dirt oval (1912 - 7/04/15) / ran motorcycles

Hartington Fairgrounds - see: Cedar County Raceway

Hastings Fairgrounds - Hastings / located at the old Adams County Fairgrounds
   1/2 mile dirt oval (c.1928 - 1931) (c.6/03/51 - c.1955)

Hastings Raceway - Hastings / located at the new Adams County Fairgrounds
   1/2 mile dirt oval (10/14/56 - c.1956) / A.J. Shepherd won the first race
   1/4 mile dirt oval (c.1956 - c.1975)

Hemingford Fairgrounds - Hemingford / located at the Box Butte Co. Fairgrounds
   1/2 mile dirt oval (1950 - late 1960's)

Holdrege Fairgrounds - Holdrege / located at the Phelps County Fairgrounds
   1/2 mile dirt oval (1924) (early 1930's) (1952)

Humboldt Fairgrounds - Humboldt / located at the Richardson Co. Fairgrounds
   dirt oval (early 1950's)

I-80 Speedway - Greenwood - 3/8 mile dirt oval (May, 1994 - present)
   located 1/4 mile north of the former Nebraska Int'l Raceway

Imperial Fairgrounds - Imperial - dirt oval (1953) / at the Chase Co. Fairgrounds

Irish Village Speedway - Omaha - dirt oval (8/12/39)

Jaycees Dragstrip - Grand Island - 1/4 mile paved dragstrip (c.1962 - c.1965)

K & P Raceway - see: Cornhuskers Raceway Park

Kam Raceway - Hastings - 1/8 mile dirt oval (1979 - present) / runs Mini-sprints

Kartwheels Speedway - Norfolk - 1/7 mile dirt oval (c.1991 - 1993)
   Kart track that ran Modified-midgets for three years, too small for them

Kearney - 1/2 mile dirt oval (1930's)

Kearney Raceway - Kearney - 1/2 mile dirt oval (late 1950's - c.1972)

Kearney Raceway Park - Kearney - 1/4 mile paved dragstrip (c.1964 - 1983)
  1/4 mile paved dragstrip (1984 - present) / (aka: Kearney Dragway)
  located on former airstrip runways / moved to a different runway in 1984

Key Amusement Raceway - Sargent - 3/8 mile dirt oval (c.1959- c.1960)(1977-1985)

Kimball - dirt oval (c.1953)

King's Speedway - see: Riviera Raceway

Landis Field - Lincoln - 1/5 mile dirt tri oval (5/24/40 - c.1941) (1946 - c.1949)
  (aka: Union Airport) / located 1 mile north of Havelock Ave. on US Hwy 77

League Park - Omaha - 1/4 mile dirt oval (c.8/18/35 - c.10/06/35) / ran midgets

Lexington Fairgrounds - see: Platte Valley Speedway

Lincoln Air Force Base Dragstrip - see: Shaundos Dragstrip

Lincoln County Raceway - North Platte / located at the Lincoln Co. Fairgrounds
  1/2 mile dirt oval (c.1951 - c.1957) / NASCAR sanctioned 1950's
  only NASCAR GN race ever in Nebraska was held here on 7/26/53
  3/8 mile dirt oval (c.1986 - present) / (aka: Lincoln County Speedway)
  (aka: North Platte Speedway)

Lincoln Fairgrounds - see: Nebraska State Fairgrounds

Lincoln Speedway - Lincoln / located at 14th & Cornhuskers Highway
  1/4 mile dirt oval (1963 - 1966) / (aka: Raceway Park)
  the grandstands were from the Capitol Beach Amusement Park track

Lincoln Speedway - Lincoln / located at Capitol Beach Amusement Park
  3/8 mile dirt oval (1953 - 1962) / (aka: Capitol Speedway)

Lincoln - Eagle, Landis Field, Micro, Midwest, Pershing, Rocket

McCook Fairgrounds - McCook / located at the Red Willow County Fairgrounds
  1/4 mile dirt oval (8/13/37) (1967 - 1989) (1992)

The cars are lined up at the Nebraska State Fairgrounds. - Bob Stolze photo.

Merriman Speedway - Merriman - 1/4 mile paved oval (1965 - c.1985)

Micro Raceway - Lincoln - 1/8 mile dirt oval (c.1954 - c.1961)

Mid-Continent Race Track - Doniphan / (aka: Mid-Continent Raceway)
3/8 mile dirt oval (6/24/72 - present) / located south of Grand Island

An aerial view of Mid-Continent Race Track. - Official track photo.

Midwest Speedway - Lincoln - 3/8 mile dirt oval (c.7/04/63 - 9/05/87)
located north of Superior St. on 27th St. / north of downtown
the property is now the site of a housing development

Nebraska City - 1/2 mile dirt oval (1910) / ran motorcycles in 1915

Nebraska City - see: I-29 Speedway - Iowa chapter

Nebraska Int'l Raceway - Greenwood - 1/5 mile dirt oval (5/03/86 - 1986)
1/4 mile dirt oval (1987) / located northeast of Lincoln

Nebraska Motorplex - Scribner / (aka: Scribner Raceway)
1/4 mile paved dragstrip (1980 - present)

Nebraska State Fairgrounds - see: State Fair Park Speedway

Neligh Fairgrounds - Neligh / located at the Antelope County Fairgrounds
1/2 mile dirt oval (1915) (1930) (1934 & 1935) (1937) (1957)

Neligh Speedway - Neligh - 3/8 mile dirt oval (c.1957 - 1973)
located at Riverside Park

Nelson Fairgrounds - Nelson / located at the Nuckolls County Fairgrounds
1/2 mile dirt oval (1936) (c.1950 - 1956) (c.1975) (1977)
1/8 mile dirt oval (1984 - 7/15/87) / new grandstands in 1977

Norfolk - dirt oval (1955)

Norfolk Fairgrounds - Norfolk / located at the old Madison County Fairgrounds
dirt oval (9/15/14 & 9/16/14)

Norfolk - also see: Kartwheel Speedway, Riviera Raceway

North Platte Fairgrounds (Speedway) - see: Lincoln County Speedway

North Platte Valley Raceway - see: Rebel Raceway

Offutt Air Force Base - Bellevue - 3.0 mile paved road course (1952 - 7/04/54)

Ogallala Fairgrounds - Ogallala / located at the Keith County Fairgrounds
    1/4 mile dirt oval (early 1950's)

Omaha Civic Auditorium - Omaha
    1/8 mile indoor concrete oval (12/31/57 - 1959) (10/07/89 - 11/11/89)

Omaha Dragway - Omaha - 1/4 mile paved dragstrip (c.1961 - c.1969)
    this was a different track then Cornhusker

Omaha Driving Park - Omaha - 1.0 mile dirt oval (8/23/04)

Omaha Speedway - Omaha - 1.25 mile wood oval (7/05/15) (7/15/16) (7/04/17)
    designed by Jack Prince / turns were banked 41 degrees
    (aka: Omaha Auto Derby) / the track broke up severely during the 1917 race

Omaha Stadium Speedway - Omaha - 1/3 mile wood oval (7/05/15) / motorcycles

Omaha - also see: Ak-Sar-Ben, Cornhuskers, Irish Village, League Park, Ralston,
    Riverside, Spick's Cabin, Sunset

Ord Fairgrounds - Ord / located at the Valley County Fairgrounds
    1/2 mile high banked dirt oval (1926 - c.1941) (1946 - c.1955)
    1/4 mile dirt oval (8/30/55) / site is now a shopping center
    the 1/2 mile track was a high banked oval similar to Belleville, Kansas

Oregon Trail Raceway - Gering / (aka: Oregon Trail Speedway) / near Scottsbluff
    1/4 mile paved oval (July, 1957 - 1987) (1992 - present)

Oshkosh - 1/2 mile dirt oval (1930's)

Oxford Fairgrounds - Oxford - 1/2 mile dirt oval (c.7/19/57 - c.10/07/57)

Pawnee City Fairgrounds - Pawnee City / located at the Pawnee Co. Fairgrounds
    1/2 mile dirt oval (early 1950's)

Pershing Auditorium - Lincoln - 1/12 mile indoor concrete oval (1989 & 1990)

Platte Valley Speedway - see: Dawson County Speedway

Raceway Park - Lincoln - see: Lincoln Speedway

Raceway Park - South Sioux City - 1/2 mile dirt oval (1962 - 1974)

Ralston Race Track - Omaha (Ralston) - 1/8 mile dirt oval (7/15/51 - 1956)

Rebel Raceway - Columbus - 1/4 mile dirt oval (1961 - 1973)
    (aka: Skylark Speedway) / (aka: North Platte Valley Raceway)

Riverside Speedway - Omaha - 1/4 mile dirt oval (c.9/08/52 - c.1956) south of town

Riviera Raceway - Norfolk - 3/10 mile dirt oval (March, 1963 - present)
    (aka: King's Speedway)

Rocket Speedway - Lincoln - 1/4 mile dirt oval (c.8/25/57 - c.1957)

Scottsbluff - 1/2 mile dirt oval (c.1950 - c.1953) / located near the old airport

Scottsbluff Dragway - Scottsbluff - 1/4 mile paved dragstrip (c.1963 - c.1970)

342   *Nebraska*

Scribner Raceway - see: Nebraska Motorplex

Shaundos Dragstrip - Lincoln - 1/4 mile paved dragstrip (c.1963 - c.1965)
  (aka: Lincoln Air Force Base Dragstrip)

Sidney Fairgrounds - Sidney / located at the Cheyenne County Fairgrounds
  dirt oval (c.1953 - c.1954) / (aka: Sidney Speedway)

Skylark Speedway - see: Rebel Raceway

Speed Bowl - Red Cloud - 3/8 mile dirt oval (1972 - 1979) (c.1988 - c.1992)

The Speed Bowl in Red Cloud, Nebraska. - Official track photo.

Spick's Cabin Camp - Omaha - dirt oval (5/24/36 - c.1936)

Stanton Fairgrounds - Stanton / located at the Stanton County Fairgrounds
  1/2 mile dirt oval (c.7/04/49 - c.1951) / (aka: Fireman's Celebration)

Stapleton Fairgrounds - Stapleton / located at the Logan County Fairgrounds
  1/4 mile dirt oval (early 1950's)

State Fair Park Speedway - Lincoln / at the Nebraska State Fairgrounds
  1/2 mile dirt oval (9/10/15 - 9/01/40) (7/04/46 - 9/01/58)
  1/4 mile dirt oval (c.5/26/39 - 1939) (c.7/11/41 - 8/31/41)
  5/8 mile dirt oval (9/06/59 - 9/11/77) / was a horse track from 1978 to 1994
  Doug Wolfgang won the last race on the 5/8 mile track
  3/8 mile dirt oval (8/14/94 - present)

Stuart Community Track - Stuart / located at the Stuart Community Park in town
  1/5 mile dirt oval (1953 - 1986) (1988 - present)

Sunset Speedway - Omaha - 1/4 mile dirt oval (5/19/57 - 9/18/66)
  3/80 mile dirt oval (5/07/67 - present) / located northwest of town

Twin Arrows Speedway - Fort Calhoun - 1/8 mile dirt oval (1968 - 1984)

U.S. 30 Speedway - Columbus - 1/3 mile dirt oval (April, 1986 - present)

Walthill Fairgrounds - Walthill / located at the Thurston County Fairgrounds
  1/2 mile dirt oval (early 1950's)

The 5/8 mile track at the Nebraska State Fairgrounds. - Courtesy of I.M.C.A.

Wayne Fairgrounds - Wayne / located at the Wayne County Fairgrounds
    1/2 mile dirt oval (9/16/50)

Western States Speedway - Chadron - 1/2 mile dirt oval (c.1964 - c.1965)
    1/2 mile paved oval (early 1970's)

Ymada Speedway - David City - 1/12 mile dirt oval (c.1981 - 1988)

York Speedway - York - 1/2 mile dirt oval (c.1950 - c.1954)
    1/3 mile dirt oval (c.1972 - 1973) / at the York County Fairgrounds

NEVADA

Battle Mountain Raceway - Battle Mtn. - 1/4 mile dirt oval (May 1982 - present)

Black Springs - 1/5 mile dirt oval (1938) / ran midgets on a dog track
    parimutuel betting was allowed on the midget races

Bob Ruud Memorial Speedway - see: Pahrump Valley Speedway

Bob Van Norman Memorial Speedway - see: Las Vegas Int'l Speedway

Bristlecone Race Track - Ely - 1/4 mile dirt oval (1960's - 1971) (1982)

Caesar's Palace Grand Prix - Las Vegas / races in Caesar's Palace parking lot
    2.268 mile paved road course (1980 - 9/25/82) / ran Formula One
    1.125 mile paved modified oval (10/06/83 & 1984) / ran Indy Cars on oval

Craig Road Speedway - North Las Vegas - 1/4 mile paved oval (1966 - 12/05/82)

Douglas-Tahoe Airport - Minden - 4.3 mile paved road course (8/02/58)
    (aka: Gardnerville Airport)

Fallon Fairgrounds - Fallon / located at the Churchill County Fairgrounds
    1/8 mile dirt oval (1970)

Fernley Speedway Park - Fernley - 1/4 & 3/8 mile dirt ovals (July, 1984 - c.1986)

Gardnerville Airport - see: Douglas-Tahoe Airport

Hawthorne Centennial Speedway - Hawthorne / (aka: Hawthorne Speedway)
    1/4 mile dirt oval (c.1977 - present)

Las Vegas Park - Las Vegas / formerly the Las Vegas Jockey Club (horse track)
    1.0 mile dirt oval (11/14/54) (10/16/55) (11/29/59)
    ran AAA champ cars 1954 / only NASCAR GN race in Nevada ran in 1955
    USAC Late models 1959 / the site is now the Las Vegas Hilton

Las Vegas Speedway Park - North Las Vegas / (aka: Las Vegas Int'l Speedrome)
    1.6 mile paved road course (c.1959 - present) / north of Nellis Air Force Base
    1/4 mile paved dragstrip (c.1981 - present) / (aka: Las Vegas Int'l Speedway)
    3/8 mile paved oval (1985-present) / (aka: Bob Van Norman Mem. Speedway)

Las Vegas - also see: Caesar's Palace, Craig Road, Last Frontier, Silver Slipper,
    Speed Bowl, Stardust Int'l

Last Frontier Sportsdrome - Las Vegas / behind the Frontier Hotel (Casino)
    1/4 mile paved oval (8/31/47 - c.1958)

Lemmon Valley Speedway - see: Stead Air Force Base

Lovelock Speedway - Lovelock / located at the Lovelock Rodeo Grounds
    3/10 mile dirt oval (c.1973 - 1988) (1994 - present)

Mount Diablo Speedway - see: Summit Raceway

Nevada State Fairgrounds - Reno / also known as the Washoe County Fairgrounds
    1.0 mile dirt oval (1950 - c.1952) / (aka: Reno Rodeo Grounds)
    3/8 mile paved oval (c.1955 - c.1967) / (aka: Reno Raceway)
    1/8 mile dirt oval (1971 - 1984)

Outlaw Speedway - Carson City - 1/8 mile dirt oval (1991 - present)

Pahrump Valley Speedway - Pahrump - 1/4 mile dirt oval (1985 - present)
    (aka: Pahrump Speedway) / (aka: Bob Ruud Memorial Speedway)

Aerial view of Pahrump Valley Speedway from 1986. - Official track photo.

Rattlesnake Speedway - Fallon - 1/4 mile dirt oval (c.1974 - present)
    on top of a hill overlooking the town / (aka: Rattlesnake Raceway)

Reno - 1/2 mile dirt oval (1926)

Reno Fairgrounds - see: Nevada State Fairgrounds

Reno Hilton Grand Prix - Reno / races ran on the parking lot of the Reno Hilton
    1.3 mile paved parking lot road course (6/06/93)

Reno Livestock Events Center - Reno - 1/6 mile indoor dirt oval (3/12/88 - 1990)

Reno - paved road course (1952) / ran on downtown city streets (around a lake)

Reno Raceway - Reno - 1/4 mile dirt oval (1952 - 1954) / at the Reno Airport

Reno Raceway - see: Nevada State Fairgrounds

Reno Rodeo Grounds - see: Nevada State Fairgrounds

Reno Speedway - Reno (Lawton) - 1/5 mile dirt oval (7/03/37 - 7/05/37)

Rod Squad Raceway - Hawthorne - 1/4 mile paved dragstrip (c.1972)

Silver Slipper Speedway - Las Vegas - oval (1960's)

Silver State Raceway - Carson City / (aka: T-Car Speedway)
    1/3 mile paved oval (1964 - present) / (aka: Tahoe-Carson Speedway)
    had parimutuel betting in July, 1967 / the winner had a 35 to 1 odds
    1/6 mile dirt oval (1988) / (aka: Silver State Speedway)

Speed Bowl - Las Vegas - 1/5 mile paved oval (c.1950)

Stardust Int'l Raceway - Las Vegas - 3.0 mile paved road course (10/02/65 - 1969)
    1/4 mile paved dragstrip (1965 - 1969)

Stead Air Force Base - Reno-Stead / the site of the annual Reno Air Races
    5.33 mile paved road course (10/17/53 & 10/18/53) (6/01/63)
    1/4 mile paved dragstrip (1961 - 1965) / located 10 miles northwest of Reno
    1/3 mile dirt oval (1961 - 1965) / (aka: Lemmon Valley Speedway)
    (aka: Lemmon Valley Dragway)

Steamboat Springs - (location unknown) - oval (1930's) / maybe located near Reno

Summit Raceway - Elko - 1/4 mile dirt oval (1987 - present)
    (aka: Mount Diablo Speedway)

T-Car Speedway - see: Silver State Speedway

Tahoe-Carson Speedway - see: Silver State Speedway

Tonopah Speedway - Tonopah - 1/4 mile dirt oval (1983 - present)
    the grandstands are from Craig Road Speedway

Walker Lake Speedway - Hawthorne - 1/4 mile dirt oval (1974 - c.1975)
    this track was located eight miles south of Hawthorne

Winnemucca Fairgrounds - Winnemucca / located at the Tri-County Fairgrounds
    3/8 mile dirt oval (early 1950's - 1963)

346

Winnemucca Municipal Airstrip - Winnemucca
1/4 mile paved dragstrip (1992 - present)

Winnemucca Speedway - Winnemucca - 3/8 mile dirt oval (1981 - 1986)
the track was converted into a horse track in 1986

Yerrington - 1/4 mile dirt oval (1950's)

Yerrington Fairgrounds - Yerrington / located at the Lyons County Fairgrounds
1/10 mile dirt oval (1977) / only ran one year

NEW HAMPSHIRE

Amherst Speedway - Amherst - 1/5 mile paved oval (5/28/39 - c.6/30/40)

Bedford Speedway - Bedford - 1/5 mile dirt oval (5/21/39 - 1939)
probably Amherst Speedway / the towns are only a few miles apart

Belknap Recreation Area - Gilford (Laconia) / (aka: Lake Region Race Track)
1/4 mile paved oval (c.1949 - c.1956) / (aka: Gilford Bowl)
.875 mile paved road course (9/24/50 - c.1956) / the first turn was dirt

Brookline Super Speedway - Brookline - 1/4 mile paved oval (4/28/57 - c.1962)
paved road course (1960's)

Bryar Motorsports Park - Loudon - 1/4 mile paved dragstrip (1970's)
1.6 mile paved road course (c.1967 - 1989)
1/5 mile dirt oval (early 1960's) / later used as a motorcycle track
4/10 & 5/8 mile paved oval (1965 - 1988)
sold to Bob Bahre in 1989 / also see: New Hampshire Int'l Speedway

Canaan U.S.A. Speedway - Canaan / located at the Canaan Fairgrounds
1/4 mile dirt oval (1950's) (1981 - 1984) (1987 - present)
(aka: Mascoma Valley Speedway)

Canobi Lake - Salem - dirt oval (1910's or 1920's) / was at an amusement park

Cheshire Fairgrounds - see: Safford Park Fairgrounds

Claremont Speedway - Claremont - 1/5 mile dirt oval (October, 1947 - 1972)
1/3 mile paved oval (1973 - present)

Dover Speedway - Dover - 1/4 mile dirt oval (c.1934 - 1942) (1945)
1/4 mile paved oval (c.1946 - 1950) (1953 - c.1961) (c.1965)

Dover - also see: Granite State Park Speedway

Exeter Fairgrounds - Exeter - dirt oval (years unknown)
maybe located in Exeter, Maine at the Fairgrounds instead

Farmington Speedway - Farmington - dirt oval (1941) (late 1940's)

Franklin - 1/4 mile dirt oval (c.1946)

Franklin - 1/4 mile high banked paved oval (early 1960's)

Gilford Bowl - see: Belknap Recreation Area

Granite State Park Speedway - Dover / located 5 miles north of town on St Rt 16
    1.0 mile dirt oval (c.9/16/34 - c.6/16/35) (10/05/41 - 11/16/41)
    1/2 mile dirt oval (5/10/42 - mid-1942) (6/16/46 - c.9/07/48)
    located at a fairgrounds / (aka: Granite Trotting Park)

Hannahan Farm - West Swanzey - 1/2 mile dirt oval (1940) / ran only two events

Hi-Groove Speedway - Winchester - 1/8 mile dirt oval (c.1984 - present)
    (aka: Rattlesnake Mountain Speedway)

Hinsdale Airport Speedway - Hinsdale - steeple chase road course (1950)
    1/4 mile dirt oval (c.1951 - c.1953)

Hudson Speedway - Hudson - 1/4 mile paved oval (1946 - present)

Keene Fairgrounds - see: Safford Park

Lake Region Race Track - see: Belknap Recreation Area

Lee USA Speedway - Lee - 1/3 mile paved tri-oval (1965 - 1983)
    3/8 mile high banked paved oval (10/27/83 - present)
    (aka: Lee Raceway) / (aka: Lee County Raceway)
    Note: the track is actually in Strafford County / no Lee County in NH

Littleton - dirt oval (1965)

Log Cabin Speedway - Lancaster - 1/2 mile dirt oval (c.1949 - c.1955)

Manchester Motordrome - Londonderry / located south of Manchester
    1/4 mile paved oval (c.8/10/47 - c.1962) / later became a Go-Kart track

Mascoma Valley Speedway - see: Canaan U.S.A. Speedway

Monadnock Speedway - Winchester - 1/4 mile dirt oval (1971 - c.1974)
    1/4 mile paved oval (c.1975 - present) / (aka: Monadnock Motor Speedway)
    Bronson Speedway in Florida was patterned after this track

Monroe - 1/5 mile dirt oval (early 1950's)

Nashau - 1/2 mile dirt oval (1923)

New England Dragway - Epping - 1/4 mile paved dragstrip (1966 - present)

New Hampshire Int'l Speedway - Loudon / also see: Bryar Motorsports Park
    1.0 mile paved oval (7/14/90 - present) / new track built by Bob Bahre
    1.063 mile paved road course (1991 - present)
    1st NASCAR Winston Cup race on 7/11/93 / former site of Bryar Mtspt Park

Newmarket Speedway - Newmarket / formerly a horse track
    1/2 mile dirt oval (1927 - 5/03/42) (c.1952)

Nor-Way Pines Raceway - Wentworth (West Rumney)
    1/5 mile dirt oval (mid-1960's) / the track is located in a woods
    1/4 mile dirt oval (1971 - present)

Pittsfield Fairgrounds - Pittsfield - 1/2 mile dirt oval (1948)

Plymouth State Fairgrounds - Plymouth - 1/2 mile dirt oval (1947 - 1957)

Rattlesnake Mountain Speedway - see: Hi-Groove Speedway

Riverside Speedway - Groveton - 1/4 mile dirt oval (1964 - 1976)
    1/4 mile paved oval (1977 - present) / (aka: Riverside Int'l Speedway)

Rochester Fairgrounds - Rochester - dirt oval (c.1939)

Rockingham Speedway - Salem - 1.0 mile dirt oval (1912) (1915) (9/07/31- 6/26/32)
    1.25 mile dirt oval (7/04/25 - 7/11/25) / (aka: Rockingham Motor Speedway)
    1.25 mile wood oval (10/31/25 - 10/12/28) / turns were banked 38 degrees
    The first race on the board track scheduled for 10/17/25 was rained out.
    Wood track built by Jack Prince / grandstands burned down in the 1970's.
    72,000 fans watched Peter DePaolo win the first race on the board track.
    Last board track race was shortened by Fred Comer fatality on 11/12/28.
    The tracks were located at a horse track and is still a horse track

The board track at Rockingham Speedway in New Hampshire. The site is
currently a horse track called Rockingham Park. - Phil Harms collection.

Safford Park Fairgrounds - Keene / located at the Cheshire County Fairgrounds
    1/2 mile dirt oval (c.8/04/35 - 5/10/42) (5/19/46 - c.1961)
    1/3 mile dirt oval (6/10/54 - c.1961) / (aka: Cheshire Fairgrounds)
    1/5 mile dirt oval (8/04/94 - present) / Modified-Midgets on small track

Salem - see: Canobi Lake, Rockingham Speedway

Star Speedway - Epping - 1/4 mile paved oval (1966 - present)
    home of the "Star Classic" for supermodifieds

Sugar Hill Speedway - Weare - 1/8 mile dirt oval (1979 - 1993)
    1/5 mile dirt oval (1994 - present)

Ten Rod Speedway - Farmington - 1/8 mile dirt oval (7/22/85 - 1987)

White Mountain Motorsports Park - North Woodstock
    1/4 mile paved oval (5/29/93 - present)

Woodstock Speedway - Woodstock - 1/5 mile dirt oval (early 1950's)

NEW JERSEY

Acella Speedway - see: East Windsor Speedway

Airport Junction Speedway - see: Hightstown Speedway

Airport Speedway - Camden (Palmyra) - 1/4 mile dirt oval (c.1934 - c.1939)
    near the site of the U.S.A.'s very first drive-in movie theater

Alcyon Speedway - Pitman / located at the Gloucester County Fairgrounds
    1/2 mile dirt oval (1909) (1919 - 1925) (10/26/35 - 1942) (5/30/46 - 1960)
    (aka: Pitman Stadium) / the track was D-shaped similar to Daytona
    bought by Charles Nocco and then sold to developers for a housing complex,
    so as to eliminate the competition for his own Vineland Speedway

*A racer gets the green flag in time trials at Alcyon Speedway in Pitman, New
Jersey. - Jon H. Clifton collection.*

Amatol (board track) - see: Atlantic City Speedway - Hammonton

Arney Mount Speedway - Mount Holly / 5 miles east town in Springfield Township
    1/3 mile paved oval (4/24/55 - 1958) / (aka: Mount Holly Speedway)
    1/8 mile paved dragstrip (1957 & 1958)

Asbury Park High School - Asbury Park - 1/4 mile dirt oval (1934 & 1935)

Atco Raceway - Atco - 1/4 mile paved dragstrip (5/30/60 - present)
    located six miles from Atco Speedway on Jackson Road / (aka: Atco Dragway)
    Don Garlits turned first ever 200 mph run (201.34) here in 1964

Atco Speedway - Atco - 1/3 mile dirt oval (c.5/20/50 - 1954)
    3/8 mile paved oval (c.5/14/55 - c.1960) / (aka: White Horse Pike Raceway)
    located on the White Horse Pike behind the Chesilhurst Fire Department

Atlantic City Convention Hall - Atlantic City / (aka: Municipal Stadium)
    1/5 mile indoor concrete oval (9/09/39 - 1941) (1946 - 1981)
    site is where the annual Miss America pageant is held

The line up for a stock car race on the board track at Atlantic City Speedway on September 5, 1927. - Phil Harms collection.

Atlantic City Speedway - Hammonton - 1.5 mile wood oval (5/01/26 - 9/16/28)
    built by Jack Prince & Art Pillsbury / turns were banked 45 degrees
    first race was won by Harry Hartz at an average speed of 134.091 mph
    fastest of the board tracks / 147.727 mph set by Frank Lockhart in 1927
    Ralph DePalma won a couple of stock car races on 5/30/28 in a Mercedes
    the track was built on the old site of the Amatol Arsenal where TNT
    explosives were made for use by the U.S. Government during World War I
    site is now the site of Troop A of the New Jersey State Police

Atlantic City Speedway - Pleasantville - 1/2 mile dirt oval (9/03/50 - 1955)
    1/2 mile paved oval (1956 - 1979) / (aka: Powell Speedway) < first name
    1/8 mile paved dragstrip (1960's) / (aka: Pleasantville Speedway)
    the property was sold for casino parking, but is now a vacant lot
    1956 to 1963 promoter: George Stockinger > (Pleasantville Speedway)
    1964 to 1979 promoter: Ken Butler > (Atlantic City Speedway)

Augusta Fairgrounds - Augusta / located at the Sussex County Fairgrounds
    1/8 mile dirt oval (6/07/92 - 1992) / ran Micro-stocks

Bader Field - Atlantic City - dirt oval (scheduled for 7/30/38 but didn't run)

Bayonne Speedway - see: Veterans Stadium

Bridgeport Raceway - Bridgeport / the grandstands were from Langhorne, PA
    5/8 mile dirt oval (10/22/72 - present) / Kenny Brightbill first winner
    (aka: Statewide Speedway) / (aka: Bridgeport Fair Speedway)
    (aka: Bridgeport Speedway) / the track was originally proposed in 1967

Bridgeton Fairgrounds - Bridgeton / located at the Cumberland Co. Fairgrounds
    1/2 mile dirt oval (1925) (1930) (c.1934 - c.5/02/36)
    (aka: Garden State Fairgrounds)

Camden Convention Hall - Camden - 1/10 mile indoor wood oval (4/05/52)

Camden - also see: Airport, Delaware Township, Pennsauken Speedway

Cape May Court House - 1/2 mile beach oval (9/04/05 - 4/28/06)
    the races were held on the beach

Cape May Court House Fairgrounds - Cape May Court House
    1/2 mile dirt oval (1922) (7/06/40)

Capital City Speedway - Trenton / located at Princeton Ave. & Spruce St.
1/5 mile dirt oval (July, 1936 - 1936)

Central Jersey Speedway - Hightstown - see: Hightstown Speedway

Central Jersey Speedway - New Egypt - see: New Egypt Speedway

Clark Township Speedway - Westfield - 1/5 mile dirt oval (5/19/35 - c.9/08/35)

Coytesville - 1/4 mile dirt oval (years unknown) / 2 midget races / near Fort Lee
built as a dog track, but gambling was not approved / races unsuccessful

Delaware Township Speedway - Camden / township is now Cherry Hill Township
5/8 mile dirt oval (1937 - c.1937)

Dover Speedway - Dover / (aka: New Dover Speedway) / located on US 46
1/2 mile dirt oval (6/11/33 - 1935) (7/04/47 - 1952) (c.6/12/54 - 7/10/54)
the grandstands reportedly collapsed on two different occasions

They're off in the feature at Dover Speedway on July 20, 1947. - Frank Smith photo (Len Ashburn collection).

East Windsor Speedway - Hightstown / on the same site as Hightstown Speedway
1/2 mile dirt oval (6/11/65 - present) / (aka: Acella Speedway)
(aka: East Windsor Fairgrounds) / the new track was built by Don Jones

Elkwood Park - see: Monmouth Fairgrounds

Flemington - 1/8 mile paved dragstrip (1950's) / not at Flemington Speedway

Flemington Speedway - Flemington / Ira Vail won first auto race in 1915
1/2 mile dirt oval (1910) (8/13/15 - 9/01/41) (6/16/46 - 1966)
5/8 mile dirt oval (square) (5/06/67 - 1990) / ran motorcycles in 1910
5/8 mile paved oval (1991 - present) (aka: Flemington Fair Speedway)
Chet Gardner (9/03/38) & Dick Tobias (6/23/78) were fatally injured here
the fairgrounds was originally called the Hunterdon County Fairgrounds
the track owner, Paul Kuhl, was the 1991 RPM Promoter of the Year

Fort Dix Speedway - see: New Egypt Speedway

Freehold - 1/2 mile dirt oval (c.8/06/27 - c.1940) / was a horse track

Garden State Fairgrounds - see: Bridgeton Fairgrounds

Garfield Stadium - see: Long Branch Speedway

Guttenberg - 1.0 mile dirt oval (September, 1911)

Hammonton - see: Atlantic City Speedway - Hammonton

Harmony Raceway - Harmony - 5/8 mile dirt D-shaped oval (6/07/63 - 1972)
1/4 mile paved dragstrip (1960's)

Hightstown Speedway - Hightstown - 1/5 mile dirt oval (1951 - 10/17/51)
1/5 mile paved oval (5/03/52 - 1960) / (aka: Central Jersey Speedway)
(aka: Airport Junction Speedway) / Wally Dallenbach Sr. started here 1952
the track site is on the same property as current East Windsor Speedway
the site was the former Hightstown Airport / torn down in 1965

Hinchliffe Stadium - Paterson - 1/5 mile cinder oval (c.8/10/34 - c.6/14/35)
1/5 mile paved oval (1939 - 1942) (1945 - c.11/04/51)
the track was reopened and paved when the Nutley Velodrome closed
the track surface was painted by Neil Cole in a checkered board design so
when the races were televised it gave a better sensation of speed

Neil Cole had the Hinchliffe Stadium painted checkerboard so when the races were televised in the early 1950's the black and white surface would give a better sensation of speed for the TV viewers. - Bruce Craig collection.

Ho-Ho-Kus Speedway - Ho-Ho-Kus / (aka: Bergen County Park)
1/2 mile dirt oval (c.1910 - 7/04/38) / a famous big car track
Chris Economaki attended his first auto race here

Hope Chapel Oval - Lakewood - dirt oval (4/16/50 - 10/18/51)
(aka: Hope Road Oval) / located in a gravel pit on County Line Road

Irvington - see: Olympic Park Stadium, Tri-City Stadium

Island Dragway - Great Meadows - 1/4 mile paved dragstrip (July, 1960 - present)

Jersey City Speedway - see: Roosevelt Stadium

Lakewood - see: Hope Chapel Oval

Launch Haven Boardwalk - Somers Point - wood track (race schedule for 6/11/10)
the race was to be held on the boardwalk, but was never held

Lincoln Field - Trenton - 1/4 mile dirt oval (1938 - c.9/17/39)
located at a picnic grounds on Klockner Road

Linden Airport - Linden - 2.2 mile paved road course (8/21/49 - c.1950)
2.0 mile paved road course (c.1951 - 6/13/54) / races held on runways
the last race was a NASCAR Grand Nat'l race won by Al Keller in a Jaguar
(the only NASCAR Grand Nat'l race ever won in a foreign car)
1/4 mile paved dragstrip (1954 - c.1955)

Lodi Municipal Stadium - Lodi - 1/5 mile paved oval (c.7/13/47 - c.1950)

Long Branch Speedway - Long Branch / (aka: Long Branch Memorial Stadium)
1/5 mile cinder oval (6/25/37 - 1939) / formerly a dog racing track
Ronney Householder won the first race (he won the night before in Detroit
and drove all night to get to New Jersey (pre-expressway days)
1/5 mile paved oval (6/25/49 - c.1951) / (aka: Garfield Stadium)
the property is now the site of retail businesses

Long Branch - also see: Monmouth Fairgrounds

Longport Speedway - Longport - 2.5 mile beach track (9/04/05)
the track went from 24th St. in Longport to Fredericksburg Ave. in Ventnor

Madison Township Raceway Park - see: Old Bridge Township Raceway Park

Manahawkin Speedway - Manahawkin - 1/2 mile dirt oval (c.4/23/50 - 1951)
the track was located in a gravel pit

Manahawkin Speedway - Manahawkin / same property as above Manahawkin
1/2 mile paved oval (4/20/52 - 1954) / owned by John Earlin
the track was located about 800 yards from the other track
organized boxing matches were held in the infield in 1952

This beautiful 1956 Chevy is called "Engine-uity". - Allan E. Brown collection.

Manville Airport - Manville - 1/4 mile paved dragstrip (c.1951 - c.1964)

Maple Grove Park - Trenton - dirt oval (1935)

McAfee Fairgrounds - McAfee - 1/2 mile dirt oval (5/18/52 - 1953)
    (aka: McAfee Speedway)

Meadowlands Grand Prix - East Rutherford / at the Meadowlands Sports Complex
    1.8 mile paved road course (7/01/84) / races on parking lot
    1.6 mile paved road course (1985 - 1987) / ran Indy Cars
    1.217 mile paved road course (1988 - 1991)

Merchantville - 1/2 mile dirt oval (11/11/34 - 1935)
    located on West Maple Ave. / five miles east of the Camden Bridge

Miller Stadium - West New York / (aka: West New York Stadium)
    1/5 mile dirt oval (8/08/34 - c.1940) / ran auto races in 1934 & 1935
    (aka: Municipal Stadium) / ran motorcycles races until 1940

Monmouth County Airport - Belmar - 1/2 mile dirt oval (1948 - 1950)

Monmouth Fairgrounds - Long Branch / near Oceanport / (aka: Elkwood Park)
    1.0 mile dirt oval (9/01/02) (8/20/04) (8/19/05) (7/04/08) (9/06/17)
    near Red Bank / the site is now the Monmouth Park Race Track (horse track)

Morristown Speedway - Morristown (Morris Plains) / (aka: Soranno Park)
    1/2 mile dirt oval (6/30/50 - 10/25/55) / built by Joe Soranno
    now the site of the Mennen Ice Skating Arena / (aka: Morristown Raceway)
    ran four NASCAR GN races (8/24/51) (7/10/53) (7/03/54) (7/15/55)

Morristown Airport - Morristown - small oval (1945 - 1948) / ran T.Q. midgets

Mount Holly Fairgrounds - Mount Holly / at the Burlington County Fairgrounds
    1/2 mile dirt oval (c.1922 - 7/04/27) (5/19/37 - 6/23/40)
    the site later became a shopping center / (aka: Mount Holly Speedway)
    it had the only double-deck grandstands at a fairgrounds on the East Coast

Mount Holly Speedway - see: Arnies Mount Speedway

Municipal Stadium - see: Atlantic City Convention Hall

New Egypt Speedway - New Egypt - 1/5 mile dirt/sand oval (1954)
    1/5 mile paved oval (c.7/18/54 - 1987) (1990) / (aka: Central Jersey Speedway)
    (aka: Fort Dix Speedway) / the track was called Fort Dix from 1960 to 1968
    (aka: Ocean County Speedway) / runs Go-Karts on 1/4 mile paved road course

New Jersey State Fairgrounds - see: Trenton Int'l Speedway

New Market Speedway - Dunellen (New Market)
    1/2 mile dirt oval (7/01/28 - 10/05/34) / maybe last race was 10/12/34
    located on Stelton Road between the Hadley Airport & Dunellen
    now the site of Somerset County Bus Garage

New Woodbridge Speedway (board track) - see: Woodbridge Speedway

Newark Fairgrounds - see: Weequahic Park

Newark - also see: Olympic Park, Ruppert, Tri-City, Veteran Stadium

Newfoundland Speedway - Newfoundland / ran motorcycles only
1/3 mile dirt oval (1949 - 1951)

Nutley Velodrome - Nutley / opened 6/04/33 for bicycle racing
1/7 mile high banked wood oval (4/03/38 - 8/26/39) / built by Joe Miele
Paul Russo was the first auto race winner / turns were banked 45 degrees
three drivers were killed in 60 race dates / torn down in March of 1942

The view of the grandstands from the pit area at the Nutley Velodrome in 1939.
Phil Harms collection.

Ocean County Speedway - see: New Egypt Speedway

Old Bridge Stadium - Old Bridge - 1/2 mile paved oval (8/21/53 - 8/25/68)
1/5 mile paved oval (c.1959 - 1968) / ran six NASCAR GN races (8/17/56)
(8/16/57) (4/27/58) (7/19/63) (7/10/64) and (7/09/65)
1/8 mile paved dragstrip (1960's) / not to be confused with other dragstrip
the site is now Whispering Pines housing development

Old Bridge Township Raceway Park - Englishtown / (aka: Raceway Park)
1/4 mile paved dragstrip (7/04/64 - present) / home of "SpringNationals"
(aka: Madison Township Raceway Park)

Olympic Park Stadium - Irvington (Newark) / built in 1909 as a harness track
1/2 mile dirt oval (1909 - c.1911) (7/24/15 - 1917)
at the Becker Grove Amusement Park / ran motorcycle races 1909 - 1911
the race on 7/24/15 was an IMCA race under the lights won by Art Klein
1/5 mile cinder oval (6/10/34 - 10/07/34) (5/04/36 - 6/29/36) / cycles 1935
the cinder surface had ground up Coca Cola bottles mixed with the cinders
the 6/10/34 race was the first ever race for midgets on the East Coast

Paterson - 1/4 mile paved dragstrip (1950's)

Paterson Velodrome - Paterson - 1/6 mile wood oval (July, 1908) / motorcycles

Paterson - also see: Hinchliffe Stadium

Pennsauken Speedway - Camden (Pennsauken) / located in a gravel pit
1/2 mile dirt oval (9/03/34 - 10/21/34) / was not Airport Speedway

Pine Brook Stadium - Pine Brook - 1/10 mile paved oval (7/06/62 - 1989)
Micro-Stock racing started here in 1982

356

Pitman Stadium - see: Alcyon Speedway

Pleasantville Speedway - see: Atlantic City Speedway

Powell Speedway - see: Atlantic City Speedway

Raceway Park - see: Old Bridge Township Raceway Park

Red Bank - see: Monmouth Fairgrounds

Roosevelt Stadium - Jersey City - 1/4 mile shale oval (7/03/51 - 8/09/51)
    1/4 mile paved oval (10/07/51 - 9/17/55) / (aka: Jersey City Speedway)
    located at a baseball diamond / the stadium was torn down in 1984

Ruppert Stadium - Newark - 1/5 mile paved oval (5/06/50 - 1952)
    races scheduled for 4/23/50 & 4/30/50 were both rained out
    located at 258 Wilson Ave. / the site is now the Ruppert School Stadium

Singac - see: Wayne

Soranno Park - see: Morristown Speedway

South Orange Bowl - South Orange - wood oval (1910's) / ran motorcycles

Statewide Speedway - see: Bridgeport Raceway

Strato Rods Dragway - Wrightstown - 1/4 mile paved dragstrip (c.1966 - c.1982)
    located on runways at McGuire Air Force Base

Sussex County Fairgrounds - see: Augusta Fairgrounds

Teaneck Armory - Teaneck
    1/10 mile indoor concrete oval (1/12/52 - 2/13/54) (2/01/58 - c.1962)

Toms River Speedway - Tom River - 1/4 mile dirt oval (March, 1950 - Oct., 1950)
    the track was located on Route 37

Trenton - 1/4 mile dirt oval (1950 & 1951) / built by D. Natale Bros / SE of town

Buzzie Reutimann from Tampa, Florida is one of the most popular drivers in the Northeast on the modified circuits. - John Grady photo.

The 1/2 mile track at the Trenton Fairgrounds. - Jon H. Clifton collection.

Trenton Speedway - Trenton / located at the Trenton Inter-State Fairgrounds
   1/2 mile dirt oval (9/24/1900) (c.1912 - 10/12/41) (1945)
   the fairgrounds became the New Jersey State Fairgrounds in 1936
   1.0 mile dirt oval (5/05/46 - 9/30/56) / (aka: Trenton Int'l Speedway)
   1.0 mile paved oval (6/23/57 - 1968) / a promoter was Sam Nunis
   ran USAC Indy Cars, NASCAR GN, Modifieds, Sprints & Midgets
   Jimmy Reece (9/28/58) & Dick Linder were fatally injured here
   Fireball Roberts won 500 mile NASCAR GN race 5/30/58
   1.5 mile peanut shaped paved oval (7/19/69 - 1980) / fairgrounds built 1888
   torn down in 1983 / the site is now an industrial park and housing

Trenton - also see: Capital City, Lincoln Field, Maple Grove.

Tri-City Stadium - Irvington (Newark) / opened on 7/26/33 for motorcycle racing
   1/5 mile cinder oval (5/04/38 - 1939) / on Mill Road & Union Avenue
   1/5 mile paved oval (5/29/40 - 10/05/41) / maybe ran in 1942 as well
   torn down during World War II / a bowling alley was built on site in 1958

Troy Hills Speedway - Parsippany (Troy Hills)
   1/3 mile oiled dirt oval (c.1931 - c.1934)

Tuckerton Speedway - Tuckerton - dirt oval (5/30/50 - 10/21/51)
   located about eight miles from Manahawkin Speedway

Union Speedway - Union / located off County Road 29 on Springfield Road
   1/2 mile dirt oval (5/10/36 - 9/22/40) / ran a motorcycle race on 5/10/36
   first auto race 5/15/36 / site of an Army Camp during World War II
   1/5 mile paved oval (5/03/42 - 7/28/42) / Pappy Hough won the last race
   torn down in 1946 / now the site of an industrial park

Veteran Stadium - Bayonne / (aka: Bayonne Speedway) / near Newark Bay
   1/5 mile paved oval (5/16/49 - 1950) / located on West 25th Street

Vineland Fairgrounds - Vineland - 1/2 mile dirt oval (1930's)

Vineland Speedway - Vineland - 1/2 mile dirt oval (4/03/55 - 10/20/57)
   built by Charles Nocco / now the site of the Cumberland County College
   1/10 mile dirt oval (1956) Pappy Hough won micro-midget race on 1/10 mile
   1/2 mile paved oval (4/12/58 - 7/30/65) / located on Route 57
   1.5 mile paved road course (10/26/58 - c.1965)
   Roger Penske & Mark Donohue used to drive sports cars on the road course
   1/4 mile paved dragstrip (8/02/58 - 1967)

Wall Stadium - Belmar - 1/3 mile paved oval (5/26/50 - present)
patterned after Lonesdale Sports Arena (RI) or a bicycle track
Frankie Schneider won the first feature race in 1950
the Jersey Sharks (a pro football team) played in the infield 1957 & 1958
   ran the first ever NASCAR midget race here on 6/27/53
ran a NASCAR GN race here on 7/26/58 which was won by Jim Reed

Waverly Fairgrounds (Park) - see: Weequahic Park

Wayne (Singac) - 1/2 mile dirt oval (1920's) / between Little Falls & Fairfield
1/5 mile dirt oval (1931) / ran motorcycles under lights on small track

Weequahic Park - Newark - 1/2 mile dirt oval (9/03/06) (11/06/06) (early 1920's)
at the Essex County Fairgrounds / (aka: Newark Fairgrounds)
also referred to as the Waverly Fairgrounds or Waverly Park

West New York Stadium - see: Miller Stadium

White Horse Pike Speedway - see: Atco Speedway

Wildwood - beach oval (1910 - 1911) (8/27/26) / races around barrels on beach

Woodbine - 1/4 mile paved dragstrip (c.1951 - c.1955) / first dragstrip in NJ

Woodbridge Speedway - Woodbridge / (aka: New Woodbridge Speedway)
1/2 mile dirt oval (7/04/26) (8/28/32 - 1941) / built by Wilbert Baine
1/2 mile wood oval (7/21/28 - 10/18/31) / turns were banked 38 degrees
   the first race on wood track scheduled for 7/04/28 was rained out
three drivers, Johnny Rohrer (10/27/29), Bob Robinson (7/27/30), and
   Bernie Katz (5/10/31) were fatally injured on the board track
Bert Karnatz won the very last ever major board track race on 10/18/31
wood track ran AAA races, but never a AAA National Championship race
Fred Farmer was fatally injured on the dirt track on 8/28/32
the site is now the Woodbridge High School Stadium / uses old grandstands

Woodstown - dirt oval (8/04/37)

*Big cars tour the banks of Woodbridge Speedway. A race on October 18, 1931
was the last race on the famous board tracks. - Bruce Craig collection.*

NEW MEXICO

66 Drive-Inn - Albuquerque - 1/8 mile dirt oval (late 1950's) / ran 1/2 midgets

Albuquerque Coliseum - Albuquerque - 1/10 mile concrete indoor oval (1989)

Albuquerque National Dragway - Albuquerque / (aka: Road Runner Dragway)
1/4 mile paved dragstrip (1960 - present) / south of town off Broadway
(aka: New Mexico Motorsports Dragway) / (aka: Albuquerque Dragway)

Albuquerque Raceway - see: Duke City Raceway

Albuquerque - also see: 66 Drive-Inn, All American, Cormit, Coronada,
First American, Hell's Half Acre, Rio Grande Sports Bowl

All American Speedway - Albuquerque - 1.0 mile dirt oval (8/29/26) (1946)

Aztec Speedway - Aztec - 1/2 mile dirt oval (c.1949 - 1958)
(aka: Legion Speedway)

Aztec Speedway - Aztec - 3/8 mile dirt oval (c.1959 - present)
1/5 mile dirt oval (1989 - present) / different site than as old track

Bottomless Lakes State Park - Roswell - 8.0 mile paved road course (1964- c.1967)

Cannon Speedway Park - Clovis - 1/3 mile dirt oval (1990 - 1993)
located near Cannon Air Force Base

Carlsbad Dragway - Carlsbad - 1/8 mile paved dragstrip (1980 - present)
located south of town on Old Cavern Road

Carlsbad - paved road course (late 1950's)

Carlsbad Speedway - Carlsbad - 1/2 mile dirt oval (c.4/04/48 - c.1952)

Carlsbad Speedway - Carlsbad - 1/4 mile dirt oval (1984 - present)
located south of town / across the street from Carlsbad Dragway

Carlsbad - also see: Cavern City Dragway, Jaycees Speedway

Cattle Capitol Speedway - see: Clovis Speedway

Cavern City Dragway - Carlsbad - 1/8 mile paved dragstrip (c.1963)

Chaparral Raceway - see: Southern New Mexico Speedway

Clovis Speedway - Clovis / located at the Curry County Fairgrounds
1/2 mile dirt oval (c.4/16/50 - 1956) / (aka: Cattle Capitol Speedway)

Cormit Speedway - Albuquerque - 1/4 mile high banked dirt oval (1/26/47 - c.1951)
(aka: Sandia Stadium) / located near Speedway Park on Wyoming St.

Coronada Speedway - Albuquerque - 1/4 mile dirt oval (1970's) / near the airport

Deming Speedway - Deming - 1/8 mile dirt oval (1980's)

Drag Club - Alamogordo - 1/4 mile paved dragstrip (1976 - present)
located near the Holloman Air Force Base

360

Duke City Raceway - Albuquerque / built by A.L. Smith
    1/4 & 1/2 mile dirt ovals (4/13/68 - 1984) / (aka: Valley Raceway)
    7/16 mile dirt oval (1985 - present) / (aka: Albuquerque Raceway)
    (aka: Seven Flags Raceway) / south of town at Broadway & Murray Road

Espanola Raceway - Espanola - dirt oval (early 1970's)

First American Grounds - Albuquerque - 1/5 mile dirt oval (8/27/39 - c.1939)

Fort Sumner - 2.7 mile paved road course (c.1957 - 1960's) / an old Air Force Base

Gallup - dirt oval (1938)

Gallup - dirt oval (c.1947 - c.1949)

Gallup Raceway Park - Gallup - 3/8 mile dirt oval (c.1986 - present)
    located northeast of town

Hell's Half Acre Speedway - Albuquerque - 5/8 mile dirt oval (5/30/39 - c.1939)

Hobbs - 1/2 mile dirt oval (1956) / only ran one race

Hobbs Dragway - Hobbs - 1/4 mile paved dragstrip (1956 - present)
    located at the old Hobbs Air Force Base / northwest of town

Hobbs - also see: Lea County Speedway, Roadrunner Speedway

Jaycees Dragstrip - Raton - 1/4 mile paved dragstrip (c.1963 - c.1965)
    (aka: Raton Dragstrip)

Jaycees Speedway - Carlsbad - 1/8 mile dirt oval (c.11/18/57 - c.1958)

Las Cruces - 1/5 mile dirt oval (1939) / only ran one race (midgets)

Las Cruces Speedway - see: Southern New Mexico Speedway

The car in the middle is driven by Casey Luna, who currently is the Lieutenant Governor of New Mexico and owns one of the fastest sprint cars in the land. Casey Luna collection.

Las Cruces - also see: New Mexico State University, Porter & Sims Drag-O-Way

Lea County Speedbowl - Hobbs - 1/4 mile dirt oval (1965 - 1982)

Legion Speedway - see: Aztec Speedway

Lion's Speedway - see: Roswell Speedway

Midway Speedway - see: Portales Speedway

Navajo Speedway - Elkins - 1/5 mile dirt oval (8/21/39)

New Mexico Motorsports Dragway - see: Albuquerque National Dragway

New Mexico State Fairgrounds - Albuquerque - 1.0 mile dirt oval (1989 & 1990)
    south of I-40 on Louisiana Blvd / ran AMA National motorcycles events only

New Mexico State University Dragstrip - Las Cruces / on the NM State campus
    1/4 mile paved dragstrip (c.1977)

Pecos Valley Raceway - Roswell / (aka: Roswell Super Speedway)
    3/8 mile dirt oval (c.1984 - 1987) (1991 - present)

Pecos Valley Raceway - see: Rosell Dragway

Porter & Sims Drag-A-Way - Las Cruces - 1/4 mile paved dragstrip (1970)
    formerly the municipal airport

Portales Speedway - Portales - 1/4 mile dirt oval (1964 - 1966)
    (aka: Midway Speedway) / (aka: Roosevelt County Speedway)
    now site of an anthropology museum / probably the Roosevelt Co. Museum

Raton Dragstrip - see: Jaycees Dragstrip

Rio Grande Sports Bowl - Albuquerque - 1/4 mile dirt oval (1947 - 1949)
    near junction I-25 & I-40 / Buddy Taylor started his driver career here

Roadrunner Dragway - see: Albuquerque National Dragway

Roadrunner Speedway - Hobbs - 1/4 mile dirt oval (1984 - present)

Roosevelt County Speedway - see: Portales Speedway

Roswell Airport - Roswell - paved road course (1960's)

Roswell Dragway - Roswell - 1/4 mile paved dragstrip (c.1970 - present)
    located at a former airport

Roswell Speedway - Roswell - 1/2 mile dirt oval (c.3/26/48 - 1959)
    (aka: Lion's Speedway) / Bobby Unser started his racing career here 1949

Roswell Super Speedway - see: Pecos Valley Raceway

Sandia Stadium - see: Cormit Speedway

Santa Fe Speedway - Santa Fe - 1/4 mile dirt oval (years unknown)

Sermota Raceway - see: Southern New Mexico Speedway

Coming down for a start of a roadster race at Gallup, New Mexico in 1949. Bob Roe collection (courtesy of Don Radbruch).

Southern New Mexico Speedway - Las Cruces (Mesilla)
   5/16 mile dirt oval (1967 - present) / (aka: Mesilla Valley Raceway)
   (aka: Las Cruces Speedway) / at the Southern N.M. State Fairgrounds
   also known as the Dona Ana County Fairgrounds / (aka: Sertoma Raceway)
   (aka: The Speedway, Inc.) / (aka: Chapparral Raceway)

Speedway Park - Albuquerque / located two miles south of I-40 on Eubanks Blvd.
   3/8 mile dirt oval (c.10/01/50 - 1981) / (aka: Albuquerque Raceway)

The Drag Club - see: Drag Club

Truth or Consequences - dirt oval (1970's)

Truth or Consequences Raceway - Truth or Consequences
   3/8 mile dirt oval (1981 & 1982) (c.1985 - 1992)
   1/8 mile dirt oval (1993 - present)

Uranium Capital Speedway - Grants - 3/8 mile dirt oval (1971 - present)

Valley Raceway - see: Duke City Raceway

NEW YORK

105th Field Artillery Regiment Armory - Bronx / located at Franklin Ave. & 166th
   1/10 mile paved indoor oval (12/08/36 - 1/19/37)
   Bill Schindler won the first feature race

106th Regiment Armory - Brooklyn / located at Bedford & Atlantic
   1/7 mile flat wood indoor oval (12/02/38) (12/05/38) (12/09/38)
   Bill Schindler won the first feature race here too

Accord Speedway - Accord / (aka: Fastland USA)
  1/4 mile dirt oval (1963 - Sept., 1987) (1992 - present)

Addison - 1/4 mile dirt oval (c.7/05/53 - c.1953)

Adirondack Park - see: Airborne Park Speedway

Afton Raceway Park - Afton / at the Afton Fairgrounds / (aka: Afton Speedway)
  Bob Sall was the first winner
  1/2 mile dirt oval (8/20/33 - 8/16/41) (1946 - 9/06/48)
  1/3 mile dirt oval (1990 - present)

Airborne Int'l Speedway - Plattsburgh / (aka: Plattsburgh Int'l Raceway)
  1/2 mile dirt oval (1954 - 1960) / (aka: Adirondack Park)
  1/2 mile paved oval (1961 - 1981) (1990 - present)
  4/10 mile dirt oval (1982 - 1989) / (aka: Airborne Park Speedway)

Airport Speedway - Big Flats - 1/4 mile dirt oval (c.9/07/52 - 1953)

Airport Speedway - New Springville (Staten Island) - 1/4 mile dirt oval (c.1953)

Airport Stadium Speedway - Rochester - 1/4 mile paved oval (6/09/39 - c.7/26/40)

Akron Motor Speedway - Akron - 1/2 mile dirt oval (1934 - 5/30/41) (1946 - c.1948)
  (aka: New Afton Speedway) / Bill Rafter started his driving career here

Albany Riding Club - Albany (Wemple) - 1/2 mile dirt oval (9/08/34)

Albany-Saratoga Speedway - Malta / originally to be called Albany-Troy Speedway
  4/10 mile paved oval (5/01/65 - 1975) (9/29/91) / built by Joe Lesik
  4/10 mile dirt oval (1977 - present) / (aka: Malta Speedway)
  scrapped dirt off and exposed old paved track to run the 9/29/91 race

Albion Fairgrounds - Albion - 1/2 mile dirt oval (1919) (1929) (1932)

The Albion Fairgrounds in 1919. - Courtesy of Reel Racing photos.

Alexandria Bay Speedway - Alexandria Bay / (aka: Edgewood Raceway)
1/3 mile dirt oval (c.1950 - c.1954)

Altamont - dirt oval (1932) / around a barn / Lee Wallard started his career here

Altamont Fairgrounds - Altamont / located at the Tri-County Fairgrounds
1/2 mile dirt oval (7/09/32- c.7/04/41)(9/15/45)(1948)(1951)(7/04/53 - 1955)
(aka: Albany-Schenectady Fairgrounds) / (aka: Altamont Speedway)

Amenia Fairgrounds - Amenia - 1/2 mile dirt oval (9/20/36)

American Legion Speedway - Woodstock - 1/4 mile dirt oval (1937 - 1941)
(aka: Woodstock Legion Speedway)

Angelica Raceway - Angelica / located at the Allegheny County Fairgrounds
1/3 mile dirt oval (1958 - 1964)

Apple Valley Speedway - Williamson - 1/2 mile paved oval (1955 - c.1961)
1/2 mile paved oval (1963 - present) / (aka: Spencer Speedway)
1/10 mile paved dragstrip (1959 - present) / NASCAR dragway at one time

Arlington Raceway - Poughkeepsie (Arlington) - 1/4 mile paved dragstrip (1950's)
possibly at Arlington Speedway

Arlington Speedway - Poughkeepsie - 1/4 mile dirt oval (c.8/04/51 - 9/07/62)
located 1/2 mile north of the Howard Johnson Inn on Van Wagner Road
(aka: Poughkeepsie Airport Speedway) / radio station tower now on site
the Southern New York Racing Association ran here in 1956 & 1957

Ashland Park Speedway - Warrensburg - 1/4 mile dirt oval (c.1949 - c.1954)
1/2 mile dirt oval (c.1952) / possibly at the fairgrounds

Averill Park - see: Burden Lake Speedway

Avon Fairgrounds - Avon - 1/2 mile dirt oval (1918) (1946) / horse training track

B & K Track - Altamont - 1/4 mile dirt oval (9/03/50)

Hauling your race car on a trailer was traveling first class in the 1950's. Pete Corey heads down the New York Thruway towards Fonda. - John Grady photo.

Baldwinsville - dirt oval (1935) / located northwest of Syracuse

Ballston Spa Fairgrounds - Ballston Spa / located at the Saratoga Co. Fairgrounds
    1/2 mile dirt oval (9/03/32) (9/08/40)

Batavia Fairgrounds - Batavia / located at the old Genesee County Fairgrounds
    1/2 mile dirt oval (1920-1929) (7/04/35-1942) (8/10/46-c.1952) (c.1962-c.1972)
    1/4 mile dirt oval (7/02/38 - 8/05/38)

Early race cars motor around the Batavia Fairgrounds in 1921. The races were held during the annual fair. The ferris wheel is in the top left of the picture. courtesy of Reel Racing Photos.

Batavia Motorsports Park - see: Kelly's Motorsports Park

Bath Speedway - Bath / located at the Steuben County Fairgrounds
    1/2 mile dirt oval (1952 - 1954) / not only did Dutch Hoag start his career
    at this track, but he was also the track champion all three years

Bay Ridge Oval Stadium - Brooklyn (Bay Ridge)- 1/5 mile dirt oval (8/11/38 - 1939)
    located at 15th Ave. & 86th St. / old motorcycle track at Dyker Beach Park

Bearsville Speedway - Woodstock - 1/2 mile dirt oval (1920's or 1930's)

Belden Hill - (location unknown) - dirt oval (1984) / ran Mini-sprints
    maybe located northeast of Binghamton

Bennett's Field Speedway - Utica - 1/4 mile dirt oval (5/14/50 - c.1950)

Berkshire Park - Gloversville - 1/2 mile dirt oval (10/02/37)

Big Flats - 1/2 mile dirt oval (1938)

Binghamton Fairgrounds - Binghamton - dirt oval (1914) (9/01/40)

Bolton Landing - see: Trout Lake

Boyce's Speedway - see: South Seneca Speedway

Bray Brook Oval - Staten Island (exact location unknown) - oval (years unknown)

Brentwood Airport - Brentwood (Long Island) - dirt oval (11/13/49)
    ran an exhibition stock car race when Islip Speedway was rained out

Brewerton Int'l Speedway - Brewerton - 1/4 mile dirt oval (7/04/49 - c.1955)
  1/4 mile paved oval (c.1956 - 1972) / (aka: Brewerton Speedway)
  1/3 mile dirt oval (1973 - 1984) (1986 - 1990) (1992 - present)
  (aka: Route 11 Raceway) / (aka: Brewerton Int'l Raceway)

Brewster Speedway - Brewster - 1/3 mile dirt oval (1949 - 1951)
  home of the SNYRA club before they moved to Danbury Fair Speedway, CT
  now the site of a housing development

Briarcliff Manor - 3.17 mile city street road course (11/11/34 - c.6/23/35)
  these races were run by the American Auto Racing Club

Briarcliff Manor - 30.0 mile road course on city streets (4/24/08)
  Ralph DePalma started his driving career at this race

Bridgehampton Cup - Bridgehampton
  city street road courses (1915 - 1920) (1949 - 5/26/53)

Bridgehampton Race Circuit - Bridgehampton / ran NASCAR GN race on 8/03/58
  2.85 mile paved road course (9/28/57 - 1983) (1987 - present)

Brighton Beach - Brooklyn (Coney Island) / located just east Coney Island
  1.0 mile dirt oval (8/10/02 - c.7/10/15) / was a trotter horse track
  ran a 1000 mile race on 5/06/05 & 5/07/05
  also held a 24 hour race and Ralph Mulford won, and went 1196 miles

Brighton Fairgrounds - Rochester (Brighton) - 1/2 mile dirt oval (early 1950's)

Brockport - dirt oval (1919)

Bronx Coliseum - Bronx / (aka: New York Coliseum) / now a bus repair garage
  built in 1926 in Philadelphia shipped to NY in 1928 / at Starlite Park
  1/10 mile indoor cinder oval (1/06/35 - 4/21/35) / Sig Haugdahl 1st winner
  located at East 177th St. & West Farmington
  1/7 mile indoor wood oval (1/08/38 - 4/26/42)
  wood track designed by Bill Heiserman
  Jimmy McCaron fatally injured, probably first indoor fatality

Many-time NASCAR modified champion Richie Evans. - John Grady photo.

Bronx - also see: 105th Field, Castle Hill, Kingsbridge, Morris Park, Yankee Stdm

Brookfield Fairgrounds - Waterville / at the new Madison County Fairgrounds
1/2 mile dirt oval (c.1949 - 1954) (c.1960) / (aka: Brookfield Speedway)
1/3 mile dirt oval (5/14/78 - 6/14/81) (1983) (1985)

Brooklyn Sports Arena - Brooklyn - 1/5 mile dirt oval (1933) / motorcycles only

Brooklyn - also see: 106th Regiment, Bay Brook, Brighton Beach, Coney Island,
Floyd Bennett, Sheepshead Bay

Brown Farm - Olean - dirt oval (6/02/40) / ran jalopies / located on Portville Rd

Buffalo Armory - Buffalo - 1/8 mile indoor paved oval (Dec., 1950 - 1/14/51)
located at the corner of Best St. & Masten Ave.

Buffalo Civic Stadium - Buffalo / (aka: Jopp Stadium) / located on Jefferson Ave.
1/4 mile cinder oval (5/30/40) / now called the War Memorial
1/4 mile paved oval (Aug., 1940 - 7/30/42) (8/30/45 - 1959)
ran a NASCAR GN race here on 7/19/58 won by Jim Reed
where the Buffalo Bills (pro football team) used to play

Buffalo Convention Center - Buffalo - 1/6 mile indoor oval (5/03/42 - 5/10/42)

Buffalo - dirt oval (1921) / maybe Keniworth Park

Buffalo - see: Cheektowago, Great Lakes, Keniworth, Legion, Niagara Falls Blvd

Burden Lake Speedway - Averill Park - 1/4 mile dirt oval (1948 - c.1955)
Pete Corey & Ken Shoemaker both started their driving careers here

Byberry Fairgrounds - (location unknown) - dirt oval (1920's)

Cairo Fairgrounds Speedway - Cairo / located at the Greene County Fairgrounds
1/2 mile dirt oval (8/18/74 - 9/22/74)

Caledonia Speedway - Caledonia / located at the Caledonia Fairgrounds
1/2 mile dirt oval (5/30/36 - 1942) (5/05/46 - c.1949)

Cambridge Fairgrounds - Cambridge / located on SR 372 / now a horse pasture
1/2 mile dirt oval (1929) (1932 - 5/30/40) (1942)

Camp Ma-Na-Vu - (location unknown) - .076 mile paved oval (8/12/84)

Campville Speedway - see: Triple Cities Speedway

Can-Am Int'l Speedway - LaFargeville (Watertown)
5/8 mile dirt oval (July, 1974 - 1982) / (aka: LaFargeville Speedway)
1/2 mile dirt oval (1983 - present) / (aka: Can-Am Winners Circle)

Can-Am Speedway - see: Kelly's Speedway

Canandaigua Speedway - Canandaigua / at the Ontario County Fairgrounds
1/2 mile dirt oval (1920) (c.7/25/53 - 1964)(1972 - 1975) (1977 - present)
1/8 mile dirt dragstrip (1960's) / (aka: Big C Speedway)

Canastota - 1/2 mile dirt oval (1930's)

Capital City Speedway - Albany - 1/4 mile dirt oval (8/07/38 - 1939)

368   *New York*

Cardiff - see: LaFayette Speedway

Carmel Race Track - Carmel - 1/2 mile dirt oval (1929) / old harness horse track
    the track was located near the center of town

Carroll's Grove Speedway - Troy - dirt oval (c.6/25/50)

Castle Hill Speedway - Bronx - 1/4 mile dirt oval (6/10/38 - 10/10/39)
    the first race scheduled for 6/07/38 was rained out
    1/4 mile paved oval (5/14/40 - 10/17/41) / promoter was Bill Heiserman
    the track torn down in 1942 for construction of a defense project

Cayuga County Fair Speedway - Weedsport - 1/3 mile dirt oval (Aug, 1955-c.1960)
    3/8 mile dirt oval (c.1975 - present) / at the Cayuga County Fairgrounds
    home of the DIRT Museum & Hall of Fame & DIRT Headquarters
    track president, Glenn Donnelly, was the 1985 RPM Promoter of the Year

Cedarhurst Speedway - Cedarhurst (long Island) / promoter was Walter Stebbins
    1/4 mile paved oval (5/09/38 - 9/20/41) / 1st A.R.D.C. midget race 5/15/40
    the site would be near where Kennedy Int'l Airport is now located

Champion Park Speedway - Syracuse / (aka: Fairmont Midget Track)
    1/5 mile dirt oval (7/02/39 - c.7/10/40) / 4 miles west on Genesee (Rt 5)

Champion Speedway - see: Owego Motorsports Park

Champlain Speedway - Ticonderoga - dirt oval (1950's)

Chariot Park - Sloansville - 1/4 mile dirt oval (1978) (1980)
    ran motorcycles in 1978 / ran mini-stocks in 1980

Chatham Fairgrounds - Chatham - 1/2 mile dirt oval (1922) / ran motorcycles 1978

Cheektowago Dog Track - Buffalo - 1/4 mile dirt oval (9/26/37) / ran midgets

Chemung Speedway - Chemung - 1/3 mile dirt oval (c.5/15/51 - 1969)
    1/3 mile paved oval (1970 - 1978) (1988)
    Geoff Bodine & Brett Bodine (1976) started their driving career here
    their father Junie Bodine owned the track at that time
    Dick O'Brien promoted a race here on 10/05/77

Chittenango - 1/2 mile dirt oval (1922)

Circle Hill Speedway - LeRoy - 1/2 mile dirt oval (1940 - 10/26/41)
    1/4 mile dirt oval (10/19/41 - 1941)

Circle K Speedway - Whitesville - 1/3 mile dirt oval (1981 - c.1987)

Clearview Speedway - South Westerlo / located 25 miles SW of Albany on Rt 32
    1/3 mile dirt oval (1949 - c.1953) / (aka: Clearview Thrillway)

Clearview Speedway - Troy (Eagle Mills) - 1/3 mile dirt oval (8/18/35 - 5/16/37)
    1/2 mile dirt oval (c.8/01/37 - 10/24/37) / located south of Troy

Cobleskill Fairgrounds - Cobleskill - 1/2 mile dirt oval (1932)

Columbiaville Speedway - Columbiaville - dirt oval (maybe early 1950's)

Commack Arena - Commack (Long Island) / at Jericho Turnpike & Veterans Hwy
1/10 mile indoor oval (11/05/60 - 10/27/61) / (aka: Long Island Arena)

Coney Island Velodrome - Brooklyn (Coney Island) / built for bicycle racing
1/8 mile wood oval (1932) (5/28/39 - c.8/10/40) / ran midgets
ran motorcycles in 1932 / the corners were banked 45 degrees

Coon Road Speedway - see: Westfield Speedway

Corning War Memorial Stadium - Corning - 1/4 mile dirt oval (1949-1950) (c.1961)

Cortland Fairgrounds - Cortland / located at the Cortland County Fairgrounds
1/2 mile dirt oval (1932 - 8/23/41) (c.5/28/50 - 1953)
the fairgrounds was built in 1839 / sold for a grocery store in 1953

County Line Speedway - Broadalbin - dirt oval (1992)

Coxsackie Speedway - Coxsackie - 1/4 mile dirt oval (6/01/52)
1/4 mile paved oval (6/08/52 - c.1953)

Crossbay Int'l Speedway - Queens (Ozone Park) / located on the Sunrise Highway
1/2 mile dirt oval (5/20/34 - 1939) / (aka: Crossbay Sunrise Speedway)
possibly the first track to have a handicap system, approximately in 1936
sold for real estate in 1939

Cuba Lake Raceway - Cuba - 1/4 mile dirt oval (c.1953 - c.1959)

Deer Park Speedway - Deer Park (Long Island)
1/2 mile dirt oval (c.5/12/29 - 7/04/41)
1/4 mile dirt oval (8/10/41) / (aka: Deer Park Speedrome)
1/4 mile paved oval (July, 1946 - 1948)

*The quarter mile paved track at Deer Park Speedway in 1947. - Frank Smith
photo (Len Ashburn collection).*

Dexter Bowl Motordrome - Queens (Ridgewood) - dirt oval (c.1910) / motorcycles

Dexter Park - Queens (Woodhaven) - 1/3 mile paved oval (4/30/51 - 9/22/55)
sold for housing project / maybe first race on 4/15/51

Dodge City Speedway - Cobleskill - 1/8 mile dirt oval (1989) / ran mini-sprints
active Kart track since c.1984 / still running Karts on weekly basis

Dongan Hills Fairgrounds - Dongan Hills (Staten Island) (aka: Staten Island Fair)
1/2 mile dirt oval (1898 or 1899) (c.5/31/27 - c.1928)

Doty Hill - Elmira - dirt oval (1950's) / possibly Glider City Speedway

Dover Dragstrip - Wingdale - 1/4 mile paved dragstrip (c.1965 - c.1970)

Dragway 36 - see: New York Int'l Raceway Park

Drum Raceway - Allentown - 1/3 mile dirt oval (c.1969 - 1980) / west of Wellsville
closed down when someone broke into the track and was seriously hurt when
they flipped their car hot lapping the track. They sued and won.

Dundee Raceway - Dundee / (aka: Dundee Raceway Park) / at a fairgrounds
1/3 mile dirt oval (1957 - present) / (aka: Dundee Speedway)

Dunkirk Airport - Dunkirk - paved road course on runways (c.1957 - c.1958)
1/4 mile paved dragstrip (c.1959) / (aka: Dunkirk Dragway)
the dragstrip held the first NASCAR drag Nationals

Dunkirk Fairgrounds - Dunkirk / located at the Chautauqua County Fairgrounds
1/2 mile dirt oval (c.1923 - c.9/10/32) (9/07/40 - 6/21/42) (1945 - 1952)
1/3 mile dirt oval (c.1956)

Dutchess Kartways - Hyde Park - 1/8 mile dirt oval (1988) / ran mini-sprints
active Kart track since c.1986 / still running Karts on weekly a basis

Dutchess Speedway - Sharps Corner (town unknown) - dirt oval (c.1952)

E.J. Murray Memorial Center - Yonkers - 1/10 mile paved indoor oval (8/13/61)

East Greenbush Speedbowl - East Greenbush (Schodack Center) / near Albany
1/4 mile dirt oval (1955) / owned by Morris Mermelstein
(aka: Schodack Center Speedbowl)

Eastport Dragway (Dragstrip) - see: Long Island Dragway

Ebenezer Speedway - see: Legion Speedway

Edgerton Park - Rochester - 1/4 mile dirt oval (1941)

Edgewood Raceway - see: Alexandria Bay Speedway

Ellenville Fairgrounds - Ellenville / located at the Ulster County Fairgrounds
1/2 mile dirt oval (c.1921)

Elmira Driving Park - Elmira - 1.0 mile dirt oval (1910's)

Elmira Fairgrounds - Elmira - 1/2 mile dirt oval (c.7/04/38 - c.1941)

Elmira - also see: Doty Hill, Glider City, Silver Speedway, Southport Speedway

Elmsford Fairgrounds - Elmsford - 1/2 mile dirt oval (1950's)
located at the Greenburgh County Fairgrounds

Empire City Speedway - Yonkers - 1.0 mile dirt oval (1900 - 5/30/07)
Isaac D. Plank won 1st race / (aka: Empire Horse Track)
now Yonkers Raceway (horse track)

Empire Dragway - see: New York Int'l Raceway Park

Empire Raceways - Menands / (aka: Menands Raceway) / located near Troy
1/4 mile paved oval (6/12/47 - c.1961) / now the site of a shopping center

Empire Speedway - Brewerton - 1/8 mile dirt oval (1986) 1/4 mile dirt oval (1987)

Erie County Fairgrounds - see: Hamburg Fairgrounds

ESTA Safety Park Dragstrip - Bridgeport- 1/4 mile paved dragstrip (1960-present)
(aka: Empire State Timing Association) / proposed 1958 by Schmidt family

Evans Mills Speedway - Watertown (Evans Mills) / (aka: Evans Mills Raceway)
1/3 mile paved oval (1967 - 1979) / seven miles northeast of Watertown
3/8 mile dirt oval (1981 - 1983) (1988 - 1993)

Expo Park Speedway - see: Rochester Expo Fairgrounds

F & M Speedway - see: Perth Speedway

Fairmont Midget Speedway - see: Champion Park Speedway

Farmers Oval Speedway - Queens (Glendale) / located at 68th Ave. & 65th Place
1/5 mile dirt oval (7/04/38- 1939) / (aka: Ridgefield Park) / ball diamond

Fastland USA - see: Accord Speedway

Fishkill - dirt oval (1951)

Five Mile Point Speedway - Binghamton (Kirkwood) / built by Irving Heath
1/4 mile dirt oval (7/11/51 - present) / rained out on 7/04/51

Floyd Bennett Field - Brooklyn - 4.2 mile paved road course (8/30/53) / an airport
this was the first sports car race in the area since 1915

Fonda Speedway - Fonda / located at the Montgomery County Fairgrounds
1/2 mile dirt oval (c.1926 - 1939) (1948) (5/30/53 - present)
the track was moved slightly in 1953 from its original position
(aka: Fonda-Fultonville Speedway) / first called Fonda Speedway in 1953
1/8 mile paved dragstrip (c.1957 - c.1968) / (aka: Thruway Speedway)
Shirley Muldowney started her career here in 1958

*Danny Johnson (#10) dices it out with Will Cagle (#24) at the Henrietta
Fairgrounds in 1981. - Kim Jennejohn photo (Allan E. Brown collection).*

372

Fort Covington Speedway - Fort Covington - 1/2 mile dirt oval (1956 - 1975)
reportedly turns 1, 3 & 4 were in the U.S.A. and turn 2 was in Canada
the track was on an Indian Reservation and operated by the Indians

Fort Hardy Park - Schuylerville - dirt oval (c.1947 - c.1948)

Frankfort Speedway - Frankfort - dirt oval (c.1950)

Freedom Raceway - Delevan / (aka: Tri-County Speedway)
1/3 mile dirt oval (May, 1983 - 1985) (1987) (1989 - present)

Freeport Speedway - Freeport (Long Island) / (aka: Freeport Municipal Stadium)
1/5 mile dirt oval (4/08/34 - 6/20/34) / ran motorcycle races 1933 & 1934
1/5 mile paved oval (5/04/35 - 1942) (8/30/45 - 1974)
1/4 mile paved oval (1975 - 9/24/83) / first promoter was Bill Heiserman
the property is now the site of the Caldor's Department Store

Frogtown Int'l Speedway - Hogansburg - 3/8 mile dirt oval (8/15/87 - present)
the track is operated by Indians and parimutuel betting is allowed

Fulton Airport - Fulton - 1/4 mile paved dragstrip (1955)

Fulton Speedway - Fulton - 1/3 mile paved oval (6/24/61 - 1978)
1/3 mile dirt oval (1979 - present) / track built by Millard Benway
1/8 mile dragstrip (1960's - c.1971)

Gardenville Speedway - see: West Seneca Speedway

Genesee Speedway - Batavia / located at the new Genesee County Fairgrounds
1/3 mile dirt oval (1983 - present) / the new fairgrounds was built 1979
(aka: Genesee Country Speedway)

Glen Aubrey Raceway - Conklin - 1/4 mile dirt oval (1950 - 1968)

Glen - oval (years unknown)

Glider City Speedway - Elmira - dirt oval (1950's)

Good Time Park - see: Goshen

Goodle Speedway - Little Falls - 1/3 mile dirt oval (1953 - 1956)

Goshen - 1.0 mile dirt tri-oval (1908) (6/20/36 - 10/03/36) (10/06/46 - 8/17/47)
(aka: William H. Cane's Good Time Speedway) / (aka: Good Time Park)
ran AAA championship race on 6/20/36

Goshen - 1/2 mile dirt oval (years unknown) / ran auto races a couple of times
the track is still a horse track

Gouverneur Fairgrounds - Gouverneur / at the St. Lawrence Co. Fairgrounds
1/2 mile dirt oval (1932)

Grahamsville - 1/4 mile dirt oval (1946 - 1950)

Grand Island - paved road course (c.8/30/52 - 1953) / (Grand Prix of Niagara Falls)
1.75 mile paved road course (6/12/88) / between Buffalo & Niagara Falls

Grand Prix of Niagara Falls - see: Grand Island

Grand Sport Speedway - see: Owego Motorsports Park

Great Lakes Speedway - Buffalo - 1/2 mile dirt oval (1936)

Great Neck (Long Island) - dirt oval (1900's or 1910's) / maybe in Jamaica

Greenport Airport - Greenport (Long Island) - road course on runways (1965)

Greenport Speedway - Greenport - dirt oval (1948) (1952)

Hamburg Fairgrounds - Hamburg / located at the Erie County Fairgrounds
1/2 mile dirt oval (c.1929 - 8/23/41) (1946 - 1960) (1962 - present)
runs AMA motorcycle race annually / last auto race was in 1983
built as a horse track in the 1840's / still used as a horse track

Hannibal Speedway - Hannibal - 1/4 mile dirt oval (8/21/83 - 1983)

Hemlock Fairgrounds - Hemlock - 1/2 mile dirt oval (1947 - 1953)

The roadsters kick up the dust at the Hemlock Fairgrounds in 1949. - Len Campagno photo (Bob Chaddock collection courtesy of Don Radbruch).

Henrietta Fairgrounds - Henrietta / located at the Monroe County Fairgrounds
1/2 mile dirt oval (c.5/31/48 - 1969) (1981)
1/4 mile paved dragstrip (c.1959) / NASCAR dragstrip

Herkimer - dirt oval (1930's)

Hill Crest Speedway - McLean - paved road course (1990) / ran Micro-stocks
1/10 mile paved oval (6/15/91) / ran Micro-stocks

Holland Int'l Speedway - Holland - 3/8 mile dirt oval (1960 - 1967)
3/8 mile paved oval (6/20/68 - present)

Hollywood Bowl - see: Route 66 Speedway

Holmes Airport Speedway - Queens (Jackson Heights) - 1/2 mile dirt oval (1932)
1/5 mile dirt oval (7/29/34 - 9/02/34)

Hornell Raceway - Hornell - 1/3 mile dirt oval (1962)

Horseheads - 1/2 mile dirt oval (1930's) / possibly at Chemung Co. Fairgrounds

Hudson Falls - 1/2 mile dirt oval (1929) (5/30/34)

Hunt Speedway - Dalton (Hunt) - 1/4 mile dirt oval (c.1956 - c.1960)

Ida Mae Speedway - Schodack - 1/4 mile dirt oval (c.1939 - 1941)
ran jalopies / was connected with the Ida Mae Diner on US Highway 9

Innisfail - New York City - 1/5 mile dirt oval (1934) / ran motorcycles
possibly at the Manhattan College Football Stadium

Island Gardens - West Hempstead (Long Island) / at 500 Hempstead Turnpike
1/10 mile indoor concrete oval (12/13/59 - 2/13/65) / now shopping center

Islip Speedway - Islip (Long Island) - 1/5 mile paved oval (8/02/47 - 9/08/84)
1/8 mile paved dragstrip (c.1961 - c.1962)
ran annual "World Figure 8 Championship" on ABC Wide World of Sports
held NASCAR GN races on 7/15/64, 7/14/65, 7/16/66, 7/15/67 & 7/07/68
the property is now the site of a cookie factory

Ithaca-Dryden Speedway - Dryden - 1/3 mile dirt oval (1951 - c.1966)

Jackson's Dragway - see: King's Dragway

Jamaica - 1.0 mile dirt oval (6/05/08)

Jamestown Speedway - Jamestown (Gerry) / located of CR 380 northwest of town
1/2 mile dirt oval (c.8/29/37 - 1940) (c.1949 - c.1953)

Jamestown - also see: Stateline Speedway, Ted's Torture Track

Johnnies Speedway - see: North Collins Speedway

Holland Int'l Speedway. - Official track photo.

Johnstown Fairgrounds - Johnstown / located at the Fulton County Fairgrounds
   dirt oval (1930's)

Kelly's Motorsports Park - Batavia - 1/4 mile dirt oval (1990)
   (aka: Batavia Motorsports Park) / (aka: Can-Am Speedway)

Keniworth Park - Buffalo - 1.0 mile dirt oval (8/12/04 - 8/19/05) / horse track

King's Dragway - Savannah - 1/8 mile paved dragstrip (1959 - c.1983)
   (aka: Jackson's Dragway) / promoters were Ed Otto & Paul Jackson

Kingsbridge Armory Speedrome - Bronx / at Jerome Ave & Kingsbridge Road
   1/5 mile concrete indoor oval (12/04/46 - c.1962) Midgets & NASCAR stocks

The Knightsbridge Armory. - Frank Smith photo (Len Ashburn collection).

Kingston Fairgrounds - Kingston - dirt oval (c.1950)

Kirkwood Speedway - Kirkwood - 1/2 mile dirt oval (8/28/38 - c.6/22/41)

LaFargeville Speedway - see: Can-Am Int'l Speedway

LaFayette Speedway - LaFayette (Cardiff) - 1/2 mile dirt oval (c.1950 - 1955)

Lancaster Speedway - Lancaster (Bowmansville) - 1/2 mile dirt oval (5/30/59-1962)
   1/8 mile paved dragstrip (1960 - present) / (aka: New Lancaster Speedway)
   1/2 mile paved oval (1963 - 1975) / (aka: Lancaster Nat'l Speedway)
   1/4 mile paved oval (1969 - c.1972) / 5/8 mile paved oval (1976 - present)

Lawrenceville - dirt oval (1970's)

Lebanon Valley Speedway - West Lebanon / at the former Lebanon Valley Airport
   1/2 mile high banked dirt oval (6/28/53 - 1955) (1957 - present)
   1/4 mile paved dragstrip (1961 - present)
   the original property owners were Lou and Harry Spanier
   current track owner, Howard Commander, 1989 RPM Promoter of the Year
   1/4 mile paved oval (June, 1994 - present) / runs legend cars on paved oval

Legion Speedway - Buffalo (Ebenezer) / located on Union Road near West Seneca
   1/2 mile dirt oval (c.5/17/36 - c.5/22/38) (1946 - c.1947)
   (aka: Ebenezer Speedway) / the site is now the Southgate Shopping Plaza

LeRoy Jalopy Track - LeRoy - dirt oval (2/23/41) / ran jalopies in a wheat field

LeRoy - also see: Circle Hill, Limerock, Pebble Hill

Limerock Speedway - LeRoy - 1/8 mile paved oval (1964 - 1981) / karts on paved
1/8 mile dirt oval (1982 - present) / mini-sprints & karts on dirt track
ran T.Q. midgets on paved track in 1967

Limerock Speedway - Allan E. Brown photo.

Little Valley Fairgrounds - Little Valley / at the Cattaraugus County Fairgrounds
1/2 mile dirt oval (8/26/32 - 8/28/37) (7/06/41) (1946 - 1975) (1977)

Lockport Fairgrounds - Lockport / located at the Niagara County Fairgrounds
1/2 mile dirt oval (c.5/30/27 - 1935) (10/01/39) (6/28/42) (1945 - c.1949)
held the first ever URC sprint car race here in 1948
1/4 mile dirt oval (6/06/46 - c.1950)

Long Island Arena - see: Commack Arena

Long Island Dragway - Westhampton (Long Island) (aka: Westhampton Speedway)
1/4 mile paved dragstrip (1956 - present) / (aka: Eastport Dragstrip)
2.5 mile paved road course (1960) / (aka: Westhampton Beach Speedway)
1/4, 4/10 & 1/2 mile paved ovals (8/05/60 - c.1975)
(aka: Suffolk County Raceway)

Long Island Motor Parkway - Long Island / in Queens, Nassau & Suffolk Counties
23.46 mile city street paved road course (10/11/08) (10/24/08)
22.75 mile city street paved road course (9/29/09)
ran a race called the Long Island Stock Car Derby on 9/29/09
12.64 mile city street paved road course (10/30/09) (10/01/10)
ran prestigious Vanderbilt Cup Races here 1908, 1909 & 1910

Long Island - the circuit went through towns of Westbury, Jericho & Hempstead
28.44 mile country road & city street road course (10/08/04)
28.3 mile country road & city street road course (9/23/05 - 10/14/05)
29.71 mile country road & city street road course (9/22/06 - 10/06/06)
held prestigious Vanderbilt Cup Races here on 10/08/04, 10/14/05, 10/06/06
reportedly had appx. 200,000 spectators for the 1905 Vanderbilt Cup Race
(aka: Hicksville-Hemstead-Jericho Circuit)

Long Meadow Speedway - Rexford - 1/4 mile dirt oval (1947 & 1948) / ran jalopies
located off Route 146, north of Schnenactady / now a housing development

Lowville Fairgrounds - Lowville / located at the Lewis County Fairgrounds
1/2 mile dirt oval (c.1949 - early 1950's) / ran roadsters

Lyons - 1/2 mile dirt oval (1920)

MacGreagor Speedway - Saratoga Springs - 1/2 mile dirt oval (c.1929)

Madison Square Gardens Bowl - Queens (Long Island City)
    1/5 mile paved oval (5/27/36 - 9/23/36) / Curly Mills first winner
    Curly Mills seriously injured here on 8/19/36 / he died on 12/24/36

Madison Square Gardens - New York City (Manhattan) / different than above
    1/10 mile indoor paved oval (1971) / ran a T.Q. midget race

Malone Fairgrounds - Malone - dirt oval (1933) / at Franklin County Fairgrounds

Maple Grove Speedway - Waterloo / located at the Seneca County Fairgrounds
    1/2 mile dirt oval (c.1921 - c.1941) (c.1946 - 1971) (1976 - 1977)
    (aka: Waterloo Speedway) / (aka: Seneca County Fair Speedway)

Maspeth Fairgrounds - Queens (Maspeth) / located near Metropolitan Heights
    1/2 mile dirt oval (1927 - 5/30/29) / (aka: Metropolitan Speedway)

McKown's Grove Speedway - Guilderland - 1/4 mile dirt oval (c.1938 - 1942)
    located on US 20, just west of Albany

Meadowdrome - Dunkirk - dirt oval (1950's) / (aka: Silver Creek Speedway)

Mellenville - 1/4 mile paved oval (c.6/11/50 - c.1950)

Menands Raceway - see: Empire Raceways

Metowee Speedway - North Granville - dirt oval (1953)

Metropolitan Speedway - see: Maspeth Fairgrounds

Mid-State Speedway - see: Morris Fairgrounds

Middletown Fairgrounds - see: Orange County Fair Speedway

Millbrook - dirt oval (1931) / ran motorcycles

Millerton - 1/2 mile dirt oval (1919) / possibly the Amenia Fairgrounds

Milray Speedway - see: Fulton Speedway (Dragway)

Mineola Fairgrounds - Mineola (Long Island) / Bill Schindler lost a leg in accident
    1/2 mile dirt oval (c.1925 - c.9/13/41) (6/08/46 - c.1949)

Moffits Park - Moffitsville - dirt oval (years unknown)

Montauk Point - 2.0 mile road course (7/09/39) / around sand dunes
    3.03 mile city street road course (7/06/40) / called "Light of Bust" races

Montgomery Air Force Base - Montgomery / (aka: Stewart Air Force Base)
    1.85 mile concrete road course (8/19/56 - 8/07/60)
    1.9 mile concrete tri oval on runways (7/17/60) / NASCAR GN race on oval
    1/4 mile paved dragstrip (c.1958 - c.1960) / located west of White Plains

Morris Fairgrounds - Morris / at Otsego Co. Fairgrounds / (aka: Morris Speedway)
    1/2 mile dirt oval (c.5/30/49 - 1972) / (aka: Mid-State Speedway)

Morris Park - Bronx - 1.0 mile dirt oval (5/20/05 - 7/30/05)
  1.25 mile road course (9/27/07) (9/28/07) / (aka: Allen Course)
  1st race won by Louis Chevrolet / both races in 1907 were 24 hour events

Motor City Raceway - see: New York Int'l Raceway Park

Naples Speedway - Naples - 1/3 mile dirt oval (c.1950 - 1951)

Nassau Coliseum - Uniondale (Long Island) - 1/7 mile indoor oval (1983)

Nassau Victory Speedway - Nassau - 1/4 mile dirt oval (6/08/46 - 1946) / Midgets
  located at the Nassau Fairgrounds / was a dog track in the mid 1930's
  also had a 1/2 mile dirt oval used for horse races only

National Dragway - see: New York Nat'l Dragway

New Legion Speedway - Pine Plains / (aka: Pine Plains Speedway)
  1/2 mile dirt oval (5/30/36 - 9/18/38)

New Paltz Fairgrounds - New Paltz - dirt oval (years unknown)
  located at the Ulster County Fairgrounds

New Utica-Rome Speedway - Vernon - 1/4 mile paved oval (8/06/61 - 1962)
  1/3 mile paved oval (1963 - 1975) (1977 - 1978) / built by Joe Lesik
  1/8 mile paved dragstrip (c.1963 - c.1977) / (aka: Utica-Rome Speedway)
  1/2 mile dirt oval (1979 - 1982) (1985 - 1987)
  1/3 mile dirt oval (1989 - present) / (aka: New Venture Speedway)

New Venture Speedway - see: New Utica-Rome Speedway

New York City / (aka: Cosmopolitan Race) / second auto racing in the U.S.A.
  30 mile city street road course (5/30/1896) / won by J. Frank Duryea
  from Bronx's Kingsbridge City Hall to Irvington and back to City Hall

New York City - also see: Innisfail, Madison Square Gardens, Polo Grounds

New York Coliseum - see: Bronx Coliseum

New York Int. Raceway Park - Leicester (aka: Empire Dragway)(aka: Dragway 36)
  1/4 mile paved dragstrip (c.1970 - present) (aka: Motor City Raceway)

New York Nat'l Dragway - Center Moriches (Long Island) / (aka: Nat'l Dragway)
  1/4 mile paved dragstrip (c.1970 - 1979) / closed by environmentalists
  Leroy Goldstein drove to first six second run in a Funny Car on 6/20/70

New York State Fairgrounds Arena - Syracuse / located northeast of downtown
  1/20 mile indoor concrete oval (late 1980's)

New York State Fairgrounds - Syracuse / built as a horse track in 1880
  1.0 mile dirt oval (9/18/09 - 9/16/11) (Sept., 1919 - 9/01/41) (1946)
  (9/10/49 - present) / maybe ran 1903 & 1905 / home of "Syracuse Nationals"
  Lee Oldfield crashed through the fence and into the crowd (1911), killing 11
  spectators in one of the USA's worst auto racing accidents in history
  Jimmy Murphy (9/15/24) & Jimmy Gleason (9/12/31) fatally injured here
  Ira Vail was an early promoter / oldest state fair, first held in 1841
  currently promoter is Glenn Donnelly

Gary Balough (#112) dominated the 1980 "Schaefer 200" at the New York State Fairgrounds with the "Lincoln Continental" built by Kenny Weld and Don Brown. The car incorporated a wing in the roof. - Rolland Rickard photo.

New York World's Fair - Queens (Flushing) / the last ARCA sports car events
    3/4 mile paved road course (10/06/40) / circuit went through the fair

Newburgh Armory - Newburgh - 1/16 mile indoor oval (1983)

Niagara Dragstrip - Niagara Falls - 1/4 mile paved dragstrip (c.1963 - c.1972)
    (aka: Niagara Int'l Dragway) / (aka: Niagara Airport Drag Strip)

Niagara Falls Boulevard Speedway - Buffalo - dirt oval (1930's)

Niagara Falls Convention Center - Niagara Falls
    1/8 mile indoor concrete oval (12/29/84 - present)

The Can-Am T.Q. midgets are the featured attraction at the Niagara Falls Convention Center. - 1989 photo by Nancy Brown.

Niagara Falls - paved city street road course (1980)

North Collins Speedway - North Collins - 1/4 mile dirt oval (c.1960)
    1/3 mile dirt oval (c.1960 - c.1968) / (aka: Johnnies Speedway)
    the track was in a shale pit / the site is still a gravel/sand pit

North County Speedway - see: Sandy Creek Speedway

North Ridge Raceway - Argyle - 4/10 mile dirt oval (4/29/90 - 1990)
    the track was closed by a injunction by irate neighbors
    the track builder Gerald Durkee then moved to Florida and reopened the
    former Lake City Speedway and renamed it South Ridge Raceway

Norwich Fairgrounds - Norwich / located at the Chenango County Fairgrounds
    1/2 mile dirt oval (c.8/13/38 - 1940) (1950) / ran before 1938 as well

Noto Speedway - Otisville - 1/4 mile dirt oval (5/29/83) (6/05/83)

Olean Speedway - Olean - 1/3 mile dirt oval (c.8/09/58 - c.1969)
    (aka: Olean Raceway) / Merv Triechler started his driving career here

Olivebridge Speedway - see: Onteara Speedway

Onteara Speedway - Olivebridge / (aka: Olivebridge Speedway)
    1/2 mile dirt oval (8/14/60 - c.1966) / maybe 1/3 mile as well

Opp Stadium - see: Buffalo Civic Stadium

Orange County Fair Speedway - Middletown / at the Orange County Fairgrounds
    1/2 mile dirt oval (8/15/19 - 9/28/41) (10/13/45 - c.10/23/67)
    1/5 mile dirt oval (1942) (9/23/45 - 1945) / (aka: Victory Speedway)
    1/5 mile paved oval (1945 - 9/12/53) (5/18/57 - 6/24/61)
    the small 1/5 mile track was patterned after Danbury Fair Speedway
    5/8 mile dirt oval (c.1968 - present)

Ossining - 1/4 mile paved dragstrip (1953 - 1954)

*The covered grandstands of the Orange County Fair Speedway in Middletown,
New York. - Rolland Rickard photo.*

Oswego Speedway is one of the premier oval tracks in New York. It is the home of the supermodifieds. - Official track photo.

Oswego Speedway - Oswego - 1/2 mile dirt oval (8/10/51 - 7/04/52)
    1/2 mile paved oval (1952 - 1960) / (aka: Wine Creek Race Track)
    5/8 mile paved oval (1961 - present) / formerly a horse track
    Jimmy Shampine fatally injured here on 9/04/82 in a modified
    Dick & Linda O'Brien were the 1981 RPM Promoters of the Year
    home of the annual "Oswego Classic" for supermodifieds

Ovid Speedway - Ovid - 1/4 mile dirt oval (c.1951)

Ovid - also see: South Seneca Speedway

Owego Fairgrounds - Owego / located at the Tioga County Fairgrounds
    1/2 mile dirt oval (8/29/36 & 8/30/36)

Owego Motorsports Park - Owego - 1/6 mile dirt oval (c.1987 - 1993)
    (aka: Grand Sport Speedway) / built as a motorcycle track
    (aka: Champion Speedway) / Mini-sprints 1992 & 1993

Palmyra - 1/3 mile dirt oval (1959) / not at the fairgrounds

Palmyra Speedway - Palmyra / located at the Wayne County Fairgrounds
    1/2 mile dirt oval (1922) (1929) (c.4/22/48 - c.1954) (1958) (1960)
    1/3 mile paved oval (1950's) (aka: Greater Palmyra Fairgrounds)

Paradise Speedway - Phelps / located northwest of Geneva
    1/5 mile dirt oval (1958 - 1971) (c.1985 - present)

Patterson Speedway - Patterson - 1/4 mile dirt oval (1950 - 1952)

Pebble Hill Speedway - LeRoy - 1/4 mile dirt oval (1936) / built in a quarry
    the promoters were the Morrison Brothers / admission price $.30

Peekskill - dirt oval (late 1930's)

Peekskill Speedway - Peekskill / (aka: Peekskill Stadium) / an old baseball park
    1/5 mile paved oval (5/04/51 - 9/27/57) / (aka: New Victory Speedway)

Speedsters wait for the start of a race at the Penn Yan Fairgrounds in 1920. courtesy of Reel Racing Photos.

Penn Yan Fairgrounds - Penn Yan - 1/2 mile dirt oval (1918 - 1921)

Penn Yan Speedway - Penn Yan - 1/3 mile dirt oval (c.1957)
     now the site of the new Yates County Fairgrounds

Pennellville - 1/4 mile gravel dragstrip (1954 - c.1958)

Penny Royal Speedway - Leon / located at the Fireman's Fairgrounds
     dirt oval (c.1949 - late 1950's) / now an Amish sawmill & farm

Penny Royal Speedway ran the roadsters in 1949. - Lou Ensworth collection (courtesy of Don Radbruch).

Perry - dirt oval (1922) / possibly the Silver Lake Fairgrounds

Perry Int'l Speedway - Perry - 1/3 mile dirt oval (1959 - 1967) (1985 - present)
     1/3 mile paved oval (1968 - 1974) (1976 - 1982) (1984 - June, 1985)
     1/4 mile dirt oval (6/07/85 - 6/28/85) / 1/4 mile inside of paved track
     (aka: Perry Speedway)

Perth Speedway - Perth / (aka: F & M Speedway)
     1/2 mile dirt oval (1949 & 1950) / (aka: Fulton-Montgomery Speedway)

Philmont - dirt oval (1922)

Pine Bowl Speedway - Troy (Snyders Corners)
     1/3 mile paved oval (7/01/50 - c.1963) / race on 6/24/50 was rained out

Pine Plains Speedway - see: New Legion Speedway

Plattsburgh Int'l Raceway - see: Airborne Park Speedway

Pocantico Hills - see: Sleepy Hollow Ring

Polo Grounds - New York City / where the N.Y. Giants (baseball) use to play
  1/4 mile dirt oval (c.1940 - 1942) / races on the warning track of field
  1/5 mile wood oval (6/05/48) (6/08/48) / 25,000 spectators on 6/05/48
  built of aluminum & wood / Alexis Thompson was promoter of wood track
  1/4 mile paved oval (8/28/58 - 9/12/59) / Ed Otto promoter in 1950's
  the paved track was built after the baseball team moved to San Francisco

Poughkeepsie - 1.0 mile dirt oval (9/16/04)

Poughkeepsie Airport Speedway - see: Arlington Speedway

Poughkeepsie - also see: Arlington

Queens - see: Crossbay, Dexter, Farmers Oval, Holmes Airport, Madison Square
  Garden Bowl, Maspeth, New York World's Fair

Raceway Park - see: White's Beach Speedway

Ransomville - 1/4 mile dirt oval (May, 1955 - 1955) / located in a field on Route 53
  operated by the Slow Poke Car Club / they built other Ransomville tracks
  the track was on the Ortiz's property and had to be moved a little

Ransomville - 1/4 mile dirt oval (1955 - 1957) / 100 yards west of the first track

Ransomville Speedway - Ransomville - 1/3 mile dirt oval (1958 - 1976)
  1/2 mile dirt oval (1977 - present) / replaced other tracks

Rhinebeck Speedway - Rhinebeck / located at the Dutchess County Fairgrounds
  1/2 mile dirt oval (9/12/04) (1932 - 1936) (8/30/41) (c.9/16/47 - c.1955)
  1/5 mile paved oval (1947 - 9/08/62) / north of Poughkeepsie

Richfield Springs Speedway - Richfield Springs / (aka: Richfield Speedway)
  1/2 mile dirt oval (c.1954 - c.1955)

Richmondville - dirt oval (7/05/53 - c.1954)

Riverhead Fairgrounds - Riverhead / located at the Suffolk County Fairgrounds
  1/2 mile dirt oval (1920) (1926 - 1928) (1932 - 1936) (9/01/41)

Riverhead Raceway - Riverhead - 1/5 mile dirt oval (5/30/52 - 1954)
  1/4 mile paved oval (1955 - present) / (aka: Vimco-Riverhead Speedway)

Riverhead - road course on city streets (9/29/09) / Louis Chevrolet was the winner

Rochester - 1/5 mile dirt oval (Sept. 1938) / probably Rochester Expo Fairgrounds

Rochester - Airport Stadium, Brighton, Edgerton Park, Sportsman Park

Rochester Driving Park - Rochester - 1.0 mile dirt oval (5/30/1898 - 5/31/1900)

Rochester Expo Fairgrounds - Rochester / located on Dewey Ave.
  1/2 mile dirt oval (1923 & 1924) / (aka: Rochester Expo)
  1/5 mile dirt oval (5/26/39) / (aka: Expo Park Speedway)

Rochester Fairgrounds (new) - see: Henrietta Fairgrounds

Rochester War Memorial Auditorium - Rochester - indoor wood oval (1963 - 1967)

Rock Age Colonie Speedway - Colonie - 4/10 mile dirt oval (c.1950)

Rock & Roll Speedway - Frewsburg - dirt oval (c.1958 - early 1960's)
    the track was leveled and the property is now a field on Oak Hill Road

Roll-O-Bowl - Panama (Watts Flats) - 1/4 mile dirt oval (1950's)
    located on Button Valley Road

Rolling Wheels Raceway - Elbridge - 5/8 mile dirt oval (8/17/69 - present)
    built by Robert Petocci, who was killed when a car crashed into the pits
    at Spencer Speedway in 1970 / his sons Bob (age 19) and Don (only 16)
    took over and ran the track until the mid 1980's

Roosevelt Speedway - Westbury (Long Island) / (aka: Roosevelt Field)
    4 mile paved road course (10/12/36) designers Art Pillsbury & Mark Linentral
    this was the airfield Charles Lindberg took off from on flight to England
    3.33 mile paved road course (7/05/37 - 1939) / George Robertson manager
    ran the prestigious "Vanderbilt Trophy" races on 10/12/36 & 7/05/37
    1.87 mile paved road course (Sept., 1937) / had 16 turns in 1936
    1/2 mile paved oval (1936 - c.1941) (c.1946 - 1960)
    once ran a 300 lap midget race / once ran a race with sand covering track
    1/5 mile dirt oval (7/09/38 - c.10/02/39) / (aka: Roosevelt Raceway)

Roosevelt Speedway - Westbury (Long Island) - continued
    held parimutuel betting on oval track auto races here in 1938
    1.5 mile paved parking lot road course (6/19/60) / site now a horse track

Round The Houses Road Race - Alexandria Bay - city street road course (1936)
    road course on city streets (8/07/37) / the race was 86.2 miles long
    1.33 mile road course on city streets (8/06/38) / 60 lap race in 1938
    road course on city streets (1939) / the race was 70.0 miles long

Route 20 Speedway - Nassau - 1/4 mile dirt oval (August, 1950 - c.1950)

Route 66 Speedway - Albany (Troy) / located four miles south of Troy on SR 66
    1/3 mile dirt oval (c.1960 - c.1963) / (aka: Hollywood Bowl)

Saint Lawrence Valley Speedway - Canton - dirt oval (1951)
    Bill Wimble started his driving career here in 1951

Salamanca - 1/4 mile paved oval (1953)

Sandy Creek Speedway - Sandy Creek / at the Oswego County Fairgrounds
    1/2 mile dirt oval (1950 - c.5/11/55) / (aka: North County Speedway)

Saranac Lake Speedway - Saranac Lake - 1/2 mile oiled dirt oval (1958 - 1968)
    the track was always a NASCAR sanctioned track

Satan's Bowl-O-Death - Busti - dirt oval (c.1939 - c.1941) (c.1946 - 1950's)
    (aka: Sugar Grove Raceway) / located on CR 69

Schaghticoke Fairgrounds - Schaghticoke / at the Rensselaer Co. Fairgrounds
    1/2 mile dirt oval (late 1920's - early 1930's) (1950's) / ran cycles in '50s

New York

Schodack Center Speedbowl - Schodack Center - 1/4 mile dirt oval (1955)
    located five miles from East Greenbush Speedbowl / (aka: Ups and Downs)
    closed by New York State Police as they raced on Sundays (blue law)

Seneca Falls Speedway - Seneca Falls - 1/3 mile dirt oval (8/15/48 - 1952)

Shangri-La Speedway - see: Tioga Speedway

Sharon Raceway - Sharon Springs - 1/4 mile dirt oval (6/27/52 - 1957)

Sheepshead Bay Speedway - Brooklyn (Sheepshead Bay) / a horse track
    1.0 mile dirt oval (8/25/10) / held an exhibition race between Barney Oldfield
    and Jack Johnson (the World Champion prize fighter)

Sheepshead Bay Speedway - Brooklyn (Sheepshead Bay) / site of ex-horse track
    2.0 mile wood oval (10/09/15 - 9/20/19) / (aka: Speedway Park)
    built by Blaine Miller / turns banked 17 degrees
    (the track was planned to be built of brick or concrete but with the
    success of the Chicago board track it was built of wood instead)
    Harry Harkness was chairman of corporation / Carl Fisher helped at first
    Dario Resta ran 108 mph in an exhibition run on 9/18/15
    Harry Grant fatally injured in a practice run in October of 1915
    Carl Limberg fatally injured 5/13/16 / later became a housing development

Sherman Raceway - Sherman - dirt oval (1950's) / located in a gravel pit

Sidney Speedway - Sidney - 1/2 mile dirt oval (c.1937 - c.1941) (1946 - c.1953)

Silver Creek Speedway - see: Meadowdrome

Silver Lake Fairgrounds - Silver Springs - 1/2 mile dirt oval (early 1900's)

Silver Lake Speedway - Silver Springs - 1/4 mile dirt oval (c.1957)

Silver Speedway - Elmira - 1/3 mile dirt oval (c.1984 - 1985)

Sky High Speedway - Schenevus - 1/2 mile dirt oval (7/05/53 - 1954)
    located on top of a mountain southwest of Cobleskill

Skyline Speedway - Cortland (Blodgett Mills) / located on top of a hill
    3/8 mile dirt oval (1962 - 1976) (1980) (1988 - present)

Sleepy Hollow Ring - Tarrytown (Pocantico Hills) / located in a farmers field
    3/4 mile dirt road course (7/08/34) (7/14/34) (7/29/34) / had 10 corners
    the sports cars were referred to as foreign midgets
    these races were the first ARCA races / later to become SCCA
    the races were organized by Miles Collier, son of Barron Collier

Smyrna Speedway - Sherburne - 3/8 mile dirt oval (c.1953 - c.1956)
    located on Hank Dexter's farm on Route 80

Somers Speedway - Somers - 1/4 mile dirt oval (1949) / in cow pasture on SR 22
    birthplace of the Southern New York Racing Association

South Dayton - dirt oval (late 1930's)

South Glen Falls Dragway - South Glen Falls
    1/4 mile paved dragstrip (c.1964-1970's)

386

South Seneca Speedway - Ovid - 3/8 mile dirt oval (May, 1952 - 1954)
    (aka: Boyce's Speedway)

Southport Speedway - Elmira (Southport) - dirt oval (1957 & 1958)

Speedway Park (board track) - see: Sheepshead Bay Speedway

Spencer - dirt oval (years unknown) / located northwest of Owego

Spencer Speedway - see: Apple Valley Speedway

Speonk Stadium - Speonk (Long Island) - dirt oval (1951 - 9/28/52)
    this was a primitive race track with no grandstands

Sportsman Park - Rochester - 1/2 mile dirt oval (Aug., 1939 - Sept., 1939)

Springfield Gardens - 50 mile city street road course (4/18/1900) / on Merrick Rd
    the race ran from Springfield Gardens to Babylon and then back again

Stapleton Speedway - see: Thompson Stadium

State Line Speedway - Hoosick Falls - see: Vermont chapter

Stateline Speedway - Jamestown (Busti) - 1/3 mile dirt oval (7/21/56 - present)
    ran a NASCAR GN race here on 7/16/58 won by Shorty Rollins

Staten Island - see: Airport, Bray Brook, Dongan Hills, Thompson, Weissglass

Stewart Air Force Base - see: Montgomery Air Force Base

Stormsville - 1/2 mile dirt oval (c.1933 - c.1939)

Suffolk County Air Force Base - Westhampton Beach
    2.0 mile paved road course (5/07/50) (5/09/54)

Suffolk County Raceway - see: Long Island Dragway

Sullivan County Speedway - White Lake / (aka: White Lake Speedway)
    1/4 mile paved oval (1960 - present) / Robb Griggs was once the promoter

Sulphur Springs Speedway - Mina - 1/4 mile dirt oval (1956 - 1959)

Syracuse Army Air Base - Syracuse - 1/4 mile paved dragstrip (1958)

Syracuse Fairgrounds - see: New York State Fairgrounds

Syracuse - also see: Champion Park, War Memorial

Ted's Torture Track - Jamestown - dirt oval (1950's) / located on Route 60

Thompson Stadium - Stapleton (Staten Island) / (aka: Stapleton Speedway)
    1/5 mile dirt oval (5/24/39 - 1942) (1945 - 9/27/48)

Thunder Mountain Speedway - Center Lisle - 3/8 mile dirt oval (5/24/92 - present)

Ticonderoga - dirt oval (early 1930's)

Tioga Speedway - Owego - 1/2 mile paved oval (7/28/46 - present)
    1/4 mile paved oval (5/25/51 - c.1951) / grandstands once burned down
    (aka: Shangri-La Speedway) / ran a NASCAR GN race on 7/04/52

Tri-Cities Drag-Way - Endicott - 1/4 mile paved dragstrip (c.1962 - 1969)
    located on an airport

Tri-County Speedway - see: Freedom Raceway

Triple Cities Speedway - Endicott (Campville) / (aka: Campville Speedway)
    1/2 mile dirt oval (5/16/37 - 7/31/38) / Kenneth Basley first winner
    three miles NW of Endicott on Owego Road near the Triple Cities Airport

Triple State Speedway - Johnson City - 1/2 mile dirt oval (1933 - c.6/27/37)

Trout Lake - Bolton Landing - 1/4 mile dirt oval (c.1948) / near Lake George

Troy - dirt oval (9/26/14)

Troy Speedway - Troy - dirt oval (1952)

Troy - also see: Carroll's Grove, Clearview, Pine Bowl, Route 66

Twin State Speedway - West Lebanon (Cornish Flats) - dirt oval (early 1950's)
    possibly Route 20 Speedway or Lebanon Valley Speedway

Twin Valley Speedway - Chenango Forks - 1/2 mile dirt oval (Oct., 1970 - 1974)

Ups & Downs - see: Schodack Center Speedbowl

Utica - 1/2 mile dirt oval (1919)

Utica - also see: Bennett's, War Memorial, Yorkville

Utica-Rome Speedway - see: New Utica-Rome Speedway

Valhalla Speedway - Valhalla - 1/4 mile dirt oval (1948)

Van's Speedway - Arkwright / located on Center Road
    1/4 mile dirt oval (c.1957 - 1962)

Vernon Fairgrounds - Vernon - 1/2 mile dirt oval (c.5/29/49 - c.1951)
    promoter was Ed Otto / now training track for Vernon Downs horse track

Victoria Speedway - Duanesburg (Guilderland) 12 miles west of Albany on US 20
    1/2 mile dirt oval (8/19/60 - 6/29/66)
    first event rained out after hot laps / first feature was on 8/26/60

Victory Speedway - see: Orange County Fair Speedway

Walden - 1/2 mile dirt oval (c.1928) / Bob Sall started his driving career here

War Memorial Auditorium - Syracuse - indoor paved oval (c.1958) / T.Q. midgets

War Memorial Auditorium - Utica - wood oval (1963 - c.1970)

Warrensburg Speedway - Warrensburg - dirt oval (1960) / maybe at a fairgrounds
    (aka: Warrensburg Stadium)

Warsaw - dirt oval (1922)

Washington Hollow Speedway - Washington Hollow
    3/10 mile dirt oval (8/13/39 - c.6/16/40) / 12 mile east of Poughkeepsie

388

The above photo shows that streamlining was on the mind of Walter C. Baker in 1903. The white car (second from right) was called the "Torpedo Kid" and was powered by electric. - Allan E. Brown collection.

Waterloo Speedway (Fairgrounds) - see: Maple Grove Speedway

Watertown Speedway - Watertown - 1/2 mile dirt oval (c.1920 - 1936) (8/22/40)
    1/4 mile dirt oval (1936) / located at the Jefferson County Fairgrounds
    3/5 mile dirt oval (1956 - 1974) (one race in the 1980's)

Watertown - also see: Can-Am Int'l Speedway, Evans Mills Speedway

Watkins Glen - 6.6 mile paved city street road course (10/02/48 - 9/20/52)
    the first race was the first ever SCCA sports car race ever held
    Sam Collier was fatality injured here on 9/23/50

Watkins Glen (Dix) - 4.6 mile paved road course (9/19/53) (9/18/54) (9/17/55)
    replaced the other street circuit as it had become too dangerous

Watkins Glen Dragway - Watkins Glen - 1/4 mile paved dragstrip (c.1970)
    located adjacent to Watkins Glen Grand Prix course

Watkins Glen Int'l - Watkins Glen / (aka: Watkins Glen Grand Prix)
    2.3 mile paved road course (9/15/56 - 10/04/70)
    3.4 mile paved road course (1971 - 1981) (7/07/84 - present)
    held its first NASCAR Grand National (Winston Cup) race was 8/04/57
    ran U.S. Grand Prix (Formula One) here from 1961 to 1980
    1/4 mile paved dragstrip (1957 - 1959)
    1/5 mile paved oval (6/11/93 - present) / (aka: Inner Oval)
    had 750,000 fans here for a rock concert in 1973

Webb Island - Oneonta - 1/2 mile dirt oval (10/09/49 - 1949)

Weedsport Fairgrounds - see: Cayuga County Fair Speedway

Weedsport Speedway - see: Cayuga County Fair Speedway

Weissglass Stadium - Port Richmond (Staten Island) / torn down in 1973
    1/5 mile paved oval (1952 - 1972) / site is now a sewage treatment plant

One of the world's best sports car drivers was Juan Manuel Fangio. This picture was taken at Sebring (FL) in the 1950's. - Len Ashburn photo

Wellsville - 1/2 mile dirt oval (1919) / probably at a fairgrounds

Wellsville Stock Car Speedway - Wellsville - 1/2 mile dirt oval (c.8/27/50 - c.1955)

West Seneca Speedway - West Seneca (Gardenville) / (aka: Gardenville Speedway)
    1/4 mile dirt oval (c.10/01/50 - 1952) / located on SR 277
    the property is now the site of a the Gardenville Shopping Plaza

Westfield Speedway - Westfield (Chautauqua) - 1/2 mile dirt oval (early 1950's)
    (aka: Coon Road Speedway) / actually located closer to Chautauqua

Westhampton Speedway - see: Long Island Dragway

Westport Fairgrounds - Westport - 1/2 mile dirt oval (years unknown)
    located at the Essex County Fairgrounds

West Sheridan Speedway - Arkwright - 1/4 mile dirt oval (c.1955) / Lakeview Road

White Lake Speedway - see: Sullivan County Speedway

White Plains - 1.0 mile dirt oval (8/16/13)

White's Beach Speedway - Ballston Spa - 1/4 mile dirt oval (1952 - 1961)
    (aka: Raceway Park)

Whitney Point Fairgrounds - Whitney Point / at the Broome County Fairgrounds
    1/2 mile dirt oval (8/15/14) (8/07/38) (9/18/38) (1960's)
    motorcycle race on 8/15/14

Williamson Microd Club - Wallington - dirt oval (years unknown) / Old Ridge Rd

Woodhull Speedway - Woodhull - 1/3 mile dirt oval (6/13/65 - present)

Woodstock Legion Speedway - see: American Legion Speedway

Woodstock - also see: Bearsville Speedway

Yankee Stadium - Bronx - 1/5 mile cinder oval (1931) (1934 - 1937) / motorcycles

Yonkers - see: Empire City Speedway

Yorkville (Utica) - 1/2 mile dirt oval (1930's)

Zoar Valley Speedway - Gowanda - dirt oval (years unknown)

NORTH CAROLINA

311 Speedway - see: Three-Eleven Speedway

Ace Speedway - Altamahaw - 1/4 mile dirt oval (1953 - 1981) (1984 - 1989)
   3/8 mile paved oval (1990 - present) / (aka: Southern Speedway)
   (aka: Ace Short Track) / (aka: Southern Int'l Speedway)

Ahoskie Fairgrounds - Ahoskie / located at the Atlantic District Fairgrounds
   1/2 mile dirt oval (5/11/52) / rain out after heat & semi feature races

Airport Speedway - Charlotte - 1/2 mile dirt oval (10/03/35 - 7/04/36)
   Doc MacKenzie won the first race / the site is now the airport

Angola Speedway - Jacksonville - oval (years unknown)

Antioch Speedway - Morganton / (aka: Lenoir Burke Speedway)
   1/2 mile dirt oval (c.1962 - c.1966) (8/05/88 - present)

Asbury Speedway - Westfield - 1/2 mile dirt oval (late 1960's)

Asheville Airport Speedway - Asheville - 1/4 mile dirt oval (maybe ran in 1961)
   1/4 mile paved dragstrip (1960's) / paved road course (1960's)

Asheville Fairgrounds - Asheville - dirt oval (1940)

Asheville Motor Speedway - see: New Ashville Speedway

Asheville-Weaverville Speedway - Weaverville / (aka: Skyline Speedway)
   1/2 mile dirt oval (5/20/50 - c.3/31/57) / the owner was Eugene Sluder
   1/2 mile paved oval (c.6/29/58 - 1969) / the promoter was Enoch Staley

Asheville - also see: McCormick Field, Fairview

Belmont - 1/8 mile dirt (late 1940's) / ran jalopies

Bennett Speedway - Bennett - 1/4 mile dirt oval (mid 1950's) / ran stock cars

Bi-State Speedway - see: Draper Speedway

Biscoe Speedway - Biscoe - dirt oval (c.1962)

Bladen County Speedway - Dublin / (aka: Dublin Race Track)
   5/8 mile dirt oval (May, 1979 - 1986) (1988 - 1989) (1993)

Blair Speedway - High Point - 1/2 mile dirt oval (6/29/47 - 11/07/54)

Boone Fairgrounds - see: Fairgrounds Raceway

Bowman Gray Stadium - Winston-Salem - 1/4 mile paved oval (6/06/47 - present)
   track is a flat asphalt oval that is around a high school football field

Brewer's Speedway - Rocky Mount - 1/8 mile paved dragstrip (7/04/76 - present)

Broad-Slab Speedway - Benson - 3/8 mile dirt oval (c.1962)

Bullard's Dragway - Whiteville - 1/8 mile paved dragstrip (1962 - 1991)
   (aka: Columbus County Dragstrip)

Butner Speedway - Butner - 3/8 mile paved oval (mid 1960's) maybe Tri-City

Cape Fear Motor Speedway - Leland - 4/10 mile dirt oval (1964 - c.1981)
(aka: Leland Speedway) / (aka: CMK Speedway)

Capella Speedway - Winston-Salem - oval (1948)

Caraway Speedway - Asheboro - 1/2 mile dirt oval (1966 - 1974)
1/2 (.455) mile paved oval (1975 - present)

Carolina Beach Speedway - Wilmington - dirt oval (1963 - c.1965)

Carolina Speedway - Gastonia - 4/10 mile dirt oval (1961 - present)
(aka: Gaston Speedway)

Chadbourn Speedway - Chadbourn - dirt oval (years unknown) / near Cerro Gordo

Champion Speedway - Brinkleyville - 3/10 mile dirt oval (5/30/87 - present)

Champion Speedway - Fayetteville / built by Harold Brasington
1/4 mile dirt oval (early 1950's)
1/3 mile paved oval (5/10/53 - 1959) / Marvin Panch was the last promoter

Chantilly Speedway - Roanoke Rapids - 3/10 mile dirt oval (c.1965 - c.1978)

Charlotte Coliseum - Charlotte - 1/10 mile indoor concrete oval (12/22/90)

Charlotte - dirt oval (1950's) / located on Beatties Ford Road

Charlotte Fairgrounds - Charlotte / at the Southern State Fairgrounds
located at Sugar Creek Road & Tyron / (aka: Charlotte Agricultural Fair)
1/2 mile dirt oval (c.1926 - 11/02/41) (1945 - 11/06/60) / a horse track
1/5 mile dirt oval (10/20/36 - 10/24/36) / ran a series of 10 midget races
(two races each day) / Henry Banks won the first race on the small track
promoters in the late 1940's until 1960 were Bill France & Bruton Smith
Richard Petty won his first NASCAR GN race here on 2/27/60
the site is now a shopping center

Bowman Gray Stadium - Official track photo.

Coming down for a start of the NASCAR Busch Grand National cars at Charlotte Motor Speedway in 1993. - Nancy Brown photo.

Charlotte Motor Speedway - Harrisburg (Charlotte) / designed by Curtis Turner
    1.5 mile paved oval (1960 - present) / turns banked 24 degrees
    Fireball Roberts crashed here in 5/24/64 / he died from burns on 7/02/64
    1/8 mile paved dragstrip (c.1961 - c.1970) / promoter is "Humpy Wheeler"
    1.7 & 2.25 mile paved road courses (5/22/71 - present) / home of "World 600"
    1/4 mile paved oval (1988 - present) / < in front of main grandstands
    1/4 mile dirt oval (1992 - 1993) / < outside turn three of the big track
    1/4 mile paved oval (Sept., 1993 - present) / (aka: Outback Speedway)

Charlotte Speedway - Charlotte / located at Little Lock & Wilkinson Ave.
    3/4 mile dirt oval (6/06/48 - c.10/14/56) / (aka: New Charlotte Speedway)
    the first ever NASCAR GN (Winston Cup) race was held here 6/19/49
    won by Jim Roper / the promoter was Bill France / the purse was $5,000
    1/4 mile dirt oval (c.1953) / tracks built by Harvey & Pat Charles

Charlotte Speedway - Charlotte (Pineville) / built by Jack Prince
    1.25 mile wood oval (10/25/24 - 9/19/27) / turns were banked 40 degrees
    Earl Antersberg was killed in an exhibition run on 10/24/24
    Earl Cooper was inadvertently announced the winner of the first race,
    but when the tapes were rechecked the win was awarded to Tommy Milton
    The surface had deteriorated by 1928 and the owners decided not to fix it

Charlotte's Sunset Speedway - see: Metrolina Speedway

Charlotte - also see: Airport Speedway, Queen City Speedway, Shuffletown

Chase City - dirt oval (1950's)

Chimney Rock Hill Climb - Chimney Rock - 1.8 mile hill climb (c.1946 - 1970's)

Clingman Speedway - Ronda - 3/10 mile dirt oval (c.1977 - 1983)

Clinton Fairgrounds - Clinton / located at the Sampson County Fairgrounds
    1/2 mile dirt oval (10/30/36 - 1937)

CMK Speedway - see: Cape Fear Motor Speedway

Coastal Plains Dragway - Jacksonville - 1/4 mile dragstrip (c.1970 - present)
    (aka: Hi Way 258 Dragstrip) / (aka: Highway 258 Dragstrip)

Columbus County Dragstrip - see: Bullard's Dragway

Concord Dragstrip - Concord - 1/4 mile paved dragstrip (c.1959 - c.1960)

The pace lap of the 1956 "National Championship" modified race at Concord International Speedway. - Len Ashburn photo.

Concord Fairgrounds - Concord / located at the Cabarrus District Fairgrounds
   1/2 mile dirt oval (1925 - 10/14/34) / formerly a horse track on US 29
   now the site of the S & D Coffee Co.

Concord Int'l Speedway - Concord / (aka: Harris Super Speedway)
   1/2 mile dirt oval (c.5/06/55 - 1978) / (aka: New Concord Speedway)
   (aka: Concord Speedway) / Bruton Smith was the promoter in the 1950's

Concord Motor Speedway - Concord - 4/10 mile dirt oval (1981 - 1986)
   4/10 mile paved oval (9/06/86 - present) / (aka: New Concord Speedway)
   (aka: Concord Speedway)

Concord - also see: Harris Super Speedway, Two Flags Speedway

County Line 311 Speedway - see: Three-Eleven Speedway

County Line Raceway - Rocky Mount - 3/8 mile dirt oval (1988 - present)

Craven County Dragstrip - see: New Bern Dragstrip

Cumberland County Speedway - see: Fayetteville Motor Speedway

Cumberland Int'l Dragway - Fayetteville - 1/4 mile dragstrip (1962 - present)
   same location as New Fayetteville Speedway

Diamond Speedway - Stokesdale - dirt oval (1960's)

Dixieland Speedway - Elizabeth City - 3/8 mile dirt oval (May, 1983 - present)

Dixieland Speedway - Raleigh - see: Southland Speedway

Dogtrack Raceway - Moyock / 1/4 mile dirt oval (Aug., 1960 - c.1964)
   formerly a dog racing track / (aka Dogtrack Speedway)
   (aka: Moyock Speedway) / 1/4 mile paved oval (c.1966 - c.1969)

Draper Speedway - Eden (Draper) - 1/4 mile dirt oval (c.1949 - c.6/11/50)
   1/4 mile paved oval (c.7/08/51 - 1960) / (aka: Bi-State Speedway)
   the towns of Draper, Spray & Leaksville merged to become Eden in 1970

Dublin Race Track - see: Bladen County Speedway

Dunn Benson Dragstrip - Dunn - 1/8 mile paved dragstrip (1960 - present)

Dunn Legion Speedway - Dunn - 3/8 mile dirt oval (c.1949 - c.1971)
(aka: Dunn Speedway)

East Bend Dragstrip - East Bend - 1/8 mile dragstrip (c.1981 - c.1984)

East Bend Raceway - East Bend - 4/10 mile dirt oval (c.1985 - c.1986)

East Carolina Motor Speedway - Robersonville
3/8 mile paved oval (1990 - present)

An aerial view of East Carolina Motor Speedway. - Official track photo.

East Lincoln Motor Speedway - Lowesville - 3/8 mile dirt oval (1990 - present)

Easy Street - see: Kinston Dragstrip

Elkin Super Speedway - see: Jonesville Speedway

Fairgrounds Raceway - Boone - 1/4 mile dirt oval (1988 - present)
located at the High Country Mountain Fairgrounds

Fairview - Asheville - dirt oval (1949) / (aka: Hollywood)

Farmington Dragway - Farmington / (aka: Sportsman Park Dragstrip)
1/8 mile paved dragstrip (April 1962 - present)

Fayetteville - 1/2 mile high banked dirt oval (1948)

Fayetteville - dirt oval (1937)

Fayetteville Motor Speedway - Fayetteville / (aka: Cumberland County Speedway)
1/2 mile paved oval (c.1973 - June, 1980)
1/2 mile dirt oval (8/23/80- present) / (aka: New Fayetteville Speedway)
same site as Cumberland County Dragway

Fayetteville Speedway - Fayetteville - 3/8 mile dirt oval (c.1972 - c.1979)

Fayetteville - also see: Champion Speedway, Cumberland, Northside Speedway

Franklin County Speedway - Franklinton - 1/2 mile dirt oval (c.1952 - c.1967)
sometimes referred to as Templeton

Franklin Speedway - Franklin - 1/4 mile dirt oval (c.1968 - c.1975)

Franklinton Micro-Midget Speedway - Franklinton - 1/10 mile dirt oval (1956)

Friendship Speedway - Elkin - 4/10 mile dirt oval (4/20/84 - present)

Gaskey Speedway - see: Queen City Speedway

Gaston Speedway - see: Gastonia Fairgrounds & Carolina Speedway

Gastonia Fairgrounds - Gastonia (Lowell) / (aka: Spindle Center Fairgrounds)
1/3 mile dirt oval (c.1953 - 1964) / (aka: Lowell Fairgrounds)
(aka: Spindale City Speedway) / (aka: Gaston Speedway)

Gastonia - also see: Robbinwood Speedway

Goldsboro Speedway - Goldsboro - 1/2 mile dirt oval (1952 - c.1955)

Greenhill Speedway - Mount Airy - 1/4 mile dirt oval (c.7/15/56 - 1956)

Greensboro - dirt oval (1957) / located on Highway 220

Greensboro Fairgrounds - Greensboro / at the Central Carolina Fairgrounds
1/2 mile dirt oval (c.1926 - 10/04/41) (10/07/45 - 1953)
1/3 mile dirt oval (6/04/53 - c.4/28/57) / grandstands burned down 5/01/55
Herb Thomas started his driving career here

Guilford Tobacco Warehouse - Greensboro - 1/10 mile indoor cement oval (1/05/57)

NASCAR Late Model Sportsman star Jack Ingram. - David Allio photo.

396

Hammer Down Speedway - Red Springs - 1/8 mile dirt oval (1990 - present)
same location as Thunder Valley Raceway Park (dragstrip)

Harnett County Speedway - Spring Lake - 1/2 mile dirt oval (1952 - c.1970)

Harrells Raceway - Harrells - 1/8 mile paved dragstrip (9/20/89 - present)

Harris Speedway - Harris (Forest City) / (aka: Tri-City Motor Speedway)
3/10 mile paved oval (c.1964 - c.1978) / located next to Hillview Speedway
3/8 mile dirt oval (c.1981 - c.1984) (1989 - present)
(aka: Harris Motor Speedway)

The twin tracks of Hillview Speedway (right) and Harris Speedway (left).
Hillview was dirt and Harris was pavement. - Official track photo.

Harris Super Speedway - Concord - 3/8 mile dirt oval (4/06/49 - c.1951)

Hendersonville Fairgrounds - Hendersonville / (aka: Hendersonville Speedway)
1/2 mile dirt oval (c.1946 - c.1955)

Hi Way 258 Dragstrip - see: Coastal Plains Dragway

Hickory Fairgrounds - Hickory / located at the Catawba County Fairgrounds
1/2 mile dirt oval (c.1946)

Hickory Speedway - Hickory - 4/10 mile dirt oval (1951 - 1967)
3/8 mile paved oval (8/05/67 - present)
Harry Gant (1964) & Dale Jarrett (1977) both started their careers here

High Point Motor Speedway - High Point / (aka: Tri-City Speedway)
1.0 mile dirt (liquid asphalt) oval (10/20/40 - 1942) / C.N. Baity built

Hillside Speedway - Mount Airy - 3/10 mile dirt oval (1991 & 1992)
a Go-Kart track running since c.1983 which ran Mini-sprints in 1991 & 1992

Hillview Speedway - Harris - 1/2 mile dirt oval (c.1956 - late 1960's)
was located next to Tri-City Motor Speedway
now used as the parking lot for Harris Speedway

Hollywood - see: Fairview

Hooker Speedway - Sparta - dirt oval (mid 1970's)

Hudson Dragstrip - Hudson - 1/8 mile paved dragstrip (c.1981) (c.1991 - present)

Hudson - also see: Saw Mill Speedway, Tri-County Motor Speedway

J & J Speedway - see: Saw Mill Speedway

Jacksonville Speedway - Jacksonville - 1/2 mile dirt oval (1952 - 11/06/64)
(aka: Onslow Speedway)

Jacksonville - also see: Angola Speedway, Coastal Plains Dragway, Surf City

Jet Motor Speedway - Stem - 1/2 mile dirt oval (1968) / located in a cow pasture

Jonesville Speedway - Jonesville - 1/2 mile dirt oval (c.1947 - c.1950)
located behind the Jonesville School / (aka: Elkin Super Speedway)

Kannapolis Fairgrounds - see: Salisbury Fairgrounds

King - 1/8 mile dirt oval (1957) / ran Micro-midgets / maybe at a fairgrounds

Kings Kountry Motor Speedway - see: Tar Heel Speedway

Kings Mountain Speedway - Kings Mountain - 3/8 mile dirt oval (11/06/54 - c.1956)

Kinston - 1/2 mile dirt oval (c.1921) / probably at the Kinston Fairgrounds

Kinston Dragstrip - Kinston - 1/4 mile paved dragstrip (June, 1960 - present)
(aka: Easy Street) / built on an old section of highway

Kinston Speedway - Kinston - 1/2 mile dirt oval (late 1960's)

Lakeview Speedway - Lexington - 5/8 mile dirt oval (5/02/48 - 1949)

Lakewood Speedway - Denver - 3/4 mile dirt tri-oval (late 1940's - 1952)
near Lake Norman / promoter was Bruton Smith / now housing development

Laurinburg - 1/2 mile dirt oval (11/29/34)

Legion Speedway - see: Wilson Fairgrounds

Legion Speedway - Wilmington - dirt oval (7/25/54) / maybe at the fairgrounds

Leland Raceway - see: Cape Fear Motor Speedway

Lenoir Burke Speedway - see: Antioch Speedway

Lincoln County Speedway - Lincolnton - 3/8 mile dirt oval (c.1988 - present)

Lincoln Speedway - Lincolnton - 1/2 mile dirt oval (c.1965)

A Corvair and a Maverick warm their tires as two Novas are waiting out the "Christmas Tree" at Mooresville Dragway. - Official track photo.

398

Lowell Fairgrounds - see: Gastonia Fairgrounds

Lumberton - dirt oval (c.1954)

Marion Speedway - Marion - dirt oval (August, 1957 - early 1970's)

McCormick Field - Asheville / ran a NASCAR GN race around a baseball diamond
    1/4 mile dirt oval (late 1940's or early 1950's)
    1/4 mile paved oval (7/28/56 - 1959) / also ran NASCAR midgets

McKenzie Race Track - Hallsboro - 1/8 mile paved dragstrip (c.1986 - present)

Metrolina Speedway - Charlotte / located at the Metrolina Fairgrounds
    1/2 mile dirt oval (July 1968 - 1973)(1977 - 1987) (1989) (1991 - present)
    1/2 mile paved oval (1972 - 1977) / Ned Jarrett was promoter 1974 - 1977
    (aka: Queen City Speedway) / (aka: Speedworld) / (aka: Sunset Speedway)
    (aka: Charlotte's Sunset Speedway)

Midland Dustbowl - Midland - 1/2 mile dirt oval (c.1948 - early 1950's)
    Bruton Smith promoted his first race here

Mooresville Dragway - Mooresville - 1/8 mile paved dragstrip (1960 - present)

Morehead City - 1/2 dirt (June, 1955 - c.1955) / located on US Highway 70

Mount Airy - 1/2 mile dirt oval (July, 1946 - 1947)
    Curtis Turner started his driving career here

Mount Airy - also see: Greenhill Speedway, Hillside Speedway

New Asheville Speedway - Asheville / built by Jim Harrin
    1/3 mile dirt oval (1961) / (aka: New Asheville Motor Speedway)
    1/3 mile paved oval (1962 - present) / (aka: Asheville Motor Speedway)

New Bern Dragstrip - New Bern - 1/4 mile paved dragstrip (c.1963 - present)
    (aka: Craven County Dragstrip) / (aka: New Bern Motorsports)

New Bern Speedway - New Bern - dirt oval (years unknown)

New Dublin Speedway - see: Bladen County Speedway

New Fayetteville Speedway - see: Fayetteville Motor Speedway

North Carolina Motor Speedway - Rockingham / located 10 miles NE of town
    1.017 mile paved oval (10/31/65 - present) / turns banked 25 degrees
    the first race was a NASCAR GN (Winston Cup) race / (aka: The Rock)
    1.5 mile paved road course (1960's) (c.1992 - present)
    located across the street from Rockingham Int'l Dragway

North Carolina State Fairgrounds Arena - Raleigh / (aka: State Fair Coliseum)
    1/10 mile paved indoor oval (11/10/56 - 12/14/56) / ran T.Q. midgets

North Carolina State Fairgrounds - Raleigh / (aka: State Fair Speedway)
    1.0 mile dirt oval (c.1926 - c.1941) (c.1946 - 1951)
    1/2 mile dirt oval (c.1940 - c.1941) (10/19/46 - 9/30/70)
    the last race was also the last NASCAR GN race ever held on a dirt track

North Davidson - Midway - 1/8 mile dirt oval (1985 - 1990) / in Davidson County

North Wilkesboro Dragway - see: Wilkesboro Dragway Park

North Wilkesboro Speedway - North Wilkesboro
5/8 mile dirt oval (5/18/47 - c.4/07/57) / built by Enoch Staley
Fireball Roberts 5/18/47 & Tim Flock 1948 started their driving careers here
5/8 mile paved oval (9/22/57 - present) / turns banked 14 degrees

North Wilkesboro Speedway. - Official track photo.

Northside Speedway - Fayetteville - 1/4 mile paved oval (c.1994 - present)

Occoneechee Speedway - see: Orange Speedway

Onslow Speedway - see: Jacksonville Speedway

Orange County Speedway - Rougement - 1/4 mile dirt oval (c.1966 - c.1967)
5/8 mile dirt oval (c.1968 - c.1972) / (aka: Trico Speedway)
3/8 mile paved oval (c.1973 - present) / new grandstands in 1983
ran the "Independent 250" here on 11/25/73 / NASCAR independent drivers
ran in this non sanctioned event

Orange Speedway - Hillsborough / (aka: Occoneechee Speedway)
9/10 mile dirt oval (6/17/48 - c.1965) / listed as 1.0 mile at first
1/4 mile dirt oval (7/15/55 - 1956) / Fonty Flock started his career here

Outback Speedway - see: Charlotte Motor Speedway

Peace Haven Speedway - Winston-Salem - 1/2 mile dirt oval (7/05/48 - c.1957)
promoters were Bill France & Bruton Smith (aka: Winston-Salem Speedway)
Curtis Turner won the first race at this track on 7/05/48

Pender County Speedway - Rocky Point / built by Richard Brickhouse
1/2 mile dirt oval (May, 1979 - 1987)

Piedmont Dragway - Greensboro / (aka: Piedmont Motorsports Park)
1/4 mile paved dragstrip (1957 - present)

400

Queen City Speedway - Charlotte / (aka: Gaskey Speedway)
    1/2 mile dirt oval (1968) / closed down because of a dust problem
    had a massage parlor in   concession stands after the track closed
    located near the airport / bought by Lee Petty / torn down in 1971

Queen City Speedway - see: Metrolina Speedway

Rainbow Speedway - Reidsville - 3/8 mile dirt oval (1977 & 1978)

Raleigh Fairgrounds - see: North Carolina State Fairgrounds

Raleigh Speedway - see: Southland Speedway

Raleigh - also see: Wake County Speedway

Roanoke Rapids - dirt oval (1936)

Roaring River Speedway - Roaring River - 3/8 mile dirt oval (c.1978 - 1986)

Robbinwood Speedway - Gastonia - dirt oval (c.1947 - 1954) (1958)
    Bob Harkey started his driving career here in 1949
    "Humpy" Wheeler was a promoter here

Rock Rest Speedway - Monroe - 1/8 mile dirt oval (c.1982 - 1988) / T.Q. midgets

Rockingham Dragway - Rockingham / (aka: Rockingham Int'l Dragway)
    1/4 mile paved dragstrip (1969 - present)
    located across the street from North Carolina Motor Speedway

Rockingham - see: North Carolina Motor Speedway

Rockingham Speedway - Rockingham - 1/4 mile dirt oval (c.1956 - c.1963)
    1/4 mile paved oval (1963 - c.1964) / near the town of Hamlet

Rocky Mount Fairgrounds - Rocky Mount
    1/2 mile dirt oval (11/07/36 - c.1941) (c.1946 - 1952)

Roxboro Dragway - Roxboro - 1/8 mile dirt dragstrip (c.1962 - 1968)
    1/8 mile paved dragstrip (1969 - present)

Rutherford County Speedway - see: Spindale Fairgrounds

Salisbury Fairgrounds - Salisbury / at the Rowan County Fairgrounds
    1/2 mile dirt oval (c.1932 - June, 1941) / located north of Kannapolis

Salisbury Sports Arena - Salisbury - 1/2 mile dirt tri-oval (mid 1960's)

Salisbury Super Speedway - Salisbury / located on US Highway 29
    5/8 mile dirt oval (c.10/05/58 - 1961)

Sanford Dragway - Sanford - 1/8 mile paved dragstrip (c.1981 - 1987)

Sanford Motor Speedway - Sanford - 1/4 mile dirt oval (late 1960's)

Saw Mill Speedway - Hudson - 1/4 mile dirt oval (years unknown)
    (aka: J & J Speedway)

Shadyside Dragway - Boiling Springs - 1/8 mile dragstrip (c.1981 - present)

Shelby Dragway - Shelby - 1/4 mile paved dragstrip (c.1968 - c.1970)

Shelby Fairgrounds - Shelby / located at the Cleveland County Fairgrounds
1/2 mile dirt oval (1924 - 10/04/41) (c.1946 - c.1976)
(aka: Shelby Motor Speedway)

Shuffletown Dragway - Charlotte - 1/4 mile paved dragstrip (1958 - 1993)

Silver City Micro Midget Speedway - Silk Hope - dirt oval (1957)

Skyline Speedway - see: Asheville-Weaverville Speedway

Smoky Mountain Speedway - Waynesville - 1/4 mile dirt oval (c.1959 - c.1962)
now the site of a mobile home park

Smoky Mountain Speedway - Whittier - 5/16 mile dirt oval (8/11/90 - present)

South Side Park - Winston-Salem - 1/4 mile dirt oval (c.8/08/35)

Southern (Int'l) Speedway - see: Ace Speedway

Southern National Speedway - Kenly - 4/10 mile paved oval (1993 - present)

Southland Speedway - Raleigh / one mile north of Raleigh / (aka: Dixie Speedway)
1.0 mile paved oval (7/04/52 - 7/04/58) / corners were banked 16 degrees
the first race, an AAA Championship car event, was won by Troy Ruttman
1/4 mile paved oval (6/19/53 - 1958) / (aka: Raleigh Speedway)

Speedworld - see: Metrolina Speedway

Spindale Fairgrounds - Spindale (Forest City) / at the Rutherford Co. Fairgrounds
1/2 mile dirt oval (c.1925 - c.1941) (c.1946 - c.1970)
(aka: Rutherford County Speedway) / (aka: Rutherfordton Speedway)

Spindle Center Fairgrounds (Speedway) - see: Gastonia Fairgrounds

Sportsman Park Dragstrip - see: Farmington Dragway

Sportsman Park - Elizabeth City - 1/4 mile dirt oval (1950's)
(aka: Elizabeth City Track)

Starlite Speedway - Monroe - 4/10 mile dirt oval (June, 1962 - c.1975)

State Fair Coliseum - see: North Carolina State Fairgrounds Arena

State Fair Speedway - see: North Carolina State Fairgrounds

Statesville Speedway - Statesville - 1/2 mile dirt oval (4/04/48 - 1949)
Curtis Turner won the first feature race on 4/04/48

Sunset Speedway - see: Metrolina Speedway

Surf City - Jacksonville - 2.5 mile beach/road oval (5/30/64) (5/31/64)

Tar Heel Speedway - Randleman / (aka: Kings Kountry Motor Speedway)
1/4 mile paved oval (5/26/57 - c.1959) (1962 - c.1967) (1975)
built by Harold Brasington who also built Darlington Raceway, SC

Taylorsville Speedway - Taylorsville - 1/4 mile dirt oval (1985 - 1991)

Templeton - see: Franklin County Speedway

The Rock - see: North Carolina Motor Speedway

Three-Eleven (311) Speedway - Madison (Pine Hall) / (aka: 311 Speedway)
1/2 mile dirt oval (April, 1965 - present)
(aka: U.S. 311 Motor Speedway) / (aka: County Line 311 Speedway)

Thunder Valley Raceway Park - Red Springs - 1/8 mile dragstrip (c.1985 - present)
same location as Hammer Down Speedway / (aka: Thunder Valley Speedway)

Thunder Valley Speedway - Lawndale - 4/10 mile dirt oval (1991 - present)

Tri-City Motor Speedway - see: Harris Speedway

Tri-City Speedway - Creedmore - 4/10 mile dirt oval (c.1952 - c.1968)

Tri-City Speedway - High Point - see: High Point Motor Speedway

*Tri-County Motor Speedway is one of the first smaller tracks to have a tunnel
large enough to drive semi-trailers through. - Official track photo.*

Tri-County Motor Speedway - Hudson - 4/10 mile dirt oval (4/26/85 - 1988)
4/10 (.416) mile paved oval (7/16/88 - present)
(aka: Tri-County Speedway) / the track has a tunnel to get into the pits

Tri-County Raceway - Brasstown - 1/4 mile dirt oval (c.1964 - present)

Tri-County Speedway - see: Harris Speedway

Tri-State Motor Speedway - Greensboro - dirt oval (c.1934 - 1935)

Trico Speedway - see: Orange County Speedway

Twin City Speedway - Kannapolis - 1/4 mile dirt oval (c.1964)

Two Flags Raceway - Concord - 1/8 mile dirt oval (1986 - 1991) / now a Kart track

U.S. 311 Motor Speedway - see: Three-Eleven Speedway

Union County Speedway - Weddington - 1/4 mile dirt oval (mid 1960's)

Victory Lane Speedway - Ronda - 2/10 mile dirt oval (1987 - 1992)
active Go-Kart track that ran mini-sprints from 1987 to 1992

Wadesboro - 1/2 mile dirt oval (5/09/48 - c.1953) / a horse track / SE on SR 52

Wadesboro - 3/8 mile dirt oval (1956 - 1958)

Wake County Speedway - Raleigh - 1/4 mile dirt oval (1962 - 1986)
1/4 mile paved oval (1987 - present)

Wake County Speedway in Raleigh started as a dirt track in 1962. It was asphalted in 1986. - Official track photo.

Walker Heights Dragway - (location unknown) - 1/4 mile dirt oval (1960's)

Washington - dirt oval (c.1950 - 1952)

Earl Moss in a 1937 Ford at the beach course in Daytona Beach (FL) in 1958 during the modified race. - Len Ashburn photo.

Wayne County Speedway - Official track photo.

Wayne County Speedway - Pikeville - 1/3 mile dirt oval (1990 - 1991)
1/3 mile paved oval (1992 - present)

Weaverville - see: Asheville-Weaverville Speedway

Whiteville Fairgrounds - Whiteville / located at the Columbus County Fairgrounds
1/2 mile dirt oval (1964 - c.1965) / (aka: Whiteville Speedway)

Wilkesboro Dragway Park - North Wilkesboro / (aka: North Wilkesboro Dragway)
1/8 mile paved dragstrip (c.1981 - present)

Williamston Fairgrounds - Williamston - 1/2 mile dirt oval (c.10/02/34 - 10/03/36)

Wilmington Fairgrounds - Wilmington / at the New Hanover County Fairgrounds
3/4 mile dirt oval (10/02/37 - c.1941) (c.1946 - c.1949)
(aka: Wilmington Coastal Fairgrounds)

Wilson Fairgrounds - Wilson / located at the new Wilson County Fairgrounds
1/2 mile dirt oval (1934 - 1941) (1946 - c.1989)
opened in 1933 for horse racing / located south edge of town
(aka: Wilson County Speedway) / (aka: Legion Speedway)

Wilson Fairgrounds - Wilson / located at the old Wilson County Fairgrounds
1/2 mile dirt oval (c.1924 - c.1932)

Winston-Salem - 1/8 mile dirt oval (1957)

Winston-Salem Fairgrounds - Winston-Salem / at Forsythe County Fairgrounds
1/2 mile dirt oval (c.1929-10/11/41)(1945-1946)(c.5/29/55-10/11/58)(10/12/63)
1/8 mile paved dragstrip (1959 - c.1960)
(aka: Dixie Classic Fairgrounds) / oval track was a horse track

Winston-Salem Memorial Coliseum - Winston-Salem
1/10 mile paved indoor oval (10/18/57 - 12/10/57) / ran Micro-midgets

Winston-Salem Speedway - see: Peace Haven Speedway

Winston-Salem - also see: Bowman Gray Stadium, Capella, South Side Park

Woodland - 1/2 mile dirt oval (10/27/34)

NORTH DAKOTA

All Season Arena - Minot - oval (years unknown)

Badlands Speedway - see: Southwest Speedway

Beulah Fairgrounds - Beulah / located at the Mercer County Fairgrounds
   3/8 mile dirt oval (c.1971 - c.1975) / (aka: Beulah Speedway)

Binford Speedway - Binford - 1/4 mile dirt oval (c.1972 - 1973)

Bismarck - 1/4 mile dirt oval (1950's) / this track was not Bismarck Speedway

Bismarck Fairgrounds - Bismarck / located at the old Missouri Valley Fairgrounds
   1/2 mile dirt oval (1929)

Bismarck Fairgrounds (new) - see: Missouri Valley

Bismarck Speedway - Bismarck / (aka: Capital City Speedway) / (aka: Fast Track)
   1/4 mile dirt oval (1951 - 1989) / (aka: Central State Race Track)
   (aka: Bismarck Capital Raceway) / appx. two miles east of town near I-94

Blue Ribbon Speedway - Langdon - 1/4 mile dirt oval (5/15/91 - present)
   located at an old snowmobile track

Buffalo City Speedway - see: Jamestown Speedway

Cando Fairgrounds - Cando / located at the Towner County Fairgrounds
   1/4 mile dirt oval (1953) (6/28/84) (1989)

Capital City Speedway - see: Bismarck Speedway

Central Raceway - Carrington - 1/4 & 1/2 mile dirt ovals (c.1968 - 1975)

Central State Race Track - see: Bismarck Speedway

Crosby Fairgrounds - Crosby - 1/4 mile dirt oval (1989)
   located at the Divide County Fairgrounds

Dacotah Speedway - Mandan - 3/8 mile dirt oval (1989 - present)
   located at a city park on the southeast side of town

Fargo Fairgrounds - Fargo / located at the old Red River Valley Fairgrounds
   1/2 mile dirt oval (1908 - 8/26/41) (8/30/46 - c.8/25/56)
   (aka: North Dakota State Fairgrounds) / located on the north side of town

Fargo Fairgrounds - see: Red River Valley Speedway

Fargo Motor Speedway - Fargo - 1/4 mile dirt oval (c.6/29/56)

Fargo Speedway Park - Fargo - 1/4 mile dirt oval (c.1964 - 1971)

Fast Track - see: Bismarck Speedway

Fesseden Fairgrounds - Fesseden / located at the Wells County Fairgrounds
   1/2 mile dirt oval (c.1948 - c.1952)

406   *North Dakota*

Geographical Center Speedway - Rugby / located at the Pierce Co. Fairgrounds
1/2 mile dirt oval (early 1950's) (1988 - present)

Grand Forks Airport - Grand Forks - paved road course on runways (1965)

Grand Forks Speedway - Grand Forks / at the Greater Grand Forks Fairgrounds
1/2 mile dirt oval (c.7/24/15 - 6/28/42) (6/29/46 - c.1952)
1/4 mile dirt oval (c.1963 - present)

Hamilton Speedway - Hamilton - 1/2 mile dirt oval (early 1950's)
1/4 mile dirt oval (1987 - present) / at the Pembina County Fairgrounds

Interstate Dragways - see: Minnesota chapter

Jamestown Speedway - Jamestown / located at the Stutsman County Fairgrounds
1/4 mile dirt oval (c.8/03/51 - present) / (aka: Buffalo City Speedway)

Langdon Fairgrounds - Langdon / located at the Cavalier County Fairgrounds
1/2 mile dirt oval (1950's - c.1966) / site became a housing project

Lisbon Fairgrounds (Speedway) - see: Sheyenne River Speedway

Mandan Fairgrounds - Mandan - 1/2 mile dirt oval (1929)

McLean County Speedway - Underwood / located at the McLean Co. Fairgrounds
3/8 mile dirt oval (1992 - present)

Minot Fairgrounds - see: Nodak Speedway

Missouri Valley Speedway - Bismarck - 3/8 mile dirt oval (1990 - present)
located at the new Missouri Valley Fairgrounds

Nodak Speedway - Minot / located at the North Dakota State Fairgrounds
1/2 mile dirt oval (c.1917 - 8/26/41) (c.7/19/47 - c.1967)
1/4 mile dirt oval (c.1966 - 1977) / (aka: Northwest Fairgrounds)
3/8 mile dirt oval (1978 - present)

North Dakota State Fairgrounds - see: Nodak Speedway or Fargo Fairgrounds

Park River Speedway - Park River - dirt oval (1970's) (1983)

Queen City Speedway - see: Southwest Speedway

Red River Valley Speedway - West Fargo / at the Red River Valley Fairgrounds
1/2 mile dirt oval (1972 - present) / track designed by Jimmy Thomas

Richmond Speedway - (location unknown) - dirt oval (c.1953)

Rugby Fairgrounds - see: Geographical Center Speedway

Sheyenne River Speedway - Lisbon / located at the Ransom County Fairgrounds
1/4 mile dirt oval (c.1973 - present) / (aka: Lisbon Speedway)

Southwest Speedway - Dickinson / (aka: Queen City Speedway)
1/3 mile dirt oval (1974 - 1975) (1980 - present) / (aka: Badlands Speedway)

Thunder Mountain Speedway - Bottineau - 1/4 mile dirt oval (6/11/94 - present)

Tri-County Speedway - Wishek / located at the Tri-County Fairgrounds
1/4 mile dirt oval (c.1973 - c.1983) (1986 - present)

Turtle Mountain Speedway - Belcourt - 1/4 mile dirt oval (August, 1991 - present)

Valley City Fairgrounds - Valley City / located at the Barnes County Fairgrounds
1/2 mile dirt oval (1918)

West Fargo Fairgrounds - see: Red River Valley Speedway

Williston Basin Speedway - Williston - 1/4 mile dirt oval (1971 - 1982)
3/8 mile dirt oval (1983 - present) / at Upper Missouri Valley Fairgrounds
(aka: Upper Missouri Valley Fairgrounds Race Track)

Williston Fairgrounds - Williston / at the old Upper Missouri Valley Fairgrounds
1/2 mile dirt oval (c.1914 - c.1915)

Wishek Fairgrounds - see: Tri-County Speedway

OHIO

339 Raceway - Watertown - 1/4 mile dirt oval (1960's) / (aka: Dobbie's Speedway)
Watertown is located five miles from Barlow / located on SR 339

Ace High Speedway - Conneaut - 3/8 mile dirt oval (1970 - 1990) (1992 - present)
(aka: Raceway 7) / (aka: Speedway 7) / located south of I-90 on SR 7

Ada Speedway - Ada - 1/8 mile dirt oval (1986 - 1990)
plowed under when co-owners couldn't agree

Airway Speedway - Dayton - 1/5 mile oiled dirt oval (7/22/36 - c.1937)
formerly a dog track / located at south Broadway & River Road

Akron - 1/4 mile paved dragstrip (1952 - c.1954)

Akron - 1/5 mile dirt oval (8/13/44 & 8/27/44)   was four miles from Rubber Bowl
these were outlaw races as there was a ban on auto racing during WWII

*Larry Dickson in the Lay's Transmission sprinter at Terre Haute in 1970.
John Mahoney photo.*

408

Akron Bowl (board track) - see: Akron-Cleveland Speedway

Akron - dirt oval (c.1915 - c.5/30/16) / maybe Fountain Park or Northampton

Akron Municipal Airport - Akron - paved road course (10/10/54) (7/01/56)

Akron Rubber Bowl - Akron - 1/5 mile dirt oval (6/11/41 - 7/29/42) (8/25/45 - 1948)
    (c.6/05/53 - 1954) (1957 - 1958) / Paul Russo won the first race
    the stadium is still used for football games / east end of airport

Akron Speedway - Akron - 1/2 mile dirt oval (6/22/30)

Akron Speedway - Akron - 1/2 mile dirt oval (7/01/34 - c.8/26/34)
    this track was advertised as a new speedway in 1934 race paper

*Ohio resident Eddie Richenbacher at San Francisco on February 27, 1915.
Phil Harms collection.*

Akron-Cleveland Speedway - Akron - 1/2 mile wood oval (9/06/26 - 9/28/30)
    built by Paul Turtin / turns banked 45 degrees (aka: Akron Bowl)
    track was located 7 miles north of Akron / 30 miles south of Cleveland
    ran only one AAA Nat'l Championship race (6/22/30) won by Shorty Cantlon
    (during the Great Depression the wood track completely vanished within
    five years. It wasn't sold, burned or given away, it was stolen piece
    by piece and used for building or was burned as heat in nearby homes) the
    track was actually in Northampton Township (since incorporated to Akron)

Akron - also see: Brimfield, Firestone Test Track, Fountain Park, Northampton

Al's Sportsmans Speedway - Ashland (Olivesburg) - 1/4 mile dirt oval (1946-c.1947)

Alderman Speedway - see: Saint Clairsville Speedway - Saint Clairsville

Allentown (Family) Speedway - see: Limaland Speedway

Alliance - 1/6 mile dirt oval (Oct., 1942) (6/16/44)/ (aka: Harnar's Track)
    the 1944 race was held illegally / ban on auto racing during World War II

American Legion Raceway - Southington - 3/8 mile dirt oval (1947 & 1948)

Argonne Forest Speedway - Dayton - dirt oval (c.10/15/39) / maybe Forest Park

Ascot Park - see: Northampton Track

Ashland Coliseum - Ashland - 1/8 mile indoor dirt oval (1/24/54 - 1954)
    located at the Ashland County Fairgrounds / ran T.Q. midgets races

Ashland County Fairgrounds - Ashland / (aka: Ashland Speedway)
    1/2 mile dirt oval (c.1932 - July, 1942) (5/26/46 - c.1959)

Athen County Fairgrounds - Athens - 1/2 mile dirt oval (7/04/54)

Athens County Speedway - see: Skyline Speedway

Atomic Speedway - see: K-C Raceway

The tracks at Attica Raceway Park. - Official track photo.

Attica Raceway Park - Attica / located at the Attica Independent Fairgrounds
    1/2 mile dirt oval (1951 - c.1956) (1959 - c.8/27/76)
    1/3 mile dirt oval (May, 1988 - present) / (aka: Attica Speedway)

Bainbridge Fairgrounds - Aurora / the site is 1.2 mile north of Sea World
    1.0 mile dirt oval (6/07/46- 1948)(5/07/50- c.1951) / ran AAA race 7/13/47
    the promoter was Vincent Frattone / ran NASCAR GN race on 7/08/51
    the track became the Grandview Race Track for horse racing in 1950's
    the track is still visible but overgrown with weeds / grandstands removed

Barberton Speedway - Norton / (aka: Rubber City Speedway)
    1/4 mile paved oval (c.7/09/48 - present)

Bear Creek Speedway - Canton - 1/8 mile dirt oval (1988 - 1992)
    ran Mini-sprint from 1988 - 1992 / now only runs Go-Karts

Bellefontaine Fairgrounds - Bellefontaine / at the Logan County Fairgrounds
    1/2 mile dirt oval (c.1948 - c.1955)

Benore Speedway - Toledo - 1/5 mile dirt oval (1935) (7/21/39 - 8/18/39)
    formerly a dog track / located 1/4 mile east of Toledo Speedway

410

Berea Fairgrounds - Berea - 1/2 mile dirt oval (c.1934 - c.1941) (9/03/45)
1/4 mile dirt oval (4/21/46 - c.1948) / at the Cuyahoga County Fairgrounds
also known as the Cleveland Fairgrounds

Beulah Park - Columbus (Grove City) - 1/2 mile dirt oval (late 1920's) (c.1934)
3/4 mile dirt oval (7/14/35) / also see: Grove City Speedway

Big Oak Speedway - McConnelsville - 1/4 mile dirt oval (1947 & 1948)
located two mile south of SR 78 on SR 377

Blevin's Speedway - see: Valley Speedway - (c.10/29/50 - c.1955)

Bond Speedway - see: Skyline Speedway

Boone Hill Speedway - Troy - 1/4 mile dirt oval (c.1950 - c.1955)

Bowling Green Fairgrounds - Bowling Green / at the Wood County Fairgrounds
5/8 mile dirt oval (c.5/29/54 - 1956) (1960) / (aka: Bowling Green Speedway)
1/4 mile dirt oval (c.8/11/56 - 1956)

Bradford - 1/2 mile dirt oval (1932) / only year races were held at this site

Brimfield Speedway - Akron - 1/4 mile dirt oval (1947 - 1955) / a former dog track
the site is at the northwest corner of I-76 & Talmadge Road

Brookpark Speedway - Cleveland / located at Brookpark & West 139th
1/2 mile dirt oval (1933 - 1935)

Brown County Speedway - Russellville - 1/4 mile dirt oval (c.1971 - present)

Brush Run Park - Saint Clairsville - 1/8 mile paved dragstrip (1960's - present)
located on an old airport runway / (aka: Cherokee Dragway)
the same location as the old Saint Clairsville Speedway

Bryan Raceway - Bryan - 3/8 mile paved oval (c.1970 - 1982)
1/2 mile dirt oval (5/26/72 - c.1984) / track may have opened in 1949
7/16 mile dirt oval (c.1985 - present) / (aka: Bryan Motor Speedway)

Bryan Speedway - Bryan - 1/2 mile dirt oval (c.1929 - c.8/04/29)

Buck's Racing Grounds - Athens - 1/4 mile dirt oval (c.9/12/48)

Wally Arkkelin in his roadster in 1947. - Cora Arkkelin collection.

Buckeye Speedway - Orrville / (aka: Wayne County Speedway)
   3/8 mile dirt oval (1965 - present)

Bucyrus Fairgrounds - Bucyrus / located at the Crawford County Fairgrounds
   1/2 mile dirt oval (1932) (c.1952 - c.6/18/60)

Burton Fairgrounds - Burton / located at the Great Geauga County Fairgrounds
   1/4 & 1/2 mile dirt ovals (c.5/23/53 - c.1967) / (aka: Burton Speedway)

Budde Field Speedway - Steubenville - 1/2 mile dirt oval (c.8/17/41) (1946 - 1954)
   (aka: Fort Steuben Speedway)

Cadiz Race Track - Cadiz - 1/2 mile dirt oval (c.7/04/25 - c.1940)
   probably at the Cadiz Fairgrounds off US 22

Caldwell Fairgrounds - Caldwell / located at the Noble County Fairgrounds
   1/2 mile dirt oval (early 1950's)

Cambridge Speedway - Cambridge - dirt oval (c.1948 - c.1950) / near fairgrounds

Canfield Fairgrounds - Canfield / located at the Mahoning County Fairgrounds
   1/2 mile dirt oval (c.1929 - c.7/20/41) (5/25/46 - 1950)
   1/4 mile dirt oval (c.9/24/39 - 1942) (5/25/46 - 1973)
   Bud Miller held a big open competition sprint car race here in 1970

Canton Fairgrounds - Canton / located at the Stark County Fairgrounds
   1/2 mile dirt oval (c.1938 - 1940) / (aka: Lewis Midget Auto Speedway)
   1/3 mile dirt oval (8/12/39 - c.8/24/40) (1946 - c.1948)
   (aka: Canton Super Midget Motor Speedway)

Canton Motor Speedway - Canton - 1/4 mile dirt oval (c.6/27/52 - 1953)
   1/4 mile paved oval (1954 - 1992) / (aka: Canton Speedway)
   made into a gravel pit in late 1992

Canton - also see: Bear Creek, Municipal Auditorium

Carrollton Fairgrounds - Carrollton / located at the Carroll County Fairgrounds
   1/2 mile dirt oval (early 1930's) (early 1950's)

Carthage Fairgrounds - Cincinnati (Carthage) / at the Hamilton Co. Fairgrounds
   1/2 mile dirt oval (c.5/14/36 - c.6/25/36) / town no longer exist
   Carthage was incorporated into Cincinnati / fair still active but track gone

CCC Auto Derby Track - Columbus / (aka: CCC Auto Derby Speedway)
   1/4 mile dirt oval (c.8/25/40 - c.1940)

Celina Fairgrounds - Celina - 1/2 mile dirt oval (1930's) (6/22/47)
   1/4 mile dirt oval (c.1947 - c.1956) / at the Mercer County Fairgrounds

Champion Speedway - Kitts Hill - 1/4 mile dirt oval (1968 - 1970)
   the track is still there but overgrown with weeds

Cheek's Super Speedway - Portsmouth - 1/4 mile dirt oval (c.1958 - 1968)
   located 17 miles east of Portsmouth on CR 13, near Gephart

Cherokee Dragway - see: Brush Run Park

Chestnut Grove Speedway - Geneva-on-the-Lake - dirt oval (1951 & 1952)
   the promoter was Wally Arkkelin

412   *Ohio*

Chillicothe Fairgrounds - Chillicothe / located at the Ross County Fairgrounds
1/2 mile dirt oval (c.7/18/48 - c.1956)

Chillicothe Speedway - Chillicothe - 1/4 mile dirt oval (1954 - 1956)
track layout is still visible off Lunbeck Road / located south of town

Chippewa Lake Park Speedway - Medina - dirt oval (1938 - 1940)

Cincinnati - 7.9 mile road course on city streets (1954)

Cincinnati - 7.9 mile road course on city streets (9/09/11) / AAA championship race

Cincinnati Gardens - Cincinnati / Duke Cook was the last promoter
1/10 mile indoor concrete oval (3/28/51 - 1968) (1/14/79)

Cincinnati Motor Speedway - Cincinnati (Sharonville) / track was proposed in 1914
2.0 mile wood oval (9/04/16 - 10/12/19) / built by Harry Hake
turns were banked 17 degrees / rumored 65,000 fans at 5/30/17 race
the track was a near exact copy of the Chicago board track
last event was a 48 hour endurance run for Essex autos in December, 1919
the site is currently a U.S. Post Office among other businesses
the track was dismantled and the lumber was shipped to Chillicothe to be
used in the construction of Camp Sherman during World War I

Cincinnati Race Bowl - Cincinnati (Reading)
1/4 mile paved oval (May, 1948 - c.8/27/58)
1/5 mile dirt oval (c.7/03/51 - c.1951) / (aka: Cincinnati Speedway)
1/8 mile dirt oval (Sept., 1956 - c.1956) / (aka: Milford Speedway)
located at Reading Road & Glendale-Milford Road in Hamilton Township
sold for commercial and industrial use, the site is now a housing development

Cincinnati-Hamilton Speedway - Cincinnati / (aka: Jeff's Speedway)
1/2 mile dirt oval (c.1929 - c.1941) / Frank Funk promoter at one time
1/4 mile dirt oval (4/23/39 - c.8/27/39)
(aka: Cincinnati-Hamilton Midget Speedway)

Cincinnati - also see: Carthage, Coney Island, Edgewater, Fairfield, Gleneste,
Northside Ballpark, Oakley Park, Queen City & Springdale

Circleville Coliseum - Circleville - 1/15 mile paved indoor oval (12/05/53 & 1954)

Circleville Fairgrounds - Circleville / located at the Pickaway County Fairgrounds
1/2 mile dirt oval (c.9/08/49 - c.1959) / (aka: Circleville Speedway)
1/8 mile dirt oval (c.7/20/57 - 1959) / ran T.Q. midgets on smaller track

Circleville - also see: Salt Creek Valley Speedway

Cleveland - 1/2 mile dirt oval (5/29/22) (6/02/29)

Cleveland Arena - Cleveland - 1/10 mile indoor oval (11/26/54 - c.1963)
torn down in 1977 / now the site of the Red Cross Building

Cleveland Grand Prix - Cleveland / located at the Burke Lakefront Airport
2.369 mile concrete road course on runways (7/04/82 - present)
(aka: Cleveland Budweiser 500) / (aka: Budweiser Cleveland Grand Prix)
the promoter is Roger Penske / runs CART Indy Cars

Cleveland Luna Park - Cleveland - 1/5 mile dirt oval (c.1928) / ran motorcycles
the track, located at an amusement park, was called a Motodrome
on Woodland Ave & Woodhill Rd. / torn down in 1931
the site is now Woodhill Homes public housing project

Cleveland Municipal Stadium - Cleveland / former home of the Cleveland Indians
1/4 mile dirt oval (5/24/35) (6/14/47 - 8/02/47) / located near downtown

Cleveland - also see: Brookpark, Cloverleaf, Columbus Township, Cranwood,
Equestrian, Glenville, Maple Heights, Public Square, Randall Park,
Sportsmen Park, Thistledowns

Cloverleaf Stadium - Cleveland (Valley View) / (aka: Cloverleaf Speedway)
1/4 mile paved oval (5/20/60 - 1990) / the site is used for gravel storage
the former home of the Cleveland Bulldogs (a semi-pro football team)
the track operator for a number of years was George Eisenhart
(Eisenhart was the 1980 RPM Promoter of the Year)

Columbia Station Speedway - Columbia Station / at Royalton Rd & Station Rd
1/5 mile paved oval (years unknown)

Columbus - 1/4 mile dirt oval (c.1949 - c.1950) / maybe Columbus Motor or Devil's

Columbus - 1/5 mile dirt oval (7/18/41) / maybe CCC, Mock Road or Powell

Columbus Ballpark - Columbus - 1/5 mile dirt oval (1935 & 1936)

Columbus Driving Park - Columbus - 1.0 mile dirt oval (7/04/03 - 1925)
Barney Oldfield ran an exhibition race here on 7/02/03
Eddie Rickenbacker lived one block from this track when he was young
held a 24 hour endurance race here in 1905
was a horse track / torn down in 1926 / site is now a housing development

Columbus Fairgrounds - see: Ohio State Fairgrounds

Columbus Grand Prix - Columbus / ran IMSA GT on downtown circuit
2.3 mile paved city street road course (10/04/84 - 1988)

Columbus Motor Speedway - Columbus - 1/3 mile dirt oval (9/21/47 - 6/16/57)
1/10 mile paved oval (7/28/56 - 1956) / T.Q. midgets on 1/10 mile track
1/3 mile paved oval (1957 - present)
started out as the Indian Motorcycle Club track before World War II

Columbus - also see: Beulah Park, CCC, Devil's, Grove City, Harrisburg, Mock
Road, Morse, Neil Park, Norway, Ohio State Fairgrounds, Powell, Walker

Columbus Township - Cleveland (Bedford) - 3/16 mile paved oval (1962) / TQs

Community Arena - Steubenville - 1/8 mile indoor oval (11/28/65 - c.2/27/66)

Coney Island Speedway - Cincinnati (Sharonville) / located 10 miles NE of town
1.0 mile dirt oval (1/28/28) / same site as Cincinnati (wood) Speedway
1/7 mile cinder oval (5/30/35) / was located at an amusement park

Conley Speedway - McDermott - 1/4 mile dirt oval (9/27/59 - c.1960)
located on the eastern edge of McDermott in a gravel pit

Conneaut - dirt oval (1939) / ran roadsters

414

Cornstalk Speedway - Pleasant Hill - dirt oval (years unknown)

Cortland Fairgrounds - Cortland / at the new Trumbull County Fairgrounds
    1/2 mile dirt oval (1970 - c.1983) / (aka: Expo Motor Speedway)

Coshocton Speedway - Coshocton - 1/4 mile dirt oval (c.1975 - 1987)
    now the site of Boyd Gravel Co. / now a gravel pit

Courtney Road Speedway - Alliance - 1/8 mile dirt oval (c.1966)

Cranwood Raceway - Warrensville Heights / corner of Miles & Cranwood Pkwy
    1/4 mile oiled dirt oval (7/12/40 - 1941) / now site is a Value City store

Dahio Drag Strip - Dayton - 1/4 mile paved dragstrip (8/17/57)

Darke County Speedway (Fairgrounds) - see: Greenville Motor Speedway

Davey Beef Arena - see: Ohio State Fair Coliseum

Dayton Fairgrounds - Dayton - 1/2 mile dirt oval (1902) (7/04/04) (9/29/13)
    (9/29/18) (1924) (1929) (5/16/59 - 1961) / at the Montgomery Co. Fairgrounds

USAC sprint cars at Dayton Speedway in 1979. - Rolland Rickard photo.

Dayton Speedway - Dayton - 5/8 mile flat square dirt oval (6/03/34 - 1938)
    1/2 mile high banked dirt oval (1939 - 7/26/42) (9/09/45 - 1959)
    Frank Funk changed the track from the square 5/8 mile to a 1/2 mile
    1/4 mile paved oval (6/20/47 - c.1954) / (aka: Greater Dayton Speedway)
    3/8 mile flat dirt oval (1959) / inside of the 1/2 mile track
    1/2 mile paved oval (1960 - 1970) (8/17/75 - 1982) / now a land fill

Dayton - also see: Airway, Argonne, Ervin Nutter, Forest, Hara, Mock, Westwood

Debo Speedway - Rayland - 1/4 mile dirt oval (5/30/47 - c.1965) / located on Rt 7
    (aka: Steubenville Motor Speedway) / now site of the Ohio Coal Co. yard

Deerfield Speedway - Deerfield - 3/16 mile dirt oval (1986) / ran Micro-sprints

Defiance Speedway - Defiance / (aka: Taylor's Speedway)
    1/3 mile dirt oval (c.5/15/54 - 1961)

DeGraff Nat'l Speedway - see: Shady Bowl Speedway

Delaware Fairgrounds - Delaware / located at the Delaware County Fairgrounds
1/4 mile dirt oval (c.8/17/52 - 1954) / (aka: Indian Valley Speedway)
1/2 mile dirt oval (8/24/52) / where Little Brown Jug harness race is held

Delphos Fairgrounds - see: Landeck Speedway

Devil's Speedway - Columbus - dirt oval (1948)
located one mile east of Big Walnut Creek on Livingston Ave.

Dick Willings Motorcycle Track - Ashtabula - 1/3 mile dirt oval (1947)
ran roadsters and motorcycles / on US 20 near North Bend Road

Dobbie's Speedway - see: 339 Raceway

DORA Speedway - Lancaster / (aka: Forest Rose Ranger's Track)
1/4 mile dirt oval (c.1952 - c.1953) / four miles from R.A.F. Speedway

Dover Fairgrounds - Dover / located at the Tuscarawas County Fairgrounds
1/2 mile dirt oval (c.7/06/47 - c.1953) / (aka: Dover Speedway)
currently holds an annual vintage race car convention

Dragway 42 - West Salem - 1/4 mile paved dragstrip (1961 - present)

Dunaway's 93 Raceway - Oak Hill - 1/4 mile dirt oval (April, 1992 - 1993)
3/8 mile dirt oval (1994 - present)

East Palestine - 1/2 mile dirt oval (1920's) / destroyed by a tornado

Eaton Fairgrounds - Eaton / located at the Preble County Fairgrounds
1/2 mile dirt oval (8/28/38) (5/16/54)

Edgewater Sports Park - Cincinnati (Cleves) / alongside the Greater Miami River
1/4 mile paved dragstrip (May, 1954 - present)

Eldora Speedway - Rossburg (New Weston) - 1/4 mile dirt oval (1953 - 1955)
3/8 mile dirt oval (1956 & 1957) / (aka: El Dora Speedway)
1/2 mile high banked dirt oval (1958 - present) / built by Earl Baltes
held the first ever $100,000 to win sprint car race on 8/14/93
home of the "World 100", "Kings Royal", "The Big One", & "The Dream"
also has a 1.0 mile dirt track that was carved out but never ran on
owner and promoter Earl Baltes was the 1993 RPM Promoter of the Year

Eldora Speedway during the first annual "Historic Big One" in 1993. A packed crowd awaits the start of the $100,000 to win sprint car race. Panoramic photo by Nancy Brown.

416

Elyria Fairgrounds - Elyria - 1/2 mile dirt oval (c.1932 - 7/05/37)
(aka: Riverside Park) / located on 2nd St. / now site of a trailer park
the track was at the old Lorain County Fairgrounds

Equestrium Hall - Cleveland - 1/10 mile paved indoor oval (3/22/35)
locate at 6800 Denison / later became the site of a supermarket (now closed)

Ervin J. Nutter Center - Dayton - 1/8 mile indoor concrete oval (1/09/94 - present)
located at the Wright State University on the east side of town

Expo Motor Speedway - see: Cortland Fairgrounds

Fairfield (Cincinnati) - 1/5 mile dirt oval (c.6/13/35 - c.7/10/35) / ex-dog track

Findlay Fairgrounds - Findlay / located at the Hancock County Fairgrounds
1/2 mile dirt oval (6/03/28 - 8/26/28) (early 1950's - 9/01/82)

Findlay Speedway - see: Millstream Motor Speedway

Firestone Test Track - Akron - 7.712 mile paved oval / maybe in Texas
Jim McElreath turned 183 mph plus here in an Indy car in 1963

Forest Park - Dayton - 1/5 mile dirt oval (1949 - 1956)
formerly an amusement park / now the site of a shopping center

Fort Defiance Speedway - Defiance - 1/2 mile dirt oval (9/02/28)

Fort Miami Speedway - Toledo / located on Key Street (south of Ohio Turnpike)
1.0 mile dirt oval (10/28/02) (c.1918 - 1942) (1945 - 8/04/46) (7/04/56)
1/4 mile dirt oval (7/22/36 - 7/31/42) (c.9/13/45 - c.1949)
1/2 mile dirt oval (9/28/41) (7/06/47 - c.7/04/56)
3/8 mile dirt oval (c.6/30/57 - 8/11/57)
at the old Lucas Co. Fairgrounds / now site of Lucas Co. Recreation Center
promoters included Gerald Good / Don Zeiter / Jim White / Jechura Brothers

Fort Steuben Speedway - see: Budde Field

Fountain Park - Akron / formerly an amusement park / (aka: Forge Field)
1/2 mile dirt oval (mid 1920's - early 1930's)

Franklin Park - see: Strasburg Speedway

Fremont Speedway - Fremont / located at the Sandusky County Fairgrounds
1/2 mile dirt oval (6/07/36) / has a covered grandstand
1/3 mile dirt oval (1941) (c.1948 - present)

Gleneste Speedway - Cincinnati (Glenseste) - 1/4 mile dirt oval (c.1951 - c.1972)
(aka: Greater Cincinnati Race Bowl) / (aka: Gleneste Speed Bowl)

Glenville Driving Track - Cleveland - 1.0 mile dirt oval (5/30/1897 - c.1908)
torn down in 1909 / southside of St. Clair Ave. between E. 88th & 101
formerly a harness horse track / was in the old town of Glenville
closed when betting was declared illegal by mayor Frederick Goff
the harness racing shifted to Randall Park were it was legal

Glouster Speedway - Glouster - 1/4 mile dirt oval (c.1949 - c.1953) / now hayfield

Grabits' Speedway - Bloomingdale (Hopedale) - 1/4 mile dirt oval (c.1955 - 1976)
Stanley Grabits proposed a 1.0 dirt track in the 1970's / never built

Grand Lake Speedway - Mendon - 1/4 mile dirt oval (c.1964 - c.1992)
    a motorcycle track since mid 1960's / ran Mini-sprints 1988 / Midgets 1989
    (aka: Lake St. Mary) / located southeast of Celina

Greater Cincinnati Speed Bowl - see: Gleneste Speedway

Greene - 1/4 mile dirt oval (1948 - c.1949) / between Lockwood and Gustavus
    3/8 mile dirt oval (c.1950 - 1953) / built by Ike Jewitt
    the track was located near the intersection of SR 87 & SR 46 on a side road

Greenville - 1/2 mile dirt oval (8/27/21) / not Greenville Motor Speedway

Greenville Motor Speedway - Greenville / at the Darke County Fairgrounds
    1/2 mile dirt oval (c.10/13/21 - c.5/20/42) (8/03/47 - 1948)(6/17/51 - 1955)
    (aka: Darke County Speedway) / a drive-in theater was built in the infield
    possibly opened on 8/27/21 / Ralph D. Ormsby won the race on 10/13/21

Grove City Speedway - Columbus (Grove City) - dirt oval (c.1953)
    the track was next to Buelah Park (horse track) / now horse barns on site

Grove Speedway - Jackson - 1/4 mile dirt oval (c.1953) / was in a picnic grounds

Guernsey Speedway - Byesville - 1/4 mile dirt oval (5/10/53 - 1953)
    1/4 mile paved oval (late 1953 - 1954) / now site of a housing development

Hamilton Fairgrounds - Hamilton / located at the new Butler County Fairgrounds
    1/2 mile dirt oval (c.1920 - 9/28/41) / (aka: Hamilton Speedway)

Hara Arena - Dayton - 1/10 mile indoor concrete oval (1983) (1/26/85) / Midgets

Harrisburg Speedway - Columbus - 1/6 mile dirt oval (1962) / ran T.Q. midgets

Haydenville - dirt oval (years unknown) / two miles north of town

Hicksville Fairgrounds - Hicksville / located at the Defiance County Fairgrounds
    1/2 mile dirt oval (8/07/20) (7/11/48 - c.1955) (aka: Hicksville Speedway)

Hilliard Fairgrounds - Hilliard - 1/2 mile dirt oval (years unknown)
    located at the Franklin County Fairgrounds

Hilltop Speedway - Marietta (Gravel Banks) / (aka: Marietta-Belpre Speedway)
    1/4 mile dirt oval (c.1967 - 1985) / (aka: Marietta Speedway) / on SR 7

Hocking Valley Speedway - Logan - 1/2 mile dirt oval (c.5/22/49 - 1966)
    located on the southeast edge town on CR 4 / site is now a cornfield

Holbart Arena - Troy - 1/10 mile indoor oval (1949 - c.1959) / ran T.Q. midgets

Holmes County Speedway - see: Lakeville Speedway

Holmes Hilltop Speedway - Millersburg - 1/4 mile dirt oval (early 1970's)
    Hilltop Motors & Auto Parts now occupy track's parking lot / track intact

Hyde Park Dragway - Hebron - 1/4 mile paved dragstrip (1958 - 1962)

Indian Lake - Russells Point - 1/4 mile dirt oval (1960) / ran T.Q. midgets

Indian Valley Speedway - see: Delaware Fairgrounds

Ironton - dirt oval (1930's - c.1940) / this was not Southern Speedway

418

Jeff's Speedway - see: Cincinnati-Hamilton Speedway

Jefferson Fairgrounds - Jefferson - 1/2 mile dirt oval (c.1932- c.1935)(1952 & 1953)
    1/4 mile dirt oval (1953 - 1958) / at the Ashtabula County Fairgrounds

Jockey Park - Maple Heights - dirt oval (1930's) / near Cleveland off Rockside Rd
    the site is behind the First National Supermarket warehouse / ex-horse track

Jones Boy Speedway - Zanesville / seven miles south on SR 77 (now SR 60)
    1/5 mile dirt oval (7/09/39 - c.6/02/40) / (aka: Zanesville Speedway)
    the site is now Shelly's & Sam's constructon yard

Jones Speedway - see: London Fairgrounds

K.D. Dragway - South Webster - 1/8 mile paved dragstrip (9/01/89 - present)

K-C Raceway - Chillicothe (Alma) - 1/3 mile dirt oval (c.6/28/53 - 9/16/69)
    3/8 mile dirt oval (1970 - present) / (aka: Atomic Speedway)

Kenton Fairgrounds - Kenton / located at the Hardin County Fairgrounds
    1/2 mile dirt oval (9/26/58 - c.1966)

Kettlersville Dragstrip - Kettlersville - 1/5 mile paved dragstrip (1961)

Kil-Kare Speedway. - Official track photo.

Kil-Kare Speedway - Xenia - 1/5 mile dirt oval (1951 - 1955)
    1/3 mile paved oval (7/01/55 - present) / also has a 1/4 mile paved oval
    1/4 mile paved dragstrip (1956 - present)

Kinsman Fairgrounds - Kinsman - 1/2 mile dirt oval (c.1926) (1952)
    the site is now the Kinsman Car Wash and Laundromat on SR 7

Kiser Lake Sportsman's Speedway - see: Saint Paris Speedway

Knox-Vernon Speedway - Mount Vernon - 1/3 mile dirt oval (June, 1958 - 1961)

Lake Milton Speedway - Lake Milton - 1/4 mile dirt oval (c.6/08/52 - c.1952)

Lakeland Speedway - see: Painesville Speedway

Lakeville Speedway - Lakeville / (aka: Holmes County Speedway)
    1/3 mile dirt oval (1964 - 1992) (1994 - present)
    (aka: Tri-C Motor Speedway)

Lancaster Motor Speedway - Lancaster / (aka: R.A.F. Speedway)
    1/4 mile dirt oval (c.10/26/52 - c.1956) / may have been at the fairgrounds
    located west of town on US 33 / site is now the Fairfield Career Center

Lancaster Motor Speedway - Lancaster / located close to downtown
1/4 mile dirt oval (6/25/83 - 1986) / closed because of too much noise

Landeck Speedway - Delphos (Landeck) - 1/2 mile dirt oval (c.5/30/47 - 1953)
1/4 mile dirt oval (5/16/54 - c.1954)
3/8 mile paved oval (6/29/56 - 1963) / ten miles southeast of Van Wert

Lebanon Fairgrounds - Lebanon / located at the Warren County Fairgrounds
1/2 mile dirt oval (5/04/47 - 1949)

Lebanon Raceway - Lebanon - 1/2 mile dirt oval (c.1922-c.1929) (1953) horse track

Legion Speedway - see: Sharon Speedway

Lewis Midget Auto Speedway - see: Canton Fairgrounds

Lima Fairgrounds - Lima / located at the Allen County Fairgrounds
1/2 mile dirt oval (7/04/16 - 8/31/17) (1961 - 1992)
1/4 mile dirt oval (8/24/61 - 1962) / running motorcycles only since 1961

Limaland Speedway - Lima (Allentown) - 1/3 mile dirt oval (c.8/23/39 - c.9/10/39)
1/4 mile flat dirt oval (4/28/40- c.9/03/40) (8/23/46 - 6/22/47)
(7/15/50 - 1950) (c.7/26/54 - 1966) / race scheduled for 6/06/48 rained out
1/4 mile banked dirt oval (July 1967 - 1983) (1986- 1987) (1989 - present)
(aka: Limaland Motor Speedway) / (aka: Allentown Speedway)
(aka: Allentown Family Speedway) / on West North St & Dutch Hollow

Lockbourne Air Force Base - Lockbourne / now called the Rickenbacker A.N.G.B.
3.5 mile paved road course on runways (8/09/53 & 4/04/54)

London Fairgrounds - London / located at the Madison County Fairgrounds
1/2 mile dirt oval (c.6/13/48 - early 1950's) / (aka: Jones Speedway)

Lorain Speedway - South Amherst - 1/3 mile dirt oval (7/03/49 - c.1956)
3/8 mile paved oval (c.1957 - present) / (aka: Lorain County Speedway)

Lucasville Fairgrounds - Lucasville / located at the Scioto County Fairgrounds
1/2 mile dirt oval (1939) (10/05/47) (c.5/31/53 & 1954)

Magnolia Dragway - Magnolia - 1/4 mile paved dragstrip (1970's)

Manchester - dirt oval (c.1937) / located in Adams County

Mansfield Fairgrounds - Mansfield / located at the Richland County Fairgrounds
1/2 mile dirt oval (mid 1930's - 7/26/42)

Mansfield Raceway Park - Mansfield - 3/8 mile dirt oval (1959 - 1967)
1/4 mile dirt oval (1968) / located north of town near the airport
1/2 mile dirt oval (1968 - 7/06/88) (5/28/93 - present)
(aka: Mansfield Raceway)

Marietta Fairgrounds - Marietta - 1/2 mile dirt oval (1921 - 1930)
1/4 mile dirt oval (early 1950's) / at the Washington County Fairgrounds

Marietta Speedway - see: Hilltop Speedway

Marion Co. Int'l Raceway - LaRue - 1/4 mile paved dragstrip (May, 1969 - present)

420

Marion Fairgrounds - Marion / located at the Marion County Fairgrounds
1/2 mile dirt oval (c.7/12/36 - 1941)(1946 - 1968)(1972- 1973)(1978)(1984)
Shorty Templeman fatally injured in a midget crash on 8/24/62

Marion Speedway - Marion - 3/8 mile dirt oval (1948 - c.1955)
1/4 mile dirt oval (9/06/48 - c.1950) / (aka: New Marion Speedbowl)

Marysville Fairgrounds - Marysville / located at the Union County Fairgrounds
1/4 & 1/2 mile dirt ovals (1946 - 10/27/47) (1951) (1955) (1966)

Mason Beach Speedway - Bryan / built by Don Zieter in a Quarry
1/2 mile dirt oval (5/30/31 - c.1941) (1946 - c.1955)
1/4 mile dirt oval (c.7/18/52 - c.1952)

Mathias Raceway - New Philadelphia - 1/4 mile dirt oval (1990)

McConnelsville - see: Big Oak Speedway

McCutchenville Speedway - McCutchenville / (aka: Quad City Speedway)
3/8 mile dirt oval (1971 - 1984) (1986) / (aka: Mohawk Speedway)
(aka: O.K. Corral Speedway) / (aka: Mid-America Raceway Park)

McDermott Speedway - see: Rushtown Speedway

Miami County Raceway - Troy - 1/4 mile dirt oval (1960) / maybe at fairgrounds

Mick's Speedway - Athens - dirt oval (years unknown)

Mid-American Raceway Park - see: McCutchenville Speedway

Mid-Ohio Sports Car Course - Lexington / (aka: Mid-Ohio Race Track)
2.4 mile paved road course (1964 - present)

Midvale Speedway - Midvale - 3/10 mile dirt oval (1953 - c.1965)
3/10 mile paved oval (c.1966 - present)

Midway Speedway - Crooksville / (aka: Silver Dollar Speedway)
3/8 mile dirt oval (c.1963 - 1974) (1988 - present)

Midway Speedway - Lexington - dirt oval (c.1953)

Milford Speedway - see: Cincinnati Race Bowl

Millstream Motor Speedway - Findlay - 5/8 mile dirt oval (c.7/03/54 - 1959)
3/8 mile dirt oval (1960 - present) / (aka: Findlay Speedway)

Mock Oval - Dayton - 1/5 mile dirt oval (mid 1930's)

Mock Road Speed Bowl - Columbus - 1/4 mile dirt oval (c.1939 - c.1941)
located one mile east of Cleveland Avenue

Montpelier Fairgrounds - Montpelier / located at the Williams County Fairgrounds
1/2 mile dirt oval (1946) (c.1959 - c.1964)

Montville - see: Ziegler's Speedway

Morse Road Airport - Columbus - 1/4 mile paved dragstrip (1960's)

Mount Gilead Fairgrounds - Mount Gilead / at the Morrow Co. Fairgrounds
1/2 mile dirt oval (c.8/20/55 - c.8/18/72)

Mount Orab - 1/5 mile dirt oval (c.7/11/54)

Mount Vernon Fairgrounds - Mount Vernon - 1/2 mile dirt oval (c.1938 - 1939)
1/4 mile dirt oval (8/16/40 - 1940) (1956) / (aka: Knox Fairgrounds Speedway)

Mount Vernon - also see: Vernon Speedway, Knox-Vernon Speedway

Moxie Speedway - Zanesville (Moxahala Park)
1/4 mile dirt oval (c.7/21/49 - c.1956) / now site of Nolan Bros. Amusement
1/4 mile paved oval (1960's) / (c.1981 - c.1982) / the track is still intact

Municipal Auditorium - Canton - indoor oval (1/20/57) / ran T.Q. midgets

Muskingum County Speedway - Zanesville / south of town of Dresden on SR 60
1/4 mile dirt oval (6/28/42) (c.1946 - 1954) / built by Louie Morosco
1/4 mile paved oval (1955 -1970) / (aka: Zanesville Speedway)
3/8 mile dirt oval (Oct., 1970 - 1981) (1983 - 1987) (1989 - 1990)
(1993 - present) / Butch Hartman started driving career here in 1964 a the
new track and grandstands were built in 1983 / (aka: New City Speedway)

Nat'l Trail Raceway - Newark - 1/4 mile paved dragstrip (7/04/64 - present)

Neil Park Speedway - Columbus - 1/5 mile dirt oval (6/14/35 - c.1936)
at the Columbus Red Bird's baseball diamond / torn down in 1942

Nelson Ledges Race Track - Garretsville / (aka: Steel City Int'l Raceway)
2.1 mile paved road course (4/18/64 - present)

New Bremen Speedway - New Bremen
1/2 mile dirt oval (1926 - 9/20/31) (8/31/47 - 1966) (1979 - 1981)
the grandstands were burned down by Shorty Wolfe during a riot on 9/31/31
1/2 mile paved oval (1967 - 1978) / the pavement was removed in 1979

New City Speedway - Zanesville - 1/4 mile dirt oval (9/02/51) / outside city limits

New Concord Speedway - New Concord - 1/4 mile dirt oval (May,1964- June,1968)
the track was lengthened to a 1/3 mile and later to a 1/2 mile

New Waterford - dirt dragstrip (1970's)

Mario Andretti in the Wynn's sprinter at Eldora. - Alden Jamison collection.

422

North Randall - see: Randall Park

Northampton Track - Akron / located just south of wood track / (aka: Ascot Park)
   3/4 mile dirt oval (1920's - c.7/21/31) (1940) / now Ascot Industrial Park

Northside Ballpark Speedway - Cincinnati - 1/5 mile dirt oval (c.6/20/35-c.7/11/35)

Norwalk Fairgrounds - Norwalk / located at the Huron County Fairgrounds
   1/2 mile dirt oval (1923 - 9/14/41) (c.5/16/48)

Norwalk Raceway Park - Norwalk - 1/4 mile paved dragstrip (1962 - present)

*Two "rails" head down the dragstrip of Norwalk Raceway Park. The track
holds an annual IHRA National event. - Official track photo.*

Norway Dragstrip - Columbus - 1/4 mile paved dragstrip (c.1957)

O.K. Corral Speedway - see: McCutchenville Speedway

Oak Harbor Fairgrounds - Oak Harbor - dirt oval (1963)
   located at the Ottawa County Fairgrounds

Oakley Park - Cincinnati - 1.0 mile dirt oval (11/25/01) (8/18/05 - 1907) (1909)
   southeast corner of the city / the site is now ballfields

Oakshade Raceways - Wauseon (Oakshade) - 3/8 mile dirt oval (c.1976 - present)

Ohio State Fair Coliseum - Columbus - 1/10 mile indoor oval (11/03/56 - 1963)
   (aka: Ohio State University Beef & Cattle Building)
   (aka: Davey Beef Arena) / 1/4 midget and kart racing / dismantled in 1994

Ohio State Fairgrounds - Columbus - 1/2 mile dirt oval (5/22/55 - c.1970)
   1/10 mile dirt oval (5/30/57 - c.1957) / on front stretch of big track
   new fairgrounds to replace old one / located I-71 & 17th Avenue North
   the grandstands still remain but track is now horse arena and parking

Ohio State Fairgrounds - Columbus / this was not the Columbus Driving Park
   1/2 mile dirt oval (1919 - 9/01/30) (1932) (c.1939)
   1/4 mile dirt oval (6/19/40 - c.8/31/41) (c.8/24/46 - c.1946)

Ottawa Fairgrounds - Ottawa / located at the Putnam County Fairgrounds
   1/2 mile dirt oval (5/30/48) (9/26/59 - c.1965) (1979) (1983)

Pacemakers Dragway - Mt. Vernon - 1/4 mile paved dragstrip (1956 - present)

Painesville Fairgrounds - Painesville / located at the Lake County Fairgrounds
1/2 mile dirt oval (early 1930's) (8/21/41) (1946) (8/27/60 - c.1962)

Painesville Speedway - Painesville / (aka: Lakeland Speedway)
1/5 mile paved oval (7/11/58 - present)

Pattenville Speedway - see: Walker Speedway

Paulding Fairgrounds - Paulding / located at the Paulding County Fairgrounds
3/8 mile dirt oval (1950 - 1952) (c.1954) (1960)

Pickaway Speedway - see: Salt Creek Valley Speedway

Piketon Fairgrounds - Piketon / located at the Pike County Fairgrounds
1/2 mile dirt oval (years unknown)

Plain City Fairgrounds - Plain City - 1/2 mile dirt oval (c.9/03/50 - c.1952)

Pomeroy Fairgrounds - Pomeroy / located at the Meigs County Fairgrounds
1/2 mile dirt oval (c.7/06/47 - c.1951)

Portsmouth - Cheek's Super, Raven Rock Dragstrip, South Ohio Speedway

Portsmouth Fairgrounds - see: Lucasville Fairgrounds

Portsmouth Football Stadium - see: Spartan Stadium

Portsmouth Raceway Park - Portsmouth - 1/4 mile dirt oval (9/22/90 - 1993)
the track is located next to the Ohio River, and the grandstands floated
away when the river overflowed on 11/15/90, a boat had to be taken out to
lasso the stands and retrieve them, the track was 20 foot under water
1/3 mile dirt oval (1994 - present)

Portsmouth Speedway - Portsmouth (Friendship) - 1/4 mile dirt oval (early 1950's)
1/4 mile paved oval (c.1953 - c.1963) / located west of town on Highway 52
the site is the Shawnee Village Campgrounds / track used as camping sites

Powell Motor Speedway - Columbus (Powell) - 1/2 mile dirt oval (June 1939- 1941)
the first track ran in the opposite direction than later tracks
1/2 mile dirt oval (6/30/46 - 1959) / (aka: Powell Speedway)
1/4 mile dirt oval (7/25/53 - c.5/30/54) / located on SR 750
1/4 mile paved oval (c.6/16/54 - 1959)
1/2 mile paved oval (5/29/60 - 1965) < 3140 foot long, two foot from inside
1/3 mile dirt oval (1960 - 1965) / the track is still intact

Proctorville Fairgrounds - Proctorville / at the Lawrence County Fairgrounds
1/4 mile dirt oval (c.10/26/47 - c.1967)

Public Square - Cleveland - city street oval (c.1955) / ran stocks cars downtown

Put-In-Bay - South Bass Island / on an island on Lake Erie (near Sandusky)
paved city street road course (1952 - 1963)

Quad City Speedway - see: McCutchenville Speedway

Quaker City Dragway - Salem - 1/4 mile paved dragstrip (1957 - present)

424

Queen City Speedway - Cincinnati (Westchester) / (aka: Tri-County Speedway)
1/2 mile dirt oval (4/27/68 - 5/06/72) / first promoter was Bill Redwine
Chuck McWilliams won first race / Jim Cushman won first race on pavement
Rodney Combs started his driving career here in 1968
1/2 mile paved oval (5/20/72 - 1987) / became a truck driving school

R.A.F. Speedway - see: Lancaster Motor Speedway

R & R Speedway - Zanesville - 3/8 mile dirt oval (1988 - present)

Raceway 7 - see: Ace High Speedway

Randall Park Raceway - Cleveland (North Randall) / was a horse track
1/2 mile dirt oval (9/25/27 - c.6/13/37) / 3/4 mile east of Cranwood Raceway
1/5 mile dirt oval (7/10/38) / now the site of the Randall Mall
the track was located at the northwest corner of SR 43 & SR 8

Raven Rock Dragstrip - Portsmouth - 1/4 mile paved dragstrip (1960's)

Ravenna Fairgrounds - Ravenna / located at the old Portage County Fairgrounds
1/2 mile dirt oval (c.1926 - c.1929) (8/30/36) (6/09/47)
the site is now the Woodgate Apartments on SR 88

Richwood Fairgrounds - Richwood / located at the Union County Fairgrounds
1/2 mile dirt oval (c.1952) / (aka: Richwood Independent Fairgrounds)
1/4 mile dirt oval (c.1953 - 1966) / (aka: Richwood Speedway)

Riverside Park - see: Elyria Fairgrounds

Riverside Raceway - Chesapeake (Proctorville) - 1/4 mile dirt oval (late 1960's)
1/4 mile paved oval (1970 & 1971) / located two miles east on Old Hwy 17
1/4 mile paved dragstrip (late 1960's - 1972) / (aka: Riverside Dragway)
forced out of business by a nearby hospital that complained about noise
the track is still visible / a coal company now occupies the property

Rubber Bowl - see: Akron Rubber Bowl

Rubber City Speedway - see: Barberton Speedway

Rushtown Speedway - McDermott - 1/4 mile dirt oval (1973 - 1974)
located on SR 104 (McDermott Pike) / site now behind Adkins Used Cars

Saint Clairsville Speedway - Morristown / built to replace other track
3/8 mile dirt oval (7/27/75 - 1987)

Saint Clairsville Speedway - Saint Clairsville / (aka: Wheels Speedway)
1/4 mile dirt oval (May, 1958 - Sept., 1973) / closed to strip mine property
located on Airport Road / and just off of US Highway 40
the site is now part of Alderman Field airport / (aka: Alderman Speedway)

Saint Paris Speedway - Saint Paris / (aka: Kiser Lake Sportsman's Speedway)
1/8 mile dirt oval (5/24/58 - c.1961) / ran T.Q. midgets

Salt Creek Valley Speedway - Circleville / (aka: Pickaway Speedway)
1/2 mile dirt oval (late 1950's) (1965 - 1968) (1975) (1984) (8/03/90)
located on SR 56 / part of the track is now a cornfield

Sandusky Fairgrounds - Sandusky / located at the Erie County Fairgrounds
1/2 mile dirt oval (1930's) / fairgrounds still exist but track is gone

Tim Richmond was a standout supermodified driver before he moved on to Indy Cars and the NASCAR Winston Cup circuit. - Rolland Rickard photo.

Sandusky Speedway - Sandusky - 1/4 mile dirt oval (1948 - 1954)
    1/2 mile paved oval (1955 - present) / (aka: Sandusky Int'l Speedway)
    promoters included Dick Decker / Bill Bader / Larry Boos / Bentley Warren
    Nolan Johncock fatally injured here in a supermodified crash on 10/03/71

Shady Bowl Speedway - DeGraff - 3/10 mile dirt oval (1946)
    located over the hill from the present Shady Bowl Speedway

Shady Bowl Speedway - DeGraff - 3/10 mile paved oval (1947-1990)(1992- present)
    (aka: DeGraff Nat'l Speedway) / owner arrested in 1990 for drug dealing

Sharon Speedway - Hartford / named after closest large city (Sharon, PA)
    1/2 mile dirt oval (1929 - 1942) (8/11/46 - c.1958)(1969 - 7/06/70)
    1/4 mile dirt oval (6/04/53 - 8/02/70) / (aka: Legion Speedway)
    1/2 mile paved oval (5/09/71 - 9/07/80) / called Legion in 1930's
    1/2 mile dirt oval (1981 - present) / pavement torn out in 1981
    Deb Snider started his career here

Sharonville - see: Cincinnati Motor Speedway

Sidney Fairgrounds - Sidney / located at the Shelby County Fairgrounds
    1/2 mile dirt oval (late 1920's) (Sept., 1938 - c.1941) (1945 - c.1961)

Silver Dollar Speedway - see: Midway Speedway

Skyline Speedway - Athens (Stewart) / (aka: Athens County Speedway)
    1/4 mile dirt oval (1965 - present) / (aka: Bond Speedway)

Smithfield Fairgrounds - Smithfield / located at the Jefferson County Fairgrounds
    1/2 mile dirt oval (c.1926 - 1927) (1954) / located in Friendship Park
    1/3 mile dirt oval (1941 - 7/04/41) (c.1947 - c.1960)

Snook Speedway - Antwerp - dirt oval (7/28/29) (8/25/29) (10/06/29)

Southern Ohio Raceway - Portsmouth (Fair Oaks) / located on CR 242
    3/8 mile dirt oval (c.1967 - c.1974)
    1/2 mile dirt oval (c.1975 - 1985) (1988 - 1992)

Southern Speedway - Ironton - oval (c.6/03/51 - c.1951)

426

Spartan Stadium - Portsmouth - dirt oval (mid 1930's) / eastside of town
(aka: Portsmouth Football Stadium) / (aka: Brick Stadium) / walls of brick
running track in semi-pro football stadium / now used for high school games

Speedway 21 - Beach City - 1/4 mile dirt oval (1960's) / built by Russ Draime
located near Dover on SR 21 / site is now partially covered by I-77

Speedway 250 - Cadiz - 1/4 mile dirt oval (c.1965 - 1970's) (1992)
(aka: Wide Oval Speedway) / the promoter in the 1960's was Tom Coultrap

Speedway 7 - see: Ace High Speedway

Sportsmen Park - Cleveland (Bedford) / located southeast of Cleveland on SR 8
1/4 mile dirt oval (10/18/36 - 7/26/42) (8/26/45 - 1955)
1/4 mile paved oval (c.6/24/56 - c.9/09/56) / the promoter was Earl Clay
Originally built by Al Capone for dog racing. The grandstands were built
in two counties in hopes of one or the other would legalize gambling -
neither did / turns 1 & 2 in Summit Co. / turns 3 & 4 in Cuyahoga Co.
now the site of Northfield Park (a horse track)

Springdale Amusement Park - Cincinnati - 1/4 mile dirt oval (9/08/34 - c.1934)

Springfield - 1/2 mile dirt oval (c.1951) / at an abandoned airport

Springfield Fairgrounds - Springfield / located at the Clark County Fairgrounds
1/2 mile dirt oval (1938) (9/23/51 - 5/30/76) / (aka: Clark Co. Speedway)

Springfield Speedway - see: Springfield Springs Speedway

Springfield Springs Speedway - Springfield / located two miles east of town
1/4 mile dirt oval (c.5.30/54 - 1957) / (aka: Springfield Speedway)

Steel City Int'l Raceway - see: Nelson Ledges Race Track

Steel Valley Dragway - Smithfield - 1/8 mile paved dragstrip (c.1994 - present)

Steubenville Fairgrounds - see: Smithfield Fairgrounds

*John Mickle was so disgusted with his race car at Chestnut Grove Speedway
that he abandoned the car and left it at the track at the end of the 1951 season.
Cora Arkkelin collection.*

Strasburg Speedway - Strasburg / (aka: Franklin Park Football Field)
    1/4 mile dirt oval (c.9/20/51 - 1953) (5/18/56) / now a running track

Swayne Field - Toledo / home of the Toledo Braves (minor league baseball team)
    1/5 mile dirt oval (6/11/35 - 10/27/35) / first midget races in Toledo
    now the site of Swayne Field Shopping Center / at corner of SR 25 & SR 51

Sycamore Kartway - Sycamore - 1/8 mile dirt oval (1987 & 1988) / ran Mini-sprints

Taylor's Speedway - see: Defiance Speedway

Thirty-Five (35) Raceway - Frankfort - 1/5 mile dirt oval (1990 - present)

An aerial view of Thirty-Five (35) Raceway. - Official track photo.

Thistledowns Race Track - Cleveland - 1.0 mile dirt oval (9/16/28)
    still a horse track / across from Randall Park Mall on Emery Road

Thompson Drag Raceway - Thompson / (aka: Thompson Dragway)
    1/4 mile paved dragstrip (1958 - present) / also has a Go-Kart track

Tiffin Fairgrounds - Tiffin / located at the Seneca County Fairgrounds
    1/2 mile dirt oval (1920's) (1938) (c.5/12/40 - 4/26/42) (c.1946 - c.1952)
    1/8 mile dirt oval (c.9/21/47 - c.1959) / southwest side of town on CR 594

Tiffin Raceway - Tiffin / (aka: Tiffin Speedway) / northeast of town on CR 21
    3/8 mile dirt oval (c.1947 - c.1959) / site is now a farmer's field

Toledo Fairgrounds - see: Fort Miami Speedway

Toledo Raceway Park - Toledo - 5/8 mile dirt oval (7/21/50 - 1958)
    Rollie Beale started his driving career here in 1950
    1/4 mile dirt oval (c.10/07/50 - c.1950)
    1/3 mile dirt oval (1955) / the track was located at 5555 Detroit Avenue
    1/2 mile dirt oval (1959 - c.1961) / the track was torn down in 1960's
    the site is now a harness track with the same name

Toledo Speedway - Toledo - 1/2 mile dirt oval (6/08/60 - 1961)
    1/5 & 1/2 mile paved ovals (1962 - present) / near I-75 on Benore Road
    the track was near the site of the old Benore Kart Track

Toledo Sports Arena - Toledo / ran mini-stocks (Crosleys) in 1950's / midgets 1973
1/10 mile indoor concrete oval (11/10/50 - 2/09/52) (1/02/73 & 1/07/73)

Toledo - also see: Benore, Fort Miami and Swayne Field

Torch Speedway - Torch (Coolville) - 1/5 mile dirt oval (c.9/04/48 - 1959)
located on CR 62, just south of SR 32 / site now a construction company

Track 42 - Mason - dirt oval (c.1954 - c.1955) / location on US 42

Tri-C Motor Speedway - see: Lakeville Speedway

Tri-County Speedway - see: Queen City Speedway

Tri-State Dragstrip - Hamilton - 1/4 mile paved dragstrip (c.1969 - present)

Tri-State Speedway - Forestdale - 1/4 mile dirt oval (5/30/50 - c.1953)
located one mile east of Coal Grove on SR 243

Trojan Speedway - Elden (location unknown) - 1/4 mile dirt oval (early 1950's)
may have been in the towns of either Eldean, Elden or Eldon

Troy Fairgrounds - Troy / located at the Miami County Fairgrounds
1/2 mile dirt oval (c.1954)

Upper Sandusky Fairgrounds - Upper Sandusky / at the Wyandot Co. Fairgrounds
1/2 mile dirt oval (1937) (1940 - c.1941) (c.5/05/46 - c.1958) (c.1983)

Urbana Fairgrounds - Urbana - 1/2 mile dirt oval (1939 & 1940) (1960 & 1961)
1/4 mile dirt oval (1957 - c.8/08/60) / at the Champaign Co. Fairgrounds

Vacationland Speedway - Port Clinton - 1/4 mile dirt oval (6/08/46 - 1946)

Valley Speedway - Middletown - dirt oval (c.10/29/50 - c.1955)
(aka: Blevin's Speedway) / location unknown (not Wellston or Middleton)

Van Wert Speedway - Van Wert - 1/2 mile dirt oval (years unknown) / on US 127
at Van Wert Co. Fairgrounds / sometimes confused with Landeck Speedway

Vernon Speedway - Mount Vernon - 1/4 mile dirt oval (1953 - c.1954)
there were no grandstands at this track

Vinton Raceway Park - Vinton - 1/4 mile dirt oval (1992 - present)

Vinton Raceway Park in southern Ohio. - Ron Garske photo.

Walker Speedway - Columbus - 1/5 mile dirt oval (6/16/50 - 1950)
   located at Agler & Stelzer Roads

Walker Speedway - Pattenville - dirt oval (1951) (1955) / located near Logan
   (aka: Pattenville Speedway)

Wapakoneta Fairgrounds - Wapakoneta / located at the Auglaize Co. Fairgrounds
   1/2 mile dirt oval (1939) (c.1956 - c.1969)

Warren Fairgrounds - Warren / located at the old Trumbull County Fairgrounds
   1/2 mile dirt oval (early 1930's) (9/04/50) / located near downtown
   now the site of the Athletic Fields at Warren Harding High School

Washington Court House Fairgrounds - Washington Court House / CORA midgets
   1/2 mile dirt oval (8/28/65) / west side of town at Fayette Co. Fairgrounds

Washington Court House Speedway - Washington Court House (Jonesboro)
   1/2 mile dirt oval (c.9/06/52 - 1962) / now site of 84 Lumber yard on US 22

Wauseon Fairgrounds - Wauseon / located at the Fulton County Fairgrounds
   1/4 & 1/2 mile dirt ovals (1951 - c.1956) / (aka: Wauseon Raceway)
   currently holds vintage auto racing events

Wayne County Speedway - see: Buckeye Speedway

Wayne Trail Dragway - Delphos - 1/8 mile paved dragstrip (c.1981 - 1985)

Wellington Fairgrounds - Wellington / located at the Lorain County Fairgrounds
   1/2 mile dirt oval (1948) (1954)

Wellston Fairgrounds - Wellston / located at the Jackson County Fairgrounds
   1/4 mile dirt oval (c.1946 - c.1954) / (aka: Wellston Speedway)

West Branch Speedway - Newton Falls - 1/7 mile dirt oval (c.1960 - 1962)
   1/7 mile paved oval (c.1963 - c.1964) / north of town off SR 5

Westwood Ballpark - Dayton - 1/6 mile dirt oval (8/10/35)

Wheels Speedway - see: Saint Clairsville Speedway - Saint Clairsville

Wide Oval Speedway - see: Speedway 250

Wilkesville Raceway - Wilkesville
   1/4 mile dirt oval (8/15/92 - c.9/13/92) (1994 - present)

Williston - dirt oval (1953) / located in Ottawa County / east of Northwood

Wilmington Fairgrounds - Wilmington / located at the Clinton County Fairgrounds
   1/2 mile dirt oval (Sept., 1938 - 1940) (c.8/10/57 - c.8/14/65)

Winchester - 1/2 mile semi-banked dirt oval (1948) / near junction SR 322 & 136
   located at a fairgrounds in Adams County

Xenia Fairgrounds - Xenia / located at the Greene County Fairgrounds
   1/2 mile dirt oval (1928)

Youngstown Drag City - Youngstown - 1/4 mile paved dragstrip (1964 - present)
   started construction on the strip in 1961

430   *Ohio*

Zanesville - 1/2 mile dirt oval (c.5/30/35)

Zanesville Speedway - see: Jones Boy Speedway or Muskingum County Speedway

Zanesville - also see: Jones Boy, Moxie, Muskingum, New City Speedway, R & R

Ziegler's Speedway - Hambden (Montville) - 1/5 mile dirt oval (1951 - c.1970)
    ran jalopies in beginning / ran T.Q. midgets & Micro-midgets after 1954

Jalopy stock car racing was rough and tumble. This is the aftermath of an accident at Ziegler's Speedway. - Cora Arkkelin collection.

OKLAHOMA

66 Raceway Park - see: Sixty-Six (66) Raceway Park

Ada Raceway - Ada / (aka: Echo Ranch Speedway) / (aka: Ada Speedway)
    3/8 mile dirt oval (c.1972 - c.1980) (1985 - 1987)

Ada Raceway - see: Sun Valley Speedway

Airport Speedway - Oklahoma City - 1/10 mile dirt oval (c.1956)

Altus - 1/4 mile dirt oval (c.1961 - 1962)

Altus Speedway - Altus - 1/3 mile dirt oval (8/04/73) / near Sooner Int'l Speedway
    1/3 mile paved oval (Sept., 1973 - present)
    this track's sister track is Pleasant Valley Speedway in Texas

Altus - also see: Quartz Mountain, Sooner Int'l

Alva - 1/4 mile dirt oval (1937) (c.1950 - c.1951)

Anadarko Fairgrounds - Anadarko / located at the Caddo County Fairgrounds
    1/2 mile dirt oval (early 1950's) / (aka: Caddo County Speedway)

Arbuckle Speedway - Ardmore - 3/8 mile dirt oval (3/26/89 - present)

Ardmore - 1/2 mile dirt oval (c.1919 - c.1925) / probably at Carter Co. Fairgrounds

Ardmore Airport - see: Gene Autry Municipal Airport

Ardmore Raceway - Ardmore - 1/4 mile paved dragstrip (c.1977 - present)

Bartlesville Speedway - see: Mid-America Speedway

Beaver Speedway - Beaver / located at the Beaver County Fairgrounds
3/8 mile dirt oval (1991 - present)

Black Widow Raceway - Lexington - 1/8 mile dirt oval (4/07/84 - 1989)
1/5 mile dirt oval (1990 - present) / (aka: River City Speedway)
(aka: Lexington 77 Speedway) / located north of town on US Highway 77

Blackwell Fairgrounds - Blackwell / located at the Kay County Fairgrounds
dirt oval (c.9/10/47 - c.9/12/47)

Buddy Cagle Speedway - Tulsa (Vera) - dirt oval (late 1970's)

Byerly's Speedway - Oklahoma City / located at a softball park
1/5 (.181) mile dirt oval (9/15/38 - 10/20/38)

Caddo County Speedway - see: Anadarko Fairgrounds

Capitol Hill High School Stadium - Oklahoma City
1/5 mile dirt oval (1937 - 7/22/38)

Chandler Fairgrounds - Chandler / located at the Lincoln County Fairgrounds
dirt oval (early 1950's)

Cherokee Dragstrip - Frederick - 1/4 mile paved dragstrip (c.1965 - c.1976)
located at an airport

Chickasha - 1/2 mile dirt oval (c.1925 - c.1935)
1/5 mile dirt oval (5/15/42) / maybe at the Grady County Fairgrounds

Chili Bowl - see: Tulsa Expo Center

Cimarron Raceway - Tulsa - 1/4 mile dirt oval (1991) / located west of Tulsa

Circle A Speedway - Guthrie - dirt oval (late 1970's)

*Altus Speedway is across the street from Sooner International Speedway.
Official track photo.*

Claxton Speedway - Meeker - 1/4 mile dirt oval (c.1986 - present)
(aka: County Line Speedway)

Cleveland - 1/2 mile dirt oval (5/29/51)

Coalgate Speedway - see: Oklahoma State Fairgrounds (old)

Colbert Raceway - Colbert - 3/8 mile dirt oval (c.1974 - 1975)

Colbert - also see: Jack Rabbit Speedway, Red River Valley Speedway

County Line Speedway - see: Claxton Speedway

Cratersville Speedway - see: Quartz Mountain Speedway

Creek County Speedway - see: Sixty-Six (66) Raceway Park

Crystal Beach Speedway - see: Woodward Fairgrounds

Cushing - 1/2 mile dirt oval (c.11/25/21 - c.1934) / maybe at a fairgrounds

Cushing Dragstrip - Cushing - 1/4 mile paved dragstrip (c.1964 - c.1965)

Deckerville - (location unknown) - dirt oval (1970's)

Devil's Bowl - Oklahoma City / located at Northeast 13th & Eastern
1/4 mile dirt oval (4/06/47 - 6/11/47) / ran jalopies

Dewey Fairgrounds - Dewey - 1/2 mile dirt oval (early 1930's) (6/11/47- c.11/11/47)

Dewey Speedway - Dewey / (aka: Lakeside Speedway)
1/4 mile dirt oval (c.1972 - c.1982) / (aka: Dewey America)

Duncan - 1/2 mile dirt oval (1929)

Duncan Dragway - Duncan - 1/4 mile paved dragstrip (c.1956 - c.1964)

Duncan Speedway - Duncan - dirt oval (1950)

Dutton Speedway - Fort Cobb - 1/5 mile dirt oval (1986 - present)

Echo Ranch Speedway - see: Ada Speedway

Elk City Speedway - Elk City / (aka: I-40 Speedway)
3/8 mile dirt oval (1971 - present) / on old US 66 behind the new Wal-Mart

Elmwood Speedway - Oklahoma City - dirt oval (c.5/18/47 - c.6/08/47)

Enid - 1/5 mile dirt oval (12/03/37 - c.1941) (c.1946 - c.1949)
probably at the Lake Helliums Park

Enid - 5/8 mile dirt oval (c.10/06/56) / probably Enid Speedway

Enid Speedway - Enid / located at the Garfield County Fairgrounds
3/8 mile dirt oval (c.8/23/48 - present) / (aka: Thunderbird Speedway #2)

Enid - also see: Lake Helliums Park, Phillips Stadium, Vance Air Force Base

Fairgrounds Speedway - see: State Fair Speedway

Faxon Speedway - Lawton - 1/5 mile dirt oval (1986 - present)
located next to Lawton Motorsports Park (dragstrip)

Four Seasons Raceway - Guthrie - dirt oval (1966)

Frederick - 1/2 mile dirt oval (early 1930's) / maybe at the Tillman Co Fairgrounds

Frederick Dragstrip - Frederick - 1/4 mile paved dragstrip (c.1963)

Gene Autry Municipal Airport - Ardmore / (aka: Ardmore Airport)
    2.6 mile paved road course (1988)

Grand Lakes Speedway - Grove - 1/4 mile dirt oval (1980 - 1986)

Hallett Motor Racing Circuit - Hallett / (aka: Hallett Motor Speedway)
    1.89 mile paved road course (c.1977 - present)

Hallett Motor Racing Circuit is a regular stop on the American IndyCar Series. This picture was from 1990. - Nancy Brown photo.

Hobart - 1/2 mile dirt oval (1925) (1946) / probably at a fairgrounds

Hollis - 1/4 mile dirt oval (1950's)

I-35 Speedway - Washington - 1/4 mile dirt oval (1971 - 1980)

I-40 Speedway - see: Elk City Speedway

Idabel Speedway - Idabel - 1/4 mile dirt oval (c.1974 - c.1975)

Jack Rabbit Speedway - Colbert - 1/4 mile dirt oval (1983 - 1985) (1987 - 1991)

Jaycees Speedway - see: Woodward Fairgrounds

L.A. Dragway - Lawton (Geronimo) / (aka: Motorsports Park)
    1/8 mile paved dragstrip (1960 - c.1970) (c.1973 - present)
    (aka: Lawton Dragstrip) / located next to Faxon Speedway (oval track)
    (aka: Red River Dragway) / town is referred to as Little Los Angeles (L.A.)
    (aka: Lawton Motorsports Park) / south of Lawton on Route 36

L.A. Speedway - Lawton - 1/4 mile dirt oval (1961 - present)
    L.A. stands for Los Angeles / (aka: Lawton Speedway)

Lake Helliums Park - Enid - 1/5 mile dirt oval (8/28/38)

Lake Ponca Park - see: Ponca City Grand Prix

Lakeside Speedway - see: Dewey Speedway

Lawton Bowl - Lawton - 1/2 mile dirt oval (c.1934 - c.1941) (c.1946 - c.1952)
    Rodger Ward started his driving career here / was a horse track

434

Lawton Speedway - see: L.A. Speedway

Lawton - also see: Faxon Speedway

Lexington 77 Speedway - see: Black Widow Raceway

MacArthur Park Speedway - Oklahoma City - 1/6 mile dirt oval (1980 - 1982)

Mannford - dirt oval (years unknown)

Mannford - also see: War Bonnet Park

Marietta Speedway - Marietta - 1/4 mile dirt oval (1975)

Martha Speedway - Martha - 1/5 mile dirt oval (1992 - present)

McAlester - 1/2 mile dirt oval (early 1930's) / maybe at Pittsburg Co. Fairgrounds

Miami Fairgrounds - Miami / located at the Ottawa County Fairgrounds
    1/2 mile dirt oval (c.1946 - c.1952)

Mid-America Speedway - Bartlesville / (aka: Bartlesville Speedway)
    1/8 mile dirt oval (1950's) (1970 - c.1988) / (aka: Phillips 66 Speedway)
    1/8 mile paved oval (late 1950's - mid 1960's)

Mid-America Speedway - South Coffeyville - 3/8 mile dirt oval (1993 - present)

Midway Speedway - Grove - 1/4 mile dirt oval (1978 & 1979)

Mighty Mouse Speedway - see: Tri-State Speedway

Motorsports Park - see: L.A. Dragway

Muskogee - 1/5 mile dirt oval (c.1940 - c.1941) (c.1946 - c.1952)
    probably not at the Muskogee Speedway

Muskogee Speedway - Muskogee / located at the Muskogee State Fairgrounds
    1/2 mile dirt oval (10/08/15 - 10/02/41) (10/01/46 - present)
    1/4 mile dirt oval (1948 - present) / (aka: Thunderbird Speedway)
    (aka: Oklahoma State Fairgrounds) / (aka: Oklahoma Free Fairgrounds)

Northwest Speedway - Oklahoma City - dirt oval (c.10/28/51)

Oklahoma City - 1/4 mile paved dragstrip (c.8/30/57 - c.1958)
    probably was the Oklahoma City Jaycees Dragstrip

Oklahoma City - 2.404 mile city street road course (4/29/15)
    race on 4/29/15 was a AAA Championship race won by Bob Burman
    6.65 mile city street road course (5/01/15)

Oklahoma City Coliseum - Oklahoma City / (aka: Stockyards Coliseum)
    1/10 mile indoor dirt oval (11/23/37 - 1/05/40) (1949 - 1950) (3/20/65)

Oklahoma City Fairgrounds - see: State Fair Speedway

Oklahoma City Int'l Raceway - Oklahoma City / (aka: Willow Run Raceway)
    1/4 mile paved dragstrip (c.1972 - c.1986)
    (aka: Pebble Creek Motorsports Park)

Oklahoma City Jaycees Dragstrip - Oklahoma City / possibly at the fairgrounds
1/4 mile paved dragstrip (c.1961 - c.1963)

Oklahoma State Fairgrounds - Oklahoma City / (aka: Mar-Car Twin Speedway)
1/2 mile dirt oval (c.1913 - 9/27/41) (9/23/46 - 1954)
1/5 mile dirt oval (8/01/37 - c.6/16/39) / (aka: Coalgate Speedway)
1/4 mile dirt oval (5/18/48 - 1954) / at old Oklahoma City Fairgrounds

Oklahoma State Fairgrounds (new) - see: State Fair Speedway

Oklahoma City - also see: Airport, Byerly's, Capitol Hill, Devil's Bowl, Elmwood,
MacArthur Park, Northwest, Sports Arena, Sportsman's Park, Taft

Okmulgee Airport - Okmulgee - paved road course (c.1952 - early 1970's)

Pebble Creek Motorsports Park - see: Oklahoma City Int'l Raceway

Phillips 66 Speedway - see: Mid-America Speedway

Phillips Stadium - Enid - 1/5 mile dirt oval (5/04/39 - 1939)

Picher - dirt oval (1919) / probably at a fairgrounds

Ponca City - 1/5 mile dirt oval (1947 - 8/03/47) / 2 miles north of town on US 77
closed when the grandstands collapsed on 8/03/47

Ponca City Auto Speedway - Ponca City - 3/8 mile dirt oval (4/14/40) (5/05/40)

Ponca City Grand Prix - Ponca City / (aka: Lake Ponca Park)
1.5 mile paved city street road course (1961 - 1980) (1987 - present)

Pond Creek Speedway - Pond Creek - 1/8 mile dirt oval (1989)

Port City Raceway - Tulsa / located east side on town on Pine & East 161th Ave.
1/8 mile dirt oval (1975 - 1987) (1990 - present) / (aka: Ru-Jo Raceway)

Quartz Mountain Speed Drome - Altus / (aka: Cratersville Speedway)
3/8 mile dirt oval (c.1965 - 1992) / (aka: Quartz Mountain Speedway)
at the entrance to the Quartz Mountain State Park & Resort

Red River Dragway - see: L.A. Dragway

Red River Valley Speedway - Colbert - 1/4 mile dirt oval (1981 & 1982) (1986)

River City Speedway - see: Black Widow Raceway

Riverside Raceway - Woodward / located four miles northwest of town on US 183
3/8 mile dirt oval (1980 - 1983)

Rodeo Stadium - see: Woodward Fairgrounds

Roland - 1/4 mile dirt oval (c.1959 - c.1962)

Route 66 Raceway Park - see: Sixty-Six (66) Raceway Park

Ru-Jo Raceway - see: Port City Raceway

Salina - 3/8 mile dirt oval (1994 - present)

Sallisaw - dirt oval (c.1967 - 1974)

Seminole - 1/10 mile dirt oval (3/06/38) / ran midgets

Sixty-Six (66) Raceway Park - Sapulpa - 1/8 mile dirt oval (11/10/85 - 1987)
　　1/5 mile dirt oval (1987 - 1990) / (aka: Creek County Speedway)
　　1/4 mile dirt oval (1991 - present) / (aka: Route 66 Raceway Park)

Sooner Int'l Speedway - Altus - 1/4 mile dirt oval (early 1983) / one race only
　　1/2 mile paved oval (4/17/83 - 1984) (1987) (1992 - present)
　　across the street from Altus Speedway

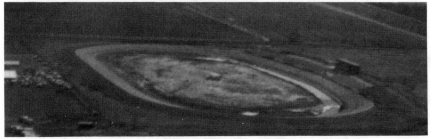

The 1/2 mile Sooner Int'l Raceway. - Official track photo

Sooner Raceway - Ringwood - 1/4 mile paved dragstrip (c.1972)

Southwest Oklahoma Dragway - Clinton - 1/4 mile paved dragstrip (1970's)

Sports Arena - Oklahoma City - 1/10 mile dirt oval (1975)

Sportsman's Park - Oklahoma City - 1/5 mile oiled dirt oval (8/27/39 - 10/22/39)

State Fair Speedway - Oklahoma City / at the new Oklahoma State Fairgrounds
　　1/2 mile dirt oval (c.9/30/54 - present) / located at 5th & May Ave.
　　1/4 mile dirt oval (c.10/24/54 - present)
　　paved parking lot road course (late 1950's) / (aka: Fairgrounds Speedway)
　　maybe had a parking lot dragstrip / (aka: Oklahoma State Fair Speedway)

State Lodge - Tulsa - dirt oval (years unknown)

Stillwater Municipal Airport - Stillwater
　　3.5 mile paved road course (1953 - 9/15/57)

Stockyards Coliseum - see: Oklahoma City Coliseum

Sun Valley Speedway - Ada - 3/8 mile dirt oval (1981) (1986)
　　(aka: Ada Raceway) / maybe same as Echo Ranch Speedway

Taft Stadium - Oklahoma City / located at Northwest 27th & May Ave.
　　1/4 mile dirt oval (7/29/46 - 10/27/47) (5/01/50 - 1964)
　　promoter was Ray Lavely / (aka: Ray Lavely's Taft Stadium)
　　built by O.D. Lavely around a football field

Taloga Fairgrounds - Taloga / located at the Dewey County Fairgrounds
　　1/2 mile dirt oval (early 1950's)

Texoma Speedway - Thackersville - 3/8 mile dirt oval (1977)

Thackersville Speedway - Thackersville - 1/4 mile dirt oval (1960's)

Thunder Valley Raceway Park - Norman
　　1/4 mile paved dragstrip (4/25/92 - present)

Thunderbird Speedway (#1) - see: Muskogee Speedway

Thunderbird Speedway (#2) - see: Enid Speedway

Thunderbird Speedway (#3) - see: Woodward Fairgrounds

Tri-State Speedway - Pocola / located two miles west of Fort Smith, Arkansas
　　1/2 mile paved oval (March, 1971 - 1978) / (aka: Mighty Mouse Speedway)
　　1/2 mile dirt oval (1979 - present)

Tulsa Airport Dragstrip - Tulsa - 1/4 mile paved dragstrip (c.1963 - c.1965)

Tulsa Assembly Center - Tulsa - indoor oval (3/21/65) / ran TQ midgets

Tulsa Expo Center - Tulsa / at the Tulsa State Fair / (aka: Tulsa IPE Building)
　　1/4 mile indoor dirt oval (1/10/87 - present) / home of the "Chili Bowl"

Tulsa Fair Pavilion - Tulsa / (aka: Tulsa Midget Oval)
　　1/8 mile dirt oval (11/09/38 - 11/23/38) (10/22/49) / (aka: Horse Show)

Tulsa Int'l Raceway - Tulsa - 1/4 mile paved dragstrip (1967 - present)
　　also had proposed 1.5 mile paved oval & 2.5 mile road course in 1966

Tulsa Speedway - Tulsa (Owasso) / located north of town on US 75 & 66th St.
　　3/8 mile dirt oval (1985 - present)

Tulsa State Fairgrounds - Tulsa / south of downtown between 15th St. & 21st St.
　　1/2 mile dirt oval (c.10/17/14 - 9/01/41) (9/21/46 - 10/09/53)
　　1/5 mile dirt oval (6/02/39 - 7/25/42) (9/15/45 - 1972)
　　3/8 mile dirt oval (c.1954 - 1972) / (aka: Tulsa Speedway)
　　a new grandstands was built and the tracks were moved slightly in 1973
　　3/8 & 5/8 mile dirt ovals (1973 - 1984) / also see: Tulsa Expo Center

Tulsa - also see Buddy Cagle, Cimarron, Port City, State Lodge

Vance Air Force Base - Enid - 1/4 mile paved dragstrip (c.1964)

War Bonnet Park - Mannford
　　2.7 & 5.7 mile paved road courses (October, 1966 - c.1969)

Watonga Fairgrounds - Watonga / located at the Blaine County Fairgrounds
　　1/4 mile dirt oval (early 1950's)

West Siloam Springs Speedway - West Siloam Springs
　　3/8 mile dirt oval (1987 - present) / just west of the Arkansas State line

Willow Run Raceway - see: Oklahoma City Int'l Raceway

Woodward Fairgrounds - Woodward / located at the Woodward Co. Fairgrounds
　　1/2 mile dirt oval (c.1948 - c.1961) / located at 1900 South 2nd St.
　　1/4 mile dirt oval (c.4/30/50) / aka: Rodeo Stadium)
　　1/4 mile dirt oval (1960's - 1973) / inside of 1/2 mile track
　　3/8 mile dirt oval (1974 - 1982) (1986 - c.1987) (1989)
　　(aka: Crystal Beach Park Speedway) / (aka: Jaycees Speedway)
　　(aka: Thunderbird Speedway #3) / (aka: Crystal Beach Speedway)

OREGON

Alamedo Speedway - see: Klamath Raceway

Albany Speedway - see: Asbury Park Speedway

Asbury Park Speedway - Albany - 1/4 mile dirt oval (August, 1966 - c.1975)
(aka: Albany Speedway)

Baker Fairgrounds - Baker - 1/4 mile dirt oval (7/04/51) (5/19/63 - c.1966)
1951 race held during "Oregon Trail Day Celebration"
located at the Baker County Fairgrounds

Balboa Park Raceways - Eugene - dirt oval (7/05/68 - c.1968)
1/8 mile paved dragstrip (May, 1967 - c.1968)

Banks Sunset Park - Banks - 1/4 mile dirt oval (1987 - present)

Base Line Speed Bowl - Portland - dirt oval (1934)

Bend Fairgrounds - Bend - 1/4 mile dirt oval (c.1987)
located at the Deschutes Co. Fairgrounds / (aka: Redmond-Bend Speedway)

Bend Rodeo Grounds - Bend - 3/8 mile dirt oval (late 1930's or early 1940's)

C.O.M.A. Raceway - see: Madras Speedway

Cascade Raceways - see: Medford Speedway or White City

Chetco Rodeo Grounds - Brookings - 1/13 mile dirt oval (June, 1957)

City of Roses Speedway - see: Portland Speedway

Clatsop Speedway - Seaside - 1/4 mile dirt oval (c.5/10/87 - present)
(aka: Clatsop County Speedway) / promoted by North Shore Racing Assoc.

Columbia County Speedway - see: River City Speedway

Hershel McGriff (#01) has been racing for six decades. The ex-logger is a popular driver on the West Coast. He also won four NASCAR Grand National races in 1954. - Allan E. Brown collection.

Coos Bay Int'l Speedway - Coos Bay / (aka: Ken-Kel Park)
1/4 mile paved oval (1972 - c.1982) (1987 - 1988) (1992 - present)
1/8 mile paved dragstrip (1991 - present) / (aka: Coos Bay Speedway)

Coos Bay - also see: Laping Track

County Stadium - Eugene - 1/5 mile dirt oval (9/11/46) / was a baseball park

Delta Park Speedway - see: Portland International Raceway

Douglas County Fair Speedway - Roseburg - 1/2 mile dirt oval (1951)
1/4 mile paved oval (1965 - 7/04/87) / (aka: Roseburg Speedway)
1/3 mile paved oval (1987 - present)

Earlington - 1.0 mile dirt oval (1920's or 1930's)

Emerald Speedway - see: Eugene Speedway

Enterprise - dirt oval (1961)

Eugene Fairgrounds - Eugene / located at the Lane County Fairgrounds
1/2 mile dirt oval (c.6/16/35 - c.8/09/41) (c.1946 - c.1950)

Eugene Speedway - Eugene - 3/8 mile dirt oval (1953 - 1954)
3/8 mile paved oval (1955 - present) / (aka: Universal Speedway)
(aka: Emerald Speedway)

Eugene - also see: Balboa Park, County Stadium, West-Pacific Dragway

Grants Pass Fairgrounds - Grants Pass - 1/2 mile dirt oval (c.1935)
1/4 mile dirt oval (1947) / located at the Josephine County Fairgrounds

Gresham Fairgrounds - Gresham / located at the Multnomah County Fairgrounds
5/8 mile dirt oval (1939)

Gresham Speedbowl - Portland / (aka: Twelve Mile Speedbowl)
1/2 mile dirt oval (1928 - 9/26/37) (1950's) / located on 12 Mile Road

Hermiston Speedway - see: Race City USA

Hollywood Bowl - Salem - 1/4 mile paved oval (1946 - c.1953)
this track was not located at the fairgrounds

Independence - 1/6 mile dirt oval (1936 & 8/28/37)

Jackson Co. Sports Park - Medford - 1/4 mile paved dragstrip (c.1981 - present)
located on a sports complex including ball diamonds and a go-kart track

Jantzen Beach Bowl - Portland - 1/5 mile dirt oval (c.1935 - c.6/18/41)
1/5 mile paved oval (9/08/45 - Sept. c.1970) / torn down in 1970
later known as Jantzen Beach Arena

Kelley Field - Oregon City - 1/4 mile dirt oval (May 1939 - June c.1939)

Ken-Kel Park - see: Coos Bay Int'l Speedway

Klamath Falls Fairgrounds - Klamath Falls / at the Klamath County Fairgrounds
3/8 mile dirt oval (1940) (1952)

Klamath Raceway - Klamath Falls - 5/8 mile dirt oval (1960 - 1969)
    3/8 mile dirt oval (c.1965 - 1969) / (aka: Alamedo Speedway)
    1/4 mile paved oval (1970 - 1982) (c.1987 - 1993) / (aka: CJ Speedway)
    (aka: Community Park Raceway) / (aka: Alamedo Park Speedway)
    (aka: Klamath Speedway)

LaGrande - dirt oval (9/07/63) / also ran motorcycles / maybe at a fairgrounds

LaGrande Speedway - LaGrande - 1/4 mile dirt oval (1984) (1986 - present)

Lakeview Fairgrounds - Lakeview / located at the Lake County Fairgrounds
    3/8 mile dirt oval (maybe ran in 1971)

Laping Track - Coos Bay - 1/4 mile dirt oval (mid 1950's)

Lebanon Fairgrounds - Lebanon - 5/8 mile dirt oval (1930's) (1954) (1957 - 1963)
    (aka: Lebanon Meadows)

Lebanon Speedway - see: Willamette Speedway

Libby - dirt oval (1959)

Lone Oak Speedway - see: Oregon State Fairgrounds

Madras Raceway Park - Madras - 1/8 mile paved dragstrip (c.1961 - present)
    (aka: Madras Airport) / located north of town at an old airport

Madras Speedway - Madras - 3/8 mile dirt oval (1983 - present)
    (aka: C.O.M.A. Speedway) / located north of town / 1/2 mile from dragstrip

McMinnville - 1/2 mile dirt oval (1930's)

McMinnville Dragstrip - McMinnville - 1/4 mile paved dragstrip (c.1960 - c.1963)
    operated by the Columbia Timing Association

Medford - 1/2 mile dirt oval (1913) (late 1930's)
    possibly located at the Jackson County Fairgrounds

Medford - city street road course (7/03/11 & 7/04/11)

Medford Raceway - Medford / (aka: Rogue Valley Raceway)
    1/4 mile dirt oval (1951 - 1989) / (aka: Medford Speedway)
    located at the Posse Ground on Sage Road / maybe called Cascade Raceways

Medford - also see: Jackson County Sports Park

Molalla Buckaroo Arena - Molalla - 1/10 mile indoor dirt oval (1989)

Moro - 1/2 mile dirt oval (1934)

Myrtle Point - 1/2 mile dirt oval (1950's) / maybe at the Coos County Fairgrounds

Newport Municipal Airport - Newport - paved road course (9/16/63 - c.1968)

Norway - 1/4 mile dirt oval (late 1950's)

Nyssa - dirt oval (late 1940's or early 1950's)

Ontario Fairgrounds - Ontario - 1/4 mile paved oval (c.1962 - c.1971)
    located at the Malhuer County Fairgrounds

Oregon Int'l Raceways - Goshen - road course (6/04/64 - 1966)

Oregon State Fairgrounds - Salem - 1.0 mile dirt oval (c.1927 - c.1929)
1/2 mile dirt oval (c.1933 - c.7/05/37) (1946 & 1947) (1951)
1/4 mile paved oval (c.1952 - 1973) / (aka: Lone Oak Speedway)
1.0 mile dirt oval originally built for horse racing / (aka: Salem Speedway)

Pendleton - dirt oval (1953) / possibly same track as Pendleton Rodeo Grounds

Pendleton Rodeo Grounds - Pendleton - 3/8 mile dirt oval (1940)

Portland - 14.6 mile city street road course (1907 - 6/12/09)
held first AAA Championship race here on 6/12/09

Portland Bowl - Portland - 1/2 mile dirt oval (5/30/37 - c.8/08/37)
maybe Portland Speedway

Portland Drive-In Speedway - see: Portland Speedway

Portland Int'l Raceway - Portland / (aka: West Delta Park Track)
1.915 mile paved road course (c.1966 - present)
1/4 mile paved dragstrip (c.4/22/67 - present) / (aka: Delta Park Track)

*Derek Bell (#4) leads Porsche teammate Al Holbert (#14) through turn nine
at Portland Int'l Raceway during a 1985 IMSA GT race. - David Allio photo.*

Portland Meadows - Portland / is a horse track located near Portland Speedway
1.0 mile dirt oval (Sept., 1949) (1950) (9/07/53) (9/04/55) (7/14/68)
ran motorcycles only in 1968

Portland Memorial Coliseum - Portland - 1/10 mile indoor oval (11/17/62- 12/12/62)

The unusual design in the infield of the little track at Portland Speedway was the parking spaces for the drive-in theater. - Official track photo.

Portland Speedway - Portland / (aka: Union Avenue Speedway)
    5/8 mile dirt oval (c.1923 - c.1941) (c.1947 - c.1950) / (aka: Rankin Field)
    1/4 mile paved oval (5/19/42 - July 1942) (c.1951 - present)
    5/8 mile paved oval (c.4/06/51 - 1951) / track shortened in 1952
    1/2 mile paved oval (4/06/52 - present) / (aka: City of Roses Speedway)
    (aka: Rose City Speedway) / (aka: Portland Drive-In Speedway)
    track infield was parking for a drive-In theater / screen off backstretch
    located north of town on Union Ave. (street now called M.L. King Blvd.)
    (aka: Rankin Airport) / Rebel Jackson, Sr. fatality injured here 6/25/94

Portland - also see: Base Line, Gresham, Jantzen Beach and Rose City Speedway

Prineville - 1/2 mile dirt oval (1920's or 1930's)

Race City USA - Hermiston - 1/4 mile paved oval (4/30/67 - present)
    (aka: Umatilla Speedway) / (aka: Hermiston Speedway)

Rankin Airport - see: Portland Speedway

Redmund-Bend Speedway - see: Bend Fairgrounds

Reith - dirt oval (c.1962)

River City Speedway - Saint Helens - 1/4 mile dirt oval (1985 - present)
    located at the new Columbia Co. Fairgrounds / (aka: Columbia Co. Speedway)

River City Speedway - Saint Helens - 5/8 mile dirt oval (1964 - 1968) located at the old Columbia County Fairgrounds

Riverside Speedway - Cottage Grove - 1/4 mile dirt oval (1949 - present) built by JC's for motorcycle racing / first auto race was in 1954

Rocket Speedway - Pilot Rock - 1/4 mile paved oval (5/03/64 - 1967)

Rogue Valley Raceway - see: Medford Raceway

Rose City Speedway - Portland - 1.0 mile dirt oval (7/11/14 & 7/12/14)

Rose City Speedway - see: Portland Speedway

Roseburg (Fairgrounds) Speedway - see: Douglas County Fair Speedway

Roseburg Speedway - Roseburg - 1/4 mile dirt oval (c.1963 - mid 1963) 1/4 mile paved oval (mid 1963 - 1964) / not at the fairgrounds

Saint Helens - 1/4 mile dirt oval (c.1936) / possibly old Columbia Co Fairgrounds

Saint Helens Fairgrounds - see: River City Speedway

Salem (Fairgrounds) Speedway - see: Oregon State Fairgrounds

Salem - also see: Hollywood Bowl

Siletz Valley Speedway - Toledo - 1/4 mile dirt oval (c.1975 - 1977) (aka: Siletz Valley Fairgrounds) / proposed for construction in 1972

The Dalles - 1/4 mile paved dragstrip (1961) / maybe ran in 1962 as well

The Dalles - dirt oval (late 1930's) / probably at an old fairgrounds

Tillamook - 1/2 mile dirt oval (1930's) (1950) / maybe Tillamook Co. Fairgrounds

Toledo Fairgrounds - see: Siletz Valley Speedway

Twelve Mile Speedbowl - see: Gresham Speedbowl

Umatilla Rodeo Grounds - Umatilla - dirt oval (1951)

Umatilla Speedway - see: Race City USA

Union Avenue Speedway - see: Portland Speedway

Universal Speedway - see: Eugene Speedway

West-Pacific Dragway - Eugene - 1/4 mile paved dragstrip (c.1977)

Western Oregon Dragway - Port Orford - 1/4 mile paved dragstrip (c.1963- c.1970)

White City - 1/4 mile dragstrip (c.1959 - 1962) / located north of Medford

White City - dirt oval (1964) / north of Medford / maybe called Cascade Raceways

Willamette Speedway - Lebanon - 1/4 mile dirt oval (7/05/64 - present) (aka: Lebanon Speedway) / located one mile from the Lebanon Fairgrounds

Woodburn Dragstrip - Woodburn - 1/8 mile paved dragstrip (June, 1961 - c.1966) 1/4 mile paved dragstrip (c.1967 - present)

PENNSYLVANIA

Academy High School Stadium - Erie / (aka: Erie Veterans Memorial Stadium)
1/5 mile dirt oval (6/24/47 - 1948) (1953 - 1960)
ran on a high school running track / the track was located on US 20

Ackerly Fairgrounds - see: Scranton Fairgrounds

Adventure Park Speedway - Clearfield - 1/5 mile dirt oval (c.1986 - 1987)

Airport Speedway - Brockway - 1/4 mile dirt oval (c.1954)
(aka: Brockway Speedway)

Airport Speedway - see: Susquehanna Speedway

Albion Horse Track - Albion - 1/2 mile dirt oval (1950)

Now doesn't this look fun. The jalopies rounding a turn at the Albion track in 1950. - Cora Arkkelin collection.

Allentown Agricultural Hall - Allentown - indoor oval (1962 - 1966)
ran T.Q. midgets & Micro-Midgets

Allentown Fairgrounds - Allentown / Ira Vail was the first winner in 1919
1/2 mile dirt oval (1919 - 1942) (9/22/45 - 8/10/68) (8/14/76)
Bill Schindler (9/20/52) & Johnny Thomson (9/24/60) fatally injured here
1/8 mile dirt dragstrip (c.1964)
1/8 mile dirt oval (1989) / ran Mini-sprints on 1/8 mile dirt

Allentown - also see: Convair Airstrip, Dorney Park Speedway

Allison Park - dirt oval (early 1940's)

Altoona Fairgrounds - Altoona - 1/2 mile dirt oval (1913 - 1916) (1920)
(aka: Plank Road Speedway) / occasionally referred to as a 3/8 mile

The famous board track of Altoona Speedway. Altoona lasted longer than any other board track because it was resurfaced. - Greg Fielden collection.

Altoona Speedway - Tipton (Tyrone) - 1.25 mile wood oval (9/04/23 - 9/07/31)
    built by Jack Prince & Art Pillsbury / turns banked 32 degrees
    located 12 miles north of Altoona on US 220 / manager was W.W. Morgan
    Howard Wilcox (9/04/23); Joe Boyer (9/01/24); and Ray Keech (6/15/29)
    were fatally injured in separate accidents at the Altoona board track
    1.125 mile dirt oval (9/07/35) inside of wood track (9/06/37) (6/11/38)
    1.125 mile paved oval (9/05/38) / a fire destroyed wood track 5/19/36
    (aka: Altoona-Tyrone Speedway) / site is now   ballfields and parking

American Legion Speedway - Houtzdale - see: Houtzdale Speedway

American Legion Speedway - see: Claridge Speedway

Anthracite Raceway - Pottsville (Port Carbon) - 3/8 mile dirt oval (1955 - 1975)
    closed because of a driver strike / the site is now a cemetery

Arden Downs Speedway - see: Washington Raceway

Armstrong Speedway - see: Kittanning Fairgrounds

Athens Fairgrounds - Athens / located at the Interstate Fairgrounds
    1/2 mile dirt oval (7/04/35) / may have ran in previous years

Auburn Speedway - see: Circle M Ranch Speedway

Bakerstown - dirt oval (early 1940's)

Banana Speedway - Lewistown - 1/8 mile dirt oval (c.1980 - 1990) (1993 - present)
    Go-Kart track / ran only Karts in 1991 & 1992

Baumstown Jalopy Track - Baumstown - 1/2 mile dirt oval (c.7/16/39 - c.7/28/40)
    located southeast of Reading

Beaver - dirt oval (1948) / maybe New Brighton

Beaver Falls Speedway - Beaver Falls - 1/4 mile dirt oval (1951) / motorcycles only
Crocky Wright won all four feature races held at this track

Beaver Springs Dragway - Beaver Springs - 1/4 mile dragstrip (5/30/71 - present)

Bedford Fairgrounds - Bedford - 1/2 mile dirt oval / (aka: Bedford Speedway)
(c.9/08/36 - c.8/23/41) (8/11/46 - 1978) (1980 - 1983) (1985 - present)
located at the Greater Bedford County Fairgrounds

Belmont Estates - Narberth (Philadelphia) - 1/2 mile dirt oval (1924)

Berks Micro-Midget Racing Club Speedway - see: Leesport Speedway

Berne Speedway - Hamburg - dirt oval (August, 1955 - c.1955)

Berwick - paved road course (7/18/58 & 7/19/58)

Berwick-Beach Haven Park Speedway - Berwick / began building in 1963
1/2 mile dirt oval (1972) (8/22/76)
built by George Perluke / grandstands from Palisades Park in NJ

Big Diamond Raceway - Minersville - 1/3 mile dirt oval (1972 - 7/08/94)
3/8 mile dirt oval (8/26/94 - present)

Bird-In-Hand Speedway - Bird-In-Hand / (aka: Central Raceway)
1/2 mile dirt oval (c.7/21/35 - 10/09/38)

Blakeslee Speedway - Blakeslee - 1/2 mile dirt oval (7/16/50 - 1951)
(aka: Pocono Mountains Sunrise Speedway)

Blanket Hill Speedway - Kittanning - 1/4 mile paved oval (6/03/53 - 1953)
1/4 mile dirt oval (c.1953 - 6/27/70) (1973) / Go-Karts only 1987 to 1993
1/8 mile dirt oval (1984 - 1986) (1994 - present)

Bloomsburg Fairgrounds - Bloomsburg / at the Columbia County Fairgrounds
1/2 mile dirt oval (c.1927 - 9/27/41) (c.9/27-47 - 1985) (1987)

Bone Stadium - Pittston - 1/4 mile paved oval (c.6/01/48-1955) George Bone built

*An accident at Bone Stadium in Pittston, Pennsylvania. The paved track was
built by George Bone. - Bruce Craig collection.*

Bowling Green Speedway - Jefferson - 1/2 mile dirt oval (1953 - 1956)
probably had a small track too, as T.Q. midgets ran there 8/27/56

Bowman Creek Speedway - Tunkhannock - 1/4 mile dirt oval (9/07/52 - 1953)

Bradford - 1/4 mile dirt oval (1955 - 1957) / about 1/2 mile from current track
maybe at the Rodeo Grounds

Bradford Rodeo Grounds - Bradford - 1/4 mile dirt oval (c.1953 - c.1957)

Bradford Speedway - Bradford - 1/4 mile dirt oval (6/12/58 - present)

Brecknock Speedway - Reading / now the site of Maple Grove Dragway
1/2 mile dirt oval (5/08/38 - c.5/11/41)

Bridgeville Speedway (board track) - see: Pittsburgh-Bridgeville Speedway

Brockway Arena - Brockway - indoor oval (c.1953 - 1955) / now a city park

Brockway Speedway - see: Airport Speedway - Brockway

Brookville Speedway - Brookville (Coder) - dirt oval (1962)

Brunots Island - Pittsburgh - 1.0 mile dirt oval (c.10/03/04 - Sept., 1907)
located on an island in a Ohio River / was a horse track

Brynfan Tyddyn - Wilkes-Barre / on the private estate of senator Newell Wood
3.5 mile paved road course (1952 - 1956)
Note: Brynfan Tyddyn is Welsh for "Farm on the Hill"

Buehler Stadium - Brandonville - 1/5 mile dirt oval (7/01/35 - 8/23/35)
located southwest of Hazleton

Bully Hill Speedway - Franklin - 1/4 mile dirt oval (late 1950's)
located two miles east of Franklin

Butler Fairgrounds - Butler - 1/2 mile dirt oval (c.1916 - 1941) (1946 - 1955)
1/4 mile dirt oval (4/21/50 - 1955) / now the site of Butler High School

Butler Fairgrounds - Butler (Prospect) / replaced old Butler Fairgrounds
3/8 mile dirt oval (1956 - 9/07/73) / (aka: Butler Speedway)

Byberry - North Philadelphia - 1/2 mile dirt oval (1920's & 1930's) / on US 1

Cambria County War Memorial Building - Johnstown / ran T.Q. midgets
1/10 mile indoor concrete oval (11/26/50) (1/31/53 - 2/21/53)

Camp Hill - dirt oval (1938)

Carlisle Fairgrounds - Carlisle - 1/2 mile dirt oval (9/02/46 - c.1963)
the site is now the Carlisle Flea Market

Cedar Hill - Birdsboro (Gibralter) - dirt oval (1960's)

Central Speedway - see: Bird-In-Hand Speedway

Challenger Raceway - Kent - 1/4 mile dirt oval (5/02/92 - present)
4/10 mile dirt oval (1993 - present)

Charleston Raceway Park - see: Sunset Dragstrip

Chelsea Speedway - Chester (Chelsea) - 1/2 mile dirt oval (1930 - 1941)

Chester Fairgrounds - Chester - 1/2 mile dirt oval (1920's) / 12th St. & Engle St.

Circle M Ranch Speedway - Auburn / the track is still there, now a landfill
 1/4 mile dirt oval (May, 1955 - c.1956) / (aka: Auburn Speedway)

Claridge Speedway - Claridge / (aka: American Legion Speedway)
 1/4 mile dirt oval (c.1953 - c.1958) / located in Westmoreland County
 the site is now the PTSC Soccer Complex on SR 4022

Clarion Fairgrounds - Clarion - 1/2 mile dirt oval (1920's - 9/19/38)
 the site is now the Clarion University Football Stadium on US 322

Clarion Raceway Park - Clarion - dirt oval (c.1947 - c.1957) / maybe Pine Grove

Clarksburg - 1/2 mile dirt oval (1937)

Clearfield - 1/4 mile dirt oval (late 1950 - c.1963) / site is now I-80 near SR 879
 owned by the father of the current Hidden Valley Speedway promoters

Clearfield Fairgrounds - Clearfield / located at the Clearfield County Fairgrounds
 1/2 mile dirt oval (1936 - 9/25/37) (1941) (1950's)
 1/3 mile dirt oval (1964) / the site is now used as a running track

Clearfield Mountain Speedway - Clearfield - 1/2 mile dirt oval (5/29/70 - 1986)
 1/2 mile paved oval (1987 - present) / (aka: Mt. Zion Speedway)
 (aka: Clearfield Speedway)

One of the nation's nicest tracks is Clearfield Mountain Speedway. The 1/2 mile track was paved in 1987. - Official track photo.

Clearfield - also see: Adventure Park Speedway, Hidden Valley Speedway

Clearview Speedway - Ridgway - dirt oval (1953)

Clinton County Speedway - Lock Haven - 1/3 mile dirt oval (4/28/89 - present)
 located at the Clinton County Fairgrounds

Clyde Martin Memorial Speedway - Brickerville
  1/8 mile dirt oval (1957 - present) / (aka: Lanco Track)

Connellsburg Airport - Connellsburg - road course on runways (c.7/04/59 - c.1965)

Convair Airstrip - Allentown - 1.58 mile paved road course (1951 & 8/03/52)

Cooperstown - see: Penn Speedway

Country Club Speedway - Lebanon - dirt oval (1936) / ran midgets

Cumberland Valley Speedway - see: Shippensburg Speedway

Darby - dirt oval (1935) / Bill Holland started here / the track was in a field

Davis Lane Speedway - Hustontown - 1/2 mile dirt oval (1955 - 1960)
  (aka: Big Track) / located about five miles from Hustontown Speedway

Dawson Fairgrounds - Dawson - 1/2 mile dirt oval (1920's) / not sure if operated

Dayton Fairgrounds - Dayton (Milton) - 1/2 mile dirt oval (1952)
  (aka: Tri-County Speedway) located on SR 839 / the site is now an open field

Delco Speedway - (location unknown) - 1/2 (.45) mile dirt oval (7/11/37 - 11/13/38)
  town listed as Twin Oaks / probably in Delaware County

Dickey-Ben Speedway - Warren (Grunderville) / (aka: Warren Speedway)
  3/8 mile dirt oval (1962 - c.1970) / located on Grunderville Road

Dickey-Ben Speedway - Warren (Starbrick) - 1/3 mile dirt oval (c.1947 - 1960)
  named after the track builder and his son / later became a drive-in theater

Dorney Park Speedway - Allentown / located at Dorney Park Amusement Park
  1/5 mile paved oval (5/28/39 - 6/21/42) (1945 - 1986)
  1/10 mile paved oval (6/11/52 - c.1952)
  the oldest active amusement park in the nation / built in 1884
  the exact track location is the site of the Hercules amusement ride

*Dave Randolph slides his midget through a corner at Dorney Park Speedway
in this 1939 photo. - Mick Ringo photo (Larry Jendras, Jr. collection).*

450

Dreamland Park - Reading - oval (1953) / ran Micro-midgets

Drive-In Speedway - Fassett - 1/4 mile dirt oval (6/03/51 - c.1951)
    located east of town on SR 4030 in a cornfield

DuBois Airport - DuBois - paved road course (1964) / ran SCCA regional

DuBois Fairgrounds - DuBois / located at the Gateway Fairgrounds
    1/2 mile dirt oval (c.1916 - c.1941) (1946) / now an athletic field

Dunbar Fairgrounds - Dunbar - 1/2 mile dirt oval (1947)
    located at Dunbar 4-H Fairgrounds

Dunn-Hill Raceway - Monroeton - 1/4 mile dirt oval (1991 - present)

Dysart Park - Hollidaysburg - 1/5 mile oval (5/27/48 - 1948)
    Ottis Stine was the first winner

East Smethport Fairgrounds - see: McKean County Fairgrounds Raceway

Ebensburg Fairgrounds - Ebensburg / located at new Cambria County Fairgrounds
    1/2 mile dirt oval (1932 - c.1938) / (aka: Ebensburg Speedway)
    1/4 mile dirt oval (6/09/47 - 1949) (c.1982) (1994 - present)
    grandstands burned down in 1953 / (aka: Cambria County Fair Speedway)

Elmwood Track - Philadelphia - dirt oval (1904)

Emporium Speedway - Emporium - 1.0 mile paved road course (1983 & 10/07/84)
    1/8 mile dirt oval (1991 - present) / Micro-stocks around a ball diamond

Ephrata Speedway - Ephrata - 1/8 mile dirt oval (1957 - c.1962)
    ran Micro midgets / (aka: M-M Speedway) / (aka: Garden Sport Airport)

Erie Expo Grounds - see: Silver Speedway

Erie Speedway - see: Sportsman's Field

Erie Veterans Memorial Stadium - see: Academy High School Stadium

Eriez Speedway - Erie - 3/8 mile dirt oval (July, 1961 - present)

Everett Speedway - see: South Penn Speedway

Evergreen Raceway - Hazleton (Saint Johns) / (aka: Evergreen Park Speedway)
    1/3 mile dirt oval (c.1949 - 1951)
    1/3 mile paved oval (Oct., 1952 - 1962)(1977 - 1982)(Apr., 1988 - present)
    (aka: New Evergreen Speedway) / (aka: Evergreen Speedway)

Fairmount Park - Philadelphia / reportedly had 400,000 fans at a race on 10/08/10
    7.8 mile city street road course (10/10/08) (10/09/09)
    8.1 mile road course on city streets (10/08/10) (10/09/11)

Fairview Speedway - Swarthmore - 1/2 mile dirt oval (1927 - 1935)
    located on Fairview Road

Farm Show Arena - see: Harrisburg Farms Show Arena

Fireball Stadium - Reynoldsville (Wishaw) - dirt oval (c.1962 - c.1965)
    (aka: Wishaw-Reynoldsville Speedway) / located east of SR 310 on SR 2027

Flying Dutchman Speedway - Lebanon - 1/8 mile dirt oval (1986)

Ford City - see: Kittanning Fairgrounds

Fort Lebanon - Deer Lake - dirt oval (August, 1955)

Forty Fort Airport - Wilkes-Barre - 1/4 mile paved dragstrip (7/20/58)

Franklin Speedway - see: Tri-City Speedway

Fredericksburg Stadium Speedway - Fredericksburg / located on US 22
    1/4 mile paved oval (1960) / located at a baseball diamond
    1/4 mile dirt oval (1965 - June, 1976) / the site is now a junkyard

Gable Hill Speedway - Meadville - dirt oval (9/08/40)

Garden Sport Airport - see: Ephrata Speedway

Gayland Speedway - see: South Penn Speedway

Gilbert Fairgrounds - see: West End Fairgrounds

Gilpin Field - Kittanning - 1/5 mile dirt oval (10/24/36) / ran midgets

Gold Mine Speedway - Tower City - 1/4 mile dirt oval (May, 1952 - 1964)

Grandview Speedway - Bechtelsville / (aka: Grandview Hi Speedway)
    1/3 mile dirt oval (8/11/63 - present) / home of "Freedom 76"

Granville Speedway - Troy (Granville) - 1/5 mile dirt oval (August, 1988 - c.1993)

Gratz Fairgrounds - Gratz / located at the Dauphin County Fairgrounds
    1/2 mile dirt oval (1945 - c.1955)

Greater Johnstown Speedway - Johnstown - 1/3 mile dirt oval (7/06/58 - 1961)

Greater Latrobe Speedway - see: Latrobe Speedway

Greater Pittsburgh Speedway - Clinton / located west of town off US 30
    1/4 mile dirt oval (6/13/58 - 1967)
    1/4 mile paved oval (7/06/68 - 8/20/70) / referred to as G.P.S.

Green Valley Speedway - see: North Hills Motorsports Park

Greensburg Fairgrounds - see: Westmoreland Fairgrounds

Greenwood Kart Track - Thompsontown - 1/8 mile dirt oval (1993 - present)
    a Go-Kart track / ran Micro-stocks & Champ-Karts in 1993

Greenwood Valley Action Track - Millville (Rohrsburg) / runs Mini-sprints
    1/5 mile dirt oval (1989 - present) / Go-Kart track running since 1980

Harborcreek Raceway - Harborcreek - 1/2 mile dirt oval (1957) / held one race

Harrisburg Fairgrounds - Harrisburg - 1/2 mile dirt oval (9/10/28)

Harrisburg Farm Show Arena - Harrisburg / at the Pennsylvania Farm Show
    1/10 mile indoor concrete oval (11/08/40 & 11/22/40) (1980 - 11/27/82)
    1/10 mile indoor dirt oval (c.1985 - present)
    1/10 mile indoor concrete oval (1993) < in a different building

452

Hatfield Speedway - Hatfield - 1/2 mile dirt oval (1922 - 6/08/41) (6/15/47 - 1951)
    1/4 mile dirt oval (1952 - 8/11/53) / at the Montgomery County Fairgrounds
    1/2 mile paved oval (5/27/54 - 5/29/59) / (aka: Hatfield Hi-Speedway)
    1/3 mile high banked dirt oval (6/12/59 - 1967)
    1/8 mile paved dragstrip (1960's) / site is now a housing development

Heidelberg Raceway - Carnegie (Pittsburgh) / now site of a Montgomery Wards
    1/4 & 1/2 mile dirt ovals (5/31/48 - 10/16/66)
    Lee Petty won his first NASCAR Grand National race here on 10/02/49
    1/4 mile paved oval (5/28/67 - 9/18/66) / home of the "Pittsburgher 250"
    1/2 mile paved oval (6/25/67 - 10/07/73) / Ed Howe won the last race

Herb Harvey Speedway - Tunkhannock - 1/3 mile dirt oval (1973 - 1977)
    (aka: Harvey Speedway) / located on SR 29 / now a auto junkyard

The Hershey Stadium held 16,000 people. It was owned by the Hershey's Chocolate factory. - Allan E. Brown collection.

Hershey Stadium - Hershey / owner Milton Hershey (Hershey's Chocolate fame)
    1/5 mile flat paved oval (5/18/39 - 9/11/41)
    Doc Shanebrook won the first race / built around a football field
    1/5 mile banked paved oval (4/28/67 - 1969) (1982 - 1983)

Hesston Speedway - Huntingdon - 1/2 mile dirt oval (1962 - 1979) (1993 - present)

Hickory Motor Speedway - New Castle / (aka: Old Hickory Speedway)
    1/4 mile dirt oval (8/13/59 - 1967) / (aka: Hickory Speedway)
    1/4 mile paved oval (1968 - 1980) (1984 - 1991) (aka: Tri-State Speedway)
    1/4 mile dirt oval (1992 - present) / 3 miles east of town on Route 108

Hidden Valley Speedway. - Nancy Brown photo.

Hidden Valley Speedway - Clearfield - 1/4 mile dirt oval (7/11/92 - present)
   patterned after the design of Mahaffey Speedway

Highland Raceway - Kane - dirt oval (c.9/24/54 - c.1955) / southeast of Warren
   the track site is behind the Highland Motel on SR 948

Hill Top Ranch Speedway - Lebanon - 1/4 mile dirt oval (8/24/47 - 8/26/56)

Hill Valley Speedway - Shirleysburg - 1/4 mile dirt oval (5/10/86 - present)

Hilltop Speedway - Albion - dirt oval (1952) / located on US 6-N

Hilltop Speedway - Myerstown / located one mile north of town near Route 422
   1/4 mile dirt oval (c.6/23/49 - c.1958) / next to Zellers Grove Speedway

Honesdale Fairgrounds - Honesdale / located at the Wayne County Fairgrounds
   1/2 mile dirt oval (c.1950 - 9/16/55) (1968)

Honey Brook Speedway - Phoenixville - small dirt oval (c.1984 - present)
   runs half-midgets & quarter-midgets

Houtzdale Speedway - Houtzdale / (aka: Park Hill Race Course)
   1/2 mile dirt oval (1937) (1953) / (aka: American Legion Speedway)
   the site was south of town on SR 2007 / site is now a state prison

Hughesville Fairgrounds - Hughesville / at the Lycoming Valley Fairgrounds
   1/2 mile dirt oval (c.1929 - 9/06/41) (Sept., 1945 - c.1952)

Hull Hill Speedway - Youngsville - dirt oval (early 1960's)
   located north of town on SR 4013 / the site is now a grass field

Hummingbird Speedway - Reynoldsville - 1/3 mile dirt oval (c.1962 - c.1977)
   located north of town (near Falls Creek) / has since been strip mined

Huntingdon Fairgrounds - Huntingdon / at the Huntingdon County Fairgrounds
   1/2 mile dirt oval (1956) (1970)

Hustontown - 1/4 mile dirt oval (1956 - 1960) / (aka: Little Track)

Hustontown - also see: Davis Lane Speedway

Indiana Fairgrounds - Indiana / located at the Indiana County Fairgrounds
   1/2 mile dirt oval (c.1916 - c.1941) (c.1947 - c.1964)

J.F.K. Stadium - see: Philadelphia Municipal Stadium

The newly paved Jennerstown Speedway. - Official track photo.

Jennerstown Speedway - Jennerstown / probably at an old fairgrounds
1/2 mile dirt oval (1927- 1941) (1946 - c.1948)
1/3 mile dirt oval (c.1966 - 1967) / located on the south edge of town
1/2 mile dirt oval (6/15/68 - 1985)   /   1/2 mile paved oval (1987 - present)
1/5 mile paved oval (1994 - present)

Jenny's Goat Farm - Erie - dirt oval (late 1940's) / ran roadsters

Johnstown Fairgrounds - see: Ebensburg Fairgrounds

Johnstown - also see: Cambia County, Greater Johnstown, Luna Park

Kent Field - Clifton Heights - 1/5 mile dirt oval (c.8/14/36 - c.6/26/38)

Keystone Raceway Park - New Alexandria - 1/4 mile dragstrip (1967 - present)
Tommy Ivo turned first 5 second run (5.97) here on 10/22/72

Kittanning Fairgrounds - Kittanning / located at the Armstrong Co. Fairgrounds
1/2 mile dirt oval (1948) (1954 - 1955) / (aka: V.F.W. Speedway)
(aka: Armstrong Speedway) / located south of Kittanning on SR 66
now housing development / the track was actually in Ford City

Kittanning - also see: Blanket Hill Speedway, Gilpin Field

Kocher's Speedway - Shickshinny / the promoter was George Perluke
1/2 mile dirt oval (c.1937 - c.1939) / located on US Highway 11

Kuhl Speedway - see: Thunderbowl Speedway

Kutztown Fairgrounds - Kutztown / (aka: Kutztown Speedway) / maybe 1920's too
1/2 mile dirt oval (8/17/35 - c.1941) (Sept., 1945 - c.1947)

L.A.M. Speedway - Norristown - 1/5 mile dirt oval (c.7/07/39 - 1939)

Lackawanna Speedway - see: Scranton Fairgrounds

Lake Hill Speedway - (location unknown) - dirt oval (1954)

Lancaster Airport - Lancaster - 1/2 mile dirt oval (1932) / ran jalopies

Lancaster Fairgrounds - Lancaster / (aka: Lancaster Speedway)
1/2 mile dirt oval (7/09/27 - 1936)

Lancaster Speedway - Lancaster / located six miles south of town
1/3 & 1/2 mile dirt ovals (6/30/46 - 1953) (6/14/58)

Lanco Track - see: Clyde Martin Memorial Speedway

Landisville - 1/2 mile dirt oval (c.1932 - 9/15/37) / located in a field

Langhorne Speedway - Langhorne / (aka: Langhorne Int'l Speedway)
1.0 mile dirt oval (5/24/26 - 5/10/42) (6/30/46 - 10/11/64)
the track's first name was New Philadelphia Speedway
built in 1925 for Philadelphia's Sesqui-Centennial
ran weekly big car races in 1941 / only 1.0 mile track to run weekly
Mike Nazaruk (5/01/55) & Jimmy Bryan (6/19/60) were fatally injured here
1/4 mile dirt oval (5/11/51 - 8/24/51) / (aka: Yellow Jacket Speedway)
1/8 mile paved dragstrip (7/04/58 - c.1959)
1.0 mile paved oval (6/20/65 - 10/17/71)   / now a shopping center

The circular-shaped Langhorne Speedway. - Walt Chernokal collection.

Lansdale - 1/2 mile dirt oval (1950) / located two miles north of town
possibly Hatfield Speedway

Large - 1/2 mile peanut shaped dirt oval (1946 - 1947) / ran jalopies
the town of Large is located near Clairton

Latimore Valley Fairgrounds - York Springs - 1/2 mile dirt oval (c.1933 - 1939)
the track was built in 1923 / was located at a fairgrounds
now the site of the Williams Grove Auto Racing Library & Museum

Latrobe Speedway - Latrobe / located near the airport / located on SR 981
1/4 mile dirt oval (c.8/03/52 - c.1965) / (aka: Schmuckers Speedway)
1/2 mile dirt oval (7/15/67 - 7/21/81) / (aka: Greater Latrobe Speedway)

Lauer's Park - Reading - 1/5 mile dirt oval (6/15/37)

Laureldale - 1/2 mile dirt oval (1937) / ran Big Cars on 1/2 mile track
1/4 mile dirt oval (1939) / ran Midgets on 1/4 mile track

Lawrence Park - 1/3 mile dirt oval (late 1950's) / located in a dump

Lebanon Fairgrounds - Lebanon - 1/2 mile dirt oval (c.1924) (1934 - 1941)
the promoter in the track's later years was Mark Light

Lebanon - also see: Country Club, Flying Dutchman, Hill Top Ranch, & Sunset

456   *Pennsylvania*

Leesport Speedway - Leesport - 1/8 mile dirt oval (1954 - c.1963)
  (aka: Berks Micro-Midget Racing Club Speedway)
  located at the Leesport Auction Grounds

Legion Speedway - see: Sharon Speedway in Ohio chapter

Lehighton Fairgrounds - Lehighton / located at the Carbon County Fairgrounds
  1/2 mile dirt oval (c.1922-9/04/37)(1939-1941)(1945-1958)(c.1982-1987)
  a high school is scheduled to be built on the race track site

*The midgets are entering turn one at the Lehighton Fairgrounds. - Frank
Smith photo (Len Ashburn collection).*

Lernerville Speedway - Sarver - 1/4 mile dirt oval (9/23/67 - 1970)
  1/3 mile dirt oval (1971 - 1982) / same location as old track
  1/2 mile dirt oval (1983 - present) / the tracks were built by the late
  Don Martin, who was the 1983 RPM Promoter of the Year

Lernerville Speedway - Sarver / the former site of an amusement park
  1/4 mile dirt oval (1938 - 1939) / the track was in a cow pasture

Lewisburg Fairgrounds - Lewisburg - 1/2 mile dirt oval (late 1920's - c.8/27/32)
  located at the Union County Fairgrounds / the site is now an empty lot

Lewistown Fairgrounds - Lewistown - 1/2 mile dirt oval (c.1929 - 1939)
  the site is now the Lewistown Area Senior High School

Liberty Race Track - Liberty - 1/4 mile dirt oval (1984 - c.1993)

Ligonier Speedway - Ligonier - 1/2 mile dirt oval (1950) / ran only one race

Lincoln Speedway - Hanover - 4/10 mile dirt oval (1951 - present)
  ran a NASCAR Grand National race here on 6/10/55, won by Junior Johnson

Linda's Speedway - Jonestown - 1/3 mile dirt oval (1976 - c.1983)
  1/4 mile dirt oval (c.1984 - present) / (aka: Interstate Speedway)
  1/8 mile dirt oval (c.1984 - c.1985)

Linglestown Fairgrounds - Linglestown - 1/2 mile dirt oval (5/09/36)

Little Washington - Washington - 1/2 mile dirt oval (early 1930's

Lock Haven - 1/2 mile dirt oval (5/22/48)

Lock Haven Fairgrounds - see: Clinton County Speedway

Lowville Drag Raceway - Lowville / (aka: Wattsburg Dragway)
1/8 mile paved dragstrip (c.1964 - c.1965) (c.1993 - present)

Luna Park - Johnstown - 1.0 mile dirt oval (1910's) / was a park from 1895 - 1921
now the site of Roxbury Park Ballfield / at the old Cambria Co. Fairgrounds

Luzerne County Airport - Forty Fort - 1/4 mile paved dragstrip (c.1954)

M-M Speedway - see: Ephrata Speedway

Mahaffey Speedway - Mahaffey - 1/4 mile dirt oval (May, 1959 - c.1971)
located south of town on SR 3023

Mahanoy City Fairgrounds - Mahanoy City / at the New Schuylkill Fairgrounds
1/3 mile dirt oval (c.1947 - c.1952) / (aka: Township Stadium Speedway)
(aka: Mahanoy Township Speedway)

Mahoning Valley Speedway - Lehighton - 1/4 mile dirt oval (1960's)
1/4 mile paved oval (1971) (1976 - 5/21/77) (1987 - present)

Maple Grove Dragway - Reading / same site as Brecknock Speedway (oval track)
1/4 mile paved dragstrip (August, 1962 - present)
Scott Kalitta went 308.958 mph here on 9/18/94 in a Top Fuel dragster

Maple Grove Speedway - Lancaster - 1/5 mile dirt oval (7/16/36-10/23/38)(7/14/40)

Marion Center Speedway - Marion Center - 1/4 mile dirt oval (1966 - present)

Mason-Dixon Speedway - Wakefield - 1/2 mile dirt oval (1949 - c.1955)
1/3 mile dirt oval (1949 - 1958) / located 100 yards from Maryland border
1/2 mile paved oval (5/30/57) / (aka: Milford Speedway)
1/3 mile paved oval (1959 - c.1962)
the town was listed as Sylmar / also referred to near Conowingo, Maryland

McConnellsburg Fairgrounds - McConnellsburg - dirt oval (years unknown)

McCormack's Park - Wilkes-Barre (Ashley) - 1/5 mile paved oval (1938 - c.4/26/39)
promoter was George Perluke / Chris Economaki drove his first race car here
the track was in a parking lot

McKean County Fairgrounds Raceway - East Smethport
1/3 mile dirt oval (9/17/83 - present) / maybe Smethport Fairgrounds

Meadow Race Track - see: Washington Raceway

Meadville Fairgrounds - Meadville - 1/2 mile dirt oval (7/04/47 - 1953)
1/4 mile dirt oval (1952 - c.1986) / at the Crawford County Fairgrounds

Media - oval (years unknown) / only rumors that a track existed in the town

Mercer Raceway - Mercer / the grandstands burned down in 1975
1/4 mile dirt oval (c.8/02/51 - 1982) (8/26/84) (5/08/88 - 1989) (1994 - present)

Meyersdale Fairgrounds - see: Somerset County Speedway

Middletown - dirt oval (1934)

Midway Speedway - see: Susquehanna Speedway

Mifflin County Speedway - see: Reedsville Speedway

Mill Park Track - see: Pottstown Fairgrounds

Mills - dirt oval (years unknown) / located west of town off of SR 49

Minnooka Park - Scranton - dirt oval (9/04/11)

Moc-A-Tek Speedway - Lakeville / (aka: Lake Moc-A-Tek Speedway)
1/4 mile dirt oval (c.1973 - present) / north side of Lake Wallenpaupack
(aka: Paupack Speedway)

Mon City Speedway - Monongahela / (aka: Monongahela Speedway)
5/8 mile dirt oval (c.1933 - c.7/04/38) / horse track built appx. 1908
(aka: Monongahela Driving Park) / now site of Mon-Valley Rodeo Grounds

Mon-Duke Amphitheatre - see: William Penn Speedway

Motordrome 70 Speedway - Smithton - 1/2 mile dirt oval (5/28/72 - 1989)
1/2 mile paved oval (1990 - present) / replacement for Motordrome Speedway

Motordrome Speedway - Ruffsdale - 1/3 mile dirt oval (August, 1966 - 10/02/70)

Mount Carbon - 1/3 mile dirt oval (c.1950 - c.1955) / now a housing development

Mount Joy Speedway - Mount Pleasant - 1/4 mile dirt oval (1960's) / on Route 31
the track was located southeast of Pittsburgh / the site is now a pond

Mount Zion Speedway - see: Clearfield Mountain Speedway

Muncy - dirt oval (1950's) / located between Muncy and Turbotville

Myerstown - see: Hilltop Speedway & Zellers Grove Speedway

National Speedway - Philadelphia / located at Broad St. & Lehigh Ave.
1/5 mile paved oval (6/28/39 - 7/31/42) / (aka: Philadelphia Gardens)
was an old Philadelphia ball park

Nazareth Raceway - Nazareth / located at the Northampton County Fairgrounds
1.0 mile dirt oval (9/24/10) / (aka: Nazareth Speedway)
1/2 mile dirt oval (c.9/03/27 - 1932) (6/29/47 - 1988)
1/8 mile paved oval (early 1970's) / now site of Laneco Department Store

The modifieds get the green flag at Nazareth Raceway. The 1/2 mile track closed in 1988. - Bruce Craig collection.

Nazareth Speedway - Nazareth / (aka: Nazareth Nat'l Motor Speedway)
  1.125 mile dirt oval (10/15/65 - 6/03/71) / built by Jerry Fried
  1.0 mile dirt tri-oval (1982 - c.7/29/84) / (aka: Nazareth Nat'l Speedway)
  1.0 mile paved tri-oval (1987 - present) / (aka: Pennsylvania Int'l Raceway)
  currently owned by Roger Penske / next to Nazareth Raceway

Neffsville - dirt oval (1937) / located north of Lancaster

New Brighton Speedway - New Brighton / the site is now commercial businesses
  1/2 mile dirt oval (c.1935 - c.1941) (c.1946 - c.1948)

New Castle Fairgrounds - New Castle / located at the Lawrence Co. Fairgrounds
  1/2 mile dirt oval (early 1930's)

New Castle Speedway - New Castle / (aka: Speedway Park) / located on SR 65
  3/4 mile dirt oval (9/27/53) (10/17/53) (5/31/54)
  the first race was won by Jim Romine / the site is now a shopping plaza

New Castle - also see: Hickory Motor Speedway, Pulaski Speedway

New Evergreen Speedway - see: Evergreen Raceway

New Kensington - 1/2 mile dirt oval (c.1931 - 9/03/34) / now housing development
  1/4 mile dirt oval (5/30/39 - 5/30/41) (1948 & 1949)
  Herb Scott started his driving career here in 1948

New Susquehanna Speedway - see: Susquehanna Speedway

New Uniontown Speedway - Uniontown / 2 miles from old Uniontown Speedway
  1/4 mile paved oval (1950 - c.5/30/57) / (aka: Uniontown Speedway)
  closed when the son of the owner was killed in a accident at the track
  now the site of a baseball field

North Bedford Speedway - Bedford (Belden) - 1/4 mile dirt oval (1957 - 1959)
  located five miles north of town / ran jalopies

North Hills Motorsports Park - Pittsburgh (Mount Nebo Church)
  1/3 mile dirt oval (late 1950's) (7/07/68 - 1978) (1981 - 9/13/81)
  (aka: Green Valley Speedway) / (aka: North Hills Motorsports Speedway)
  the track had a creek running along the back stretch

Numidia Dragway - Catawissa - 1/4 mile paved dragstrip (c.1964 - present)

O'Hara Anthracite Speedway - Brandonville
  1/2 mile dirt oval (late 1920's - early 1930's) (9/08/35)

Oakford Park - (near Pittsburgh) - dirt oval (1950's)

Oaklane Speedway - Trumbauersville - small paved oval (late 1980's - present)
  runs 1/2 & 1/4 midgets / located near Quakerstown

Old Hickory Speedway - see: Hickory Motor Speedway

Oswego Speedway - see: Troy Fairgrounds

Pagona Motorcycle Club Track - Birdsboro - 1/8 mile dirt oval (2/02/92 - present)
  located at an active motorcycle track / run junker stock cars occasionally

Park Hill Race Course - see: Houtzdale Speedway

Path Valley Speedway - Spring Run - 1/4 mile dirt oval (1987 - present)

Paupack Speedway - see: Moc-A-Tek Speedway

Paxtang Speedway - Paxtonia - 1/2 mile dirt oval (1926) / located near Harrisburg

Peckville Speedway - Peckville - 1/4 mile dirt oval (c.1938 - c.4/23/39)
(aka: Wilson Stadium) / located near Scranton

Peckway Speedway - Peckway - dirt oval (1954) / located near Lancaster

Penn Can Speedway - Susquehanna - 3/8 mile dirt oval (1949 - present)

Penn National Speedway - Grantville / (aka: Penn National Auto Track)
1/2 mile dirt oval (7/17/71 - present) / adjacent to the horse track

Penn Speedway - Cooperstown (McBride) - 3/8 mile dirt oval (1950 - 1952)
north of town on SR 8 / now the site of the Steppe housing development

Pennsylvania Farm Show Building - see: Harrisburg Farms Show Arena

Pennsylvania Int'l Raceway - see: Nazareth Speedway

Pennsylvania Motor Speedway - Imperial (Pittsburgh)
1/2 mile dirt oval (6/10/79 - present) / stands from Heidelberg Raceway
proposed as a 1.0 mile dirt oval and to be called Parkway Int'l Raceway

Pennsylvania Motor Speedway opened in 1979. - Official track photo.

Peterson Memorial Dragway - Altoona - 1/4 mile paved dragstrip (c.1970 - c.1977)

Philadelphia Civic Center - Philadelphia - 1/10 mile indoor concrete oval (1/14/89)

Philadelphia Gardens - see: National Speedway

Philadelphia Municipal Stadium - Philadelphia / (aka: J.F.K. Stadium)
  1/4 mile cinder oval (6/09/36 - c.7/21/36) / at South Broad & Terminal
  53,632 spectators watched Duke Nalon win first race in a midget
  it was estimated that 20,000 fans were turned away that day
  (aka: Sesqui-Centennial Stadium) / promoter in 1936's was Ralph Hankinson
  1/5 mile paved oval (6/27/52 - 1958) / where Army/Navy play football game
  1/4 mile paved oval (6/05/64 - 7/03/73) (1987)
  ran "Crown 100" (USAC midget race) in 1972 won by Gary Bettenhausen
  George Marshman was the promoter from 1952 - 1973 / torn down in 1992

Philadelphia - also see: Belmont, Byberry, Elmwood, Fairmount, Kent Field,
  National Speedway, Point Breeze, Saint Mary's Stadium, Southwest Airport,
  Toppi, Village Green, Willow Grove, and Yellow Jacket

Ralph Mulford winning at 1911 Fairmont Park. - Allan E. Brown collection.

Phillies Ball Park - Philadelphia - 1/5 mile dirt oval (c.1951)
  ran midgets here after Yellow Jacket Speedway closed

Pine Grove Speedway - Clarion (Shippenville) / maybe Clarion Raceway Park
  1/4 & 1/2 mile dirt ovals (1950 - 1955) (1957) (early 1960's)

Pinevalley Speedway - Frostburg - 1/4 mile dirt oval (c.1970 - 1971) / on SR 536

Pittsburgh (Charlerio) - dirt oval (9/30/14) / ran an AAA race

Pittsburgh Civic Arena - Pittsburgh - 1/10 mile indoor oval (1964 - 1966)

Pittsburgh - dirt oval (5/30/29)

Pittsburgh Int'l Dragway - Bridgeville - 1/4 mile paved dragstrip (c.1965 - c.1971)

Pittsburgh Speedway - Pittsburgh - 1/4 mile dirt oval (8/31/47 - 1948)
  the track had a dip and a hill in it / track located in Jefferson (Boro)
  the site later became the Colonial Drive In Theater

Pittsburgh-Bridgeville Speedway - Bridgeville / (aka: Bridgeville Speedway)
  1/2 mile wood oval (5/30/27 - c.7/04/30) / turns banked 35 degrees
  built by Paul Tustin / maybe ran a non-sanctioned race on 5/30/31
  ran only one AAA Nat'l Championship race (7/04/30) - won by Wilbur Shaw
  west edge of town on SR 50 / site is now Burgunder Motors car dealership

462

Pittsburgh - also see: Allison Park, Brunots, Greater Pittsburgh, Heidelberg, Large, New Kensington, North Hills, Penn. Motor, Turnpike, or South Park

Pittsfield - 1/4 mile dirt oval (1948 or 1949) / 2 miles west of town on US 6

Pittston - 1/4 mile dirt oval (years unknown) / maybe Bone Stadium

Plank Road Speedway - see: Altoona Fairgrounds

Pleasant Hills (Jefferson Boro) - 1/4 mile dirt oval (c.1939 - 1941) / on SR 51
    now the site of the Southland Mall / located just south of Pittsburgh

Pleasantville Speedway - Pleasantville - 1/4 mile dirt oval (1983)
    3/8 mile dirt oval (5/06/84 - 1984)

Pocono Drag Lodge - Bear Creek - 1/4 mile paved dragstrip (c.1963 - c.1964)

Pocono Int'l Raceway - Long Pond / proposed in 1960
    3/4 mile paved oval (5/04/69 - 9/15/91) / Jim Shampine first winner
    first race scheduled for 3/4 mile track was on 10/20/68 - rained out
    1.5 1.79 & 2.8 mile paved road courses (Sept. 1969 - present)
    2.5 mile paved tri-oval (7/03/71 - present)
    first race on 2.5 mile track was a USAC Indy car race won by Mark Donohue
    the first NASCAR Winston Cup race was on 8/04/74
    1/8 mile paved dragstrip (c.1970) / used front stretch of oval track
    ran annual "Race of Champions" for modifieds on 3/4 mile track

Pocono Mountains Sunrise Speedway - see: Blakeslee Speedway

Point Breeze - Philadelphia - 1.0 mile dirt oval (5/30/04 - 8/08/10)
    1/3 mile wood oval (early 1910's) / ran motorcycle on wood track

Polk Fairgrounds - Polk - 1/2 mile dirt oval (early 1930's) / near Franklin

Port Royal Speedway - Port Royal / located at the Juniata County Fairgrounds
    1/2 mile dirt oval (9/10/38 - c.1941) (c.1946 - present)
    (aka: Z & O Speedway) / Russ Campbell was the first winner

Pottstown (Sanatoga) - 1/4 mile paved dragstrip (1958 - c.1959)
    same site as Sanatoga Speedway

Pottstown Speedway - Pottstown / (aka: Mill Park Track)
    1.1 mile dirt oval (c.9/02/11 - 1934)

Pottsville Fairgrounds - Pottsville (Cressona) / at the Schuylkill Co. Fairgrounds
    1/2 mile dirt oval (c.1918 - c.1941) / became an Alcoa plant during WW II
    the site is presently a Cressona Aluminum Company Plant

Pulaski Speedway - New Castle (Pulaski) - 1/2 mile dirt oval (7/15/51 - 1957)
    located west of Pulaski in a cornfield

Punxsutawney Speedway - Covode - dirt oval (years unknown)
    not Pinevalley Speedway / the track was behind Gaston's Lumber Mill

Quakertown - 1/6 mile dirt oval (1983)

Quakertown Fairgrounds - Quakertown / located at the Bucks County Fairgrounds
    1/2 mile dirt oval (c.1928 - 1941) / site is now the Quakertown Hill School
    the property was nearly destroyed by angry drivers in 1935

Queen Speedway - Titusville - 1/4 mile dirt oval (c.1954 - c.1958)

Reading Airport - Reading - road course on runways (1962 - 1968)

Reading - dirt oval (1920's) / site is now a Post Office on North 10th St.

Reading - dirt oval (early 1900's) / located in city park where band shelter is now

Reading Fairgrounds Speedway - Reading / now the site of the art mall
    1/2 mile dirt oval (9/20/24 - 1942) (5/26/46 - 6/29/79)
    Grady Garner won first race / Tommy Hinnershitz started in 1930
    Promoters: Ralph Hankinson (1924 - 1942) / Sam Nunis (1946 - 1954)
    Russ Moyer (1955 - 1962) / John S. Giles (1963 - 1966)
    Lindy Vicari (1967 - 1979) / ran ARDC stock cars here in 1953
    1/16 mile dirt dragstrip (1960's) / Bobby Marshman started here in 1954
    Jud Larson & Red Reigel fatally injured here on 6/11/66
    Mike Grbac seriously injured in a crash here on 10/29/78 / he died 11/29/78

The Reading Fairgrounds was one of the most famous dirt tracks in Pennsylvania. This photo is from 1968. - Rolland Rickard photo.

Reading - also see: Brecknock, Dreamland Park, Lauer's Park, Maple Grove Dgwy

Reamstown - 1/2 mile dirt oval (1932)

Reedsville Speedway - Reedsville - 1/4 mile dirt oval (5/30/47 - c.1950)
    (aka: Mifflin County Speedway) / formerly a fairgrounds off of US 322

Riverview Speedway - Williamsport - 1/2 mile dirt oval (c.1952 - c.9/05/54)

Rochester - see: Valley Downs Speedway

Rose Speedway - Harrison City (Jeannette) - 1/4 mile dirt oval (c.1952)
    1/4 mile paved oval (c.5/30/53 - c.1954) / turns dirt - straights paved
    the property is now the site of a housing development

Roseland Speedway - (location unknown) - dirt oval (1969)

464   *Pennsylvania*

Roulette Raceway - Roulette - 1/4 mile dirt oval (c.1953 - 1954) (1985)

Saint Joseph College - (location unknown) - 1/4 mile cinder oval (7/30/38 - 1939)
    located at 54th & City Line

Saint Mary's Stadium - South Philadelphia - 1/4 mile dirt oval (1938)

Saint Marys Speedway - Saint Marys - dirt oval (c.1953 - c.1957)
    on the southern edge of town / later became a school bus parking lot

Saint Marys Speedway - Saint Marys - dirt oval (c.1958 - c.1959)
    the site later became Saint Marys Salvage on SR 255, just south of SR 948

Saint Thomas Speedway - Saint Thomas - 1/4 mile dirt oval (c.1960 - c.1975)
    (aka: Chambersburg-Saint Thomas Speedway) / now a baseball diamond

Sanatoga Speedway - Pottstown (Sanatoga) / 2 miles east of Pottstown on US 422
    1/5 mile paved oval (May, 1939 - 10/12/41) (c.6/20/48 - c.5/30/58)
    (aka: Sanatoga Park Speedway) / George Marshman was the last promoter
    the track was torn out to build a dragstrip / also see: Pottstown

Schmuckers Speedway - see: Latrobe Speedway

Scranton - 1.0 mile dirt oval (1907) / probably Minnooka Park

Scranton Athletic Field - Scranton - 1/5 mile dirt oval (6/03/37)
    possibly the Memorial Stadium near the Lackawanna River

Scranton Fairgrounds - Scranton (Waverly) / (aka: Lackawanna Speedway)
    1/2 mile dirt oval (c.1924 - c.1941) (c.1946 - c.1953)
    ran a Figure 8 race in 1946 / (aka: Ackerly Fairgrounds)
    site is now a ball field / located south of SR 632 (north of Clarks Summit)

Selinsgrove Speedway - Selinsgrove / (aka: Snyder's Fairgrounds)
    1/2 mile dirt oval (9/15/46 - 1959) (1963 - present)
    the track was designed by Joie Chitwood

Sesqui-Centennial Stadium - see: Philadelphia Municipal Stadium

Sharon Speedway - see: Sharon Speedway in Ohio chapter

Shenandoah - 1/2 mile dirt oval (10/12/35) / ran midgets

Shillington - dirt oval (years unknown) / maybe Sinking Spring Speedway

Shippensburg Speedway - Shippensburg - 1/7 mile dirt oval (c.1988 - present)
    (aka: Cumberland Valley Speedway) / a Go-Kart track since c.1985

Silver Speedway - Erie - 1/2 mile dirt oval (c.1917 - c.5/22/27) (5/30/38)
    1/4 mile dirt oval (5/30/38 - c.7/08/39) / (aka: Erie Expo Grounds)

Silver Spring Speedway - Mechanicsburg
    3/8 mile dirt oval (1953 - present) / called 2/5 mile in 1953

Sinking Spring Speedway - Sinking Spring - dirt oval (1947 - 1949)

Skyline Speedway - Perrysville - 1/4 mile dirt oval (9/16/51 - c.1952)

Skyline Speedway - Sugar Grove - 1/3 mile dirt oval (1953 - 1956) / east of town

Sleepy Hollow Ranch - Quakertown / located near Pennsburg
1/10 mile dirt oval (9/09/51 - 1952) / ran T.Q. midgets

Slippery Rock Raceway - Slippery Rock - 1/8 mile dirt oval (1992)
an active Go-Kart track since c.1992 / ran Micro-sprints in 1992

Smethport Fairgrounds - Smethport - 1/2 mile dirt oval (c.1955 - c.1971)
located at the McKean County Fairgrounds

Snow Shoe Speedway - Snow Shoe - 1/3 mile paved oval (July, 1953 - 1954)
the site is now a recreational complex on SR 144

Snyder's Fairgrounds - see: Selinsgrove Speedway

Snydersville Speedway - Snydersville - 1/5 mile dirt oval (5/27/94 - present)
runs Micro-Stocks / located at a rodeo grounds
Somerset County Speedway - Meyersdale / at the Somerset County Fairgrounds
1/2 mile dirt oval (c.8/27/49 - c.1968) (1990 - present)

South Mountain Dragway - Boiling Springs - 1/8 mile dragstrip (1962 - present)

South Park Speedway - Library - 1/4 mile dirt oval (5/28/53 - 7/13/68)
located four miles south of Pittsburgh on Brownsville Road
the track was just south of the South Park Fairgrounds

South Penn Speedway - Everett / located 1 mile south of town on Route 26 (70)
1/3 mile dirt oval (1956 - c.1965) / (aka: Gayland Speedway)
1/2 mile dirt oval (May, 1966 - 1974) / (aka: Everett Speedway)
opened as Gayland Speedway / the site is now an athletic field

Southwest Airport Speedway - Philadelphia - 1/5 & 1/2 mile dirt ovals (1952)

Speedway Park - see: New Castle Speedway

Sportsman's Field - Erie / located west of town on Hwy 90 / (aka: Erie Speedway)
1/4 mile dirt oval (6/07/49 - 1952) / built to replace   Erie Stadium
located at 26th St. & East Pittsburgh Ave. / torn down in 1952
the site is under the I-79 Expressway

Sportsman's Speedway - Knox - 1/3 mile dirt oval (1973 - 1977) (1983 - present)
Allan E. Brown saw a race at a 500th different track here on 8/11/91

Spring Church - 1/4 mile dirt oval (1950's) / located five miles east of Apollo
now the site of the Apollo-Spring Church Sportsman Club on SR 56

Spring City - 1/2 mile dirt oval (c.1937)

Square Timber Speedway - Emporium - dirt oval (1954)

Stoneboro Fairgrounds - Stoneboro - 1/2 mile dirt oval (1954)
located at the Greater Stoneboro Fairgrounds

Stroudsburg Fairgrounds - East Stroudsburg / (aka: New Stroudsburg Speedway)
1/5 & 1/2 mile dirt ovals (c.7/08/51 - 1959) / (aka: Stroudsburg Speedway)
the track was located next to the airport on US Highway 209

Summerton Fairgrounds - (location unknown) - 1/2 mile dirt oval (1928)
maybe Summit Station where the Sckuykill County Fairgrounds was

Sunbury Raceway Park - Sunbury - 1/8 mile dirt oval (1991)

Sunset Dragstrip - Sharon - 1/8 & 1/4 mile paved dragstrips (1959 - present)
(aka: Charleston Raceway Park)

Sunset Speedway - Lebanon - 1/4 mile dirt oval (9/21/51 - 1952)
(aka: Sunset's Market Speedway) / ran T.Q. midgets

Super 66 Speedway - North Washington / located on SR 66 & SR 380
1/4 mile dirt oval (race scheduled for 5/15/66) / probably never ran

Susquehanna Speedway - Newberrytown / (aka: Midway Speedway)
3/8 mile dirt oval (c.1958 - 1961) / (aka: New Susquehanna Speedway)
1/2 mile dirt oval (1962 - present) / (aka: Airport Speedway)

Swarthmore - see: Fairview Speedway

Sycamore Springs Speedway - Hanover - 1/4 mile dirt oval (1976)
different track than either Lincoln Speedway or Trailways Speedway

Three Point Raceway - Wrightsville - 1/2 mile dirt oval (1959 - c.1964)
located west of town on US 6

Thunderbowl Speedway - Wesleyville - 1/4 mile dirt oval (c.1957 - c.1959)
(aka: Kuhl Speedway)

Tioga Fairgrounds - Tioga / located at the Tioga County Fairgrounds
1/4 mile dirt oval (early 1950's)

Tipton Bowl (board track) - see: Altoona Speedway

Toppi Stadium - Philadelphia / located at Broad Street & Packer Avenue
1/10 mile paved oval (5/01/52 - 5/29/52) / ran T.Q. midgets

Towanda Fairgrounds - Towanda (Wysox) / at the Bradford County Fairgrounds
1/2 mile dirt oval (c.1933 - c.1940) (c.1947 - c.1960)
(aka: V.F.W. Fairgrounds) / now the site of a gravel pit

Township Stadium Speedway - see: Mahanoy City Fairgrounds

*Bobby Abel after a win at Dorsey (MD) Speedway in 1966. - Bob Williams photo
(Larry Jendras, Jr. collection).*

The aerial view of Trail-Way Speedway. - Official track photo.

Trail-Way Speedway - McSherrystown - 1/3 mile dirt oval (c.1973 - present)

Tri-City Speedway - Franklin - 1/4 mile dirt oval (1954 - 1968)
    1/2 mile dirt oval (1969 - c.1980) (1986 - 1987)/ (aka: Franklin Speedway)

Tri-County Speedway - see: Dayton Fairgrounds

Tri-State Speedway - see: Hickory Motor Speedway

Troy Fairgrounds - Troy - 1/4 mile dirt oval (c.5/30/52 - c.1952)
    (aka: Oswego Speedway)

Tunkhannock Fairgrounds - Tunkhannock - 1/2 mile dirt oval (c.7/04/39 - c.8/12/39)

Turnpike Speedway - East McKeesport - 1/3 mile dirt oval (1951 - 1955)
    the site is now the WPCB TV 40 station and antenna

Tyrone Speedway - see: Altoona Speedway

Uniontown Fairgrounds - Uniontown / located at the Fayette County Fairgrounds
    1/2 mile dirt oval (c.1934 - c.1941) (c.1946 - c.1953)
    1/10 mile dirt oval (8/05/77)

Uniontown Speedway (new) - see: New Uniontown Speedway

Uniontown Speedway - Uniontown (Hopwood) / built by Jack Prince
    1.125 mile wood oval (11/27/16 - 6/17/22) / turns banked 34 degrees
    first race scheduled for 11/25/16 was rained out
    Hughie Hughes and Frank Calvin were fatally injured here on 12/02/16
    50,000 fans watch Tommy Milton win a 200 lap race on 6/19/20
    also see next listing / site later became a golf driving range

Uniontown Speedway - Uniontown (Hopwood) / site of Uniontown board track
    1/2 mile oiled dirt oval (7/04/40 - c.1941) (8/25/46 - c.9/12/47)

V.F.W. Fairgrounds - see: Towanda Fairgrounds

V.F.W. Speedway - see: Kittanning Fairgrounds

Valley Downs Speedway - Rochester - 1/4 mile dirt oval (1947 - 1948)

Van Gorder's Speedway - Beach Lake - 1/4 mile dirt oval (1955 - c.1966)
    located on SR 652 / site is behind current Carousel Amusements

Van Ormer Speedway - Van Ormer - 1/8 mile dirt oval (c.1959 - c.1962)

Vargo Dragstrip - Perkasie - 1/4 mile paved dragstrip (c.1963 - 1969)

VFW Speedway - Sayre - dirt oval (early 1950's)

Village Green Jalopy Track - Aston - 1/2 mile dirt oval (Sept, 1936 - 11/26/36)
    located near the cities of Village Green and Chester

Walnut Bottom - Shippensburg - 5/8 mile dirt oval (maybe ran in the late 1960's)

Warren Speedway - see: Dickey-Ben Speedway

Warren Sports Speedway - Warren - 1/2 mile dirt oval (9/06/65 - 1966)

Washington Raceway - Washington / (aka: Arden Downs Speedway)
    1/2 mile dirt oval (9/02/35) (c.1947 - c.1960) / located at a fairgrounds
    was the Arden Downs Horse Track / fair still held, horse track closed

Washington Raceway - Washington / at the Washington County Fairgrounds
    1/2 mile dirt oval (1934 - c.1941) / (aka: Meadows Race Track)
    was a horse track / maybe same track as other Washington Raceway

Wattsburg Dragway - see: Lowville Drag Raceway

Wattsburg Fairgrounds - Wattsburg - 1/2 mile dirt oval (1936)
    3/8 mile dirt oval (c.1968 - c.1971) / at the Erie County Fairgrounds
    (aka: Wattsburg Speedway) / located on SR 8 on the north side of town

Waverly Fairgrounds - see: Scranton Fairgrounds

Waynesburg - 1/2 mile dirt oval (1938) (c.9/01/47 - 1948) / Greene Co Fairgrounds

West Chester Fairgrounds - West Chester / at the Goshen Country Fairgrounds
    1/2 mile dirt oval (1920's - c.1937)

West End Fairgrounds - Gilbert - 1/6 mile dirt oval (6/10/94 - present)

Westfield Fairgrounds - Westfield - 1/2 mile dirt oval (1941)
    the site is now a high school on SR 49, just west of SR 349

Westmoreland Fairgrounds - Greensburg - 1/6 mile dirt oval (8/24/94 - present)

White Hall Speedway - White Hall - dirt oval (1938)

Wilkes-Barre Armory - Wilkes-Barre / (aka: Calgary Armory)
    1/12 mile indoor paved oval (12/12/35) / ran midgets

Wilkes-Barre - dirt oval (1917)

William Penn Speedway - Murrysville / (aka: Mon-Duke Export Amphitheatre)
    1/2 mile dirt oval (c.1954 - c.1962) / east of Pittsburgh on US Highway 22

The midget race in front of the old covered grandstands at Williams Grove. Frank Smith photo (Len Ashburn collection).

Williams Grove Speedway - Mechanicsburg (Williams Grove)
    1/2 mile dirt oval (5/31/39 - 5/10/42) (9/09/45 - present)
    originally proposed to be a 1.0 mile dirt oval / at an amusement park
    (aka: Ascot of the East) / patterned after Legion Ascot Speedway, California
    (aka: Williams Grove Park & Speedway) / built by Roy R. Richwine
    27,000 fans in 1940 for a jalopy stock car race
    Tony Willman won the first midget race at the "Grove" here on 10/05/41
    31,374 fans here for a big car race in 1942
    promoter Jack Gunn was 1979 RPM Promoter of the Year

Winged super sprints at Williams Grove on their pace lap before the start of a feature. - Walt Chernokal photo.

Willow Grove Park - Philadelphia - 1/8 mile dirt oval (6/13/52 - 8/27/52)

Wilson Stadium - see: Peckville Speedway

Wind Gap - 1/4 mile paved dragstrip (c.1993 - present)

Windber Speedway - Windber / track has a high school football field in the infield
1/4 mile dirt oval (c.1965 - c.1967) / (aka: Windber Stadium Speedway)
3/8 mile dirt oval (7/25/85 - present)

Windham Speedway - Windham - 3/8 mile dirt oval (1982)

Wrightsville - 1/4 mile dirt oval (1950) / operated by the Wrightsville Firemen

Yellow Jacket Speedway - Langhorne - see: Langhorne Speedway

Yellow Jacket Speedway - Philadelphia - 1/5 mile dirt oval (c.7/12/38 - 10/09/39)
1/5 mile paved oval (c.6/10/40 - 7/29/42) (Sept., 1945 - 10/13/50)
located at Erie Ave. & G Street / the track is now the site of a factory

Yellow Jacket Stadium - Philadelphia / located at Frankford & Deveroux
1/5 mile cinder oval (6/25/35 - 1939) / (aka: Yellow Jacket Speedway)
1/5 mile paved oval (1939) / promoter Bill Heiserman / (aka: Trojan Field)
former home of the Philadelphia Yellow Jackets football team
(aka: Yellow Jacket Field)

York Fairgrounds - York / located at the York Inter-State Fairgrounds
1/2 mile dirt oval (c/7/04/11 - 1934) (5/30/41) (1946 - 1953) (7/04/60 - 6/15/80)

York Springs Speedway - York Springs / located on US Highway 15
1/4 mile dirt oval (7/19/36 - c.7/03/38) / (aka: Griest Field)

York U.S. 30 Dragway - York - 1/4 mile paved dragstrip (c.1961 - c.1977)
Arnie Beswick drove to the 1st 9 second run in a Funny Car here on 4/17/65
(aka: York Drag-O-Way)

Zellers Grove Speedway - Myerstown - 4/10 mile dirt oval (c.6/29/47 - 1952)
located next to Hilltop Speedway

RHODE ISLAND

Aquidneck Trotter Park - see: Newport Fairgrounds

Barnyard Raceway - Chepachet - 1/4 mile dirt oval (1993 - August, 1994)
the first oval track running stock cars in Rhode Island since 1956

Charlestown Dragway - Charlestown - 1/4 mile paved dragstrip (c.1957 - c.1964)
located on a Naval Air Station

Coyote Raceway - North Scituate - 1/12 mile paved oval (c.1985) / Go-Karts only

Cranston Stadium - Cranston - 1/5 mile dirt oval (6/04/37 - 7/09/37)
located at a football field / appx. site as Narragansett Park's 1st & 2nd turn

Kingston Fairgrounds - Kingston - 1/2 mile dirt oval (5/19/48 - 9/21/51)
located at the new Rhode Island State Fairgrounds

The Lonsdale Sports Arena had grandstands that encircled the 1/3 mile track. R.A. Silva collection.

Lonsdale Sports Arena - Lonsdale / two miles north of Pawtucket on Highway 22
  1/3 mile high banked paved oval (8/13/47 - 9/30/56) / now a shopping center
  a race on 10/26/47 was the first race promoted by future NASCAR officials
  Wall Stadium in New Jersey was patterned after this track

Narragansett Park - Cranston / located at the old Rhode Island State Fairgrounds
  1.0 mile dirt oval (9/07/1896 - 10/13/13) / was a horse track built in 1867
  Harry B. Morris won the first ever oval track auto race here on 9/07/1896
  an entry fee of $100 was charged and 50,000 fans came for the 9/11/1896 race
  1.0 mile concrete oval (9/18/15 - 8/04/23) / Milt McBride won the last race
  torn down in 1925 for housing development / built Cranston Stadium on site
  present Fiat St. in Cranston is the same location as the old backstretch

Newport - dirt oval (1951) / ran jalopies

Newport Fairgrounds - Newport / (aka: Aquidneck Trotter Park)
  1/2 mile dirt oval (8/31/1900 - 7/30/1904) (1937) (1940 & 1941)
  the first winner was William Vanderbilt / now the site of the airport

Pascoag - 1/2 mile dirt oval (9/11/38 - 9/29/40) (1950)
  1/8 mile dirt dragstrip (1957) / drags were on the old front straightaway
  now the site of Burrillville Industrial Park

Ponta Delgada Motor Speedway - Tiverton / became a drive-in theater in 1958
  1/5 mile dirt oval (1939 - 1940) / (aka: Ponta Delgada Motor Stadium)
  1/5 mile paved oval (6/22/41 - 7/26/42) (9/16/45 - 7/27/47) (1952 - 1953)
  maybe the first race in New England after World War II was held here
  (aka: Tiverton Speedway) / now the site of a social club

Ponta Delgada Stadium - Tiverton - 1/10 mile indoor concrete oval (11/11/52)

Providence Arena - Providence / (aka: Rhode Island Auditorium)
    1/11 mile flat indoor wood oval (1/22/37 & 2/02/37)
    the track consisted of wood planks laid over the ice on a hockey arena
    1/11 mile indoor concrete oval (3/23/51) (3/24/52) (4/05/52)
    ran micro-midgets / ran T.Q. midgets on (4/04/59) (4/11/59) (4/18/59)
    Jerry Wall (Wallenburg) won the last race on 4/18/59

Rhode Island Auditorium - see: Providence Arena

Rhode Island State Fairgrounds - see: Kingston Fairgrounds or Narragansett Park

Tiverton Speedway - see: Ponta Delgada Motor Speedway

Warwick - dirt oval (1920's & 1930's) / motorcycle race on a horse track

Woonsocket Fairgrounds - Woonsocket / now the site of a park
    1/2 mile dirt oval (11/02/24)

SOUTH CAROLINA

Abbeville Airport Speedway - Abbeville / located west of Greenwood
    1/4 mile dirt oval (c.11/26/53 - Oct., 1956) / maybe opened in Oct., 1953

Aiken County Speedway - Aiken - 1/2 mile dirt oval (1953 - 1954)
    located two miles south of town on State Highway 19

Airbase Speedway - see: Textile Speedway

Anderson - 1/2 mile dirt oval (5/03/47)

Anderson Motor Speedway - Anderson - 3/8 mile dirt oval (1963 - 1986)
    3/8 mile paved oval (1987 - present) / (aka: Anderson Speedway)
    located north of town on State Highway 81

Red Byron was NASCAR's first champion. This photo was taken in 1948.
Frank Smith photo (Len Ashburn collection).

Anderson - also see: Eastside Speedway

Andrews Speedway - see: Black River Speedway

Ashwood Speedway - Bishopville - 1/2 mile dirt oval (c.1957 - c.1968)

Batesburg Dragstrip - Batesburg - 1/4 mile paved dragstrip (early 1960's - c.1969)
   a concrete track with a dirt shut down area / (aka: Mid-Carolina Drag Strip)

Bennettsville - 1/2 mile dirt oval (1930's)

Bennettsville Dragstrip - Bennettsville / owned by S.C. Governor Wallace
   1/4 mile paved dragstrip (10/18/57 - c.1958)

Black River Speedway - Andrews / (aka: Andrews Speedway)
   4/10 mile dirt oval (c.1961 - c.1963)

Blaney Dragstrip - Columbia (Elgin) - 1/4 mile paved dragstrip (c.1961 - 1985)

Buffalo Motor Speedway - Union (Buffalo) / (aka: Gault's Motor Speedway)
   1/4 mile dirt oval (1980 - c.1983) (1986 - 1987) / on State Highway 215

Caesar's Head Race Track - Greer - dirt oval (years unknown) / ran motorcycles
   located 25 miles northeast of Greenville on Greer Road

Carolina Dragway - Jackson / (aka: Jackson Dragstrip)
   1/4 mile paved dragstrip (July, 1957 - present)

Charleston Speedway - Charleston / (aka: Charleston Rebel Speedway)
   3/8 mile dirt oval (1964 - 1976)

Charleston - also see: Coastal Speedway, County Hall

Cheraw Speedway - Cheraw - dirt oval (1955)

Cherokee Speedway - Gaffney - 4/10 mile dirt oval (1957 - 1959)
   1/2 mile dirt oval (1960 - present) / Mike Duvall started here

Glen "Fireball" Roberts slides through a corner on the beach course at Daytona Beach, Florida in a Ford. - Len Ashburn photo.

474

Cherry Grove Beach - beach/road oval (years unknown) / near No. Myrtle Beach

Chester Airport - Chester - 2.4 mile paved road course (1956 - c.1958)
1/4 mile paved dragstrip (1957 - c.1959) / (aka: Chester Airport Dragstrip)
Don Garlits was seriously burned here in an accident in 1959

Chester Speedway - Chester / (aka: I-77 Speedway)
3/8 mile dirt oval (1981 - 1986) (1988 - 1991) (1994 - present)

Coastal Speedway - Charleston - 1/2 mile dirt oval (4/09/50)
located one mile south of town

Coastal Speedway - Myrtle Beach - 1/2 mile dirt oval (c.1955 - c.8/26/57)
Ray Tilley started here in 1955 / site is now the Convention Center

Columbia Fairgrounds - Columbia / at the South Carolina State Fairgrounds
1.0 mile dirt oval (11/20/10 - 1916) (11/28/29) (10/26/40 - 10/25/41)
the track was built for auto racing but mostly ran horse from 1917 to 1940

Columbia Speedway - Cayce - 1/2 mile dirt oval (1932 - 1941) (1946 - 1970)
1/4 mile dirt oval (c.1953) / (aka: Palmetto Speedway)
located at the new South Carolina State Fairgrounds
.510 mile paved oval (1971 - 1977) / (aka: New Columbia Speedway)
first race as Palmetto Speedway was on 3/20/53 and was listed in a
press release as a brand new track in Nat'l Speed Sports News

Columbia Speedway - Columbia (Gaston) / (aka: New Columbia Speedway)
3/8 mile dirt oval (8/12/83 - present)

Columbia - also see: Blaney Dragstrip

Confederate Motor Speedway - Woodruff - 1/4 mile dirt oval (1952 - 1957)
David Pearson started his career here in 1953 / (aka: Woodruff Speedway)
located three miles south on Lauren Highway, near current track

Confederate Motor Speedway - Woodruff / located south of town on US 221
3/8 mile dirt oval (May, 1970 - 1988) (1992 - present)
(aka: Woodruff Speedway) / was near site of old Confederate Speedway

Conway Raceway - Conway - 3/8 mile dirt oval (1963 - 1986) / now only Go-Karts

Seven-time NASCAR Winston Cup champion Dale Earnhardt at Indianapolis Motor Speedway during practice in 1993. - Nancy Brown photo.

Cooper River Speedway - Moncks Corner - dirt oval (1963 - 1969)
1/8 mile paved dragstrip (c.1976 - c.1990) / (aka: Cooper River Dragway)

County Hall - Charleston - indoor oval (1/23/59) / ran T.Q. midgets

Cowpens - 3/8 mile dirt oval (c.1949 - c.1960) / located northeast of Spartanburg

Darlington Int'l Dragway - Darlington - 1/4 mile paved dragstrip (1957 - present)
six miles west on SR 151 / same site as Hartsville-Darlington Speedway

Darlington Raceway - Darlington / built by Harold Brasington
1.25 mile paved oval (9/04/50 - 9/01/50) / first race was a "Southern 500"
1.366 mile paved oval (7/04/53 - present) / turns banked 26 degrees

Tony Bettenhausen leading the AAA Championship race at Darlington Raceway. Walt Faulkner ended up winning the 250 mile race on July 4, 1951. Don O'Reilly photo (Allan E. Brown collection).

Dillon County Raceway - Dillon / located west of town
4/10 (.426) mile dirt oval (c.1961 - c.1970) (1977 - 1980)

Dixie Speedway - Laurens - see: Laurens Speedway

Dixie Speedway - Orangeburg / located at the Orange County Fairgrounds
1/2 mile dirt oval (1937) / (aka: Stacy Speedway)
3/8 mile dirt oval (1965 - 1979)

Dorchester Dragway - Dorchester - 1/8 mile paved dragstrip (c.1986 - present)

Dorchester Speedway - see: Summerville Speedway

Duncan Park - Spartanburg - 1/5 mile dirt oval (9/22/39 - 10/05/41) / ball field

East Park Speedway - Anderson - 1/4 mile dirt oval (Apr., 1954 - 1958) / US 29

Florence I-95 Speedway - Timmonsville / (aka: Timmonsville Speedway)
4/10 mile dirt oval (1982 - 1987) / (aka: Raceland Timmonsville)
3/8 mile paved oval (1988 - present) / located on US Highway 76 near I-95

Florence Speedway - Florence / (aka: New Florence Speedway)
1/2 mile dirt oval (5/28/50 - 1951) / located on Timmonsville Road

Florence-Darlington Dragstrip - Florence - 1/8 mile dragstrip (1962 - present)

Flower Bowl Speedway - see: (old) Summerville Speedway

Fort Mill Speedway - Fort Mill - dirt oval (c.1954)

Gaffney Speedway - Gaffney - 3/4 mile dirt oval (late 1940's)

Gaffney - also see: Cherokee Speedway, Service-Stephens Speedway

Gamecock Speedway - Sumter / (aka: Sumter Rebel Speedway)
    1/4 mile dirt oval (c.1955 - 1984) (1987 - present) / (aka: Rebel Raceway)
    Cale Yarborough started his career here in 1955 / (aka: Sumter Speedway)

Gator Speedway - Goose Creek - dirt oval (years unknown)

Gault's Motor Speedway - see: Buffalo Motor Speedway

Golden Strip Speedway - Fountain Inn - 3/8 mile dirt oval (1954 - 1988)
    the site is now part of a National Guard Base

Graniteville - 1/4 mile paved dragstrip (1960's) / control tower was torched

Greenville Fairgrounds - see: Greenville-Pickens Speedway

Greenville - indoor oval (1959) / ran T.Q. midgets

Greenville Memorial Auditorium - Greenville
    1/9 mile concrete indoor oval (1/02/59 - c.1959)

Greenville-Pickens Speedway - Greenville
    1/2 mile dirt oval (1940 - c.1941) (7/04/46 - 1952) (1954 - 1969)
    located at the Upper South Carolina State Fairgrounds
    1/2 mile paved oval (April, 1970 - present)

Greenville-Textile Speedway - see: Textile Speedway

Greenville - also see: Meadow Brooke, Parker Stadium

Greenwood Speedway - Greenwood / located at the Greenwood Fairgrounds
    1/2 mile dirt oval (11/01/47 - 1949) / built as a horse track in 1935
    1/4 mile dirt oval (1949) / small tracks were adjacent to horse track
    1/4 mile dirt oval (1950 - 1954) (1956 - 1957) (1959 - 1968)
    1/4 mile paved oval (c.5/06/54 - 1954) / (aka: Greenwood Stadium Speedway)
    races on the small track in 1949 were around a football field

Greer Dragway - Greer - 1/8 mile paved dragstrip (c.1969 - present)
    (aka: Jaycee Dragstrip)

Greer - also see: Caesar's Head Race Track, Highway 14 Raceway, I-85 Raceway

Hanging Rock Speedway - (located unknown) - 1/4 mile dirt oval (1993)

Hartsville Speedway - Hartsville - 1/3 mile dirt oval (c.1956 - c.1962)

Hartsville-Darlington Speedway - Darlington - 3/8 mile dirt oval (7/07/78 - 1986)
    six miles west of town on SR 151 / same site as Darlington Int'l Dragway

Hemingway Speedway - Hemingway - 1/4 mile dirt oval (c.1956 - c.1963)

Highway 14 Raceway - Greer - dirt oval (c.1974)

Hub City Speedway - see: Spartanburg Fairgrounds

I-20 Speedway - Batesburg - 3/8 mile dirt oval (1987 - 1990) (1992 - present)
located north of I-20 on US Highway 178

I-77 Speedway - see: Chester Speedway

I-85 Raceway - Greer - 1/2 mile dirt oval (1985 - present) / (aka: I-85 Speedway)

I-95 Speedway - see: Florence I-95 Speedway

Jackson Dragstrip - see: Carolina Dragway

Jaycee Dragstrip - see: Greer Dragway

Keowee Speedway - Walhalla - 1/4 mile dirt oval (1963 - c.1964)

Lake City Speedway - Lake City - 1/2 mile dirt oval (c.1949)

Lake View Speedway - Lake View - 3/8 mile dirt oval (4/11/81-1988)(1992-present)

Lancaster Speedway - Lancaster / located at the Lancaster County Fairgrounds
1/2 mile dirt oval (c.9/11/54 - present) / (aka: Lancaster Raceway)

Lando Speedway - Lando - 4/10 mile dirt oval (1962) / (aka: Suicide Circle)

Landrum Speedway - Landrum - dirt oval (8/13/49)

Laurens Speedway - Laurens / (aka: Dixie Speedway)
3/8 mile dirt oval (1952 - present)

Laurens-Clinton Speedway - dirt oval (1947)

Leesville - dirt track / built next to Thunder Valley Speedway / never used

Little River Speedway - North Myrtle Beach / site is now Eagle Nest Golf Course
3/8 mile high banked dirt oval (c.1963 - 1971)

Loris - dirt oval (years unknown) / not Twin City Speedway

Marion - dirt oval (c.1957)

Meadow Brooke Park Speedway - Greenville - 1/4 mile dirt oval (4/19/56 - 3/26/88)
the site is now a recreation complex

Mid-Carolina Drag Strip - see: Batesburg Dragstrip

Modoc Speedway - Modoc / confiscated by US Government in a drug bust
4/10 mile dirt oval (6/22/84 - 1991) (1993 - present)

Mount Zion - (location unknown) - dirt oval (1957)

Myrtle Beach Speedway - Myrtle Beach - 1/2 mile dirt oval (1957 - 1974)
6/10 mile paved oval (1975 - mid-1976) / (aka: Rambi Race Track)
6/10 mile dirt oval (late 1976) pavement covered over with clay
6/10 mile paved oval (1977 - 6/01/78) / the clay was removed
6/10 mile dirt oval (7/01/78 - 9/05/81) (7/18/86 - 1987) pavement torn up
6/10 mile paved oval (1987 - present) / repaved again
currently listed as a 1/2 mile track again

Myrtle Beach - also see: Cherry Grove, Coastal, Little River, North Myrtle Beach

New Columbia Speedway - see: Columbia Speedway

Newberry Speedway - Newberry - 1/2 mile dirt oval (8/16/52 - c.1961)
     1/4 mile dirt oval (c.1961 - c.1979)

North Myrtle Beach Dragstrip - N. Myrtle Beach - 1/8 mile paved dragstrip (1991)

North Speedway - North - 5/8 mile dirt oval (1963 & 1964)

Orangeburg Drag Strip - Orangeburg - 1/8 mile paved dragstrip (c.1981- present)

Orangeburg Fairgrounds - see: Dixie Speedway - Orangeburg

Pageland - 1/4 mile dirt oval (7/04/50 - 1951)

Palmetto Nat'l Dragway - North Augusta - 1/4 mile paved dragstrip (c.1969- 1982)

Palmetto Speedway - see: Columbia Speedway

Parker Stadium - Greenville - dirt oval (7/04/50) / ran Micro-midgets

Pelion - 1/4 mile paved dragstrip (c.1968 - c.1971)

Pickens - 1/4 mile paved dragstrip (1960's) / located on SR 183
     the site is currently the Bargain Exchange Flea Market

Piedmont Interstate Fairgrounds - see: Spartanburg Fairgrounds

Raceland Timmonsville - see: Florence I-95 Speedway

Rambi Race Track - see: Myrtle Beach Speedway

Rebel Raceway - see: Gamecock Speedway

Riverside Speedway - Travelers Rest / located on State Highway 11
     3/8 mile dirt oval (1976 - 1985) (1988 - present) / ran cycles 1986 & 1987

Rock Hill Speedway - Rock Hill / located at the York County Fairgrounds
     1/4 mile dirt oval (4/17/54 - c.1962) / ran by Rock Hill American Legion

Service-Stephens Speedway - Gaffney - 1/4 mile dirt oval (1953) / ran by JC's

South Carolina State Fairgrounds - see: Columbia Fair & Columbia Speedway

Southside Speedway - Seneca - 1/4 mile dirt oval (1960 - c.1962)

Spartanburg - 1.8 mile paved road course (1964)

Spartanburg Dragway - Spartanburg - 1/8 mile dragstrip (c.1965 - c.1982)
     (aka: Spartanburg Int'l Dragway)

Spartanburg Fairgrounds - Spartanburg - 1/2 mile dirt oval (1932 - 10/17/36)
     located at a different location than the Piedmont Interstate Fairgrounds

Spartanburg Fairgrounds - Spartanburg / at the Piedmont Interstate Fairgrounds
     1/2 mile dirt oval (10/17/37 - 1941) (10/13/45 - c.1986)
     this was a new fairgrounds built in 1937 / ran Big Cars before WWII
     (aka: Hub City Speedway) / ran stock cars during the fair after WWII

Spartanburg - also see: Duncan Park

Speedway Park - Travelers Rest - 3/8 mile dirt oval (4/17/71 - 1977)
    Butch Lindley's driving career started here / located on Stamey Valley Rd.

Stacy Speedway - see: Dixie Speedway - Orangeburg

Stamey Valley Race Track - Travelers Rest - dirt oval (October, 1949 - 1950)

Starlite 25 Dragway - see: Ware Shoals Dragway

Sugar Creek Motor Speedway - Union (Buffalo) / south of Union on SR 215
    3/8 mile dirt oval (9/03/79 - c.1984) (1991 - 1993)

Suicide Circle - see: Lando Speedway

Summerville Speedway - Summerville - 9/16 mile dirt oval (9/18/48 - 1955)
    (aka: Flower Bowl Speedway)

Summerville Speedway - Summerville - 4/10 mile dirt oval (Sept., 1964 - 1986)
    4/10 mile paved oval (1987 - present) / (aka: Dorchester Speedway)

Sumter - 1/4 mile dirt oval (early 1950's)

Sumter (Rebel) Speedway - see: Gamecock Speedway

Sumter Road Race - Sumter - 3.625 mile road course (11/22/04)

Textile Speedway - Greenville - 1/2 mile dirt oval (c.1941) (c.1946 - c.1951)
    located 10 miles south of town on US 25 near old Donaldson Air Force Base
    (aka: Greenville-Textile Speedway) / ran motorcycles in July of 1949
    1/4 mile dirt oval (October, 1950) / (aka: Airbase Speedway)

Thunder Valley Speedway - Leesville / located 3 miles NE of town on Gilbert Road

    4/10 mile dirt oval (1968 - c.1986) (1988 & 1989) (1991)

Timmonsville Speedway - see: Florence I-95 Speedway

Travelers Rest - see: Riverside, Speedway Park, Stamey Valley

Tucker Midget Speedway - Williamston - 1/5 mile dirt oval (c.9/13/47)

Twin City Speedway - Loris - 4/10 mile dirt oval (1965 - 1966) / at the airport

Walterboro Army Air Base - Walterboro - 2.0 mile paved road course (1955)
    3.5 mile paved road course (3/10/56 - c.1959)

Ware Shoals Dragway - Ware Shoals - 1/8 mile paved dragstrip (c.1969 - present)
    (aka: Starlite 25 Dragway) / (aka: Starlite 25 Dragstrip)

Westminster Speedway - Westminster
    1/4 mile dirt oval (1956 - 1961) (1988 - 1990)
    4/10 mile dirt oval (1991 - present)

York-Clover Speedway - York - 1/4 mile dirt oval (c.1963 - c.1964)

480   *South Carolina*

SOUTH DAKOTA

Aberdeen - also see: Brown County (Fairgrounds) Speedway, Tacoma Park Spwy

Airport Speedway - Stevens - 1/2 mile dirt oval (c.8/01/37 - c.9/26/37)
    1/5 mile dirt oval (c.9/19/37 - c.10/17/37) (town is now North Sioux City)

Alpena Speedway - Alpena - 1/6 mile dirt oval (7/04/83) / ran Mini-sprints

Black Hills Dragway - see: Dakota Intermountain Dragway

Black Hills Speedway - Rapid City - 1/2 mile dirt oval (c.1949 - present)
    (aka: Rapid Valley Race Track) / (aka: Rapid Valley Speedway)
    was a NASCAR sanctioned track in the 1950's / maybe opened in 1952

You could enjoy steak, seafood, or a cocktail while watching the races from the "Crows Nest Restaurant" at Black Hills Speedway. - Official track photo.

Bonesteel - 1/4 mile dirt oval (early 1950's)

Brandon Speedway - see: Huset's Speedway

Brookings Speedway - Brookings - 3/8 mile dirt oval (5/14/67 - 7/30/76)

Brown County Speedway - Aberdeen / located at the Brown County Fairgrounds
    1/2 mile dirt oval (1922 - c.1941) (c.1946 - c.1955)
    3/8 mile dirt oval (1971 - present) / smaller track inside of horse track
    (aka: Brown County Raceway)

Buckmiller Race Track - see: Sioux Empire Fairgrounds

Caseys Speedway - Yankton - 3/8 mile dirt oval (c.1949 - c.1954)

Casino Speedway - Watertown / (aka: Lake Park Speedway)
    1/4 mile dirt oval (1955 - present)

Central Speedway - see: Miller Central Speedway

Central States Fairgrounds - see: Rapid City Fairgrounds

Central U.S. Dragway - Pierre - 1/4 mile paved dragstrip (c.1963 - c.1964)

Chamberlain - 1/5 mile dirt oval (6/21/38 - 6/23/38) (c.1956)

Clear Lake Fairgrounds - Clear Lake - 1/2 mile dirt oval (early 1950's)
   at the Deuel County Fairgrounds / track site is now baseball diamonds

Custer - dirt oval (1940)

Dakota Intermountain Dragway - Belle Fourche / (aka: Black Hills Dragway)
   1/4 mile paved dragstrip (1975 - present)

Dawson Creek Speedway - Scotland / Doug Wolfgang started here in 1970
   1/4 mile dirt oval (1969 - 1973) (1976)

Day County Raceway - see: Webster Fairgrounds

Delta Speedway - Alexandria - dirt oval (1968 - 1973)

Edgemont Fairgrounds - Edgemont / located at the Fall River County Fairgrounds
   1/5 mile dirt oval (early 1950's) / held only one race

Empire Dragway - see: Sioux Empire Fairgrounds

Estelline - dirt oval (1951 - late 1950's) / the site is now a junkyard

Eureka Fairgrounds - Eureka - 1/2 mile dirt circle (c.1923 - c.1932)
   located at the McPherson County Fairgrounds

Flandreau - dirt oval (1930's)

Fred Buckmiller Race Track - see: Sioux Empire Fairgrounds

Gregory Raceway - Gregory - 1/4 mile dirt oval (mid 1950's - 1962)
   located next to the airport on SR 18

Hartford Speedway - see: Red Devil Speedway

Huron - also see: Northwest Speedway, Valley Speedway, State Fair Speedway

Huset's Speedway - Sioux Falls (Brandon) / built by Tilman Huset
   3/8 mile dirt oval (5/23/54 - August, 1955) (late 1958 - present)
   1/5 mile dirt oval (Sept. 1955 - July, 1958) / Paul Stogsdill won the first race
   sometimes referred to as Brandon Speedway, but never officially called that

Igloo Raceways - Edgemont - 2.0 mile paved road course (late 1960's)
   located on runways of an abandoned Army air base

Interlakes Speedway - see: Lake County Speedway

Interstate Speedway - Jefferson / across the street from Park Jefferson Speedway
   3/8 mile dirt oval (June, 1970 - 1988) (1991 - present)

Interstate Speedway - Stevens - see: Sioux City Speedway

James Valley Speedway - Huron - 3/8 mile dirt oval (5/09/65 - 8/28/70)
   (aka: Valley Speedway)

482   *South Dakota*

Marshall Gardner was the 1954 Soo Speedway champion. He won 14 features in his 1938 Plymouth coupe in 1954. - Tom Savage collection.

Kimball Fairgrounds - Kimball - 1/2 mile dirt oval (1920's & 1930's)
   located at the Brule County Fairgrounds

Lake Andes Speedway - Lake Andes / (aka: Randall Valley Speedway)
   1/4 mile dirt oval (1970 - 1974) (May, 1987 - present)

Lake County Speedway - Madison / (aka: Interlakes Speedway)
   3/8 mile dirt oval (1960 - 1973) (1976 - present)

Lake Park Speedway - see: Casino Speedway

Lemmon Fairgrounds - Lemmon / located at the Perkins County Fairgrounds
   1/2 mile dirt oval (c.1922 - c.1931)

Letcher - 1/2 mile dirt oval (1920's - 1930's) / maybe the Sanborn Co. Fairgrounds

Madison - 1/2 mile dirt oval (c.1913 - c.1938) / located west of town

Huset's Speedway in 1993. - Nancy Brown photo.

McLaughlin Fairgrounds - McLaughlin / located at the Corson County Fairgrounds
1/2 mile dirt oval (c.1924 - c.1930)

Milbank Fairgrounds - Milbank / located at the Grant County Fairgrounds
1/2 mile dirt oval (1922 - c.1933) (1950's)

Miller Central Speedway - Miller - 3/8 mile dirt oval (1965 - 1985) (c.1987 - 1989)
(aka: Central Speedway)

Mitchell Speedway - Mitchell - 3/8 mile dirt oval (c.1953 - 6/02/56)

Mobridge Fairgrounds - Mobridge / located at the Walworth County Fairgrounds
3/8 mile dirt oval (1950's or 1960's) / site is now a cow pasture

New Oahe Speedway - Pierre / located at the Hughes County Fairgrounds
1/4 mile dirt oval (1971 - 1972) / track built in 1971 by Tony Dean
4/10 mile dirt oval (1974 - 1975) / lights were from James Valley Speedway

Northwest Speedway - Huron - 1/5 mile dirt oval (6/24/62 - 7/09/65) / near airport

Oahe Speedway - Pierre - 3/8 mile dirt oval (1960 - 1973) (1976 - 1979)

Park Jefferson Speedway - Jefferson - 1/2 mile dirt oval (1986 - present)
formerly a horse track / across the street from Interstate Speedway

Parker Fairgrounds - Parker / located at the Turner County Fairgrounds
1/4 mile dirt oval (c.1968 - c.1975) (1985 - present)

Pierre - also see: Central U.S., New Oahe (Fairgrounds), Oahe Speedway

Plankinton Fairgrounds - Plankinton / located at the Aurora County Fairgrounds
1/2 mile dirt oval (c.1923 - c.1932)

Randall Valley Speedway - see: Lake Andes Speedway

Rapid City Fairgrounds - Rapid City / located at the Pennington Co. Fairgrounds
1/2 mile dirt oval (c.9/07/52 - c.1980) (1986 - present)
(aka: Central States Fairgrounds) / only runs during the annual fair

Rapid Valley - also see: Black Hills Speedway, South 79 Speedway

Red Devil Speedway - Hartford - 1/2 mile dirt oval (1976 - 1982)
3/8 mile dirt oval (1988 - present) / (aka: Hartford Speedway)

Renner - 1/2 mile dirt oval (c.1928 - c.1934) / ran weekly Big Car races

Roll-N-Wheel Raceway - Mitchell - 1/4 mile dirt oval (1985 - present)

Ruskin Park - Forestburg - 1.0 mile dirt oval (1914 - 1931)
1/4 mile dirt oval (1951 - 1956) / grandstands later used as a corn crib

Sioux City Speedway - Stevens (the town is now called North Sioux City)
2.0 mile dirt oval (10/18/11, 6/06/13, 7/05/13, 7/06/13, 9/01/13, 9/02/13, 6/30/14,
7/04/14, 9/01/14, 7/03/15, 7/08/16 & 7/04/17)
(aka: Woodland Park) / (aka: Interstate Speedway) built by W.W. Stevens
ran 300 mile AAA championship races in 1914 & 1915
later became the Eddie Rickenbacker Airfield / the airfield is now defunct
(the grandstand were torn down during World War I, the numbered boards
became rafters in many houses built in the area shortly thereafter)

The Sioux Empire Fairgrounds in 1953. - Bob Stolze collection.

Sioux Empire Fairgrounds - Sioux Falls / (aka: Fred Buckmiller Race Track)
 1/2 mile dirt oval (8/21/39 - 8/23/41) (8/20/46 - 10/03/93)
 1/4 mile paved dragstrip (c.1970 - c.1989) / (aka: Empire Dragway)
 (aka: Thunderdome Dragway) / located at the Minnehaha County Fairgrounds
 the fairgrounds, race track and grandstands were built in 1939. This track
  is on the same property as the old Sioux Falls 3/4 mile track
 (see next listing) / Doug Wolfgang won the last race (also his last win)
 (aka: Lion's Fairgrounds)

Sioux Falls - 3/4 mile dirt oval (1929 - 1936) / later the site of Sioux Empire Fair

Sioux Falls - paved road course (1960)

Sioux Falls Speedway - see: Soo Falls Speedway

Soo Falls Speedway - Sioux Falls - 3/4 mile dirt oval (5/30/36 - 7/25/37)
 1/5 mile dirt oval (c.7/25/37 - c.1940) / (aka: Sioux Falls Speedway)
 (aka: West Sioux Speedway)

Soo Speedway - Sioux Falls - 3/8 mile dirt oval (5/30/54 - July, 1958) (May 1972)
 near Huset's Speedway, but on SR 38 / now site of Arndt's Salvage

South 79 Speedway - Rapid City - dirt oval (c.1965 - 1969) / ran motorcycles 1974

South Dakota State Fairgrounds - see: State Fair Speedway

Speedy Hollow Speedway - Bath - 3/8 mile high banked dirt oval (1956 - c.1970)
 (aka: Sleepy Hollow Speedway)

State Fair Speedway - Huron / located at the South Dakota State Fairgrounds
 1/2 mile dirt oval (1913 - 9/04/41) (9/03/46 - present)
 the South Dakota State Fairgrounds was built on this site in 1905

Sturgis Dragway - Sturgis - 1/8 mile paved dragstrip (1986 - present)
 holds Harley-Davidson motorcycle drag racing during "Sturgis Rally"

Sturgis Fairgrounds - Sturgis / located at the Meade County Fairgrounds
 1/2 mile dirt oval (1925) / location where the "Sturgis Rally" is held

Sturgis Rally - Sturgis - 1/5 mile dirt oval (1970's - present)
a motorcycle track / ran mini-sprints in 1970's

Tacoma Park Speedway - Aberdeen - 3/8 mile dirt oval (c.1953 - July, 1957)

Thunder Valley Dragway - Marion - 1/4 mile paved dragstrip (c.1967 - present)

Thunderdome Dragway - see: Sioux Empire Fairgrounds

Tomahawk Speedway - Wagner - 3/8 mile dirt oval (5/04/90 - present)
same location as the old Wagner Fairgrounds

Tripp Fairgrounds - Tripp / located at the Hutchinson County Fairgrounds
1/2 mile dirt oval (1928 - 1938) (early 1950's)

Forrest Hurd broadslides in front of the fans at the Winner Fairgrounds in
1950. - Johansson-Hurd collection (courtesy of Don Radbruch).

Turner County Fairgrounds - see: Parker Fairgrounds

Tyndall - 1/2 mile dirt oval (1920's or 1930's)

Valley Park Speedway - Milbank - 3/8 mile dirt oval (6/10/56 - c.1959)

Valley Speedway - see: James Valley Speedway

Vermillion Fairgrounds - Vermillion / located at the Clay County Fairgrounds
1/5 mile dirt oval (5/01/38 - c.1938)
1/8 mile dirt oval (1983) / ran one Mini-sprint race

Wagner Fairgrounds - Wagner / located at the Charles Mix County Fairgrounds
1/2 mile dirt oval (c.1922 - c.1931) / (aka: Tomahawk Speedway)
1/4 mile dirt oval (1954 - 1956) / same site as current Tomahawk Speedway
Paul Stogsdill used to practice on the 1/2 mile track in the early 1950's

486

Webster Fairgrounds - Webster - 1/2 mile dirt oval (c.1923 - c.1933)
  1/5 mile dirt oval (5/01/38 - c.1938) / at the Day County Fairgrounds
  1/4 mile dirt oval (1959) (1967 - 1969) (1975) / (aka: Day County Speedway)

Wessington Springs - 1/4 mile dirt oval (1970's - 1980's) / ran mini-sprints

West Sioux Speedway - see: Soo Falls Speedway

Westside Raceway - Yankton - 1/4 mile dirt oval (early 1950's - 1971)

Wildcat Speedway - Corsica - 1/4 mile dirt oval (1971 - 1976)

Winner Fairgrounds - Winner - dirt oval (1950) / at the Tripp Co. Fairgrounds

Winner Speedway - Winner / (aka: Winner Stock Car Track)
  1/4 mile dirt oval (1968 - 1971) (1987 - present)

TENNESSEE

411 Speedway - see: Four-Eleven Motor Speedway

Alton Park - Chattanooga - 1/2 mile dirt oval (years unknown)

American Legion Speed Bowl - Nashville / (aka: Nashville Speedway)
  1/4 mile dirt oval (1950 - 1956)

American Legion Speedway - Memphis / (aka: Legion Speed Bowl)
  1/4 mile dirt oval (5/06/49 - 1950)

Appalachian Speedway - Kingsport / built by Paul Dykes
  1/2 mile dirt oval (4/18/69 - 1972) (1974 - 1975)
  Robert Smawley was the promoter in the last years

Ashway Speedway - Strawberry Plains - 1/2 mile dirt oval (c.1954 - c.1980)

Atomic Speedway - Knoxville (Oak Ridge) - 1/3 mile dirt oval (1970 - present)

Atomic Speedway near Oak Ridge, Tennessee. The track is home to a number of short track late model special events. - Official track photo.

Austin Springs Park - Johnson City - 1/2 mile dirt oval (5/30/32)

Beechnut Speedway - Blountville - 1/8 mile dirt oval (c.1982 - 1983)

Big Oak Speedway - Spring Hill - dirt oval (years unknown)

Blankenship Motorsports Park - see: Memphis Dirt Trax

Boyd's Speedway - see: Georgia chapter

Brainerd's Raceway - Lebanon - 1/4 mile dirt oval (early 1960's)
    located between Lebanon and Murfreesboro / later became a junkyard

Bristol Int'l Dragway - Bristol / (aka: Thunder Valley Dragway)
    1/4 mile paved dragstrip (1962 - present) / next to Bristol Int'l Raceway

Bristol Int'l Raceway - Bristol / (aka: Bristol Int'l Speedway)
    1/2 (.533) mile asphalt oval (7/30/61 - 1991) / turns banked 29 degrees
    first race was a NASCAR Grand National (Winston Cup) event
    1/2 (.533) mile concrete oval (1992 - present)

Broadway Speedway - Knoxville - 1/4 & 1/2 mile dirt ovals (4/10/49 - c.1958)
    site later became a shopping center

Buena Vista Speedway - Clarksville - 3/10 mile dirt oval (c.1954)

Buffalo Valley Speedway - see: Middle Tennessee Dragway

Camp Gordon - Chattanooga / the track was located on Ringgold Road
    3/4 mile dirt oval (c.8/11/40 - c.1941)

Chattanooga Fairgrounds - Chattanooga / at the Tri-State Fairgrounds
    1/2 mile dirt oval (c.1917 - c.9/24/36)

Memphis' Sammy Swindell in the Kodiak sponsored sprint car at Ascot Speedway (CA) in 1987. Swindell is a two-time World of Outlaw champion. - Phil Dullinger photo.

488

Chattanooga Int'l Speedway - Chattanooga / (aka: Warner Park)
1/2 mile dirt oval (c.1935 - 1936) (7/27/47 - c.1955)

Chattanooga - also see: Alton Park, Camp Gordon & Moccasin Bend

Cherokee Dragway - Rogersville - 1/8 mile paved dragstrip (1965 - present)

Chickopin Raceway - Bluff City - dirt oval (1950's or 1960's) / maybe Tri-City

Clarksville Speedway - Clarksville - 1/4 mile dirt oval (1961 - present)
1/8 mile dirt oval (c.1983 - c.1984) / small track used for T.Q. midgets
1/4 mile paved dragstrip (1960 - present) / (aka: Raceway Park)

Clarksville - also see: Buena Vista Speedway

Clay Hill Motorsports - Atwood - 3/8 mile dirt oval (April, 1994 - present)

Cleveland Fairgrounds - Cleveland - dirt oval (May, 1968) / 6 miles east on US 64

Cleveland Speedway - Cleveland / current promoter is Joe Lee Johnson
1/3 mile dirt oval (c.1955 - c.1958) (c.1965 - present)

Columbia Speedway - Columbia - dirt oval (1954)

Cotton Carnival Road Race - Memphis - 8.0 mile road course (May, 1936)

Crossville Int'l Dragway - see: I-40 Dragway

Crossville Raceway - Crossville - 1/3 mile dirt oval (1986 - present)

*The red clay, high-banked Crossville Speedway. The track was built in 1986
by J.Paul Smith. - Official track photo.*

Crossville - also see: Cumberland County Speedway(s)

Crump Stadium - Memphis - 1/4 mile dirt oval (8/28/46 - c.1946)

Cumberland County Speedway - Crossville - dirt oval #1 (late 1940's)

Cumberland County Speedway - Crossville - dirt oval #2 (late 1940's)

Cumberland County Speedway - Crossville - dirt oval (#3) / three different tracks
1/4 mile dirt oval (5/01/49 - c.1950)

Cumberland Park - see: Nashville Motor Speedway

Cumberland Speedway - Nashville - paved road course (late 1940's - mid 1950's)
1/4 mile paved dragstrip (1950's) / located at an airport

Dallas Ricker Racing Complex - Greeneville - 1/3 mile dirt oval (1991 - present)
1/8 mile paved dragstrip (June, 1992 - present)
the oval track originally was a Go-Kart track running since c.1990
(aka: Northeast Tennessee Raceway)

Davy Crockett Speedway - see: Rogersville Speedway

Decherd - 1/4 mile dirt oval (1983) / the only event was rained out

Del Monte Speedway - (location unknown) - dirt oval (years unknown)

Dixie Speedway - see: Georgia chapter

Duck River Speedway - Wheel - 1/4 mile dirt oval (1973 - present)
(aka: Duck River Motor Speedway)

Dumplin Valley Raceway - Kodak - 1/4 mile dirt oval (1992) / TQ midgets races
an active Go-Kart track that has been running since c.1989

Dyersburg Speedway - Dyersburg - 3/8 mile dirt oval (September, 1986 - present)

Edgemoor - see: Oak Ridge Sportsdrome

English Mountain Dragway - Newport / (aka: New English Mountain Dragway)
1/8 mile paved dragstrip (c.1959 - 1990) (1994 - present)

Fairgrounds Speedway - see: Nashville Speedway

Fayetteville - 5/8 mile dirt oval (c.1981 - 1983)

Finger - 1/4 mile dirt oval (early 1960's)

Flat Rock Speedway - see: Hot Rod Speedway

Four-Eleven (411) Motor Speedway - Knoxville (Seymour) / near Shooks Gap
3/8 mile dirt oval (c.1969 - 1973) (1988 - 1992)
1/8 mile paved dragstrip (c.1962 - present) / (aka: 411 Int'l Raceway)
1/8 mile dirt oval (1980 - 1983) / ran TQ midgets on 1/8 mile track
3/8 mile paved oval (1993 - present) / (aka: Tennessee Motor Speedway)

Gadsden Speedway - Gadsden - 1/4 mile dirt oval (1960's - early 1970's)

Gallatin Fairgrounds - Gallatin / located at the Sumner County Fairgrounds
1/8 mile dirt oval (c.4/19/52 - c.1953) / ran TQ midgets

Gardner - 1/2 mile dirt oval (late 1950's - early 1960's)

Greeneville Fairgrounds - Greeneville / located at the Greene County Fairgrounds
1/4 mile dirt oval (1953 - 1955)

Halls Dragway - Halls - 1/4 mile paved dragstrip (1954 - c.1970) / old airstrip

Halls Speedbowl - Halls - 1/4 mile dirt oval (mid 1960's)

Harriman Speedway - Harriman / (aka: Roane County Speedway)
1/4 mile dirt oval (1951 - 1968) (1984)

490

Henry County Speedway - Paris - 1/4 mile dirt oval (1960's)

Highland Park Speedway - see: Hohenwald Motorsports Speedway

Highland Rim Speedway - Goodlettsville - 1/4 mile paved oval (1963 - present)

Hodges Field - Memphis - 1/5 mile dirt oval (1937 - c.10/01/39)

Hohenwald Motorsports Speedway - Hohenwald / (aka: Highland Park Speedway)
1/4 mile dirt oval (early 1950's - 1965) (9/15/90 - present)

Hot Rod Speedway - Pulaski / (aka: Pulaski Speedway) (aka: Flat Rock Speedway)
1/4 mile dirt oval (1982 - 1985) (1987 - 1988) (1990 - 1992)

Huntingdon Speedway - Huntingdon - 1/4 mile dirt oval (1950's)

I-40 Dragway - Crossville / (aka: Crossville Int'l Dragway)
1/8 mile paved dragstrip (c.1981 - present)

Inskip Speedway - see: Knoxville Motor Speedway

Jackson - 1/2 mile dirt oval (1950's) / the site is now Casey Jones Museum Store

Jackson Dragway - Jackson - 1/8 mile paved dragstrip (c.1970 - present)

An aerial view of Jackson Dragway. - Official track photo.

Jackson Fairgrounds - Jackson / located at the West Tennessee State Fairgrounds
1/2 mile dirt oval (9/16/39) / (aka: Raceland Park Motor Speedway)
1/4 mile dirt oval (5/19/78 - 1980)

Jackson - also see: Northside Speedway

Kingsport Speedway - see: MARCA Motorsports Community

Kingsport - also see: Appalachian Speedway

Knoxville Dragway - Knoxville - 1/8 mile paved dragstrip (August, 1984 - present)
same location as Knoxville Raceway (oval track)
the site was used as an off road course in the late 1970's

Knoxville Fairgrounds - Knoxville / located at the Knox County Fairgrounds
1/2 mile dirt oval (10/13/35) / now called Tennessee Valley Fairgrounds

Knoxville Motor Speedway - Morristown / (aka: Inskip Speedway)
3/4 mile dirt oval (c.5/30/28 - 9/08/35)

Knoxville Raceway - Knoxville - 3/8 mile dirt oval (c.1959 - c.1970)
3/8 mile paved oval (c.1971 - 1975) / same site as Knoxville Dragway

Knoxville - also see: Atomic, Broadway, Four-Eleven, Oak Ridge

Claude Donovan (#6), Bill Corum (#21), and Wayne Fielden (#2) at the paved track at Knoxville Raceway in 1971. - John D. Moore photo.

Lake Winnepansaukie - see: Georgia chapter

Lakeland Speedbowl - Memphis - 1/3 mile dirt oval (1960) (1968)
3/8 mile paved oval (9/08/60 - 1968) / (aka: Lakeland RaceWay Park)
1/4 mile paved dragstrip (c.1972 - c.1973) / (aka: Lakeland Speedway)
the site later became an amusement park / site is now a shopping center

Laurel Mountain Speedway - Madisonville - 1/3 mile dirt oval (4/22/94 - present)

Lawrenceburg - dirt oval (early 1960's)

Legion Speedbowl - see: American Legion Speedway - Memphis

Liberty Hill Speedway - Bethpage - 1/4 mile dirt oval (early 1960's - mid 1970's)
this was a very primitive track with no rest rooms or concessions

Madison Speedway - Nashville (Madison) - oval (1952 & 1953) / ran TQ midgets

MARCA Motorsports Community - Kingsport / (aka: Kingsport Speedway)
3/8 (.337) mile paved oval (c.1967 - 1983) / (aka: Raceland Kingsport)
3/8 mile dirt oval (4/28/84 - present) / (aka: Kingsport Motor Speedway)
(aka: Tri-Cities Speedway) / (aka: New Kingsport Speedway)
(aka: Kingsport Int'l Speedway) / held NDRA's Strohs Invitational in 1985.

Maury County Raceway - Mt. Pleasant - dirt oval (years unknown)

McKenzie - 1/4 mile dirt oval (1960's)

McMinnville Speedway - McMinnville - 1/4 mile dirt oval (1950's - 1969)

McMinnville Speedway - McMinnville - 1/4 mile dirt oval (1977 - 1983) (1987)
(aka: Warren County Speedway) / (aka: Outlaw City Speedway)

Memorial Stadium - Johnson City - 1/4 mile paved oval (1956) / was a ballpark

Memphis Dirt Trax - Memphis (Millington) - 1/2 mile dirt oval (1987 - 1989)
3/8 mile dirt oval (1990 - present) / (aka: Blankenship Motorsports Park)
1/8 mile dirt oval (1992) / (aka: Memphis Round Track)
located next to Memphis Motorsports Park

Memphis Fairgrounds - Memphis / located at the Mid-South Fairgrounds
1/2 mile dirt oval (c.9/26/14 - 11/18/41) (c.1946 - c.1953)
1/4 mile dirt oval (c.9/23/52 - c.1952)
(aka: Cotton Carnival Fairgrounds) / (aka: Tri-State Fairgrounds)

Memphis Motorsports Park - Memphis - 1/4 mile paved dragstrip (1987 - present)
1.77 mile paved road course (1987 - present) / near town of Millington
(aka: Memphis Int'l Motorsports Park) / located next to Memphis Dirt Trax

Memphis-Ark Speedway - see: Arkansas chapter

Memphis - also see: American Legion, Cotton Carnival, Crump, Hodges Field,
Lakeland, Midsouth Coliseum, Shelby

Mid-South Coliseum - Memphis - 1/10 mile indoor concrete oval (11/09/91)
at the Memphis Fairgrounds / maybe the Shelby Farms Showplace Arena

Middle Tennessee Dragway - Cookeville - 1/8 mile paved dragstrip (1965 - present)
1/4 mile dirt oval (1975 - 1981) / (aka: Middle Tennessee Speedway)
(aka: Buffalo Valley Speedway)

Midway Speedway - Athens - 1/4 mile dirt oval (c.1953)

Milan Raceway - Milan - 1/4 mile dirt oval (1960 - 1981) / (aka: Milan Speedway)
3/8 mile dirt oval (1982 - present) / (aka: Milan Int'l Speedway)
the grandstands for the 3/8 mile are from Raceland Park Motor Speedway

These cars were called "Modified Specials" at Nashville Speedway in the late 1960's. - Len Hayden photo.

Moccasin Bend Speedbowl - Chattanooga - 1/4 mile dirt oval (c.8/01/54)

Morristown - 1/4 mile dirt oval (c.1953 - c.1958)
  now the site of a Tobacco Warehouse / located near a Chevrolet dealership

Mount Vernon - dirt oval (1985)

Murfreesboro Fairgrounds - Murfreesboro - dirt oval (1938)

Murfreesboro - oval (1970's)

Music City Raceway - Nashville / (aka: Union Hill Dragway)
  1/8 mile paved dragstrip (1957 - present) / (aka: Music City Dragway)
  (aka: Music City Int'l Raceway)

Nashville Motor Speedway - Nashville / at the Tennessee State Fairgrounds
  1.0 mile dirt oval (1907 - 9/20/41) (9/21/46 - 9/21/57)
  Bobby Grim in an IMCA sprint car was last winner on the 1.0 mile track
  (aka: Cumberland Park) / originally built in 19th century as a horse track
  1/2 mile semi-banked paved oval (8/10/58 - 1969)
  1/4 mile paved oval (1958 - present) / (aka: Fairgrounds Speedway)
  5/8 mile high banked paved oval (7/25/70 - 1972) / turns banked 35 degrees
  ultra high banked track very dangerous as 3 drivers were fatally injured
  5/8 mile high banked paved oval (1973 - present) / turns banked 24 degrees
  (aka: Nashville Int'l Speedway) / the grandstands burned down in 1965
  (aka: Nashville Speedway)

Nashville Motor Speedway before the crowd arrives for the ASA race in 1993. Nancy Brown photo.

Nashville Municipal Auditorium - Nashville / located downtown Nashville
  1/12 mile indoor concrete oval (1987 - 10/15/88)

Nashville Speedway - see: American Legion Speed Bowl

Nashville - also see: American Legion, Madison, Music City, Old Hickory,
  Pleasant Valley, Riverside, Sulphur Dell

New English Mountain Dragway - see: English Mountain Dragway

New Kingsport Speedway - see: Kingsport Speedway

494

Newport Fairgrounds - Newport / (aka: Tennessee-Carolina Speedway)
1/2 mile dirt oval (6/23/56 - 1967) / at the Cocke County Fairgrounds
the first race was an IMCA sprint car race won by Jud Larson

Newport Raceway - 4/10 mile dirt oval (1977 - 1988)
4/10 mile paved oval (1988 - present)

Northeast Tennessee Raceway - see: Dallas Ricker Complex

Northside Speedway - Jackson - 1/4 mile dirt oval (1977)

Northwest Tennessee Motorsports - Dresden / between Dresden and Gleason
1/8 mile paved dragstrip (8/11/93 - present)

Oak Ridge Sportsdrome - Knoxville (Oak Ridge) - 1/4 mile dirt oval (1953 - c.1954)
1/4 mile paved oval (c.1954 - c.1962) / (aka: Oak Ridge Speedway)

Obion Fairgrounds - Obion / located at the Obion County Fairgrounds
3/8 mile dirt oval (4/04/80 - 1980) / (aka: Obion County Raceway)

Old Hickory Speedway - Nashville - oval (c.1955 - 1956)

Outlaw City Speedway - see: McMinnville Speedway

Overton County Speedway - Livingston - dirt oval (years unknown)

Pleasant Valley Speedway - Nashville - 1/8 mile dirt oval (c.1982 - c.1983)

Powder Branch Speedway - Elizabethton - 1/4 mile dirt oval (late 1950's - c.1964)

Raceland Kingsport - see: Kingsport Speedway

Raceway Park - see: Clarksville Speedway

Rhea County Raceway - Spring City - 1/4 mile dirt oval (1986 - 1993)

Rhea County Speedway - Dayton - dirt oval (1965 - 1968)

Riverside Park - Bluff City - dirt oval (5/01/93)

Riverside Raceway Park - Nashville - 1/4 mile paved dragstrip (c.1965 - 1988)

Roane County Speedway - see: Harriman Speedway

Rockwood - dirt oval (1953)

Rogersville Speedway - Rogersville - 3/10 mile dirt oval (c.1972 - 1976)
(aka: Davy Crockett Speedway)

Scott County Speedway - Sunbright (Glenmary) - dirt oval (years unknown)
(aka: Sunbright Speedway)

Shelby County Int'l Raceway - Memphis / nine miles from town on Canada Road
1.7 mile paved road course (1969) / ran a USAC late model race

Shelby Farms Showplace Arena - Memphis / runs Mini-sprints, Go-Karts & Cycles
1/10 mile indoor dirt oval (11/21/92 - present)

Smoky Mountain Speedway - Maryville / (aka: Smoky Mountain Race Track)
    1/2 mile dirt oval (c.1965 - 4/06/67) (9/30/78 - 1987)
    1/2 (.52) mile paved oval (June, 1968 - 7/30/78)
    4/10 mile dirt oval (1988 - present) / (aka: Smoky Mountain Raceway)

Smyrna Speedway - Smyrna / now the site of the Nissan Truck Plant
    1/4 mile paved oval (c.1969 - 1978) / owned by Marty Robbins at one time

Sparta Speedway - Sparta - 3/8 mile dirt oval (c.1959 - 1982)

Sportsman Speedway - Johnson City - 3/8 mile dirt oval (c.1960 - 1974)
    the site is now a warehouse

Stateline Speedway - Guys - 1/4 mile dirt oval (c.6/18/93 - present)

Sulphur Dell Speedway - Nashville - 1/5 mile asphalt oval (mid 1960's)
    built around a baseball field

Sunbright Speedway - see: Scott County Speedway

Tazewell Speedway - Tazewell / reopened in 1993 when 411 paved their track
    1/4 mile dirt oval (1965 - 1987) (1989) (1993 - present)

Tennessee Motor Speedway - see: Four-Eleven Speedway

Tennessee State Fairgrounds - see: Nashville Motor Speedway

Tennessee-Carolina Speedway - see: Newport Fairgrounds

Thunder Hill Raceway - Summertown - 1/4 mile dirt oval (1988 - present)

Thunder Valley Dragway - see: Bristol Int'l Dragway

Trenton Speedway - Trenton - 1/4 mile dirt oval (early 1950's)

Tri-Cities Speedway - see: Kingsport Speedway

Tri-City Speedway - Bluff City - 1/3 mile dirt oval (c.4/01/51 - c.1955)

Tuckassee Raceway Park - White House - 1/8 mile dirt oval (1985 - 1988)

Tullahoma Speedway - Tullahoma - 3/8 mile paved oval (c.1975 - 1980)

U.S. 43 Dragway - Lawrenceburg - 1/8 mile paved dragstrip (1956 - present)

Union Hill Dragway - see: Music City Int'l Raceway

Volunteer Speedway - Bulls Gap - 4/10 mile high banked dirt oval (1975 - present)

Warner Park - see: Chattanooga Int'l Speedway

Warren County Speedway - see: McMinnville Speedway

Wartburg Speedway - Wartburg - 1/4 mile dirt oval (1964 - 1968) (1985 - present)

Winchester Fairgrounds - Winchester / located at the Franklin Co. Fairgrounds
    1/4 mile dirt oval (8/21/55 - c.1955)

Winchester Speedway - Winchester - 1/4 mile dirt oval (1951 - present)

TEXAS

85 Speedway - see: Eighty-Five (85) Speedway

AA Dragway - see: Wall Dragway

Abilene - 5/8 mile dirt oval (c.1949 - c.1952)

Abilene Dragway - Abilene - 1/4 mile paved dragstrip (c.1965 - c.1970)
(aka: Big Country Raceway) / located five miles south of town

Abilene Fairgrounds - Abilene / located at the West Texas Fairgrounds
5/8 mile dirt oval (c.1925 - c.1931)

Abilene Motor Speedway - Abilene - 1/4 mile dirt oval (1960 - 1962)
1/4 mile paved oval (1963 - 1980) / (aka: Armadillo Competition Speedway)
3/8 mile dirt oval (1980 - present) / (aka: Abilene Speedbowl)
(aka: Big Country Speedway) / (aka: Abilene Speedway)

Abilene Municipal Airport - Abilene - 1.69 mile paved road course (1989 - present)

Abilene - also see: I-20 Motor Speedway & Johnson's

Air Park - Midland - paved road course (late 1950's)

Airport Speedway - Amarillo - 3/8 mile paved oval (1974 - c.1988)
(aka: Southwest Speedway)

Alamo Downs Raceway - San Antonio / was located on Culebra Rd at horse track
1/5 mile dirt oval (10/06/40 - c.1941)

Alamo Dragway - San Antonio - 1/4 mile paved dragstrip (1973 - present)
1/4 mile dirt oval (6/03/94 - present) / located behind San Antonio Speedway
the dirt track is called Texas Dirt Speedway

Alamo Speedway - Seguin / (aka: San Antonio Midget Speedway) old dog track
East of San Antonio / 1/5 mile dirt oval (1/02/36 - c.12/14/41)(c.1947)
1/6 mile dirt oval (12/25/37 & 12/26/37) / (aka: Seguin Highway Track)

Almedo Speedway - Houston - small dirt oval (1970) / ran midgets

Aloe Field - Victoria - 2.0 mile paved road course (early 1970's)

Aloe Speedway - Victoria - 1/4 mile dirt oval (1974 - 1975) / maybe at Aloe Field

Amarillo Dragway - Amarillo - 1/4 mile paved dragstrip (1960 - present)

Amarillo Fairgrounds - Amarillo - 5/8 mile dirt oval (c.1926 - c.1929) (1940)

Amarillo Micro Midget Speedway - Amarillo - 1/8 mile dirt oval (c.1970 - present)
the track may have been paved at one time

Amarillo Speedbowl - see: Dirt Track Speedway

Amarillo - also see: Airport, Buffalo Park, Curly, Dirt Track & Helium

Angelo Speedway - see: Road Runner Speedway

Angleton Fairgrounds - Angleton - dirt oval (years unknown)
  located at the Brazoria County Fairgrounds

Arena Park Raceway - see: Lubbock Speedway

Arlington - 1/2 mile dirt oval (c.1929) / between Fort Worth & Dallas

Arlington Downs Raceway - Arlington - 1.0625 mile dirt oval (11/02/47 - c.9/30/51)

Armadillo Competition Speedway - see: Big Country Speedway

Arnold Speedway - Waco - 3/8 mile dirt oval (c.1948 - c.1952)
  paved in later years

Arrowhead Park Speedway - Houston - 1/4 mile paved oval (August, 1947 - 1954)
  1/2 mile dirt oval (8/14/47 - c.9/30/51) / built as a horse track
  at Old Spanish Trail & South Main / now site of Marriott Motor Motel
  A.J. Foyt won his first race here 7/11/53 (a trophy dash)

Ascarate Park - El Paso - 1.9 mile paved road course (10/11/59 - 1960)

Ascarate Speedway - El Paso - 1/4 mile dirt oval (c.6/17/50 - c.1953)

Astrodome - Houston / home of the Houston Oilers (football) & Astros (baseball)
  1/5 mile dirt oval (3/08/69 - 1970) (1992) / the stadium opened in 1965
  Tom Bigelow won the first race (USAC midgets) before 31,000 fans
  ran Dwarf Cars in November of 1992

Austin Raceway Park - Austin - 1/4 mile paved dragstrip (c.1968 - c.1970)
  paved road course (late 1960's)

Austin Speed-O-Rama - see: Longhorn Speedway

Austin Speedway - Austin - 1/2 mile dirt oval (c.1925 - c.1939)
  Jud Larson started his driving career here in 1939

Austin - also see: Bastrop AFB, Bergtrom AFB, Capital City, Fredericksburg,
  Longhorn, Oak Hill, Pan American, River City

Bass Speedrome - Beaumont - 1/4 mile dirt oval (August, 1946 - 1948)
  (aka: Beaumont Speedrome)

Bastrop Speedway - Austin - 1/2 mile dirt oval (6/30/46 - 1946)

Battleground Speedway - Houston (Highland) - 3/8 mile dirt oval (3/31/84-present)

Beaumont - 1/2 mile dirt oval (1953)

Beaumont - 1/2 mile dirt oval (c.1926 - c.1929) / possible at the fairgrounds

Beaumont Dragstrip - Beaumont - 1/4 mile paved dragstrip (c.1965)

Beaumont - also see: Bass Speedrome, H & B Speedway & Speedway 90

Bell County Speedway - Temple (Belton) - 3/8 mile dirt oval (1971)

Bellaire (Houston) - 1.5 mile dirt oval (c.1926 - 1929)
  1/2 mile dirt oval (c.1924 - c.11/10/35) / site would be near Astrodome
  located on Stella Link Road, between Holcomb Blvd. & Braes Bayou

498

Bergstrom Air Force Base - Austin / (aka: Lone Star)
     4.48 mile paved road course on runways (c.4/12/53 - 3/30/54)

Betty Dragstrip - Betty (Gilmer) / (aka: Pools Dragstrip)
     1/4 mile paved dragstrip (c.1957 - c.1965)

Big Country Speedway - see: Abilene Speedway

Big H Speedway - see: Houston Speedway

*Steve Kinser (#11) leads Cris Eash (#17) at Big H Speedway in 1990 at a
World of Outlaws event. - Nancy Brown photo.*

Big Spring Raceway - Big Spring - 1/4 mile dirt oval (1974 - 1975)

Big Valley Dragway - Edinburg / (aka: Edinburg Dragway)
     1/4 mile paved dragstrip (c.1974 - present
     1/4 mile dirt oval (c.1975 - c.1982) / (aka: Edinburg Speedway)

Blue Bonnet Speedway - (location unknown) - 1/4 mile dirt oval (1987)

Borger - 1/10 mile dirt oval (early 1950's) / ran T.Q. midgets

Boyd's Raceway - Boyd - 1/4 mile dirt oval (1987 - present)
     built in 1982 for ATVs / the first auto race was in 1987

Brady Fairgrounds - Brady - 1/2 mile dirt oval (1936) / McCulloch Co Fairgrounds

Brazos Valley Dragstrip - Mineral Wells - 1/4 mile paved dragstrip (c.1965)

Breckenridge - 1/2 mile dirt oval (1926 - 1927)

Brownsville Speedway - Brownsville / (aka: St. Joseph Park)
     1/5 mile dirt oval (late 1930's) (c.1948 - 1949)

Bryan - 1/5 mile dirt oval (late 1940's) / ran midgets

Bryan Air Force Base - Bryan - paved road course on runways (1960's)

Buffalo Lake Dirt Track - Amarillo (Canyon) - dirt oval (1950)

Buffalo Park Speedway - Dallas (Carrollton) - 1/4 mile dirt oval (1975 - 1986)

Buffalo Stadium - Houston - 1/5 mile dirt oval (c.1937 - 1942) / ran midgets
    ball diamond on San Bernard Street (the street is now called Cullen St.)

Burkburnett - 1/2 mile dirt oval (1938)

C C Performance Center - see: Speedway Park

C. C. Speedway - Corpus Christi - 1/4 mile dirt oval (5/09/48 - c.1949)
    the track was located on Robstown Road

Cabaniss N.A.S. (Aux) - Corpus Christi / at the Naval Air Station Auxiliary
    2.6 mile paved road course (1968) (1981 - 1985) (1991 - present)
    1/4 mile paved dragstrip (1994 - present)

Caddo Mills Airport Dragstrip - Caddo Mills - 1/4 mile dragstrip (1950 - c.1964)
    in 1961 this track claimed to be the oldest dragstrip in the United States

Cameron - 1/5 mile dirt oval (June, 1939 - c.1939)

Camp Gary Air Force Base - San Marcos - 2.2 mile paved road course (1960's)
    1.6 mile paved road course (1988) / (aka: San Marcos Airport)

Capital City Speedway - Austin - 1/4 mile paved oval (1971) / on Lockhart Hwy

Carswells Air Force Base Dragstrip - Fort Worth - 1/4 mile paved dragstrip (1990)

Cedar Creek Dragway - Kemp - 1/8 mile concrete dragstrip (1976 - present)

Cen-Tex Speedway - Killeen - 1/4 mile dirt oval (c.1976 - present)
    (aka: Stars & Stripes Speedway) / (aka: Central Texas Speedway)

Central Texas Speedway - see: Waco Fairgrounds

Channelview - 1/4 mile paved oval (early 1952) / located east of Houston
    1/4 mile dirt oval (3/29/52 - c.1952) / located on Market Street Road

Childress Fairgrounds - Childress - 1/2 mile dirt oval (c.1913 - c.1929)

Chili Bowl Grand Prix - Terlingua - paved road course (c.1964 - 11/28/65)

Clarendon - dirt oval (1915)

Cleveland Speedway - Cleveland - dirt oval (1966)

Coastal City Speedway - Corpus Christi / (aka: Callallen Speedway)
    1/2 mile dirt oval (7/21/46 - c.1953)

Colonel C's Speedrome - see: Thunder Hill Speedway

Commerce - 1/4 mile paved dragstrip (1958)

Como Dragway - Silver Springs - 1/4 mile paved dragstrip (1970's - c.1980)

Concho Speedway - San Antonio - 1/2 mile dirt oval (c.7/04/46 - 1948)

Conroe - dirt oval (years unknown) / probably at Montgomery County Fairgrounds

Corpus Christi - 1/5 mile dirt oval (9/30/39) / ran midgets

Corpus Christi Raceway - see: Cuddihy Speedway

Corpus Christi Speedway - Corpus Christi / (aka: Speedway Park)
  1/4 mile dirt oval (1948 - 1950) / (aka: CC Performance Center)
  1/2 mile dirt oval (1950) / (aka: GO Center Speedway)
  1/4 mile paved oval(11/05/50 - present) / maybe old C C Speedway
  Terry Labonte started his career here in 1974

Corpus Christi - also see: C.C., Cabaniss, Coastal City, Cuddihy, Ocean, Riverside

Corsicana Speedway - Corsicana - 1/5 mile dirt oval (May, 1939 - 1939)
  1/2 mile dirt oval (c.8/27/49)

Cowboy Speedway - Dallas - 1/2 mile dirt oval (c.1946 - c.1952) / on NW Highway
  Jim McElreath started his career here / (aka: Cowboy Cannon's)

Cowtown Speedway - Fort Worth (Kennedale) - 1/4 mile dirt oval (c.1963-present)
  located next to Texas Raceway

Cuddihy Speedway - Corpus Christi / (aka: Corpus Christi Raceway)
  1/8 mile paved dragstrip (c.1969 - c.1977)
  3/8 mile dirt oval (June, 1969 - c.1975) / located at Cuddihy Field

Curly Speedway - Amarillo - dirt oval (1954)

Dallas - 1.0 mile dirt oval (1909)

Dallas - 1/4 mile paved dragstrip (c.1956)

Dallas Fairgrounds - see: Texas State Expo

Dallas Grand Prix - see: Grand Prix of Dallas

Dallas Int'l Motor Raceway - Lewisville - 1/2 mile paved oval (1970's)
  2.5 mile paved road course (7/05/70 - c.1971) / located in North Dallas
  1/4 mile paved dragstrip (c.1965 - c.1971) / (aka: Dallas Int'l Raceway)
  Eddie Hill turned first ever 4 second (4.990) run here on 4/09/88

Dallas - road race on city streets (12/09/09) / ran a 50 mile race

Odessa, Texas' John Foster (#99) races California's Jim Robinson (#78).
Allan E. Brown collection.

Dallas - also see: Buffalo Park, Cowboy, Devil's Bowl, DFW, Gold Mine, Industrial, Lions Field, Love Field, North Star, Pan American Grounds, Sportsman, Suicide, Texas State Expo, Walnut Hill, Yello Belly

Devil's Bowl - San Antonio - 1/2 mile dirt oval (c.12/05/45 - c.1946)

Fred Elbel in his roadster at San Antonio's Devil's Bowl Speedway in 1946. Charles McQueen collection (courtesy of Don Radbruch)

Devil's Bowl Speedway - Dallas / located on John West Road & Buckner Blvd.
  1/4 mile dirt oval (1937 - c.10/26/41) (c.1946 - 1963)
  1/2 mile dirt oval (1964 - 1966) / (aka: Big D Speedway)
  there was a big dip in the track and a Cliff in the backstretch
  promoter was Roy Carter / Johnny Rutherford started his career here 1955

Devil's Bowl Speedway - Dallas (Mesquite) / built to replace old Devil's Bowl
  3/8 mile dirt oval (April, 1967 - c.1973)
  1/2 mile dirt oval (c.1973 - present)

DFW Speedway - Dallas (Grand Prairie) - 1/5 mile dirt oval (1981 - present)
  located halfway between Dallas & Fort Worth / next to Yello Belly Drags

Dirt Track Speedway - Amarillo / (aka: Amarillo Speedbowl)
  1/4 mile dirt oval (8/02/46 - 1993) / (aka: Amarillo Speedway)
  1/3 mile dirt oval (1994 - present)

Dirt Track Speedway - Odessa - see: I-20 West Speedway

Dixieland Speedway - Victoria - 1/4 mile dirt oval (3/15/86 - c.1986)

Double A Dragway - see: Wall Dragway

Dragon Speedway - San Antonio
  1/2 mile dirt oval (c.1/26/36 - c.12/05/37) (11/16/41)

Sports car racing at Eagle Mountain in the 1950's. - Len Ashburn photo.

Eagle Mountain Nat'l Guard Base - Newark - 2.9 mile paved road course (1953)
    3.3 mile paved road course on runways (1955) (1/22/56)
    2.7 mile paved road course (6/03/56) (January, 1957) (6/02/57) (1/19/58)
    (aka: Frostbite Sports Car Races)

Eagle Pass - 1/4 mile paved dragstrip (1970)

Eagle Speedway - see: Silsbee Speedway

Eastex Dragway - Porter - 1/4 mile paved dragstrip (c.1962 - 1992)

Edinburg Dragway (Speedway) - see: Big Valley Dragway

Eighty-Five (85) Speedway - Ennis - 1/4 mile dirt oval (1985 - present)
    some of the track's buildings were destroyed in a tornado in June, 1994

El Paso Dragway - El Paso - 1/4 mile paved dragstrip (c.1977 - present)
    (aka: Sun City Dragway) / (aka: West Texas Motorsports Park)

El Paso Rodeo Grounds - El Paso - 1/5 mile dirt oval (5/22/38 - c.1941)

El Paso Speedway Park - El Paso - 3/8 mile dirt oval (7/15/79 - present)

Play day at El Paso Speedway Park on July 15, 1979. The track hadn't officially opened as yet. - Official track photo.

El Paso - also see: Ascarate, Evans, Fastrack, Horizon, Sunland, Washington Park

Elumison Oval - San Angelo - 1/2 mile dirt oval (8/25/46)

Epson Downs - Houston - 1.0 mile dirt oval (3/02/41) / a former horse track
    1/5 mile dirt oval (c.4/11/37 - 3/02/41)

Evans Oval - El Paso - dirt oval (c.1957 - 1958)

Exposition Speedway - Victoria - dirt oval (1931 - 1933) / probably at fairgrounds

Family Park Speedway - see: Idalou Motorsports

Fastrack - El Paso / (aka: Sunbowl Speedway)
    1/4 mile dirt oval (c.1972 - c.1986) / (aka: Sun City Speedway)

Firestone Test Track - Fort Stockton - 7.7 mile paved oval (1964)
    Fred Lorenzen turned a lap at 170 plus mph here in a stock car

Fort Hood Dragway - Killeen - 1/4 mile paved dragstrip (c.1972 - c.1990)
    run by the Timing Association of Fort Hood

Fort Worth - 1/2 mile dirt oval (1920)

Fort Worth - 1/4 mile dirt oval (5/23/39 - c.9/03/40)

Fort Worth - 1/4 mile dirt oval (early 1960's)

Fort Worth - 1/4 mile paved dragstrip (c.1961)

Fort Worth Speedway - Fort Worth - 1/2 mile dirt oval (9/01/35 - c.10/20/36)

Fort Worth Speedway - Fort Worth / maybe same as other Fort Worth Speedway
    1/6 mile egg shaped dirt oval (10/06/38 - 10/11/38) (7/15/41 - c.8/05/41)

Fort Worth - also see: Arlington, Carswells, Cowtown, Green Valley, Jeff-Davis,
    Riverside Drive, Sportsman Park, Texas Raceways, Will Rogers

Franklin Street Speedway - see: Trellis Court Speedway

Fredericksburg Hiway Track - Austin - 1/2 mile dirt oval (c.1946 - 6/16/46)

Freeway Drag Strip - see: Houston Drag Raceway

Galveston Beach - 1/4 & 1/2 mile dirt ovals (6/19/38) / located at Five Mile post

Galveston Beach (Denver Beach) - 2.5 mile beach oval (7/28/13)
    5.0 mile beach oval (7/30/14) (8/03/14)
    the site of earlier speed runs on the beach in 1900

Galveston Horse Track - Galveston - dirt oval (1910 - 1912)

Galveston Municipal Airport - Galveston / (aka: Scholes Field)
    2.8 mile paved road course (July, 1957 - 1958)

Galveston - also see: Mazuma & Moody

Gold Mine Race Bowl - Dallas - 1/2 mile dirt road course (5/03/42 - 1942)
    1/4 mile dirt oval (5/03/42 - c.6/21/42) (9/16/45 - 1945)

Golden Triangle Speedway - see: Speedway 90

504

Goodyear Test Track - San Angelo - 5.0 mile paved oval (1963)
   A.J. Foyt turned the track at an unofficial speed of 200.4 mph
   it was the first over 200 mph average lap on a closed course

Graham Fairgrounds - Graham / located at the Young County Fairgrounds
   1/2 mile dirt oval (c.10/09/24 - 10/23/37)

Grand Prix of Dallas - Dallas - 2.58 mile paved road course (7/08/84)
   location at the Texas State Expo / ran Formula One race in 1984
   1.2 mile paved road course (1988)

Grand Prix of Dallas - Dallas (Addison) / located at the airport in Addison
   1.57 mile paved road course (1989 - 1991) / (aka: Grand Prix of Addison)

Grand Prix of Dallas - Dallas - 1.3 mile paved road course (9/17/93 - present)
   located on city streets in downtown Dallas

Gravy Bowl - San Antonio - 1/4 mile dirt oval (years unknown) / probably 1950's

Grayson County Speedway - Sherman (Bells) - 1/4 mile dirt oval (1975 - present)

Greater Southwest Airport - (location unknown) - paved road course (1970's)

Green Valley Raceway - North Richland Hills / located northeast of Fort Worth
   1.1 & 1.6 mile paved road courses (c.1961 - c.1977) (10/27/84 - c.1985)
   1/4 mile paved dragstrip (c.1981 - c.1989) / (aka: Green Valley Race City)

Greenbriar Raceway - Houston (Greenbriar) - 1/4 mile paved dragstrip (1987)
   check other Houston strips that ran in 1987

Greenville Speedway - Greenville - 1/4 mile dirt oval (years unknown) / Hwy 69

Groesbeck - 1/2 mile dirt oval (c.1926 - early 1930's) / probably at the fairgrounds

Gulf Coast Speedway - Houston - 1/2 mile dirt oval (1/07/23)

H & B Speedway - Beaumont - 1/4 mile dirt oval (1971)
   located eight miles northwest of town on Highway 105

Houston's A.J. Foyt at Terre Haute, Indiana in 1970. - John Mahoney photo.

H & B Speedway - see: Silsbee Speedway

Hale County Speedway - see: Plainview Speedway

Hallsville Drag Strip - Longview - 1/4 mile paved dragstrip (c.1972 - present)
(aka: Hallsville Raceway)

Hannegan Speedway - (location unknown) - 1/4 mile dirt oval (1951)
the town was listed as Whatcom in race papers

Harbenito Devil's Bowl - see: Harlingen Speedway

Harlingen - 1/2 mile dirt oval (c.1926)

Harlingen - 1/4 mile paved dragstrip (c.1963)

Harlingen - 1/5 mile dirt oval (1939)

Harlingen Motor Speedway - Harlingen - dirt oval (1934 - 1935)

Harlingen Speedway - Harlingen / (aka: Harbenito Devil's Bowl)
1/5 mile dirt oval (3/23/47 - c.1950)

Haskell Speedway - Haskell - 5/8 mile dirt oval (c.1925 - 1928) (11/01/36 - c.1938)

Heart O' Texas Speedway - Waco - 1/4 mile dirt oval (4/01/66 - present)
located at Elm Mott & Dallas Highway

Heart O' Texas Speedway - Waco - 1/4 mile dirt oval (c.1955 - 1965)

Helium City Speedway - Amarillo - 1/2 mile dirt oval (1948)
located on Highway 66 / the track was destroyed by a tornado

Hell's Half Acre - Lubbock - 1/2 mile oiled dirt oval (1938 - 1940)
located two miles north of town on Plainview Highway / ran jalopies

Hi-Way Raceway - see: San Antonio Speedway

Hillsboro Speedway - Hillsboro - 1/4 mile dirt oval (1971 - c.1982) (1985 - 1986)

Hondo - 1/4 mile paved dragstrip (1970) / maybe at the Hondo Air Force Base

Hondo Air Force Base - Hondo - paved road course (1/30/60)

Hondo - dirt oval (c.10/13/35 - c.1940) / probably at the Medina Co. Fairgrounds

Horizon Speedway - El Paso - 3/8 mile dirt oval (c.1968 - 1970)

Houston - 3/4 mile dirt oval (5/12/35)

Houston Drag Raceway - Houston - 1/4 mile paved dragstrip (c.1958 - c.1970)
(aka: Freeway Drag Strip)

Houston - indoor oval (12/11/38)

Houston Int'l Dragway - Dickinson - 1/4 mile paved dragstrip (c.1976 - c.1988)

Houston Motordrome - Houston - 1/3 mile wood oval (1912) / ran motorcycles

Houston Raceway Park - Baytown - 1/4 mile paved dragstrip (1988 - present)

Houston Speed Bowl - Houston / (aka: Houston Speedway) / torn down in 1943
1/5 mile dirt oval (10/31/37 - 7/30/42) / built by O.D. & Ray Lavely
located on the northeast side of Houston across from Buffalo Stadium
the track was partially destroyed by a hurricane in September of 1941

Houston Speedway - Houston - 1/4 mile dirt oval (March, 1979 - present)
(aka: Texas National Speedway) / (aka: Big H Speedway)

Houston - also see: Almedo, Arrowhead, Astrodome, Battleground, Bellaire,
Big H, Buffalo, Channelview, Epson Downs, Gulf Coast, Meyers, Playland,
Port American, Sam Houston, San Jacinto, South Main, West End

Howard County Industrial Park - see: West Texas Grand Prix

Hub City Speedway - Lubbock - 1/2 mile dirt oval (c.1950 - c.1952)

Hub City Speedway - Lubbock - 3/8 mile dirt oval (4/03/92 - present)
located on the southeast side of Lubbock

I-20 Dragway - Tyler - 1/4 mile paved dragstrip (c.1970 - 1983)
1/4 mile dirt oval (1982 - 1983) / (aka: I-20 Speedbowl)
(aka: Interstate 20 Raceway)

I-20 Motor Speedway - Abilene - 1/4 mile dirt oval (1977 - 1981)
the site is now an industrial park

I-20 West Speedway - Odessa / (aka: Dirt Track Speedway)
1/4 mile dirt oval (c.1986 - 1987) (1989 - present) / next to Penwell Raceway

Idalou Motorsports - Lubbock (Idalou) / (aka: Lubbock Int'l Dragway)
1/4 mile dirt oval (1972 - 1978) (1982) / (aka: Lubbock Speedbowl)
1/4 mile paved dragstrip (1972 - present) / (aka: Lubbock Dragway)

Industrial Speedway - Dallas - 5/8 mile dirt oval (c.10/10/34 - c.5/16/37)

Interstate Raceway - see: Rosebowl Speedway

Jack Rabbit Speedway - see: Rosebowl Speedway

*The NHRA sanctioned "Slick 50 Nationals" are held at Houston Raceway Park.
This beautiful dragstrip was built in 1988. - Official track photo.*

Jacksboro Speedway - Jacksboro - dirt oval (late 1940's - early 1950's)

Jeff-Davis Speedway - Fort Worth - 1/4 mile dirt oval (November, 1945 - 1947)

Johnson's Race Track - Abilene - 1/4 mile dirt oval (c.1949 - c.1958)

Killeen - dirt oval (late 1930's) / ran midget

Lake Cypress Speedway - Winnsboro - 1/4 mile dirt oval (1988 - present)

Lakeshore Speedway - see: Trellis Court Speedway

Lions Field - Dallas - 1/5 mile dirt oval (9/11/40 - 9/25/40)
    same site as Industrial Speedway

Little River Raceway - Holland - 1/7 mile paved dragstrip (c.1992 - present)

Livestock Arena - see: Pan American Grounds

Lockhart - 1/2 mile dirt oval (c.1929)

Lone Star Dragstrip - Prairie Hill - 1/4 mile paved dragstrip (c.1965)

Lone Star Road Course - see: Bergstrom Air Force Base

Lone Star Speedway - Longview (Kilgore) / (aka: Lone Star Motor Speedway)
    3/8 mile dirt oval (3/09/84 - c.8/25/84) (1986) (May, 1991 - present)

Lone Star Speedway in Kilgore - Allan E. Brown collection

Longhorn Speedway - Austin - 1/4 mile paved oval (4/08/60 - present)
    (aka: Paramount Austin Speedway) / (aka: Austin Speed-O-Rama)

Longhorn Speedway - Bellmead - see: Texas All Star Speedway

Longview Airport - Longview - paved road course on runways (1937)
    Sam Nunis' first promotion was this race for strictly stocks

Longview Racing Bowl - Longview - dirt oval (1967)

Longview - also see: Hallsville & Lone Star

Loop Speedway - Waco - 1/2 mile dirt oval (2/24/35)

Love Field - Dallas - paved road course (1960's)

Love Field Speedway - Dallas - 1/2 mile dirt oval (1930 - 4/05/36)

Lubbock Dragway (Speedbowl) - see: Idalou Motorsports

Lubbock Municipal Airport - Lubbock - 1/4 mile paved dragstrip (1955)
   paved road course (late 1950's)

Lubbock Speedway - see: West Texas Speedway

Lubbock - also see: Hell's Half Aces, Hub City, Idalou, Micro & West Texas

Mansfield Speedway - Mansfield - 1/4 mile dirt oval (c.1965 - c.1972) (1982)
   torn down in the mid 1980's

Mazuma Speedway - Texas City - 1/2 mile dirt oval (7/04/48-1948)

Meyer Speedway - Houston / (aka: Joseph F. Meyer Speedway)
   1/2 mile paved oval (10/11/59 - 1979)
   A.J. Foyt won the opening day USAC sprint car feature

Micro Speedway - Lubbock - 1/8 mile dirt oval (4/08/56) / ran Micro-midgets

Miller's Cove Speedway - Winfield - 1/4 mile dirt oval (1986 - 1992)

Mineral Wells Fairgrounds - Mineral Wells / at the Mineral Wells Co. Fairgrounds
   dirt oval (1909 - 1910)

Mission - dirt oval (1939) / ran midgets

Monahans - dirt oval (1938)

Moody Clary Speedway - see: Thunder Road Speedway

Moody Stadium - Galveston - 1/5 mile dirt oval (1939) (6/01/41 - c.7/20/41)
   located at a baseball diamond / held first midget race in Galveston

Motorama Speedway - see: Speedway 90

Mount Selman Speedway - Mt. Selman - 1/4 mile dirt oval (c.1975 - c.1977)

Nash - dirt oval (years unknown) / located near Texarkana

Navasota Dragway - Navasota - 1/4 mile paved dragstrip (1993 - present)

Navasota Speedway - see: Thunder Road Speedway

New Braunfels Fairgrounds - New Braunfels / at the Comal County Fairgrounds
   1/2 mile dirt oval (c.11/28/20 - c.1926)

North Star Speedway - Dallas (Garland) - 1/4 mile dirt oval (1971)

North Texas Motor Speedway - Royse City
   1/3 mile dirt oval (5/08/87 - 1991) (1993 - present)

Oak Hill Downs Speedway - Austin - 1/4 mile dirt oval (6/09/50 - 1951)

Oak Hill Raceway - Henderson - paved road course (c.1977 - present) motorcycles

Ocean Drive Speedway - Corpus Christi - dirt oval (1933)

Odessa - 1/5 mile dirt oval (9/08/46 - c.1947)

Odessa Speedbowl - see: Twin Cities Speedway

Odessa - also see: Dirt Track, Penwell, Twin Cities

Pampa - dirt oval (c.1938) / ran midgets

Pan American Grounds - Dallas / located at the Texas State Expo
  1/10 mile indoor oval (12/04/37 - 1/11/38) / (aka: Livestock Arena)

Pan American Speedway - San Antonio / now the site of a housing development
  1/4 mile paved oval (5/08/65 - c.1977)

Pan American Speedway - San Antonio / on Jackson Road (old Austin Highway)
  1/5 mile dirt oval (1/27/46 - 1956)
  1/5 mile paved oval (1956 - 1964) / now the site of a shopping center

Paramount Austin Speedway - see: Longhorn Speedway

Paris - 1/2 mile dirt oval (1930)

Paris Dragstrip - Paris - 1/4 mile paved dragstrip (1964 - 1992)
  1/8 mile paved dragstrip (1993 - present) / promoted by Jerry Stephens

Pattonville - dirt oval (c.1951)

Penwell Raceway - Odessa (Penwell)- 1/4 mile paved dragstrip (Sept,1966-present)
  (aka: Penwell Dragway) / (aka: Odessa Raceway Park)
  paved road course (1960's) / also see: Dirt Track Speedway

Pittsburg Fairgrounds - Pittsburg - 1/2 mile dirt oval (11/14/16 & 11/16/16)

Plainview Speedway - Plainview - dirt oval (1976) (1986) (aka: Hale Co Speedway)

Playland Park - Houston - 1/4 mile dirt oval (6/03/48 - c.1956) / at 920 S. Main
  1/3 mile B-shaped road course (12/17/50)
  1/4 mile paved oval (c.1957 - 1960) / (aka: Lavely's Playland Park)
  built by O.D. & Ray Lavely / the last promoter was Ed Hamblen
  A.J. Foyt started his career here in 1953 / built by Sam Fox

Pleasant Valley Speedway - Wichita Falls (Pleasant Valley)
  1/3 mile paved oval (5/31/74 - 1978) (1989)
  sister track to Altus Speedway, Oklahoma

Pools Dragstrip - see: Betty Dragstrip

Port America Speedway - Houston - 1/4 mile paved oval (1974)

Princeton Race Track - Princeton - dirt oval (c.1966 - c.1972)

Raceway Park - San Angelo / (aka: San Angelo Raceway Park)
  1/4 mile paved oval (c.1956 - c.1975) / possibly Three Rivers Raceway

Ram Speedway - San Angelo - 1/4 mile dirt oval (c.11/21/48)

Rattlesnake Raceway - Midland - 2.0 mile paved road course (10/11/59 - 1963)
  bought by Jim Hall for his personal test track

Red River Speedrome - Wichita Falls - dirt oval (1962)

Red River Speedway - Bonham - dirt oval (years unknown)

510

Red River Valley Dragstrip - see: Wichita Dragstrip

Rio Grande Speedway - McAllen - 1/4 mile dirt oval (1983 - present)

Rio Grande Valley Dragstrip - Rio Grande - 1/4 mile paved dragstrip (c.1965)

Rio Speedway - Pharr - 1/5 mile dirt oval (10/05/47 - c.1951)

River City Road Course - Austin - 1.0 mile city st. paved road course (1977 - 1980)
    at the Texas Expo & Heritage Center

Riverside Drive Speedway - Fort Worth - 1/4 mile dirt oval (c.1949 - c.1955)
    (aka: Riverside Speedway)

Riverside Speedway - Corpus Christi - 1/4 mile dirt oval (1983 - 1986)

Road Runner Speedway - San Angelo - 3/8 mile dirt oval (1983 - 1988)
    (aka: Angelo Speedway)

Rosebowl Raceway - Tyler (aka: Interstate Raceway)(aka: Jack Rabbit Speedway)
    3/8 mile dirt oval (6/30/72 - 1993) / (aka: Rosebowl Speedway)

Rosebowl Speedway - Owentown - 1/2 mile dirt oval (years unknown)

Rosenburg - dirt oval (6/13/37) / possibly a the Fort Bend County Fairgrounds

Saint Joseph Park - see: Brownsville Speedway

Sam Houston Coliseum - Houston - 1/10 mile indoor oval (12/18/41 - 1942)

San Angelo - 1/4 mile paved dragstrip (c.1956) / this was not Wall Dragway

San Angelo Raceway Park - see: Raceway Park

San Angelo Speedbowl - San Angelo - 1/4 mile dirt oval (c.1949)
    maybe Raceway Park

San Angelo Speedway - San Angelo - dirt oval (1935 - 1936)

San Angelo - also see: Elumison, Goodyear, Raceway Park, Ram, Road Runner,
    Three Rivers, Wall Dragway

Wichita Falls' Lloyd Ruby at Langhorne in 1960. - Len Ashburn collection.

San Antonio - 1/4 mile paved dragstrip (c.1963 - c.1970)

San Antonio - 2.0 mile dirt oval (c.1920 - 11/03/22)

San Antonio Fairgrounds - San Antonio - 1/2 mile dirt oval (c.1929 - c.12/06/36)

San Antonio Grand Prix - San Antonio / (aka: San Antonio Street Circuit)
    1.67 mile paved city street road course (9/06/87 - 1990)

San Antonio Midget Speedway - see: Alamo Speedway

San Antonio - paved road course (1974)

San Antonio Raceway - San Antonio - 1/2 mile paved oval (1977 - present)
    (aka: Hi-Way 16 Raceway) / located adjacent to Alamo Dragway

San Antonio Speedrome - San Antonio - 1/5 mile dirt oval (1/20/46 - c.2/24/46)

San Antonio Speedway - San Antonio / maybe same location as 2.0 mile track
    1.0 mile dirt oval (1909 - 1909) (4/17/20) / Ira Vail the 1920 race

San Antonio Spill-Way - San Antonio - paved oval (c.7/11/47 - 1948)

San Antonio - also see: Alamo, Concho, Devil's Bowl, Dragon, Gravy Bowl,
    Pan American, Sequin, Shadowland, Sportsman Park, Story-Woods

San Jacinto Monument - Houston - paved road course (1960's)

San Marcos Airport - see: Camp Gary Air Force Base

Sand Hill Micro Speedway - Sand Hill - 1/8 mile dirt oval (c.10/26/58)

Schulenburg - 5/8 mile dirt oval (1910's) / built as a horse track
    built by Texas State Senator, Dr. I.E. Clark

Scorpion Dragstrip - McKinney - 1/4 mile paved dragstrip (c.1960 - c.1970)

Seguin - 1/2 mile dirt oval (c.1929) / located east of San Antonio
    possibly at the Guadalupe County Fairgrounds / also see: Alamo Speedway

Shadowland Speedway - San Antonio - dirt oval (12/07/47 - c.1949)

Shady Oaks Speedway - Goliad - 3/8 mile dirt oval (6/21/86 - present)

Silsbee Speedway - Silsbee - 1/4 mile dirt oval (1986 - present)
    (aka: H & B Speedway) / (aka: Eagle Speedway)

Six Flags Dragway - see: Victoria Dragway

South Main Speedrome - Houston - 1/5 mile dirt oval (4/07/46 - c.7/10/47)
    (aka: South Main Track) / located at South Main & Eagle Ave.

South Main Track - Houston / possibly Arrowhead Park Speedway
    1/2 mile dirt oval (c.1929) (1937 - c.5/25/41) (1946 - 1947)

Southwest Speedway - see: Airport Speedway

Speed Bowl - see: Houston Speed Bowl

Speedorama - Lufkin - 1/4 mile dirt oval (1974 - 1975)

Speedway 90 - Beaumont / (aka: Golden Triangle Motor Speedway)
   1/4 mile dirt oval (June, 1970 - 1988) (1993 - present)
   (aka: Motorama Speedway) / (aka: Beaumont Tri-Plex)
   converted to a fish pond from 1989-1992 / (aka: Golden Triangle Speedway)

Speedway Park - see: Corpus Christi Speedway

Sportsdrome Speedrome - Dallas (Grand Prairie)
   1/4 mile dirt oval (1959 - 10/01/83) / now parking for an auto auction

Sportsman Park - San Antonio - (c.1/27/46)

Sportsman Park Speedway - Fort Worth - 1/2 mile dirt oval (8/01/37 - c.6/12/38)
   1/5 mile dirt oval (7/27/38 - 10/26/41)

Star Speedway - Round Rock - dirt oval (c.1950 - 1951)

Stars & Stripes Speedway - see: Cen-Tex Speedway

Stateline Speedway - see: Arkansas chapter

Stephenville 281 Speedway - Stephenville - 1/4 mile dirt oval (1989 - present)

Storey-Wood Park Speedway - San Antonio / an old horse track on Jackson Road
   1/2 mile dirt oval (1937) (4/06/47 - 1948)

Suicide Bowl - Dallas - dirt oval (c.1952 - c.1953)

Suicide Bowl - Odessa - dirt oval (c.4/20/58)

Suicide Bowl - Waco - 1/5 mile dirt oval (late 1940's - c.1953)
   Gordon Wooley started his driving career here

Sun City (Sunbowl) Speedway - see: Fastrack

Sunland Auto Raceway - El Paso - 1.5 mile dirt oval (January, 1962)
   1/4 mile paved dragstrip (c.1962 - c.1963) / small paved oval (mid 1960's)

Super Bowl Speedway - Greenville - 1/4 mile dirt oval (1968 - 1993)
   (aka: Super Bowl of Greenville)

TAMU Riverside Circuit - College Station / located at the Texas A & M University
   3.4 mile paved city street road course (1989 - present)

Taylor - dirt oval (1919)

Temple - 1/2 mile dirt oval (1915) (c.1927 - c.1932) / motorcycles in 1915

Temple Academy Dragway - Temple - 1/4 mile paved dragstrip (1957 - present)

Texana Raceway - Edna - 1/4 mile dirt oval (1988 - c.1989) (c.1991 - present)

Texarkana - 1/4 mile dirt oval (late 1930's)

Texarkana Speedbowl - Texarkana (Leary) / located on US 82
   1/4 mile dirt oval (c.1956 - 1982)

Texas All Star Speedway - Waco (Bellmead) - 1/4 mile dirt oval (1987 - present)
   (aka: Longhorn Speedway)

Texas Dirt Speedway - see: Alamo Dragway

Texas Expo & Heritage Center - see: River City Road Course Austin

Texas Motor Speedway - Alvin - 1/8 mile dirt oval (c.1987 - present)
   (aka: Triple C Raceway)

Texas Motorplex - Ennis - 1/4 mile paved dragstrip (8/01/86 - present)
   Mike Dunn drove to the first 280 mph run in a Funny Car here 10/02/87
   the track was built and owned by Billy Meyer

Texas National Speedway - see: Big H Speedway

Texas Raceway - Fort Worth (Kennedale) / located next to Cowtown Speedway
   1/8 mile paved dragstrip (1961 - present) (aka: S & N Dragway)

Texas State Expo - Dallas - 1.0 mile dirt oval (1914 - c.1929)
   1/2 mile dirt oval (1938) / 1/2 mile torn down to build the Cotton Bowl
   1/5 mile dirt oval (8/18/39 - c.9/24/41) (6/12/46 - 1957)
   1/5 mile track was razed to build the Livestock Coliseum
   (aka: Fair Park Speedway) / (aka: State Fairgrounds of Texas)
   also see: Grand Prix of Dallas & Pan American Grounds

Texas World Speedway - College Station / (aka: Texas Int'l Speedway)
   2.0 mile paved oval (12/07/69 - 1973) (1976 - 1986) (1991 - present)
   Bobby Isaac won the first race (a NASCAR GN race)
   2.75 & 3.0 mile paved road courses (11/07/69 - 1973) (1976 - 1989)
   1.8 & 1.9 mile paved road courses (1991 - present)
   sister track to Michigan Int'l Speedway

Texhoma Speedway - see: Thunder Hill Speedway

Texoma Dragway - Whitesboro - 1/4 mile paved dragstrip (c.1965)

Three Rivers Raceway - San Angelo - oval (1963 - 1964)

Thunder Hill Speedway - Wichita Falls / (aka: Wichita Falls Speedway)
   1/4 mile dirt oval (c.1970 - 1985) (1987 - present)
   (aka: Colonel C's Speedrome) / (aka: Texhoma Speedway)

Thunder Road Speedway - Navasota / (aka: Moody Clary Speedway)
   1/4 mile dirt oval (c.1969 - 1980) / (aka: Navasota Speedway)

Thunderbird Speedway - Crandall - 1/4 mile dirt oval (7/19/59 - present)

Top Of Texas Dragway - Pampa - 1/4 mile paved dragstrip (c.1963 - c.1976)

Trellis Court Speedway - Waco / located next to Lake Waco on Franklin St.
   1/5 mile dirt oval (c.6/27/38 - 1941) / (aka: Franklin Street Speedway)

Triple C Raceway - see: Texas Motor Speedway

Twin Cities Speedway - Odessa / (aka: Odessa Speed Bowl)
   1/4 mile paved oval (c.1959 - 1986)

Twin Cities Speedway - Odessa - 3/8 mile paved oval (1987 - present)
   built by John Foster to replace the old Twin Cities Speedway

Twin City Speedway - Denison - 1/2 mile dirt oval (6/04/50 - mid-1954)

Twin City Speedway - Denison - 1/4 mile dirt oval (late 1954) / different location

514

Tyler - 1/5 mile dirt oval (c.9/11/49) / maybe at the East Texas Fairgrounds

Tyler - dirt oval (1924) / probably at the East Texas Fairgrounds in Tyler

Tyler - also see: I-20 Dragway & Rosebowl

Valley (Int'l) Dragway - see: Wall Dragway

Victoria - 9/16 mile dirt oval (1952) / maybe Exposition Speedway

Victoria Dragstrip - Victoria - 1/4 mile paved dragstrip (c.1963 - c.1971)
(aka: Aloe Field) / (aka: Six Flags Dragway)

Victoria - also see: Aloe, Dixieland, Exposition

Waco Fairgrounds - Waco - 1/2 mile dirt oval (10/10/16 - c.1919) (c.1926 - 1936)
1/4 mile dirt oval (5/06/47 - late 1950's) / (aka: Central Texas Speedway)
located at the Texas Cotton Palace

Waco - also see: Arnold, Heart O' Texas, Loop, Suicide, Texas All Star, Trellis

Wall Dragway - San Angelo / (aka: Sportsman's Park Dragway)
1/4 mile paved dragstrip (1962 - present) / (aka: Valley Int'l Dragway)
(aka: Valley Dragway) / (aka: Double A Raceway)

Walnut Hill Track - Dallas - dirt oval (1930)

Washington Park - El Paso - 1.0 mile dirt oval (c.4/10/15 - c.1924)

West End Ball Park - Houston - dirt oval (January, 1942)

West Texas Grand Prix - Big Springs - 2.0 mile paved road course (1986 - 1987)
(aka: Howard County Industrial Park)

West Texas Motorsports Park - see: El Paso Dragway

West Texas Speedway - Lubbock / (aka: Arena Park Speedway)
3/8 mile dirt oval (c.1967 - present) / (aka: Lubbock Speedway)

Wichita Dragstrip - Wichita Falls / (aka: Red River Valley Dragstrip)
1/4 mile paved dragstrip (1952 - 1993) / (aka: Wichita Falls Dragstrip)

Wichita Falls - 1/2 mile dirt oval (c.1925 - c.1939)

Wichita Falls - 1/5 mile dirt oval (6/19/38) / ran midgets

Wichita Falls - dirt oval (1950's) / located on the north side of town

Wichita Falls Speedrome - Wichita Falls / built by Abe Rabin
1/4 mile dirt oval (4/13/46 - c.1955)
Rodger Ward & Lloyd Ruby started their driving careers here

Wichita Falls Speedway - see: Thunder Hill Speedway

Wichita Falls - also see: Pleasant Valley, Red River Speedrome

Will Rogers Auditorium - Fort Worth - 1/10 mile indoor oval (11/17/37 & 11/24/37)

Yello Belly Dragstrip - Dallas (Grand Prairie) - 1/4 mile paved dragstrip (c.1973)
located next to DFW Speedway

UTAH

Bonneville Raceway Park - Salt Lake City - 1/4 mile dragstrip (c.1965 - present)
    1/3 mile paved oval (1972 - present) / not at the Bonneville Salt Flats
    1.7 mile paved road course (late 1960's) / located in West Valley City
    1.4 mile paved road course (8/16/91 - 1992) / ran AIS Indy Cars

Bonneville Salt Flats - Wendover / where many land speed records are set
    home of the annual "Speed Week" for land speed records (1949 - present)
    10.0 mile salt circular oval (1956) / ran an exhibition event in 1956

Carbon County Speedway - Price - 3/8 mile dirt oval (1982 - 1985) (1992 - present)

Dixie Speedway - see: Saint George Raceway Park

Fairgrounds Speedway - Salt Lake City / located at the Utah Centennial Expo
    1/2 mile dirt oval (9/27/15 - c.10/09/24) / (aka: Utah State Fairgrounds)
    1/4 mile dirt oval (1940 - 7/31/42) / (aka: Intermountain Speedway)
    1/4 mile paved oval (c.1946 - 9/04/72)

Grand Valley Dragstrip - Moab - 1/4 mile paved dragstrip (1964 - present)

Intermountain Speedway - see: Fairgrounds Speedway

Odgen Raceway - Odgen - 1/4 mile dirt oval (1987)

Prairie Dog Speedway - Roosevelt - 3/8 mile dirt oval (1977 - 1983)

Price Fairgrounds - Price / located at the Carbon County Fairgrounds
    3/10 mile dirt oval (1974 - 1981)

Provo - 1/4 mile dirt oval (1947)

Red Rock Speedway - Moab - 1/4 mile dirt oval (1975 - 1987) (1991 - present)

Roundabout Raceway - Pleasant Grove - 1/4 mile dirt oval (1975 - 1982)
    located at a Rodeo Grounds

Saint George Raceway Park - St. George - 1/4 mile paved dragstrip (c.1973 - present)
    (aka: Dixie Speedway)

Salt Bowl - Salt Lake City - dirt oval (c.1951) / probably not at the fairgrounds

Salt Lake City - 1/4 mile paved dragstrip (1952)

Salt Lake City Fairgrounds - see: Fairgrounds Speedway

Salt Palace - Salt Lake City - 1/10 mile indoor oval (1970's)

Suntana Raceway - Provo - 3/8 mile dirt oval (1965 - 1969) / (aka: Turpin Speedway)
    4/10 mile paved oval (1970 - 1990) (1992 - present)

Turpin Speedway - see: Suntana Raceway

Wandemere Speedway - Salt Lake City - 1/6 mile wood oval (1910) / ran motorcycles

West Jordan - Salt Lake City - paved road course (c.6/02/57 - c.5/22/60)

VERMONT

Barton - 1/2 mile dirt oval (1939)

Bear Ridge Speedway - Bradford - 1/4 mile dirt oval (1968 - present)

Boltonville - 1/5 mile dirt oval (early 1950's)

Brattleboro Speedway - West Brattleboro - 1/3 mile dirt oval (July 1950 - c.1955)

Burgess Field - Bennington - dirt oval (late 1930's)

Can-Am Speedway - Newport - 1/4 mile dirt oval (1981 - 1987) / now a land fill

Catamount Stadium - Milton / (aka: Catamount Int'l Speedway)
   1/3 mile paved oval (6/11/65 - 1987) / site is now an industrial park

Champaign Valley Exposition - see: Essex Junction Fairgrounds

Davis Speedway - Enosburg Falls - oval (years unknown)

Devil's Bowl Speedway - Fair Haven - 4/10 mile dirt oval (1967 - 1970)
   1/2 mile paved oval (1971 & 1972) / (aka: West Haven Speedway)
   1/2 mile dirt oval (1972 - present)

Dog River Speedway - Northfield / located at the Northeastern Fairgrounds
   1/2 mile dirt oval (10/02/49 - c.1962)

East Concord - 1/5 mile dirt oval (1956)

East Montpelier - dirt oval (1950)

Essex Junction Fairgrounds - Essex Junction / at Champaign Valley Exposition
   1/2 mile dirt oval (1932) (c.1939 - 8/30/41) (c.1946 - 9/03/77)
   Ira Vail was the promoter for a number of years

Fairmont Park Motor Speedway - Fair Haven - 1/2 mile dirt oval (c.7/30/50 - 1966)

Green Mountain Speedway - see: Pico Raceway

Huntington - 1/2 mile dirt oval (October, 1937)

Mallets Bay Race Track - Colchester - 1/5 mile dirt oval (c.1950 - c.1961)

Manchester - dirt oval (1950)

Middle Granville Speedway - Granville - dirt oval (1950's)

Morrisville Fairgrounds - Morrisville / located at Lamoille Valley Fairgrounds
   1/2 mile dirt oval (8/09/41) (1950)

Newport - dirt oval (1950)

Northeastern Speedway - West Waterford / (aka: Waterford Speedbowl)
   1/5 mile dirt oval (late 1950's - 1960) / located near St. Johnsbury
   1/5 mile paved oval (1961 - 1965)

Northfield Fairgrounds - see: Dog River Speedway

Otter Creek Speedway - Vergennes (Waltham) - 1/2 mile dirt oval (1961 - 1963)
1/3 mile dirt oval (1963 - c.1971) / (aka: Rainbow Ridge Speedway)

Pico Raceway - Rutland / (aka: Green Mountain Speedway)
1/2 mile dirt oval (8/26/51 - c.1955) / near the junction of US 7 & US 4
the site became a housing development in 1957

Rainbow Ridge Speedway - see: Otter Creek Speedway

Rutland Fairgrounds - see: Vermont State Fairgrounds

State Line Speedway - North Bennington - 1/2 mile dirt oval (8/24/47 - c.1958)
Joie Chitwood was the first winner on 8/24/47
The track was located in Vermont, but the grandstands were in New York,
because of this the track could run on Sundays in 1950 even though the
other tracks in Vermont could not run because of a blue law

Thunder Road Int'l Speedbowl - Barre - 1/4 mile paved oval (June, 1959 - present)

Vermont State Fairgrounds - Rutland / ran AAA big cars in 1920's & 1930's
1/2 mile dirt oval (c.9/08/28 - c.1932) (9/04/38 - c.1941) (1946 - c.1970)

Waterford Speedbowl - see: Northeastern Speedway

West Haven Speedway - see: Devil's Bowl Speedway

VIRGINIA

301 Speedway - see: New Richmond Speedway

A & N Speedway - Tasley - dirt oval (1920's - c.1941) (c.1946 - c.1977)

Airport Speedway - see: Winchester Speedway

Amelia Motor Raceway - Amelia - 1/4 mile dirt oval (1989 - present)
(aka: Amelia Kart Track) / started out as a Kart track in c.1988

Ararat Speedway - Ararat - 1/2 mile dirt oval (6/22/58 - c.1960) / SW of Stuart

Atlantic Rural Exposition Fairgrounds - see: Richmond Fairgrounds Raceway

Big Al's Dragway - Richlands - 1/8 mile paved dragstrip (Spring, 1966 - present)
1/4 mile dirt oval (c.1975 - c.1980) / (aka: Richlands Motor Speedway)
(aka: Richlands Int'l Dragstrip) / (aka: Thunder Mountain Dragway)

Brunswick Speedway - Lawrenceville / (aka: Lawrenceville Speedway)
3/8 mile dirt oval (c.1955 - c.1971) / located in Brunswick County
(aka: New Brunswick Speedway) / the track was circular in shape
(aka: Lawrence Speedway)

Callaway Speedway - Callaway - 1/3 mile dirt oval (c.1964 - c.1969)

Cavalier Speedway - see: Hilltop Speedway

Chinese Corner Speedway - see: Joe Weatherly Speedway

Cockade Speedway - Petersburg - dirt oval (c.1953 - c.1954)

518

Colonial Beach Dragway - Colonial Beach - 1/4 mile dragstrip (c.1975 - present)
1/4 mile dirt oval (1950's) / (aka: Colonial Beach Speedway)

Covington - 1/2 mile dirt oval (1920's)

Craigsville Motor Speedway - Craigsville - dirt oval (years unknown)

Danville Fairgrounds - Danville / located at the Danville Fairgrounds
1/2 mile dirt oval (c.8/02/47 - c.1954) (1969) / (aka: Danville Speedway)
Wendell Scott started his driving career here

Danville Speedway - Danville - 4/10 mile dirt oval (1992 - present)

Dinwiddie Speedway - Petersburg - 3/8 mile dirt oval (c.1954 - c.1965)
the track was located in Dinwiddie County

Dixie Speedway - Norfolk - 1/2 mile dirt oval (c.5/30/24 - c.5/04/34)
was not at the Norfolk Fairgrounds / both tracks ran on 5/30/24

Douglas - (location unknown) - dirt oval (1953)

Dude Ranch Speedway - see: Langley Raceway

East Lexington Speedway - Lexington - dirt oval (1970)

Eastside Speedway - Waynesboro - 4/10 mile dirt oval (c.10/20/57 - present)
1/8 mile paved dragstrip (c.1967 - present) / (aka: Waynesboro Speedway)
located at the Greater Shenandoah Valley Fairgrounds
the fairgrounds was formerly called the Augusta County Fairgrounds

*The third and fourth turn of Eastside Speedway. The road between the oval
track and the grandstands is the dragstrip. - Official track photo.*

Edmonds Speedway - Galax - 1/4 mile dirt oval (early 1950's)

Elk Creek Dragway - Elk Creek - 1/8 mile paved dragstrip (July, 1968 - present)

Emporia Dragstrip - Emporia - 1/8 mile paved dragstrip (c.1961 - c.1963)

Fairmount Park - see: Norfolk Fairgrounds

Fairy Stone Speedway - Bassett - dirt oval (1967 & 1968)

Floyd Speedway - Floyd - 4/10 mile dirt oval (c.7/25/54 - 1955)
    Curtis Turner was the promoter in 1954

Franklin County Speedway - Callaway - 3/8 mile paved oval (1969 - present)

Fredericksburg Fairgrounds - Fredericksburg
    1/5 mile paved oval (c.8/13/53 - c.1961) / (aka: Fredericksburg Speedway)

Freedom 7 Dragway - see: Virginia Beach Motorsports Park

Hillbilly Speedway - Spencer - 1/4 mile dirt oval (1960's - early 1970's)

Hilltop Speedway - Charlottesville / (aka: Cavalier Speedway)
    dirt oval (c.8/17/52 - c.1954)

Hybla Valley Speedway - Fort Belvoir (Ashburn) / near the Ashburn Airport
    1/2 mile dirt oval (4/17/49 - c.8/06/50) (6/15/52 - 1959)

James River - dirt oval (c.1950) / maybe Jamesville instead

Joe Weatherly Speedway - Virginia Beach / (aka: Virginia Beach Speedway)
    3/8 mile dirt oval (1948 - 1955) (1957 - 1960)
    (aka: Chinese Corner Raceway) / located on Virginia Beach Blvd.
    built by Paul Sawyer / in later years the promoter was Jim Creech
    the site became a department store in the mid 1960's

Stock cars at Virginia Beach Speedway in 1948. The track was later called Joe Weatherly Speedway. - Len Ashburn photo.

Keller Fairgrounds - Keller / located at the Great Keller Fairgrounds
    1/2 mile dirt ova (c.1947 - c.1956)

Langley Raceway - Hampton - (aka: Dude Ranch Speedway)
    1/3 mile dirt oval (c.1949 - 1953)
    4/10 mile dirt oval (8/03/63 - 1968) / (aka: Langley Field)
    4/10 (.395) mile paved oval (1968 - present) / (aka: Langley Speedway)

520

Lawrenceville Speedway - see: Brunswick Speedway

Log Cabin Raceway & Park - Rocky Mount - 1/2 mile dirt oval (1981 - 1985)

Logansville - dirt oval (1923) / maybe Locustville or Lowesville instead

Lonesome Pine Int'l Raceway - Coeburn
  3/8 mile paved oval (7/22/72 - 1976) (6/05/82 - 8/13/83) (1990 - present)

Alan Kulwicki (#97) and Dick Trickle (#99) pace a American Speedway Assn.
(ASA) race at Lonesome Pine Int'l Raceway in 1982. - David Allio photo.

Longview Speedway - see: Old Dominion Speedway

Lynchburg Speedway - Lynchburg - 1/4 mile dirt oval (7/03/48 - 1953)
  1/4 mile paved oval (1954 - c.1956) / (aka: Schrader Field)

Marion - 1/2 mile dirt oval (1946)

Tim Flock's #90 Oldsmobile at Occoneechee Speedway in North Carolina.
Flock finished seventh in the August 7, 1949 race. - Len Ashburn photo.

An aerial view of Martinsville Speedway. - Official track photo.

Martinsville Speedway - Martinsville - 1/2 mile dirt oval (7/04/47 - c.6/26/55)
1/2 (.526) mile paved oval (c.10/02/55 - present) / builder: H. Clay Earles
has been running annual NASCAR GN (Winston Cup) races since 9/25/49

Mooers Field - Richmond / located on Belt Blvd. & Broad St. (Hwy 161)
1/5 mile paved oval (c.3/28/54 - c.1955)

Morris Speedway - Martinsville - dirt oval (c.1951 - 1953)
the track was located near Martinsville in the town of Horse Pasture

Natural Bridge Speedway - Natural Bridge
1/2 mile dirt oval (c.1971 - 1982) (1985) (1987 - present)
1/8 mile dirt dragstrip (c.1981 - c.1982)
1/8 mile paved dragstrip (c.1993 - present)

New Brunswick Speedway - see: Brunswick Speedway

New London Dragstrip - Lynchburg - 1/8 mile paved dragstrip (c.1963 - present)

New Richmond Speedway - Richmond / 4 miles north of town on Hwy 301
1/4 mile dirt oval (4/17/51 - 1954) / (aka: 301 Speedway)

New River Speedway - Ivanhoe - 1/2 mile dirt oval (early 1950's)

New River Valley Speedway - Radford / same site as old Pulaski County Speedway
4/10 (.416) mile paved oval (May, 1988 - present)

Norfolk Civic Center - Norfolk - 1/10 mile wood oval (1950's)

Norfolk Fairgrounds - Norfolk - 1/2 mile dirt oval (c.5/30/24 - c.5/23/37)
(aka: Fairmount Park)

Norfolk Speedway - Norfolk - 4/10 mile dirt oval (1949) (8/22/56 - 7/24/57)

Norwalk - 1/2 mile dirt oval (c.1951 - c. 1952) / maybe at a fairgrounds

Norfolk - also see: Dixie Speedway, Princess Anne Speedway, Scope Arena

522   Virginia

Old Dominion Speedway - Manassas - 3/8 mile dirt oval (c.9/12/48 - 1952)
3/8 mile paved oval (8/02/52 - present) / (aka: Longview Speedway)
1/8 mile paved dragstrip (1954 - present)

Peanut City Speedway - see: Suffolk Fairgrounds

Petersburg Fairgrounds - 1/2 mile dirt oval (early 1950's) (1961)

Petersburg -also see: Cockade, Dinwiddie, Virginia Motorsports Park

Pilot Speedway - Radford (Pilot) - dirt oval (early 1970's)

Princess Anne Speedway - Norfolk - 1/2 mile dirt oval (1930's)
1/4 mile paved oval (1946 - c.9/20/49) (8/14/51 - c.7/25/54)
1/2 mile dirt oval (1950 - c.1954) / located on Water Works Road
1/4 mile dirt oval (4/02/50 - 1951) / at the old Agricade Fairgrounds
sold for housing development in 1955 / now the site of a shopping center

Pulaski County Speedway - Radford - dirt oval (c.1954 - 7/04/69)
New River Valley Speedway was built on this same property in 1988

Pungo Dragstrip - Pungo - 1/4 mile concrete dragstrip (1950's)
home of the Cam Twisters Car Club / located on an old airstrip

Richlands Motor Speedway (Dragway) - see: Big Al's Dragway

Richmond City Stadium - Richmond - 1/4 mile paved oval (8/14/46 - 1946) (5/05/73)

Richmond Coliseum - Richmond - 1/10 mile wood oval (1993 - present)

Richmond Dragway - Richmond - 1/4 mile paved dragstrip (1963 - present)
(aka: Virginia Dragway)

Jimmy Spencer leads the pack of modifieds at Martinsville Speedway. The track is one of the first tracks to be sanctioned by NASCAR. - David Allio photo

The newly enlarged Richmond Int'l Raceway. In the summer of 1988 it was expanded from a 1/2 mile to a 3/4 mile. - Official track photo.

Richmond Int'l Raceway - Richmond / at the Atlantic Rural Exposition (first name)
  1/2 mile dirt oval (c.10/19/46 - 3/24/68) / (aka: Richmond Fair Speedway)
  1/2 (.542) mile paved oval (9/08/68 - 2/21/88) / fairgrounds built 1945
  3/4 mile paved oval (9/10/88 - present) / (aka: Strawberry Hill Raceway)
  (aka: Strawberry Hill Speedway) / (aka: Richmond Fairgrounds Raceway)
  (aka: Richmond Super Speedway) / (aka: Virginia State Fairgrounds)

Richmond - also see: Mooers Field, New Richmond, Southside Speedway

Roanoke - 1/4 mile paved dragstrip (c.1960)

Roanoke Fairgrounds - Roanoke - 1/3 mile dirt oval (c.1934) / ran a AAA race

Roanoke Speedway - see: Starkeys Speedway

Roanoke - also see: Victory Stadium

Rosells Virginia Raceway - Saluda - 1/2 mile dirt oval (10/04/70 - present)

Route 58 Speedway - Danville - dirt oval (early 1970's) / on US Highway 58

Royall Speedway - see: Southside Speedway

Salem Civic Center - Salem - 1/12 mile indoor concrete oval (11/29/85 - c.1986)

Schrader Field - see: Lynchburg Speedway

Scope Arena - Norfolk - 1/10 mile indoor paved oval (1973 - 1/17/74) (1/08/77)

South Boston Speedway - South Boston - 1/4 mile dirt oval (August, 1957 - 1961)
  3/8 mile (.357) paved oval (1962 - 1993)
  4/10 mile paved oval (1994 - present)

Southampton Speedway - Branchville - 3/8 mile dirt oval (c.1967 - c.1971)

Southampton Speedway - Capron - 3/8 mile dirt oval (3/29/92 - present)

Southside Speedway - Richmond - 1/5 mile dirt oval (c.5/28/47 - 1947)
1/5 mile paved oval (7/21/48 - 10/23/49) / built by Nelson Royall
1/3 mile dirt oval (4/09/50 - 6/29/51) / (aka: Royall Speedway)
1/3 mile paved oval (7/06/51 - present)

Starkeys Speedway - Roanoke - 1/4 mile paved oval (10/29/50 - c.5/15/58)
4/10 mile dirt oval (c.7/31/54 - c.1966) / (aka: Roanoke Raceway)
1958 promoter was Marvin Panch / track was located 3 miles south of town
Tim Sullivan was a promoter / (aka: Roanoke Speedway)

Staunton - dirt oval (1920's)

Strawberry Hill Speedway - see: Richmond Int'l Raceway

Suffolk Army Air Field - Suffolk - 1.55 mile concrete road course (1954)
same site as Suffolk Raceway (dragstrip)

Suffolk Fairgrounds - Suffolk / located at the Four County Fairgrounds
1/2 mile dirt oval (1936) (9/26/46) (1949) (mid-1950's)
3/8 mile dirt oval (1960) / (aka: Peanut City Speedway)
the 3/8 mile track was put in by Jim Creech and called Peanut City

Suffolk Raceway - Suffolk - 1/4 mile concrete dragstrip (c.1970 - 1991)
an old airstrip / same site as the Suffolk Army Air Field (road course)

Sumerduck Dragway - Culpeper - 1/8 mile paved dragstrip (c.1961 - present)

Tazewell Fairgrounds - Tazewell / located at the Tazewell County Fairgrounds
1/2 mile dirt oval (early 1950's)

Thunder Mountain Speedway - see: Big Al's Dragway

Unionville Speedway - Unionville - 1/3 mile dirt oval (7/27/52 - 1952)

Valley Speedway - Staunton - 1/2 mile dirt oval (c.5/29/48 - c.1955)

Victory Stadium - Roanoke - 1/3 mile paved oval (1970) (1991 - present)
located near downtown at a football stadium / (aka: Victory Speedway)

Victory Stadium - Roanoke - 1/4 mile dirt oval (5/29/47 - c.1949)
possible the same as the previous listing

Virginia Beach Motorsports Park - Creeds / (aka: Freedom 7 Dragway)
1/8 mile paved dragstrip (1961 - c.1985) / an old WWII Army Airfield
named Freedom 7 after first manned space craft (piloted by Alan Shepard)

Virginia Beach Speedway - see: Joe Weatherly Speedway

Virginia Dragway - see: Richmond Dragway

Virginia Int'l Raceway - Danville / ran first IMSA GT race here on 4/18/72
3.23 mile paved road course (8/03/57 - c.1973) / the farmer who owned the
property closed the track because he didn't want people on his land

Virginia Motorsports Park - Petersburg / owned and built by Don Beverly
1/4 mile paved dragstrip (3/12/94 - present)

Virginia Raceway - see: Rosells Virginia Raceway

Virginia Sports Arena - Doswell - 1/8 mile indoor paved oval (c.8/19/94 - present)
located across from Kings Dominion / runs Champ Karts & Mini Winston cars

Virginia State Fairgrounds (new) - see: Richmond Int'l Raceway

Virginia State Fairgrounds - Richmond - 1.0 mile dirt oval (1907 - c.1919)
1/2 mile dirt oval (1929 - 9/27/41) (c.1946 - c.1947)
site became Parker Field (AAA ballpark) in 1954 / site is near I-95

Waynesboro Fairgrounds - see: Eastside Speedway

Wayside Speedway - Patrick Springs - dirt oval (c.1968 - 1970)

Winchester Fairgrounds - Winchester / located on the west side of town
1/2 mile dirt oval (1920 - late 1930's) / the purse in 1920 was $12.00

Winchester Speedway - Winchester / (aka: Airport Speedway) / built in 1936
3/8 mile dirt oval (1938 - c.1941) (9/29/46 - present)

Wise Fairgrounds - Wise / located at the Virginia-Kentucky District Fairgrounds
1/2 mile dirt oval (early 1950's) / (aka: Wise County Fairgrounds)

Wythe Raceway - Rural Retreat - 1/2 mile dirt oval (4/04/71 - present)

WASHINGTON

Aberdeen Municipal Field - Aberdeen - 1/5 mile dirt oval (6/25/37 - 1937)

Airport Dragstrip - Ellensburg - 1/4 mile paved dragstrip (c.1961 - c.1964)

Alan Speedway - Spokane - 1.0 mile dirt oval (7/04/16) / formerly a horse track

Albie's Speedway - Spokane / (aka: Joe Albie's Stadium)
1/4 mile dirt oval (years unknown) / located at a football field

Arlington Timing Assn. - Arlington - 1/4 mile paved dragstrip (c.1961 - c.1968)

ASCRA Speedway - Port Angeles - dirt oval (9/18/66 - 1969)
(aka: Port Angeles Speedway)

Athletic Park - Tacoma - 1/5 mile dirt oval (5/12/36 - 7/21/36)
1/4 mile paved oval (7/28/36 - 1942) (10/06/45 - 6/08/49)
at 14th and Sprague / (aka: Speedway Royale) / (aka: Athletic Speedway)

Atomic Speedway - Pasco - 1/4 mile paved oval (1946) (1951)

Auditorium Race Track - Seattle - dirt oval (1936)

Aurora Speedway - Seattle - 5/8 mile dirt oval (1936 - 1942)
just north of the King County line / replaced the Olympic View track

Aurora Stadium - Seattle (aka: Playland Park) / formerly a dog track
1/4 mile dirt oval (7/21/41 - 7/25/42) (1945) / (aka: Aurora Speedway)
Allen Heath won first race in 1941 / located at Aurora Ave. & 136th
1/4 mile paved oval (4/14/46 - 8/31/47) (4/19/49 - c.9/21/58)

526

Bagley Race Track - Vancouver - dirt oval (c.1923 - c.1941)
   grandstands were destroyed in a fire in 1940

Bayview Airport - Bayview - 1/4 mile paved dragstrip (c.1956)

Bayview - dirt horse track (c.1948)

Bellingham - 1/2 mile dirt oval (7/04/15) / ran motorcycles

Bellingham Airport - Bellingham - 5.5 mile paved road course (1952)

Blue Mountain Speedway - Walla Walla - 1/4 mile dirt oval (c.7/04/51 - 1952)

Bonanza Raceway - Walla Walla - 1/4 mile paved dragstrip (c.1970 - c.1972)

Bremerton Raceway - Bremerton - 1/4 mile paved dragstrip (March 1949- present)
   the Handlers Racing Association / also see: Kitsap County Airport

Castle Rock Fairgrounds - Castle Rock - 1/2 mile dirt oval (1957 - present)
   holds annual AMA Grand Nat'l TT motorcycle race
   ran autos from 1962 to 1964

Centralia Fairgrounds - see: Chehalis Fairgrounds

Chehalis Fairgrounds - Chehalis (Centralia) / (aka: Borst Park)
   1/2 mile dirt oval (1920's) (c.1952) (1963 - 1972)
   1/4 mile dirt oval (1938) / (aka: Southwest Washington Fairgrounds)
   1/5 mile dirt oval (c.1973) / (aka: Centralia Fairgrounds)

City Park - Wenatchee - 1/3 mile dirt oval (1950's) / located in a gully

Civic Arena - see: Seattle Civic Arena

Colville - 1/4 mile dirt oval (1975)

Concrete - dirt oval (c.1948) / located in a plowed field

Roadster action at Aurora Stadium in 1949. - Gordy Sutherland collection
(courtesy of Don Radbruch)

Curlew - 1/4 mile dirt oval (years unknown)

Dayton Fairgrounds - Dayton - dirt oval (6/18/16)

Deer Park - Spokane - 1/4 mile paved dragstrip (c.1961 - c.1972)
    paved road course (1960's) / ran ICSCC sports cars / maybe had oval track

Deming Speedway - 1/8 mile dirt oval (1976 - 1983)
    1/6 mile dirt oval (1984 - present)

Eagle Track Raceway - Republic - 3/8 mile dirt oval (1979 - 1983) (1991 - present)
    (aka: Eagle Race Trac)

Echo Valley Speedway - Colville - 3/8 mile dirt oval (1981 - 1984)

Ellensburg Dragstrip - Ellensburg - 1/4 mile paved dragstrip (c.1970)

Ellensburg Fairgrounds - Ellensburg - 1/4 & 1/2 mile dirt ovals (1946 - c.1951)

Elma Nat'l Raceway - Elma / located at the Grays Harbor County Fairgrounds
    1/2 mile dirt oval (c.1930 - c.1941) (c.1946 - 1979) / (aka: Harbor Raceway)
    3/8 mile dirt oval (1980 - present) / (aka: Elma Speedway)
    (aka: Elma Fairgrounds Speedway)

Ephrata Speedway - see: State Central Speedway

Everett - 1/4 mile dirt oval (late 1930's) / was not Silver Lake Speedway

Everett - also see: Paine Air Force Base, Silver Lake Speedway.

Evergreen Saucer - Seattle / (aka: Evergreen Midget Speedway)
    1/4 mile dirt oval (7/15/36 - 1937) (5/22/39 - c.7/24/39)
    built by Mr. Peterson, one block from Olympic View Speedway

Evergreen Speedway - Monroe - 5/8 mile dirt oval (1954 - 1962) / horse track
    5/8 mile paved oval (5/30/63 - present) / runs annual "Motorcraft 500"
    1/5 mile paved oval (1966 - present) / (aka: Evergreen Fairgrounds)
    dirt figure eight course (1965) / paved figure eight course (1966 - present)
    3/8 mile paved oval (8/27/72 - present)

Ferndale Horse Track - Ferndale - 1/2 mile dirt oval (c.1949 - c.1952)

Five Mile Lake - Federal Way - dirt oval (late 1940's) / located near Tacoma

Forks - dirt oval (7/04/60)

Fort Lewis - Tacoma - paved road course (1952)

Gold Creek Indoor Track - Woodinville - oval (1968) / located at Gold Creek Park

Gonzaga Stadium - Spokane - 1/5 mile dirt oval (7/11/36 & 7/12/36)

Graham Fairgrounds - Graham - dirt oval (years unknown)
    located at the Pierce County Fairgrounds / maybe ran motorcycles only

Hannegan Speedway - Bellingham / also used as a motorcycle track
    1/4 mile dirt oval (1929 - c.1941) (c.1946 - 1950's) (1983 - present)

Harbor Raceway - see: Elma Nat'l Raceway

528

Holiday Hills - Liberty Lake - 1/4 mile dirt oval (c.1974 - c.1975)

Ione - 1/4 mile dirt oval (1966 - 9/11/66)

Kennewick Speedway - Kennewick / located at the Benton County Fairgrounds
    1/4 mile dirt oval (c.1954 - c.5/03/57)

Kitsap County Airport - Bremerton / (aka: Sea Fair Races)
    1.25 mile dirt oval (1945 - c.1948) / (aka: Thunderbird Stadium)
    1/4 mile concrete oval (1950) / ran midgets around cones on airport runway
    1/4 mile dirt oval (1958) (6/13/64) (7/24/65) (August, 1971)
    .9, 2.0 & 4.0 mile paved road courses on runways (c.7/31/55 - 8/04/57)
    ran NASCAR GN race on 8/04/57 won by Parnelli Jones on .9 mile track
    also see: Bremerton Raceway

Leavenworth - dirt oval (c.1951)

Lilac City Speedway - see: Spokane Interstate Fair Speedway

Longview Speedway - Longview / located at the Cowlitz County Fairgrounds
    1/4 mile dirt oval (1957 - 1962) / (aka: Timberline Speedway)
    3/8 mile paved oval (7/27/63 - 1965)
    1/4 mile paved oval (5/16/66 - 1977) / (aka: Columbia Empire Fairgrounds)

Madison Park - Seattle - 1/2 mile dirt oval (1915) maybe Seattle Motor Speedway

Mansfield Int'l Raceway - Mansfield - 1/4 mile dirt oval (1992 - present)

Mariners Pageant - Anacortes - 1/5 mile dirt oval (1948)
    Jim Raper started his racing career here

Mead Speedway - Spokane (Mead) - 5/8 mile dirt oval (c.1946 - c.1951)

Meadows - Seattle - 1/2 mile dirt oval (1910) / located on Marginal Way
    the site is now the Boeing Development Center

Mile B Speedway - Spanaway / near the site of present-day Spanaway Speedway
    1/2 mile dirt B shaped oval (late 1930's - 1940's)

Montesano - 1/10 & 1/4 mile dirt ovals (c.7/24/55)

Moses Lake - 1/4 mile dirt oval (1953)

Mount Vernon - 1/4 mile dirt oval (1930's) / track was in a plowed field

Mukilteo Speedway - Mukilteo - dirt oval (years unknown)

Natatiorum Park - see: Spokane Amusement Park

No Bar Ranch - Auburn - dirt oval (c.1950 - c.1955)

Norman A. Welches Mem. Speedway - Connell - 1/6 mile dirt oval (1992 - present)

Northport Int'l Raceway - Northport - 3/8 mile dirt oval (1954 - present)
    (aka: Northport Int'l Speedway)

Okanogan County Raceway - Omak - 3/8 mile dirt oval (4/21/84 - June, 1984)
    1/4 mile dirt oval (c.6/30/84 - 1985)

Olympia Airport - Olympia - paved road course on runways (years unknown)

Olympia - dirt oval (c.1925)

Olympia TQ Midget Speedway - Olympia - 1/10 mile dirt oval (c.7/23/54 - c.1960)

Olympia-Tenino Raceway - see: South Sound Speedway

Olympic View Speedway - Seattle / located at 125th & Greenwood
3/8 mile liquid asphalt oval (c.9/11/35 - c.9/18/35) / site became housing

Omak Fairgrounds - Omak - dirt oval (years unknown)

Othello Fairgrounds - Othello - 1/4 mile paved oval (5/07/67 - 9/28/68)

*Ernie Olson and Jimmy Murphy stop their work to pose for the camera in this
1920 photo at Pacific Coast Speedway. - Greg Fielden collection.*

Pacific Coast Speedway - Tacoma / located seven miles south of town
2.0 mile dirt oval (7/03/14 & 7/04/14) / (aka: Tacoma Speedway)
2.0 mile plank (wood) oval (7/04/15 - 7/04/22) / turns banked 21 degrees
Dave Lewis turned 100 mph plus in an exhibition run on 5/24/15
Billy Carlson and his riding mechanic were fatally injured 7/04/15
(the track was planned to have liquid asphalt placed over the planks, as
the 2x4 boards were laid flat with 3/8' gaps between them to allow the
asphalt to flow between them) / (aka: Montamarathon Races)
the site became an airport in 1935 / now site of a vocational school

Pacific Raceways - see: Seattle Int'l Raceway

Paine Air Force Base - Everett - paved road course (1954)
    the airport is currently called Paine Field / (aka: Sea Fair Races)

Peterson Speedway - Seattle - 5/16 mile D-shaped dirt oval (7/30/38 - c.1940)

Playland Park - see: Aurora Stadium

Point Roberts Speedway - Point Roberts - 1/2 mile dirt oval (years unknown)

Port Angeles Fairgrounds - Port Angeles / at the Clallam County Fairgrounds
    1/2 mile dirt oval (early 1950's)

Port Angeles Speedway - Port Angeles - 3/8 mile dirt oval (1940's)
    probably was located at the Port Angeles Fairgrounds

Port Angeles Speedway - Port Angeles - 3/8 mile paved oval (1972 - present)
    different location as other Port Angeles Speedways or ASCRA Speedway)

Port Angeles Speedway - see: ASCRA Speedway

Port Townsend - 1/2 mile dirt oval (1930's)

Puyallup Fairgrounds - Puyallup / at the Western Washington State Fairgrounds
    1/2 mile dirt oval (1935) / ran a midget race

Puyallup Raceway Park - Puyallup - 1/4 mile paved dragstrip (c.1961 - c.1970)
    dirt oval (1975) / ran midgets on oval track / (aka: Puyallup Dragway)

Ranier's Stadium - Renton - 1/5 mile dirt oval (8/02/40 - 8/09/40) / a ballpark

Renegade Raceway - Yakima - 1/4 mile paved dragstrip (c.1981 - present)

Republic Fairgrounds - Republic - 1/2 mile dirt oval (years unknown)

Roosevelt Stadium - Bremerton - 1/4 mile dirt oval (9/08/45)
    Shorty Templeton started here / was at a baseball stadium

Sea Fair races - see: Kitsap County Airport & Paine Air Force Base

Sea-Tac Speedway - Midway - 1/4 mile paved oval (1949 - 10/04/64)
    located at 254th & Pacific Highway / built by Lee Madsen & Lee Donovan
    property sold in February of 1965 / now the site of a shopping center

Seattle Civic Arena - Seattle - indoor oval (years unknown)

Seattle Civic Auditorium - Seattle - dirt oval (8/70/31 - 10/06/32) / a ballpark
    there were two fatalities at the last race, and the Seattle City Council passed
    an ordinance banning auto racing within the city limits

Seattle Coliseum - Seattle - 1/8 mile indoor oval (1/08/65 - 5/22/65)

Seattle Int'l Raceway - Kent - 2.25 mile paved road course (7/17/60 - present)
    1/4 mile paved dragstrip (7/03/60 - present) / (aka: Pacific Raceways)
    the name changed from Pacific to Seattle Int'l in 1968

Seattle Kingdome - Seattle / home of the Seattle Mariners (baseball)
    1/5 mile indoor concrete oval (March, 1977 - 1985)

Seattle Motor Speedway - Seattle - dirt oval (7/19/14) / possibly at Madison Park
    was on the 1914 AAA schedule / race may not have been held

Seattle Speedbowl - Seattle - 1/2 mile dirt oval (7/29/37 - c.8/15/37)

Seattle - also see: Auditorium, Aurora, Evergreen Saucer, Madison Park,
    Meadows, Olympic View, Peterson Speedway

Shelton Airport - Shelton - paved road course (8/02/59 -1962) (1967 - 1968)
    1/4 mile paved dragstrip (c.1966 - c.1967)

Shelton Fairgrounds - Shelton / located at the Mason County Fairgrounds
    3/8 mile dirt oval (5/30/68 - 9/29/68) / 3 miles north of town on Hwy 101

Silver Lake Speedway - Everett / located at a fairgrounds
    1/2 mile dirt oval (c.1927 - late 1930's) (4/29/51 - 5/30/51)
    Jimmy Wilburn's career started here (1934) / site now a mobile home park

Silverdale Speedway - Silverdale / (aka: Silverdale Airport)
    3/8 & 1/2 mile dirt ovals (c.7/20/58 - c.1973)
    paved road course on runways (1950's) / tracks were located at the airport

Skagit Speedway - Alger - 3/10 mile dirt oval (1954 - present)
    formerly the site of a junk yard / promoter for many years was Jim Raper
    home of the annual "Jim Raper Memorial Dirt Cup"

*The race cars are arriving at Washington's Skagit Speedway for the 1991 "Jim
Raper Memorial Dirt Cup". - Allan E. Brown photo.*

Sky Valley Speedway - Monroe - 1/4 mile dirt oval (5/30/57 - 1957)

Sky Valley Speedway - Monroe - 1/4 mile dirt oval (5/30/58 - 1977)
    built to replace old Sky Valley Speedway / different location

Smitty's Speedway - Kennewick - 1/10 & 5/16 mile paved ovals (1946)

Soap Lake Speedway - Soap Lake - 1/4 mile paved oval (c.1954 - 6/20/70)
    (aka: Sun Basin Speedway) / Ephrata Speedway was built as its replacement

South Sound Speedway - Tenino / (aka: Olympia-Tenino Int'l Raceway)
    3/8 mile paved oval (5/14/72 - present) / (aka: Olympia-Tenino Raceway)

Spanaway Speedway - Spanaway - 1/2 mile dirt oval (1956 - 1958)
    1/4 mile paved oval (1959 - present) / also has a figure 8 track inside
    (aka: Tacoma Raceways) / called Tacoma in 1964 & 1965 / Dick Boness built

Speedway Royale - see: Athletic Park

Spokane - 1/4 mile dirt oval (early 1950's) / located at Francis & Division
   ran midgets / now the site of the Eagle's Club

Spokane Amusement Park - Spokane - 1/4 mile paved oval (1951)
   (aka: Natatiorium Park) / located at Boone St. & Spokane River

Spokane Coliseum - Spokane - 1/10 mile indoor oval (11/18/62)

Spokane Grand Prix - Spokane - 1.65 mile paved road course (1987 - 1988)

Spokane Interstate Fair Speedway - Spokane / the fairgrounds opened in 1894
   horse track built in 1897 / converted back to a horse track in 1984
   1.0 mile dirt oval (c.8/11/09 - early 1920's) / (aka: Lilac City Speedway)
   the 8/11/09 date was the second auto race at the fairgrounds
   5/8 mile dirt oval (1930's - c.1941) (c.1946 - c.1950)
   3/8 mile paved oval (5/16/65 - 1983) / Tom Sneva started here in 1968

Spokane Raceway Park - Spokane / this complex was proposed in 1970
   1/4 mile paved dragstrip (May, 1974 - present) / back to back grandstands
   1/2 mile paved oval (6/03/78 - present) / has an unfinished road course

Spokane - also see: Alan, Albie's, Deer Park, Gonzaga, Mead, Sunset.

State Central Speedway - Ephrata / (aka: Ephrata Speedway)
   1/4 mile paved oval (6/27/70 - present) / sister track is Stateline, Idaho
   built to replace Soap Lake Speedway

Steilicoom Bowl - Tacoma / near the site of the old Pacific Coast Speedway
   1/5 mile dirt oval (c.1940 - 1942) (c.1946 - 1947)

Sumas Fairgrounds - Sumas - 1/4 mile dirt oval (1939)

Sun Basin Speedway - see: Soap Lake Speedway

Sunnygrand Speedway - Sunnyside - 1/2 mile paved oval (1953 - 1967)
   3/8 mile dirt oval (1969 - 1970)

Sunset Speedway - Spokane (Airway Heights) - 3/8 mile dirt oval (1960's)
   was to be called Spokane Raceway in 1969

Tacoma - 2.0 mile liquid asphalt oval on city streets (7/03/14 & 7/04/14)

Tacoma - 5.0 mile road course on city streets (7/05/12 - 7/07/12)
   3.423 mile road course on city streets (1913) / (aka: Lakeview)

Tacoma Grand Prix - Tacoma / located in the parking lot of the Tacoma Dome
   1.6 mile paved road course (8/10/83 - 1987)

Tacoma Raceways - see: Spanaway Speedway

Tacoma Speedway (board track) - see: Pacific Coast Speedway

Tacoma Sports Arena - Tacoma - 1/5 mile dirt oval (1940's - 1950)
   located at 99th & South Tacoma Way / located at a rodeo grounds

Tacoma Sports Arena - Tacoma / ran T.Q. midgets
   1/16 mile indoor dirt oval (11/17/62 - 1963) (1966) (1970)

Tacoma - also see: Athletic Park, Fort Lewis, Pacific Coast, Steilicoom.

Tenino Speedway - Tenino - 3/8 mile dirt oval (June, 1966 - 10/08/67)
(aka: Tenino Fairgrounds) / different location than South Sound Speedway

Three Lakes Camp - Wenatchee - dirt oval (c.1951)

Thun Midget Speedway - Puyallup / (aka: Thunder Midget Raceway)
1/5 mile oval (1961 - c.1962)

Timberline Speedway - see: Longview Speedway

Trails Inn Arena - Olympia - 1/12 mile dirt indoor oval (12/03/65)

Tri-City Raceway - West Richland - 1/2 mile paved tri-oval (4/28/68 - present)
(aka: Tri-City Raceways)

Tri-City Speedway - Kelso / track was located on old Highway 99
5/16 mile dirt oval (c.7/28/62 - 1964)

Vancouver Saddle Club - Vancouver - 1/10 mile indoor dirt oval (1/26/63)

Walla Walla Fairgrounds - Walla Walla - 1/2 mile dirt oval (5/30/17)

Walla Walla - also see: Blue Mountain Speedway, Bonanza Raceways.

Washington State Fairgrounds - see: Yakima Fairgrounds

Waterville Fairgrounds - Waterville - 1/2 mile dirt oval (1916) (early 1950's)
located at the North Central Washington Fairgrounds

Wenatchee Valley Raceway - East Wenatchee / (aka: East Wenatchee Speedway)
1/4 mile paved oval (5/03/70 - present)

Wenatchee - also see: City Park, Three Lake Camp.

White Salmon - 1/4 mile dirt oval (c.1954) / probably was a school running track

Woodinville Rodeo Track - Woodinville - 1/4 mile dirt oval (1950's)

*Garrett Evans from East Wenatchee, Washington was the 1985 and 1989
NASCAR Northwest Tour champion. - David Allio photo.*

Yakima Fairgrounds - Yakima / (aka: Washington State Fairgrounds) / horse track
  1.125 mile dirt oval (c.1926 - c.1941) (c.1946 - 1955) / built in 1896
    listed as a 1.0 mile track most of the time
  1/5 mile dirt oval (8/23/38 - 9/20/38) / (aka: Central Washington Fairgrounds)
  1/4 mile dirt oval (4/30/39 - c.1939) (c.1946 - 1950)

Yakima Speedway - Yakima - 1/2 mile dirt oval (8/05/56 - 1960)
  1/2 mile paved oval (7/10/60 - present) / (aka: Yakima Speedbowl)
  (aka: Yakima Apple Bowl Speedway) / called Speedbowl in 1958

WEST VIRGINIA

AJ's Speedway - see: Ohio Valley Speedway

Beckley - 1/4 mile dirt oval (7/05/48)

Beckley Motor Speedway - Beckley / (aka: Beckley Speedway)
  3/8 mile dirt oval (1957 - 1985) (1987 - present)

Bluefield - 1/2 mile dirt oval (c.1924 - 1932) / maybe Littleburg Speedway

Brennan's Raceway - see: Interstate 79 Speedway

Buckhannon - dirt oval (1953)

Camden Park - Huntington - 1/5 mile dirt oval (years unknown)
  located at an amusement park

Charleston Fairgrounds - Charleston (Dunbar) / at the Kanawha Co. Fairgrounds
  1/2 mile dirt oval (5/30/32 - c.6/23/35) (6/11/39 - 1941) (1946 - c.1955)
  1/4 mile dirt oval (1949 - c.1955) / (aka: Dunbar Speedway)
  located on SR 64 / now the site of a Shoney's and a Subway restaurant

Charleston Speedway - Charleston / (aka: West Virginia Auto Speedway)
  1/3 mile dirt oval (1946 - 1973) (8/06/83 - 1985)
  1/5 mile dirt oval (1953) / track may have been paved at one time

Charleston - also see: Saint Albans, Skyline

Clarksburg Fairgrounds - Clarksburg / at the Central West Virginia Fairgrounds
  1/2 mile dirt oval (c.7/21/21 - c.1940) / (aka: Clarksburg Speedway)
  (aka: Harrison County Fairgrounds)

Clarksburg - also see: Interstate 79, Lumberton, Norwood, Nutter, Shinnston

Danville Motor Speedway - Danville - 1/4 mile dirt oval (1980)

Dunbar (Fairgrounds) Speedway - see: Charleston Fairgrounds

Eldora Raceway Park - see: Fairmont Dragway

Elkins Fairgrounds - Elkins / located at the Randolph County Fairgrounds
  1/2 mile dirt oval (1920's & 1930's)

Elkins Motor Speedway - Elkins / (aka: Elkins Speedway)
  1/4 mile dirt oval (6/15/52 - late 1950's) (5/30/68 - present)
  (aka: Mountain State Motor Speedway) / Monty Ward first winner

Evans Fairgrounds - Evans / maybe located at the old Jackson Co. Fairgrounds
1/3 mile dirt oval (c.1946 - mid 1950's) / (aka: Evans Speedway)

Fairmont Dragway - Fairmont - dirt oval (c.1950 - c.1953)
1/8 mile paved dragstrip (c.1970 - present) / (aka: Eldora Raceway Park)

Gilbert Speedway - Gilbert - 1/3 mile dirt oval (c.9/07/53 - 1954)

Grafton Fairgrounds - Grafton / located at the Taylor County Fairgrounds
1/2 mile dirt oval (1920's)

Grandview Dragway - see: Mountaineer Dragway

Great Lakes Speedway - see: Morgantown Speedway

Green Valley Springs Speedway - Romney - 1/2 mile dirt oval (1967)

Holloway Memorial Ballpark - Wheeling - 1/4 mile dirt oval (5/14/40 - c.5/21/40)

Huntington Fairgrounds - Huntington / located at the old Cabell Co. Fairgrounds
1/2 mile dirt oval (c.7/04/23) / (aka: Tri-State Fairgrounds)

Huntington Int'l Raceway - see: West Virginia Int'l Speedway

Huntington Memorial Field House - Huntington / located at 26th St. & 5th St.
1/12 mile concrete indoor oval (3/17/51 - 11/08/53)

Huntington Motor Speedway - Huntington - 1/3 mile dirt oval (c.1952 - c.1961)

Huntington - also see: Camden Park, West Virginia Int'l Speedway

Hurricane Raceway - Hurricane - 1/5 mile dirt oval (c.1975)

Int'l Raceway Park - see: West Virginia Int'l Speedway

Interstate 79 Speedway - Clarksburg (Bridgeport) / (aka: Sirk's Super Speedway)
3/8 mile dirt oval (c.1965 - present) / (aka: Interstate Raceway)
(aka: Interstate Raceway)/ (aka: I-79 Speedway) / (aka: Brennan's Raceway)

Jackson Co. Raceway (Speedway) (Fairgrounds) - see: Mountaineer Raceway Park

Looking towards the first turn at I-79 Speedway. - Allan E. Brown photo.

Kanawha Valley Dragway Park near Charleston was built in 1994. This photo was taken before the first event was held. - Official track photo.

Kanawha Valley Dragway Park - Winfield
    1/8 mile paved dragstrip (4/23/94 - present)

Lewisburg Fairgrounds - see: West Virginia State Fairgrounds

Littleburg Speedway - Bluefield - 1/2 mile dirt oval (c.1958 - c.1961)

Lost Creek Speedway - Lost Creek / (aka: Mountaineer Speedway)
    3/8 mile dirt oval (6/29/80 - 7/26/80) / track was ruined by a flood

Lumberton Arena - Clarksburg - indoor oval (c.1953)

Marlinton Fairgrounds - Marlinton / located at the Pocahontas Co. Fairgrounds
    1/2 mile dirt oval (c.8/16/52 - c.1953)

Middlebourne Fairgrounds - see: Tyler County Speedway

Morgantown Speedway - Morgantown / (aka: Great Lakes Speedway)
    1/4 mile dirt oval (c.1953 - 9/24/78)

Moundsville Fairgrounds - Moundsville / located at the Marshall Co. Fairgrounds
    1/2 mile dirt oval (1915) (6/08/52 - c.1955) / ran motorcycles in 1915
    1/4 mile dirt oval (1952 - c.1955) / maybe ran autos in 1910's or 1920's

Mountain State Motor Speedway - see: Elkins Motor Speedway

Mountain State Raceway Park - see: Mountaineer Raceway Park

Mountaineer Dragway - Beckley - 1/8 mile paved dragstrip (c.1981 - present)
    (aka Raleigh County Dragway) / (aka: Grandview Dragway)

Mountaineer Raceway Park - Ripley / (aka: Mountain State Raceway Park)
   3/8 mile dirt oval (c.1977 - 1984) (1988 - present)
   (aka: Jackson County Speedway) / located at the Jackson Co. Fairgrounds
   (aka: Jackson County Raceway)

Mountaineer Speedway - Lost Creek - see: Lost Creek Speedway

Mountaineer Speedway - Parkersburg / (aka: West Virginia Int'l Raceway)
   1/4 mile dirt oval (possibly ran in 1971) / arena that held rock concerts
   paved road course (possibly ran SCCA events in early the 1970's)
   located four miles south of town / had a USAC championship race scheduled
   on proposed 1.0 mile paved oval for 8/08/71 / 1.0 mile track never built

Norwood Park - Clarksburg - dirt oval (c.9/30/51 - c.1953) / maybe Nutter Fort

Nutter Fort - dirt oval (c.1953)

Ohio Valley Speedway - Parkersburg / (aka: West Virginia Motor Speedway)
   3/8 mile dirt oval (c.11/16/58 - present) / (aka: Smedley's Speedway)
   (aka: AJ's Speedway) / (aka: The Valley) / (aka: Parkersburg Speedway)
   maybe former Wood Co. Fairgrounds / (aka: Parkersburg Motor Speedway)

Parkersburg Fairgrounds - Parkersburg / maybe at the Wood County Fairgrounds
   1/2 mile dirt oval (c.1924 - early 1930's)
   Slim Rutherford was a consistent winner in Big Cars here in 1924

Parkersburg (Motor) Speedway - see: Ohio Valley Speedway

Parkersburg - also see: Mountaineer, Ohio Valley, Scott Field

Pennsboro Speedway - Pennsboro / located at the Ritchie County Fairgrounds
   1/2 mile dirt oval (1920's) (c.1949 - 1987) (1989 - present)
   (aka: Ritchie County Speedway) / (aka: Ritchie Speedway)
   covered grandstands built in 1891 burned down in 1981

Petersburg - 1/4 mile paved dragstrip (c.1960)

Peytona - dirt oval (1950's)

Potomac Valley Speedway - Fort Ashby - 1/3 mile dirt oval (c.1956 - c.1959)

Princeton Speedway - Princeton - 1/8 mile paved dragstrip (1987 - present)
   4/10 mile dirt oval (1989 - present)

Pyramid Valley - (location unknown) - dirt oval (5/12/85 - 1985)
   a track that also ran Karts in 1982

Raleigh County Dragway - see: Mountaineer Dragway

Ripley County Dragway - see: Fairmont Dragway

Ripley Fairgrounds - see: Mountaineer Raceway Park

Ritchie County (Fairgrounds) Speedway - see: Pennsboro Speedway

Romney - dirt oval (c.1941)

Saint Albans - dirt oval (1950's) / maybe at the Charleston Fairgrounds

Sandyville - 1/5 mile dirt oval (late 1940's - early 1950's) / in a corn field

Scott Field - Parkersburg - 1/5 mile cinder oval (late 1930's) (c.1947 - c.1954)
was located at a baseball diamond

Shinnston - 4/10 mile dirt oval (c.1953) / maybe Norwood Park

Sirk's Super Speedway - see: Interstate 79 Speedway

Skyline Speedway - Charleston - 1/4 mile paved oval (1954)
1/4 mile dirt oval (May, 1955 - c.1961)

Smedley's Speedway - see: Ohio Valley Speedway

Spencer Fairgrounds - Spencer - dirt oval (late 1930's) / at Roane Co. Fairgrounds

Summit Point Raceway - Charles Town / (aka: Summit Point Speedway)
1.84 & 2.0 mile paved road courses (10/04/69 - present)

The Valley - see: Ohio Valley Speedway

Tri-River Dragway - Fort Gay - 300 foot paved dragstrip (1990)

Tygart Valley Speedway - (location unknown) - 1/4 mile dirt oval (9/10/88)

Tyler County Speedway - Middlebourne / located at the Tyler County Fairgrounds
1/4 mile dirt oval (c.1974 - 1985) (1988 - present)

Upper Valley - Mill Creek - 3/16 mile dirt oval (1987)

West Virginia Auto Speedway - see: Charleston Motor Speedway

West Virginia Int'l Speedway - Huntington (Ona)
7/16 mile paved oval (8/18/63 - 1973) (1975) / pavement broke up 1st race
Fred Lorenzen won the first race on 8/18/63, it was NASCAR GN race
only WV track to hold NASCAR GN races 8/18/63, 8/16/64, 7/07/70 & 7/14/71
(aka: Huntington Int. Speedway) / (aka: Int'l Raceway Park)
Lenny Waldo won the first ever USAC sprint car race in a roadster here
1/4 mile paved dragstrip (c.1970)
(aka: Dick Clark's Int'l Raceway Park) / grandstands sold to Langley, VA
the track was once owned by TV Bandstand's Dick Clark

West Virginia Motor Raceway - see: Ohio Valley Speedway

West Virginia Motor Speedway - Mineral Wells / located south of town near I-81
5/8 mile paved oval (1985 - 1989) (1991 - present)

West Virginia State Fairgrounds - Lewisburg - 1/2 mile dirt oval (years unknown)

Weston Raceway - Weston - 1/4 mile dirt oval (1968)
1/3 mile dirt oval (1968 - c.1970)

Wheeling - 1/2 mile dirt oval (9/07/29)

Wheeling Creek Speedway - Wheeling / (aka: Big Wheeling Creek Speedway)
3/8 mile dirt oval (late 1970's)

Wheeling Downs - Wheeling - 1/2 mile dirt oval (8/07/38 - c.1940) / a horse track

A-F Speedway - Friendship / located at the old Adams County Fairgrounds
1/3 mile dirt oval (mid 1950's) / (aka: Adams-Friendship Speedway)
1/4 mile paved oval (1959 - 1966) (1971 - 1972)
the track is currently across the street from a retirement home

ABC Raceway - Ashland - 1/4 mile dirt oval (10/31/65 - present)

Amery-Roller Coaster Speedway - Amery - 1.0 mile dirt road course (c.1953)

Angell Park Speedway - Sun Prairie / oldest continually running midget track
1/2 mile dirt oval (1938 - 7/26/42) (9/23/45 - 1945)
1/3 mile dirt oval (6/03/46 - present)
Rich Vogler started his career here in 1969

*Badger Midget action at Angell Park Speedway from 1953. The track is the
longest continual running midget track. - Bob Sheldon photo.*

Antigo - dirt oval (c.1947)

Antigo Fairgrounds - see: Langlade County Fairgrounds

Apple Creek Speedway - Appleton - 1/4 mile dirt oval (c.1958 - c.1969)
across the street from Gordy's Outagamie Speedway
the location is now the site of exclusive homes

Appleton Fairgrounds - Appleton - dirt oval (Aug. 1948) / at Swift Co. Fairgrounds

Baraboo Fairgrounds - Baraboo / located at the Sauk County Fairgrounds
1/2 mile dirt oval (c.1925) (6/22/47)

Beaver Dam Fairgrounds - Beaver Dam / located at the Dodge Co. Fairgrounds
1/2 mile dirt oval (c.1925 - 9/10/41) (8/04/46 - 1981) (1985 - present)

Beaver Dam Raceway - Beaver Dam / (aka: Raceway Park) / site of Raceway Park
1/3 mile dirt oval (5/29/93 - present) / new stands & track in 1993

Berlin Raceway - Berlin - dirt oval (c.1949 - early 1950's)

Black River Country Raceway - see: Neillsville Fairgrounds

Black River Falls - 1/4 mile paved oval (1963 - 1966)

Black River Falls Fairgrounds - Black River Falls
1/2 mile dirt oval (years unknown) / located at the Jackson Co. Fairgrounds

Blue Mound Dog Track - Milwaukee (Brookfield) / built in 1929 for dog racing
1/5 mile dirt (cinder) oval (c.1932 - 10/06/35) (1950)
ran motorcycles in early 1930's / the first midget race was on 7/15/34
later became the Blue Mound Outdoor Theater
the site is now the Brookfield Square Shopping Mall

Boyceville - dirt oval (c.1957 - c.1958)

Breese-Stevens Athletic Field - Madison / ran BMARA midget races
1/4 mile dirt oval (7/23/38 - 10/16/38)

Brown County Speedway - see: DePere Fairgrounds

Bruce Speedway (Race Track) - see: Racer's Raceway

Camp Randall - Madison - dirt oval (c.1938) / possibly ran midgets
the location is now the University of Wisconsin

Capital (Super) Speedway - see: Madison Int'l Speedway

A packed house watches practice for the World of Outlaws at Cedar Lake Speedway near Somerset, Wisconsin. Since this photo additional grandstands were installed. - Official track photo.

Cedar Lake Speedway - New Richmond / (aka: Cedar Lake Int'l Speedway)
1/4 mile dirt oval (6/30/57 - September, 1982)
3/8 mile dirt oval (1983 - present)

Cedarburg Fairgrounds - Cedarburg / (aka: Fireman's Park)
1/2 mile dirt oval (1914 - c.1940) / (aka: Cedarburg Speedway)
1/3 mile dirt oval (1941) (7/07/46 - 8/29/79)

Central State Speedway - see: Central Wisconsin Speedway

Central Wisconsin Speedway - Colby / (aka: Tri-County Speedway)
1/3 mile dirt oval (1970 - 1974) (1980 - 1988) (1992 - present)
(aka: Central State Speedway)

Centuria Speedway - see: Saint Croix Speedway

Chilton Speedway - Chilton / located at the Calumet County Fairgrounds
1/2 mile dirt oval (5/27/28) / (aka: Chilton Fairgrounds)
1/4 mile dirt oval (1969) (1983 - 1985) (1990 - present)

Chippewa Falls Fairgrounds - Chippewa Falls
1/2 mile dirt oval (c.1921 - c.9/27/34) (5/25/47 - 1971)
located at the Northern Wisconsin State Fairgrounds

Clintonville Bowl - Clintonville - 1/4 mile dirt oval (5/18/41 - 6/23/42)
was located on an airport grounds

Columbus 151 Speedway - Columbus - 1/4 mile dirt oval (1955 - early 1960's)
1/4 mile paved oval (1960's - present) / (aka: Red Bud Speedway)

Crandon Speedway - Crandon - 1/4 mile dirt oval (1977 - 1988)
(aka: Forest County Speedway) / located at the Forest County Fairgrounds

Crown Speedway - Wisconsin Rapids / located 3 miles east of town on Hwy 54
1/4 mile dirt oval (c.1948 - c.1952) / the promoter was Clayton Crown
the site is now the Jerre O'Days Pub

Curtis Wright Airfield - Milwaukee - 1/4 mile paved dragstrip (1950)
held only one race / the airfield is now called Timmerman Field

Dairyland Speedway - Madison (Verona) / (aka: Hell's Half Acre)
1/3 mile dirt oval (1952 - c.10/12/52) / Al Shear was the promoter

Dane County Expo Coliseum - Madison - 1/10 mile indoor oval (1990)
ran Mini-Sprints / a midget race was scheduled in 1970
but bad ventilation cancelled the race

Dane County Expo Coliseum - Madison - paved road course (1964) / in parking lot

Darlington Fairgrounds - Darlington / located at the Lafayette County Fairgrounds
1/2 mile dirt oval (c.1942) (1946 - July, 1970) / (aka: Jaycees Speedway)

Dells Motor Speedway - see: Wisconsin Dells Motor Speedway

*Dick Trickle drove this Mustang in the early 1970's. Trickle has close to 850
feature wins. He is winningest driver in modern history. - Tom DeVette photo.*

542

DePere Fairgrounds - DePere / located at the Brown County Fairgrounds
  1/2 mile dirt oval (1924 - 8/23/41) (8/23/46 - 1979) / (aka: DePere Speedway)
  1/4 mile dirt oval (1948 - c.1950) / (aka: Brown County Speedway)

Dodge County Fairgrounds - see: Beaver Dam Fairgrounds

Door County Speedway - see: Thunder Hill Raceway

Durand - 1/2 mile dirt oval (1957 & 1958)

Eau Claire - dirt oval (c.6/16/57 - c.1958)

Eau Claire Speedway - Eau Claire - 1/2 mile dirt oval (1965 - c.1966)
  3/8 mile dirt oval (c.1972 - 1977) / (aka: River City Raceway)

Edgerton Speedway - Edgerton / (aka: Raceway Park)
  1/4 mile dirt oval (c.1951 - c.1955)

Elkhart Lake - 3.35 mile road course on country roads (7/23/50)
  6.5 mile paved road course on country roads (8/26/51) (1952)

Elkhorn Fairgrounds - Elkhorn / located at the Walworth County Fairgrounds
  1/2 mile dirt oval (c.1953 - 1966)

Fireman's Park - see: Cedarburg Fairgrounds

Fond du Lac Fairgrounds - Fond du Lac / (aka: Fond du Lac Speedway)
  1/2 mile dirt oval (1920's - 8/15/41) (6/22/47 - c.1971) (1973 - c.1977)
  1/4 mile dirt oval (1952) / located at the Fond du Lac County Fairgrounds

Forest County Speedway - see: Crandon Speedway

Forty & Eight Speedway - LaCrosse / located south of town
  1/4 mile dirt oval (late 1940's - 1953)

Franksville Fairgrounds - Franksville / (aka: Racine County Speedway)
  1/2 mile dirt oval (c.1948 - c.1960)

Galesville Fairgrounds - Galesville - 1/2 mile dirt oval (1950's)
  located at the Trempealeau County Fairgrounds

Gays Mill Fairgrounds - Gays Mill / located at the Crawford County Fairgrounds
  1/2 mile dirt oval (years unknown)

Golden Sands Speedway - Plover / built by Sam Bartus
  1/3 mile paved oval (May, 1967 - 1984) (1988 - present)
  (aka: Paul's Golden Sands Speedway)

Gordy's Outagomie Speedway - Appleton - 1/4 mile paved oval (1960's - 1974)
  across the street from Apple Creek Speedway

Grant Park - South Milwaukee - 1/2 mile dirt oval (1920's) / on the lakefront

Great Lakes Drag-A-Way - Union Grove - 1/4 mile paved dragstrip (1955- present)

Griffin Park - Wisconsin Rapids / built by Sam Bartus
  1/4 mile paved oval (March, 1960 - 1970) / site is now a campground

Hales Corners Speedway - Franklin - 1/4 mile dirt oval (6/18/50 - 1973)
  1/3 mile dirt oval (1974 - present) / located in a suburb of Milwaukee

Hell's Half Acre - see: Dairyland Speedway

Horlick Athletic Field - Racine / located at Forest High & Carlisle Ave.
1/4 mile dirt oval (6/08/39 - 7/16/42)

I-43 Speedway - see: Manitowac Expo Speedway

Impact Speedway - see: Madison Int'l Speedway

Iron River Fairgrounds - Iron River - dirt oval (early 1950's)
located at the Bayfield County Fairgrounds

Iron River Speedway - Iron River - 1/4 mile dirt oval (1979 - 1984) (1986)

Janesville Airport - Janesville / (aka: Rock County Airport)
paved road course on runways (8/09/52) (1953)

Janesville - dirt oval (1920's or 1930's) / probably at the Rock County Fairgrounds

Jaycees Speedway - see: Darlington Fairgrounds

Jefferson Fairgrounds - Jefferson / located at the Jefferson County Fairgrounds
1/2 mile dirt oval (c.1925 - c.9/01/40) (1980's) / ran motorcycles in 1980's

Jefferson Speedway - Jefferson - 1/4 mile dirt oval (1952 - 1963)
1/4 mile paved oval (1964 - present) / Tom Bigelow's career started here

K G Raceway - Eagle River - 1/4 mile dirt oval (1975 - 1982)
3/8 mile dirt tri-oval (1983 - present)

Kelly Race Track - Wausau - dirt oval (1952) / was a baseball diamond

Kenosha Airport Midget Speedway - Kenosha / located at Highway 50 & 22nd St.
1/5 mile dirt oval (c.10/18/36 - 1938)

Kenosha County Fairgrounds - see: Wilmot Speedway

Kenosha County Speedway - Wilmot - 1/4 mile dirt oval (1952 - 1972)

Kenosha - also see: Olli O'Mara's Ballpark

KK Sports Arena - see: Wisconsin Int'l Raceway

LaCrosse Fairgrounds Speedway - West Salem
1/2 mile dirt oval (c.1949 - 1969) / at LaCrosse Interstate Fairgrounds
1/2 (.514) mile paved oval (7/14/70 - present)
1/4 mile paved oval (1988 - present) / (aka: LaCrosse Interstate Speedway)

LaCrosse - also see: Forty & Eight, and North LaCrosse

Ladysmith Fairgrounds - Ladysmith / located at the Rusk County Fairgrounds
1/3 mile dirt oval (c.7/24/49 - early 1950's)

Lake Front Speedway - Milwaukee / located near downtown at Wisconsin Ave.
1/5 mile dirt oval (1937) / (aka: Maitland Field)
(aka: Juneau Park) / now the site of docks for seaplanes

Lake Geneva - 1/5 mile dirt oval (1949) / ran midgets

Lake Geneva Raceway - Lake Geneva - 1/4 mile paved oval (6/02/66 - 1989)
    1/4 mile paved dragstrip (7/04/62 - 1972) / ran down middle of oval track
    1/3 mile banked paved oval (1990 - present) / (aka: Lake Geneva Dragstrip)

Lake Halles Race Track - Chippewa Falls - 1/4 mile dirt oval (c.1953)

Lancaster Fairgrounds - Lancaster / located at the Grant County Fairgrounds
    1/2 mile dirt oval (5/30/47 - 1979) / (aka: Lancaster Speedway)

Langlade County Fairgrounds - Antigo - 1/2 mile dirt oval (6/18/93 - present)

Leo's Speedway - see: Oshkosh Fairgrounds

Luxemburg Tri-Star Speedway - Luxemburg / at the Kewaunee Co. Fairgrounds
    1/3 mile dirt oval (c.1960 - 1982) (1987 - present)
    (aka: Luxemburg Speedway)

Lyndale Farms - Milwaukee - 2.7 mile paved road course (c.1963 - 1966)
    now the site of a housing sub division / in the suburb of Pewaukee

Madison - dirt oval (1911)

Madison Fairgrounds - Madison / located at the Dane County Fairgrounds
    1/2 mile dirt oval (6/22/52) (7/26/52) / maybe track that ran in 1911
    1952 races listed as first races in over 20 years / maybe was 1.0 mile
    near the location of the current Dane County Expo Coliseum

Madison Int'l Speedway - Oregon (Rutland) - 1/4 mile paved oval (1963 - 1968)
    the first track was where the pit area is of the current track
    1/2 mile paved oval (1969 - 1986) (1992 - present)
    1/4 mile paved oval (1983 - 1986) / (aka: Capital Super Speedway)
    1/2 mile dirt oval (1987 - 1989) / (aka: Sam's Capital Super Speedway)
    (dirt track aka: Impact Speedway) / (aka: Capital Speedway)

Madison - also see: Breese-Stevens, Camp Randall, Dairyland, Dane County

Manitowoc Expo Speedway - Manitowoc / located at the new Manitowoc Co. Expo
    1/2 mile dirt oval (1987 - present) / (aka: I-43 Speedway)

Manitowoc Fairgrounds - Manitowoc / at the old Manitowoc County Fairgrounds
    1/2 mile dirt oval (c.6/15/41 - 9/07/41) (8/18/46 - c.1960)

Marathon Park - see: Wausau Fairgrounds

Marengo Fairgrounds - Marengo - dirt oval (1960's) / at Ashland Co. Fairgrounds

Marinette - 1/4 mile dirt oval (early 1950's)

Marshfield - 1/4 mile dirt oval (early 1950's) / south of town at Hwy 13 & Hwy 10

Marshfield Fairgrounds - Marshfield / at the Central Wisconsin State Fairgrounds
    1/2 mile dirt oval (c.9/04/40 - 9/03/41) (c.9/03/47 - c.1982)
    1/4 mile dirt oval (early 1950's) (1985) / ran only during the fair

Marshfield Super Speedway - Marshfield / (aka: Yellow River Speedway)
    1/2 mile dirt oval (1979 - present)

Mauston - dirt oval (1948) / possibly at the Juneau County Fairgrounds

Mecca Arena - Milwaukee - 1/10 mile concrete oval (1/27/90 - 1992)
no indoor racing in Milwaukee from late 1930's until 1990 (fire codes)

Medford Stock Car Race Track - Medford - 1/4 mile dirt oval (1950's)

Menomonie Fairgrounds - see: Red Cedar Speedway

Merrill Fairgrounds - Merrill - 1/2 mile dirt oval (1935) (1949 - 1951)
located at the Lincoln County Fairgrounds

Midland Cycle Track - Milwaukee - 1/4 mile dirt oval (1934) / ran BMARA midgets

Milltown Speedway - Milltown - dirt oval (1950's)

Milwaukee Auditorium - Milwaukee - indoor paved oval (1935)

Milwaukee Mile - Milwaukee (West Allis) / at the Wisconsin State Fairgrounds
1.0 mile dirt oval (9/11/03 - 5/30/42) (6/09/46 - 9/20/53)
horse racing started 1892 / held 24 hour endurance events in 1907 and 1908
1/4 mile dirt oval (8/04/39 - c.1942) (6/07/46 - 9/06/66)
1/2 mile dirt oval (1954 - c.1955) / J.Alex Sloan was promoter in 1930's
1.0 mile paved oval (6/06/54 - present) / Marchese Bros. promoters 1950's
2.1 mile paved road course (1954 - 1958) / built in 1876 as a horse track
2.0 mile paved road course (1959 - c.1969) / sold to the state in 1891
the fairgrounds was to have moved in 1967 / second oldest active track

USAC sprints at the Wisconsin State Fairgrounds (now called the Milwaukee Mile). Parnelli Jones is on the pole. - Armin Krueger photo.

Milwaukee - also see: Blue Mound, Curtis Field, Grant Park, Hales Corners, Lake Front, Lyndale, Mecca, Midland, South Milwaukee, Wauwatosa, Wilmot Hills, Wisconsin State Fair, Wonderland Park.

Mineral Point Fairgrounds - Mineral Point / located at the Iowa Co. Fairgrounds
1/2 mile dirt oval (c.5/22/49) / (aka: Southwestern Wisconsin Fairgrounds)

Neillsville Fairgrounds - Neillsville / located at the Clark County Fairgrounds
1/2 mile dirt oval (1930's) (1973 - 1977) / (aka: Neillsville Raceway)
(aka: Black River Country Raceway) / (aka: Paul's Neillsville Speedway)

North LaCrosse Speedway - LaCrosse - 1/4 mile dirt oval (c.1954 - c.1963)
    1/3 mile paved oval (c.1964 - 1972) / (aka: North LaCrosse Speedbowl)

Oakfield - 1/4 mile dirt oval (6/03/51 - c.1960)
    the promoters were Rollie Heder & Bill Johnson, Sr.

Olli O'Mara's Ballpark - Kenosha / (aka: Sheridan Road Midget Speedway)
    1/5 mile dirt oval (5/23/37 - 1938) / located on South Sheridan Road

One-Forty-One (141) Speedway - Francis Creek - 1/2 mile dirt oval (c.1949)
    1/4 mile dirt oval (1950's) / (aka: Super 141 Speedway)
    1/2 mile paved oval (1950's) (1984)
    1/4 mile paved oval (c.1959 - 1987) (1990)

Oshkosh Fairgrounds - Oshkosh / located at the Winnebago County Fairgrounds
    1/2 mile dirt oval (1936) (7/11/48) / (aka: Oshkosh Fair Park)
    1/4 mile dirt oval (late 1940's - 1973)
    1/3 mile dirt oval (1974 - 1978) / (aka: Leo's Speedway)

Owen-Withee Speedway - Owen - 1/4 mile dirt oval (1953)

Paul's Golden Sands Speedway - see: Golden Sands Speedway

Paul's Super Speedway - see: DePere Fairgrounds

Phillips Fairgrounds - Phillips / located at the Price County Fairgrounds
    1/2 mile dirt oval (early 1950's)

Plymouth (Fairgrounds) Speedway - see: Sheboygan County Fair Speedway

Portage Fairgrounds - Portage / located at the Columbia County Fairgrounds
    1/3 mile dirt oval (c.1963 - c.1965) (1993 - present)

Racer's Raceway - Bruce - 1/4 mile dirt oval (c.1972 - c.1976)
    (aka: Bruce Speedway) / (aka: Bruce Race Track)

Raceway Park - Beaver Dam / became site of Beaver Dam Raceway Park in 1993
    1/3 mile dirt oval (c.1963 - 1982)

Racine County Speedway - see: Franksville Fairgrounds

Racine - see: Horick Athletic Field

Rangeline Speedway - Marshfield - 1/3 mile dirt oval (c.1963 - 1975)

Red Bud Speedway - see: Columbus 151 Speedway

Red Cedar Speedway - Menomonie / located at the Dunn Co. Recreational Park
    1/4 mile dirt oval (Aug., 1941) (7/05/48) / (aka: Dunn County Fairgrounds)
    3/8 mile dirt oval (c.1975 - present)

Rhinelander - 1/2 mile dirt oval (1965 & 1966)

Rib Lake - oval (years unknown)

Rice Lake Fairgrounds - Rice Lake / located at the Barron County Fairgrounds
    1/2 mile dirt oval (7/06/41) (7/06/46 - c.1949)

Rice Lake Speedway - Rice Lake - 1/4 mile dirt oval (c.1952 - 1991)
    1/3 mile dirt oval (1992 - present)

Richland Center - 1/2 mile dirt oval (c.1925) / probably at Richland Co Fairgrounds

Ripon - dirt oval (1920's or 1930's)

River City Raceway - see: Eau Claire Speedway

River Raceway Tri-Oval - Fountain City / (aka: Tri-Oval Speedway)
    3/8 mile dirt tri-oval (Sept., 1968 - present) / (aka: River Raceway Park)

Riverside Speedway - Phillips - dirt oval (late 1960's - 1972) (1985)

Road America - Elkhart Lake / holds the annual "June Sprints" for sports cars
    4.0 mile paved road course (9/10/55 - present)

Rock County Airport - see: Janesville Airport

Rock Falls Raceway - Eau Claire - 1/4 mile paved dragstrip (May, 1969 - present)

Saint Croix Speedway - Centuria - 1/2 mile dirt oval (1981 - 1986) (1988 - 1989)
    1/4 mile dirt oval (1991 - present) / (aka: Centuria Speedway)

Sam's Capital Super Speedway - see: Madison Int'l Speedway

Sam's Super Speedway - Wausau / built by Sam Bartus
    1/4 mile dirt oval (late 1950's) / located south of town

Seymour Tri-Oval Raceway - Seymour - 1/4 mile dirt oval (c.1946 - late 1950's)
    1/2 mile dirt oval (1966 - 1977) (1982 - 1987) / (aka: Seymour Speedway)
    1/3 mile dirt oval (1988 - present) / at the Outagamie County Fairgrounds

Shannon - dirt oval (1954)

Shawano Speedway - Shawano / located at the Shawano County Fairgrounds
    1/2 mile dirt oval (August, 1940) (9/06/46 - present)
    1/4 mile dirt oval (early 1950's) / the old grandstands blew down in 1941

Sheboygan - 1/4 mile dirt oval (late 1950's) / south of town / now part of I-43

Sheboygan County Fair Speedway - Plymouth / at the Sheboygan Co. Fairgrounds
    1/2 mile dirt oval (1920's - c.1941) (c.1946 - late 1950's)
    1/4 mile dirt oval (1951 - present) / (aka: Plymouth Speedway)

Sheridan Road Midget Speedway - see: Olli O'Mara's Ballpark

Shiocton Speedway - Shiocton - 1/4 mile paved oval (early 1960's - 1973)

Slinger Super Speedway - Slinger - 1/4 mile dirt oval (c.9/15/48 - 1973)
    1/4 mile high banked paved oval (1974 - present) / (aka: Slinger Speedway)
    built by Rollie Heder & Bill Johnson, Sr.

South Milwaukee (Carrolville) - 5/8 mile dirt oval (c.1928 - 1931)
    the promoter was Grover Horn / located near the shore of Lake Michigan
    the site is now a water filtration plant

Spooner - dirt oval (early 1960's)

Most people would never recognize this track as Slinger Speedway. The track is now paved an high banked. - Armin Krueger photo (Don Fischer collection).

Spring Green - 1/4 mile dirt oval (late 1940's)

State Park Speedway - Wausau / (aka: Sam's Super Speedway)
    1/5 & 1/4 mile dirt ovals (1951 - late 1950's)
    1/4 mile paved oval (1959 - present) / (aka: Wausau Speedway)

Stratford Speedway - Stratford - 1/4 mile dirt oval (c.1958 - 1960)
    Dick Trickle, Tom Reffner & Marv Marzofka careers started here in 1958
    1/4 mile paved oval (1961 & 1962)

Sturgeon Bay Fairgrounds - see: Thunder Hill Raceway

Super 141 Speedway - see: One-Forty-One (141) Speedway

Superior Speedway - Superior / located at the Head of the Lakes Fairgrounds
    1/2 mile dirt oval (c.8/04/16 - 8/17/41) (8/12/46 - c.1953)
    3/8 mile dirt oval (6/24/62 - present) / (aka: Tri-State Speedway)
    (aka: Douglas County Tri-State Fairgrounds

Thunder Hill Raceway - Sturgeon Bay / at the Door County Fairgrounds
    1/3 mile dirt oval (c.1970 - 1985) (1987 - present)
    (aka: Door County Speedway)

Tomah Fairgrounds - Tomah / located at the Monroe County Fairgrounds
    1/2 mile dirt oval (7/03/38 - 1939)

Tomah/Sparta Speedway - Tomah / (aka: Wild Bill's Track-N-Trail)
    1/4 mile paved oval (1964 - 1969) (1971) (1981 - 1984) (1987 - present)
    (aka: Tomah Speedway)

Tomahawk Speedway - Tomahawk - 1/4 mile paved oval (1963 - present)

Tri-County Speedway - see: Central Wisconsin Speedway

Tri-Oval Speedway - see: River Raceway Tri-Oval

Tri-State Speedway - see: Superior Speedway

Valley Raceways - Waumandee - 1/4 mile dirt oval (c.1964 - c.1967)

Viroqua Fairgrounds - Viroqua / located at the Vernon County Fairgrounds
   1/2 mile dirt oval (early 1950's)

Watertown - dirt oval (1920's or 1930's)

Waupaca - dirt oval (years unknown)

Wausau - dirt oval (years unknown) / located on the east side of town

Wausau Fairgrounds - Wausau / located at the Wisconsin Valley Fairgrounds
   1/2 mile dirt oval (1924) (c.8/14/47 - 1982) / (aka: Marathon Park)

Wausau - also see: Kelly, Sam's Super Speedway, State Park

Wauwatosa (Milwaukee) - 7.88 mile city street road course (10/01/12 - 10/05/12)
   (aka: Milwaukee Grand Prix) / (aka: PBR Trophy Race) < held on 10/03/12
   David Bruce-Brown fatally injured in a practice run on 10/01/12

West Bend - 1/2 mile dirt oval (1920's)

Westfield Fairgrounds - Westfield / located at the Marquette County Fairgrounds
   1/2 mile dirt oval (c.1963 - c.1965)

Wild Bill's Track-N-Trail - see: Tomah Speedway

Wilmot Hills - Milwaukee - 1.5 mile paved road course (5/26/53 - 1965)

Wilmot Speedway - Wilmot / located at the Kenosha County Fairgrounds
   1/3 mile dirt oval (1973 - present) / replaced old Kenosha County Speedway

Wisconsin Dells Motor Speedway - Wis. Dells - 1/4 mile paved oval (5/30/63 - 1970)
   1/3 mile paved oval (1971 - present) / (aka: Dells Motor Speedway)

Wisconsin Int'l Raceway - Kaukauna - 1/4 mile dirt oval (1964)
   1/4 mile paved dragstrip (1964 - present) / (aka: KK Sports Arena)
   1/4 mile paved oval (1965 - present)   /   1/2 mile dirt oval (1967)
   1/2 mile paved oval (1968 - present)
   Larry Detjens was fatally injured in an ARTGO race here on 8/01/81

Wisconsin Rapids - see: Crown Speedway & Griffin Park

Wisconsin State Fair Coliseum - Milwaukee (West Allis) / at State Fairgrounds
   1/10 mile indoor dirt oval (10/10/35 - 11/25/37) (10/20/39 - 12/15/39)

Wisconsin State Fairgrounds Ballpark - Milwaukee (West Allis)
   1/5 mile dirt (cinder) oval (9/06/34 - 7/21/39)
   built for midget racing / was located at a football stadium

Wisconsin State Fairgrounds - see: Milwaukee Mile

Wonderland Park - Milwaukee - dirt oval (1910 - 1914)
   held motorcycle races in a district of Milwaukee known as Blue Mound

Yellow River Speedway - see: Marshfield Super Speedway

550

WYOMING

Bar-Nunn Dragway - Casper - 1/4 mile paved dragstrip (c.1964)

Basin Fairgrounds - Basin - 1/4 mile dirt oval (1950's) / (aka: Big Horn Co. Fair)

Big Country Speedway - Cheyenne - 1/5 mile dirt oval (1949 - c.1964)
1/5 mile paved oval (c.1965 - present) / (aka: Intermountain Speedway)

Big Horn Dragway - Greybull - 1/4 mile paved dragstrip (c.1963 - c.1969)

Casper - dirt oval (late 1960's - early 1970's) / located 15 miles from town

Casper Fairgrounds - Casper / located at the Central Wyoming Fairgrounds
1/2 mile dirt oval (c.7/15/51 - c.1966)

Casper Rodeo Grounds - Casper - 1/4 mile dirt oval (1938)

Casper Speedway - Casper / (aka: Central Wyoming Speedway)
1/2 mile dirt oval (1977 - present) / located north of town

Cheyenne Dragway - Cheyenne - 1/4 mile paved dragstrip (c.1961 - c.1970)

Douglas Fairgrounds - see: Wyoming State Fairgrounds

Douglas Int'l Raceway - Douglas - 1/4 mile paved dragstrip (1985 - present)

Gillette Speedway - Gillette / (aka: Thunder Speedway)
3/8 mile dirt oval (1974 - present)

Goekins Speedway - Rock Springs - 3/8 mile dirt oval (1968 - 1972)

Green River - 3/8 mile dirt oval (mid-1970's) / located near downtown

Guernsey - 1/2 mile dirt oval (1964)

Hudson Speedway - Hudson - 1/3 mile dirt oval (c.1955 - c.1957)

Interstate Speedway - Sheridan - 3/8 mile dirt oval (1973 - 1978)

Jericho Raceway - Green River - 1/4 mile dirt oval (c.1977 - 1979)

Laramie - dirt oval (late 1940's)

Moorcroft Speedway - Moorcroft - 3/8 mile dirt oval (c.1974 - 1975)

Rawlins Speedway - Rawlins - 1/4 mile dirt oval (1991 - present)

Riverton Speedway - Riverton - 3/8 mile dirt oval (1971 - present)

Rocky Mountain Int'l Raceway - see: Sweetwater Speedway

Sheridan - 1/2 mile dirt oval (1908)

Sweetwater Speedway - Green River / at the Sweetwater County Fairgrounds
3/8 mile dirt oval (1981 - present) / (aka: Rocky Mountain Int'l Raceway)

Wheatland - dirt oval (years unknown) / ran motorcycles

Wyoming State Fairgrounds - Douglas - 1/2 mile dirt oval (1910's)

CANADIAN TRACKS

ALBERTA

Battle River Stock Car Track - see: Tri Way Oval Raceway

Blairmore - dirt oval (1970) / maybe Lundbreck or Burmis

Border City Raceway - see: Saskatchewan chapter

Breckenridge Speedway - Edmonton - dirt oval (1950 - c.1951)
    this track was possibly at the same location as the Edmonton Expo

Bridge County Raceway - Lethbridge - 3/8 mile dirt oval (6/01/91 - present)

Brooks - 1/2 mile dirt oval (c.1946 - c.1950)

Brooks - dirt oval (1950's & 1960's) / second track in Brooks

Brooks Speedway - Brooks / (aka: Brooks Raceway)
    3/8 mile dirt oval (c.1977 - 1984) / third track in Brooks

Burmis - dirt oval (c.1964 - c.1970) / maybe Blairmore or Lundbreck

Calgary - dirt oval (1960's) / not the same track as Circle 8 Speedway

Calgary Int'l Raceway - Calgary / 1/4 mile paved dragstrip (c.1967 - c.1984)
    paved road course (c.1967) / (aka: Shepherd Raceways)
    same site as Race City Speedway Motorsports Park

Calgary Stampede - Calgary / (aka: Calgary Industrial Exhibition)
    1/2 mile dirt oval (1915 - c.1935) (1946 - 1947) (7/31/50) / (aka: Victoria Park)

Calgary - also see: Circle 8, Race City, Springbank, Stampede.

Calmar Raceway - Calmar - 3/10 (1/4) mile dirt oval (1983 - 1990)

Capital Raceway - Edmonton - 1/4 mile paved dragstrip (8/23/92 - present)
    3/8 mile dirt oval (1991 - present) / (aka: Capital City Raceway Park)
    1.7 mile paved road course (1994 - present)

Chinook Speedway - Lethbridge - dirt oval (1955 & 1956) (1961 - 1963)

Circle 8 Speedway - Calgary - 1/4 mile dirt oval (1966)
    1/4 mile paved oval (1967 - 1981) / (aka: Stampede Speedway)

Cobra Raceway - see: Edmonton Int'l Speedway

Colinton - dirt oval (1929)

Crossroads Speedway - Red Deer / (aka: Red Deer Speedway)
    1/4 mile dirt oval (7/12/64 - 1977)

Edmonton Exhibition - Edmonton / possibly called Breckenridge Speedway
    1/2 mile dirt oval (c.1917 - c.1920) (1926) (1934 & 1935) (1949 & 1950)

Edmonton Int'l Speedway - Edmonton - 1/4 mile paved oval (c.1954 - 1983)
     1/4 mile paved dragstrip (5/21/67 - 1983) / (aka: Speedway Park)
     1.5, 2.0 & 2.46 mile paved road course (7/03/65 - 1983)
     proposed 7/8 mile paved oval in 1971 / (aka: Cobra Raceway)
     ran SCCA TA races on road course in 1971 & 1973

Edmonton - paved dragstrip (c.1962) / organized drag racing on a public highway

Edmonton - also see: Breckenridge, Capital City, Westwind Oval

Fort Macleod - paved road course (1965) / probably ran on airport runways

Fort McMurray Raceway - Fort McMurray - 5/16 mile dirt oval (1976 - c.1990)
     (aka: Fort McMurray Stock Car Track)

Grande Prairie Speedway - Grande Prairie - 3/8 mile dirt oval (1973 - present)

High Level - dirt oval (1960's)

High River - dirt oval (c.1950)

Lacombe - 1/2 mile dirt oval (c.1950)

Lethbridge Expo Grounds - Lethbridge / (aka: Lethbridge Expo Speedway)
     1/2 mile dirt oval (c.1926) (c.7/20/49 - c.6/20/51) (1966 & 1967)
     1/4 mile paved oval (1968 - c.1971)

Lethbridge - also see: Bridge County Raceway, Chinook Speedway

Lundbreck - dirt oval (c.1964 - c.1970) / maybe Blairmore or Burmis

M.H.B.R.A. Raceway - Medicine Hat - 1/4 mile paved dragstrip (c.1987 - 1990)

McMurray Raceway Park - Fort McMurray - dirt oval (year unknown)

Medicine Hat - dirt oval (1950's or 1960's)

Medicine Hat Motor Plex - Medicine Hat / (aka: M.H.B.R.A. Raceway)
     1/8 mile paved dragstrip (1990 - present) / (aka: Medicine Hat Speedway)
     3/10 mile dirt oval (8/14/93 - present) / old oval track about 1/4 mile away

Medicine Hat Speedway - Medicine Hat - 1/4 mile dirt oval (1986 - 1993)
     (aka: Medicine Hat Race Track) / The EPA was concerned because the track
     was located next to a chemical plant / so the chemical plant bought
     the property and the track was rebuilt at the Medicine Hat Motor Plex

Mountain View Raceway - see: Yellowhead Raceway

Nanton - 1/2 mile dirt oval (c.1950)

Prairie Trail - Coronation - 1/4 mile dirt oval (c.1986 - c.1989)

Race City Speedway Motorsports Park - Calgary / (aka: Race City Speedway)
     1/4 mile paved dragstrip (5/01/86 - present)
     1/2 mile paved oval (1985 - present) / same site as Calgary Int'l Raceway
     2.0 mile paved road course (1985 - present)

Red Deer - 1/2 mile dirt oval (c.1946 - c.1950)

Red Deer Speedway - see: Crossroads Speedway

Sanguda Speedway - Sanguda - 3/8 mile dirt oval (May, 1991 - present)

Semons - 1/2 mile dirt oval (1919) / Emory Collins won his first race here

Shepherd Raceways - see: Calgary Int'l Raceway

Speedway Park - see: Edmonton Int'l Speedway

Springbank Speedway - Calgary - dirt oval (1950 - 1958)

Stampede Speedway - Calgary - 3/8 mile dirt oval (c.1981 - 1987)
    bleachers burned down in 1987

Stampede Speedway - see: Circle 8 Speedway

Standard Speedbowl - Standard - 1/4 mile dirt oval (mid-1960's - 1982)

Sunset Speedway - Wetaskiwin - 1/4 mile dirt oval (1969 - present)

Taber Speedway - Taber - dirt oval (1970)

Tailcreek Speedway - Alix - 3/8 mile dirt oval (1988 - present)

Three Hills - dirt oval (c.1950)

Tri Way Oval Raceway - Sedgewick - 3/8 mile dirt oval (1988 - present)
    (aka: Battle River Stock Car Track)

Victoria Park - see: Calgary Stampede

Vulcan - dirt oval (years unknown)

Westwind Oval - Edmonton / site is now a housing development
    1/3 mile paved oval (c.7/05/69 - c.1977)

Yellowhead Raceway - Hinton / (aka: Mountain View Raceway)
    1/2 (3/8) mile dirt oval (1974 - present)

*The Race City Speedway Motorsports Park complex. The track has a dragstrip,
road course and an oval track. - Official track photo*

BRITISH COLUMBIA

Abbotsford Airport - Abbotsford - paved dragstrip (1953 - 1957)
2.0 mile paved road course (c.1956 - 4/07/57) / races were on runways

Abbotsford Expo - Abbotsford / located at the Central Fraser Valley Exhibition
1/4 mile dirt oval (1992 - present) / Mini-stocks & Figure Eights

Action Raceway - see: Langley Speedway

Agassiz Speedway - see: Kent Raceway

Agrodome - Vancouver - 1/8 mile indoor oval (11/27/65 - 1969) (1971)

Ashcroft - 1/4 mile dirt oval (1983)

Big Horn Speedway - Keremeos - 3/8 mile dirt oval (1983 - 1985)

Billy Foster Memorial Speedway - Westbank - paved oval (5/22/67 - c.1968)

Boundry Bay Int'l Raceway - Delta - 1/4 mile paved dragstrip (c.1972 - c.1975)
located at the Boundry Bay Airport

Calameda Raceway - Castlegar - 1/2 mile dirt (c.1962 - c.1964)

Callister Park - Vancouver - dirt oval (late 1940's) / race midgets
located next to Pacific National Expo / held demo-derbies in 1960's

Caribou Motorsports Club Track - see: Lake Auto Race Track

Cassidy Airport - Nanaimo - paved road course on runways (1955)

Cassidy Speedway - Nanaimo - 3/8 mile dirt oval (1983 - present)
300 foot dirt dragstrip (1972 - present)

*Cassidy Speedway opened in 1983 and runs weekly sprint car races on the 3/8
mile dirt oval. - Official track photo.*

Central Fraser Valley Expo - Abbotsford - 1/4 mile dirt oval (1993)

Clearwater Stock Car Track - Clearwater - 6/10 mile dirt oval (1989 - present)

Cloverdale Expo Grounds - Cloverdale - 1/2 mile dirt oval (1950's)

Cloverdale Speedway - Cloverdale - 1/4 mile dirt oval (June, 1946 - 1946)

Colwood Race Track - Victoria / was a horse track
    1.125 mile dirt oval (1933 & 1934) (Labour Day, 1960)

Con Jones Park - Vancouver - 1/5 mile dirt oval (c.7/25/39 - c.8/19/39)

Cranbrook Int'l Speedway - Cranbrook - 3/8 mile paved oval (1970 - present)
    (aka: Echo Field Raceway)

Digney Speedway - Burnaby - 1/4 mile paved oval (c.7/08/48 - c.1958)

Duncan Int'l Raceway - see: Van Isle Dragways

Echo Field Raceway - see: Cranbrook Int'l Speedway

False Creek Speedway - Vancouver - 1/4 mile paved oval (1957 - 9/01/62)
    now the location of a city park / the track is used as a jogging track

Gold Pan Speedway - Quesnel - 1/4 mile paved oval (7/23/72 - present)
    (aka: Quesnel Speedway)

Grandview Bowl - Nanaimo - 3/10 mile paved oval (1958 - 1973) (1976 - 1986)

Look close at this jogging track in a city park in Vancouver and you can see the people strolling on the asphalt track. This track was the former False Creek Speedway that ran from 1957 to 1962. - Robert G. Hunter photo.

Haney Speedway - Haney - 1/4 mile dirt oval (1959 - 1961)
1/4 mile paved oval (1961 - c.7/19/64)

Har-Win Speedway - Kamloops - dirt oval (c.1961 - c.1962) / possibly Schiedam

Hasting's Park - Vancouver - 1.0 mile dirt oval (1913) (1924 - 8/20/27)
the track was a horse track

Hasting's Park - Vancouver / (aka: Pacific National Expo)
1/8 mile paved parking lot oval (c.1975 - present) / old horse track
ran mini-stocks during the World's Fair on a square shaped track

Intervalley Speedway - see: Schiedam Raceway

Kamloops Expo Grounds - Kamloops - dirt oval (6/07/47 & 6/08/47)

Kamloops - paved dragstrip (1970's) / on roads in an industrial park

Kelowna Motor Sport Park - Kelowna / (aka: Siemalt Speedway Park)
1/8 mile paved dragstrip (c.1983 - 1989) (1992)

Kent Raceways - Agassiz - 1/4 mile dirt oval (1970 - c.1977)
1/4 mile paved oval (1978 - present) / (aka: Agassiz Speedway)

Kimberly - 1/4 mile paved dragstrip (c.1967) / East Kootenay Timing Association

Lake Auto Race Track - Williams Lake (aka: Caribou Motorsports Club Track)
3/8 mile dirt oval (1959 - 1970) / located five miles south of town
3/8 mile paved oval (1971 - 1992) / to moved to new location in 1994

Lake Auto Race Track - Williams Lake / located two miles west of town
3/8 mile paved oval (1994 - present)

Langford Speedway - Victoria - 3/8 mile dirt oval (1936) / built in 1936
3/8 mile paved oval (1937 - c.8/17/41) (May, 1946 - 1950)
closed in 1950 for enlargements to a nearby school / (aka: Langford Track)

Langley Speedway - Surrey / (aka: Action Raceway)
3/8 mile paved oval (6/13/65 - 9/15/84)

Lansdowne Park - Richmond - dirt oval (teens or 1920's) / was a horse track

Mahon Park - North Vancouver - 1/4 mile dirt oval (8/24/46 - 9/02/46)

Merritt Stock Car Track - Merritt - 1/4 mile dirt oval (June, 1992 - present)

Mile "Zero" Speedway - Dawson Creek - 3/8 mile dirt oval (1989 - present)

Millstream - Victoria - 3/8 mile paved oval (c.1957 - c.9/15/57)
this track was possibly Western Speedway

Mission Raceway - Mission - 1/4 mile paved dragstrip (8/26/65 - 10/01/78)
about a quarter mile from current Mission Raceway / now an industrial park

Mission Raceway Park - Mission - 300 foot sand dragstrip (1980's - 1991)
1/6 mile dirt oval (1990 - 1993) / (aka: Mission Dragway)
1/4 mile paved dragstrip (3/15/92 - present)
1.2 mile paved road course (1993 - present) / (aka: Mission Raceway)
the oval was dismantled to make room for more dragstrip parking

Molson Indy Vancouver - Vancouver / located at British Columbia Place Stadium
   1.7 mile paved city street road course (Sept., 1990 - present) / runs IndyCars

Mountain Side Raceways - Lillooet - 1/4 mile dirt oval (1983 - present)

Moyer Park - Cranbrook - 1/4 mile dirt oval (1950's - 1960's)

Nanaimo Speedway - Nanaimo - 3/8 mile dirt oval (c.1932)

Nanaimo - also see: Cassidy, Grandview Bowl

Nl'Akapxm Eagle Motorplex - Ashcroft / located on an Indian Reservation
   1/4 mile paved dragstrip (c.1987 - present) / located near Cache Creek

North Central Raceway - Prince George - 1/4 mile dragstrip (c.1981 - present)

North Island Exhibition Grounds - Port Hardy / (aka: Triport Expo Grounds)
   1/4 mile dirt oval (1991 - present)

Oyster River Raceway - see: Saratoga Speedway

Oyster River Speedway - Campbell River - dirt oval (5/22/66 - 1968)

P.G.A.R.A. Speedway Park - Prince George - 3/8 mile paved oval (1959 - 1984)
   located 2 miles west of town on Highway 16 / moved to new location in 1985

P.G.A.R.A. Speedway Park - Prince George - 3/8 mile paved oval (1985 - present)
   located three miles east of town on Highway 16

Patterson Park - Ladner - 1/2 mile dirt oval (1954) / a horse track

Penticton - dirt oval (1966) / not the same as Penticton Speedway

Penticton Speedway - Penticton / (aka: Queens Park Speedway)
   1/3 mile dirt oval (1969 - 1971) / (aka: (Penticton Raceway)
   1/4 mile paved oval (1971 - c.1981) (c.1987 - 1994) / (aka: Sun Bowl)

Piston Pilots Speedway - Agassiz - 3/10 mile dirt oval (1957 & 1958)

Port Hardy Expo - see: North Island Exhibition Grounds

Powell River - 1/4 mile dirt oval (c.1971 - c.1975)

Prince Rupert - dirt oval (years unknown)

Queens Park Speedway - see: Penticton Speedway

Quesnel - 1/4 mile dirt oval (1973 - 1974) / located on an old highway

Quesnel Speedway - Quesnel - dirt oval (1950's - late 1960's)

Quesnel Speedway - see: Gold Pan Speedway

Rocky Mountain Raceway - Valemount - 1/4 mile dirt oval (1993 - present)
   (aka: Valemount Stock Car Track)

Salmo - 3/8 mile dirt oval (1970's)

Salmon Arm - paved dragstrip (1970's) / possibly on public roads

San Cobble Dragway - Cobble Hill - 1/4 mile paved dragstrip (1960 - 4/09/67)
    operated by the Quarter Milers Club of Victoria / used an industrial road

Saratoga Speedway - Courtenay / (aka: Oyster River Raceway)
    5/16 mile paved oval (1966 - present) / drags used front straight of oval
    300 foot paved dragstrip (c.1984 - c.1986)

Schiedam Raceway - Kamloops - 1/4 mile paved oval (c.1971 - c.1972) (1976 - 1978)
    (aka: Intervalley Speedway)

Shearing Speedway - Cobble Hill - 1/4 mile paved oval (c.10/12/52 - c.9/11/54)

Siemalt Speedway Park - see: Kelowna Motor Sports Park

Smithers - oval (c.1971)

Sun Bowl - Penticton - 1/4 mile dirt oval (c.5/24/50 - c.1950)
    possible the same as the current Penticton Speedway

Sun Bowl - see: Penticton Speedway

Terrace Speedway - Terrace - 3/8 mile dirt oval (1966 - 1975)
    1/3 mile paved oval (1976 - present)

Tillicum Raceway - Vernon - 3/8 mile paved oval (c.1970 - c.1975)

Triport Expo Grounds - see: North Island Exhibition Grounds

Valemount Stock Car Track - see: Rocky Mountain Raceway

Van Isle Dragways - Mill Bay - 1/4 mile paved dragstrip (5/07/67 - 9/24/72)
    (aka: San Cobble Raceways) / (aka: Duncan Int'l Raceway)
    the shutdown area was uphill (15 degrees)

Vancouver Pavilion - Vancouver - indoor oval (late 1930's)

Vancouver - also see: Agrodome, Callister, Con Jones, False Creek, Hasting's,
    Mahon Park, Molson Indy

Victoria Expo - Victoria / located at the Willows Expo Grounds
    1/2 mile dirt oval (1910's & 1920's) (1934 & 1935) (1946 - 1948)

Victoria - also see: Colwood, Langford, Millstream, Western

Western Speedway - Victoria - 1/2 mile dirt oval (5/22/54 - June, 1957)
    4/10 mile paved oval (June, 1957 - present) / built by Andre Cottyn
    1/5 mile paved oval (c.1968 - c.1971) / dragstrip uses part of oval track
    1/8 mile paved dragstrip (May, 1984 - present)
    1.0 mile paved road course (6/12/66 - 1983) / road course now a waterslide

Westwood Motorsports Park - Port Coquitlam / (aka: Westwood)
    1.8 mile paved road course (7/26/59 - 10/08/90) / SCCA TA races 1977-1980

Wonderland Speedway - Langley - 1/4 mile dirt oval (1950's)

MANITOBA

Austin Raceway and Park - Austin - 3/8 mile dirt oval (1980)

BG's Speedway - Treherne - 1/2 mile dirt oval (1982)

Bison Dragway - Bison - 1/4 mile paved dragstrip (c.1965 - c.1975)
(aka: Keystone Dragway) / located about 32 miles east of Winnipeg

Brandon Expo Grounds - Brandon / (aka: Brandon Provincial Exhibition)
1/2 mile dirt oval (c.1917 - 7/31/18) (c.1926 - 1927) (7/07/50)
1/4 mile dirt oval (1974) / ran one race on 1/4 mile track

Brookland Stadium - Winnipeg - 1/4 mile paved oval (c.1958 - c.1971)

Centenial Speedway - Thompson - 1/2 mile dirt oval (1967 - present)

Chater Raceway - Brandon - 1/3 mile dirt oval (c.1967 - c.1974)

Crown Valley Raceways - New Bothwell - 1/8 mile dirt oval (1980 - 1989)

Dragways International - see: Viking Dragway

Gimli Motorsports Park - Gimli - 1.33 mile paved road course (1973 - present)
same site as Viking Dragway / located at an airport

Great Plains Speedway - Portage la Prairie - 1/4 mile dirt oval (late 1960's) (1983)

Keystone Dragway (Raceway) - see: Bison Dragway

McDonald Airport - Winnipeg - paved road course (c.1966 - c.1971)
formerly a Royal Canadian Air Force World War II airbase

Pacemakers Motor Speedway - Dauphin - 1/4 mile dirt oval (1989 - 1991)

Portage la Prairie Expo - Portage la Prairie - 1/2 mile dirt oval (7/27/51)

Rapid City Speedway - Rapid City - 1/2 mile dirt oval (1968 - 1986)

Saint Francios Xavier Speedway - (location unknown) - dirt oval (early 1960's)

Salt Plains Raceway - Gladstone - 1/2 mile dirt oval (1969 - 1980)

Souris Speedway - Souris - 5/16 mile dirt oval (5/31/92 - present)

Swan Valley Speedway - Swan River - 1/4 mile dirt oval (1986 - present)
(aka: Swan River Stock Car Track)

Turtle Mountain Raceway - Boissevain - 1/4 mile dirt oval (early 1970's)

Valley West Speedway - The Pas - 1/4 mile dirt oval (1968 - present)

Victory Lane Speedway - Winnipeg - 1/4 mile dirt oval (1994 - present)

Viking Dragway - Gimli - 1/4 mile paved dragstrip (c.1972 - present)
(aka: Dragways International) / located at Gimli Motorsports Park

Whittier Park Speedway - Winnipeg - dirt oval (6/27/52)

Winnipeg Expo - Winnipeg / at the Winnipeg Industrial & Agri Exhibition
1/2 mile dirt oval (c.7/10/15 - c.1925) (1936)

Winnipeg - also see: Brookland Stadium, Victory Lane, Whittier Park

Winnipeg Speedway - Winnipeg - 1/2 mile dirt oval (July, 1973 - present)

NEW BRUNSWICK

Airport Raceway - Saint John - oval (years unknown)

Atlantic Dragway - see: Pennfield Int'l Dragway

Brookside Speedway - Nashwaaksis - 1/4 mile paved oval (1975)

Cedar Mills Int'l Speedway - Saint Stephen - 1/4 mile dirt oval (1990 - 1991)
1/4 mile paved oval (1992 - present)

Danny's Speedbowl - Bathurst - 1/4 mile paved oval (c.1967 - 1984)

Douglastown Speedways - see: McKay Speedway

Exhibition Park - Saint John - 1/4 mile oval (c.1951 - c.9/20/52)

Fredericton Speedway - Fredericton - 1/4 mile dirt oval (1994 - present)

Hammond River Raceway - Nauwigewauk - 1/4 mile paved oval (1966 - present)

McEwen's Speedway - Moncton - 1/4 mile dirt oval (1967 - 1970)

McKay Speedway - Douglastown / (aka: Douglastown Speedways)
1/3 mile paved oval (1968 - 1974) (1982 - present) / on Williston Road
(aka: Williston Speedway) / (aka: Miramichi Speedway)

*A fourth turn look at Hammond River Raceway in Niauwigewauk in 1993.
The 1/4 mile paved oval track opened in 1966. - Allan E. Brown photo.*

Renegade Raceway near Fredericton was one of the many primitive tracks that have existed over the years. There was no grandstands at this dirt track. The fans sat on the hillside. - Allan E. Brown photo.

Miramichi Speedway - see: McKay Speedway

New Brunswick Int'l Speedway - Fredericton
1/3 mile asphalt oval (1994 - present)

Pennfield Int'l Dragway - Pennfield - 1/4 mile paved dragstrip (c.1963 - present)
paved road course (early 1970's) / (aka: Atlantic Dragway) / an old air base
(aka: Pennfield Dragway)

Petty Raceway - Moncton - 1/3 mile paved oval (10/09/83 - present)

Renegade Raceway - Fredericton - 1/4 mile dirt oval (1993) / northeast of town

River Glade Speedway - River Glade - 1/4 mile dirt oval (1964)
1/4 mile paved oval (June, 1965 - present)

Scoudouc Dragway - Moncton - 1/4 mile paved dragstrip (c.1967 - c.1970)
paved road course (early 1970's) / on an old military base

Williston Speedway - see: McKay Speedway

NEWFOUNDLAND

Argentia Circuit - St. John's - 2.5 mile paved road course (1960's - 1980)
located on an old naval air base

Cornerbrook - 1/4 mile paved dragstrip (1960's)
paved oval (1960's)

St. John's - 1.1 mile paved city street road course (7/28/74)

NOVA SCOTIA

Atlantic Motorsports Park - Halifax
    1.6 mile paved road course (August, 1974 - present)

Atlantic Speedway - Hammond Plains / (aka: Dartmouth Int'l Speedway)
    1/2 mile paved oval (c.1973 - c.1980) / now an amusement park

Beaverbank - dirt oval (early 1950's)

Bud's Speedway - see: Sydney Speedway

Chester - dirt oval (late 1940's & 1950's)

Dartmouth Int'l Speedway - see: Atlantic Speedway

Diebert - paved road course (early 1970's) / on a military air base

Drag City Dragway - see: Sackville Int'l Raceway

Green Acres - Nine Mile River - 1/4 mile dirt oval (years unknown)

Greenwood - 1/4 mile dirt oval (c.1963 - c.1970)

Havre Boucher Speedway - Pictou - 1/5 mile paved oval (c.1967)

Halifax-Dartmouth Int'l Speedway - see: Sackville Int'l Raceway

Island Speedway - see: Sydney Speedway

Lawrencetown - 1/4 mile paved oval (1965 - 1968)

Liverpool Raceway - Liverpool - 1/4 mile dirt oval (1992 - present)

MacDonald Speedway - Port Hood - 1/4 mile dirt oval (1992)

MacDonald Speedway had a short life-span as it only ran during the 1992 season. Although the track was overgrown with weeds in 1993 when this picture was taken this sign held up well. - Allan E. Brown photo.

Scotia Speedworld as seen from the air. The track is located a few miles north of Halifax. - Official track photo.

Maitland Dragway - Maitland
    1/4 mile paved dragstrip (1986 - 1990) (1992 - present)

Moosehead Grand Prix - Halifax / located in the Citadel Hill Park
    1.9 km paved city street road course (10/08/90 - 1992) / ran AIS IndyCars
    1.4 km paved city street road course (1993 - present)

Mountain Raceway - New Glasgow - dirt oval (early 1960's)

North River - oval (c.1958 - c.1962)

Onslow Speedway - Truro - 1/4 mile dirt oval (c.1965 - 1978)
    1/4 mile paved oval (1979 - 1984) (1986 - 1989) (1992)

Port Hood - 1/4 mile dirt oval (c.1962 - c.1965)

Riverside Speedway - Antigonish - 1/3 mile paved oval (1973 - present)

Sable Raceway - Sable River - 1/4 mile dirt oval (1989 - 1992)

Sackville Int'l Raceway - Sackville - 1/4 mile paved dragstrip (c.1969 - c.1989)
    1/4 mile paved oval (1982) / (aka: Drag City Dragway)
    (aka: Halifax-Dartmouth Int'l Speedway)

Scotia Speedworld - Halifax - 1/4 mile paved oval (1988 - present)

Sydney Speedway - Sydney / (aka: Bud's Speedway) / (aka: Island Speedway)
    1/4 mile paved oval (1975 - 1985) (1987 - present)

Yarmouth - 1/3 mile dirt oval (c.1952 - 1965)
    1/3 mile paved oval (1966 - c.1969)

ONTARIO

Acton Ospringe Speedway - Acton - 1/4 mile paved oval (c.1968 - c.1971)
locate north of Guelph

Ailsa Craig - dirt oval (early 1950's)

Ancaster Fairgrounds - Ancaster - 1/2 mile dirt oval (1952)

Ascot Park Speedway - Tillsonburg - 1/3 mile dirt oval (c.6/30/52 - c.1952)

Atherton Speedway - Simcoe - 1/2 mile dirt oval (c.1955 - c.1958)

Aylmer Fairgrounds - Aylmer - dirt oval (1952) / located on Highway 3

Barker Memorial Raceways - Geraldton - 5/16 mile dirt oval (1980 - 1983)

Barrie Speedway - Barrie - 1/4 mile paved oval (1965 - present)
(aka: Twin Cities Speedway)

Beamsville Fairgrounds - Lincoln (Beamsville) - 1/5 mile dirt oval (c.1949 - 1950)

Bell City Speedway - Lakefield - 1/4 mile dirt oval (6/04/67 - mid 1970)

Bismarck Speedway - Bismarck - 1/2 mile dirt oval (early 1950's) (c.1981)

Blue Water Speedway - see: Port Elgin Speedway

Bluebird Speedway - Windsor - oval (years unknown)

Brantford Speedway - Brantford / (aka: Mohawk Speedway)
1/4 mile paved oval (5/21/49 - c.1962)

Bridgeport Speedway - Kitchener - 1/4 mile paved oval (c.1950 - 1960)

*Two of the best Canadian drivers. Junior Hanley (#72) and arch rival Don
Biederman (#3) in 1978. Both drivers have won countless main events in
Canada as well as in the "States". - Dave Franks photo.*

*Earl Ross (#52) is the only Canadian to win a NASCAR Winston Cup race.
Here he races with Gary Bettenhausen at Michigan Int'l Speedway in 1974. -
Rolf Loss photo (Dave Franks collection).*

Brighton Speedway - Brighton - 1/4 mile dirt oval (1959 & 1960)
    1/4 mile paved oval (1961 - 1963)

Brighton Speedway Park - Brighton - 1/3 mile dirt oval (c.1969 - present)
    located next to the old Brighton Speedway / (aka: Brighton Speedway)

Brockville Ontario Speedway - Brockville / (aka: Brockville Speedway)
    1/4 mile dirt oval (1969 - 1984) (1986) (1992 - present)
    (aka: Brockville National Speedway) / (aka: Brockville Motor Speedway)

Burks Falls - dirt oval (c.1955)

C.N.E. - see: Canadian National Expo

Campbellford - 1/4 mile dirt oval (early 1960's)

Canadian National Expo (C.N.E.) - Toronto / built at a horse track
    1/2 mile dirt oval (1904) (1917 - c.1934) (1948) / ran IMCA from 1920-1928
    1/3 mile dirt oval (c.4/22/52 - c.1955)
    1/4 mile paved oval (c.1956 - c.1966) / ran a NASCAR GN 7/18/58
    Richard Petty started his very first race here on 7/18/58
    Lorne Greene (Bonanza TV fame) was the announcer here in 1950's

Capital City Speedway - Ottawa - 3/8 mile paved oval (1961 - present)
    3/8 mile dirt oval (mid 1970's) / pavement covered over with clay
    (aka: Ottawa Valley Speedway)

Cargill - 1/4 mile dirt oval (1971)

Carp Airport - Ottawa - paved road course on runways (8/27/55)

Cayuga Motorplex Park - Cayuga / (aka: Dragway Park) / (aka: Kohler Airfield)
    1/4 mile paved dragstrip (5/19/59 - present) / formerly a WWII airstrip
    (aka: Cayuga Motorsports Park) / (aka: Kohler Super Boss Dragway)
    (aka: Cayuga 1320 Dragway)

Cayuga Speedway is the largest active track in Ontario. The 5/8 mile track opened in 1967. - Official track photo.

Cayuga Speedway - Nelles Corners - 5/8 mile dirt oval (6/04/67 - 1967)
   5/8 mile paved oval (6/02/68 - present) / Chuck Boos won on 6/02/68
   1/5 mile paved oval (1970's - present) / Bob Slack was the promoter
   (aka: Cayuga Int'l Speedway)

Cedar Speedway - Petersborough - dirt oval (c.1969 - c,1970)
   (aka: Island Speedway)

Charlesbourg - (location unknown) - 1/3 mile paved oval (years unknown)
   possibly Charleston

Chatham - 1/2 mile dirt oval (5/24/36)

Checker Flag Motor Speedway - Windsor / (aka: Checker Flag National Speedway)
   3/8 mile dirt oval (1961 - 10/02/72) / (aka: Windsor Speedway)
   3/8 mile paved oval (1973 - 1992) / (aka: Checker Flag Int'l Speedway)
   property sold in late 1992 for a housing development

Chippewa Hills - 1/4 mile dirt oval (early 1950's)

Colborne - 1/4 mile dirt oval (early 1960's) / maybe Brighton Speedway

Conn - 1/4 mile dirt oval (years unknown)

Cornwall Motor Speedway - Cornwall / (aka: Cornwall Speedway)
   1/4 mile dirt oval (1969 - present) / (aka: Power Dam Speedway)

Dayus Stadium - Windsor - 1/3 mile dirt oval (5/24/46 - c.1950)
   1/3 mile paved oval (c.1953 - c.1955) / (aka: Windsor Motor Speedway)

Delaware Speedway Park - Delaware / (aka: Brodie's Delaware Raceway)
1/4 mile dirt oval (1949 - 1968) / (aka: Delaware Int'l Speedway)
1/2 mile paved oval (8/22/69 - present) / (aka: Delaware Raceway Park)

Dorchester Fairgrounds - Dorchester - 1/4 mile dirt oval (1986)

Dragway Park - see: Cayuga Motorsports Park

Dutch's Speedway - Tilbury - 1/3 mile dirt oval (June, c.1952 - c.1957)

East York Stadium - York - oval (7/31/52)

Edenvale Airport - see: Stayner Speedway

Elmwood Speedway - Sarnia - 1/4 mile paved oval (1958 & 1959)

Emo Speedway - Emo / at the Emo District Fairgrounds / west of Fort Francis
1/4 mile dirt oval (c.1975 - 1984) (1986 - present)

Essex - 1/2 mile dirt oval (c.8/01/38 - c.7/01/39)

Exhibition Place Stadium - Toronto - 1/3 mile paved oval (1990) / at the C.N.E.
this track was inside stadium the Toronto Blue Jays abandoned in 1989 when
the new Skydome was built a few blocks away / (aka: Canadian Nat'l Expo)

Fifth Line Speedway - see: Northern Raceways

Flamboro Speedway - Freelton - 1/3 mile paved oval (1962 - present)

Fort Erie - Fort Erie - 1.0 mile dirt oval (9/26/01 - 1909) / near Niagara Falls
was a horse track, but is not the same as later Fort Erie horse track
the 9/26/01 date was possibly the first auto race in Canada

The aerial view of Flamboro Speedway. The grandstands are packed on the
1/3 mile paved oval. - Official track photo.

568

Gasport Int'l Speedway - Port Colborne - 1/4 mile dirt oval (1957 - 1967)
1/3 mile dirt oval (1968 - 1983) / (aka: Humberstone Int'l Speedway)
4/10 mile dirt oval (1984 - present) / maybe paved at one time

Glendale Speedway - Sarnia - paved oval (c.7/18/52 - 1960's)
located on Murphy Road / the site is now housing

Golden Horseshoe Dragway - Georgetown - 1/4 mile paved dragstrip (c.1970)

Grand Bend Dragway - Grand Bend - 1/4 mile paved dragstrip (c.1963 - c.1969)

Grand River Speedway - Elora - 1/4 mile paved oval (1968 - 1971)

Green Acres - Goderich - paved road course (1958 & 1959)

Guelph - 1/4 mile paved oval (1952) / site is now the General Electric Building

Hamilton - paved road course on city streets

Harewood Acres - Jarvis / site is now a Texaco refinery / located near Nanticoke
3.0 mile paved road course (1951 - c.1970)

Harwich Speedway - see: Ridge Raceway

Hawkesbury - 1/4 mile dirt oval (8/23/83) / spectator killed at track's only race
maybe Maple Grove Speedway

Hayden Speedway Park - Sault Ste. Marie / located 20 miles north on Hwy 17
1/4 mile dirt oval (1968 & 1969) / the track had lots of rocks in it

Hide-A-Way Speedway - New Hamburg - 1/5 mile dirt oval (1968)
1/5 mile paved oval (1968 - c.1972)

Hockley Valley Speedway - (location unknown) - dirt oval (1969)

Humberstone Int'l Speedway - see: Gasport Int'l Speedway

Hurricane Speedway - Sudbury - 1/4 mile dirt oval (c.1974)

Island Speedway - see: Cedar Speedway

Jackpot Speedway - see: Model T Speedway

Kawartha Downs - Peterborough - 5/8 mile dirt oval (7/01/91) / at a horse track
ran a motorcycle race on the horse track

Kingston Speedway - Kingston / (aka: Kingston Int'l Speedway)
1/4 mile dirt oval (c.7/26/52 - 1976)

Kohler Super Boss Dragway (Airfield) - see: Cayuga Motorsports Park

Lambeth - dirt oval (late 1940's) / possibly Delaware Raceway Park

Lansdowne Park - Ottawa - 1/3 mile paved oval (1957 & 1958)

Leamington Fairgrounds - Leamington
1/2 mile dirt oval (5/24/37 - 5/24/39) (c.1980 - 1981)

Lions Head - oval (years unknown)

Lip-N-John Speedway - Holstein - 1/8 mile dirt oval (1969 & 1970)

London Fairgrounds - London / located at the Western Fairgrounds
　　1/2 mile dirt oval (8/30/47) (7/02/51) (1964) / ran IMCA sprints in 1947
　　(aka: Queens Park Speedway) / (aka: Western Fair Raceway)

London Motorsports Park - St. Thomas (Sparta) / (aka: St. Thomas Dragway)
　　1/4 mile paved dragstrip (5/27/62 - present)

Maple Grove Speedway - Hawkesbury - 1/4 mile dirt oval (c.1987 - 1989)

Maxville - dirt oval (1969)

Merrittville Speedway - Thorold - 1/3 mile dirt oval (7/01/52 - present)

Milverton Fairgrounds - Milverton - dirt oval (1952)

Model T Speedway - Williamsford - 1/2 mile dirt oval (1968 - 1972)
　　(aka: Jackpot Speedway) / located near McCullough Lake

Mohawk Dragway - Belleville (Deseronto) / (aka: Quinte Dragway)
　　1/4 mile paved dragstrip (c.1963 - c.1984)

Mohawk Speedway - see: Brantford Speedway

Molson Indy Toronto - Toronto - 1.78 mile paved road course (1986 - present)
　　CART Indy Car races on the streets in the Canadian National Expo

Mosport International Speedway - Mosport / (aka: Mosport Park)
　　2.459 mile paved road course (6/24/61 - present)
　　held Canadian G.P. (Formula One) here 1967, 1971, 1972, 1973, 1976 & 1977
　　1/2 mile dirt oval (1989) / ran practice only, but track was too sandy
　　1/2 mile paved oval (9/16/89 - present)

Mosquito Speedway - Nolalu - 1/4 mile clay oval (1994 - present)

Murillo Speedway - Murillo - 3/8 mile dirt oval (early 1970's)

Navan Speedway - Navan - 1/2 mile dirt oval (1975)

Nelson Int'l Speedway - see: Shannonville Motorsports Park

Nilestown Speedway - Nilestown - 1/4 mile paved oval (c.8/22/52 - 1974)
　　now the site of the Polish Canadian Recreation Centre, north of town

North Bay Motor Speedway - Sudbury - 1/5 mile dirt oval (early 1950's)
　　1/4 mile paved oval (June, c.1952 - c.1954) (1976 - 1984) (1987 - c.1992)
　　(aka: Sudbury Speedway) / (aka: Sunnydale Speedway)

Northern Raceways - Sault Ste. Marie / (aka: Fifth Line Speedway)
　　1/4 mile paved oval (1974 - 1987)

Northwood Raceway - Dryden - 1/4 mile dirt oval (1991 - present)

Norwich Fairgrounds - Norwich - 1/3 mile dirt oval (years unknown)

Norwood - 1/2 mile dirt oval (c.1927)

Oakwood Stadium - Toronto - 1/4 mile dirt oval (c.5/29/51 - c.10/20/51)
　　sold in May of 1952 for a food market to be erected on the site

Orillia - 1/3 mile dirt oval (c.7/05/52- c.1956) / flagman died in crash on 7/05/52

Oshawa Motor Speedway - Oshawa - 1/2 mile dirt oval (c.8/13/52 - c.1952)

Ottawa Auditorium - Ottawa - 1/10 mile indoor concrete oval (4/29/51)
1/10 mile indoor wood oval (12/12/58 & 12/13/58) / at Landsdowne Park

Ottawa Fairgrounds - Ottawa / located at the Central Canada Exhibition
1/2 mile dirt oval (1917 - 7/06/18) (10/17/34 - 8/24/35)
Ralph Hankinson was the promoter in 1934 & 1935

Ottawa Valley Speedway - see: Capital City Speedway

Ottawa - also see: Carp Airport, Lansdowne, Rockcliffe Airport

Paris Fairgrounds Speedway - Paris - 1/4 mile dirt oval (1985 - c.1990)

Paris Horse Track - Paris - dirt oval (years unknown) / possibly the Paris Fair

Peterborough Speedway - Peterborough - 1/4 mile paved oval (5/28/67 - 1992)
1/3 mile paved oval (1993 - present) / (aka: Westgate Speedway)

Pinecrest Speedway - Toronto (Maple) / torn down in 1977
1/4 mile paved oval (c.5/31/52 - August, 1976)
Don Biederman's started his driving career here

Port Elgin Speedway - Port Elgin - dirt oval (7/05/52 - 1960's)
(aka: Blue Water Speedway)

Powassan Track - Powassan - 1/4 mile dirt oval (years unknown)

Power Dam Speedway - see: Cornwall Motor Speedway

Queens Park Speedway - see: London Fairgrounds

Quinte Dragway - see: Mohawk Dragway

Raceland Speedway - see: South Buxton Speedway

Raleigh Raceway - see: South Buxton Speedway

Ridge Raceway - Ridgetown / (aka: The Ridge Raceway) (aka: Harwich Speedway)
1/3 mile dirt oval (1949 - c.1954) (1969 - 1978) (9/10/83 - present)

Riverview Raceway - Thunder Bay - 3/8 mile dirt oval (1967 - present)

Riverview Speedway - Trenton - 1/4 mile dirt oval (c.1962 - c.1971)

Rockliffe Airport - Ottawa - paved road course (1970)

Saint Thomas Dragway - see: London Motorsports Park

Saint Thomas Speedway - St. Thomas - oval (June, 1952 - 1952)

Sandy's Speedway - Warsaw - 1/3 mile dirt oval (c.1968 - c.1969)

Sarnia - 1/2 mile dirt oval (c.5/24/36 - 1938)

Sarnia - also see: Elmwood, Glendale

Satellite Speedway - see: Speedway Park

Sauble Speedway - Sauble Beach - 1/4 mile dirt oval (c.1962 - 1970)
1/4 mile paved oval (1971 - present)

Seymour Speedway - Hoards - dirt oval (1969)

Shakell's Sunset Speedway - see: Sunset Speedway

Shannonville Motorsports Park - Belleville / (aka: Nelson Int'l Speedway)
1/4 mile dirt oval (late 1960's) / (aka: Shannonville Speedway)
1.1 mile paved road course (1977 - present)
road course originally smaller for motorcycles & go-karts before 1977
1.4 & 2.5 mile paved road courses (1988 - present)
1/4 mile paved dragstrip (1988 - present)

Skydome Grand Prix - Toronto - 1/5 mile indoor concrete oval (1/16/93)
ran a midget race inside the new baseball stadium used by the Blue Jays

South Buxton Speedway - Merlin / (aka: Raleigh Raceway Park)
3/8 mile dirt oval (1972 - present) / (aka: Raceland Speedway)

Speedway Park - Toronto (Stoney Creek) - 1/2 mile dirt oval (1949 - c.1976)
3/8 mile dirt oval (1958 - c.1970) / (aka: Satellite Speedway)
3/8 mile paved oval (6/04/71 - c.1976)

Stamford Park - Niagara Falls / site was a horse track
1/2 mile dirt oval (c.7/01/50 - 7/01/53) / ran NASCAR GN race on 7/01/52

Stayner Speedway - Stayner / located at the Edenvale Airport (Stayner Airport)
1.5 mile paved road course on runways (c.1951 - c.1959)

Stockport Speedway - Teviotdale (Arthur) - 1/4 mile paved oval (c.1955 - 1973)

Stoney Creek - 1/4 mile dirt oval (late 1940's - early 1950's) / on Barton St.
referred to as the "Dust Bowl" / was not Speedway Park / near Toronto

Stratford Speedway - Stratford - 1/4 mile dirt oval (1954 - 1956)

The NASCAR North Tour on their pace lap at Cayuga Speedway in 1983. Wes Rosner is on the pole with Bob Dragon starting outside. Dale Earnhardt won the race after starting 21st spot. - Dave Franks photo.

572   *Ontario*

Strathroy - oval (1952)

Streetsville - (location unknown) - 1/4 mile oval (1948 - 1953) / maybe Stittsville

Sudbury Speedway - see: North Bay Motor Speedway

Sunnydale Speedway - see: North Bay Motor Speedway

Sunset Speedway - Stroud - 1/4 mile dirt oval (c.1969 - 1971)
1/3 mile dirt oval (1971) / (aka: Shakell's Sunset Speedway)
1/3 mile paved oval (1972 - present) / (aka: New Sunset Speedway)

Sutton Speedway - Sutton - oval (1970) / (aka: South Sutton Speedway)

Thunder Bay Expo Grounds - Fort Williams / at the Canadian Lakehead Expo
1/2 mile dirt oval (c.1935) (1947 - c.1963)
the town of Fort Williams is now called Thunder Bay

Timmins - 1/4 mile dirt oval (1982)

Timmins - dirt oval (c.1955)

Toronto Ball Park - Toronto - 1/5 mile dirt oval (1937)

Toronto Expo - see: Canadian National Expo

Toronto Maple Leaf Gardens - Toronto / located at the C.N.E.
indoor concrete oval (1965) / (aka: Toronto Maple Leafs Hockey Stadium)

Toronto - also see: Canadian National Expo, Exhibition Place, Molson Indy,
Oakwood, Pinecrest, Skydome, Speedway Park, Stoney Creek

Tweed Speedway - Tweed - 1/3 & 1/2 mile dirt ovals (early 1960's - c.1969)

Twin Cities Speedway - see: Barrie Speedway

Varney Speedway - Durham - 1/4 mile paved oval (1970 - present)

Wallace Speedway - Listowel - 1/4 mile paved oval (1969 - 1974)

Warwick Speedway - Warwick / (aka: Warwick Raceway)
dirt oval (c.1952) / site is now a lumbermill

Wasaga Speedway - Wasaga Beach - 1/2 mile dirt oval (c.8/27/55 - c.1973)

Welland County Speedway - Welland - 1/4 mile oval (1971)
possibly the Welland Co. Motorcycle Club that ran motorcycle races in 1991

Westgate Speedway - see: Peterborough Speedway

Windsor Arena - Windsor - 1/10 mile indoor concrete oval (11/25/53)

Windsor Dragway - Windsor - 1/4 mile paved dragstrip (c.1969 - c.1972)

Windsor Driving Park - Windsor - dirt oval (1906)

Windsor Motor Speedway - see: Dayus Stadium

Windsor Speedway - see: Checker Flag Motor Speedway

Windsor - also see: Bluebird

PRINCE EDWARD ISLAND

Covehead Speedway - Charlottetown - 1/4 mile dirt oval (1967)

East River Speedway - Dunnstaffnagle - 1/4 mile dirt oval (c.1986 - 1989)

Freetown Speedway - Summerside - 1/4 mile dirt oval (c.1967 - c.1974)

Prince Edward Island Dragway - see: Raceway Park

Raceway Park - Charlottetown - 1/4 mile paved dragstrip (1971 - present)
   1/4 mile dirt oval (c.1966 - 1986) / (aka: Prince Edward Island Dragway)
   1/4 mile paved oval (1987 - present) / maybe Covehead Speedway in 1967

QUEBEC

Accelerarama St-Eugene - see: Autodrome St-Eugene

Allumette Speedway - Allumette (location unknown) - dirt oval (late 1970's)

Alvan Dragway - St-Tite - 1/4 mile paved dragstrip (1970's - 1981)
   (aka: Piste D'Acceleration Alvan)

Ancienne Piste de Vae Report de St-Francois - St-Francois
   1/4 mile paved dragstrip (1990) / located near Ste-Francois-de-Macham

Angers Speedway - Angers - 1/3 mile dirt oval (1968) / located east of Gatineau

Autodrome 117 Nord - see: Autodrome St-Jovite

Autodrome Amqui - see: Autodrome St-Tharcius

Autodrome Californien - Sept-Iles - 1/2 mile dirt oval (1994 - present)

Autodrome Chandler - Chandler - dirt oval (1989)

Autodrome de Beauce - see: Autodrome St-Come

Autodrome de Chibougamau - Chibougamau - dirt oval (1989)

Autodrome de l'Amiante - see: Autodrome de Robertson

Autodrome de l'est - Victoriaville - 1/2 mile paved oval (c.8/12/51 - 1954)
   1/2 mile dirt oval (1985)

Autodrome de Lanaudierre - St-Damien - 1/2 mile dirt oval (c.1985 - c.1992)
   (aka: Autodrome Lanaudierre)

Autodrome de Laval - Laval / (aka: Riverside Speedway)
   1/3 mile paved oval (1958 - 1985) / (aka: Autodrome St-Paul)

Autodrome de Moisie - Moisie - 1/2 mile dirt oval (1980's) (Oct., 1993 - present)
   (aka: Sept-Iles Speedway)

Autodrome de Mont-Laurier - Mont-Laurier - 1/3 mile paved oval (c.1961 - 1985)
   1/4 mile paved dragstrip (1970's & 1980's) / (aka: Mont-Laurier Speedway)

Autodrome de Montmagny - St-Pierre-Montmagny / (aka: Le Pista Mustang)
1/3 mile dirt oval (c.1968 - 1978)
1/2 mile dirt oval (c.1979 - present)

Autodrome de Rimouski - Ste-Blandine - 1/3 mile dirt oval (c.1981 - present)

Autodrome de Robertson - Robertsonville / (aka: Robertsonville Speedway)
1/3 mile dirt oval (c.1979 - 1981) (c.1984 - present)
(aka: Autodrome de l'Amiante)

Autodrome de Val-Belair - Quebec City (Val-Belair) / (aka: Autodrome de Quebec)
1/3 mile paved oval (1961 - 1987) / (aka: Quebec Modern Speedway)

Autodrome Drummond - Drummondville - 1/2 mile dirt oval (7/15/51 - present)

Autodrome du Rang Double - St-Felicien - 1/3 mile dirt oval (1984 - 1985)

Autodrome Edelweiss Speedway - Cantley - 3/8 mile dirt oval (1980 - present)
(aka: Edelweiss Speedway) / in a small community called Wilson Corner

Autodrome Granby - Granby / (aka: Granby Rebel Speedway)
1/2 mile dirt oval (c.1964 - present) / (aka: Rebel Speedway)

Autodrome la Chaudiere - see: Circuit la Chaudiere

Raymond Beadle in one of his famous "Blue Max" funny cars. Sanair Super Speedway hosted an annual NHRA "Le Grand Nationals" from 1971 to 1992. The Canadian government created a controversy about using leaded-gasoline, which ultimately stopped the event. - Allan E. Brown collection.

Autodrome Mont-Carmel - Mont-Carmel / located near Shawinigan
4/10 mile dirt oval (1968 - 1976) (1988 - 1989)
4/10 mile paved oval (1977 - 1987)

Autodrome Rive Sud - St-Philippe (LaPrairie) - 1/4 mile dirt oval (c.1987 - c.1992)
(aka: Marcel Turcolte Speedway)

Autodrome Riviere-du-Loup - St-Patrice / (aka: Piste Club de Romaine)
1/2 mile dirt oval (1968) (c.1985 - 1988) (1994 - present)

Autodrome Rouyn - Rouyn-Noranda - 1/4 mile dirt oval (1982)
1/2 mile dirt oval (1991 - 1993)

Rock Poulin after a win at Autodrome Montmagny. - Christian Genest photo.

Autodrome Saguenay - see: Circuit Plain Gazagurnay

Autodrome Sherbrooke - Sherbrooke - oval (c.1965 - c.1969) / maybe Lennoxville
(aka: Sherbooke Motordrome) / (aka: Piste de Cookshire)

Autodrome Sorel - Rang St-Robert (Sorel) - 1/2 mile dirt oval (c.1977 - c.1989)

Autodrome Soulanges - St-Clet - 1/4 mile dirt oval (c.1980 - c.1984)
located near Coteau-du-Lac

Autodrome St-Adalbert - St-Adalbert - 1/2 mile dirt oval (1981 & 1982)

Autodrome St-Calixte - St-Calixte - 1/4 mile dirt oval (c.1982 - 1984) (1987)

Autodrome St-Come - St-Come (Beauce) - 1/3 mile dirt oval (c.1968 - 1988)
(aka: Autodrome de Beauce) / (aka: St-Come de Beauce Ranch Poulin)

Autodrome St-Eugene - St-Eugene - 1.5 mile paved road course (1983)
1/8 mile paved dragstrip (1983) / (aka: Accelerama St-Eugene) / near L'Islet

Autodrome St-Eustache - St-Eustache / (aka: Sportsman Speedway)
4/10 mile paved oval (c.1965 - 1983) (1986 - present)
1.1 mile paved road course (c.1977 - present)
1/8 mile paved dragstrip (1983 - present)
(aka: Circuit Deux-Montagnes) / (aka: Two Mountain Circuit)

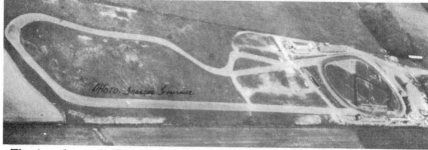

The Autodrome St-Eustache complex. It includes a 4/10 mile oval, a 1/4 mile dragstrip and a 1.1 mile road course. - Official track photo.

576

Autodrome St-Felicien before they expanded the oval track to a 1/2 mile in 1974. - Official track photo.

Autodrome St-Felicien - St-Felicien - 1/3 mile paved oval (1972 - c.1987)
    paved road course (1970's - 1990)
    1/4 mile paved dragstrip (June, 1973 - present)
    1/2 mile paved oval (1974 - present)

Autodrome St-Francois - St-Francois Xavier de Brompton
    1/3 mile dirt oval (1984 - 1986) / located near Bromptonville

Autodrome St-Gregoire - see: Autodrome Trois-Rivieres

Autodrome St-Joachim - St-Joachim-de-Tourelles - 1/3 mile dirt oval (1982 - 1987)

Autodrome St-Jovite - St-Jovite - 1/3 mile dirt oval (c.1982 - 1984)
    (aka: Autodrome 117 Nord)

Autodrome St-Juste - St-Juste-de-Bretenieres
    1/3 mile dirt oval (c.1986 - 1990) (1993 - present)

Autodrome St-Lambert - St-Lambert - 4/10 mile paved oval (1981 - 1983)

Autodrome St-Marcel - St-Marcel / (aka: Royal Raceway)
    1/2 mile dirt oval (c.1952 - c.1954) (c.1984 - 1989) / located southeast of Sorel
    1/4 mile dirt oval (9/16/93 - present) / (aka: Circuit St-Marcel)
    (aka: Motordrome St-Marcel) / (aka: Circuit Grand Prix St-Marcel)

Autodrome St-Pascal - St-Pascal (Kamouraska) - 1/3 mile dirt oval (1979)

Autodrome St-Paul - see: Autodrome de Laval

Autodrome St-Prosper - St-Prosper - 1/3 mile dirt oval (1970 - 1971)
    located near Trois-Rivieres on Route 159

Autodrome St-Tharcius - Amqui - 1/3 mile dirt oval (c.1983 - present)
    (aka: Autodrome Amqui)

Autodrome Ste-Therese - Ste-Therese-de-Lisieux - 1/2 mile dirt oval (1959 - 1968)
    1/2 mile paved oval (1968 - 1971) / located near Quebec City

Autodrome Thetford - Thetford-Mines - 1/2 mile dirt oval (c.1952 - c.1968)
    1/3 mile dirt oval (c.1980 - 1984) (1987 - 1991) (1994 - present)

Autodrome Trois-Rivieres - St-Gregoire (Nicolet) / located SE of Trois-Rivieres
1/2 mile dirt oval (c.1972 - 1985) / (aka: Autodrome St-Gregoire)

Beamishill Stock Car Track - Hull - dirt oval (c.5/25/53 - c.1965)
located 10 miles west of Hull / maybe built by A.D. Beamishill

Berthelet Speedway - Berthierville / was a NASCAR sanctioned track in 1953
1/2 mile dirt oval (7/19/53 - c.1953) (1966 - 1968)

Cantley Speedway - Cantley - 1/3 mile dirt oval (1968 - 1971)

Cedars Dragway - Pierrefonds - 1/4 mile paved dragstrip (c.1967 - c.1968)

Chalet des Sports - Issoudum - dirt oval (1986 - present) / near Ste-Croix

Champion Speedway - Bedford - 1/3 mile dirt oval (1968 - 1974)
1/3 mile paved oval (1974 - 1975) / located near Stanbridge-East

Charlevoix Speedway - Clermont - 1/3 mile dirt oval (1968)

Circuit Alma - Alma - 1.3 mile paved road course (1993 - present) / motorcycles

Circuit de Courses du Bas St-Larent - Rimouski - 1/3 mile dirt oval (1968)

Circuit de Courses Portneuf - Portneuf - 1/2 mile dirt oval (1967 - 1968)

Circuit de Ile Notre Dame - see: Circuit Gilles Villeneuve

Circuit Degelis - Degelis - 1/3 mile dirt oval (1981 - 1987)
(aka: Circuit de Courses Ste-Rose de Degelis)

Circuit Deux Montagnes - see: Autodrome St-Eustache

Circuit Gilles Villeneuve - Montreal / (aka: Circuit de Ile Notre Dame)
2.74 mile paved road course (9/24/78 - 1987) (1989 - present)
Gilles Villeneuve was the first winner / located on city streets
The Canadian Formula One Grand Prix held here from 1978 to present
track was renamed after the Canadian superstar after his death in 1983

Canadian star Gilles Villeneuve at Long Beach (CA) Grand Prix. He had six wins in 67 Grand Prix starts before he was tragically killed in a practice accident before the 1982 "Belgium Grand Prix." - Phil Harms collection.

578

Circuit Grand Prix Automobile de Quebec - Quebec City
1.3 mile paved road course (1979 & 1980) / at Parc D'Exposition de Quebec

Circuit Ile Notre Dame - see: Circuit Gilles Villeneuve

Circuit la Chaudiere - Vallee-Jonction - 1/4 mile dirt oval (1992 - present)
(aka: Autodrome la Chaudiere) / (aka: Chaudiere River Race Track)

Emilien Bergeron wins at Circuit la Chaudiere. - Christian Genest photo.

Circuit Mont-Trinite - St-Michel-des-Saints - 1/3 mile dirt oval (1984)

Circuit Plein Gazsagurnay - Chicoutimi - 1/3 mile dirt oval (c.1968 - c.1973)
1/2 mile paved oval (c.1985 - 1986) / (aka: Club de Courses de Chicoutimi)
(aka: Autodrome Saguenay)

Circuit Quebec - see: Circuit Ste-Croix

Circuit Road Runner - Clermont (Charlevoix) - 1/3 mile dirt oval (1994 - present)

Circuit St-Edmond - St-Edmond - 1/3 mile dirt oval (years unknown)

Circuit St-Esprit - St-Roch-de-l'Achigan - 1/2 mile dirt oval (1968)

Circuit St-Marcel - see: Autodrome St-Marcel

Circuit Ste-Croix - Ste-Croix (Lotbiniere) / (aka: Circuit Quebec)
1.5 mile paved road course (c.1971 - c.1990)
5/8 mile paved oval (c.1984 - present)
1/4 mile paved dragstrip (8/08/92 - present)

Circuit Trois-Rivieres - see: Grand Prix Trois-Rivieres

Club de Courses de Chicoutimi - see: Circuit Plein Gazsagurnay

Club Rimouski - Rimouski - 1/4 mile paved dragstrip (c.1989)

Coaticook Dragway - Coaticook - 1/4 mile paved dragstrip (1968)

Deslormiers Park - see: Montreal Expo

Dosquet Speedway - Dosquet - 1/3 mile dirt oval (1968)

Dun Burke Speedway - see: Piste St-Denis

Edelweiss Speedway - see: Autodrome Edelweiss Speedway

Farnham Speedway - Farnham - 1/3 mile dirt oval (1967 - 1968)

Fireburg Speedway - see: Maniwaki Speedway

Fury Speedway - Laval (Fabreville) / built by Paul Deslauriers
    1/3 mile high banked paved oval (1952 - c.1962)

Gatineau Raceway Park - La Peche (St-Francois-de-Masham)
    1/4 mile dirt oval (c.1968 - c.1975)/ (aka: Piste de Ste-Cecile-de-Masham)

Gentilly Speedway - Gentilly - dirt oval (1968)

Grand Prix de Granby - Granby - 1.8 mile paved road course (7/28/84)(1985)(1991)

Grand Prix Trois-Rivieres - Trois-Rivieres / races include SCCA CA, TA & FA
    .75 mile paved road course (1967) / 1967 races at the Exhibition Grounds
    1.3 mile paved road course on city streets (1968 - 1972)
    1.5 mile paved road course on city streets (1973 - 1976)
    2.0975 mile paved road course on city streets (1977 - 1985)
    1.6 mile paved road course on city streets (1989 - present)

Hippodrome Quebec - Quebec City - 1/2 mile dirt oval (1978 - 1980) (1983)

Kempton Park - LaPrairie - dirt oval (c.7/16/50)

Lac St-Jean - 1/2 mile dirt oval (c.1952) / probably the Roberval Track

Lac-Megantic Speedway - Nantes - dirt oval (1968)

LaPrairie - dirt oval (c.1957) / site is now a market / probably Kempton Park

LaSarre Speedway - dirt oval (1968) / located near Lake Abitibi

Le Circuit Mont-Tremblant - St-Jovite - 1.6 mile paved road course (1964)
    2.65 mile paved road course (1964 - 1971) (1974 - present)
    2.8 mile paved road course (1965) / located northwest of St-Jovite
    held Canadian Grand Prix (Formula One) here in 1968 & 1970
    ran first ever SCCA Can-Am race here in 1966, won by John Surtees

Le Piste Mustang - see: Autodrome de Montmagny

Luskville Dragway - Aylmer - 1/4 mile paved dragstrip (1969 - present)

Maniwaki Speedway - Maniwaki - dirt oval (1968) / (aka: Fireburg Speedway)

Marcel Turcolte Speedway - see: Autodrome Rive Sud

Maskinonge Stock Cars - Maskinonge - dirt oval (1968)

Montreal Expo - Montreal - dirt oval (c.1917 - 7/04/18) / (aka: Deslormiers Park)

Montreal - indoor concrete oval (1937) / ran midgets

580

Motordrome - see: Stadiaume St-Guillaume

Motordrome St-Marcel - see: Autodrome St-Marcel

Mustang Speedway - Philipsburg - 1/5 mile dirt oval (c.1964)

Napierville Dragway - Napierville / (aka: Napierville Int'l Speedway)
1/4 mile paved dragstrip (July, 1962 - present)

Noel Raceway - Bosseau Station (location unknown)
dirt oval (July, 1953 - c.1954)

Papineauville Speedway - Papineauville - 1/3 mile dirt oval (1968)

Piste Belvedere - Rouyn-Noranda - 1/3 mile dirt oval (1968)
maybe Autodrome Rouyn

Piste Club de Domaine - see: Autodrome Riviere-du-Loup

Piste Colombourg - Colombourg - dirt oval (1968) / probably LaSarre Speedway

Piste D'Acceration Pont Rouge - Pont Rouge / located southwest of Quebec City
1/4 mile paved dragstrip (1966 - present) / (aka: Quebec Dragway)

Piste de Cookshire - see: Autodrome Sherbrooke

Robert Hamel, the owner and driver of this beautiful Camaro, works at tuning his high-powered engine while a spectator looks on. Drag racing is a unique sport as many fans purchase pit passes and are then able to wander through the pit area to watch the competitors working on their cars. The photo was taken at Piste D'Acceleration Pont Rouge. - Christian Genest photo.

Piste de Course du Ranch Moco - Val-des-Monts (Perkins)
1/4 mile dirt oval (c.1979 - c.1986) (1989 - 1990) (1992)
(aka: Moco Ranch Speedway) / near Buckingham

Piste de Courses St-Charles - St-Charles - 1/2 mile dirt oval (1966 - 1968)

Piste de Dalhousie - see: Riviere-Beaudette Speedway

Piste de Lantier - Lantier - dirt oval (1968) / near Ste-Agathe-des-Monts (Rt 329)

Piste de Malartic - LaSarre - 1/3 mile dirt oval (1972) / located near Lake Abitibi
possibly LaSarre Speedway

Piste L'Etang du Nord - Iles de la Madeleine - 1/4 mile dirt oval (1967 - 1968)
located on an Island in Golfe-du-St-Laurent

Piste Lemieux - Plessisville - 1/3 mile dirt oval (1966 - 1969)

Piste Pointe-Lebel - Baie-Comeau - 1/3 mile dirt oval (1968)

Piste Rodeo d'Auto - Batiscan - 1/3 mile dirt oval (1966 - 1969)

Piste St-Athanase - St-Athanase - dirt oval (1968)

Piste St-Denis - St-Hyacinthe (St-Denis) - 1/3 mile dirt oval (1968)
(aka: Dun Burke Speedway)

Piste St-Etienne - St-Etienne-des-Gres - dirt oval (1968) / near Trois Rivieres

Piste Ste-Anne-des-Monts - Ste-Anne-des-Monts - 1/4 mile dirt oval (1968)

Piste Ste-Cecile-des-Masham - see: Gatineau Raceway Park

Piste Ste-Marthe - Ste-Marthe - dirt oval (1968)

Piste Vallee-Jonction - Tring-Jonction - 1.5 mile dirt road course (1985)

Quebec City Winter Carnival - Quebec City / (aka: ESSO Grand Prix)
paved road course in the park Plaines d'Abraham (1970's - 1980's)

Quebec Dragway - see: Piste D'Acceration Pont Rouge

Quebec Modern Speedway - see: Autodrome de Belair

Quebec Provincial Exhibition Park - Quebec City - dirt oval (7/20/18 - c.1918)

Rebel Speedway - see: Autodrome Granby

Rigaud - dirt oval (July, 1953 - c.1953)

Riverside Speedway - see: Autodrome de Laval

Riviere-Beaudette Speedway - Riviere-Beaudette - dirt oval (1968)
(aka: Piste de Dalhousie)

Robertsonville Speedway - see: Autodrome de Robertson

Roberval Track - Roberval - dirt oval (early 1950's)

Royal Raceway - see: Autodrome St-Marcel

An aerial view of Sanair Super Speedway - Official track photo.

Sanair Super Speedway - St-Pie / (aka: Sanair International)
  1/3 mile paved oval (June, 1971 - present) / CART IndyCars 1984, 1985, 1986
  1.25 mile paved road course (c.1971 - present) / SCCA TA in 1972 & 1973
  1/4 mile paved dragstrip (c.1971 - present)
  1.33 kilometer (9/10) mile paved tri-oval (8/07/83 - present)

Sept-Ile Speedway - see: Autodrome de Moisie

Shawinigan - dirt oval (c.1952) / Jean Paul Cabana started his career here

Sherbrooke Motordrome - see: Autodrome Sherbrooke

Sherrington Speedway - Sherrington - oval (years unknown) / near Barrington

South Shore Speedway - see: Autodrome Rive Sud

St-Come de Beauce Ranch Poulin - see: Autodrome St-Come

St-Henri Speedway - St-Henri - 1/3 mile paved oval (1966 - 1970)
  located near Levis-Lauzon

St-Jean-sur-Richelieu - 1/2 mile dirt oval (c.1952) / possibly Kempton Park

St-Prime - dirt oval (1978 - 1980) / located between Roberval and St-Felicien

Stadiaume St-Guillaume - St-Guillaume (Yamaska) / located southeast of Sorel
  1/2 mile dirt oval (c.1981 - c.1984) (c.1992 - present)

Ste-Agathe (Rang Bois-Franc) - dirt oval (1986) / located near Lac St-Jean

Ste-Monique des Saules - 1/2 mile dirt oval (c.1952 - 1954) / near Quebec City

Temiscaming - 1/4 mile dirt oval (1982)

SASKATCHEWAN

Battlesford Speedway - Battlesford - 1/3 mile dirt oval (1974 & 1975)

Bienfait - 1/4 mile paved dragstrip (c.1968)

Bienfait - dirt oval (late 1960's)

Big River Stock Car Track - Big River - 3/8 mile dirt oval (c.1986 - c.1990)
(aka: Big River Speed Oval)

Biggar Stock Car Track - Biggar - 1/3 mile dirt oval (c.1986 - present)

Border City Motorsports - Lloydminster - 1/3 mile dirt oval (c.1986 - present)

Bridge City Speedway - Saskatoon - 1/3 mile paved oval (May, 1971 - present)

Carrot River Race Track - Carrot River - 3/8 mile dirt oval (1984 - 1987)

Dafoe Airport - Dafoe - paved road course on airport runways (mid 1960's)

Davidson Airport - Davidson - paved road course on airport runways (1965- 1967)

Elstow Stock Car Track - Elstow - 1/3 mile dirt oval (c.1986 - 1988)

Esterhazy - dirt oval (c.1970 - c.1972)

Estevan Airport Speedway - Estevan - 1/4 mile dirt oval (1978 - c.1990)

Estevan Expo Grounds - Estevan - 1/2 mile dirt oval (c.1959 - c.1960)
1/4 mile dirt oval (c.1964 - 1966) / site is now a housing development

Estevan Speedway - Estevan - 1/4 mile dirt oval (1966 - 1972)

Grenfell - dirt oval (1966)

Gull Lake Stock Car Track - Gull Lake - 3/8 mile dirt oval (1985 - 1991)

Kings Park Speedway - Regina - 1/3 mile paved oval (1967 - present)

Lampman Speedway - Lampman - 1/4 mile dirt oval (1970 - 1979)

LaRonge Stock Car Track - LaRonge - 3/8 mile dirt oval (c.1986 - 1987)

Lloydminster Expo - Lloydminster - 1/2 mile dirt oval (6/28/51)

Lost Mountain Raceway - Raymore - 1/3 mile dirt oval (c.1980 - c.1990)
(aka: Lost Mountain Stock Car Track)

Manitou Speedway - Watrous - 1/3 mile dirt oval (c.1976 - 1987)

Melfort - dirt oval (c.1970)

Moose Jaw Expo Grounds - Moose Jaw
1/4 mile dirt oval (c.1926) (9/16/49) (1971) (c.1975 - c.1985)

Nipawin Agri Expo - Nipawin - 1/4 mile dirt oval (1988)

Outlook - 1/4 mile dirt oval (1970's)

Outlook Stock Car Track - Outlook - 1/3 mile dirt oval (1987 - present)

Parkland Raceway - Prince Albert - 4/10 mile dirt oval (c.1980 - present)

Pinto Creek Stock Car Track - Kincaid - 3/8 mile dirt oval (c.1987 - present)

Prince Albert - dirt oval (c.1970)

Radville Stock Car Track - Radville - 1/4 mile dirt oval (1972 - 1982)

Regina Exhibition Grounds - Regina / Emory Collins started his career here 1919
   1/2 mile dirt oval (c.1917 - 1937) (c.7/01/49 - c.1968)

Riverside Speedway - Nipawin - 1/4 mile dirt oval (1989 - present) / north of town

Saskatoon Exhibition Grounds - Saskatoon
   1/2 mile dirt oval (1917) (8/03/18) (c.1926) (1949) (c.1956 - c.1970)

Saskatoon - ice-covered dragstrip (winters 1957 & 1958) / raced on a slough

Saskatchewan Int'l Raceway - Saskatoon / (aka: Saskatoon Int'l Raceway)
   1/4 mile paved dragstrip (1966 - present) / (aka: Southwinds Dragway)

Semans - 1/2 mile dirt oval (1920 & 1921)

Southwinds Dragway - see: Saskatchewan Int'l Raceway

Swift Current - dirt oval (mid 1960's)

Swift Current Motor Speedway - Swift Current
   1/4 mile dirt oval (1993 - present) / check to see if opened in 1993

Wadena Stock Car Track - Wadena - 1/3 mile dirt oval (1989 - present)

Weyburn - dirt oval (1960's)

Wheatbelt Stock Car Track - Rosetown - 1/3 mile dirt oval (1969 - 1987)

Willow Bunch Speedway - Willow Bunch - 1/4 mile dirt oval (1979 & 1980)

Windthorst - 1/4 mile peanut shaped dirt oval (1983)

YUKON

Carmacks - dirt oval (early 1970's - 1974)

Dawson - dirt oval (early 1970's)

KARA Speedway - Whitehorse - 3/8 mile dirt oval (1969 - 1985)
   KARA was short for Klondike Auto Racing Association

Various race tracks: (top) Eldora Speedway (OH). - Track photo; Joplin (MO) 66 Speedway. - Allan E. Brown photo; Veteran Stadium (NJ). - Bruce Craig collection; Circuit la Chaudiere (Quebec). - Christian Genest photo.

586

Road racing: (top) An early road race at Mines Field (CA) in 1934. - Bruce
Craig collection; (middle) Club racing is an important element in SCCA. Here
a Porsche 911 leads his competitors. - Allan E. Brown collection; (bottom) The
Ford GT Mark IIs driven by Bruce McLaren & Chris Amon (#2) won the 1966
24 Hours of LeMans (France). Teammates Ken Miles, Dennis Hulme, Ronnie
Bucknum and Dick Hutcherson drove the other two Mark IIs in this photo and
finished second and third. - Official Ford Motor Company photo.

Championship cars: (top) Bob Burman in a Keeton from 1913. - Allan E. Brown collection; (middle) The roadsters of Jim Rathmann (#4), Bob Grim (#18), and Parnelli Jones (#98) battle with the rear-engined car of Dan Gurney at Indianapolis in 1962. - Len Ashburn collection; (bottom) Bobby Rahal in the 7-Eleven/Red Roof Inn March-Cosworth at Mid-Ohio during tire tests. - Photo courtesy of Goodyear Tire Company.

Dirt track championship cars: (top) Rex Mays in Bowes Seal Fast Special at Langhorne in 1947. - Frank Smith photo (Len Ashburn collection); (middle) Johnny Rutherford kicks up dirt clods in this 1971 photo by Ken Coles (Len Ashburn collection); (bottom) Jeff Swindell (#12) leads Jack Hewitt (#63). - Todd Hunter photo.

Sprint cars: (top) D.D. Morris poses with Gus Tieri in 1926 picture. -Wilson Davis collection; (middle) The great Tommy Hinnershitz from the late 1940's. - Frank Smith photo (Len Ashburn collection); (bottom) USAC champion Steve Butler in a winged sprint from 1987. - Robert G. Hunter photo.

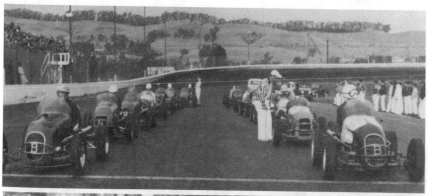

Three types of open wheel racers: (top) Midgets at Oakland (CA) Speedway in 1949. - Dick Downes collection (courtesy of Don Radbruch); (middle) George Tichenor (#K9) at Mount Lawn Speedway (IN) in 1940. - George Tichenor collection; (bottom) Gordon Johncock at Kalamazoo (MI) Speedway in 1961. - Allan E. Brown collection.

Modifieds: (top) From left to right Jimmy Griggs poses with his #709, Bob Harmon, Red Farmer, and Friday Hassler are in the back ground. - Len Heyden photo; (middle) Satch Worley (#07) and Tom Baldwin (#7) lead the pavement modifieds at Orange County Speedway (NC) in 1988. - David Allio photo; (bottom) Dirt track stars Jack Johnson (#12a) and Brian Stevens (#44) at Five Mile Point Speedway (NY) in 1982. - Michael J. Marrer photo.

NASCAR late models: (top) Billy Myers on the beach course at Daytona Beach (FL) in a Bill Stroppe prepared 1957 Mercury convertible. He finished third in the 1957 race. - Len Ashburn photo; (middle) Cale Yarborough (#28), Dale Earnhardt (#15), Ricky Rudd (#3); and Bobby Allison (#22) dice it out on the high banks in 1983. - Dave Franks photo; (bottom) Johnny Benson in the Staff American NASCAR Busch Grand National car won his first Grand National race at Dover (DE) Speedway in 1994. - Johnny Benson, Jr. Fan Club photo.

Late models: (top) The NASCAR sportsmen race on the banks of Daytona Beach (FL). Nelson Stacy (#29) leads Cale Yarborough (#50) and Bobby Johns (#7-A). - Len Heyden collection; (bottom) Mark Martin (#2) and Bob Senneker (#84) in a ASA race at Winchester (IN). - Tom DeVette photo.

Dragsters: (top) A promotional shot of the U.D.R.A. "slingshots" from the late 1960's. - Michigan Motor Sports Hall of Fame collection; (bottom) Eddie Hill in his Pennzoil sponsored dragster. - Official Atlanta (GA) Dragway photo.

Various motor sports: (top) Wilbur Shaw in 1932 at the Muroc Dry Lakes trying to set a world's record in speed trials. - Bruce Craig collection; (middle) Motorcycle road racing is a popular sport. - Autodrome St-Eustache photo; (bottom) One of the newest motor sports is Monster Trucks. These four-wheel drive trucks with huge tires can do a variety of stunts. - St-Eustache photo.